CHOCTAW OF MISSISSIPPI
INDIAN CENSUS 1933, 1934 & 1937,
SUPPLEMENTAL ROLLS TO 1934 & 1935
WITH
BIRTHS & DEATHS 1932 - 1938
AND MARRIAGES 1936 - 1938
VOLUME II

TRANSCRIBED BY
JEFF BOWEN

NATIVE STUDY
Gallipolis, Ohio
USA

Copyright © 2022
by Jeff Bowen

ALL RIGHTS RESERVED
No part of this publication may be reproduced,
distributed, or transmitted in any form or by any means,
without the prior written permission of the publisher.

Originally published:
Signal Mountain, Tennessee
1997

Santa Maria, California
2020

Reprinted by:

Native Study LLC
Gallipolis, Ohio
www.nativestudy.com

Library of Congress Control Number: 2022905968

ISBN: 978-1-64968-158-4

Title Page Image:
Moshulatubbee (He-who-puts-out-and-kills)
by Geo. Catlin, 1834

Made in the United States of America.

This series is dedicated to the people within these pages and their ancestors.

The reason both sets of Instructions that came with these records are included with this text is because the persons dealing with the records involved did not always follow their own set of rules. These Instructions, in most situations, hopefully will bring you an understanding in reading the text. As the transcriber finds so many times the rules change according to the agent or assistants at the time. As mentioned before in different volumes involving different tribes it is only hoped that the person researching will find their ancestors and personally fill in a piece of their puzzle.

INSTRUCTIONS

(*A*) A separate roll is to be made of each reservation; also, of each *rancheria* or reserve, and a separate roll of Indians allotted on the public domain or homesteading. The roll is to be based on enrollment and not on residence.

(*B*) Persons are to be listed by families alphabetically; that is, not only by the first letter of the surname, but also by the second and subsequent letters when the first letter or letters are the same. For example: Ab*a*lon, Ab*b*ott, Ab*c*on, Ab*e*nd, Ab*i*ct; B*a*ll, B*e*ll, B*i*ll, B*o*ll, B*u*ll; ...etc. Families having the same surname are also to be listed in this way, e.g.; Brown, *A*nson; Brown, *B*ill; Brown, *C*harles; Brown, *D*avid. In the case of English translations of Indian names, such as John *Flying-Elk*, Flying-Elk is the surname and is to be listed under F. In such cases the first word of the translated Indian name determines the alphabetical position. The best way to accomplish this will be to write the names of each family group on a separate card; then, arrange the cards alphabetically and type the names therefrom onto the census roll.

Members of a family are to be listed in the following order: Head, first; wife, second; then children, whether sons or daughters, *in the order of their ages*; and lastly, all other relatives and persons living with the family who do not constitute another family group.

Annuity and per capita payment rolls are also to be prepared in the same manner.

(*C*) A family is composed of the following members:
1. Both parents and their unmarried children, if any, living with them; all other relatives and persons living with the family who do not constitute another family group.
2. Either parent and the unmarried children, if the other parent is dead; all other relatives and persons living with the family who do not constitute another family group.
3. A single person over 21 years of age, not living with a relative.

(*D*) For each person the following information is to be furnished:
1. NUMBER. – A number is to be assigned in serial order. Thus, the first person listed is to be numbered as "1," the second, as "2," and so on until the census is completed.
2. NAME. – If there are both an Indian and an English name, the allotment or annuity roll name is to be given. First, the last or surname;

then, the given name in full. Ditto marks are to be used under the surname of the head for the surnames of the other members of one family.
3. SEX. – "M" for male; "F" for female.
4. AGE AT LAST BIRTHDAY. – Age in completed years at last birthday is to be shown. For infants under 1 year, age in completed months, expressed as twelfths of a year. Thus, 3 months as 3/12 yr.
5. TRIBE. – Care is to be taken that tribe, not band or local name, is given. Thus, Ute tribe, not Pahvant, which is a band of Ute. Likewise, Hupa tribe, not Bear River, which is a local name for the members of the Hupa tribe living near Bear River.
6. DEGREE OF BLOOD. – "F" for full blood; "1/4+" for one-fourth or more Indian blood; "-1/4" for less than one fourth Indian blood.
7. MARITAL STATUS. – "S" for a single or unmarried person; "M" for a married person; and "Wd" for widowed of either sex.
8. RELATIONSHIP TO HEAD OF FAMILY. – The head, whether husband or father, widow or unmarried person of either sex, is to be designated as such. For the other members, the appropriate term which designates the particular relationship the person bears to the head is to be used.
9. RESIDENCE. –
   (*a*) At *jurisdiction* where enrolled: Yes or no. The term jurisdiction includes all reservations and public domain allotments under the agency.
   (*b*) *Or* at another jurisdiction. The name of the jurisdiction is to be given.
   (*c*) *Or* elsewhere:
     1. Post office: Both the proper name of the post office and the class by which it is known (city, town, village, etc.) are to be given. Thus, Lewiston, city.
     2. County.
     3. State.
10. WARD. – Yes or no. Wardship depends primarily upon the ownership of individual property held in trust or upon membership in a tribe living on a Federal reservation.
11. ALLOTMENT, ANNUITY, AND IDENTIFICATION NUMBERS. —"Al", for allotment; "An", for annuity; and "Id", for identification, before the appropriate number or numbers. All numbers are to be shown.

(*E*) Rolls not prepared in strict conformity with the above instructions will be returned for correction.

INSTRUCTIONS FOR COMPLETION

Names are to be listed by families alphabetically. Members of each family, in the following order:
First, head; second, wife; then children, whether sons or daughters, in order of their age; and lastly, all other relatives and persons living with them, who do not constitute another family group.

1. A family is composed of the following members:
    (*a*) Both parents and their unmarried children, if any, living with them. In the case of plural wives, the oldest with her unmarried children is to be listed first; the others, in order of their ages.
    (*b*) Either parent and the unmarried children, if the other is dead or permanently residing elsewhere.
    (*c*) A single person over 18 years of age, not living with any relatives.

2. For each person the following information is to be furnished:
    (*a*) Census numbers, both present and last.
    (*b*) Name, Indian and English, if any. First the surname, then the given. Care is to be exercised in their spelling and ditto marks are to be used when the surname is the same as that of the person in the preceding line.
    (*c*) Allotment, annuity, and identification numbers. Write "Al" for allotment, "An" for annuity, and "Id" for identification, before the appropriate number or numbers.
    (*d*) Date of birth by month, day, and year.
    (*e*) Degree of blood. If full blood use "F", if mixed, "M."
    (*f*) Marital condition. "S" for a single or unmarried person of whatever age, "M" for married, and "Wd" for widowed of either sex.
    (*g*) Relation to head of family. The head, whether husband or wife or unmarried person of either six, is to be designated by the word, "head." For the other members of the family use wife, son, daughter, etc., according to the peculiar relationship which the person bears to the head.

"...General Andrew Jackson and General Thomas Hinds, with free liquor to bribe and soften the Choctaw hearts, had, first by honeyed inveigling, difficult for even the most sophisticated to contest, them by threats and at the last by fits of vociferous anger, frightened the beleaguered Choctaws into giving up five million acres. Jackson had called the expanse 'that useless little slip of land,' but within two weeks the Port Gibson "Correspondent" described it as 'fine as any in the United States,...exhibiting at once the most pleasing variety of hill and dale, prairie and grove, and furnishing a variety of soil, and a salubrity of air, not surpassed by any other region.' The thirteen million acres in the West the Choctaws were promised could not even be identified until a new treaty was held five years later in Washington. It was the treaty, Luther Cashdollar had told Jesse Furver, that cost the Choctaws the lives of their most notable chiefs. The great Pushmataha died in Washington before the treaty was signed. Puckshunubbee died in route."

Will D. Campbell, *Providence*, p. 250-251, para. 6

"Of the 370 Indian Treaties the U.S. Senate has ratified, provisions in every single one have been violated. Since 1849 the Department of Interior has been a party to each broken one."

Will D. Campbell, *Providence*, p. 252, para 1

Table of Contents

Introduction	xiii
Treaty of Dancing Rabbit Creek	
(Original)	xxiii
(Transcription)	xlix
1933 Census	3
1934 Census	81
Supplement to the 1935 Census	175
1937 Census	185
Births	281
Deaths	299
Transfer or Adjustment Roll	315
Marriages as of January, 1936	319
Marriages 1937	321
Marriages 1939	322
Index	327

Introduction

An introduction for the Choctaw couldn't be written without mentioning the famed Choctaw Chief Pushmataha on the front of this book by Charles Bird King in 1824. This is a man that actually tried to help Andrew Jackson like the Cherokee during the uprising of the Creek Indians in the early 1800's; only to later receive from Jackson a decisive blow to what would finish the Choctaw's lives as they knew them. The Treaty of Dancing Rabbit Creek would be that tool of destruction like a Communist taking what you worked for your whole life and giving it to their elitist friends. Even though Pushmataha during a time of hardship for General Jackson needing an army to defeat the Creeks he was there for a young Republic. It was said, "His personal bravery in battle proved his leadership for both Choctaws and whites. He led Choctaw troops under Andrew Jackson in the War of 1812 and the Creek War. He was welcomed at Fort Madison in 1813, wearing the full military regalia of the U.S. army--dress uniform, gold braid and epaulets, and silver medal. He joined the evening promenade of officers with his wife on his arm. Pushmataha personifies the forces acting on the full-blood Choctaws of his time. He fought with the valor of a traditional Choctaw warrior, but on the side of the white leader, Andrew Jackson, against the Creek tribe."[1] Interestingly Pushmataha wasn't at home with his family on Christmas Eve of 1824 but was in Washington trying to negotiate with the powers that be in a government that would eventually take the land of his people. Not knowing that six years later through a treaty only to eventually be broken as so many others, that evening Pushmataha not willingly, died of what has been thought of as pneumonia. His final resting place surely not of his choice, buried in a strange place, the Congressional Cemetery. "Laid among thieves", he would likely say.

The so called civilized probably thought these are Indians. But the commentary spoken of them when approached by the whites wasn't what most would think, "As farmers the Choctaws had few peers. After clearing the land around their villages, by burning the underbrush and girdling the trees, they planted maize (their staple crop), beans, pumpkins, and melons. William Bartram, the English botanist who visited the Gulf Coast of Mississippi in 1777, said they were the 'most ingenious

---

[1] Kidwell, Choctaws and Missionaries in Mississippi 1818-1919, p. 18, para.2

Introduction

and industrious husbandmen, having large plantations, or country farms, where they employ much of their time in agricultural improvements, . . . by which means their territories are more generally cultivated, and better inhabited, than any other Indian republic that we know of."[2]

The Choctaw were a self-sustaining people not just as crop farmers but as producers of beef cattle. Whatever corn they didn't use as their daily staple they used in feeding their beef. They were so capable in their livestock skills that they were able to finance their endeavors through the sales of newly bred cattle. Most whites when approaching the Choctaw found an uncommon vision before them unlike most Native tribes they had seen. They said, "Their homes were permanent type structures, log and stucco houses grouped together near their farm land in concentrations so large that the early white explorers and settlers who made contact with the Choctaws spoke of the settlements as towns. The settlements were normally located around the edge of the district as a protective barrier against potential enemies; inland, the district was sparsely settled and resembled extensive plantations with cabins or homes "a gunshot distant from each other."[3]

One hundred years prior to this census, the Choctaw of Mississippi were being betrayed and driven from a home they had known their whole lives. Not many realize that the Choctaw Tribe of Mississippi was one of the largest tribes east of the river ranging possibly from 18,000 to 21,000 people. Also they were one of the first to be forcibly removed in the early time period of 1831-1833 previous to others who were considered the Five Civilized Tribes. This removal unfortunately brought forth a perilous pattern for the rest of the decade, causing the irrational deaths of thousands of Native Americans from numerous tribes. The loss of the Choctaw homeland and a civilized people as large and deadly as it turned out to be was only a portion of unspeakable crimes that would be thrust upon the Native American during our nation's early history. In the years surrounding the early 1800's or even to this day as we stand enamored looking up at a man's face in marble thinking he must have been a

---

[2] DeRosier, The Removal of the Choctaw Indians, p. 9-10, para. 4

Introduction

marvelous creature. But you have to think again when reading his own words, and learning about his dark under lying motives. Suddenly opinions change, the statue we are staring at proudly suddenly breaks your heart. Thinking of him as humane while we stand at the base of this National monument we have no idea of who he really was and what he did until reading Native American history. As firmly stated, "The reason must be that he never actually intended to allow his wiser and more humane policies to prevail. Evidence of this hypothesis is found in the letters he wrote to Indian agents and influential frontier leaders, advocating Indian agriculture strictly as a means of confining the Indians to a small plot of land so that the government could buy up the large surplus and sell it cheaply to frontier settlers. His motives can also be interpreted from a letter he wrote to Andrew Jackson on February 16, 1803, in which he asserted that the basic reason for keeping agents among the Indians was to obtain their land. 'Toward effecting this object, we consider leading the Indian to agriculture . . . .When they shall cultivate small spots of earth, and see how useless their extensive forests are, they will sell . . . .' Each Indian agent 'shall be estimated by us in proportion to the benefits he can obtain for us,' Jefferson said, and he ended his letter with the demand that his views 'be pursued unremittingly.' During that same year Jefferson also wrote Willian Henry Harrison that he was not interested in the particular method used to secure large holdings of Indian lands, but rather that he was solely concerned with the end result."[4] History like this makes a person weary.

    Mentioned previously in this Introduction and the years surrounding the early 1800's, what could be called the first removal of the Choctaw they were being convinced that they needed to sign a treaty that was supposed to be to their advantage. Only to be broken before the ink was even dry. They were called negotiations only really they were threats from politicians of the day like Harrison, Monroe, Jefferson and Jackson to name a few or even to this day we find stories for example; in a book called, *Providence*, how it points out that things never change. The author tells of a place in Mississippi called Providence Farm or Section 13 that once belonged to the

---

[3] DeRosier, The Removal of the Choctaw Indians, p. 11, para.2
[4] DeRosier, The Removal of the Choctaw Indians, p. 25-26, para.4

Introduction

Choctaw. The author Will D. Campbell tells of how he met two men in 1955 and listened to their story or dilemma of how 32 years later their land and broken dreams devastates them with what he calls the second removal. They are trying to decide what to do with the property all these years later. Their board for Providence was having to decide what to do with this beloved land, likely a painful experience that had gone on for years. But finally a suggestion had been given with a possible answer being money was never a factor because of a few people and their dedication in a purpose to help others they decided to give the land back to the Choctaws. They brought this idea to the Choctaw Chief at the time, 1987. Only to receive a letter, "Two weeks after my visit and conversation with Chief Martin, the Providence board received a letter from the U.S. Department of Interior. They wanted 540 acres of Providence land for a game management program. They offered almost three hundred thousand dollars for it."[5] A few lines after Campbell states, "It was incredulous news. Why now? After all these years? The Department of Interior, the agency that dogged not only the Choctaw but every other native tribe and nation since it took over their management in 1849. Of the 370 Indian treaties the U.S. Senate has ratified, provisions in every single one have been violated. Since 1849 the Department of Interior has been a party to each one broken."[6]

Reading can be a curse but shouldn't be left to a dusty shelf. It only creates ignorance and a future of hopelessness or victimization. As Mr. Campbell so aptly quotes Arthur DeRosier, Jr., "Jefferson had encouraged the Choctaws to run deeply in debt at the trading posts because, he said, they were then willing to lop off the debts with cessions of land. He openly called it bribery and said bribery was preferable to war. No doubt it was, but in addition to his advocacy of extortion, he later said if that policy did not work he was prepared to push a constitutional amendment to remove the Indians by force to the West."[7]

---

[5] Campbell, Providence, p. 251, para. 5
[6] Campbell, Providence, p. 251-252, para. 6-7
[7] Campbell, Providence, p. 29, para. 2

Introduction

People might think that 186 years ago the Choctaw didn't have far to travel for their removal but they did. They were being marched out on foot, their children with them. They weren't getting in their cars and taking a couple hours' drive. They were being torn from their homes. They were leaving almost everything in their world behind. The homes they had built the land they had cleared and planted their whole lives, gone. Their cattle and other animals, gone. They had to walk for the most part to a land filled with forests, brush, brambles, and swampy land having to cross unknown water during treacherous times. This is a description of what they faced and when. Think of how we complain about a little inconvenience and what these people put up with let alone burying their loved ones along the way in strange ground by the side of some dirt path if that. The Choctaws' history says, "The main removals took place during 1831, 1832, and 1833. The sufferings of the emigrants were almost beyond belief. It was a difficult journey at best--350 miles through a wild unsettled country of vast swamps, dense forests, impenetrable canebrakes, and swollen rivers. Added to this was a great deal of blundering and inefficiency on the part of the War Department. Additional suffering and loss of life was caused by one of the worst blizzards in the history of that region, which broke upon the emigrants who were removed during the Winter of 1831-32; and the cholera epidemic, which swept down the Mississippi and caught those who were crossing the following Summer. The population of the tribe was permanently decreased by the losses sustained during this terrible experience. White Americans, with their more mobile habits, have never been able to appreciate the hopeless grief of this despoiled people when they abandoned their ancient homes, and in a strictly literal sense, the bones of their beloved dead."[8]

It is always a goal to give a little history in each introduction so you'll have a chance to understand what your ancestors went through and possibly where. Hopefully to understand who you are and where to look while conducting your genealogical hunt for those sometime elusive family members. It's always good to understand who your tribal family is today and below you can read about them in today's world. As previously mentioned the book *Providence*, would be worth

---

[8] Debo, The Rise and Fall of the Choctaw Republic, p. 56, para. 1-2

Introduction

reading with an amazing story let alone great references to read in searching Choctaw history. The Mississippi Band of Choctaw Indians current location is Mississippi with approximately 28,402 acres and a tribal enrollment of 9,483 members. "The Choctaw Reservation encompasses nine communities: Pearl River, Bogue Chitto, Tucker, Red Water, Standing Pine, Conehatta, Crystal Ridge, Bogue Homa, and Ocean Springs. Choctaw people lived throughout the Mississippi and Alabama region, hunting game and farming the area's rich soil for subsistence. The Choctaw's name is an anglicized version of Chahta, the name of a chief. At least 90 percent of the Mississippi Band of Choctaw Indians' tribal members continue to speak the indigenous Muscogean language, while English serves as the second language. Tribal members continue to practice traditional cultural elements. The Choctaw's first interaction with European explorers occurred in 1540 when the de Soto Expedition marched northwest across the continent--an encounter that resulted in the deaths of 1,500 to 3,000 Choctaw people. In 1786, the Choctaws signed the Treaty of Hopewell, which bestowed federal recognition of their sovereignty, but white settlers continued to settle on Choctaw land. The historic Treaty of Dancing Rabbit Creek, signed in 1830, deemed removal voluntary and provided land grants and citizenship for those who chose to remain in Mississippi. Approximately 5,000 Choctaws decided to stay in Mississippi. Seven communities, which coincide with the reservation's current community centers, grew from where they congregated. The band's initial isolation largely accounts for the persistent use of their native language. Since 1979, the Choctaw have experienced phenomenal economic growth, largely due to lucrative gaming operations. In 2002, the Mississippi Choctaw Tribe was the second largest employer in the state and the single largest employer in Neshoba County."[9]

"The Mississippi Band of Choctaw Indians is one of three federally recognized tribes of Choctaw Native Americans, and the only one in this state. On April 20, 1945, this band organized under the Indian Reorganization Act of 1934. Also in 1945 the Choctaw Indian Reservation was created in Mississippi by the

---

[9] Indian Nations of North America, p. 92-96, para. 1-5

Introduction

federal government by acquisition of lands in Neshoba, Leake, Newton, Scott, Jones, Attala, Kemper, and Winston counties. Other federally recognized tribes are the Choctaw Nation of Oklahoma, the largest, and the Jena Band of Choctaw Indians, a small group located in Louisiana.

By a deed dated August 18, 2008, the state returned *Nanih Waiya* in Mississippi to the Choctaw. This ancient earthwork mound and site, built ca. 1-300 CE, has been venerated by the Choctaw since the 17th century as a sacred place of origin of their ancestors. The Mississippi Band of Choctaw have made August 18 a tribal holiday to celebrate their regaining control of the sacred site.

The historic Choctaw had emerged as a tribe and occupied substantial territory in what is now considered the state of Mississippi. In the early nineteenth century, they were under increasing pressure by European Americans, who wanted to acquire their land for agricultural development. President Andrew Jackson gained congressional passage of the Indian Removal Act in 1830 to accomplish this and extinguish Native American land claims in the Southeast.

The chiefs signed the Treaty of Dancing Rabbit Creek with the United States, which was ratified by the U.S. Senate on February 25, 1831. President Jackson was anxious to make the Choctaw removal a model for other tribes to be taken out of the Southeast to territory well west of the Mississippi River. After ceding close to 11 million acres (45,000 km^2), the Choctaw were to emigrate in three stages; the first in the fall of 1831, the second in 1832, and the last in 1833. Although the removals continued into the early 20th century, some Choctaw remained in Mississippi. They continued to live in their ancient homeland. According to the terms of removal, the nearly 5000 Choctaw who remained in Mississippi became citizens of the state and United States.

For the next ten years, they were subject to increasing legal conflict, harassment, and intimidation by white settlers. Racism against them was rampant. The Choctaw described their situation in 1849, we have had our habitations torn down and burned, our fences destroyed, cattle turned into our fields and we ourselves have been scourged, manacled, fettered and otherwise personally abused, until by such treatment some of our best men have died.

Introduction

In 2002, the United States Congress formally recognized the entire Choctaw Nation in 25 U.S.C. 1779, including those Choctaw in Mobile and Washington counties, Alabama. They were described as Full-Blooded Choctaw equally and in the same Mississippi Choctaw Jurisdictional Act of 1934, by which the Mississippi Band of Choctaw reorganized.

After nearly two hundred years, the Mississippi Band of Choctaw have retaken control of the ancient site of *Nanih Waiya*, an earthwork mound built about 300-600CE. They have traditionally venerated this site as their place of origin and the home of their ancestors. For years the state protected the site as a Mississippi state park. It returned *Nanih Waiya* to the Choctaw in 2006, under Mississippi Legislature State Bill 2803.

The deed was signed on August 18, 2008, which the Choctaw have made a tribal holiday. They have celebrated the day since, and made it an occasion for telling stories of their origin and history, serving traditional foods, and conducting related dances.

Old Choctaw country included dozens of towns, such as Lukfata, Koweh Chito, Oka Hullo, Pante, Osapa Chito, Oka Cooply, and Yanni Achukma, located in and around Neshoba and Kemper counties.

The Choctaw regularly traveled hundreds of miles from their homes for long periods of time, moving to seasonal hunting grounds in the winter. They set out early in the fall and returned to their reserved lands at the opening of spring to plant their gardens. At that time they visited the Europeans at Columbus, Mississippi; Macon, Brooksville, and Crawford, and the region where Yazoo City now is located.
Presently, the Mississippi Choctaw Indian Reservation has eight communities.

- Bogue Chitto or "Bok Cito", Mississippi
- Bogue Homa [20]
- Conehatta
- Crystal Ridge
- Henning, Tennessee
- Pearl River

Introduction

    Red Water

    Tucker

    Standing Pine

These communities are located in parts of nine counties throughout the state. The largest concentration of land is in Neshoba County, at 32°48'56"N 89°14'46"W32.81556°N 89.24611°W, which comprises more than two-thirds of the reservation's land area and holds more than 62 percent of its population, as of the 2000 census. The total land area is 84.282 km² (32.541 sq mi), and its official total resident population was 5,190 persons. The nine counties are Neshoba, Newton, Leake, Kemper, Jones, Winston, Attala, Jackson, and Scott counties."[10]

This work was originally published in 1997 and has been expanded upon through careful study by reading many sources. Also while going through the film it was made sure that nothing was left out and every piece of information placed within these pages is in the same order it was found. Other than stating everyone is human and makes mistakes the best care possible was taken to make sure you'll find what you are looking for. You will find after this introduction a copy of the Treaty of Dancing Rabbit Creek both in original form and transcribed by the author so you will be able to read it without having to work so hard while trying to understand what it says. The information contained within this two book series was obtained from National Archival Microfilm rolls M-595 Rolls 41 and 42, NATIVE AMERICAN CENSUS ROLLS 1885-1940; Volume I; Choctaw of Mississippi; 1929-1932; with Birth and Death Rolls, 1924-1932. Then in Volume II you will find numerous categories or classifications titled the Choctaw Censuses of 1933 and 1934, Supplemental Rolls for 1934-35, Addition Rolls 1934-35, Addition Roll Unreported Births 1935, Deduction Rolls 1934-35, Birth Rolls 1934, Unreported Births 1934, Death Rolls 1934-36, Supplemental Census Roll 1935 (Header 1936), Marriages 1936, Census Roll 1937, Births Roll 1, (2 missing), and 3 as of 1936 Unreported Births. Births January 1 to December 31, 1936, then the same for 1934-33 and 1932. Then Death Rolls 1936, Unreported Deaths 1935-36 through 1932 (All reported backwards in years).

---

[10] Wikipedia, Mississippi Band of Choctaw Indians

Introduction

Supplemental Roll 1938 (Live Births 1937), All Other Additions 1937, Unreported Births 1937. Marriages 1937, Deaths 1937, Births 1938, Unreported Births 1938, Omissions 1938 and Marriages 1939 (No Marriages listed within material for 1938). Deaths 1938, Deaths Not Reported prior to 1938 (Occurring between 1933-37), 1938 Transfer or Adjustment Roll (Corrections in sex 1-1-1939), Added Females on account of error in sex, and finally Indians returning to jurisdiction where enrolled as of 1-1-1939. The table of contents hopefully will bring a little order to these pages but it was felt that you should know what course this material took while transcribing, since it was felt that the recorders failed in many instances to understand the term chronological order.

This piece was a mass of difficult record keeping while having to roam through each page and wonder what were the recorders thinking, while listing people's names under every circumstance. These people just wanted respect and order in their lives, they just wanted to keep their traditions and culture alive and be remembered by their people. They just wanted to take care of their loved ones. From studies made by this author it seems as though they have done a wonderful job to this point in time. This transcription is dedicated to those within these pages and their descendants.

Jeff Bowen
NativeStudy.com

[Copy of the Original]

Treaty of Dancing Rabbit Creek

1830
~~1831~~

Treaty with the Choctaws
Sep. 15. 27. 1830
And 28th Sep.r 1830
Ratified Feb.y 24th 1831.

A treaty of perpetual friendship, cession and limits entered into by John H Eaton and John Coffee for and in behalf of the Government of the United States and the Mingoes Chiefs Captains and Warriors of the Choctaw Nation begun and held at Dancing Rabbit Creek on the 15th of September in the year 1830.

Whereas the General Assembly of the State of Mississippi has extended the laws of said State to persons and property within the chartered limits of the same and the President of the United States has said that he cannot protect the Choctaw people from the operation of these laws; Now therefore that the Choctaw may live under their own laws in peace with the United States and the State of Mississippi they have determined to sell their lands east of the Mississippi & have accordingly agreed to the following articles of treaty —

Article 1st

Perpetual peace and friendship is pledged and agreed upon by and between the United States and the Mingoes, Chiefs, & Warriors of the Choctaw Nation of Red People; and that this may be considered the treaty existing between the parties all other treaties heretofore existing & unconstrued jointly the provision of other extinguished hereby declared null and void. —

Article 2nd

The United States under a grant specially to be made by the President of the U.S. shall cause to be conveyed to the Choctaw Nation a tract of Country west of the Mississippi River, beginning near Fort Smith where the Arkansas boundary crosses the Arkansas River, Running thence west to the source of the Canadian fork; if in the limits of the United States, or to those limits; thence due South to Red River, and down Red River to the West boundary of the Territory of Arkansas; thence North along that line to the beginning the boundary of the same to be agreeable, to the treaty made and concluded at Washington City in the year 1825. The grant to be executed so soon as the present treaty shall be ratified.——— Article 3rd

In consideration of the provisions contained in the several articles of this Treaty, the Choctaw Nation of Indians consent, and hereby cede to the United States, the entire Country they own and posess, East of the Mississippi River, and they agree to remove beyond the Mississippi River, early as practicable, and will so arrange thier removal, that as many as possible of thier people not exceeding one half of the whole number, shall depart during the falls of 1831 and 1832; the residue to follow during the succeeding fall of 1833; a better opportunity in this manner will be afforded the Government, to extend to them the facilities and comforts which it is desireable should be extended in conveying them to thier new Homes.——— Article 4th

The Government and people of the United States are hereby obliged to secure to the said Choctaw Nation of Red People the Jurisdiction and Government, of all the Persons & Property that may be within thier limits West, so that no territory or State shall ever have a right to pass laws for the Government of the Choctaw Nation of Red People & thier Descendants; and that no part of the land granted them shall ever be embraced in any territory or State; but the U.S. shall forever secure said Choctaw Nation from, & against, all laws except such as from time to time may be enacted in thier own National Councils, not inconsistent with the Constitution, Treaties, and laws of the United States; & except such as may, & which have been enacted by Congress, to the extent that Congress under the Constitution are required to excerscise a legislation over Indian affairs. But the Choctaws, should this treaty be ratified, express a wish that Congress may grant to the Choctaws the right of punishing by their own laws, any white man who shall come into their Nation, & infringe any of their National regulations

Article 5th

The United States are obliged to protect the Choctaws from domestic strife & from foreign enemies on the same principles that the Citizens of the United States are protected, so that whatever would be a legal demand upon the U.S, for defence or for wrongs committed by an Enemy, on a Citizen of the U.S, shall be equally binding on the favour of the Choctaws, & in all cases where the Choctaws shall be called upon by a legally authorized Officer of the U.S. to fight an Enemy, such Choctaw shall receive the pay & other emoluments, which Citizens of the U.S. receive in such cases, provided, no war shall be undertaken or prosecuted by said Choctaw Nation but by declaration made in full Council, & to be approved by the U.S. unless it be in self defence against an open rebellion or against an enemy marching into their Country, in which cases they shall defend, until the U.S. are advised thereof.

Article 6th

Should a Choctaw or any party of Choctaws commit acts of violence upon the person or property of a Citizen of the U.S, or join any war party against any neighbouring tribe of Indians, without the authority in the foreceding article; & except to oppose an actual or threatened invasion or rebellion, such person so offending, shall be delivered up to an Officer of the U.S. if in the power of the Choctaw Nation, that such Offender may be punished as may be provided in such cases, by the laws of the U.S.; but if such Offender is not within the control of the Choctaw Nation, then said Choctaw Nation shall not be held responsible for the injury done by said Offender.

Article 7th

All acts of violence committed upon persons and property of the people of the Choctaw Nation either by Citizens of the U.S. or Neighbouring tribes of Red people, shall be reffered to some authorized agent, by him to be reffered to the President of the U.S, who shall examine into such cases and see that every possible degree of justice is done to said Indian party of the Choctaw Nation —

Article 8th

Offenders against the laws of the U.S. or any individual State shall be apprehended & delivered to any duly authorized person where such Offender may be found in the Choctaw Country, having fled from any part of U.S. but in all such cases application must be made to the Agent or Chiefs & the expence of his apprehension and delivery provided for & paid by the U. States,

Article 9th

Any Citizen of the U.S. who may be ordered from the Nation by the Agent & Constituted Authorities of the Nation and refusing to obey or return into the Nation without the Consent of the aforesaid persons, shall be subject to such pains and penalties as may be provided by the laws of the U.S. in such cases. Citizens of the U.S. travelling peaceably under the authority of the laws of the U.S. shall be under the care & protection of the Nation

Article 10th

No person shall expose goods or other article for sale as a trader, without a written permit from the Constituted Authorities of the Nation, or authority of the laws of the Congress of the U.S. under penalty of forfeiting the Articles, & the Constituted authorities of the Nation shall grant no license except to such persons as reside in the Nation and are answerable to the Laws of the Nation. The U.S. shall be particularly obliged to assist in preventing ardent spirits from being introduced into the Nation

Article 11th

Navigable streams shall be free to the Choctaws who shall pay no higher toll or duty than Citizens of the U.S. It is agreed further that the U.S. shall establish one or more Post Offices in said Nation, & may establish such Military post roads, and posts, as they may consider necessary

Article 12th

All intruders shall be removed from the Choctaw Nation and kept without it: Private property to be always respected & on no occasion taken for public purposes without just compensation being made therefor to the rightful owner. If an Indian unlawfully take or steal any property from a White Man a citizen of the U.S. the offender shall be punished. And if a white Man unlawfully take or steal anything from an Indian, the property shall be restored & the offender punished. It is further agreed that, when a Choctaw shall be given up to be tried for any offence against the laws of the U.S. if unable to employ Counsel to defend him, the U.S. will do it, that his trial may be fair and impartial

Article 13th

It is consented that a qualified Agent shall be appointed for the Choctaws every four Years, unless sooner removed by the President; and he shall be removed on petition of the Constituted Authorities of the Nation the President, being satisfied there is sufficient cause shown. The Agent shall fix his residence convenient to the great body of the people; & in the selection of an Agent immediately after the ratification of this Treaty, the wishes of the Choctaw Nation on the subject shall be entitled to great respect

Article 14th

Each Choctaw head of a family being desirous to remain & become a Citizen of the States, shall be permitted to do so, by signifying his intention to the Agent within Six Months from the ratification of this Treaty, He She shall thereupon be entitled to a reservation of one Section of Six Hundred and forty Acres of Land, to be bounded by sectional lines of survey; in like Manner he shall be entitled to one half that quantity for each unmarried child which is living with him over Ten Years of Age, & a quarter Section to such child as may be under 10 years of age, to adjoin the location of the Parent. If they reside upon said lands intending to become Citizens of the States for five Years after the ratification of this Treaty in that Case a grant in fee simple shall issue; said reservation shall include the present improvements of the head of the family, or a portion of it. Persons who claim under this Article shall not loose the priviledge of a Choctaw Citizen, but if they ever remove are not to be entitled to any portion of the Choctaw Annuity; ~~~~~~

Article 15th

To each of the Chiefs in the Choctaw Nation (to wit) Greenwood Laflore, Nutackachie, and Mushulatubbe there is granted a reservation of four Sections of land; two of which shall include and adjoin their present improvements; & the other two located where they please but on unoccupied unimproved lands, such sections shall be bounded by sectional lines, & with the consent of the President they may sell the same. Also to the three principal Chiefs & their successors in office there shall be paid Two Hundred and fifty Dollars

Annually, while they shall continue in thier respective offices, except to Mushulatubbe who as he has an annuity of One Hundred &fifty Dollars for life under a former treaty, shall receive only the additional sum of One Hundred Dollars, while he shall continue in office as Chief; & if in addition to this the Nation shall think propper to elect an additional principal Chief of the whole to superintend and govern upon republican principles he shall receive annually for his services Five Hundred Dollars, which allowance to the Chiefs and thier Successors in office, shall continue for Twenty Years, At any time when in Military service, & while in service by authority of the U.S. the district Chiefs under and by selection of the President shall be entitled to the pay of Majors; the other Chief under the same Circumstances shall have the pay of a Lieutenant-Colonel. The speakers of the three districts, shall receive Twenty five Dollars a Year for four Years, & the three Secretaries one to each of the Chiefs, fifty Dollars for four years. Each Captain of the Nation, the number not to exceed Ninety nine, thirty three from each District shall be furnished upon removing to the West, with each a good suit of clothes & a broad Sword as an outfit; & for four years commencing with the first of thier removal, shall each receive Fifty Dollars a Year, for ~~four years~~ the trouble of keeping thier people ~~its~~ order in settling; & whenever they shall be in Military service by authority of the U.S. shall receive the pay of a captain

Article 14th

In waggons, & with Steam Boats as may be found necessary the U.S. agrees to remove the Indians to thier new Homes at thier expense and under the care of discreet and carefull persons, who will be kind & brotherly to them. They agree to furnish them with ample corn and beef, or pork for themselves & families for Twelve months after reaching thier new homes.

It is agreed further that the U.S. will take all thier cattle, at the valuation of some discreet person to be appointed by the President, & the same shall be paid for in Money after thier arrival at thier new homes; or in other cattle such as may be desired shall be furnished them, notice being given through thier Agent of thier wishes upon this subject before thier removal that time to supply the demand may be afforded.

Article 17th

The several Annuities and sums secured under former Treaties to the Choctaw Nation and People shall continue as tho. this Treaty had never been made. And it is further agreed that the U.S. in addition will pay the sum of Twenty thousand Dollars for Twenty Years, Commencing after thier removal to the West, of which, in the first year after thier removal, Ten thousand Dollars shall be divided and arranged to such as may not receive reservations under this Treaty.

Article 18th

The U.S. shall cause the lands hereby ceded to be surveyed, & surveyors may enter the Choctaw Country for that purpose, Conducting themselves properly & disturbing or interrupting none of the Choctaw people. But no person is to be permitted to settle within the Nation, or the lands to be sold before the Choctaws shall remove. And for the payment of the several amounts secured in this Treaty, the lands hereby ceded are to remain a fund pledged to that purpose, until the debt shall be provided for and arranged. And further it is agreed, that in the construction of this Treaty whereever well founded doubt shall arise, it shall be construed most favourably towards the Choctaws.

Article 19th

The following reservations of land are hereby admitted. To Col. David Fulsom Four sections of which Two shall include his present improvements, & two may be located elsewhere, on unoccupied, unimproved land.

To S. Garland, Col. Robert Cole, Tuppanahomer, John Pytchlyn, Charles Juzan, Tohokebetubbe, Eaychahobia, Ofehoma two sections each, to include their improvements, and to be bounded by sectional lines, & the same may be disposed of and sold with the consent of the President. And that others not provided for, may be provided for, there shall be reserved as follows.

First, One section to each head of a family not exceeding Forty in number, who during the present year, may have had in actual cultivation, with a dwelling House thereon Fifty Acres or more. Secondly three quarter sections after the manner aforesaid to each head of a family not exceeding Four Hundred and Sixty, as shall have cultivated Thirty Acres and less than Fifty, to be bounded by quarter schorn lines of survey, & to be contiguous & adjoining.

Third, One half section as aforesaid to those who shall have cultivated from Twenty to Thirty Acres the number not to exceed Four Hundred. Fourth, a quarter section as aforesaid to such as shall have cultivated from twelve to twenty Acres, the number not to exceed three hundred and fifty, and one half that quantity to such as shall have cultivated from two to twelve Acres, the number also not to exceed three hundred and fifty persons. Each of said class of cases shall be subject to the limitations contained in the first class, & shall be so located as to include that part of the improvement which contains the dwelling House. If a greater number shall be found to be entitled to reservations under the several classes of this article, than is stipulated for under the limitation prescribed, then & in that case the Chiefs separately or together shall determine the persons who shall be excluded in the respective districts. Fifth; Any Captain the number not to exceed Ninety persons, who under the provisions of this article shall receive less than a section, he shall be entitled, to an additional quantity of half a section adjoining to his other reservation. The several reservations secured under this Article, may be sold with the consent of the President of the U.S., but should any prefer it, or omit to take a reservation for the quantity he may be entitled to the U.S. will on his removing pay fifty cents an acre, after reaching their new homes, provided that before the first of January next they shall adduce to the Agent or some other authorized person to be appointed, proof of his claim & the quantity of it. Sixth; likewise children of Choctaw residing in the Nation, who have neither Father nor Mother a list of which, with satisfactory proof of Parentage and Orphanage being filed with Agent in six months to be forwarded to the War Department, shall be entitled to a quarter section of Land, to be located under the direction of the President, & with his consents the same may be sold and the proceeds applied to some beneficial purpose for the benefit of said Orphans —

Article 20th

The U.S. agree & stipulate as follows, that for the benefit and advantage of the Choctaw people, & to improve their condition, their shall be educated under the direction of the President & at the expense of the U.S. forty Choctaw Youths for Twenty years. This number shall be kept at School, & as they finish their education others to supply their places shall be received for the period stated. The U.S. agree also to erect a Council House for the Nation at some convenient central point, after their people shall be settled, & a House for each Chief, also a church for each of the three Districts, to be used also as school

Houses, until the Nation may conclude to build others; & for these purposes Ten thousand Dollars shall be appropriated; Also Fifty thousand Dollars (Viz) Twenty Five Hundred Dollars Annually shall be given for the support of three Teachers of schools for Twenty Years. Likewise there shall be furnished to the Nation, three Blacksmiths one for each District for Sixteen Years, & a qualified Mill wright for five years, Also there shall be furnished the following articles, Twenty One Hundred Blankets, To each warrior who emigrates a rifle, Moulds, Wipers and ammunition. One thousand Axes, Ploughs, Hoes, Wheels and Cards each; And four Hundred looms. There shall also be furnished One Ton of Iron & two hundred Weight of Steel Annually to each District for Sixteen years.

Article 21st

A few Choctaw Warriors yet survive who marched and fought in the Army with General Wayne the whole number stated not to exceed Twenty. These it is agreed shall hereafter while they live receive Twenty Five dollars a year. A list of them to be early as practicable, & within Six Months made out, and presented to the Agent to be forwarded to the War Department,—

Article 22d

The Chiefs of the Choctaws have suggested that their people are in a state of rapid advancement in education and refinement, and have expressed a solicitude that they might have the priviledge of a Delegate on the floor of the House of Representatives extended to them. The Commissioners do not feel, that they can under a treaty stipulation accede to the request, but at their desire, present it in the Treaty, that Congress may consider of and decide the application.

Done and Signed and executed by the Commissioners of the United States and the Chiefs Captains and Head Men of the Choctaw Nation at Dancing Rabbit Creek this 27th day of September Eighteen Hundred and Thirty.

his mark

In Presence of   Jn° H Eaton (seal)

E Breathitt Secty   Jn° Coffee (seal)
to the Commrs

William Ward   Greenwood LeFlore (seal)
for Choctaws.   Musholatubbee (seal) X
    Nittuckachee (seal) X
John Pitchlynn   Eyarhoculltubbee (seal) X
US Intr.   Iyacho hopia (seal) X
M Mackey   Offahoomah (seal) X
US Intr.   Archatatem (seal) X
Geol Gaines   Onnee hubbee (seal) X
of Alabama   Holarter hoomah (seal) X
R P Currin   Hopiauncha hubbee (seal) X
Lepe Howard   Tishomingo (seal) X
Sam S. Worcester   Captain Thlucko (seal) X
Jno N Byrn   James Shield (seal) X
John Bell   Pistiyoubbee (seal) X
Fred Ward   Tobaksuncha hubbee (seal) X
    Holubbee (seal)
    Robert Cole (seal) X
    Mokelarcharhopia (seal) X
    Lewis Perry (seal) X
    Artonamastubbee (seal) X
    Hopiaytubbee (seal) X
    Hoshahoomah (seal) X
    Chuassa hoomah (seal) X
    Joseph Kincaide (seal) X
    Artooka bee turshka (seal) X
    Ahetubbee (seal) X
    Arsarkatubbee (seal) X
    Issater hoomah X

Chohtahmatahah	(Seal)	X
Tunnuppashubbee	(Seal)	X
Okechanyer	(Seal)	X
Hoshlopia	(Seal)	X
Warshartha lopia	(Seal)	X
Moarshunchahubbee	(Seal)	X
Mistaayubbee	(Seal)	X
Daniel McCurtain	(Seal)	X
Tushkerharcho	(Seal)	X
Hoktoontubbee	(Seal)	X
Nukmaarehookmantubbee	(Seal)	X
Mingo hoomah	(Seal)	X
Pisinhocuttatubbee	(Seal)	X
Tullarhachen	(Seal)	X
Little leader	(Seal)	X
Moankutter	(Seal)	X
Cowe hoomah	(Seal)	X
Tillamoer	(Seal)	X
Immellacha	(Seal)	X
Artopulachubbee	(Seal)	X
Shushher unchahubbee	(Seal)	X
Nitter hoomah	(Seal)	X
Ockloryubbee	(Seal)	X
Pakumma	(Seal)	X
Arpalar	(Seal)	X
Hotben	(Seal)	X
Hopanmingo	(Seal)	X
Isparhoomah	(Seal)	X
Lieberhoomah	(Seal)	X
Tohoholantes	(Seal)	X
Alaarzarchubbee	(Seal)	X
Arlantes	(Seal)	X
Nittakubbee	(Seal)	X
Tihonowar	(Seal)	X
Warshar cha hooma 2	(Seal)	X

Isaac James
Hopiaintuckken X
Aryoshkanna X
Shemota X
Hopiaisketuna X
Thomas Leflore
Arnoke o hatubbee X
Shokoperlukna X
Poshenhoomah X
Robert Folsom
Arharyotubbee X
Tushonolanten X
James Vaughan
James Kanses
Tishohakubbee X
Narhnales X
Pennasha X
Inharyarken X
M. tubbee X
Nerharyubbee X
Ishmaryubbee X
Anninata James M King
Lewis Wilson
Istonerkerharcho XX
Hoskincha manterher XX
Kenneeashabbee
Oyartunstubbee X
Sam.l Garland
Thomas Wall
Sam.l Worcester
Jacob Folsom
William Foster
Ontiserharcho X
Hughes Foster
Prince Juzan

Mr. Pitchlynn Jr.	Sial	
David Folsom	Sial	
Sholohommatubbe	ad	×
Tisho	Sial	×
Lauwechubee	Sial	×
Hoshehomma	Sial	×
Ofenowa	Sial	×
Ahekoche	Sial	×
Kaloshaubee	Sial	×
Atoko	Sial	×
Ishtomeche	Sial	×
Smith tahabe	Sial	×
Silas D. Fisher	Sial	
Isaac Folsom	Sial	+
Hekatube	Sial	+
Haksehe	Sial	×
Jenny Carney	Sial	+
John Washington	Sial	×
Phipslip	Sial	×
Meshamuye	Sial	+
Ishtehera	Sial	+
Heshohomma	Sial	
John McKelbeny	Sial	+
Benjn. James	Sial	
Ikbachahambe	Sial	×
Aholiktube	Sial	✓
Walking Wolf	Sial	+
John Waiele	Sial	×
Big Ace	Sial	+
Bob	Sial	×
Tishkochaubbe	Sial	+
Atape	Sial	×
Tishowakaye	Sial	

Holatamaha	Seal x
John Garland	Seal x
Koshona	Seal x
Ishteyohomube	Seal x
Oklanowa	Seal x
Neta	Seal x
James Fletcher	Seal x
Silas D Pitchlynn	Seal
Mr William Trahern	Seal
Josh Kahemmitta	Seal x
Tethataye	Seal x
Emoklashahopie	Seal x
Ishoimuta	Seal x
Thomas The Foster	Seal
Badoc Brashears	

Levi Perkins	Seal	X
Isaac Perry	Seal	X
Ishtonocka Hoomah	Seal	w
Hiram King	Seal	
Ogla Enlah	Seal	XX
Nukelahtubbee	Seal	XX
Inska Hollattah	Seal	XX
Panshatubbee	Seal	X
P P Pitchlynn	Seal	
Sul Hosie		
Sofia Henakey	Seal	+
Fischoomma	Seal	+
William Wade	Seal	+
Pansh Stick ubbee	Seal	+
Ho lit tant chah ubbee	Seal	+
Ka want chah ubbee	Seal	
Cyarhpalubbee	Seal	X
Okentah ubbee	Seal	+
Living War Club	Seal	+
John Jones	Seal	
Charles Jones	Seal	
Isaac Jones	Seal	x
Hooklucha	Seal	+
Muscogee	Seal	+
Eden Nelson	Seal	

In the Senate of the United States
February 21st: 1831.

Resolved, (two thirds of the Senators present concurring,) That the Senate do advise and consent to the ratification of the Treaty, between the United States of America and the Mingoes, Chiefs, Captains and Warriors of the Choctaw Nation, concluded at Dancing Rabbit Creek on the 15th of September 1830, together with the supplement thereto, concluded at the same place the 28th of September 1830; with the exception of the preamble.

Attest,
Walter Lowrie

Andrew Jackson,
President of the United States of America,
To all and singular to whom these presents shall come, Greeting:

Whereas a Treaty between the United States of America, and the Mingoes, Chiefs, Captains and Warriors of the Choctaw Nation was entered into at Dancing Rabbit Creek, on the twenty-seventh day of September in the Year of our Lord one thousand eight hundred and thirty, and of the Independence of the United States, the fifty-fifth, by John H. Eaton and John Coffee, Commissioners on the part of the United

States, and the Chiefs, Captains and Head-Men of the Choctaw Nation, on the part of said Nation;— which Treaty, together with the Supplemental article thereto, is in the words following, To wit:

A Treaty

Various Choctaw persons have been presented by the chiefs of the Nation with a desire that they might be provided for, Being particularly deserving, an earnestness has been manifested that provision might be made for them, It is therefore by the undersigned Commissioners here assented to with the understanding that they are to have No interest in the reservations which are devoted and provided for under the general Treaty to which this is a Supplement.

As evidence of the liberal and Kind feelings of the President and Government of the United States the Commissioners agree to the request as follows (to wit) Pierre Suzan, Peter Pitchlynn, G. W. Harkins, Jack Pitchlynn, Israel Fulsom, Louis Laflore, Benjamin James, Joel H Nail, Hopoyuahubbee, Onahubbee, Benjamin Laflore, Michael Laflore, Peter Gates & wife, shall be entitled to a reservation of two sections of land each to include their improvement where they at present reside, with the exception of the three first named & Benj. Lefflore persons, who are authorized to locate one of their sections on any other unimproved and unoccupied land, within their respective districts.

Article 2d

And to each of the following persons there is allowed a reservation of a section and a half of land, (to wit) James L. McDonald, Robert Jones, Noah Wall, James Campbell, G. Nelson, And Vaughn Brasheans, R. Harris, Little Leader, D. Foster, J. Vaughn, L. Durant, Samuel Long, J. Magagha, Thos. Everge, Giles Thompson, Garland, John Bond, William Laflore, and Turner Brasheans; the two first named persons, may locate one section each, and one section jointly on any unimproved and unoccupied land, these not residing in the Nation, The others are to include their present residence and improvement.

Also one Section is allowed to the following persons (to wit) Middleton Mackey, Mosley Train – Charleston Moses Foster, D. McWall, Charles Scott

Molly Nail, Susan Colbert who was formerly Susan James, Saml Garland, Silas Fisher, D. McCurtain, Oaklahoma, & Polly Fillicuthey, to be located in entire sections to include their present residence and improvement, with the exception of Molly Nail & Susan Colberts, who are authorized to locate theirs, on any unimproved unoccupied land.

John Pitchlynn has long and faithfully served the Nation in character of U. States interpreter, he has acted as such for forty years, in Consideration it is agreed, in addition to what has been done for him there shall be granted to two of his Children, (to wit) Silas Pitchlynn, & Thomas Pitchlynn one Section of land each to adjoin the location of their father. Likewise to James Madison and Peter Sons of Mushulatubbee One Section of land each to include the old House and improvement of where their Father formerly lived on the old Military road, adjoining a large Prerarie.

And to Henry Groves son of the Chief Nattieache there is one Section of land given to adjoin his Fathers land.

And to each of the following persons Half a Section of land is granted on any unoccupied and unimproved lands in the Districts where they respectively live (to wit) Willis Harkins, James D Hamilton, William Juzan, Tobias Lefton, Jo Dousley, Jacob Fulsom, P. Hays, Saml. Worcester, Ge. Hunter, William Train and Robert Nail and Alexander McKee.

And there is given a quarter section of land each to Odila and her five fatherless Children, She being a Choctaw woman residing out of the Nation; also the same quantity to Peggy Trihan another Indian Woman residing out of the Nation & her two fatherless Children; & to the widows of Pushmitahoo, & Puck she nubbee, who were formerly distinguished Chiefs of the Nation and for themselves their Children four Sections of land, each in trust for themselves & their Children

All of said last mentioned reservations are to be located under and by direction of the President of the U States

Article 3

The Choctaw people now that they have ceded their lands are solicitous to get to their new Homes early as possible & accordingly they wish that a party may be permitted to proceed this fall to ascertain whereabouts will be most advantageous for their people to be located.

It is therefore agreed that three or four persons (from each of the three districts) under the guidance of some discreet and well qualified persons may proceed during this fall to the West upon an examination of the Country.

For their time and expenses the U States agree to allow the said Twelve persons Two Dollars a day each, not to exceed One Hundred days, which is deemed to be ample time to make an examination.

If necessary Pilots acquainted with the Country will be furnished when they arrive in the West.

Article 4th

John Donly of Alabama who has several Choctaw grand children, and who for Twenty years has carried the mail through the Choctaw Nation, a desire by the Chiefs is expressed that he may have a section of land, it is accordingly granted, to be located in one entire section, on any unimproved & unoccupied Land.

Allen Glover and George S Gaines licensed Traders in the Choctaw Nation, have accounts amounting to upwards of Nine thousand Dollars against the Indians who are unable to pay their said debts without distressing their families; a desire is expressed by the Chiefs that Two sections of land be set apart to be sold and the proceeds thereof to be applied toward the payment of the aforesaid debts. It is agreed that two sections of any unimproved and unoccupied land be granted to George S Gaines who will sell the same for the best price he can obtain and apply the proceeds thereof to the credit of the Indians on their accounts due to the before mentioned Glover and Gaines; & shall make the application to the poorest Indian first

At the earnest and particular request of the Chief Greenwood Leflore there is granted to David Haley One half section of land to be located in a half section on any unoccupied and unimproved land as a compensation for a journey to Washington City with dispatches to the Government and returning others to the Choctaw Nation

The foregoing is entered into, as supplemental to the treaty concluded yesterday.

Done at Dancing Rabbit Creek the 28th day of September 1830

Ind H Eaton

In presence of
E. Breathitte Secty to Com:
W. Ward Agt for Choctaws
M. Mackey U.S. Intr.
John Pitchlynn
U.S. Intr.
G Wivin
J. Pitchlynn
Bo Gaines

The following words in this supplemental were interlined before being signed "2" Article & "Allen Yates a wife" also "Benj Lafluries" "in Nercles Train" — Choctehome "person or persons"

In presence of
E. Breathitte Secty to Com?

Jno Coffee Comr
Greenwood Leflore
Nittuaachee his X mark
Mushulatubbee his X mark
Ofahoma his X mark
Eyarhocuttubbee his X mark
Iyachu Hopia his X mark
Holubbee his X mark
Enarhubbee his X mark
Robert Cole his X mark
Hopiaunchahubbee his X mark
David Folsom
John Garland his X mark
Hopiahommah his X mark
Captain Thluko his X mark
Pierre Juzan
Immastahteha his X mark
Hoshimmastarteha his X mark

Now, therefore, be it known, that I, Andrew Jackson, President of the United States of America, having seen and considered said Treaty, do, in pursuance of the advice and consent of the Senate, as expressed by their Resolution of the twenty-first day of February, one thousand eight hundred and thirty-one, accept, ratify and confirm the same, and every clause and article thereof, with the exception of the Preamble.

In Testimony whereof, I have caused the seal of the United States to be hereunto affixed, having signed the same with my hand.

Done at the City of Washington, this twenty-fourth day of February, in the Year of our Lord one thousand eight hundred and thirty-one, and of the Independence of the United States, the fifty-fifth.

Andrew Jackson

By the President,

M. Van Buren,
Sec'y of State

Treaty of Dancing Rabbit Creek

[Transcription of Original]

Treaty of Dancing Rabbit Creek

1830

~~1831~~

Treaty

with the

Choctaws

Sep. ~~15~~ 27, 1830

And 28th Sep[r] 1930
Ratified Feb[r] 24th 1831

A treaty of perpetual friendship, cession and limits entered into by John H. Eaton and John Coffee for and in behalf of the Government of the United States and the Mingoes Chiefs Captains and Warriors of the Choctaw Nation begun and held at Dancing Rabbit Creek on the 15th of September in the year 1830.

WHEREAS the General Assembly of the State of Mississippi has extended the laws of said State to persons and property within the chartered limits of the same and the President of the United States has said that he cannot protect the Choctaw people from the operation of these laws; Now therefore that the Choctaw may live under their own laws in peace with the United States and the State of Mississippi they have determined to sell their lands east of the Mississippi & have - accordingly agreed to the following articles of treaty ———

Article 1st

Perpetual peace and friendship is pledged and agreed on by and between United States and the Mingoes, Chiefs, & Warriors of the Choctaw Nation of Red People; and that this may be considered the ~~only~~ treaty existing between the parties all other treaties heretofore existing and inconsistent with the provisions of this are hereby declared null and void. ———

Article 2nd

The United States under a grant specially to be made by the President of the U. S. shall cause to be conveyed to the Choctaw Nation a tract of country west of the Mississippi River in fee simple to them & their descendants, to insure to them while they shall, exist as a nation and live on it beginning near Fort Smith where the

Arkansas boundary crosses the Arkansas River, Running thence ~~with~~ to the scource[sic] of the Canadian fork; if in the limits of the United States, or to those limits; thence due South to Red River, and down Red River to the West boundary of the Territory of Arkansas; thence North along that line to the beginning. The boundary of the same to be agreably[sic] to the treaty made and concluded at Washington City in the year 1825 The grant to be executed so soon as the present Treaty shall be ratified ———

Article 3$^{\underline{d}}$

In consideration of the provisions contained in the several articles of this Treaty, the Choctaw Nation of Indians consent and hereby cede to the United States, the entire country they own and possess, East of the Mississippi River; and they agree to remove beyond the Mississippi River, early as practicable, and will so arrange their removal, that as many as possible of thier[sic] people not exceeding one half of the whole number, shall depart during the falls of 1831 and 1832; the residue to follow during the succeeding fall of 1833; a better opportunity in this manner will be afforded the Government, to extend to them the facilities and comforts which it is desirable should be extended in conveying them to thier new Homes. ———

Article 4$^{\underline{th}}$

The Government and people of the United States are hereby obliged to secure to the said Choctaw Nation of Red People the Jurisdiction and Government of all the Persons and Property that may be within thier limits West, so that no territory or State shall ever have a right to pass laws for the Government of the Choctaw Nation of Red People and thier Descendants; and that no part of the land granted them shall ever be embraced in any territory or State; but the U. S. shall forever secure said Choctaw Nation from, & against, all laws except such as from time to time may be enacted in their own National Councils, not inconsistent with the Constitution, Treaties, and laws of the United States; & except such as may, & which have been enacted by Congress, to the extent that Congress under the Constitution are required to exerscise[sic] a legislation over Indian Affairs. But the Choctaws, should this treaty be ratified, express a wish that Congress may grant to the Choctaws the right of punishing by thier own laws, any white man who shall come into thier Nation, & infringe any of their National regulations.

Article 5$^{\underline{th}}$

The United States are obliged to protect the Choctaws from domestic strife & from foreign enemies on the same principles that the citizens of the United States are protected, so that whatever would be a legal demand upon the U. S. for defence[sic] or for wrongs committed by an Enemy, on a Citizen of the U. S, shall be equally binding

Treaty of Dancing Rabbit Creek

in favour[sic] of the Choctaws, & in all cases where the Choctaws shall be called upon by a legally authorized officer of the U. S. to fight an Enemy, such Choctaw shall receive the pay & other emoluments, which citizens of the U. S. receive in such cases, provided, no war shall be undertaken or prosecuted by said Choctaw Nation but by declaration made in full Council, & to be approved by the U. S. unless it be in self defence against an open rebellion or against an enemy marching into thier country, in which cases they shall defend, until the U. S. are advised thereof.

Article 6th

Should a Choctaw or any party of Choctaws commit acts of violence upon the person or property of a citizen of the U. S, or join any war party against any neighbouring[sic] tribe of Indians, without the authority in the preceding article; & except to oppose an actual or threatened invasion or rebellion, such person so offending shall be delivered up to an Officer of the U. S. if in the power of the Choctaw Nation, that such offender may be punished as may be provided in such cases, by the laws of the U. S.; but if such Offender is not within the control of the Choctaw Nation, then said Choctaw Nation shall not be held responsible for the injury done by said offender.

Article 7th

All acts of violence committed upon persons and property of the ~~Cho~~ people of the Choctaw Nation either by Citizens of the U. S. or neighbouring[sic] tribes of Red people, shall be referred to some authorized agent by him to be referred to the ~~U.S.~~ President of the U. S, who shall examine into such cases and see that every possible degree of justice is done to said Indian party of the Choctaw Nation.

Article 8th

Offenders against the laws of the U. S. or any individual State shall be apprehended & delivered to any duly authorized person where such offender may be found in the Choctaw Country, having fled from any part of U. S. but in all such cases application must be made to the Agent or Chiefs & the expense of his apprehension and delivery provided for & paid by the U States.

Article 9th

Any citizen of the U. S. who may be ordered from the Nation by the Agent & constituted authorities of the Nation and refusing to obey or return into the Nation without the consent of the aforesaid persons, shall be subject to such pains and penalties as may provided by the laws of the U. S. in such cases. Citizens of the U. S.

travelling peaceably under the authority of the laws of the U. S. shall be under the care and protection of the Nation.

Article 10th

No person shall expose goods or other article for sale as a trader, without a written permit from the constituted authorities of the Nation, or authority of the laws of the Congress of the U. S. under penalty of forfeiting the articles, & the constituted authorities of the Nation shall grant no license except to such persons as reside in the Nation and are answerable to the laws of the Nation. The U. S. shall be particularly obliged to assist to prevent ardent spirits from being introduced into the Nation.

Article 11th

Navigable streams shall be free to the Choctaws who shall pay no higher toll or duty than Citizens of the U. S. It is agreed further that the U. S. shall establish one or more Post Offices in said Nation, & may establish such military post roads, and posts, as they may consider necessary.

Article 12th

All intruders shall be removed from the Choctaw Nation and kept without it. Private property to be always respected & on no occasion taken for public purposes without just compensation being made therefor to the rightful owner. If an Indian unlawfully take or steal any property from a white man a citizen of the U. S. the offender shall be punished. And if a white man unlawfully take or steal any thing from an Indian, the property shall be restored & the offender punished. It is further agreed that when a Choctaw shall be given up to be tried for any offence against the laws of the U. S. if unable to employ Counsel to defend him, the U. S. will do it, that his trial may be fair and impartial.

Article 13th

It is consented that a qualified Agent shall be appointed for the Choctaws every Four Years, unless sooner removed by the President; and he shall be removed on petition of the constituted authorities of the Nation the President being satisfied there is sufficient cause shown. The Agent shall fix his residence convenient to the great body of the people; & in the selection of an Agent immediately after the ratification of this Treaty, the wishes of the Choctaw Nation on the subject shall be entitled to great respect.

Treaty of Dancing Rabbit Creek

Article 14th

Each Choctaw head of a family being desirous to remain & become a Citizen of the States, shall be permitted to do so, by signifying his intention to the Agent within Six Months from the ratification of this Treaty & he or she shall thereupon be entitled to a reservation of one section of Six Hundred and forty Acres of Land, to be bounded by sectional lines of survey; in like manner shall be entitled to one half that quantity for each unmarried child which is living with him over Ten years of Age; & a quarter section to such child as be under 10 years of age, to adjoin the location of the Parent. If they reside upon said lands intending to become Citizens of the States for five Years after the ratification of this Treaty in that case a grant in fee simple shall issue; said reservation shall include the present improvement of the head of the family, or a portion of it. Persons who claim under this article shall not lose the privilege of a Choctaw Citizen, but if they ever remove are not to be entitled to any portion of the Choctaw Annuity;

Article 15th

To each of the Chiefs in the Choctaw Nation (to wit) Greenwood Laflore Nutackachie, and Mushulatubbe there is granted a reservation of four sections of land, two of which shall include and adjoin thier[sic] present improvement, and the other two located where they please but on unoccupied unimproved lands, such sections shall be bounded by sectional lines, & with the consent of the President they may sell the same. Also to the three principal Chiefs & to their successors in office there shall be paid Two Hundred and fifty Dollars annually while they shall continue in their respective offices, except to Mushulatubbe who as he has an annuity of One Hundred & fifty Dollars for life under a former treaty, shall receive only the additional sum of One Hundred Dollars, while he shall continue in office as Chief; & if in addition to this the Nation shall think propper[sic] to elect an additional principal Chief of the whole to superintend and govern upon republican principles he shall receive annually for his services Five Hundred Dollars, which allowance to the Chiefs and their successors in office, shall continue for Twenty Years. At any time when in Military Service, & while in service by authority of the U. S. the district Chiefs under and by selection of the President shall be entitled to the pay of Majors; the other Chief under the same circumstances shall have the pay of a Lieutenant-Colonel. The speakers of the three districts, shall receive Twenty five Dollars a year for four years ~~each~~ for four years each & the three secretaries one to each of the Chiefs, fifty dollars each for four years. Each Captain of the Nation, the number not to exceed ninety nine, thirty three from each District shall be furnished upon removing to the West, with each a good suit of clothes & a broad sword as an outfit, & for four years commencing with the first of thier removal, shall each receive Fifty Dollars a Year, for the trouble of keeping thier people at order in settling; & whenever they shall be in military service by authority of the U. S. shall receive the pay of a captain.

Article 16th

In wagons; & with steam boats as may be found necessary the U. S. agree to remove the Indians to thier new Homes at thier expense and under the care of discreet and carefull[sic] persons, who will be kind and brotherly to them. They agree to furnish them with ample corn and beef, or pork for themselves & families for Twelve months after reaching thier new homes.

It is agreed further that the U. S. will take all thier cattle, at the valuation of some discreet person to be appointed by the President, & the same shall be paid for in money after thier arrival at thier new homes; or in other cattle such as may be desired shall be furnished them, notice being given through thier Agent of thier wishes upon this subject before thier removal that time to supply the demand may be afforded.

Article 17th

The several annuities and sums secured under former Treaties to the Choctaw Nation and People shall continue as tho. this Treaty had never been made. And it is further agreed that the U. S. in addition will pay the sum of Twenty thousand Dollars for Twenty Years, commencing after thier removal to the west, of which, in the first year after thier removal, Ten thousand Dollars shall be divided and arranged to such as may not receive reservations under this Treaty.

Article 18th

The U. S. shall cause the lands hereby ceded to be surveyed; & surveyors may enter the Choctaw Country for that purpose, conducting themselves properly & disturbing or interrupting none of the Choctaw people. But no person is to be permitted to settle within the Nation, or the lands to be sold before the Choctaws shall remove. And for the payment of the several amounts secured in this Treaty, the lands hereby ceded are to remain a fund pledged to that purpose, until the debt shall be provided for and arranged. And further it is agreed, that in the construction of this Treaty wherever well founded doubt shall arise, it shall be construed most favorably towards the Choctaws.

Treaty of Dancing Rabbit Creek

Article 19th

The following reservations of land are hereby admitted. To Co^l David Fulsom Four Sections of which Two shall include his present improvement, & two may be located else where, on unoccupied, unimproved land.

To I. Garland, Co^l Robert Cole, Tuppanahomer, John Pytchlynn[sic], Charles Juzan, Johokebetubbe, Eaychahobia, Ofehoma two sections, each to be include thier improvements, and to be bounded by sectional lines, & the same may be disposed of and sold with the consent of the President. And that others not provided for, may be provided for, there shall be reserved as follows:

First; One section to each head of a family not exceeding Forty in number, who during the present year, may have had in actual cultivation, with a dwelling House thereon Fifty Acres or more. Secondly three quarter sections after the manner aforesaid to each head of a family not exceeding Four Hundred and Sixty, as shall have cultivated Thirty Acres and less than Fifty, to be bounded by quarter section lines of survey, & to be contiguous and adjoining.

Third; One half section as aforesaid to those who shall have cultivated from Twenty to Thirty acres the number not to exceed Four Hundred. Fourth; a quarter section as aforesaid to such as shall have cultivated from twelve to twenty acres, the number not to exceed three hundred and fifty, and one half that quantity to such as shall have cultivated from two to twelve acres, the number also not to exceed three hundred and fifty persons. Each of said class of cases shall be subject to the limitations contained in the first class, & shall be so located as to include that part of the improvement which contains the dwelling House. If a greater number shall be found to be entitled to reservations under the several classes of this article, than is stipulated for under the limitation prescribed, then & in that case the Chiefs separeately[sic] or together shall determine the persons who shall be excluded in the respective districts.

Fifth; Any Captain the number not exceeding ninety persons, who under the provisions of this article shall receive less than a section, he shall be entitled, to an additional quantity of half a section adjoining to his other reservation. The several reservations secured under this article, may be sold with the consent of the President of the U. S; but should any prefer it, or omit to take a reservation for the quantity he may be entitled to the U. S. will on his removing pay fifty cents an acre, after reaching thier new homes, provided that before the first of January next they shall adduce to the Agent; or some other authorized person to be appointed, proof of his claim & the quantity of it. Sixth; likewise children of the Choctaw Nation residing in the Nation, who have neither Father nor Mother a list of which, with satisfactory proof of Parentage and orphanage being filed with Agent in six months to be forwarded to the War Department, shall be entitled to a quarter section of Land, to be located under the direction of the President, & with his consent the same may be sold and the proceeds applied to some beneficial purpose for the benefit of said orphans

Treaty of Dancing Rabbit Creek

Article 20th

The U. S. agree & stipulate as follows, that for the benefit and advantage of the Choctaw people, & to improve thier condition, thier[sic] shall be educated under the direction of the President & at the expense of the U. S. forty Choctaw Youths for Twenty years. This number shall be kept at school, & as they finish thier education others to supply thier places shall be received for the period stated. The U. S. agree also to erect a Council House for the Nation at some convenient central point, after thier people shall be settled; & a House for each Chief, also a church for each of the three Districts, to be used also as school Houses, until the Nation may conclude to build others; & for these purposes Ten thousand Dollars shall be appropriated; also Fifty thousand Dollars (viz) Twenty Five Hundred Dollars annually shall be given for the support of three Teachers of schools for Twenty Years. Likewise there shall be furnished to the Nation, three Blacksmiths one for each District for sixteen years, & a qualified Mill Wright for five years; Also there shall be furnished the following articles, Twenty One Hundred Blankets, To each warrior who emigrates a rifle, moulds, wipers and ammunition. One thousand axes, Ploughs, Hoes, Wheels and Cards each; and four Hundred looms. There shall also be furnished one Ton of iron & two hundred weight of steel annually to each District for sixteen years.

Article 21st

A few Choctaw Warriors yet survive who marched and fought in the Army with General Wayne the whole number stated not to exceed Twenty.
These it is agreed shall hereafter while they live receive Twenty Five dollars a year; a list of them to be early as practicable, & within six months made out, and presented to the Agent to be forwarded to the War Department.—

Article 22d

The Chiefs of the Choctaws have suggested that thier people are in a state of rapid advancement in education and refinement; and have expressed a solicitude that they might have the privilege of a Delegate on the floor of the House of Representatives extended to them. The Commissioners do not feel, that they can under a treaty stipulation accede to the request, but at thier desire, present it in the Treaty, that Congress may consider of and decide the application.

Done and signed and executed by the Commissioners of the United States and the Chiefs Captains and Head Men of the Choctaw Nation, at Dancing Rabbit Creek this 27th day of September Eighteen Hundred and Thirty.

Treaty of Dancing Rabbit Creek

			His Mark
In presence of	Jn° H. Eaton	(Seal)	
E. Breathitt Secty	Jn°. Coffee	(Seal)	
to the Commss^r =	Greenwood Leflore	(Seal)	
William Ward Agt.	Musholatubbee	(Seal)	X
for Choctaws.	Nittucachee	(Seal)	X
John Pitchlynn	Eyarhocuttubbee	(Seal)	X
US Int^r	Iyacherhopia	(Seal)	X
M Mackey	Offahoomah	(Seal)	X
US Intr.	Archalater	(Seal)	X
Geo. S. Gaines	Onnahubbee	(Seal)	X
of Alabama	Holarterhoomah	(Seal)	X
RP Currin	Hopiaunchahubbee	(Seal)	X
Luke Howard	Zishomingo	(Seal)	X
Sam. L. Worchester	Captain thalke	(Seal)	X
Jn° W Byrn	James Shield	(Seal)	X
John Bell	Pistiyubbee	(Seal)	X
Jn° Bond	Yobalarunehahubbee	(Seal)	X
	Holubbee	(Seal)	X
	Robert Cole	(Seal)	X
	Mokelareharhopin	(Seal)	X
	Lewis Perry	(Seal)	X
	Artonamarstubbe	(Seal)	X
	Hopeatubbee	(Seal)	X
	Hoshahoomah	(Seal)	X
	Chuallahoomah	(Seal)	X
	Joseph Kincaide	(Seal)	X
	Artooklubbetushpar	(Seal)	X
	Metubbee	(Seal)	X
	Arsarkatubbee	(Seal)	X
	Issaterhoomah		X
	Chohtahmatahah	(Seal)	X
	Tunnuppashubbee	(Seal)	X
	Okocharyer	(Seal)	X
	Hoshhopia	(Seal)	X
	Warsharshahopia	(Seal)	X
	Maarshunchahubbee	(Seal)	X
	Misharyubbee	(Seal)	X
	Daniel McCurtain	(Seal)	X
	Tushkerharcho	(Seal)	X
	Hoktoontubbee	(Seal)	X
	Nuknacrahookmarhee	(Seal)	X
	Mingohoomah	(Seal)	X
	Pisinhocuttubbee	(Seal)	X
	Tullarhacher	(Seal)	X
	Little leader	(Seal)	X
	Maanhutter	(Seal)	X
	Cowehoomah	(Seal)	X

Treaty of Dancing Rabbit Creek

Tillamoer	(Seal)	X
Imnullacha	(Seal)	X
Artopilachubbee	(Seal)	X
Shupherunchahubbee	(Seal)	X
Nitterhoomah	(Seal)	X
Oaklaryubbee	(Seal)	X
Pukumma	(Seal)	X
Arpalar	(Seal)	X
Holber	(Seal)	X
Hoparmingo	(Seal)	X
Isparhoomah	(Seal)	X
Tieberhoomah	(Seal)	X
Tishoholarter	(Seal)	X
Mahayarchubbee	(Seal)	X
Arlarter	(Seal)	X
Nittahubbee	(Seal)	X
Tishonouan	(Seal)	X
Warsharchaboomah	(Seal)	X
Isaac James	(Seal)	X
Hopiaintushker	(Seal)	X
Aryoshkermer		X
Shemotar		X
Hopiaisketina		X
Thomas Leflore		X
Arnokechatubbee		X
Shokoperlukna		X
Posherhoomah		X
Robert Folsom		X
Arharyotubbee		X
Kushonolarter		X
James Vaughan		X
James Karnes		X
Tishohakubbee		X
Narlanalar		X
Pennasha		X
In har yar ker		X
Motubbee		X
Narharyubbee		X
Ishmaryubbee		X
James M King		
Lewis Wilson		X
Istonarkerharcho		X
Hoshinshamartarher		X
Kinsulachubbee		X
Eyarhinstubbee		X
Sam[l] Garlands		
Thomas Wall		
Sam. S. Worcester		

Treaty of Dancing Rabbit Creek

Jacob Folsom		
William Foster		
Ontioerharcho		X
Hugh A. Foster		
Pierre Juzan		
Jno. Pitchlynn Jr.	(Seal)	
David Folsom	(Seal)	
Sholohommastube	(Seal)	X
Tesho	(Seal)	X
Lauwechubee	(Seal)	X
Hoshehammo	(Seal)	X
Ofenowo	(Seal)	X
Ahekoche	(Seal)	X
Kaloshoube	(Seal)	X
Atoko	(Seal)	X
Ishtemeleche	(Seal)	X
Emthtohabe	(Seal)	X
Silas D. Fisher	(Seal)	
Isaac Folsom	(Seal)	X
Hekatube	(Seal)	X
Hakseche	(Seal)	X
Jerry Carney	(Seal)	X
John Washington	(Seal)	X
Phiplip	(Seal)	X
Meshameye	(Seal)	X
Ish te he ka	(Seal)	X
Heshohomme	(Seal)	X
John McKelbery	(Seal)	X
Benj^m. James	(Seal)	
Tik ba cha ham be	(Seal)	X
Aholiktube	(Seal)	X
Walking Wolf	(Seal)	X
John Waide	(Seal)	X
Big Axe	(Seal)	X
Bob	(Seal)	X
Tush ko cha u bbe	(Seal)	X
It ta be	(Seal)	X
Tish o wa ka you	(Seal)	
Folehommo	(Seal)	X
John Garland	(Seal)	X
Koshona	(Seal)	X
Ish le you ham ube	(Seal)	X
Ok la no wa	(Seal)	X
Neto	(Seal)	
James Fletcher	(Seal)	X
Silus D Pitchlynn	(Seal)	
William Trahorn	(Seal)	
Tosh ka hem mit to	(Seal)	X

Treaty of Dancing Rabbit Creek

Te the ta yo	(Seal)	X
Emokloshahopie	(Seal)	X
Tishoimita	(Seal)	X
Thomas W Foster	(Seal)	
Zadoc Brashears		
Levi Perkins	(Seal)	X
Isaac Perry	(Seal)	X
Isblonocka Hoomah	(Seal)	X
Hiram King	(Seal)	
Ogla Enlah	(Seal)	X
Nu1tlahtubbee	(Seal)	X
Tuska Hollattuh	(Seal)	X
Panshastubbee	(Seal)	X
P. P. Pitchlynn	(Seal)	
Joel H. Nail	(Seal)	
Hopia Stonakey	(Seal)	X
Kocohomma	(Seal)	X
William Wade	(Seal)	X
Pansh stick ubbee	(Seal)	X
Ho lit tank chah ubbee	(Seal)	X
Ko th° ant chah ubbee	(Seal)	X
Eyarpulubbee	(Seal)	X
Oken tah ubbe	(Seal)	X
Living War Club	(Seal)	X
John Jones	(Seal)	X
Charles Jones	(Seal)	
Isaac Jones	(Seal)	X
Hocklucha	(Seal)	X
Muscogee	(Seal)	X
Eden Nelson	(Seal)	

And 28th Sept 1830
Ratified Feby 24th 1831.

In the Senate of the United States
February 21st: 1831.

Resolved, (two thirds of the Senators present concurring) That the Senate do advise and consent to the ratification of the Treaty, between the United States of America and the Mingoes, Chiefs, Captains and Warriors of the Choctaw Nation, concluded at Dancing Rabbit Creek on the 15th of September 1830, together with the Supplement thereto, concluded at the same place the 28th of September 1830: with the exception of the preamble.

Attest,   Walter Lowrie

Treaty of Dancing Rabbit Creek

Andrew Jackson,
President of the United States of America,
To all and singular to whom these presents shall come,

Greeting:

Whereas a Treaty between the United States of America, and the Mingoes, Chiefs, Captains and Warriors of the Choctaw Nation was entered into at Dancing Rabbit Creek, on the twenty-seventh day of September in the Year of our Lord one thousand eight hundred and thirty, and of the Independence of the United States, the fifty-fifth, by John H. Eaton and John Coffee, Commissioners on the part of the United States, and the Chiefs, Captains and Head-Men of the Choctaw Nation on the part of said Nation; - which Treaty, together with the supplemental article thereto, is in the words following,

To wit:

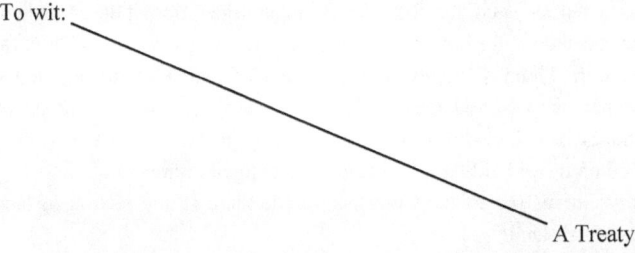

A Treaty

Various Choctaw persons have been presented by the chiefs of the Nation, with a desire that they might be provided for, Being particularly deserving, an earnestness has been manifested that provision might be made for them. It is therefore by the undersigned commissioners here assented to with the understanding that they are to have no interest in the reservations which are directed and provided for under the general Treaty to which this is a supplement.

As evidence of the liberal and kind feelings of the President and Government of the United States the Commissioners agree to the request as follows (to wit) Pierre Juzan, Peter Pitchlynn, G.W. Harkins, Jack Pitchlynn, Israel Fulsom, Louis Laflore, Benjamin James, Joel H. Nail, Hopoynjahubbee, Onorkubbee, Benjamin Laflore, Michael Laflore & Allen Yates & wife shall be entitled to a reservation of two sections of land each to include thier improvement where they at present reside, with the exception of the three first named persons & Benja. Laflore who are authorized to locate one of thier sections on any other unimproved and unoccupied land, within thier respective districts.

Article 2^d

And to each of the following persons there is allowed a reservation of a section and a half of land, (to wit) James L. McDonald, Robert Jones, Noah Wall, James Campbell, G. Nelson, and Vaughn Brashears, R. Harris, Little Leader, S. Foster, J.

Vaughn, L. Durand, Samuel Long, T. Magagha, Thos. Everge, Giles Thompson, Thomas Garland, John Bond, William Laflore, and Turner Brashears; the two first named persons, may locate one section each, and one section jointly on any unimproved and unoccupied land, these not residing in the Nation; The others are to include thier present residence and improvement.

Also one section is allowed to the following persons (to wit) Middleton Mackey, Wesley Train, Choclehomo, Moses Foster, D. W. Wall, Charles Scott, Molly Nail, Susan Colbert, who was formerly Susan James, Samuel Garland, Silas Fisher, D. McCurtain, Oaklahoma, & Polly Fillecuthey, to be located in entire sections to include thier resent residence and improvement, with the exception of Molly Nail and Susan Colbert, who are authorized to locate thiers, on any unimproved unoccupied land.

John Pitchlynn has long and faithfully served the Nation in character of U. States interpreter, he has acted as such for forty years, in consideration it is agreed, in addition to what has been done for him there shall be granted to two of his children, (to wit) Silas Pitchlynn, & Thomas Pitchlynn one section of land each to adjoin the location of thier father likewise to James Madison and Peter sons of Mushulatubbee one section of land each to include the old house and improvement ~~of~~ where thier father formerly lived on the old military road adjoining a large Prerarie[sic].

And to Henry Groves son of the Chief Natticache there is one section of land given to adjoin his father's land.

And to each of the following persons half a section of land is granted on any unoccupied and unimproved lands in the Districts where they respectively live (to wit) Willis Harkins, James D. Hamilton, William Juzan, Tobias Laflore, Jo Doake, Jacob Fulsom, P. Hays, Saml Worcester, Geo. Hunter, William Train ~~and~~ Robert Nail and Alexander McKee.

And there is given a quarter section of land each to Delila and her five fatherless children, she being a Choctaw woman residing out of the Nation; also the same quantity to Peggy Trihan, another Indian woman residing out of the Nation & her two fatherless children; & to the widows of Pushmilaha, & Puck she nubbee, who were formerly distinguished Chiefs of the Nation and for thier children four quarter sections of land, each in trust for themselves & thier children

All of said last mentioned reservations are to be located under and by direction of the President of the U States

Article 3

The Choctaw people now that they have ceded thier[sic] lands are solicitous to act to thier new homes early as possible & accordingly they wish that a party may be permitted to proceed this fall to ascertain where abouts will be most advantageous for thier people to be located.

Treaty of Dancing Rabbit Creek

It is therefore agreed that three or four persons (from each of the three districts) under the guidance of some discreet and well qualified person or persons ~~man~~ may proceed during this fall to the West upon an examination of the country.

For thier time and expenses the U. States agree to allow the said twelve persons Two Dollars a day each, not to exceed one hundred days, which is deemed to be ample time to make an examination.

If necessary Pilots acquainted with the country will be furnished when they arrive in the West.

Article 4th

John Donly of Alabama who has several Choctaw grand children, and who for Twenty years has carried the mail through the Choctaw Nation, a desire by the Chiefs is expressed that he may have a section of land, it is accordingly granted, to be located in one entire section, on any unimproved & unoccupied land.

Allen Glover and George S. Gaines licensed Traders in the Choctaw Nation, have accounts amounting to upwards of Nine thousand Dollars against the Indians who are unable to pay thier said debts without distressing thier families; a desire is expressed by the Chiefs that Two sections of land be set apart to be sold and the proceeds thereof to be applied toward the payment of the aforesaid debts. It is agreed that two sections of any unimproved and unoccupied land be granted to George S. Gaines who will sell the same for the best price he can obtain and apply the proceeds thereof to the credit of the Indians on thier accounts due to the before mentioned Glover and Gaines; & shall make the application to the poorest Indian first.

At the earnest and particular request of the Chief Greenwood Laflore there is granted to David Haley one half section of land to be located in a half section on any unoccupied and unimproved land as a compensation for a journey to Washington City with dispatches to the Government and returning others to the Choctaw Nation.

The foregoing is entered into, as supplemental to the treaty concluded yesterday.

Done at Dancing Rabbit creek the 28th day of September 1830.

In presence of	Jn° H Eaton Seal
E. Breathitt Secty to Com^r.	Jn°. Coffee Seal
W. Ward Agt. for Choctaws	Greenwood Leflore
M Mackey US Intr.	Nittucachee his x mark
John Pitchlynn	Musholatubbee his x mark
US Int^t	Ofahoomah his x mark
RP Currin	Eyarhoeuttubbee his x mark
Jn° W Byrn	Iyaeherhopia his x mark

Treaty of Dancing Rabbit Creek

Geo. S. Gaines	Holubbee his x mark
The following words in this supplement	Onarhubbee his x mark
were interlined before being signed	Robert Cole his x mark
1st Article "& Allen Yates & wife" also	Hopiaunchahubbee his x mark
& Benj^a Laflore	David Folsom
Do. Wesley Train - Choclehomo	John Garland his x mark
	Hopiahoomah his x mark
"person or persons"	Captain Thalko his x mark
	Pierre Juzan
In presence of	Immarstarher his x mark
E. Breathitt Secty to Com^r.	Hoshimhamarter his x mark

Now, therefore, be it known, that I, Andrew Jackson, President of the United States of America, having seen and considered said Treaty, do in pursuance of the advice and consent of the Senate, as expressed by their Resolution of the twenty-first day of February, one thousand eight hundred and thirty-one, accept, ratify and confirm the same, and every clause and article thereof, with the exception of the Preamble.

In Testimony whereof, I have caused the seal of the United States to be hereunto affixed, having signed the same with my hand.

Done at the City of Washington, this twenty fourth day of February, in the Year of our Lord one thousand eight hundred and thirty-one, and of the Independence of the United States, the fifty-fifth.

       Andrew Jackson

By the President,

       M. VanBuren
       Secty of State

Mississippi Choctaw Census

as of April 1, 1933

and Additional Information

taken by A. C. Hector, Superintendent

Census of the __Mississippi Choctaws__ reservation of the __Choctaw Agency__ jurisdiction, as of __April 1__, 19__33__, taken by __A. C. Hector__, Superintendent.

KEY: Surname; Census Number; Given Name; Sex; Age at Last Birthday; Tribe; Degree of Blood; Marital Status; Relationship to Head of Family; Last Census Roll Number; At Jurisdiction Where Enrolled (Yes/No); At Another Jurisdiction; Post Office, County, State (if given); Ward (Yes/No)

ALEX

1; Cooper; m; 23; Miss. Choctaw; F; S; Head; 1; Yes; Yes

2; Missie; f; 53; Miss. Choctaw; F; Wd; Head; 2; Yes; Yes
3; Nelson; m; 9; Miss. Choctaw; F; S; Son; 3; Yes; Yes

ALLEN

4; Willis; m; 38; Miss. Choctaw; F; M; Head; 5; Yes; Yes
5; Bessie; f; 38; Miss. Choctaw; F; M; Wife; 6; Yes; Yes
6; Bob; m; 16; Miss. Choctaw; F; S; Son; 7; Yes; Yes
7; Sulum; m; 12; Miss. Choctaw; F; S; Son; 8; Yes; Yes
8; Maggie; f; 10; Miss. Choctaw; F; S; Dau; 9; Yes; Yes
9; Huston; m; 9; Miss. Choctaw; F; S; Son; 10; Yes; Yes
10; Nell; f; 8; Miss. Choctaw; F; S; Dau; 11; Yes; Yes
11; Willie; f; 5; Miss. Choctaw; F; S; Son; 12; Yes; Yes
12; Wilbert; m; 8/12; Miss. Choctaw; F; S; Yes; Yes
13; Herbert; m; 8/12; Miss. Choctaw; F; S; Yes; Yes

14; Jim; m; 47; Miss. Choctaw; F; M; Head; 13; Yes; Yes
15; Manda; f; 49; Miss. Choctaw; F; M; Wife; 14; Yes; Yes
16; I. C; m; 19; Miss. Choctaw; F; S; Son; 15; Yes; Yes
17; Annie Mae; f; 19; Miss. Choctaw; F; S; Dau; 16; Yes; Yes
18; J. C; m; 18; Miss. Choctaw; F; S; Son; 17; Yes; Yes
19; R. G; m; 17; Miss. Choctaw; F; S; Son; 18; Yes; Yes
20; Will; m; 10; Miss. Choctaw; F; S; Son; 19; Yes; Yes

21; Joseph; m; 40; Miss. Choctaw; F; S; Head; 20; Yes; Yes

22; Lacey; m; 39; Miss. Choctaw; F; S; Head; 21; Yes; Yes

Census of the **Mississippi Choctaws** reservation of the **Choctaw Agency** jurisdiction, as of **April 1**, 19**33**, taken by **A. C. Hector**, Superintendent.

KEY; Surname; Census Number; Given Name; Sex; Age at Last Birthday; Tribe; Degree of Blood; Marital Status; Relationship to Head of Family; Last Census Roll Number; At Jurisdiction Where Enrolled (Yes/No); At Another Jurisdiction; Post Office, County, State (if given); Ward (Yes/No)

AMOS

23; Sebbie; f; 55; Miss. Choctaw; F; Wd; Head; 22; Yes; Yes
24; Albert; m; 29; Miss. Choctaw; F; S; Nephew; 23; Yes; Yes

25; Griffin; m; 45; Miss. Choctaw; F; M; Head; 24; Yes; Yes
26; Sallie; f; 41; Miss. Choctaw; F; M; Wife; 25; Yes; Yes
27; Beauty; f; 23; Miss. Choctaw; F; S; Dau; 26; Yes; Yes
28; Julia; f; 21; Miss. Choctaw; F; S; Dau; 27; Yes; Yes
29; Land; m; 17; Miss. Choctaw; F; S; Son; 29; Yes; Yes
30; Fulton; m; 12; Miss. Choctaw; F; S; Son; 30; Yes; Yes
31; Floyd; m; 12; Miss. Choctaw; F; S; Son; 31; Yes; Yes
32; Mose; m; 11; F; S; Son; 32; Yes; Yes

33; John; m; 19; Miss. Choctaw; F; M; Head; 28
34; Ruth; f; 15; Miss. Choctaw; F; M; Wife; 353

35; Lampkin; m; 55; Miss. Choctaw; F; M; Head; 33; Yes; Yes
36; Ann; f; 55; Miss. Choctaw; F; M; Wife; 34; Yes; Yes
37; Bonnie; f; 22; Miss. Choctaw; F; S; Dau; 35; Yes; Yes
38; Lonie; f; 16; Miss. Choctaw; F; S; Dau; 36; Yes; Yes
39; **Isom**, Mary; f; 6; Miss. Choctaw; F; S; Grand-dau; 37; Yes; Yes

ANDERSON

40; Bob; m; 48; Miss. Choctaw; F; M; Head; Yes; Yes
41; Ella; f; 45; Miss. Choctaw; F; M; Wife; Yes; Yes
42; A. J; m; 21; Miss. Choctaw; F; S; Son; 40; Yes; Yes
43; Chuty; f; 15; Miss. Choctaw; F; S; Dau; 41; Yes; Yes
44; Josephine; f; 11; Miss. Choctaw; F; S; Dau; 42; Yes; Yes
45; Sallie Mae; f; 8; Miss. Choctaw; F; S; Dau; 43; Yes; Yes
46; Burnice; f; 5; Miss. Choctaw; F; S; Dau; 44; Yes; Yes

47; John; m; 65; Miss. Choctaw; F; M; Head; 45; Yes; Yes

Census of the **Mississippi Choctaws** reservation of the **Choctaw Agency** jurisdiction, as of **April 1**, 19**33**, taken by **A. C. Hector**, Superintendent.

KEY: Surname; Census Number; Given Name; Sex; Age at Last Birthday; Tribe; Degree of Blood; Marital Status; Relationship to Head of Family; Last Census Roll Number; At Jurisdiction Where Enrolled (Yes/No); At Another Jurisdiction; Post Office, County, State (if given); Ward (Yes/No)

48; Sallie; f; 30; Miss. Choctaw; F; M; Wife; 46; Yes; Yes
49; J. C; m; 8; Miss. Choctaw; F; S; Son; 47; Yes; Yes
50; Amy; f; 24 da; Miss. Choctaw; F; S; Dau; Yes; Yes

51; Mattie; f; 63; Miss. Choctaw; F; Wd; Head; 48; Yes; Yes
52; Ike; m; 31; Miss. Choctaw; F; S; Son; 49; Yes; Yes
53; Vada; f; 27; Miss. Choctaw; F; S; Dau; 50; Yes; Yes

54; Evan; m; 29; Miss. Choctaw; F; M; Head; 51; Yes; Yes
55; Thelma; f; 17; Miss. Choctaw; F; M; Wife; 52; Yes; Yes

56; Roy; m; 37; Miss. Choctaw; F; M; Head; 53; Yes; Yes
57; Lonie; f; 33; Miss. Choctaw; F; M; Wife; 54; Yes; Yes
58; Frances B; f; 4; Miss. Choctaw; F; S; Dau; 55; Yes; Yes

59; Ollie; m; 47; Miss. Choctaw; F; M; Head; 56; Yes; Yes
60; Kate; f; 52; Miss. Choctaw; F; M; Wife; 57; Yes; Yes
61; Grace; f; 10; Miss. Choctaw; F; S; Dau; 58; Yes; Yes

62; Oliver; m; 47; Miss. Choctaw; F; M; Head; 60; Yes; Yes
63; Sallie; f; 40; Miss. Choctaw; F; M; Wife; 61; Yes; Yes
64; Hinton; m; 19; Miss. Choctaw; F; S; Son; 62; Yes; Yes
65; Lonie; f; 18; Miss. Choctaw; F; S; Dau; 63; Yes; Yes
66; Phillip; m; 14; Miss. Choctaw; F; S; Son; 64; Yes; Yes
67; Houston; m; 12; Miss. Choctaw; F; S; Son; 65; Yes; Yes
68; Lucille; f; 10; Miss. Choctaw; F; S; Dau; 66; Yes; Yes

69; Abel; m; 27; Miss. Choctaw; F; M; Head; 67; Yes; Yes
70; Nancy; f; 47; Miss. Choctaw; F; M; Wife; 68; Yes; Yes
71; **Farmer**, Sallie; f; 17; Miss. Choctaw; F; S; Step-dau; 69; Yes; Yes
72; **Farmer**, Ella Mae; f; 11; Miss. Choctaw; F; S; Step-dau; 70; Yes; Yes
73; **Farmer**, Annie Mae; f; 9; Miss. Choctaw; F; S; Step-dau; 71; Yes; Yes

Census of the **Mississippi Choctaws** reservation of the **Choctaw Agency** jurisdiction, as of **April 1**, 19**33**, taken by **A. C. Hector**, Superintendent.

KEY; Surname; Census Number; Given Name; Sex; Age at Last Birthday; Tribe; Degree of Blood; Marital Status; Relationship to Head of Family; Last Census Roll Number; At Jurisdiction Where Enrolled (Yes/No); At Another Jurisdiction; Post Office, County, State (if given); Ward (Yes/No)

BELL

74; Hugh; m; 53; Miss. Choctaw; F; Wd; Head; 72; Yes; Yes
75; Mamie; f; 7; Miss. Choctaw; F; S; Dau; 74; Yes; Yes

76; John; m; 42; Miss. Choctaw; F; M; Head; 75; Yes; Yes
77; Lillian; f; 43; Miss. Choctaw; F; M; Wife; 76; Yes; Yes
78; Hattie; f; 12; Miss. Choctaw; F; S; Dau; 77; Yes; Yes
79; Eva; f; 8; Miss. Choctaw; F; S; Dau; 78; Yes; Yes
80; Ola; f; 6; Miss. Choctaw; F; S; Dau; 79; Yes; Yes

81; Sallie; f; 43; Miss. Choctaw; F; Wd; Head; 80; Yes; Yes
82; Emma; f; 21; Miss. Choctaw; F; S; Dau; 81; Yes; Yes
83; Effie; f; 14; Miss. Choctaw; F; S; Dau; 82; Yes; Yes
84; Idie; f; 8/12; Miss. Choctaw; F; S; Dau; Yes; Yes

85; Junus; m; 36; Miss. Choctaw; F; M; Head; 83; Yes; Yes
86; Winnie; f; 31; Miss. Choctaw; F; M; Wife; 84; Yes; Yes
87; Ronie; f; 16; Miss. Choctaw; F; S; Dau; 85; Yes; Yes
88; Woods; m; 13; Miss. Choctaw; F; S; Son; 86; Yes; Yes
89; Minnie; f; 11; Miss. Choctaw; F; S; Dau; 87; Yes; Yes
90; Edmond; m; 8; Miss. Choctaw; F; S; Son; 88; Yes; Yes
91; George; m; 6; Miss. Choctaw; F; S; Son; 89; Yes; Yes

92; Evans; m; 31; Miss. Choctaw; F; M; Head; 90; Yes; Yes
93; Willie; f; 21; Miss. Choctaw; F; M; Wife; 91; Yes; Yes
94; Homer; m; 6; Miss. Choctaw; F; S; Son; 92; Yes; Yes
95; Nancy L; f; 4; Miss. Choctaw; F; S; Dau; 93; Yes; Yes
96; Hester; f; 20 da; Miss. Choctaw; F; S; Dau; Yes; Yes

97; Mack; m; 28; Miss. Choctaw; F; M; Head; 94; Yes; Yes
98; Lena; f; 19; Miss. Choctaw; F; M; Wife; 95; Yes; Yes
99; James Cook; m; 5; Miss. Choctaw; F; S; Son; 96; Yes; Yes
100; Herbert H; m; 1; Miss. Choctaw; F; S; Son; 97; Yes; Yes

Census of the **Mississippi Choctaws** reservation of the **Choctaw Agency** jurisdiction, as of **April 1**, 19**33**, taken by **A. C. Hector**, Superintendent.

KEY; Surname; Census Number; Given Name; Sex; Age at Last Birthday; Tribe; Degree of Blood; Marital Status; Relationship to Head of Family; Last Census Roll Number; At Jurisdiction Where Enrolled (Yes/No); At Another Jurisdiction; Post Office, County, State (if given); Ward (Yes/No)

101; Thompson; m; 35; Miss. Choctaw; F; M; Head; 98; Yes; Yes
102; Ellen; f; 35; Miss. Choctaw; F; M; Wife; 99; Yes; Yes
103; Frank K; m; 19; Miss. Choctaw; F; S; Son; 100; Yes; Yes

104; Nicholas; m; 33; Miss. Choctaw; F; M; Head; 101; Yes; Yes
105; Cleddie; f; 20; Miss. Choctaw; F; M; Wife; 102; Yes; Yes
106; Ruby; f; 2; Miss. Choctaw; F; S; Dau; 103; Yes; Yes
107; Bonnie K; f; 2; Miss. Choctaw; F; S; Dau; 104; Yes; Yes
108; Franklin; m; 3/12; Miss. Choctaw; F; S; Son; Yes; Yes

109; Gipson; m; 20; Miss. Choctaw; F; M; Head; 105; Yes; Yes
110; Lucy; f; 20; Miss. Choctaw; F; M; Wife; 106; Yes; Yes
111; Gipson, Jr; m; 1; Miss. Choctaw; F; S; Son; 107; Yes; Yes

112; Amon; m; 31; Miss. Choctaw; F; M; Head; 108; Yes; Yes
113; Alice; f; 30; Miss. Choctaw; F; M; Wife; 109; Yes; Yes

114; Jim; m; 63; Miss. Choctaw; F; S; Alone; 110; Yes; Yes

115; Joe; m; 41; Miss. Choctaw; F; M; Head; 111; Yes; Yes
116; Susie; f; 33; Miss. Choctaw; F; M; Wife; 112; Yes; Yes
117; Tom; m; 13; Miss. Choctaw; F; S; Son; 113; Yes; Yes
118; Bill; m; 9; Miss. Choctaw; F; S; Son; 114; Yes; Yes
119; Henry; m; 7; Miss. Choctaw; F; S; Son; 115; Yes; Yes
120; Polly Ann; f; 5; Miss. Choctaw; F; S; Dau; 116; Yes; Yes
121; Sallie; f; 56; Miss. Choctaw; F; Wd; Mother-in-law; 117; Yes; Yes

122; Boston; m; 48; Miss. Choctaw; F; M; Head; 118; Yes; Yes
123; Lela; f; 33; Miss. Choctaw; F; M; Wife; 119; Yes; Yes
124; Sophia; f; 25; Miss. Choctaw; F; S; Dau; 120; Yes; Yes
125; Ola; f; 23; Miss. Choctaw; F; S; Dau; 121; Yes; Yes
126; Effie; f; 21; Miss. Choctaw; F; S; Dau; 122; Yes; Yes
127; John; m; 11; Miss. Choctaw; F; S; Son; 123; Yes; Yes
128; Emma; f; 9; Miss. Choctaw; F; S; Dau; 124; Yes; Yes

Census of the **Mississippi Choctaws** reservation of the **Choctaw Agency** jurisdiction, as of **April 1**, 19**33**, taken by **A. C. Hector**, Superintendent.

KEY; Surname; Census Number; Given Name; Sex; Age at Last Birthday; Tribe; Degree of Blood; Marital Status; Relationship to Head of Family; Last Census Roll Number; At Jurisdiction Where Enrolled (Yes/No); At Another Jurisdiction; Post Office, County, State (if given); Ward (Yes/No)

129; Emmett; m; 8; Miss. Choctaw; F; S; Son; 125; Yes; Yes
130; Marshall; m; 3; Miss. Choctaw; F; s; Son; 126; Yes; Yes

131; Cornelius; m; 75; Miss. Choctaw; F; Wd; Head; 127; Yes; Yes
132; John; m; 26; Miss. Choctaw; F; S; Son; 128; Yes; Yes

133; Jim; m; 71; Miss. Choctaw; F; S; Alone; 129; Yes; Yes

134; Lish; m; 43; Miss. Choctaw; F; M; Head; 130; Yes; Yes
135; Martha; f; 38; Miss. Choctaw; F; M; Wife; 131; Yes; Yes
136; Willie; m; 18; Miss. Choctaw; F; S; Son; 132; Yes; Yes
137; Houston; m; 13; Miss. Choctaw; F; S; Son; 133; Yes; Yes
138; Minnie; f; 12; Miss. Choctaw; F; S; Dau; 134; Yes; Yes
139; Less C; m; 10; Miss. Choctaw; F; S; Son; 135; Yes; Yes
140; Gene D; m; 8; Miss. Choctaw; F; S; Son; 136; Yes; Yes
141; Jay; m; 6; Miss. Choctaw; F; S; Son; 137; Yes; Yes
142; Gaston; m; 24; Miss. Choctaw; F; S; Bro; 138; Yes; Yes

143; Bob; m; 23; Miss. Choctaw; F; M; Head; 139; Yes; Yes
144; Geneva; m; 22; Miss. Choctaw; F; M; Wife; 140; Yes; Yes
145; Sadie; f; 3; Miss. Choctaw; F; S; Dau; 141; Yes; Yes
146; Naomi Ruth; f; 1; Miss. Choctaw; F; S; Dau; 142; Yes; Yes

147; Lish; m; 52; Miss. Choctaw; F; M; Head; 143; Yes; Yes
148; Maggie; f; 52; Miss. Choctaw; F; M; Wife; 144; Yes; Yes
149; Minnie; f; 25; Miss. Choctaw; F; S; Dau; 145; Yes; Yes
150; Lula; f; 17; Miss. Choctaw; F; S; Dau; 146; Yes; Yes
151; Tom; m; 27; Miss. Choctaw; F; S; Son; 147; Yes; Yes
152; Bob; m; 23; Miss. Choctaw; F; S; Son; 148; Yes; Yes
153; Basin; m; 8; Miss. Choctaw; F; S; Son; 149; Yes; Yes

154; Mandy; f; 65; Miss. Choctaw; F; Wd; Head; Yes; Yes
Omitted on 1932 Census and previous reports

Census of the **Mississippi Choctaws** reservation of the **Choctaw Agency** jurisdiction, as of **April 1**, 19**33**, taken by **A. C. Hector**, Superintendent.

KEY; Surname; Census Number; Given Name; Sex; Age at Last Birthday; Tribe; Degree of Blood; Marital Status; Relationship to Head of Family; Last Census Roll Number; At Jurisdiction Where Enrolled (Yes/No); At Another Jurisdiction; Post Office, County, State (if given); Ward (Yes/No)

155; Tony; m; 18; Miss. Choctaw; F; S; Son; Yes; Yes
Omitted on 1932 Census and previous report

BEN

156; Olin; m; 33; Miss. Choctaw; F; M; Head; 150; Yes; Yes
157; Neva; f; 26; Miss. Choctaw; F; M; Wife; 151; Yes; Yes
158; Nannie Mae; f; Miss. Choctaw; F; S; Dau; 152; Yes; Yes
159; Annie Laura; f; 8; Miss. Choctaw; F; S; Dau; 153; Yes; Yes
160; Mattie Lou; f; 5; Miss. Choctaw; F; S; Dau; 154; Yes; Yes
161; **Isaac**, Coline; f; 14; Miss. Choctaw; F; S; Sister-in-law; 156; Yes; Yes

162; Wyatt; m; 65; Miss. Choctaw; F; M; Head; 157; Yes; Yes
163; Elle; f; 61; Miss. Choctaw; F; M; Wife; 158; Yes; Yes

164; Lula; f; 49; Miss. Choctaw; F; Wd; Head; 159; Yes; Yes
165; Jimpson; m; 27; Miss. Choctaw; F; S; Son; 160; Yes; Yes
166; Wilson; m; 16; Miss. Choctaw; F; S; Son; 162; Yes; Yes

167; Otho; m; 19; Miss. Choctaw; F; M; Head; 161; Yes; Yes
168; Lessie; f; 20; Miss. Choctaw; F; M; Wife; 155; Yes; Yes

169; Tom; m; 38; Miss. Choctaw; F; M; Head; 163; Yes; Yes
170; Gladys; f; 27; Miss. Choctaw; F; M; Wife; 164; Yes; Yes
171; Fannie Lou; f; 8; Miss. Choctaw; F; S; Dau; 165; Yes; Yes
172; Hubert; m; 6; Miss. Choctaw; F; S; Son; 166; Yes; Yes
173; Henry Ford; m; 4; Miss. Choctaw; F; S; Son; 167; Yes; Yes
174; Helen Marie; f; 6/12; Miss. Choctaw; F; S; Dau; Yes; Yes

175; Charlie; m; 34; Miss. Choctaw; F; M; Head; 168; Yes; Yes
176; Emeline; f;; 26; Miss. Choctaw; F; M; Wife; 169; Yes; Yes
177; Opal Grace; f; 1; Miss. Choctaw; F; S; Dau; 170; Yes; Yes

Census of the **Mississippi Choctaws** reservation of the **Choctaw Agency** jurisdiction, as of **April 1**, 19**33**, taken by **A. C. Hector**, Superintendent.

KEY; Surname; Census Number; Given Name; Sex; Age at Last Birthday; Tribe; Degree of Blood; Marital Status; Relationship to Head of Family; Last Census Roll Number; At Jurisdiction Where Enrolled (Yes/No); At Another Jurisdiction; Post Office, County, State (if given); Ward (Yes/No)

178; Jim; m; 57; Miss. Choctaw; F; Wd; Alone; 171; Yes; Yes

179; Monroe; m; 22; Miss. Choctaw; F; M; Head; 172; Yes; Yes
180; Lilly May; f; 22; Miss. Choctaw; F; M; Wife; 173; Yes; Yes

BILLY

181; Lum; m; 48; Miss. Choctaw; F; M; Head; 174; Yes; Yes
182; Minnie; f; 50; Miss. Choctaw; F; M; Wife; 175; Yes; Yes
183; **Charles**, James; m; 35; Miss. Choctaw; F; S; Brother-in-law; Yes; Yes

184; Tom; m; 22; Miss. Choctaw; F; M; Head; 177; Yes; Yes
185; Sallie; f; 23; Miss. Choctaw; F; M; Wife; 178; Yes; Yes
186; Robert; m; 5; Miss. Choctaw; F; S; Son; 179; Yes; Yes
187; James; m; 2; Miss. Choctaw; F; S; Son; 180; Yes; Yes

188; Will; m; 56; Miss. Choctaw; F; S; Alone; 181; Yes; Yes

189; Williston; m; 39; Miss. Choctaw; F; M; Head; 182; Yes; Yes
190; Jessie; f; 29; Miss. Choctaw; F; M; Wife; 183; Yes; Yes
191; Melton; m; 12; Miss. Choctaw; F; S; Son; 184; Yes; Yes
192; Beaman; m; 9; Miss. Choctaw; F; S; Son; 185; Yes; Yes
193; Maurice; m; 7; Miss. Choctaw; F; S; Son; 186; Yes; Yes
194; Horace; m; 6; Miss. Choctaw; F; S; Son; 187; Yes; Yes
195; Betty Jean; f; 2; Miss. Choctaw; F; S; Dau; 188; Yes; Yes

196; Nicy; f; 73; Miss. Choctaw; F; Wd; Head; 189; Yes; Yes
197; Leona; f; 33; Miss. Choctaw; F; S; Dau; 190; Yes; Yes
198; Earl; m; 7; Miss. Choctaw; F; S; Grand-son; 192; Yes; Yes

199; Ike; m; 23; Miss. Choctaw; F; M; Head; 191; Yes; Yes
200; Jennie; f; 21; Miss. Choctaw; F; M; Wife; 59; Yes; Yes
201; Kate; f; 6/12; Miss. Choctaw; F; S; Dau; Yes; Yes

Census of the **Mississippi Choctaws** reservation of the **Choctaw Agency** jurisdiction, as of **April 1**, 19**33**, taken by **A. C. Hector**, Superintendent.

KEY; Surname; Census Number; Given Name; Sex; Age at Last Birthday; Tribe; Degree of Blood; Marital Status; Relationship to Head of Family; Last Census Roll Number; At Jurisdiction Where Enrolled (Yes/No); At Another Jurisdiction; Post Office, County, State (if given); Ward (Yes/No)

202; Lorene; f; 23; Miss. Choctaw; F; Wd; Head; 194; Yes; Yes
203; Cicero L; m; 1; Miss. Choctaw; F; S; Son; 195; Yes; Yes

204; Johnson; m; 67; Miss. Choctaw; F; M; Head; 196; Yes; Yes
205; Belaria; f; 52; Miss. Choctaw; F; M; Wife; 197; Yes; Yes
206; Gipson; m; 22; Miss. Choctaw; F; S; Son; 198; Yes; Yes
207; Ike; m; 21; Miss. Choctaw; F; S; Son; 199; Yes; Yes
208; Maude; f; 20; Miss. Choctaw; F; S; Dau; 200; Yes; Yes
209; Wilson; m; 16; Miss. Choctaw; F; S; Son; 201; Yes; Yes
210; Greer; m; 14; Miss. Choctaw; F; S; Son; 202; Yes; Yes
211; Frank; m; 9; Miss. Choctaw; F; S; Son; 203; Yes; Yes
212; Phillip; m; 3; Miss. Choctaw; F; S; Grand-son; 204; Yes; Yes

213; Lewis; m; 28; Miss. Choctaw; F; M; Head; 205; Yes; Yes
214; Zelma; f; 28; Miss. Choctaw; F; M; Wife; 206; Yes; Yes
215; Clennie; f; 13; Miss. Choctaw; F; S; Step-dau; 207; Yes; Yes
216; Mamie; f; 11; Miss. Choctaw; F; S; Step-dau; 208; Yes; Yes
217; Frank; m; 7; Miss. Choctaw; F; S; Son; 209; Yes; Yes
218; Annie; f; 4; Miss. Choctaw; F; S; Dau; 210; Yes; Yes

219; Will; m; 45; Miss. Choctaw; F; M; Head; 211; Yes; Yes
220; Alice; f; 43; Miss. Choctaw; F; M; Wife; 212; Yes; Yes
221; William; m; 18; Miss. Choctaw; F; W; Son; 213; Yes; Yes
222; Lee; m; 17; Miss. Choctaw; F; S; Son; 214; Yes; Yes
223; Rose; f; 14; Miss. Choctaw; F; S; Dau; 215; Yes; Yes
224; Irene; f; 11; Miss. Choctaw; F; S; Dau; 216; Yes; Yes
225; Joe; m; 10; Miss. Choctaw; F; S; Son; 217; Yes; Yes
226; Will, Jr; m; 6; Miss. Choctaw; F; S; Son; 218; Yes; Yes
227; Marchie; f; 5; Miss. Choctaw; F; S; Dau; 219; Yes; Yes
228; Charlie; m; 3; Miss. Choctaw; F; S; Son; 220; Yes; Yes

229; Jordan; m; 48; Miss. Choctaw; F; M; Head; 221; Yes; Yes
230; Lillie; f; 30; Miss. Choctaw; F; M; Wife; 222; Yes; Yes
231; Sallie Mae; f; 15; Miss. Choctaw; F; S; Dau; 223; Yes; Yes

Census of the **Mississippi Choctaws** reservation of the **Choctaw Agency** jurisdiction, as of **April 1**, 19**33**, taken by **A. C. Hector**, Superintendent.

KEY; Surname; Census Number; Given Name; Sex; Age at Last Birthday; Tribe; Degree of Blood; Marital Status; Relationship to Head of Family; Last Census Roll Number; At Jurisdiction Where Enrolled (Yes/No); At Another Jurisdiction; Post Office, County, State (if given); Ward (Yes/No)

232; Nellie; f; 23; Miss. Choctaw; F; S; Dau; 224; Yes; Yes
233; Jim; m; 7; Miss. Choctaw; F; S; Son; 225; Yes; Yes
234; Mary Lou; f; 5; Miss. Choctaw; F; S; Dau; 226; Yes; Yes
235; Paul; m; 2; Miss. Choctaw; F; S; Son; 227; Yes; Yes
236; Peter Cooper; m; 11/12; Miss. Choctaw; F; S; Son; Yes; Yes

237; Richard; m; 22; Miss. Choctaw; F; M; Head; 228; Yes; Yes
238; Cassie; f; 18; Miss. Choctaw; F; M; Wife; 229; Yes; Yes
239; Duley; f; 1; Miss. Choctaw; F; M[sic]; Dau; 230; Yes; Yes
240; Sarah; f; 6 da; Miss. Choctaw; F; S; Dau; Yes; Yes

241; Wade; m; 54; Miss. Choctaw; F; M; Head; 231; Yes; Yes
242; Lina; f; 36; Miss. Choctaw; F; M; Wife; 232; Yes; Yes
243; Sienna; f; 26 da; Miss. Choctaw; F; S; Dau; Yes; Yes
244; **McMillan**, Mary; f; 13; Miss. Choctaw; F; S; Step-dau; 233; Yes; Yes

BOB

245; Simon; m; 63; Miss. Choctaw; F; S; Alone; 234; Yes; Yes

BOX

246; Illiman; m; 27; Miss. Choctaw; F; M; Head; 235; Yes; Yes
247; Rosie; f; 21; Miss. Choctaw; F; M; Wife; 236; Yes; Yes

248; Lillie; f; 45; Miss. Choctaw; F; Wd; Head; 237; Yes; Yes
249; Ollie T; m; 18; Miss. Choctaw; F; S; Son; 238; Yes; Yes
250; Bathie; f; 10; Miss. Choctaw; F; S; Dau; 239; Yes; Yes
251; Bethy; f; 8; Miss. Choctaw; F; S; Dau; 240; Yes; Yes
253[sic]; **Joe,** Emly; f; 73; Miss. Choctaw; F; Wd; Mother; 241; Yes; Yes

254; Ola; f; 18; Miss. Choctaw; F; S; Orphan; 242; Yes; Yes

Census of the **Mississippi Choctaws** reservation of the **Choctaw Agency** jurisdiction, as of **April 1**, 19**33**, taken by **A. C. Hector**, Superintendent.

KEY; Surname; Census Number; Given Name; Sex; Age at Last Birthday; Tribe; Degree of Blood; Marital Status; Relationship to Head of Family; Last Census Roll Number; At Jurisdiction Where Enrolled (Yes/No); At Another Jurisdiction; Post Office, County, State (if given); Ward (Yes/No)

255; Eula; f; 10; Miss. Choctaw; F; S; Orphan; 243; Yes; Yes

BRISCOE

256; Tom; m; 32; Miss. Choctaw; F; M; Head; 245; Yes; Yes
257; Lucy; f; 50; Miss. Choctaw; F; M; Wife; 246; Yes; Yes

258; Stephens; m; 24; Miss. Choctaw; F; M; Head; 248; Yes; Yes
259; Maggie; f; 25; Miss. Choctaw; F; M; Wife; 249; Yes; Yes
260; J. Claud; m; 1; Miss. Choctaw; F; S; Son; 250; Yes; Yes

BULL

261; Pink; m; 55; Miss. Choctaw; F; Wd; Head; 251; Yes; Yes
262; **Lewis**, Houston; m; 16; Miss. Choctaw; F; S; Orphan; Yes; Yes
Never reported on previous census

263; George; m; 59; Miss. Choctaw; F; M; Head; 252; Yes; Yes
264; Sissy; f; 51; Miss. Choctaw; F; M; Wife; 253; Yes; Yes

265; Foreman; m; 30; Miss. Choctaw; F; M; Head; 254; Yes; Yes
266; Sarah; f; 29; Miss. Choctaw; F; M; Wife; 255; Yes; Yes

CAMPBELL

267; Wiley; m; 32; Miss. Choctaw; F; Wd; Alone; 256; Yes; Yes

CATES

268; Susan; f; 55; Miss. Choctaw; F; Wd; Head; 257; Yes; Yes
269; Enis; m; 28; Miss. Choctaw; F; S; Son; 258; Yes; Yes
270; Essie; f; 25; Miss. Choctaw; F; S; Dau; 259; Yes; Yes
271; John; m; 21; Miss. Choctaw; F; S; Son; 260; Yes; Yes
272; Lonie; f; 20; Miss. Choctaw; F; S; Dau; 261; Yes; Yes

Census of the **Mississippi Choctaws** reservation of the **Choctaw Agency** jurisdiction, as of **April 1**, 19 **33**, taken by **A. C. Hector**, Superintendent.

KEY; Surname; Census Number; Given Name; Sex; Age at Last Birthday; Tribe; Degree of Blood; Marital Status; Relationship to Head of Family; Last Census Roll Number; At Jurisdiction Where Enrolled (Yes/No); At Another Jurisdiction; Post Office, County, State (if given); Ward (Yes/No)

273; Molpus; m; 19; Miss. Choctaw; F; S; Son; 262; Yes; Yes
274; Iona; f; 15; Miss. Choctaw; F; S; Dau; 263; Yes; Yes
275; John; m; 5; Miss. Choctaw; F; S; Grand-son; 264; Yes; Yes
276; Oscar; m; 23; Miss. Choctaw; F; S; Alone; 265; Yes; Yes

277; Alice; f; 28[sic]; Miss. Choctaw; F; Wd; Head; 266; Yes; Yes
278; Dock; m; 31; Miss. Choctaw; F; S; Son; 267; Yes; Yes
279; Dee m; 25; Miss. Choctaw; F; S; Son; 268; Yes; Yes

280; Ned; m; 35; Miss. Choctaw; F; M; Head; 269; Yes; Yes
281; Janie; f; 31; Miss. Choctaw; F; M; Wife; 270; Yes; Yes
282; Susan Mabel; f; 16; Miss. Choctaw; F; S; Dau; 271; Yes; Yes
283; Emma; f; 16; Miss. Choctaw; F; S; Dau; 272; Yes; Yes
284; Tubby; m; 15; Miss. Choctaw; F; S; Son; 273; Yes; Yes
285; Henry M; m; 13; Miss. Choctaw; F; S; Son; 274; Yes; Yes
286; Willie F; m; 10; Miss. Choctaw; F; S; Son; 275; Yes; Yes
287; Nannie; f; 8; Miss. Choctaw; F; S; Dau; 276; Yes; Yes
288; Julia; f; 7; Miss. Choctaw, F, S, Dau; 277; Yes; Yes

CHAPMAN

289; Will; m; 46; Miss. Choctaw; F; M; Head; 278; Yes; Yes
290; Bettie; f; 49; Miss. Choctaw; F; M; Wife; 279; Yes; Yes
291; Asa; m; 16; Miss. Choctaw; F; S; Son; 280; Yes; Yes
292; Ralston; m; 14; Miss. Choctaw; F; S; Son; 281; Yes; Yes
293; Hattie; f; 10; Miss. Choctaw; F; S; Dau; 282; Yes; Yes
294; Ronie; f; 9; Miss. Choctaw; F; S; Dau; 283; Yes; Yes
295; Lilly; f; 8; Miss. Choctaw; F; S; Dau; 284; Yes; Yes
296; Raymond; m; 7; Miss. Choctaw; F; S; Son; 285; Yes; Yes
297; Christ; m; 6; Miss. Choctaw; F; S; Son; 286; Yes; Yes
298; Minnie; f; 5; Miss. Choctaw; F; S; Dau; 287; Yes; Yes

Census of the **Mississippi Choctaws** reservation of the **Choctaw Agency** jurisdiction, as of **April 1**, 19**33**, taken by **A. C. Hector**, Superintendent.

KEY; Surname; Census Number; Given Name; Sex; Age at Last Birthday; Tribe; Degree of Blood; Marital Status; Relationship to Head of Family; Last Census Roll Number; At Jurisdiction Where Enrolled (Yes/No); At Another Jurisdiction; Post Office, County, State (if given); Ward (Yes/No)

CHARLIE

299; William; m; 82; Miss. Choctaw; F; M; Head; 292; Yes; Yes
300; Fannie; f; 68; Miss. Choctaw; F; M; Wife; 293; Yes; Yes
301; **McMillen**, Nola; f; 28; Miss. Choctaw; F; Wd; Dau; 1042; Yes; Yes
302; **McMillen**, A. J; m; 11; Miss. Choctaw; F; S; Grand-son; 1043; Yes; Yes
303; **McMillen**, Odie Mae; f; 9; Miss. Choctaw; F; S; Grand-dau; 1044; Yes; Yes
304; **McMillen**, John; m; 6; Miss. Choctaw; F; S; Grand-son; 1045; Yes; Yes
305; **McMillen**, Mattie; f; 2; Miss. Choctaw; F; S; Grand-dau; 1046; Yes; Yes

306; John; m; 39; Miss. Choctaw; F; M; Head; 294; Yes; Yes
307; Mary; f; 31; Miss. Choctaw; F; M; Wife; 295; Yes; Yes
308; Elsie; f; 14; Miss. Choctaw; F; S; Dau; 296; Yes; Yes

CHICKAWAY

309; Sim; m; 35; Miss. Choctaw; F; M; Head; 297; Yes; Yes
310; Maggie; f; 32; Miss. Choctaw; F; M; Wife; 298; Yes; Yes
311; Clemon; m; 14; Miss. Choctaw; F; S; Son; 299; Yes; Yes
312; Nellie; f; 12; Miss. Choctaw; F; S; Dau; 300; Yes; Yes
313; Agnes; f; 10; Miss. Choctaw; F; S; Dau; 301; Yes; Yes
314; Albert; m; 7; Miss. Choctaw; F; S; Son; 302; Yes; Yes
315; Maggie Kate; f; 5; Miss. Choctaw; F; S; Dau; 303; Yes; Yes
316; Kate; f; 2; Miss. Choctaw; F; S; Dau; 304; Yes; Yes
317; John Study; m; 9/12; Miss. Choctaw; F; S; Son; Yes; Yes

318; Isabell; f; 71; Miss. Choctaw; F; Wd; Head; 305; Yes; Yes
319; Ola; f; 26; Miss. Choctaw; F; S; Dau; 306; Yes; Yes

Census of the **Mississippi Choctaws** reservation of the **Choctaw Agency** jurisdiction, as of **April 1**, 19**33**, taken by **A. C. Hector**, Superintendent.

KEY; Surname; Census Number; Given Name; Sex; Age at Last Birthday; Tribe; Degree of Blood; Marital Status; Relationship to Head of Family; Last Census Roll Number; At Jurisdiction Where Enrolled (Yes/No); At Another Jurisdiction; Post Office, County, State (if given); Ward (Yes/No)

320; Jim; m; 30; Miss. Choctaw; F; M; Head; 307; Yes; Yes
321; Eunice; f; 27; Miss. Choctaw; F; M; Wife; 308; Yes; Yes
322; John Hester; m; 5; Miss. Choctaw; F; S; Son; 309; Yes; Yes
323; Henry; m; 2; Miss. Choctaw; F; S; Son; 310; Yes; Yes
324; **Grant**, Rosie Lee; f; 11; Miss. Choctaw; F; S; Step-dau; 311; Yes; Yes

325; Kelly; m; 40; Miss. Choctaw; F; M; Head; 312; Yes; Yes
326; Lilla; f; 31; Miss. Choctaw; F; M; Wife; 313; Yes; Yes
327; Micheal[sic]; m; 10; Miss. Choctaw; F; S; Son; 314; Yes; Yes
328; Anna; f; 8; Miss. Choctaw; F; S; Dau; 315; Yes; Yes
329; Jane; f; 6; Miss. Choctaw; F; S; Dau; 316; Yes;

330; Rufus; m; 31; Miss. Choctaw; F; M; Head; 317; Yes; Yes
331; Bessie; f; 28; Miss. Choctaw; F; M; Wife; 318; Yes; Yes
332; Ross C; m; 5; Miss. Choctaw; F; S; Son; 319; Yes; Yes
333; Elizabeth; f; 3; Miss. Choctaw; F; S; Dau; 320; Yes; Yes

CHITTO

334; Joe; m 33; Miss. Choctaw; F; M; Head; 321; Yes; Yes
335; Callie; f; 33; Miss. Choctaw; F; M; Wife; 322; Yes; Yes
336; Leo Clifton; m; 5; Miss. Choctaw; F; S; Son; 323; Yes; Yes

337; Pat; m; 56; Miss. Choctaw; F; Wd; Head; 324; Yes; Yes
338; Henrietta; f; 18; Miss. Choctaw; F; S; Dau; 325; Yes; Yes
339; Jefferson; m; 16; Miss. Choctaw; F; S; Son; 326; Yes; Yes
340; Erma; f; 11; Miss. Choctaw; F; S; Dau; 327; Yes; Yes
341; Isom; m; 9; Miss. Choctaw; F; S; Son; 328; Yes; Yes

342; John; m; 43; Miss. Choctaw; F; M; Head; 329; Yes; Yes
343; Sallie; f; 42; Miss. Choctaw; F; M; Wife; 330; Yes; Yes
344; Minnie; f; 22; Miss. Choctaw; F; S; Dau; 331; Yes; Yes
345; Hattie; f; 15; Miss. Choctaw; F; S; Dau; 332; Yes; Yes

Census of the **Mississippi Choctaws** reservation of the **Choctaw Agency** jurisdiction, as of **April 1**, 19**33**, taken by **A. C. Hector**, Superintendent.

KEY; Surname; Census Number; Given Name; Sex; Age at Last Birthday; Tribe; Degree of Blood; Marital Status; Relationship to Head of Family; Last Census Roll Number; At Jurisdiction Where Enrolled (Yes/No); At Another Jurisdiction; Post Office, County, State (if given); Ward (Yes/No)

346; Allie Nora; f; 13; Miss. Choctaw; F; S; Dau; 333; Yes; Yes
347; Ella; f; 11; Miss. Choctaw; F; S; Dau; 334; Yes; Yes
348; Lum Billy; m; 7; Miss. Choctaw; F; S; Son; 335; Yes; Yes

CLEMONS

349; Phillip; m; 38; Miss. Choctaw; F; S; Alone; 338; Yes; Yes

CLEMONS or COWED

350; Jim; m; 28; Miss. Choctaw; F; M; Head; 339; Yes; Yes
351; Bessie; f; 26; Miss. Choctaw; F; M; Wife; 340; Yes; Yes
352; Margie; f; 5; Miss. Choctaw; F; S; Dau; 341; Yes; Yes
353; Lewisman; m; 3; Miss. Choctaw; F; S; Son; 342; Yes; Yes

CLARK

354; Stella; f; 38; Miss. Choctaw; F; S; Alone; 343; Yes; Yes

CLEMONS

355; Jeff; m; 36; Miss. Choctaw; F; M; Head; 344; Yes; Yes
356; Cora; f; 32; Miss. Choctaw; F; M; Wife; 345; Yes; Yes
357; Mattie; f; 11; Miss. Choctaw; F; S; Dau; 346; Yes; Yes
358; Ethel; f; 10; Miss. Choctaw; F; S; Dau; 347; Yes; Yes
359; Letha; f; 8; Miss. Choctaw; F; S; Dau; 348; Yes; Yes
360; John; m; 7; Miss. Choctaw; F; S; Son; 349; Yes; Yes
361; Rena Mae; f; 5; Miss. Choctaw; F; S; Dau; 350; Yes; Yes

362; Munch; m; 50; Miss. Choctaw; F; M; Head; 351; Yes; Yes
363; Nellie; f; 43; Miss. Choctaw; F; M; Wife; 352; Yes; Yes
364; Bathia; f; 14; Miss. Choctaw; F; S; Dau; 354; Yes; Yes
365; Mollie; f; 12; Miss. Choctaw; F; S; Dau; 355; Yes; Yes

Census of the **Mississippi Choctaws** reservation of the **Choctaw Agency** jurisdiction, as of **April 1**, 19__33__, taken by **A. C. Hector**, Superintendent.

KEY; Surname; Census Number; Given Name; Sex; Age at Last Birthday; Tribe; Degree of Blood; Marital Status; Relationship to Head of Family; Last Census Roll Number; At Jurisdiction Where Enrolled (Yes/No); At Another Jurisdiction; Post Office, County, State (if given); Ward (Yes/No)

COMBY

366; Alma; f; 41; Miss. Choctaw; F; Wd; Head; 356; Yes; Yes
367; **McMillan**, Jimmie; m; 22; Miss. Choctaw; F; S; Son; 357; Yes; Yes
368; **McMillan**, Jimpson; m; 20; Miss. Choctaw; F; S; Son; 358; Yes; Yes
369; **McMillan**, Ella; f; 18; Miss. Choctaw; F; S; Dau; 359; Yes; Yes
370; **McMillan**, Jordan; m; 3; Miss. Choctaw; F; S; Grand-son; 360; Yes; Yes

371; Arbin; m; 45; Miss. Choctaw; F; Wd; Head; 361; Yes; Yes
372; Gilbert; m; 21; Miss. Choctaw; F; S; Son; 362; Yes; Yes
373; Rosella; f; 13; Miss. Choctaw; F; S; Dau; 363; Yes; Yes
374; Maudell; f; 10; Miss. Choctaw; F; S; Dau; 364; Yes; Yes

375; Seymour; m; 32; Miss. Choctaw; F; M; Head; 365; Yes; Yes
376; Edna; f; 27; Miss. Choctaw; F; M; Wife; 366; Yes; Yes
377; W. C; m; 11; Miss. Choctaw; F; S; Son; 367; Yes; Yes
378; B. C; m; 9; Miss. Choctaw; F; S; Son; 368; Yes; Yes
379; Leroy; m; 7; Miss. Choctaw; F; S; Son; 369; Yes; Yes

380; Allie; f; 28; Miss. Choctaw; F; Wd; Head; 370; Yes; Yes
381; Jonas; m; 9; Miss. Choctaw; F; S; Son; 371; Yes; Yes
382; Irene; f; 7; Miss. Choctaw; F; S; Dau; 372; Yes; Yes
252[sic]; Joyce Ann; f; 5; Miss. Choctaw; F; S; Dau; 373; Yes; Yes
383; R. L; m; 3; Miss. Choctaw; F; S; Son; 374; Yes; Yes
384; **Chitto**, Mary; f; 34; Miss. Choctaw; F; S; Sister; 375; Yes; Yes

385; Ben; m; 71; Miss. Choctaw; F; Wd; Alone; 376; Yes; Yes

386; Olmon; m; 55; Miss. Choctaw; F; M; Head; 377; Yes; Yes
387; Laura; f; 52; Miss. Choctaw; F; M; Wife; 378; Yes; Yes

Census of the **Mississippi Choctaws** reservation of the **Choctaw** **Agency** jurisdiction, as of **April 1**, 19**33**, taken by **A. C. Hector**, Superintendent.

KEY; Surname; Census Number; Given Name; Sex; Age at Last Birthday; Tribe; Degree of Blood; Marital Status; Relationship to Head of Family; Last Census Roll Number; At Jurisdiction Where Enrolled (Yes/No); At Another Jurisdiction; Post Office, County, State (if given); Ward (Yes/No)

COOPER

388; Dixon; m; 32; Miss. Choctaw; F; M; Head; 379; Yes; Yes
389; Leana; f; 25; Miss. Choctaw; F; M; Wife; 380; Yes; Yes

390; Gaston; m; 47; Miss. Choctaw; F; M; Head; 381; Yes; Yes
391; Ada; f; 49; Miss. Choctaw; F; M; Wife; 382; Yes; Yes
392; Fannie; f; 15; Miss. Choctaw; F; S; Dau; 384; Yes; Yes
393; Hubert; m; 12; Miss. Choctaw; F; S; Son; 385; Yes; Yes
394; Christine; f; 9; Miss. Choctaw; F; S; Dau; 386; Yes; Yes
395; Alma; f; 6; Miss. Choctaw; F; S; Dau; 387; Yes; Yes

COTTON

396; John; m; 23; Miss. Choctaw; F; S; Alone; 388; Yes; Yes

397; George; m; 33; Miss. Choctaw; F; M; Head; 389; Yes; Yes
398; Ellen; f; 32; Miss. Choctaw; F; M; Wife; 390; Yes; Yes
399; Minnie; f; 7; Miss. Choctaw; F; S; Dau; 391; Yes; Yes
400; **Crenshaw**, Amos; m; 21; Miss. Choctaw; F; S; Orphan; 393; Yes; Yes
401; **Crenshaw**, Austin; m; 17; Miss. Choctaw; F; S; Orphan; 393; Yes; Yes

DAN

402; Williston; m; 36; Miss. Choctaw; F; M; Head; 397; Yes; Yes
403; Dinah; f; 21; Miss. Choctaw; F; M; Wife; 398; Yes; Yes
404; Rose Ida; f; 11; Miss. Choctaw; F; S; Dau; 399; Yes; Yes

DANSBY

405; Jacob; m; 61; Miss. Choctaw; F; M; Head; 400; Yes; Yes
406; Jennie; f; 48; Miss. Choctaw; F; M; Wife; 401; Yes; Yes

Census of the **Mississippi Choctaws** reservation of the **Choctaw Agency** jurisdiction, as of **April 1**, 19**33**, taken by **A. C. Hector**, Superintendent.

KEY; Surname; Census Number; Given Name; Sex; Age at Last Birthday; Tribe; Degree of Blood; Marital Status; Relationship to Head of Family; Last Census Roll Number; At Jurisdiction Where Enrolled (Yes/No); At Another Jurisdiction; Post Office, County, State (if given); Ward (Yes/No)

407; **Tubby**, R. B; m; 26; Miss. Choctaw; F; S; Brother-in-law; 402; Yes; Yes
408; **Tubby**, Jim; m; 60; Miss. Choctaw; F; S; Brother-in-law; 403; Yes; Yes

DAVIS

409; Alyne; f; 23; Miss. Choctaw; F; M; Wife; 377; No; Ft. Definance[sic]; Ft. Definance, Ariz; Yes

410; Leona; f; 57; Miss. Choctaw; F; Wd; Head; 405; Yes; Yes
411; Hobbie; m; 27; Miss. Choctaw; F; S; Son; 406; Yes; Yes

412; Will; m; 59; Miss. Choctaw; F; M; Head; 407; Yes; Yes
413; Mattie; f; 31; Miss. Choctaw; F; M; Wife; 408; Yes; Yes
414; Annie; f; 14; Miss. Choctaw; F; S; Dau; 409; Yes; Yes
415; John; m; 11; Miss. Choctaw; F; S; Son; 410; Yes; Yes
416; Mary; f; 5; Miss. Choctaw; F; S; Dau; 411; Yes; Yes
417; Mack; m; 4; Miss. Choctaw; F; S; Son; 412; Yes; Yes
418; Lewis; m; 2; Miss. Choctaw; F; S; Son; 413; Yes; Yes
419; William; m; 8/12; Miss. Choctaw; F; S; Son; Yes; Yes

420; Sidney; m; 45; Miss. Choctaw; F; Wd; Head; 414; Yes; Yes
421; Elamer; f; 24; Miss. Choctaw; F; S; Dau; 415; Yes; Yes
422; Mabel; f; 21; Miss. Choctaw; F; S; Dau; 416; Yes; Yes
423; Anna; f; 13; Miss. Choctaw; F; S; Dau; 417; Yes; Yes
424; Johnnie; m; 11; Miss. Choctaw; F; S; Son; 418; Yes; Yes

425; Malissie; f; 63; Miss. Choctaw; F; Wd; Head; 419; Yes; Yes
426; Alice; f; 36; Miss. Choctaw; F; S; Dau; 420; Yes; Yes
427; Bessie; f; 23; Miss. Choctaw; F; S; Dau; 421; Yes; Yes
428; Sina; f; 21; Miss. Choctaw; F; S; Grand-dau; 422; Yes; Yes
429; Ada Francis; f; 13; Miss. Choctaw; F; S; Grand-dau; 423; Yes; Yes

Census of the **Mississippi Choctaws** reservation of the **Choctaw Agency** jurisdiction, as of **April 1**, 19**33**, taken by **A. C. Hector**, Superintendent.

KEY; Surname; Census Number; Given Name; Sex; Age at Last Birthday; Tribe; Degree of Blood; Marital Status; Relationship to Head of Family; Last Census Roll Number; At Jurisdiction Where Enrolled (Yes/No); At Another Jurisdiction; Post Office, County, State (if given); Ward (Yes/No)

430; Mary; f; 18; Miss. Choctaw; F; S; Grand-dau; 424; Yes; Yes

431; Tom; m; 33; Miss. Choctaw; F; Wd; Head; 425; Yes; Yes
432; Millie; f; 13; Miss. Choctaw; F; S; Dau; 426; Yes; Yes
433; Henderson; m; 11; Miss. Choctaw; F; S; Son; 427; Yes; Yes

DENSON

434; Lilly; f; 45; Miss. Choctaw; F; Wd; Head; 428; Yes; Yes
435; Hendrix; m; 16; Miss. Choctaw; F; S; Son; 429; Yes; Yes
436; Emma; f; 13; Miss. Choctaw; F; S; Dau; 430; Yes; Yes
437; Charley; m; 10; Miss. Choctaw; F; S; Son; 431; Yes; Yes
438; David; m; 8; Miss. Choctaw; F; S; Son; 432; Yes; Yes
439; **Farmer**, Eula Mae; f; 2; Miss. Choctaw; F; S; Grand-dau; 433; Yes; Yes

440; Pete; m; 45; Miss. Choctaw; F; S[sic]; Head; 434; Yes; Yes
441; Rosie; f; 32; Miss. Choctaw; F; S[sic]; Wife; 435; Yes; Yes
442; Mary; f; 17; Miss. Choctaw; F; S; Dau; 436; Yes; Yes
443; Jeffie; f; 15; Miss. Choctaw; F; S; Dau; 437; Yes; Yes
444; Edna; f; 10; Miss. Choctaw; F; S; Dau; 438; Yes; Yes
445; Nancy; f; 4; Miss. Choctaw; F; S; Dau; 439; Yes; Yes
446; Jennie E; f; 1; Miss. Choctaw; F; S; Dau; 440; Yes; Yes

447; Willie; m; 25; Miss. Choctaw; F; M; Head; 441; Yes; Yes
448; Beauty; f; 21; Miss. Choctaw; F; M; Wife; 442; Yes; Yes
449; Hector; m; 8/12; Miss. Choctaw; F; S; Son; Yes; Yes

450; Ezell; m; 21; Miss. Choctaw; F; M; Head; 443; Yes; Yes
451; Beauty; f; 21; Miss. Choctaw; F; M; Wife; 444; Yes; Yes
452; Ruth; f; 2; Miss. Choctaw; F; S; Dau; 445; Yes; Yes
453; Louise; f; 24 da; Miss. Choctaw; F; S; Dau; Yes; Yes

Census of the **Mississippi Choctaws** reservation of the **Choctaw Agency** jurisdiction, as of **April 1**, 19**33**, taken by **A. C. Hector**, Superintendent.

KEY; Surname; Census Number; Given Name; Sex; Age at Last Birthday; Tribe; Degree of Blood; Marital Status; Relationship to Head of Family; Last Census Roll Number; At Jurisdiction Where Enrolled (Yes/No); At Another Jurisdiction; Post Office, County, State (if given); Ward (Yes/No)

DIXON

454; Nannie; f; 53; Miss. Choctaw; F; Wd; Head; 446; Yes; Yes
455; **Sam**, Charlie; m; 18; Miss. Choctaw; F; S; Nephew; 447; Yes; Yes

456; Jim; m; 32; Miss. Choctaw; F; M; Head; 448; Yes; Yes
457; Sarah; f; 30; Miss. Choctaw; F; M; Wife;; 449; Yes; Yes
458; Marie; f; 10; Miss. Choctaw; F; S; Dau; 450; Yes; Yes
459; Imogene; f; 7; Miss. Choctaw; F; S; Dau; 451; Yes; Yes
460; Ellen; f; 5; Miss. Choctaw; F; S; Dau; 452; Yes; Yes
461; Mable C; f; 2; Miss. Choctaw; F; S; Dau; 453; Yes; Yes

462; Jess; m; 55; Miss. Choctaw; F; M; Head; 454; Yes; Yes
463; Callie; f; 63; Miss. Choctaw; F; M; Wife; 455; Yes; Yes
464; Young; m; 16; Miss. Choctaw; F; S; Son; 457; Yes; Yes
465; Lilly; f; 13; Miss. Choctaw; F; S; Dau; 458; Yes; Yes
466; **Thompson**, Mary Jane; f; 83; Miss. Choctaw; F; Wd; Mother-in-law; 459; Yes; Yes

467; Scott; m; 22; Miss. Choctaw; F; M; Head; 456; Yes; Yes
468; Essie; f; 26; Miss. Choctaw; F; M; Wife; 591; Yes; Yes
469; Nola; f; 6/12; Miss. Choctaw; F; S; Dau; Yes; Yes

470; Horace; m; 27; Miss. Choctaw; F; M; Head; 460; Yes; Yes
471; Esther; f; 26; Miss. Choctaw; F; M; Wife; 461; Yes; Yes
472; Calonia; f; 6; Miss. Choctaw; F; S; Dau; 462; Yes; Yes

473; Edmond; m; 25; Miss. Choctaw; F; M; Head; 463; Yes; Yes
474; Julia; f; 24; Miss. Choctaw; F; M; Wife; 464; Yes; Yes
475; Addie Mae; f; 3; Miss. Choctaw; F; S; Dau; 465; Yes; Yes
476; Anita; f; 24 da; Miss. Choctaw; F; S; Dau; 466[sic]; Yes; Yes

477; Wilson; m; 74; Miss. Choctaw; F; M; Head; 466; Yes; Yes

Census of the **Mississippi Choctaws** reservation of the **Choctaw Agency** jurisdiction, as of **April 1**, 19**33**, taken by **A. C. Hector**, Superintendent.

KEY; Surname; Census Number; Given Name; Sex; Age at Last Birthday; Tribe; Degree of Blood; Marital Status; Relationship to Head of Family; Last Census Roll Number; At Jurisdiction Where Enrolled (Yes/No); At Another Jurisdiction; Post Office, County, State (if given); Ward (Yes/No)

478; Hope; f; 47; Miss. Choctaw; F; S[sic]; Wife; 467; Yes; Yes

479; Kanis; m; 41; Miss. Choctaw; F; Wd; Head; 468; Yes; Yes
480; Esby; f; 22; Miss. Choctaw; F; S; Dau; 469; Yes; Yes
481; Lonie; f; 19; Miss. Choctaw; F; S; Dau; 470; Yes; Yes
482; Jim; m; 28[sic]; Miss. Choctaw; F; S; Son; 471; Yes; Yes
483; Wade; m; 18; Miss. Choctaw; F; S; Son; 471; Yes; Yes

EVANS

484; John; m; 58; Miss. Choctaw; F; Wd; Head; 473; Yes; Yes
485; **Wickson**, Kelly; m; 8; Miss. Choctaw; F; S; Son; 474; Yes; Yes

FARMER

486; Silmon; m; 59; Miss. Choctaw; F; Wd; Head; 475; Yes; Yes
487; Henry; m; 21; Miss. Choctaw; F; S; Son; 476; Yes; Yes
488; Bennie; f; 15; Miss. Choctaw; F; S; Dau; 477; Yes; Yes
489; Corine; f; 12; Miss. Choctaw; F; S; Dau; 478; Yes; Yes

490; Ishman; m; 88; Miss. Choctaw; F; M; Head; 479; Yes; Yes
491; Sweeter; f; 60; Miss. Choctaw; F; M; Wife; 480; Yes; Yes
492; Emma; f; 30; Miss. Choctaw; F; S; Dau; 481; Yes; Yes
493; Marshall; m; 28; Miss. Choctaw; F; S; Son; 482; Yes; Yes
494; Maggie; f; 23; Miss. Choctaw; F; S; Dau; 483; Yes; Yes
495; Lena; f; 20; Miss. Choctaw; F; S; Dau; 484; Yes; Yes
496; Bill; m; 17; Miss. Choctaw; F; S; Son; 485; Yes; Yes
497; Rainey; f; 13; Miss. Choctaw; F; S; Dau; 486; Yes; Yes

498; Moses; m; 33; Miss. Choctaw; F; M; Head; 487; Yes; Yes
499; Lottie; f; 25; Miss. Choctaw; F; M; Wife; 488; Yes; Yes
500; Mealie; f; 2; Miss. Choctaw; F; S; Dau; 489; Yes; Yes

501; Thomas; m; 67; Miss. Choctaw; F; M; Head; 490; Yes; Yes

Census of the **Mississippi Choctaws** reservation of the **Choctaw Agency** jurisdiction, as of **April 1**, 19**33**, taken by **A. C. Hector**, Superintendent.

KEY; Surname; Census Number; Given Name; Sex; Age at Last Birthday; Tribe; Degree of Blood; Marital Status; Relationship to Head of Family; Last Census Roll Number; At Jurisdiction Where Enrolled (Yes/No); At Another Jurisdiction; Post Office, County, State (if given); Ward (Yes/No)

502; Melissa; f; 60; Miss. Choctaw; F; M; Wife; 491; Yes; Yes
503; Howard; m; 21; Miss. Choctaw; F; M; Head; 492; Yes; Yes
504; Lonie; f; 19; Miss. Choctaw; F; M; wife; 4[sic]; Yes; Yes

FARVE

505; Bennett; m; 40; Miss. Choctaw; F; S; Alone; 493; Yes; Yes

506; Paul; m; 45; Miss. Choctaw; F; M; Head; 494; Yes; Yes
507; Renia; f; 28; Miss. Choctaw; F; M; Wife; 495; Yes; Yes
508; Phillip; m; 9; Miss. Choctaw; F; S; Son; 496; Yes; Yes
509; Eula Mae; f; 7; Miss. Choctaw; F; S; Dau; 497; Yes; Yes
510; Estelle; f; 5; Miss. Choctaw; F; S; Dau; 498; Yes; Yes
511; Viola; f; 3; Miss. Choctaw; F; S; Dau; 499; Yes; Yes

512; Joseph; m; 21; Miss. Choctaw; F; M; Head; 500; Yes; Yes
513; Rachel; f; 54; Miss. Choctaw; F; M; Wife; 501; Yes; Yes

514; Western; m; 43; Miss. Choctaw; F; Wd; Head; 502; Yes; Yes
515; Chester; m; 28; Miss. Choctaw; F; S; Son; 503; Yes; Yes
516; Josie; f; 25; Miss. Choctaw; F; S; Dau; 504; Yes; Yes
517; John; m; 25; Miss. Choctaw; F; S; Son; 505; Yes; Yes
518; Lillian; f; 22; Miss. Choctaw; F; S; Dau; 506; Yes; Yes
519; Ima; f; 17; Miss. Choctaw; F; S; Dau; 507; Yes; Yes
520; Hilda; f; 9; Miss. Choctaw; F; S; Dau; 508; Yes; Yes

521; Antwine; m; 56; Miss. Choctaw; F; M; Head; 509; Yes; Yes
522; Liseeda; f; 59; Miss. Choctaw; F; m; Wife; 510; Yes; Yes
523; Edna; f; 23; Miss. Choctaw; F; S; Dau; 511; Yes; Yes
524; Cecilia; f; 21; Miss. Choctaw; F; S; Dau; 512; Yes; Yes
525; Isileen; f; 20; Miss. Choctaw; F; S; Dau; 513; Yes; Yes
526; Earl; m; 15; Miss. Choctaw; F; S; Son; 514; Yes; Yes
527; Mamie; f; 13; Miss. Choctaw; F; S; Dau; 515; Yes; Yes
528; Corbrin; m; 10; Miss. Choctaw; F; S; Son; 516; Yes; Yes

Census of the **Mississippi Choctaws** reservation of the **Choctaw Agency** jurisdiction, as of **April 1**, 19**33**, taken by **A. C. Hector**, Superintendent.

KEY: Surname; Census Number; Given Name; Sex; Age at Last Birthday; Tribe; Degree of Blood; Marital Status; Relationship to Head of Family; Last Census Roll Number; At Jurisdiction Where Enrolled (Yes/No); At Another Jurisdiction; Post Office, County, State (if given); Ward (Yes/No)

529; Dave; m; 55; Miss. Choctaw; F; Wd; Head; 517; Yes; Yes
530; Lena; f; 33; Miss. Choctaw; F; S; Dau; 518; Yes; Yes
531; Sarah Alma; f; 22; Miss. Choctaw; F; S; Dau; 519; Yes; Yes
532; Georgia; f; 14; Miss. Choctaw; F; S; Dau; 520; Yes; Yes
533; John; m; 11; Miss. Choctaw; F; S; Son; 521; Yes; Yes

534; William; m; 32; Miss. Choctaw; F; Wd; Alone; 522; Yes; Yes

535; Rosine H; m; 50; Miss. Choctaw; F; M; Head; 524; Yes; Yes
536; Winoa; f; 55; Miss. Choctaw; F; M; Wife; 525; Yes; Yes

537; Charles; m; 45; Miss. Choctaw; F; M; Head; 526; Yes; Yes
538; Edwina; f; 42; Miss. Choctaw; F; M; Wife; 527; Yes; Yes
539; Retha; f; 15; Miss. Choctaw; F; S; Dau; 528; Yes; Yes
540; Alvin; m; 13; Miss. Choctaw; F; S; Son; 529; Yes; Yes
541; Irvin; m; 11; Miss. Choctaw; F; S; Son; 530; Yes; Yes
542; Audrey; f; 8; Miss. Choctaw; F; S; Dau; 531; Yes; Yes
543; Vivian; f; 7; Miss. Choctaw; F; S; Dau; 532; Yes; Yes

544; Thomas; m; 51; Miss. Choctaw; F; M; Head; 533; Yes; Yes
545; Mary; f; 35; Miss. Choctaw; F; M; Wife; 534; Yes; Yes
546; Hazel; f; 15; Miss. Choctaw; F; S; Dau; 535; Yes; Yes
547; Robert; m; 14; Miss. Choctaw; F; S; Son; 536; Yes; Yes
548; Gertrude; f; 12; Miss. Choctaw; F; S; Dau; 537; Yes; Yes
549; Ruth; f; 9; Miss. Choctaw; F; S; Dau; 538; Yes; Yes

550; Sylvester; m; 45; Miss. Choctaw; F; S; Alone; 539; Yes; Yes

551; Joe Tole; m; 68; Miss. Choctaw; F; M; Head; 540; Yes; Yes
552; Lola; f; 65; Miss. Choctaw; F; M; Wife; 541; Yes; Yes
553; Dora; f; 40; Miss. Choctaw; F; S; Dau; 542; Yes; Yes
554; Victoria; f; 33; Miss. Choctaw; F; S; Dau; 543; Yes; Yes

555; Gilmore; m; 31; Miss. Choctaw; F; M; Head; 544; Yes; Yes

Census of the **Mississippi Choctaws** reservation of the **Choctaw Agency** jurisdiction, as of **April 1**, 19**33**, taken by **A. C. Hector**, Superintendent.

KEY; Surname; Census Number; Given Name; Sex; Age at Last Birthday; Tribe; Degree of Blood; Marital Status; Relationship to Head of Family; Last Census Roll Number; At Jurisdiction Where Enrolled (Yes/No); At Another Jurisdiction; Post Office, County, State (if given); Ward (Yes/No)

556; Gertrude; f; 29; Miss. Choctaw; F; M; Wife; 545; Yes; Yes
557; Joe; m; 27; Miss. Choctaw; F; M; Head; 546; Yes; Yes
558; Lillian; f; 24; Miss. Choctaw; F; M; Wife; 547; Yes; Yes
559; Basie; m; 22; Miss. Choctaw; F; S; Alone; 548; Yes; Yes

560; Jessie; f; 21; Miss. Choctaw; F; S; Alone; 549; Yes; Yes

561; Corrine; m; 38; Miss. Choctaw; F; M; Head; 550; Yes; Yes
562; Viola; f; 36; Miss. Choctaw; F; M; Wife; 551; Yes; Yes
563; William; m; 17; Miss. Choctaw; F; S; Son; 552; Yes; Yes
564; Francis; m; 11; Miss. Choctaw; F; S; Son; 553; Yes; Yes
565; J. C; m; 9; Miss. Choctaw; F; S; Son; 554; Yes; Yes
566; Wilma; f; 7; Miss. Choctaw; F; S; Dau; 555; Yes; Yes

567; John Tole; m; 50; Miss. Choctaw; F; S; Alone; 556; Yes; Yes

568; Charles T; m; 49; Miss. Choctaw; F; M; Head; 557; Yes; Yes
569; Alfonsine; f; 35; Miss. Choctaw; F; M; Wife; 558; Yes; Yes

570; Emeline; f; 43; Miss. Choctaw; F; S; Alone; 559; Yes; Yes

571; Mary; f; 37; Miss. Choctaw; F; S; Alone; 560; Yes; Yes

572; Julia; f; 48; Miss. Choctaw; F; S; Alone; 561; Yes; Yes

573; R. C; m; 32; Miss. Choctaw; F; S; Alone; 562; Yes; Yes

574; Dennis; m; 45; Miss. Choctaw; F; S; Alone; 563; Yes; Yes

575; Western; m; 53; Miss. Choctaw; F; S; Alone; 564; Yes; Yes

576; Noah; m; 41; Miss. Choctaw; F; S; Alone; 565; Yes; Yes

577; Bennett; m; 39; Miss. Choctaw; F; S; Alone; 566; Yes; Yes

Census of the **Mississippi Choctaws** reservation of the **Choctaw Agency** jurisdiction, as of **April 1**, 19**33**, taken by **A. C. Hector**, Superintendent.

KEY; Surname; Census Number; Given Name; Sex; Age at Last Birthday; Tribe; Degree of Blood; Marital Status; Relationship to Head of Family; Last Census Roll Number; At Jurisdiction Where Enrolled (Yes/No); At Another Jurisdiction; Post Office, County, State (if given); Ward (Yes/No)

578; William; m; 35; Miss. Choctaw; F; S; Alone; 567; Yes; Yes

579; Seman; m; 67; Miss. Choctaw; F; S; Alone; 568; Yes; Yes

580; Elinor; f; 39; Miss. Choctaw; F; S; Alone; 569; Yes; Yes

581; Joe; m; 60; Miss. Choctaw; F; S; Alone; 570; Yes; Yes

582; Albert; m; 52; Miss. Choctaw; F; M; Head; 571; Yes; Yes
583; Iktial; f; 50; Miss. Choctaw; F; M; Wife; 572; Yes; Yes

584; Lucille; f; 30; Miss. Choctaw; F; S; Alone; 573; Yes; Yes

585; Ethel; f; 29; Miss. Choctaw; F; S; Alone; 574; Yes; Yes

586; Ida; f; 53; Miss. Choctaw; F; S; Alone; 575; Yes; Yes

587; Rosella; f; 57; Miss. Choctaw; F; S; Alone; 576; Yes; Yes

588; Amelia; f; 39; Miss. Choctaw; F; S; Alone; 577; Yes; Yes

589; Henrietta; f; 35; Miss. Choctaw; F; S; Alone; 578; Yes; Yes

590; Bay Turner; m; 28; Miss. Choctaw; F; S; Alone; 579; Yes; Yes

591; Ceciline; m; 27; Miss. Choctaw; F; S; Alone; 580; Yes; Yes

592; Charles; m; 53; Miss. Choctaw; F; S; Alone; 581; Yes; Yes

FORBES

593; Wesley; m; 69; Miss. Choctaw; F; M; Head; 582; Yes; Yes
594; Sallie; f; 58; Miss. Choctaw; F; M; Wife; 583; Yes; Yes
595; Ella; f; 22; Miss. Choctaw; F; S; Dau; 584; Yes; Yes

Census of the **Mississippi Choctaws** reservation of the **Choctaw Agency** jurisdiction, as of **April 1**, 19**33**, taken by **A. C. Hector**, Superintendent.

KEY; Surname; Census Number; Given Name; Sex; Age at Last Birthday; Tribe; Degree of Blood; Marital Status; Relationship to Head of Family; Last Census Roll Number; At Jurisdiction Where Enrolled (Yes/No); At Another Jurisdiction; Post Office, County, State (if given); Ward (Yes/No)

596; Clint; m; 31; Miss. Choctaw; F; M; Head; 585; Yes; Yes
597; Josey; f; 32; Miss. Choctaw; F; M; Wife; 586; Yes; Yes
598; Ida Mae; f; 16; Miss. Choctaw; F; S; Dau; 587; Yes; Yes
599; Gaston; m; 11; Miss. Choctaw; F; S; Son; 588; Yes; Yes
600; Henry; m; 3; Miss. Choctaw; F; S; Son; 589; Yes; Yes

FRAZIER

601; Mollie; f; 58; Miss. Choctaw; F; Wd; Head; 590; Yes; Yes
602; John; m; 22; Miss. Choctaw; F; S; Son; 592; Yes; Yes

603; West; m; 25; Miss. Choctaw; F; M; Head; 593; Yes; Yes
604; Nannie; f; 24; Miss. Choctaw; F; M; Wife; 594; Yes; Yes
605; Marshall; m; 4; Miss. Choctaw; F; S; Son; 595; Yes; Yes

606; Forbes; m; 32; Miss. Choctaw; F; M; Head; 596; Yes; Yes
607; Iam; f; 28; Miss. Choctaw; F; M; Wife; 597; Yes; Yes
608; Homer; m; 9; Miss. Choctaw; F; S; Son; 598; Yes; Yes
609; **Box**, Sam Davis; m; 10; Miss. Choctaw; F; S; Stepson; 599; Yes; Yes

610; Will; m; 33; Miss. Choctaw; F; M; Head; 600; Yes; Yes
611; Lavena; f; 30; Miss. Choctaw; F; M; Wife; 601; Yes; Yes

612; Seale; m; 63; Miss. Choctaw; F; M; Head; 602; Yes; Yes
613; Eliza; f; 78; Miss. Choctaw; F; M; Wife; 603; Yes; Yes
614; Willie; f; 8; Miss. Choctaw; F; S; Grand-dau; 604; Yes; Yes

615; Jim; m; 27; Miss. Choctaw; F; M; Head; 605; Yes; Yes
616; Nannie; f; 29; Miss. Choctaw; F; M; Wife; 606; Yes; Yes
617; A. B; m; 6; Miss. Choctaw; F; S; Son; 607; Yes; Yes
618; Henry; m; 7; Miss. Choctaw; F; S; Son; 608; Yes; Yes
619; Nancy; f; 4; Miss. Choctaw; F; S; Dau; 609; Yes; Yes

Census of the **Mississippi Choctaws** reservation of the **Choctaw Agency** jurisdiction, as of **April 1**, 19**33**, taken by **A. C. Hector**, Superintendent.

KEY; Surname; Census Number; Given Name; Sex; Age at Last Birthday; Tribe; Degree of Blood; Marital Status; Relationship to Head of Family; Last Census Roll Number; At Jurisdiction Where Enrolled (Yes/No); At Another Jurisdiction; Post Office, County, State (if given); Ward (Yes/No)

620; Ligman; m; 39; Miss. Choctaw; F; M; Head; 610; Yes; Yes
621; Sina; f; 24; Miss. Choctaw; F; M; Wife; 611; Yes; Yes
622; Edmond; m; 11; Miss. Choctaw; F; S; Son; 612; Yes; Yes
623; Sallie; f; 9; Miss. Choctaw; F; S; Dau; 613; Yes; Yes

624; Emma; f; 35; Miss. Choctaw; F; Wd; Head; 614; Yes; Yes
625; Susie; f; 17; Miss. Choctaw; F; S; Dau; 615; Yes; Yes
626; Simpson; f; 13; Miss. Choctaw; F; S; Dau; 616; Yes; Yes
627; Herman; m; 12; Miss. Choctaw; F; S; Son; 617; Yes; Yes
628; Frazier; m; 10; Miss. Choctaw; F; S; Son; 618; Yes; Yes
629; Velma; f; 8; Miss. Choctaw; F; S; Dau; 619; Yes; Yes

630; Henson; m; 65; Miss. Choctaw; F; M; Head; 620; Yes; Yes
631; Fenie; f; 63; Miss. Choctaw; F; M; Wife; 621; Yes; Yes
632; Lucy; f; 15; Miss. Choctaw; F; S; Dau; 622; Yes; Yes
633; Wade; m; 15; Miss. Choctaw; F; S; Son; 623; Yes; Yes
634; Jake; m; 11; Miss. Choctaw; F; S; Son; 624; Yes; Yes

635; Wesley; m; 70; Miss. Choctaw; F; Wd; Head; Yes; Yes
   Omitted on previous Census rolls
636; Ella; f; 25; Miss. Choctaw; F; S; Dau; Yes; Yes
   Omitted on previous Census rolls

GARDNER

637; Jim; m; 34; Miss. Choctaw; F; M; Head; 625; Yes; Yes
638; Celia; f; 29; Miss. Choctaw; F; M; Wife; 626; Yes; Yes
639; Arleta; f; 12; Miss. Choctaw; F; S; Dau; 627; Yes; Yes
640; Alton; m; 6; Miss. Choctaw; F; S; Son; 628; Yes; Yes

GIPSON

641; Bart; m; 57; Miss. Choctaw; F; M; Head; 629; Yes; Yes
642; Lucy; f; 53; Miss. Choctaw; F; M; Wife; 630; Yes; Yes

Census of the **Mississippi Choctaws** reservation of the **Choctaw Agency** jurisdiction, as of **April 1**, 19__33__, taken by **A. C. Hector**, Superintendent.

KEY; Surname; Census Number; Given Name; Sex; Age at Last Birthday; Tribe; Degree of Blood; Marital Status; Relationship to Head of Family; Last Census Roll Number; At Jurisdiction Where Enrolled (Yes/No); At Another Jurisdiction; Post Office, County, State (if given); Ward (Yes/No)

643; Homer; m; 20; Miss. Choctaw; F; M; Head; 631; Yes; Yes
644; Sophie; f; 20; Miss. Choctaw; F; M; Wife; 1221; Yes; Yes

645; Hensley; m; 22; Miss. Choctaw; F; M; Head; 632; Yes; Yes
646; Elizabeth; f; 22; Miss. Choctaw; F; M; Wife; 633; Yes; Yes
647; Henrietta; f; 1; Miss. Choctaw; F; S; Dau; 634; Yes; Yes

648; Andrew; m; 28; Miss. Choctaw; F; M; Head; 635; Yes; Yes
649; Esther; f; 20; Miss. Choctaw; F; M; Wife; Yes; Yes

650; Gus; m; 24; Miss. Choctaw; F; S; Alone; 637; Yes; Yes

651; Nolie; m; 31; Miss. Choctaw; F; M; Head; 638; Yes; Yes
652; Frances; f; 33; Miss. Choctaw; F; M; Wife; 639; Yes; Yes
653; Pearl; f; 8; Miss. Choctaw; F; S; Dau; 640; Yes; Yes
654; Clay; m; 7; Miss. Choctaw; F; S; Son; 641; Yes; Yes
655; Annie; f; 4; Miss. Choctaw; F; S; Dau; 642; Yes; Yes
656; Fannie; f; 11/12; Miss. Choctaw; F; S; Dau; Yes; Yes

657; Steve; m; 69; Miss. Choctaw; F; M; Head; 643; Yes; Yes
658; Jennie; f; 65; Miss. Choctaw; F; M; Wife; 644; Yes; Yes
659; Ikey; f; 30; Miss. Choctaw; F; S; Dau; 645; Yes; Yes
660; Fannie; f; 25; Miss. Choctaw; F; S; Dau; 646; Yes; Yes
661; Annie; f; 24; Miss. Choctaw; F; S; Dau; 647; Yes; Yes
662; Willie; m; 15; Miss. Choctaw; F; S; Son; 648; Yes; Yes
663; Hugh; m; 7; Miss. Choctaw; F; S; Grand-son; 649; Yes; Yes
664; Aron; m; 6; Miss. Choctaw; F; S; Grand-son; 650; Yes; Yes

HALL

665; Langford; m; Miss. Choctaw; F; M; Head; 654; Yes; Yes
666; Lou; f; 29; Miss. Choctaw; F; M; Wife; 655; Yes; Yes
667; Travis; m; 10; Miss. Choctaw; F; S; Son; 656; Yes; Yes
668; Arlone; f; 9; Miss. Choctaw; F; S; Dau; 657; Yes; Yes

Census of the **Mississippi Choctaws** reservation of the **Choctaw Agency** jurisdiction, as of **April 1**, 19**33**, taken by **A. C. Hector**, Superintendent.

KEY; Surname; Census Number; Given Name; Sex; Age at Last Birthday; Tribe; Degree of Blood; Marital Status; Relationship to Head of Family; Last Census Roll Number; At Jurisdiction Where Enrolled (Yes/No); At Another Jurisdiction; Post Office, County, State (if given); Ward (Yes/No)

669; Frank; m; 7; Miss. Choctaw; F; S; Son; 658; Yes; Yes
670; Francis; f; 1; Miss. Choctaw; F; S; Dau; 659; Yes; Yes

HARPER

671; Lena; f; 21; Miss. Choctaw; F; S; Alone; 660; Yes; Yes

HARRIS

672; Elsmore; f; 25; Miss. Choctaw; F; S; Alone; 661; Yes; Yes

HAWKINS

673; Alice; f; 51; Miss. Choctaw; F; Wd; Head; 663; Yes; Yes
674; **Shoemaker**, Mary; f; Miss. Choctaw; F; S; Dau; 664; Yes; Yes

HENRY

675; Albert; m; 55; Miss. Choctaw; F; M; Head; 665; Yes; Yes
676; Martha; f; 45; Miss. Choctaw; F; M; Wife; 666; Yes; Yes
677; Guiser; f; 29; Miss. Choctaw; F; S; Dau; 667; Yes; Yes
678; Beulah; f; 25; Miss. Choctaw; F; S; Dau; 668; Yes; Yes
679; Liege; m; 23; Miss. Choctaw; F; S; Son; 669; Yes; Yes
680; Melvin; m; 20; Miss. Choctaw; F; S; Son; 670; Yes; Yes
681; Nettie; f; 18; Miss. Choctaw; F; S; Dau; 671; Yes; Yes
682; Sis; f; 15; Miss. Choctaw; F; S; Dau; 672; Yes; Yes
683; Susie; f; 13; Miss. Choctaw; F; S; Dau; 673; Yes; Yes
684; R. D; m; 11; Miss. Choctaw; F; S; Son; 674; Yes; Yes
685; Ellen; f; 4; Miss. Choctaw; F; S; Grand-dau; 675; Yes; Yes
Daughter of Guiser Henry

686; Jim; m; 30; Miss. Choctaw; F; M; Head; 676; Yes; Yes
687; Sallie; f; 28; Miss. Choctaw; F; M; Wife; 677; Yes; Yes
688; Frank; m; 6; Miss. Choctaw; F; S; Son; 678; Yes; Yes

Census of the **Mississippi Choctaws** reservation of the **Choctaw Agency** jurisdiction, as of **April 1**, 19**33**, taken by **A. C. Hector**, Superintendent.

KEY; Surname; Census Number; Given Name; Sex; Age at Last Birthday; Tribe; Degree of Blood; Marital Status; Relationship to Head of Family; Last Census Roll Number; At Jurisdiction Where Enrolled (Yes/No); At Another Jurisdiction; Post Office, County, State (if given); Ward (Yes/No)

689; Wicks; m; 4; Miss. Choctaw; F; S; Son; 679; Yes; Yes
690; Joy June; f; 4/12; Miss. Choctaw; F; S; Dau; Yes; Yes

691; Robert; m; 59; Miss. Choctaw; F; M; Head; 680; Yes; Yes
692; Nellie; f; 49; Miss. Choctaw; F; M; Wife; 681; Yes; Yes
693; Bob; m; 25; Miss. Choctaw; F; S; Son; 682; Yes; Yes
694; Mattie; f; 22; Miss. Choctaw; F; S; Dau; 683; Yes; Yes
695; Jasper; m; 16; Miss. Choctaw; F; S; Son; 684; Yes; Yes
696; Dolphus; m; 13; Miss. Choctaw; F; S; Son; 685; Yes; Yes

HICKMAN

697; Billy; m; 47; Miss. Choctaw; F; M; Head; 686; Yes; Yes
698; Rhodie; f; 49; Miss. Choctaw; F; M; Wife; 687; Yes; Yes
699; Sim; m; 21; Miss. Choctaw; F; S; Son; 688; Yes; Yes
700; Susan; f; 15; Miss. Choctaw; F; S; Dau; 689; Yes; Yes
701; Lula; f; 13; Miss. Choctaw; F; S; Dau; 690; Yes; Yes

702; Willie; m; 23; Miss. Choctaw; F; M; Head; 691; Yes; Yes
703; Lodie Mae; f; 25; Miss. Choctaw; F; M; Wife; 692; Yes; Yes

704; Ellis; m; 63; Miss. Choctaw; F; M; Head; 693; Yes; Yes
705; Susuan[sic]; f; 57; Miss. Choctaw; F; M; Wife; 694; Yes; Yes
706; **Bell**, Burton; m; 13; Miss. Choctaw; F; S; Grand-son; 695; Yes; Yes
707; **Bell**, Henry; m; 11; Miss. Choctaw; F; S; Grand-son; 696; Yes; Yes

708; Johnkin; m; 33; Miss. Choctaw; F; M; Head; 697; Yes; Yes
709; Minnie; f; 28; Miss. Choctaw; F; M; Wife; 698; Yes; Yes

710; Enoch; m; 59; Miss. Choctaw; F; M; Head; 699; Yes; Yes
711; Malinda; f; 57; Miss. Choctaw; F; M; Wife; 700; Yes; Yes
712; Sallie; f; 23; Miss. Choctaw; F; S; Dau; 701; Yes; Yes

Census of the **Mississippi Choctaws** reservation of the **Choctaw** Agency jurisdiction, as of **April 1**, 19**33**, taken by **A. C. Hector**, Superintendent.

KEY; Surname; Census Number; Given Name; Sex; Age at Last Birthday; Tribe; Degree of Blood; Marital Status; Relationship to Head of Family; Last Census Roll Number; At Jurisdiction Where Enrolled (Yes/No); At Another Jurisdiction; Post Office, County, State (if given); Ward (Yes/No)

713; Sadie; f; 22; Miss. Choctaw; F; S; Son; 702; Yes; Yes
714; Tubby; m; 20; Miss. Choctaw; F; S; Son; 703; Yes; Yes
715; Eliza Jane; f; 19; Miss. Choctaw; F; S; Dau; 704; Yes; Yes
716; Mary Long; f; 17; Miss. Choctaw; F; S; Dau; 705; Yes; Yes
717; Annie; f; 12; Miss. Choctaw; F; S; Dau; 706; Yes; Yes
718; Wm. Penn; m; 11; Miss. Choctaw; F; S; Son; 707; Yes; Yes
719; Varderman; m; 9; Miss. Choctaw; F; S; Son; 708; Yes; Yes
720; John; m; 8; Miss. Choctaw; F; S; Son; 709; Yes; Yes

721; Wallace; m; 27; Miss. Choctaw; F; M; Head; 710; Yes; Yes
722; Dona; f; 24; Miss. Choctaw; F; M; Wife; 711; Yes; Yes
723; Robinson; m; 7; Miss. Choctaw; F; S; Son; 712; Yes; Yes
724; Pearl; f; 3/12; Miss. Choctaw; F; S; Dau; Yes; Yes

725; Stennis; m; 29; Miss. Choctaw; F; M; Head; 713; Yes; Yes
726; Winnie; f; 28; Miss. Choctaw; F; M; Wife; 714; Yes; Yes
727; Eula; f; 6; Miss. Choctaw; F; S; Dau; 715; Yes; Yes
728; Snooks; m; 5; Miss. Choctaw; F; S; Son; 716; Yes; Yes

729; Mary; f; 77; Miss. Choctaw; F; Wd; Head; 717; Yes; Yes
730; **Charlie**, Beckie; f; 16; Miss. Choctaw; F; S; Grand-day[sic]; Yes; Yes

HUDSON

731; Celia; f; 26; Miss. Choctaw; F; S; Alone; 719; Yes; Yes

ISAAC

732; Jim; m; 38; Miss. Choctaw; F; M; Head; 720; Yes; Yes
733; Bessie; f; 32; Miss. Choctaw; F; M; Wife; 721; Yes; Yes
734; Steve; m; 78; Miss. Choctaw; F; Wd; Father; 722; Yes; Yes

735; Byrd; m; 37; Miss. Choctaw; F; M; Head; 723; Yes; Yes

Census of the **Mississippi Choctaws** reservation of the **Choctaw Agency** jurisdiction, as of **April 1**, 19**33**, taken by **A. C. Hector**, Superintendent.

KEY; Surname; Census Number; Given Name; Sex; Age at Last Birthday; Tribe; Degree of Blood; Marital Status; Relationship to Head of Family; Last Census Roll Number; At Jurisdiction Where Enrolled (Yes/No); At Another Jurisdiction; Post Office, County, State (if given); Ward (Yes/No)

736; Pauline; f; 21; Miss. Choctaw; F; M; Wife; 724; Yes; Yes
737; Odie Mae; f; 17; Miss. Choctaw; F; S; Dau; 725; Yes; Yes
738; Bernice; f; 15; Miss. Choctaw; F; S; Dau; 726; Yes; Yes
739; Catherine; f; 13; Miss. Choctaw; F; S; Dau; 727; Yes; Yes
740; Edwin; m; 6; Miss. Choctaw; F; S; Son; 728; Yes; Yes
741; Jesse A; m; 1; Miss. Choctaw; F; S; Son; 729; Yes; Yes
742; **Hall**, Herbert H; m; 4; Miss. Choctaw; F; S; Stepson; Yes; Yes

743; Hickman; m; 26; Miss. Choctaw; F; S; Alone; 731; Yes; Yes

744; Simon; m; 49; Miss. Choctaw; F; M; Head; 732; Yes; Yes
745; Nannie; f; 52; Miss. Choctaw; F; M; Wife; 733; Yes; Yes
746; Effie; f; 10; Miss. Choctaw; F; S; Dau; 734; Yes; Yes
747; Lillie Mae; f; 8; Miss. Choctaw; F; S; Grand-dau; 735; Yes; Yes

748; Hugh; m; 23; Miss. Choctaw; F; M: Head; 736; Yes; Yes
749; Celia; f; 24; Miss. Choctaw; F; M; Wife; 737; Yes; Yes
750; Beneda; f; 2; Miss. Choctaw; F; S; Dau; 738; Yes; Yes

751; Isaac; m; 32; Miss. Choctaw; F; M; Head; 739; Yes; Yes
752; Maggie; f; 24; Miss. Choctaw; F; M; Wife; 740; Yes; Yes
753; Claudine; f; 11; Miss. Choctaw; F; S; Dau; 741; Yes; Yes
754; Wilbur; m; 9; Miss. Choctaw; F; S; Son; 742; Yes; Yes
755; Claud Preston; m; 5; Miss. Choctaw; F; S; Son; 743; Yes; Yes
756; Enochs; m; 4; Miss. Choctaw; F; S; Son; 744; Yes; Yes
757; Delphia; f; 11/12; Miss. Choctaw; F; S; Dau; Yes; Yes

758; Will; m; 35; Miss. Choctaw; F; M; Head; 745; Yes; Yes
759; Louisa; f; 34; Miss. Choctaw; F; M; Wife; 746; Yes; Yes
760; Annie; f; 15; Miss. Choctaw; F; S; Dau; 747; Yes; Yes
761; Cornelia; f; 6; Miss. Choctaw; F; S; Dau; 748; Yes; Yes

762; Wilson; m; 79; Miss. Choctaw; F; M; Head; 749; Yes; Yes
763; Martha; f; 66; Miss. Choctaw; F; M: Wife; 750; Yes; Yes

Census of the **Mississippi Choctaws** reservation of the **Choctaw Agency** jurisdiction, as of **April 1**, 19**33**, taken by **A. C. Hector**, Superintendent.

KEY; Surname; Census Number; Given Name; Sex; Age at Last Birthday; Tribe; Degree of Blood; Marital Status; Relationship to Head of Family; Last Census Roll Number; At Jurisdiction Where Enrolled (Yes/No); At Another Jurisdiction; Post Office, County, State (if given); Ward (Yes/No)

764;   John Day; m; 20; Miss. Choctaw; F; S; Son; 752; Yes; Yes
765;   **Sam**, Edna; f; 11; Miss. Choctaw; F; S; Orphan; 753; Yes; Yes

766;   Jackson; m; 28; Miss. Choctaw; F; M; Head; 751; Yes; Yes
767;   Eva; f; 19; Miss. Choctaw; F; M; wife; 1467; Yes; Yes

768;   David; m; 26; Miss. Choctaw; F; M; Head; 754; Yes; Yes
769;   Lesper; f; 25; Miss. Choctaw; F; M; Wife; 755; Yes; Yes
770;   Joe Day; m; 6; Miss. Choctaw; F; S; Son; 756; Yes; Yes
771;   Franklin; m; 4; Miss. Choctaw; F; S; Son; 757; Yes; Yes
772;   Wansey; f; 2; Miss. Choctaw; F; S; Dau; 758; Yes; Yes

773;   Dixon; m; 81; Miss. Choctaw; F; M; Head; 859; Yes; Yes
774;   Lou; f; 28; Miss. Choctaw; F; M; Wife; 760; Yes; Yes
775;   Elsie; f; 15; Miss. Choctaw; F; S; Dau; 761; Yes; Yes
776;   Rainey; f; 12; Miss. Choctaw; F; S; Dau; 762; Yes; Yes
777;   Manda; f; 10; Miss. Choctaw; F; S; Dau; 763; Yes; Yes
778;   Lester; m; 9; Miss. Choctaw; F; S; Son; 764; Yes; Yes
779;   **Billy**, Emma; f; 27; Miss. Choctaw; F; S; Sister-in-law; 765; Yes; Yes

ISOM

780;   Willie; m; 19; Miss. Choctaw; F; S; Alone; 766; Yes; Yes

781;   Isom; m; 33; Miss. Choctaw; F; S; Alone; 767; Yes; Yes

JACKSON

782;   Betty; f; 57; Miss. Choctaw; F; Wd; Head; 768; Yes; Yes
783;   Rose; f; 21; Miss. Choctaw; F; S; Dau; 769; Yes; Yes
784;   Nancie; f; 19; Miss. Choctaw; F; S; Dau; 770; Yes; Yes
785;   Carlson; m; 13; Miss. Choctaw; F; S; Son; 772; Yes; Yes

Census of the **Mississippi Choctaws** reservation of the **Choctaw Agency** jurisdiction, as of **April 1**, 19**33**, taken by **A. C. Hector**, Superintendent.

KEY; Surname; Census Number; Given Name; Sex; Age at Last Birthday; Tribe; Degree of Blood; Marital Status; Relationship to Head of Family; Last Census Roll Number; At Jurisdiction Where Enrolled (Yes/No); At Another Jurisdiction; Post Office, County, State (if given); Ward (Yes/No)

786; Lena; f; 45; Miss. Choctaw; F; Wd; Head; 772; Yes; Yes
787; Ella; f; 19; Miss. Choctaw; F; S; Dau; 773; Yes; Yes
789[sic]; Jackson; m; 16; Miss. Choctaw; F; S; Son; 775; Yes; Yes
789; Emmett; m; 13; Miss. Choctaw; F; S; Son; 776; Yes; Yes
790; Lucille; f; 12; Miss. Choctaw; F; S; Dau; 777; Yes; Yes

791; Tom; m; 45; Miss. Choctaw; F; M: Head; 778; Yes; Yes
792; Mamie; f; 41; Miss. Choctaw; F; M; Wife; 779; Yes; Yes
793; Woodrow; m; 14; Miss. Choctaw; F; S; Son; 780; Yes; Yes
794; Eva; f; 13; Miss. Choctaw; F; S; Dau; 781; Yes; Yes

795; Sam; m; 49; Miss. Choctaw; F; M; Head; 782; Yes; Yes
796; Martha; f; 50; Miss. Choctaw; F; M; Wife; 783; Yes; Yes

797; Tubby; m; 23; Miss. Choctaw; F; M; Head; 784; Yes; Yes
798; Missie; f; 23; Miss. Choctaw; F; M; Wife; 785; Yes; Yes

799; Prentiss; m; 30; Miss. Choctaw; F; M; Head; 786; Yes; Yes
800; Mary; f; 30; Miss. Choctaw; F; M; Wife; 787; Yes; Yes

801; Mike; m; 32; Miss. Choctaw; F; S; Alone; 788; Yes; Yes

JEFFERSON

802; Braxton; m; 27; Miss. Choctaw; F; Wd; Alone; 789; Yes; Yes

803; Amos; m; 26; Miss. Choctaw; F; M; Head; 790; Yes; Yes
804; Ida; f; 21; Miss. Choctaw; F; M; Wife; 791; Yes; Yes
805; Leon; m; 1; Miss. Choctaw; F; S; Son; 797; Yes; Yes

806; Willis; m; 58; Miss. Choctaw; F; S; Head; 792; Yes; Yes
807; Elsie; f; 46; Miss. Choctaw; F; S; Sister; 793; Yes; Yes

808; Oscar; m; 28; Miss. Choctaw; F; M; Head; 794; Yes; Yes

Census of the **Mississippi Choctaws** reservation of the **Choctaw Agency** jurisdiction, as of **April 1**, 19**33**, taken by **A. C. Hector**, Superintendent.

KEY; Surname; Census Number; Given Name; Sex; Age at Last Birthday; Tribe; Degree of Blood; Marital Status; Relationship to Head of Family; Last Census Roll Number; At Jurisdiction Where Enrolled (Yes/No); At Another Jurisdiction; Post Office, County, State (if given); Ward (Yes/No)

809; Saline; f; 26; Miss. Choctaw; F; M; Wife; 795; Yes; Yes
810; Malcolm; m; 7; Miss. Choctaw; F; S; Son; 796; Yes; Yes

811; Otis; m; 30; Miss. Choctaw; F; M; Head; 798; Yes; Yes
812; Onie; f; 28; Miss. Choctaw; F; M; Wife; 799; Yes; Yes
813; Otho; m; 8; Miss. Choctaw; F; S; Son; 800; Yes; Yes
814; Andy; m; 7; Miss. Choctaw; F; S; Son; 801; Yes; Yes

JIM

815; George; m; 65; Miss. Choctaw; F; M; Head; 802; Yes; Yes
816; Eliza; f; 55; Miss. Choctaw; F; M; Wife; 803; Yes; Yes
817; Lee; m; 27; Miss. Choctaw; F; S; Son; 804; Yes; Yes
818; Sidney; m; 17; Miss. Choctaw; F; S; Son; 805; Yes; Yes

819; Cooley; m; 63; Miss. Choctaw; F; M; Head; 806; Yes; Yes
820; Lorena; f; 35; Miss. Choctaw; F; M; Wife; 807; Yes; Yes
821; William; m; 12; Miss. Choctaw; F; S; Son; 808; Yes; Yes
822; Tom; m; 10; Miss. Choctaw; F; S; Son; 809; Yes; Yes

823; John; m; 27; Miss. Choctaw; F; M; Head; 810; Yes; Yes
824; Bessie; f; 24; Miss. Choctaw; F; M: Wife; 811; Yes; Yes
825; Susie Ann; f; 2; Miss. Choctaw; F; S; Dau; 812; Yes; Yes
826; Corrine; f; 11/12; Miss. Choctaw; F; S; Dau; Yes; Yes

827; Henry; m; 48; Miss. Choctaw; F; M; Head; 813; Yes; Yes
828; Mollie; f; 61; Miss. Choctaw; F; M; Wife; 814; Yes; Yes

829; Harvey; m; 18; Miss. Choctaw; F; M; Head; 815; Yes; Yes
830; Mattie; f; 35; Miss. Choctaw; F; M; Wife; 816; Yes; Yes
831; **Hall**, Henrietta; f; 5; Miss. Choctaw; F; S; Niece; 652; Yes; Yes
832; **Thomas**, Lula; f; 19; Miss. Choctaw; F; S; Sister-in-law; 653; Yes; Yes

Census of the **Mississippi Choctaws** reservation of the **Choctaw Agency** jurisdiction, as of **April 1**, 19 **33**, taken by **A. C. Hector**, Superintendent.

KEY; Surname; Census Number; Given Name; Sex; Age at Last Birthday; Tribe; Degree of Blood; Marital Status; Relationship to Head of Family; Last Census Roll Number; At Jurisdiction Where Enrolled (Yes/No); At Another Jurisdiction; Post Office, County, State (if given); Ward (Yes/No)

833; **Thomas**, George; m; 84; Miss. Choctaw; F; Wd; Father-in-law; 1315; Yes; Yes

834; Ben; m; 55; Miss. Choctaw; F; M; Head; 817; Yes; Yes
835; Dora; f; 43; Miss. Choctaw; F; M; Wife; 818; Yes; Yes
836; Annie Mae; f; 19; Miss. Choctaw; F; S; Dau; 819; Yes; Yes
837; Rena; f; 11; Miss. Choctaw; F; S; Dau; 820; Yes; Yes
838; Christine; f; 1; Miss. Choctaw; F; S; Dau; 823; Yes; Yes
839; Frank; m; 5; Miss. Choctaw; F; S; Grand-son; 821; Yes; Yes
840; Bobbie Sue; f; 4; Miss. Choctaw; F; S; Grand-dau; 822; Yes; Yes

841; Logan; m; 85; Miss. Choctaw; F; Wd; Alone; 824; Yes; Yes

842; Amon; m; 56; Miss. Choctaw; F; M; Head; 825; Yes; Yes
843; Lucy; f; 48; Miss. Choctaw; F; M; Wife; 826; Yes; Yes
844; Opal; f; 13; Miss. Choctaw; F; S; Dau; 827; Yes; Yes
845; Carter; m; 4; Miss. Choctaw; F; S; Son; 828; Yes; Yes
846; Wm. Murray; m; 1; Miss. Choctaw; F; S; Son; 829; Yes; Yes

847; Goodman; m; 68; Miss. Choctaw; F; M; Head; 830; Yes; Yes
848; Leona; f; 31; Miss. Choctaw; F; M; Wife; 831; Yes; Yes
849; Frank McKinley; m; 7; Miss. Choctaw; F; S; Son; 832; Yes; Yes
850; Claud Yates; m; 5; Miss. Choctaw; F; S; Son; 833; Yes; Yes
851; Betty Lou; f; 7/12; Miss. Choctaw; F; S; [blank]; Yes; Yes
852; **Farmer**, Sallie; f; 78; Miss. Choctaw; F; Wd; Sister; 834; Yes; Yes

853; Albert; m; 26; Miss. Choctaw; F; M: Head; 835; Yes; Yes
854; Dora; f; 25; Miss. Choctaw; F; M; Wife; 836; Yes; Yes
855; Grace; f; 3; Miss. Choctaw; F; S; Dau; 837; Yes; Yes
856; Gordon G; m; 6/12; Miss. Choctaw; F; S; Son; Yes; Yes

857; Henry; m; 33; Miss. Choctaw; F; M; Head; 838; Yes; Yes
858; Maggie; f; 39; Miss. Choctaw; F; M; Wife; 839; Yes; Yes

Census of the **Mississippi Choctaws** reservation of the **Choctaw Agency** jurisdiction, as of **April 1**, 19**33**, taken by **A. C. Hector**, Superintendent.

KEY; Surname; Census Number; Given Name; Sex; Age at Last Birthday; Tribe; Degree of Blood; Marital Status; Relationship to Head of Family; Last Census Roll Number; At Jurisdiction Where Enrolled (Yes/No); At Another Jurisdiction; Post Office, County, State (if given); Ward (Yes/No)

859; Winston; m; 23; Miss. Choctaw; F; S; Alone; 844; Yes; Yes

860; Victor; m; 32; Miss. Choctaw; F; M: Head; 840; Yes; Yes
861; Lena; f; 23; Miss. Choctaw; F; M; Wife; 841; Yes; Yes
862; Foy; m; 7; Miss. Choctaw; F; S; Son; 842; Yes; Yes
863; Egbert; m; 3; Miss. Choctaw; F; S; Son; 843; Yes; Yes

JIMMIE

864; Mary; f; 26; Miss. Choctaw; F; Wd; Head; 845; Yes; Yes
865; Ona C; f; 5; Miss. Choctaw; F; S; Dau; 846; Yes; Yes
866; Delores; f; 3; Miss. Choctaw; F; S; Dau; 847; Yes; Yes

867; Frank M; m; 21; Miss. Choctaw; F; S; Alone; 848; No; Chilocco; Yes

868; Ike; m; 63; Miss. Choctaw; F; S; Alone; 849; Yes; Yes

869; Will; m; 53; Miss. Choctaw; F; M; Head; 850; Yes; Yes
870; Hester; f; 51; Miss. Choctaw; F; M; Wife; 851; Yes; Yes
871; Mack; m; 27; Miss. Choctaw; F; S; Dau[sic]; 852; Yes; Yes

872; Homer; m; 24; Miss. Choctaw; F; M; Head; 853; Yes; Yes
873; Lela; f; 25; Miss. Choctaw; F; M; Wife; 394; Yes; Yes
874; **Dan**, Irene; f; 7; Miss. Choctaw; F; S; Step-dau; 395; Yes; Yes
875; **Dan**, Albert R; m; 3; Miss. Choctaw; F; S; Step-son; 396; Yes; Yes

JOE

876; Nicholas; m; 43; Miss. Choctaw; F; M; Head; 854; Yes; Yes
877; Ella; f; 38; Miss. Choctaw; F; M; Wife; 855; Yes; Yes
878; Austin; m; 19; Miss. Choctaw; F; S; Son; 856; Yes; Yes
879; Henry; m; 15; Miss. Choctaw; F; S; Son; 857; Yes; Yes

Census of the __Mississippi Choctaws__ reservation of the __Choctaw Agency__ jurisdiction, as of __April 1__, 19__33__, taken by __A. C. Hector__, Superintendent.

KEY; Surname; Census Number; Given Name; Sex; Age at Last Birthday; Tribe; Degree of Blood; Marital Status; Relationship to Head of Family; Last Census Roll Number; At Jurisdiction Where Enrolled (Yes/No); At Another Jurisdiction; Post Office, County, State (if given); Ward (Yes/No)

880; Widge; m; 12; Miss. Choctaw; F; S; Son; 858; Yes; Yes
881; Bessie; f; 10; Miss. Choctaw; F; S; Dau; 859; Yes; Yes
882; Billie Joe; m; 9; Miss. Choctaw; F; S; Son; 860; Yes; Yes
883; Mary; f; 3; Miss. Choctaw; F; S; Dau; 861; Yes;
884; Nicholas; m; 2; Miss. Choctaw; F; S; Son; Yes
Omitted on previous census rolls; [blank]
885; **Lewis**, Susie; f; 9; Miss. Choctaw; F; S; Dau; 862; Yes; Yes
886; **Lewis**, Elsie; f; 8; Miss. Choctaw; F; S; Dau; 863; Yes; Yes

887; Jasper; m; 45; Miss. Choctaw; F; M; Head; 864; Yes; Yes
888; Sallie; f; 40; Miss. Choctaw; F; M; Wife; 865; Yes; Yes
889; Lula; f; 20; Miss. Choctaw; F; S; Dau; 866; Yes; Yes
890; Houston; m; 15; Miss. Choctaw; F; S; Son; 867; Yes; Yes
891; Watkins; m; 11; Miss. Choctaw; F; S; Son; 868; Yes; Yes

892; Emily; f; 77; Miss. Choctaw; F; Wd; Alone; 869; Yes; Yes

893; John; m; 34; Miss. Choctaw; F; M; Head; 870; Yes; Yes
894; Emma; f; 33; Miss. Choctaw; F; M; Wife; 871; Yes; Yes
895; Bessie; f; 12; Miss. Choctaw; F; S; Dau; 872; Yes; Yes
896; Killie; f; 8; Miss. Choctaw; F; S; Dau; 873; Yes; Yes
897; Claud; m; 5; Miss. Choctaw; F; S; Son; 874; Yes; Yes

898; Langley; m; 86; Miss. Choctaw; F; Wd; Alone; 875; Yes; Yes

899; **Denson**, Joe; 79; Miss. Choctaw; F; W[sic]; Alone; 878; Yes; Yes

JOHN

900; Mike; m; 60; Miss. Choctaw; F; M; Head; 876; Yes; Yes
901; Lizzie; f; 75; Miss. Choctaw; F; M; Wife; 877; Yes; Yes
902; **Willis**, Dina; f; 19; Miss. Choctaw; F; S; Grand-dau; 878; Yes; Yes

Census of the **Mississippi Choctaws** reservation of the **Choctaw Agency** jurisdiction, as of **April 1**, 19**33**, taken by **A. C. Hector**, Superintendent.

KEY; Surname; Census Number; Given Name; Sex; Age at Last Birthday; Tribe; Degree of Blood; Marital Status; Relationship to Head of Family; Last Census Roll Number; At Jurisdiction Where Enrolled (Yes/No); At Another Jurisdiction; Post Office, County, State (if given); Ward (Yes/No)

903; Josh; m; 57; Miss. Choctaw; F; Wd; Alone; 879; Yes; Yes

904; Anderson; m; 56; Miss. Choctaw; F; M; Head; 881; Yes; Yes
905; Bettie; f; 44; Miss. Choctaw; F; M; Wife; 882; Yes; Yes
906; L. E; f; 18; Miss. Choctaw; F; S; Dau; 883; Yes; Yes
907; Hubert; m; 15; Miss. Choctaw; F; S; Son; 884; Yes; Yes
908; Oden; m; 12; Miss. Choctaw; F; S; Son; 885; Yes; Yes
909; Wilson; m; 5; Miss. Choctaw; F; S; Son; 886; Yes; Yes

910; Bennett; m; 24; Miss. Choctaw; F; M: Head; 887; Yes; Yes
911; Lena Pearl; f; 18; Miss. Choctaw; F; M; Wife; 888; Yes; Yes
912; Egbert; m; 2; Miss. Choctaw; F; S; Son; 889; Yes; Yes

913; Clint; m; 42; Miss. Choctaw; F; S; Alone; 890; Yes; Yes

914; Ira; m; 28; Miss. Choctaw; F; M; Head; 891; Yes; Yes
915; Ovetta; f; 20; Miss. Choctaw; F; M; Wife; 892; Yes; Yes
916; Mercy Lee; f; 3; Miss. Choctaw; F; S; Dau; 893; Yes; Yes
917; Harry; m; 6/12; Miss. Choctaw; F; S; Son; Yes; Yes

918; Bob; m; 59; Miss. Choctaw; F; M; Head; 894; Yes; Yes
919; Onie; f; 48; Miss. Choctaw; F; M; Wife; 895; Yes; Yes
920; Oliver; m; 18; Miss. Choctaw; F; S; Son; 896; Yes; Yes
921; Ruby; f; 12; Miss. Choctaw; F; S; Dau; 898; Yes; Yes
922; Rose; f; 10; Miss. Choctaw; F; S; Dau; 899; Yes; Yes

923; Otis; m; 16; Miss. Choctaw; F; M; Head; 897; Yes; Yes
924; Annie; f; 14; Miss. Choctaw; F; M; Wife; 1076; Yes; Yes

925; Jack; m; 59; Miss. Choctaw; F; M; Head; 900; Yes; Yes
926; Amanda; f; 38; Miss. Choctaw; F; M; Wife; 901; Yes; Yes
927; Jefferson; m; 11; Miss. Choctaw; F; S; Son; 902; Yes; Yes
928; Mary; f; 9; Miss. Choctaw; F; S; Dau; 903; Yes; Yes
929; **Box**, Mamie; f; 11; Miss. Choctaw; F; S; Orphan; 904; Yes; Yes

Census of the **Mississippi Choctaws** reservation of the **Choctaw Agency** jurisdiction, as of **April 1**, 19**33**, taken by **A. C. Hector**, Superintendent.

KEY; Surname; Census Number; Given Name; Sex; Age at Last Birthday; Tribe; Degree of Blood; Marital Status; Relationship to Head of Family; Last Census Roll Number; At Jurisdiction Where Enrolled (Yes/No); At Another Jurisdiction; Post Office, County, State (if given); Ward (Yes/No)

930; Betsie; f; 35; Miss. Choctaw; F; Wd; Head; 905; Yes; Yes
931; Bilbo; m; 16; Miss. Choctaw; F; S; Son; 906; Yes; Yes
932; Mable; f; 13; Miss. Choctaw; F; S; Dau; 907; Yes; Yes
933; Renie; f; 11; Miss. Choctaw; F; S; Dau; 908; Yes; Yes
934; Varderman; m; 8; Miss. Choctaw; F; S; Son; 909; Yes; Yes
935; Smith; m; 6; Miss. Choctaw; F; S; Son; 910; Yes; Yes
936; Lisette H; f; 3; Miss. Choctaw; F; S; Dau; 911; Yes; Yes

JOHNSON

937; Whitman; m; 22; Miss. Choctaw; F; M; Head; 912; Yes; Yes
938; Viola; f; 21; Miss. Choctaw; F; M; Wife; 73; Yes; Yes
939; Will; m; 61; Miss. Choctaw; F; M; Head; 913; Yes; Yes
940; Dixie; f; 39; Miss. Choctaw; F; M; Wife; 914; Yes; Yes
941; **Comby**, Gus; m; 8; Miss. Choctaw; F; S; Step-son; 916; Yes; Yes
942; Sallie; f; 78; Miss. Choctaw; F; Wd; Mother; 917; Yes; Yes

943; Afton; m; 29; Miss. Choctaw; F; M; Head; 918; Yes; Yes
944; Savannia; f; 27; Miss. Choctaw; F; M; Wife; 919; Yes; Yes
945; Callie; f; 4; Miss. Choctaw; F; S; Dau; 920; Yes; Yes
946; Ralph; m; 9/12; Miss. Choctaw; F; S; Son; Yes; Yes

947; Edgar; m; 34; Miss. Choctaw; F; M; Head; 921; Yes; Yes
948; Beatrice; f; 30; Miss. Choctaw; F; M; Wife; 922; Yes; Yes
949; Callie; f; 10; Miss. Choctaw; F; S; Dau; 923; Yes; Yes
950; Frances; f; 8; Miss. Choctaw; F; S; Dau; 924; Yes; Yes
951; Egbert; m; 6; Miss. Choctaw; F; S; Son; 925; Yes; Yes
952; Neva; f; 2; Miss. Choctaw; F; S; Dau; 926; Yes; Yes
953; Beverly; f; 2 da; Miss. Choctaw; F; S; Dau; Yes; Yes

954; Frank; m; 41; Miss. Choctaw; F; M; Head; 927; Yes; Yes
955; Lorine; f; 33; Miss. Choctaw; F; M; Wife; 928; Yes; Yes
956; Athens; m; 15; Miss. Choctaw; F; S; Son; 930; Yes; Yes
957; Sadie; f; 13; Miss. Choctaw; F; S; Dau; 931; Yes; Yes

Census of the **Mississippi Choctaws** reservation of the **Choctaw Agency** jurisdiction, as of **April 1**, 19**33**, taken by **A. C. Hector**, Superintendent.

KEY; Surname; Census Number; Given Name; Sex; Age at Last Birthday; Tribe; Degree of Blood; Marital Status; Relationship to Head of Family; Last Census Roll Number; At Jurisdiction Where Enrolled (Yes/No); At Another Jurisdiction; Post Office, County, State (if given); Ward (Yes/No)

958; Bertha; f; 11; Miss. Choctaw; F; S; Dau; 932; Yes; Yes
959; Haven; m; 9; Miss. Choctaw; F; S; Son; 933; Yes; Yes
960; Sudan; f; 7; Miss. Choctaw; F; S; Dau; 934; Yes; Yes
961; Bena; f; 5; Miss. Choctaw; F; S; Dau; 935; Yes; Yes
962; Marvin; m; 2; Miss. Choctaw; F; S; Son; 936; Yes; Yes

963; Otho; m; 17; Miss. Choctaw; F; M; Head; 929; Yes; Yes
964; Ellen; f; 17; Miss. Choctaw; F; M; Wife; Yes; [blank]
Omitted on previous census rolls

JOSHUA

965; Jennnie[sic]; f; 63; Miss. Choctaw; F; Wd; Head; 937; Yes; Yes
966; **John**, Callie; f; 22; Miss. Choctaw; F; M; Grand-dau; 938; Yes; Yes
967; **John**, Edison; m; 5; Miss. Choctaw; F; S; Grand-son; 939; Yes; Yes

KING

968; John W; m; 73; Miss. Choctaw; F; Wd; Head; 940; Yes; Yes
969; Mollie; f; 30; Miss. Choctaw; F; S; Dau; 941; Yes; Yes
970; Enis; m; 21; Miss. Choctaw; F; S; Son; 942; Yes; Yes
971; Varman; m; 21; Miss. Choctaw; F; S; Son; 943; Yes; Yes
972; John Lee; m; 19; Miss. Choctaw; F; S; Great-nephew; 944; Yes; Yes
973; Lavenia; f; 14; Miss. Choctaw; F; S; Great-niece; 945; Yes; Yes

974; Clay; m; 27; Miss. Choctaw; F; M; Head; 946; Yes; Yes
975; Alice; f; 31; Miss. Choctaw; F; M; Wife; 947; Yes; Yes

976; Betsie; f; 51; Miss. Choctaw; F; Wd; Head; 948; Yes; Yes
977; Christine; f; 23; Miss. Choctaw; F; S; Dau; 949; Yes; Yes
978; Joseph; m; 16; Miss. Choctaw; F; S; Son; 950; Yes; Yes

Census of the **Mississippi Choctaws** reservation of the **Choctaw Agency** jurisdiction, as of **April 1**, 19**33**, taken by **A. C. Hector**, Superintendent.

KEY; Surname; Census Number; Given Name; Sex; Age at Last Birthday; Tribe; Degree of Blood; Marital Status; Relationship to Head of Family; Last Census Roll Number; At Jurisdiction Where Enrolled (Yes/No); At Another Jurisdiction; Post Office, County, State (if given); Ward (Yes/No)

979; Joe; m; 14; Miss. Choctaw; F; S; Son; 951; Yes; Yes
980; Barkum; m; 12; Miss. Choctaw; F; S; Son; 952; Yes; Yes
981; Banks; m; 28; Miss. Choctaw; F; M; Son; 953; Yes; Yes
982; Betsie; f; 37; Miss. Choctaw; F; M; Dau-in-law; 954; Yes; Yes

LEBAN

983; Ben; m; 61; Miss. Choctaw; F; M; Head; 955; Yes; Yes
984; Lena; f; 60; Miss. Choctaw; F; M; Wife; 956; Yes; Yes
985; Mary; f; 32; Miss. Choctaw; F; S; Dau; 957; Yes; Yes

LEFLORE

986; John; m; 62; Miss. Choctaw; F; M; Head; 958; Yes; Yes
987; Emma; f; 53; Miss. Choctaw; F; M; Wife; 959; Yes; Yes
988; Richard; m; 40; Miss. Choctaw; F; S; Son; 960; Yes; Yes
989; S. D; m; 27; Miss. Choctaw; F; S; Son; 961; Yes; Yes
990; Willie; f; 29; Miss. Choctaw; F; S; Dau; 962; Yes; Yes
991; Bertha Lee; f; 25; Miss. Choctaw; F; S; Dau; 963; Yes; Yes
992; John; m; 22; Miss. Choctaw; F; S; Son; 964; Yes; Yes
993; Lewis; m; 21; Miss. Choctaw; F; S; Son; 965; Yes; Yes

LEWIS

994; Fannie; f; 43; Miss. Choctaw; F; Wd; Head; 967; Yes; Yes
995; **Wickson**, Alma; f; 18; Miss. Choctaw; F; Wd; Dau; 1529; Yes; Yes

996; Adam; m; 28; Miss. Choctaw; F; M; Head; 968; Yes; Yes
997; Celia; f; 27; Miss. Choctaw; F; M; Wife; 969; Yes; Yes
998; Nannie; f; 5; Miss. Choctaw; F; S; Dau; 970; Yes; Yes
999; Mamie; f; 3; Miss. Choctaw; F; S; Dau; 971; Yes; Yes
1000; Jacob; m; 6/12; Miss. Choctaw; F; S; Son; Yes; Yes
1001; Tom; m; 7; Miss. Choctaw; F; S; Step-son; 972; Yes; Yes

Census of the **Mississippi Choctaws** reservation of the **Choctaw Agency** jurisdiction, as of **April 1**, 19**33**, taken by **A. C. Hector**, Superintendent.

KEY; Surname; Census Number; Given Name; Sex; Age at Last Birthday; Tribe; Degree of Blood; Marital Status; Relationship to Head of Family; Last Census Roll Number; At Jurisdiction Where Enrolled (Yes/No); At Another Jurisdiction; Post Office, County, State (if given); Ward (Yes/No)

1002; Elon; m; 52; Miss. Choctaw; F; M; Head; 973; Yes; Yes
1003; Lula; f; 55; Miss. Choctaw; F; M; Wife; 974; Yes; Yes
1004; **Jefferson**, Nute; m; 17; Miss. Choctaw; F; S; Step-son; Yes; Yes

1005; Marshall; m; 58; Miss. Choctaw; F; M; Head; 978; Yes; Yes
1006; Martha; f; 47; Miss. Choctaw; F; M; Wife; 979; Yes; Yes
1007; Belfa; f; 17; Miss. Choctaw; F; S; Dau; 981; Yes; Yes
1008; Houston; m; 14; Miss. Choctaw; F; S; Son; 982; Yes; Yes
1009; Lee; m; 12; Miss. Choctaw; F; S; Son; 983; Yes; Yes
1010; Esther; f; 9; Miss. Choctaw; F; S; Dau; 984; Yes; Yes
1011; Hodges; m; 6; Miss. Choctaw; F; S; Son; 985; Yes; Yes
1012; Leon; m; 5; Miss. Choctaw; F; S; Son; 986; Yes; Yes
1013; Lucille; f; 3; Miss. Choctaw; F; S; Dau; 987; Yes; Yes
1014; Prentiss; m; 1; Miss. Choctaw; F; S; Son; 988; Yes; Yes
1015; **Denson**, Wintson[sic]; m; 18; Miss. Choctaw; F; M; Son-in-law; 1686; Yes; Yes
1016; **Denson**, Eliza; f; 18; Miss. Choctaw; F; M; Dau; 980; Yes; Yes

1017; Joe; m; 59; Miss. Choctaw; F; Wd; Alone; 989; Yes; Yes

1018; Lennis; m; 26; Miss. Choctaw; F; M; Head; 990; Yes; Yes
1019; Ola; f; 21; Miss. Choctaw; F; M; Wife; 991; Yes; Yes
1020; Nervie; f; 4; Miss. Choctaw; F; S; Dau; 992; Yes; Yes

1021; Edd; m; 59; Miss. Choctaw; F; M; Head; 993; Yes; Yes
1022; Edna; f; 51; Miss. Choctaw; F; M; Wife; 994; Yes; Yes
1023; Hollis; m; 17; Miss. Choctaw; F; S; Son; 995; Yes; Yes

1024; Reuben; m; 73; Miss. Choctaw; F; Wd; Head; 996; Yes; Yes
1025; Amos; m; 20; Miss. Choctaw; F; S; Grand-son; 997; Yes; Yes

1026; Albert; m; 39; Miss. Choctaw; F; M; Head; 998; Yes; Yes
1027; Mollie; f; 36; Miss. Choctaw; F; M; Wife; 999; Yes; Yes
1028; Bernice; f; 16; Miss. Choctaw; F; S; Dau; 1000; Yes; Yes

Census of the **Mississippi Choctaws** reservation of the **Choctaw Agency** jurisdiction, as of **April 1**, 19**33**, taken by **A. C. Hector**, Superintendent.

KEY; Surname; Census Number; Given Name; Sex; Age at Last Birthday; Tribe; Degree of Blood; Marital Status; Relationship to Head of Family; Last Census Roll Number; At Jurisdiction Where Enrolled (Yes/No); At Another Jurisdiction; Post Office, County, State (if given); Ward (Yes/No)

1029; Eastland; m; 14; Miss. Choctaw; F; S; Son; 1001; Yes; Yes
1030; Ivena; f; 12; Miss. Choctaw; F; S; Dau; 1002; Yes; Yes

1031; Jim; m; 30; Miss. Choctaw; F; M; Head; 1004; Yes; Yes
1032; Jennie; f; 25; Miss. Choctaw; F; M; Wife; 1005; Yes; Yes
1033; Jennie Lin; f; 4; Miss. Choctaw; F; S; Dau; 1006; Yes; Yes
1034; Willie; m; 1; Miss. Choctaw; F; S; Son; 1007; Yes; Yes

1035; Duffie; m; 37; Miss. Choctaw; F; M: Head; 1008; Yes; Yes
1036; Lilly; f; 53; Miss. Choctaw; F; M; Wife; 1009; Yes; Yes
1037; **Briscoe**, Egbert; m; 10; Miss. Choctaw; F; S; Step-son; 1011; Yes; Yes
1038; **Farmer**, Henry; m; 22; Miss. Choctaw; F; S; Nephew; 1012; Yes; Yes
1039; **Wickson**, Yates; m; 4; Miss. Choctaw; F; S; Nephew; 1013; Yes; Yes
1040; **Briscoe**, Jim; m; 18; Miss. Choctaw; F; M; Step-son; 1010; Yes; Yes
1041; **Briscoe**, Elsie Y; f; 17; Miss. Choctaw; F; M; Dau-in-law; 1669; Yes; Yes

MARTIN

1042; Willie; m; 43; Miss. Choctaw; F; M; Head; 1014; Yes; Yes
1043; Mary; f; 37; Miss. Choctaw; F; M; Wife; 1015; Yes; Yes
1044; Raymond; m; 13; Miss. Choctaw; F; S; Son; 1016; Yes; Yes
1045; Edmond J; m; 10; Miss. Choctaw; F; S; Son; 1017; Yes; Yes
1046; Phillip; m; 7; Miss. Choctaw; F; S; Son; 1018; Yes; Yes
1047; Annie Mae; f; 5; Miss. Choctaw; F; S; Dau; 1019; Yes; Yes
1048; Harry M; m; 2; Miss. Choctaw; F; S; Son; 1020; Yes; Yes

1049; Ennis; m; 24; Miss. Choctaw; F; M; Head; 1021; Yes; Yes
1050; Nancy; f; 23; Miss. Choctaw; F; M; Wife; 1022; Yes; Yes
1051; Thomas; m; 3; Miss. Choctaw; F; S; Son; 1023; Yes; Yes

Census of the **Mississippi Choctaws** reservation of the **Choctaw Agency** jurisdiction, as of **April 1**, 19**33**, taken by **A. C. Hector**, Superintendent.

KEY; Surname; Census Number; Given Name; Sex; Age at Last Birthday; Tribe; Degree of Blood; Marital Status; Relationship to Head of Family; Last Census Roll Number; At Jurisdiction Where Enrolled (Yes/No); At Another Jurisdiction; Post Office, County, State (if given); Ward (Yes/No)

1052;   **Alex**, Herbert; m; 6; Miss. Choctaw; F; S; Step-son; 1024; Yes; Yes

McMILLEN

1053;   Sorsby; m; 57; Miss. Choctaw; F; Wd; Head; 1025; Yes; Yes
1054;   Mary; f; 19; Miss. Choctaw; F; S; Dau; 1026; Yes; Yes
1055;   Emma; f; 18; Miss. Choctaw; F; S; Dau; 1027; Yes; Yes
1056;   Clarence; m; 16; Miss. Choctaw; F; S; Son; 1028; Yes; Yes
1057;   Bessie; f; 14; Miss. Choctaw; F; S; Dau; 1029; Yes; Yes
1058;   Gipson; m; 9; Miss. Choctaw; F; S; Son; 1030; Yes; Yes
1059;   Pauline; f; 5; Miss. Choctaw; F; S; Dau; 1031; Yes; Yes

1060;   Lemmie; m; 23; Miss. Choctaw; F; M; Head; 1032; Yes; Yes
1061;   Maggie; f; 24; Miss. Choctaw; F; M; Wife; 1033; Yes; Yes

1062;   Cephus; m; 51; Miss. Choctaw; F; M; Head; 1034; Yes; Yes
1063;   Mina; f; 39; Miss. Choctaw; F; M; Wife; 1035; Yes; Yes
1064;   Mary; f; 20; Miss. Choctaw; F; S; Dau; 1037; Yes; Yes
1065;   Willie; m; 17; Miss. Choctaw; F; S; Son; 1038; Yes; Yes
1066;   Enochs; m; 5; Miss. Choctaw; F; S; Son; 1039; Yes; Yes
1067;   Lurline; f; 1; Miss. Choctaw; F; S; Dau; 1040; Yes; Yes
1068;   **Billy**, Clemon; m; 19; Miss. Choctaw; F; S; Step-son; 1041; Yes; Yes

1069;   Anthony; m; 25; Miss. Choctaw; F; M; Head; 1036; Yes; Yes
1070;   Venie; f; 17; Miss. Choctaw; F; M; Wife; 915; Yes; Yes

1071;   Oscar; m; 39; Miss. Choctaw; F; M; Head; 1047; Yes; Yes
1072;   Bennie; f; 34; Miss. Choctaw; F; M; Wife; 1048; Yes; Yes
1073;   Arnold; m; 19; Miss. Choctaw; F; S; Son; 1049; Yes; Yes
1074;   Leslie; m; 11; Miss. Choctaw; F; S; Son; 1050; Yes; Yes
1075;   Bert; m; 9; Miss. Choctaw; F; S; Son; 1051; Yes; Yes
1076;   Frances; f; 7; Miss. Choctaw; F; S; Dau; 1052; Yes; Yes

Census of the **Mississippi Choctaws** reservation of the **Choctaw Agency** jurisdiction, as of **April 1**, 19**33**, taken by **A. C. Hector**, Superintendent.

KEY; Surname; Census Number; Given Name; Sex; Age at Last Birthday; Tribe; Degree of Blood; Marital Status; Relationship to Head of Family; Last Census Roll Number; At Jurisdiction Where Enrolled (Yes/No); At Another Jurisdiction; Post Office, County, State (if given); Ward (Yes/No)

1077; John; m; 4; Miss. Choctaw; F; S; Son; 1053; Yes; Yes
1078; Jean; f; 2; Miss. Choctaw; F; S; Dau; 1054; Yes; Yes

MINGO

1079; Rich; m; 28; Miss. Choctaw; F; M; Head; 1055; Yes; Yes
1080; Annie; f; 29; Miss. Choctaw; F; M: Wife; 1056; Yes; Yes
1081; Davidson; m; 10; Miss. Choctaw; F; S; Son; 1057; Yes; Yes
1082; Effie; f; 9; Miss. Choctaw; F; S; Dau; 1058; Yes; Yes

1083; John; m; 57; Miss. Choctaw; F; M: Head; 1059; Yes; Yes
1084; Hattie; f; 31; Miss. Choctaw; F; M; Wife; 1060; Yes; Yes
1085; Arch; m; 11; Miss. Choctaw; F; S; Son; 1061; Yes; Yes
1086; Otis; m; 8; Miss. Choctaw; F; S; Son; 1062; Yes; Yes
1087; Sister; f; 6; Miss. Choctaw; F; S; Daul[sic]; 1063; Yes; Yes
1088; Mary; f; 3; Miss. Choctaw; F; S; Dau; 1064; Yes; Yes

1089; Lilly; f; 55; Miss. Choctaw; F; Wd; Head; 1065; Yes; Yes
1090; Jim; m; 19; Miss. Choctaw; F; S; Son; 1066; Yes; Yes
1091; Olin; m; 15; Miss. Choctaw; F; S; Son; 1067; Yes; Yes
1092; Nettie; f; 12; Miss. Choctaw; F; S; Dau; 1068; Yes; Yes

1093; Oscar; m; 23; Miss. Choctaw; F; M; Head; 1069; Yes; Yes
1094; Linday; f; 29; Miss. Choctaw; F; M; Wife; 1070; Yes; Yes

MITCH

1095; Sarah; f; 49; Miss. Choctaw; F; Wd; Head; 1071; Yes; Yes
1096; Elea; m; 31; Miss. Choctaw; F; S; Son; 1072; Yes; Yes
1097; Divan; m; 29; Miss. Choctaw; F; S; Son; 1073; Yes; Yes
1098; Wilson; m; 27; Miss. Choctaw; F; S; Son; 1074; Yes; Yes
1099; Gilmore; m; 18; Miss. Choctaw; F; S; Son; 1075; Yes; Yes

Census of the **Mississippi Choctaws** reservation of the **Choctaw Agency** jurisdiction, as of **April 1**, 19**33**, taken by **A. C. Hector**, Superintendent.

KEY; Surname; Census Number; Given Name; Sex; Age at Last Birthday; Tribe; Degree of Blood; Marital Status; Relationship to Head of Family; Last Census Roll Number; At Jurisdiction Where Enrolled (Yes/No); At Another Jurisdiction; Post Office, County, State (if given); Ward (Yes/No)

MORRIS

1100; Julis[sic]; m; 31; Miss. Choctaw; F; M; Head; 1077; Yes; Yes
1101; Beauty; f; 28; Miss. Choctaw; F; M; Wife; 1078; Yes; Yes
1102; Eddie; m; 9; Miss. Choctaw; F; S; Son; 1079; Yes; Yes
1103; Lena; f; 6; Miss. Choctaw; F; S; Dau; 1080; Yes; Yes
1104; Water Olin; m; 3; Miss. Choctaw; F; S; Son; 1081; Yes; Yes

1105; Moseley; m; 67; Miss. Choctaw; F; M; Head; 1082; Yes; Yes
1106; Ida; f; 52; Miss. Choctaw; F; M; Wife; 1083; Yes; Yes
1107; Lilly; f; 33; Miss. Choctaw; F; S; Dau; 1084; Yes; Yes
1108; Sue; f; 31; Miss. Choctaw; F; Wd; Dau; 1085; Yes; Yes
1109; Wilson; m; 29; Miss. Choctaw; F; S; Son; 1086; Yes; Yes
1110; Joe; m; 12; Miss. Choctaw; F; S; Grand-son; 1087; Yes; Yes
1111; **Wesley**, Rufus; m; 8; Miss. Choctaw; F; S; Grand-son; 1088; Yes; Yes

1112; Dempsey; m; 32; Miss. Choctaw; F; M; Head; 1089; Yes; Yes
1113; Janie; f; 31; Miss. Choctaw; F; M; Wife; 1090; Yes; Yes
1114; Ora; f; 12; Miss. Choctaw; F; S; Dau; 1091; Yes; Yes
1115; Bethany; m; 9; Miss. Choctaw; F; S; Son; 1092; Yes; Yes
1116; Printess; m; 7; Miss. Choctaw; F; S; Son; 1093; Yes; Yes
1117; Chester; m; 3; Miss. Choctaw; F; S; Son; Yes; Yes
   Omitted on previous census
1118; Champ; m; 5; Miss. Choctaw; F; S; Son; 1094; Yes; Yes
1119; Lester; m; 7/12; Miss. Choctaw; F; S; Son; Yes; Yes

1120; Sallie; f; 64; Miss. Choctaw; F; Wd; Head; 1095; Yes; Yes
1121; Seward; m; 32; Miss. Choctaw; F; S; Son; 1096; Yes; Yes

1122; Howard; m; 26; Miss. Choctaw; F; M; Head; 1097; Yes; Yes
1123; Bertie; f; 23; Miss. Choctaw; F; M; Wife; 1098; Yes; Yes
1124; Jimmie; m; 7; Miss. Choctaw; F; S; Son; 1099; Yes; Yes

Census of the **Mississippi Choctaws** reservation of the **Choctaw Agency** jurisdiction, as of **April 1**, 19**33**, taken by **A. C. Hector**, Superintendent.

KEY; Surname; Census Number; Given Name; Sex; Age at Last Birthday; Tribe; Degree of Blood; Marital Status; Relationship to Head of Family; Last Census Roll Number; At Jurisdiction Where Enrolled (Yes/No); At Another Jurisdiction; Post Office, County, State (if given); Ward (Yes/No)

1125; Huston; m; 27; Miss. Choctaw; 1/4; M; Head; 1100; Yes; Yes
1126; Bertha; f; 25; Miss. Choctaw; 1/4; M; Wife; 1101; Yes; Yes
1127; **Hays**, Velma; f; 24; Miss. Choctaw; 1/4; M; Sister; 1104; Yes; Yes

1128; Boston; m; 30; Miss. Choctaw; 1/4; M; Head; 1102; Yes; Yes
1129; Nola; f; 28; Miss. Choctaw; 1/4; M; Wife; 1103; Yes; Yes

MOSES

1130; Alma; f; 22; Miss. Choctaw; F; S; Alone; 1105; Yes; Yes
1131; Allen; m; 27; Miss. Choctaw; F; M; Head; 1106; Yes; Yes
1132; Florence; f; 27 Miss. Choctaw; F; M; Wife; 1107; Yes; Yes

NICKEY

1133; Sam; m; 48; Miss. Choctaw; F; M; Head; 1108; Yes; Yes
1134; Malessie[sic]; f; 46; Miss. Choctaw; F; M; Wife; 1109; Yes; Yes
1135; Dora; f; 18; Miss. Choctaw; F; S; Dau; 1110; Yes; Yes
1136; Sherman; m; 11; Miss. Choctaw; F; S; Son; 1111; Yes; Yes
1137; Copeland; m; 5; Miss. Choctaw; F; S; Son; 1112; Yes; Yes

1138; Billy; m; 50; Miss. Choctaw; F; M; Head; 1113; Yes; Yes
1139; Fronie; f; 52; Miss. Choctaw; F; M; Wife; 1114; Yes; Yes
1140; Ode; f; 24; Miss. Choctaw; F; S; Dau; 1115; Yes; Yes
1141; Zelma; f; 21; Miss. Choctaw; F; S; Dau; 1116; Yes; Yes
1142; Hughie; m; 18; Miss. Choctaw; F; S; Son; 1117; Yes; Yes
1143; Zona; f; 16; Miss. Choctaw; F; S; Dau; 1118; Yes; Yes
1144; Cozette; m; 14; Miss. Choctaw; F; S; Son; 1119; Yes; Yes
1145; Thomas; m; 10; Miss. Choctaw; F; S; Son; 1120; Yes; Yes

NOAH

1146; Elizabeth; f; 61; Miss. Choctaw; F; Wd; Alone; 1121; Yes; Yes

Census of the **Mississippi Choctaws** reservation of the **Choctaw Agency** jurisdiction, as of **April 1**, 19**33**, taken by **A. C. Hector**, Superintendent.

KEY; Surname; Census Number; Given Name; Sex; Age at Last Birthday; Tribe; Degree of Blood; Marital Status; Relationship to Head of Family; Last Census Roll Number; At Jurisdiction Where Enrolled (Yes/No); At Another Jurisdiction; Post Office, County, State (if given); Ward (Yes/No)

1147; Lizzie; f; 43; Miss. Choctaw; F; Wd; Head; 1123; Yes; Yes
1148; Nancie; f; 17; Miss. Choctaw; F; S; Dau; 1124; Yes; Yes
1149; Annie; f; 14; Miss. Choctaw; F; S; Dau; 1125; Yes; Yes

NUBBY

1150; Billy; m; 73; Miss. Choctaw; F; M; Head; 1126; Yes; Yes
1151; Lilly; f; 53; Miss. Choctaw; F; M; Wife; 1127; Yes; Yes

PHILLIPS

1152; Riley; m; 26; Miss. Choctaw; F; M; Head; 1128; Yes; Yes
1153; Lester; f; 20; Miss. Choctaw; F; M; Wife; 1129; Yes; Yes
1154; Chas. Geo; m; 1/12; Miss. Choctaw; F; S; Son; Yes; Yes
1155; Edmond; m; 6; Miss. Choctaw; F; S; Son; 1130; Yes; Yes
1156; Empsey; m; 4; Miss. Choctaw; F; S; Son; 1131; Yes; Yes

POLK

1157; Henry; m; 25; Miss. Choctaw; F; M; Head; 1132; Yes; Yes
1158; Susie; f; 31; Miss. Choctaw; F; M; Wife; 1133; Yes; Yes
1159; Sula; f; 4; Miss. Choctaw; F; S; Dau; 1134; Yes; Yes
1160; Hudson; m; 2; Miss. Choctaw; F; S; Son; 1135; Yes; Yes

1161; George; m; 71; Miss. Choctaw; F; Wd; Alone; 1136; Yes; Yes

1162; Francis; m; 23; Miss. Choctaw; F; M; Head; 247; Yes; Yes
1163; Odell; f; 20; Miss. Choctaw; F; M; Wife; 383; Yes; Yes

1164; Josie; m; 52; Miss. Choctaw; F; M; Head; 1137; Yes; Yes
1165; Lennie; f; 53; Miss. Choctaw; F; M; Wife; 1138; Yes; Yes
1166; Ada; f; 15; Miss. Choctaw; F; S; Dau; 1139; Yes; Yes
1167; Frances; f; 15; Miss. Choctaw; F; S; Dau; 1140; Yes; Yes

Census of the **Mississippi Choctaws** reservation of the **Choctaw Agency** jurisdiction, as of **April 1**, 19**33**, taken by **A. C. Hector**, Superintendent.

KEY; Surname; Census Number; Given Name; Sex; Age at Last Birthday; Tribe; Degree of Blood; Marital Status; Relationship to Head of Family; Last Census Roll Number; At Jurisdiction Where Enrolled (Yes/No); At Another Jurisdiction; Post Office, County, State (if given); Ward (Yes/No)

1168; Tom; m; 55; Miss. Choctaw; F; Wd; Head; 1141; Yes; Yes
1169; Comelia[sic]; m; 23; Miss. Choctaw; F; S; Son; 1142; Yes; Yes
1170; Alma; f; 19; Miss. Choctaw; F; S; Dau; 1143; Yes; Yes
1171; Osborn; m; 17; Miss. Choctaw; F; S; Son; 1144; Yes; Yes

POULSON

1172; Allie; f; 60; Miss. Choctaw; F; S; Alone; 1145; Yes; Yes

1173; Julius; m; 26; Miss. Choctaw; F; S; Alone; 1150; Yes

1174; Frank; m; 33; Miss. Choctaw; F; M; Head; 1146; Yes; Yes
1175; Mary; f; 31; Miss. Choctaw; F; M; Wife; 1147; Yes; Yes

1176; Eddie M; m; 26; Miss. Choctaw; F; M; Head; 1148; Yes; Yes
1177; Cornelia; f; 29; Miss. Choctaw; F; M; Wife; 1149; Yes; Yes

1178; Johnnie; m; 24; Miss. Choctaw; F; S; Alone; 1151; Yes; Yes

1179; Charlie; m; 21; Miss. Choctaw; F; S; Alone; 1152; Yes; Yes

ROBINSON

1180; Thomas; m; 43; Miss. Choctaw; F; M; Head; 1153; Yes; Yes
1181; Syble; f; 38; Miss. Choctaw; F; M; Wife; 1154; Yes; Yes
1182; Jimmie; m; 19; Miss. Choctaw; F; S; Son; 1155; Yes; Yes
1183; Georgie; f; 17; Miss. Choctaw; F; S; Dau; 1156; Yes; Yes
1184; Sallie; f; 16; Miss. Choctaw; F; S; Dau; 1157; Yes; Yes
1185; Carl; m; 14; Miss. Choctaw; F; S; Son; 1158; Yes; Yes
1186; Mamie; f; 13; Miss. Choctaw; F; S; Dau; 1159; Yes; Yes
1187; Betsey; f; 11; Miss. Choctaw; F; S; Dau; 1160; Yes; Yes
1188; Homer; m; 9; Miss. Choctaw; F; S; Son; 1161; Yes; Yes
1189; Teach; m; 4; Miss. Choctaw; F; S; Son; 1162; Yes; Yes

Census of the **Mississippi Choctaws** reservation of the **Choctaw Agency** jurisdiction, as of **April 1**, 19__33__, taken by **A. C. Hector**, Superintendent.

KEY; Surname; Census Number; Given Name; Sex; Age at Last Birthday; Tribe; Degree of Blood; Marital Status; Relationship to Head of Family; Last Census Roll Number; At Jurisdiction Where Enrolled (Yes/No); At Another Jurisdiction; Post Office, County, State (if given); Ward (Yes/No)

1190; Mary; f; 3; Miss. Choctaw; F; S; Dau; Yes; Yes
   Omitted on previous census rolls

1191; Belia; f; 26; Miss. Choctaw; F; Wd; Head; 1163; Yes; Yes
1192; Campbell; m; 6; Miss. Choctaw; F; S; Son; 1164; Yes; Yes

RUTHERFORD

1193; Henrietta; f; 35; Miss. Choctaw; F; S; Alone; 1165; Yes; Yes

SAM

1194; Truman; m; 24; Miss. Choctaw; F; M; Head; 1166; Yes; Yes
1195; Sina; f; 21; Miss. Choctaw; F; M; Wife; 1167; Yes; Yes

1196; Raymond; m; 52; Miss. Choctaw; F; S; Alone; 1168; Yes; Yes

1197; Oscar; m; 79; Miss. Choctaw; F; M; Head; 1169; Yes; Yes
1198; Mattie; f; 53; Miss. Choctaw; F; M; Wife; 1170; Yes; Yes
1199; Seer; m; 19; Miss. Choctaw; F; S; Grand-son; 1171; Yes; Yes
1200; Lavade; f; 21; Miss. Choctaw; F; S; Grand-dau; 1172; Yes; Yes
1201; Ruth Ann; f; 7/12; Miss. Choctaw; F; S; Great Grand-dau; Yes; Yes Daughter of Lavade Sam

1202; Jimpson; m; 30; Miss. Choctaw; F; M; Head; 1173; Yes; Yes
1203; Lousiana; f; 28; Miss. Choctaw; F; M; Wife; 1174; Yes; Yes

1204; Walter; m; 43; Miss. Choctaw; F; Wd; Head; 1175; Yes; Yes
1205; Grace; f; 16; Miss. Choctaw; F; S; Dau; 1176; Yes; Yes
1206; Tom; f[sic]; 14; Miss. Choctaw; F; S; Son; 1177; Yes; Yes
1207; Edna; f; 11; Miss. Choctaw; F; S; Dau; 1178; Yes; Yes
1208; Manzie; f; 9; Miss. Choctaw; F; S; Dau; 1179; Yes; Yes
1209; Fontaine; m; 47; Miss. Choctaw; F; M; Head; 1180; Yes; Yes

Census of the **Mississippi Choctaws** reservation of the **Choctaw Agency** jurisdiction, as of **April 1**, 19**33**, taken by **A. C. Hector**, Superintendent.

KEY; Surname; Census Number; Given Name; Sex; Age at Last Birthday; Tribe; Degree of Blood; Marital Status; Relationship to Head of Family; Last Census Roll Number; At Jurisdiction Where Enrolled (Yes/No); At Another Jurisdiction; Post Office, County, State (if given); Ward (Yes/No)

1210; Emily; f; 43; Miss. Choctaw; F; M; Wife; 1181; Yes; Yes
1211; Leona; f; 11; Miss. Choctaw; F; S; Dau; 1182; Yes; Yes
1212; Ellis; m; 8; Miss. Choctaw; F; S; Son; 1183; Yes; Yes
1213; Fannie; f; 7; Miss. Choctaw; F; S; Dau; 1184; Yes; Yes
1214; Ella Ruth; f; 5; Miss. Choctaw; F; S; Dau; 1185; Yes; Yes
1215; Armond; m; 3; Miss. Choctaw; F; S; Son; 1186; Yes; Yes
1216; Beaman; m; 13; Miss. Choctaw; F; S; Nephew; 1187; Yes; Yes

1217; Willie; m; 34; Miss. Choctaw; F; M; Head; 1188; Yes; Yes
1218; Eva; f; 32; Miss. Choctaw; F; M; Wife; 1189; Yes; Yes
1219; Nettie; f; 12; Miss. Choctaw; F; S; Dau; 1190; Yes; Yes
1220; Abel; m; 11; Miss. Choctaw; F; S; Son; 1191; Yes; Yes
1221; Lonie; m; 9; Miss. Choctaw; F; S; Son; 1192; Yes; Yes
1222; Grisaline; f; 3; Miss. Choctaw; F; S; Dau; 1193; Yes; Yes
1223; Susan; f; 6/12; Miss. Choctaw; F; S; Dau; Yes; Yes

SCOTT

1224; Marshall; m; 63; Miss. Choctaw; F; M; Head; 1194; Yes; Yes
1225; Lonie; f; 28; Miss. Choctaw; F; M; Wife; 1195; Yes; Yes
1226; Rachel; f; 7; Miss. Choctaw; F; S; Dau; 1196; Yes; Yes

SHOEMAKER

1227; Susan; f; 33; Miss. Choctaw; F; Wd; Head; 1198; Yes; Yes
1228; Dempsey; m; 12; Miss. Choctaw; F; S; Son; 1199; Yes; Yes
1229; Layman; m; 10; Miss. Choctaw; F; S; Son; 1200; Yes; Yes
1230; Ruben; m; 7; Miss. Choctaw; F; S; Son; 1201; Yes; Yes
1231; Noleen; f; 4; Miss. Choctaw; F; S; Dau; 1202; Yes; Yes

1232; Buck; m; 48; Miss. Choctaw; F; M; Head; 1203; Yes; Yes
1233; Annie; f; 33; Miss. Choctaw; F; M: Wife; 1204; Yes; Yes
1234; Leona; f; 13; Miss. Choctaw; F; S; Dau; 1205; Yes; Yes
1235; Eliza; f; 11; Miss. Choctaw; F; S; Dau; 1206; Yes; Yes

Census of the **Mississippi Choctaws** reservation of the **Choctaw Agency** jurisdiction, as of **April 1**, 19**33**, taken by **A. C. Hector**, Superintendent.

KEY; Surname; Census Number; Given Name; Sex; Age at Last Birthday; Tribe; Degree of Blood; Marital Status; Relationship to Head of Family; Last Census Roll Number; At Jurisdiction Where Enrolled (Yes/No); At Another Jurisdiction; Post Office, County, State (if given); Ward (Yes/No)

1236; Martha; f; 9; Miss. Choctaw; F; S; Dau; 1207; Yes; Yes
1237; Daisy; f; 7; Miss. Choctaw; F; S; Dau; 1208; Yes; Yes
1238; Carrie Mae; f; 6; Miss. Choctaw; F; S; Dau; 1209; Yes; Yes
1239; Hubert; m; 2; Miss. Choctaw; F; S; Son; 1210; Yes; Yes
1240; Edmond; m; 9/12; Miss. Choctaw; F; S; Son; 1[sic]; Yes; Yes

SIMPSON

1241; John; m; 55; Miss. Choctaw; F; M; Head; 1211; Yes; Yes
1242; Sallie; f; 53; Miss. Choctaw; F; M: Wife; 1212; Yes; Yes
1243; Pauline; f; 17; Miss. Choctaw; F; S; Dau; 1213; Yes; Yes
1244; Celie; f; 15; Miss. Choctaw; F; S; Dau; 1214; Yes; Yes

SMITH

1245; George; m; 61; Miss. Choctaw; F; M: Head; 1215; Yes; Yes
1246; Mandy; g; 47; Miss. Choctaw; F; M; Wife; 1216; Yes; Yes
1247; **Farmer**, Lilly Kate; f; 13; Miss. Choctaw; F; S; Step-dau; Yes; Yes
1248; **Farmer**, Grace; f; 10; Miss. Choctaw; F; S; Step-dau; 1218; Yes; Yes
1249; **Farve**, Mary Lou; f; 16; Miss. Choctaw; F; Wd; Step-dau; 523; Yes; Yes

1250; Sebe; m; 43; Miss. Choctaw; F; M: Head; 1219; Yes; Yes
1251; Sinie; f; 42; Miss. Choctaw; F; M; Wife; 1220; Yes; Yes
1252; Clemon; m; 14; Miss. Choctaw; F; S; Son; 1222; Yes; Yes

1253; John W; m; 58; Miss. Choctaw; F; M; Head; 1223; Yes; Yes
1254; Mary; f; 73; Miss. Choctaw; F; M; Wife; 1224; Yes; Yes

1255; Minnie; f; 38; Miss. Choctaw; F; Wd; Head; 1225; Yes; Yes
1256; Melton; m; 7; Miss. Choctaw; F; S; Son; 1226; Yes; Yes
1257; Elton; m; 5; Miss. Choctaw; F; S; 1227; Yes; Yes

Census of the __Mississippi Choctaws__ reservation of the __Choctaw Agency__ jurisdiction, as of __April 1__, 19__33__, taken by __A. C. Hector__, Superintendent.

KEY; Surname; Census Number; Given Name; Sex; Age at Last Birthday; Tribe; Degree of Blood; Marital Status; Relationship to Head of Family; Last Census Roll Number; At Jurisdiction Where Enrolled (Yes/No); At Another Jurisdiction; Post Office, County, State (if given); Ward (Yes/No)

1258; **Stephens**, Phoebe; f; 13; Miss. Choctaw; F; S; Niece; 1228; Yes; Yes

1259; Clay; m; 28; Miss. Choctaw; F; M: Head; 1229; Yes; Yes
1260; Mattie; f; 31; Miss. Choctaw; F; M; Wife; 1230; Yes; Yes

SOCKEY

1261; Irvin; m; 51; Miss. Choctaw; F; M; Head; 1231; Yes; Yes
1262; Lula; f; 38; Miss. Choctaw; F; M; Wife; 1232; Yes; Yes
1263; Benny; m; 25; Miss. Choctaw; F; S; Son; 1233; Yes; Yes
1264; Homer; m; 10; Miss. Choctaw; F; S; Son; 1234; Yes; Yes
1265; Ill; m; 5; Miss. Choctaw; F; S; Son; 1235; Yes; Yes

1266; Mike; m; 31; Miss. Choctaw; F; M; Head; 1236; Yes; Yes
1267; Nephus; f; 30; Miss. Choctaw; F; M; Wife; 1237; Yes; Yes
1268; Varelia; f; 11; Miss. Choctaw; F; S; Dau; 1238; Yes; Yes
1269; Odell; m; 9; Miss. Choctaw; F; S; Son; 1239; Yes; Yes
1270; Enochs; m; 6; Miss. Choctaw; F; S; Son; 1240; Yes; Yes
1271; Reba; f; 8/12; Miss. Choctaw; F; S; Dau; Yes; Yes

SOLOMON

1272; Willie; m; 49; Miss. Choctaw; F; M; Head; 1241; Yes; Yes
1273; Onie; f; 47; Miss. Choctaw; F; M; Wife; 288; Yes; Yes
1274; **Charlie**, Beaman; m; 18; Moss; S; Step-son; 289; Yes; Yes
1275; **Charlie**, Juanita; f; 13; Miss. Choctaw; F; S; Step-dau; 290; Yes; Yes
1276; **Charlie**, Charlie C; m; 11; Miss. Choctaw; F; S; Step-son; 291; Yes; Yes

1277; Marshall; m; 29; Miss. Choctaw; F; M; Head; 1242; Yes; Yes
1278; Addie; f; 24; Miss. Choctaw; F; M; Wife; 1243; Yes; Yes
1279; Johnson; m; 7/12; Miss. Choctaw; F; S; Son; Yes; Yes

Census of the **Mississippi Choctaws** reservation of the **Choctaw Agency** jurisdiction, as of **April 1**, 19**33**, taken by **A. C. Hector**, Superintendent.

KEY; Surname; Census Number; Given Name; Sex; Age at Last Birthday; Tribe; Degree of Blood; Marital Status; Relationship to Head of Family; Last Census Roll Number; At Jurisdiction Where Enrolled (Yes/No); At Another Jurisdiction; Post Office, County, State (if given); Ward (Yes/No)

1280; Willie; m; 70; Miss. Choctaw; F; M: Head; 1244; Yes; Yes
1281; Winnie L; f; 28; Miss. Choctaw; F; M; Wife; 1245; Yes; Yes
1282; Mollie Lee; f; 4; Miss. Choctaw; F; S; Dau; 1246; Yes; Yes

1283; Raymond; m; 39; Miss. Choctaw; F; M; Head; 1247; Yes; Yes
1284; Bessie; f; 39; Miss. Choctaw; F; M: Wife; 1248; Yes; Yes
1285; Earnest; m; 17; Miss. Choctaw; F; S; Son; 1249; Yes; Yes
1286; Murphy; m; 14; Miss. Choctaw; F; S; Son; 1250; Yes; Yes
1287; Mollie; f; 11; Miss. Choctaw; F; S; Dau; 1251; Yes; Yes

STAR

1288; Lucy; f; 45; Miss. Choctaw; F; Wd; Alone; 1252; Yes; Yes

1289; Bill; m; 44; Miss. Choctaw; F; Wd; Head; 1253; Yes; Yes
1290; Summers; m; 17; Miss. Choctaw; F; S; Son; 1254; Yes; Yes
1291; Edna; f; 15; Miss. Choctaw; F; S; Dau; 1255; Yes; Yes
1292; Nannie; f; 11; Miss. Choctaw; F; S; Dau; 1256; Yes; Yes
1293; Mary; f; 10; Miss. Choctaw; F; S; Dau; 1257; Yes; Yes

STEPHENS

1294; Nathan; m; 30; Miss. Choctaw; F; M; Head; 1258; Yes; Yes
1295; Annie; f; 35; Miss. Choctaw; F; M; Wife; 1259; Yes; Yes
1296; Maxton; m; 8; Miss. Choctaw; F; S; Son; 1260; Yes; Yes
1297; Cutie Mae; f; 6; Miss. Choctaw; F; S; Dau; 1261; Yes; Yes
1298; Dorthy D; f; 5; Miss. Choctaw; F; S; Dau; 1262; Yes; Yes
1299; Bonnie B; f; 3; Miss. Choctaw; F; S; Dau; 1263; Yes; Yes
1300; Franklin; m; 6/12; Miss. Choctaw; F; S; Son; Yes; Yes

1301; Tom; m; 70; Miss. Choctaw; F; Wd; Head; 1264; Yes; Yes
1302; Cornelia; f; 27; Miss. Choctaw; F; S; Dau; 1265; Yes; Yes
1303; Willie; m; 23; Miss. Choctaw; F; S; Son; 1267; Yes; Yes

Census of the **Mississippi Choctaws** reservation of the **Choctaw Agency** jurisdiction, as of **April 1**, 19 **33**, taken by **A. C. Hector**, Superintendent.

KEY; Surname; Census Number; Given Name; Sex; Age at Last Birthday; Tribe; Degree of Blood; Marital Status; Relationship to Head of Family; Last Census Roll Number; At Jurisdiction Where Enrolled (Yes/No); At Another Jurisdiction; Post Office, County, State (if given); Ward (Yes/No)

1304; Felix; m; 28; Miss. Choctaw; F; M; Head; 1268; Yes; Yes
1305; Martha; f; 25; Miss. Choctaw; F; M; Wife; 1269; Yes; Yes
1306; Martha Lee; f; 3; Miss. Choctaw; F; S; Dau; 1270; Yes; Yes
1307; Mary Frances; f; 2; Miss. Choctaw; F; S; Dau; 1271; Yes; Yes

STEVE

1308; Murphy; m; 59; Miss. Choctaw; F; Wd; Head; 1272; Yes; Yes
1309; Helen; f; 6; Miss. Choctaw; F; S; Dau; 1274; Yes; Yes
1310; Winston; m; 3; Miss. Choctaw; F; S; Son; 1275; Yes; Yes

1311; Josie; m; 31; Miss. Choctaw; F; M; Head; 1276; Yes; Yes
1312; Maggie; f; 24; Miss. Choctaw; F; M; Wife; 1277; Yes; Yes
1313; Ruby; f; 7; Miss. Choctaw; F; S; Dau; 1278; Yes; Yes
1314; Jane; f; 6; Miss. Choctaw; F; S; Dau; 1279; Yes; Yes
1315; Joan; f; 2/12; Miss. Choctaw; F; S; Dau; Yes; Yes

1316; Ennis; m; 24; Miss. Choctaw; F; M; Head; 1285; Yes; Yes
1317; Callie; f; 21; Miss. Choctaw; F; M; Wife; 1286; Yes; Yes
1318; **Morris**, Arwin; f; 6; Miss. Choctaw; F; S; Step-dau; 1287; Yes; Yes

1319; Houston; m; 45; Miss. Choctaw; F; M; Head; 1280; Yes; Yes
1320; Lena; f; 41; Miss. Choctaw; F; M; Wife; 1281; Yes; Yes
1321; McKinley; m; 14; Miss. Choctaw; F; S; Son; 1282; Yes; Yes
1322; Yates; m; 10; Miss. Choctaw; F; S; Son; 1283; Yes; Yes
1323; Marabelle; f; 6; Miss. Choctaw; F; S; Dau; 1284; Yes; Yes

1324; Bobo; m; 26; Miss. Choctaw; F; M; Head; 1288; Yes; Yes
1325; Lucille; f; 21; Miss. Choctaw; F; M; Wife; 1289; Yes; Yes
1326; Maurice; m; 7; Miss. Choctaw; F; S; Son; 1290; Yes; Yes
1327; Audrey; f; 5; Miss. Choctaw; F; S; Dau; 1291; Yes; Yes
1328; Vivian; f; 3; Miss. Choctaw; F; S; Dau; 1292; Yes; Yes
1329; Maraurite; f; 2; Miss. Choctaw; F; S; Dau; 1293; Yes; Yes

Census of the **Mississippi Choctaws** reservation of the **Choctaw Agency** jurisdiction, as of **April 1**, 19**33**, taken by **A. C. Hector**, Superintendent.

KEY; Surname; Census Number; Given Name; Sex; Age at Last Birthday; Tribe; Degree of Blood; Marital Status; Relationship to Head of Family; Last Census Roll Number; At Jurisdiction Where Enrolled (Yes/No); At Another Jurisdiction; Post Office, County, State (if given); Ward (Yes/No)

1330; Lauratina; f; 17 da; Miss. Choctaw; F; S; Dau; 129[sic]; Yes; Yes

1331; Smith; m; 39; Miss. Choctaw; F; M; Head; 1294; Yes; Yes
1332; Winnie; f; 36; Miss. Choctaw; F; M; Wife; 1295; Yes; Yes
1333; Tonie; f; 13; Miss. Choctaw; F; S; Dau; 1296; Yes; Yes
1334; Pauline; f; 12; Miss. Choctaw; F; S; Dau; 1297; Yes; Yes
1335; Mollie; f; 8; Miss. Choctaw; F; S; Dau; 1298; Yes; Yes
1336; Aileen; f; 4; Miss. Choctaw; F; S; Dau; 1299; Yes; Yes
1337; Rebecca; f; 2; Miss. Choctaw; F; S; Dau; 1300; Yes; Yes

STOLIBY

1338; Tom; m; 30; Miss. Choctaw; F; S; Head; 1302; Yes; Yes
1339; Elum Ferum; m; 7; Miss. Choctaw; F; S; Nephew; 1303; Yes; Yes

1340; John; m; 43; Miss. Choctaw; F; Wd; Head; 1304; Yes; Yes
1341; Nancy; f; 22; Miss. Choctaw; F; S; Dau; 1305; Yes; Yes
1342; Will Banks; m; 14; Miss. Choctaw; F; S; Son; 1306; Yes; Yes
1343; Otis; m; 12; Miss. Choctaw; F; S; Son; 1307; Yes; Yes
1344; Zona Miller; f; 8; Miss. Choctaw; F; S; Dau; 1308; Yes; Yes

STRIBLING

1345; Malissie; f; 61; Miss. Choctaw; F; Wd; Alone; 1309; Yes; Yes

THOMAS

1346; Lewis; m; 49; Miss. Choctaw; F; M; Head; 1310; Yes; Yes
1347; Mamie; f; 46; Miss. Choctaw; F; M: Wife; 1311; Yes; Yes
1348; Newman; m; 14; Miss. Choctaw; F; S; Son; 1312; Yes; Yes
1349; Isaac; m; 10; Miss. Choctaw; F; S; Son; 1313; Yes; Yes
1350; Mina; f; 8; Miss. Choctaw; F; S; Dau; 1314; Yes; Yes

1351; Riley; m; 28; Miss. Choctaw; F; S; Alone; 1316; Yes; Yes

Census of the Mississippi Choctaws reservation of the Choctaw
Agency jurisdiction, as of April 1 , 19 33 , taken by
A. C. Hector , Superintendent.

KEY; Surname; Census Number; Given Name; Sex; Age at Last Birthday; Tribe; Degree of Blood; Marital Status; Relationship to Head of Family; Last Census Roll Number; At Jurisdiction Where Enrolled (Yes/No); At Another Jurisdiction; Post Office, County, State (if given); Ward (Yes/No)

1352; Cleve; m; 30; Miss. Choctaw; F; M: Head; 1317; Yes; Yes
1353; Phoebe; f; 25; Miss. Choctaw; F; M; Wife; 1318; Yes; Yes

1354; Wilman; m; 33; Miss. Choctaw; F; M; Head; 1319; Yes; Yes
1355; Sallie; f; 32; Miss. Choctaw; F; M; Wife; 1320; Yes; Yes
1356; Woodrow; m; 14; Miss. Choctaw; F; S; Son; 1321; Yes; Yes
1357; Mollie; f; 12; Miss. Choctaw; F; S; Dau; 1322; Yes; Yes
1358; Golden; m; 10; Miss. Choctaw; F; S; Son; 1323; Yes; Yes
1359; Amos; m; 8; Miss. Choctaw; F; S; Son; 1324; Yes; Yes
1360; Single; m; 4; Miss. Choctaw; F; S; Son; 1325; Yes; Yes
1361; Linnie Helen; f; 2; Miss. Choctaw; F; S; Dau; 1326; Yes; Yes

1362; Lester; m; 24; Miss. Choctaw; F; M: Head; 1327; Yes; Yes
1363; Rosie; f; 22; Miss. Choctaw; F; M; Wife; 1328; Yes; Yes

1364; Rosie; f; 38; Miss. Choctaw; F; S; Alone; 1329; Yes; Yes

1365; *Leona; f, 33; Miss Choctaw; F; M; Wife*; 1330; Yes; Yes

1366; *Evaline; f; 37; Miss. Choctaw; F; M; Wife*; 1331; Yes; Yes
Leona and Evaline Thomas listed above are married to white men-- no children.

THOMPSON

1367; Will; m; 29; Miss. Choctaw; F; M; Head; 1332; Yes; Yes
1368; Sina; f; 26; Miss. Choctaw; F; M; Wife; 1333; Yes; Yes
1369; Otis; m; 9; Miss. Choctaw; F; S; Son; 1334; Yes; Yes
1370 Claudine; f; 6; Miss. Choctaw; F; S; Dau; 1335; Yes; Yes
1371; Henry; m; 4; Miss. Choctaw; F; S; Son; 1336; Yes; Yes
1372; Oneva; f; 2; Miss. Choctaw; F; S; Dau; 1337; Yes; Yes

1373; Cephus; m; 43; Miss. Choctaw; F; M: Head; 1338; Yes; Yes
1374; Beckie; f; 28; Miss. Choctaw; F; M; Wife; 1339; Yes; Yes

Census of the **Mississippi Choctaws** reservation of the **Choctaw Agency** jurisdiction, as of **April 1**, 19**33**, taken by **A. C. Hector**, Superintendent.

KEY; Surname; Census Number; Given Name; Sex; Age at Last Birthday; Tribe; Degree of Blood; Marital Status; Relationship to Head of Family; Last Census Roll Number; At Jurisdiction Where Enrolled (Yes/No); At Another Jurisdiction; Post Office, County, State (if given); Ward (Yes/No)

1375; Dixon; m; 29; Miss. Choctaw; F; S; Son; 1340; 1340; Yes; Yes
1376; Farmer; m; 10; Miss. Choctaw; F; S; Son; 1341; Yes; Yes
1377; Alice; m; 8; Miss. Choctaw; F; S; Dau; 1342; Yes; Yes
1378; Annie; f; 5; Miss. Choctaw; F; S; Dau; 1343; Yes; Yes
1379; Daniel E; m; 4/12; Miss. Choctaw; F; S; Son; Yes; Yes

1380; Malinda; f; 68; Miss. Choctaw; F; Wd; Alone; 1344; Yes; Yes

1381; Mose; m; 36; Miss. Choctaw; F; M; Head; 1345; Yes; Yes
1382; Jean; f; 37; Miss. Choctaw; F; M; Wife; 1347; Yes; Yes
1383; Jim; m; 13; Miss. Choctaw; F; S; Son; 1348; Yes; Yes
1384; Annie; f; 10; Miss. Choctaw; F; S; Dau; 1349; Yes; Yes
1385; Therman; m; 7; Miss. Choctaw; F; S; Son; 1350; Yes; Yes
1386; Steve; m; 6; Miss. Choctaw; F; S; Son; 1351; Yes; Yes

1387; John; m; 41; Miss. Choctaw; F; M; Head; 1352; Yes; Yes
1388; Lula; f; 39; Miss. Choctaw; F; M; Wife; 1353; Yes; Yes
1389; Moline; m; 12; Miss. Choctaw; F; S; Son; 1354; Yes; Yes
1390; Onie; f; 11; Miss. Choctaw; F; S; Dau; 1355; Yes; Yes
1391; Tom; m; 6; Miss. Choctaw; F; S; Son; 1356; Yes; Yes

1392; Tommie; m; 34; Miss. Choctaw; F; M; Head; 1357; Yes; Yes
1393; Bonnie; f; 31; Miss. Choctaw; F; M; Wife; 1358; Yes; Yes
1394; Nathan; m; 2; Miss. Choctaw; F; S; Son; 1359; Yes; Yes
1395; Louise; f; 1/12; Miss. Choctaw; F; S; Dau; Yes; Yes

TUBBY

1396; Dan; m; 31; Miss. Choctaw; F; M; Head; 1360; Yes; Yes
1397; Lola; f; 37; Miss. Choctaw; F; M; Wife; 1361; Yes; Yes
1398; Mable; f; 9/12; Miss. Choctaw; F; S; Dau; Yes; Yes
1399; **Lewis**, Lum; m; 7; Miss. Choctaw; F; S; Step-son; Yes; Yes

1400; George; m; 25; Miss. Choctaw; F; M; Head; 1363; Yes; Yes

Census of the **Mississippi Choctaws** reservation of the **Choctaw Agency** jurisdiction, as of **April 1**, 19**33**, taken by **A. C. Hector**, Superintendent.

KEY; Surname; Census Number; Given Name; Sex; Age at Last Birthday; Tribe; Degree of Blood; Marital Status; Relationship to Head of Family; Last Census Roll Number; At Jurisdiction Where Enrolled (Yes/No); At Another Jurisdiction; Post Office, County, State (if given); Ward (Yes/No)

1401; Mary; f; 22; Miss. Choctaw; F; M; Wife; 1364; Yes; Yes
1402; Thomas; m; 4; Miss. Choctaw; F; S; Son; 1365; Yes; Yes
1403; Annie Lee; f; 11/12; Miss. Choctaw; F; S; Dau; Yes; Yes
1404; Jennie; f; 15; Miss. Choctaw; F; S; Sister; 1366; Yes; Yes

1405; Lefus; m; 40; Miss. Choctaw; F; M; Head; 1367; Yes; Yes
1406; Frances; f; 33; Miss. Choctaw; F; M; Wife; 1368; Yes; Yes
1407; Ina; f; 11; Miss. Choctaw; F; S; Dau; 1369; Yes; Yes
1408; Irene; f; 9; Miss. Choctaw; F; S; Dau; 1370; Yes; Yes
1409; Leona; f; 6; Miss. Choctaw; F; S; Dau; 1371; Yes; Yes
1410; Robert; m; 1; Miss. Choctaw; F; S; Son; 1373; Yes; Yes
1411; **Ben**, Rufus; m; 15; Miss. Choctaw; F; S; Step-son; 1372; Yes; Yes

1412; Sidney; m; 33; Miss. Choctaw; F; M; Head; 1374; Yes; Yes
1413; Kate; f; 32; Miss. Choctaw; F; M; Wife; 1375; Yes; Yes
1414; Rufus; m; 14; Miss. Choctaw; F; S; Son; 1376; Yes; Yes
1415; Phelia; f; 11; Miss. Choctaw; F; S; Son[sic]; 1377; Yes; Yes
1416; Eva Kate; f; 8; Miss. Choctaw; F; S; Dau; 1378; Yes; Yes
1417; Edmond; m; 5; Miss. Choctaw; F; S; Son; 1379; Yes; Yes

1418; Annis; m; 54; Miss. Choctaw; F; M; Head; 1380; Yes; Yes
1419; Annie; f; 33; Miss. Choctaw; F; M; Wife; 1381; Yes; Yes

1420; Edgar; m; 33; Miss. Choctaw; F; M: Head; 1382; Yes; Yes
1421; Annie; f; 31; Miss. Choctaw; F; M; Wife; 1383; Yes; Yes
1422; Steve; m; 12; Miss. Choctaw; F; S; Son; 1384; Yes; Yes
1423; Willie; m; 11; Miss. Choctaw; F; S; Son; 1385; Yes; Yes
1424; Odie; m; 9; Miss. Choctaw; F; S; Son; 1386; Yes; Yes
1425; Parline; f; 6; Miss. Choctaw; F; S; Dau; 1387; Yes; Yes

1426; Dick; m; 62; Miss. Choctaw; F; M; Head; 1388; Yes; Yes
1427; Eline; f; 53; Miss. Choctaw; F; M; Wife; 1389; Yes; Yes
1428; Jeff; m; 27; Miss. Choctaw; F; S; Nephew; 1390; Yes; Yes

Census of the **Mississippi Choctaws** reservation of the **Choctaw Agency** jurisdiction, as of **April 1**, 19**33**, taken by **A. C. Hector**, Superintendent.

KEY; Surname; Census Number; Given Name; Sex; Age at Last Birthday; Tribe; Degree of Blood; Marital Status; Relationship to Head of Family; Last Census Roll Number; At Jurisdiction Where Enrolled (Yes/No); At Another Jurisdiction; Post Office, County, State (if given); Ward (Yes/No)

1429; Allen; m; 77; Miss. Choctaw; F; Wd; Head; 1391; Yes; Yes
1430; Mary; f; 30; Miss. Choctaw; F; S; Dau; 1392; Yes; Yes
1431; Lilly; f; 28; Miss. Choctaw; F; S; Dau; 1393; Yes; Yes

1432; Pat; m; 39; Miss. Choctaw; F; M; Head; 1394; Yes; Yes
1433; Frances; f; 39; Miss. Choctaw; F; M; Wife; 1395; Yes; Yes
1434; Vernal; m; 21; Miss. Choctaw; F; S; Son; 1396; Yes; Yes
1435; Earnest; m; 13; Miss. Choctaw; F; S; Son; 1397; Yes; Yes
1436; Loraine; f; 11; Miss. Choctaw; F; S; Dau; 1397; Dau; 1398; Yes; Yes
1437; Alice; f; 9; Miss. Choctaw; F; S; Dau; 1399; Yes; Yes
1438; Aileen; f; 6; Miss. Choctaw; F; S; Dau; 1400; Yes; Yes

1439; Lysander; m; 45; Miss. Choctaw; F; M; Head; 1401; Yes; Yes

1440; Moley; m; 30; Miss. Choctaw; F; M; Head; 1403; Yes; Yes
1441; Sallie; f; 26; Miss. Choctaw; F; M; Wife; 1404; Yes; Yes
1442; Grace; f; 9/12; Miss. Choctaw; F; S; Dau; Yes; Yes

1443; Adam; m; 31; Miss. Choctaw; F; S; Alone; 1405; Yes; Yes

1444; Dewitt; m; 26; Miss. Choctaw; F; M; Head; 1406; Yes; Yes
1445; Katie; f; 27; Miss. Choctaw; F; M; Wife; 1407; Yes; Yes
1446; Cicero L; m; 6/12; Miss. Choctaw; F; S; Son; Yes; Yes

1447; Rainey; f; 63; Miss. Choctaw; F; Wd; Head; 1408; Yes; Yes
1448; Lena; f; 33; Miss. Choctaw; F; S; Dau; 1409; Yes; Yes
1449; Mollie; f; 28; Miss. Choctaw; F; S; Dau; 1410; Yes; Yes
1450; Herbert; m; 25; Miss. Choctaw; F; S; Son; 1411; Yes

1451; Jimpson; m; 69; Miss. Choctaw; F; Wd; Alone; 1412; Yes; Yes

1452; Anderson; m; 33; Miss. Choctaw; F; M; Head; 1413; Yes; Yes
1453; Nancy; f; 23; Miss. Choctaw; F; M; Wife; 1414; Yes; Yes

Census of the **Mississippi Choctaws** reservation of the **Choctaw Agency** jurisdiction, as of **April 1**, 19**33**, taken by **A. C. Hector**, Superintendent.

KEY; Surname; Census Number; Given Name; Sex; Age at Last Birthday; Tribe; Degree of Blood; Marital Status; Relationship to Head of Family; Last Census Roll Number; At Jurisdiction Where Enrolled (Yes/No); At Another Jurisdiction; Post Office, County, State (if given); Ward (Yes/No)

1454; Jim; m; 9; Miss. Choctaw; F; S; Son; 1415; Yes; Yes
1455; Oscar; f; 7; Miss. Choctaw; F; S; Dau; 1416; Yes; Yes
1456; Buracy; f; 5; Miss. Choctaw; F; S; Dau; 1417; Yes; Yes
1457; Etolye; f; 3; Miss. Choctaw; F; S; Dau; 1418; Yes; Yes

1458; Evan; m; 40; Miss. Choctaw; F; M; Head; 1419; Yes; Yes
1459; Jennie; f; 45; Miss. Choctaw; F; M; Wife; 1420; Yes; Yes
1460; Annie; f; 10; Miss. Choctaw; F; S; Dau; 1421; Yes; Yes

1461; Charlie; m; 37; Miss. Choctaw; F; M; Head; 1422; Yes; Yes
1462; Betsey; f; 32; Miss. Choctaw; F; M; Wife; 1423; Yes; Yes
1463; Alice; f; 10; Miss. Choctaw; F; S; Dau; 1424; Yes; Yes
1464; Jack; m; 8; Miss. Choctaw; F; S; Son; 1425; Yes; Yes
1465; J. C; m; 6; Miss. Choctaw; F; S; Son; 1426; Yes; Yes
1466; Colie; f; 4; Miss. Choctaw; F; S; Sau; 1427; Yes; Yes
1467; Bessie; f; 1; Miss. Choctaw; F; S; Dau; 1428; Yes; Yes
1468; Kate; f; 12; Miss. Choctaw; F; S; Step-dau; 1429; Yes; Yes
1469; Ellis; m; 9; Miss. Choctaw; F; S; Orphan; 1430; Yes; Yes

1470; Henderson; m; 40; Miss. Choctaw; F; M; Head; 1431; Yes; Yes
1471; Maggie; f; 29; Miss. Choctaw; F; M; Wife; 1432; Yes; Yes
1472; Otis; f; 10; Miss. Choctaw; F; S; Dau; 1433; Yes; Yes
1473; W. C; m; 8; Miss. Choctaw; F; S; Son; 1434; Yes; Yes
1474; Gladys; f; 6; Miss. Choctaw; F; S; Dau; 1435; Yes; Yes
1475; Finis; m; 4; Miss. Choctaw; F; S; Son; 1436; Yes; Yes
1476; Martha Lee; f; 2; Miss. Choctaw; F; S; Dau; 1437; Yes; Yes
1477; James H; m; 9/12; Miss. Choctaw; F; S; Son; Yes; Yes

1478; Clemon; m; 58; Miss. Choctaw; F; M; Head; 1438; Yes; Yes
1479; Alice; f; 48; Miss. Choctaw; F; M; Wife; 1439; Yes; Yes
1480; Joe; m; 24; Miss. Choctaw; F; S; Son; 1440; Yes; Yes
1481; Elias; m; 7; Miss. Choctaw; F; S; Great-nephew; 1441; Yes; Yes
1482; Sarah; f; 6; Miss. Choctaw; F; S; Great-niece; 1442; Yes; Yes

Census of the **Mississippi Choctaws** reservation of the **Choctaw Agency** jurisdiction, as of **April 1**, 19**33**, taken by **A. C. Hector**, Superintendent.

KEY; Surname; Census Number; Given Name; Sex; Age at Last Birthday; Tribe; Degree of Blood; Marital Status; Relationship to Head of Family; Last Census Roll Number; At Jurisdiction Where Enrolled (Yes/No); At Another Jurisdiction; Post Office, County, State (if given); Ward (Yes/No)

1483; Jackson; m; 25; Miss. Choctaw; F; M; Head; 1443; Yes; Yes
1484; Malissa; f; 26; Miss. Choctaw; F; M; Wife; 1444; Yes; Yes
1485; Coleman; m; 5/12; Mis; S; Son; Yes; Yes

1486; Nichols; m; 35; Miss. Choctaw; F; M; Head; 1445; Yes; Yes
1487; Esther; f; 30; Miss. Choctaw; F; M: Wife; 1446; Yes; Yes
1488; Sullivan; m; 11; Miss. Choctaw; F; S; Son; 1447; Yes; Yes
1489; Alice; f; 10; Miss. Choctaw; F; S; Dau; 1448; Yes; Yes
1490; Minnie; f; 8; Miss. Choctaw; F; S; Dau; 1449; Yes; Yes
1491; Catherine; f; 6; Miss. Choctaw; F; S; Dau; 1450; Yes; Yes

1492; Alice; f; 43; Miss. Choctaw; F; Wd; Head; 1451; Yes; Yes
1493; **Johnson**, Lee; m; 21; Miss. Choctaw; F; S; Son; 1452; Yes; Yes

1494; Tom; m; 24; Miss. Choctaw; F; M; Head; 1453; Yes; Yes
1495; Marceline; f; 26; Miss. Choctaw; F; M; Wife; 1454; Yes; Yes
1496; Inis; m; 3; Miss. Choctaw; F; S; Son; 1455; Yes; Yes
1497; Leonard; m; 6/12; Miss. Choctaw; F; S; Son; Yes; Yes
1498; Joseph; m; 5; Miss. Choctaw; F; S; Son; 1456; Yes; Yes

1499; Anderson; m; 41; Miss. Choctaw; F; M; Head; 1457; Yes; Yes
1500; Lousiana; f; 43; Miss. Choctaw; F; M; Wife; 1458; Yes; Yes
1501; Hazel; f; 19; Miss. Choctaw; F; S; Dau; 1459; Yes; Yes
1502; Smith; m; 17; Miss. Choctaw; F; S; Son; 1460; Yes; Yes
1503; Icy; f; 15; Miss. Choctaw; F; S; Dau; 1461; Yes; Yes
1504; John; m; 13; Miss. Choctaw; F; S; Son; 1462; Yes; Yes

1505; Simpson; m; 73; Miss. Choctaw; F; M; Head; 1463; Yes; Yes
1506; Minnie; f; 40; Miss. Choctaw; F; M; Wife; 1464; Yes; Yes
1507; Ike; m; 21; Miss. Choctaw; F; S; Son; 1465; Yes; Yes
1508; Henry; m; 20; Miss. Choctaw; F; S; Son; 1466; Yes; Yes
1509; Lewis; m; 16; Miss. Choctaw; F; S; Son; 1468; Yes; Yes
1510; McKinley; m; 13; Miss. Choctaw; F; S; Son; 1469; Yes; Yes
1511; Hudson; m; 10; Miss. Choctaw; F; S; Son; 1470; Yes; Yes

Census of the **Mississippi Choctaws** reservation of the **Choctaw Agency** jurisdiction, as of **April 1**, 19 **33**, taken by **A. C. Hector**, Superintendent.

KEY; Surname; Census Number; Given Name; Sex; Age at Last Birthday; Tribe; Degree of Blood; Marital Status; Relationship to Head of Family; Last Census Roll Number; At Jurisdiction Where Enrolled (Yes/No); At Another Jurisdiction; Post Office, County, State (if given); Ward (Yes/No)

1512; Sullivan; m; 9; Miss. Choctaw; F; S; Son; 1471; Yes; Yes
1513; Callie; f; 7; Miss. Choctaw; F; S; Dau; 1472; Yes; Yes
1514; Nellie; f; 6; Miss. Choctaw; F; S; Dau; 1473; Yes; Yes

TUCKALOO

1515; Frances; f; 70; Miss. Choctaw; F; Wd; Head; 1474; Yes; Yes
1516; **Tubby**, Wesley; m; 14; Miss. Choctaw; F; S; Grand-son; 1475; Yes; Yes
1517; Mason; m; 19; Miss. Choctaw; F; S; Grand-son; 1476; Yes; Yes
1518; Enia; m; 9; Miss. Choctaw; F; S; Grand-son; 1477; Yes; Yes
1519; Alice; f; 8; Miss. Choctaw; F; S; Grand-dau; 1478; Yes; Yes
1520; Sarah; f; 7; Miss. Choctaw; F; S; Grand-dau; 1479; Yes; Yes

VAUGHN

1521; John; m; 68; Miss. Choctaw; F; Wd; Alone; 1480; Yes; Yes

1522; Greer; m; 58; Miss. Choctaw; F; M; Head; 1481; Yes; Yes
1523; Jane; f; 53; Miss. Choctaw; F; M; Wife; 1482; Yes; Yes
1524; Agnes; f; 7; Miss. Choctaw; F; S; Dau; 1483; Yes; Yes

1525; Cooksie; m; 66; Miss. Choctaw; F; M; Head; 1484; Yes; Yes
1526; Susan; f; 61; Miss. Choctaw; F; M; Wife; 1485; Yes; Yes
1527; Lena; f; 38; Miss. Choctaw; F; S; Dau; 1486; Yes; Yes
1528; Ludie; f; 26; Miss. Choctaw; F; S; Dau; 1487; Yes; Yes

1529; Silmon; m; 21; Miss. Choctaw; F; M; Head; 1488; Yes; Yes
1530; Seta; f; 17; Miss. Choctaw; F; M; Wife; 1489; Yes; Yes

1531; Howard; m; 31; Miss. Choctaw; F; M: Head; 1490; Yes; Yes
1532; Bessie; f; 31; Miss. Choctaw; F; M; Wife; 1491; Yes; Yes
1533; Clifton; m; 7; Miss. Choctaw; F; S; Son; 1492; Yes; Yes
1534; Mary Rose; f; 5; Miss. Choctaw; F; S; Dau; 1493; Yes; Yes

Census of the **Mississippi Choctaws** reservation of the **Choctaw Agency** jurisdiction, as of **April 1**, 19**33**, taken by **A. C. Hector**, Superintendent.

KEY; Surname; Census Number; Given Name; Sex; Age at Last Birthday; Tribe; Degree of Blood; Marital Status; Relationship to Head of Family; Last Census Roll Number; At Jurisdiction Where Enrolled (Yes/No); At Another Jurisdiction; Post Office, County, State (if given); Ward (Yes/No)

1535; John; m; 27; Miss. Choctaw; F; M: Head; 1494; Yes; Yes
1536; Melissa; f; 40; Miss. Choctaw; F; M; Wife; 1495; Yes; Yes
1537; Mollie; f; 20; Miss. Choctaw; F; S; Step-dau; 1496; Yes; Yes
1538; Annie; f; 15; Miss. Choctaw; F; S; Step-dau; 1497; Yes; Yes

WAITER

1539; Gipson; m; 70; Miss. Choctaw; F; Wd; Alone; 1498; Yes; Yes

1540; Minnie; f; 57; Miss. Choctaw; F; Wd; Alone; 1499; Yes; Yes

1541; Lonnie; m; 28; Miss. Choctaw; F; M; Head; 1500; Yes; Yes
1542; Sue; f; 23; Miss. Choctaw; F; M; Wife; 1501; Yes; Yes
1543; Cora Mae; f; 2; Miss. Choctaw; F; S; Dau; 1502; Yes; Yes

WALLACE

1544; Comby; m; 61; Miss. Choctaw; F; M; Head; 1503; Yes; Yes
1545; Betty; f; 57; Miss. Choctaw; F; M; Wife; 1504; Yes; Yes
1546; Emma; f; 18; Miss. Choctaw; F; S; Dau; 1505; Yes; Yes
1547; Maggie; f; 16; Miss. Choctaw; F; S; Dau; 1506; Yes; Yes
1548; Tom; m; 12; Miss. Choctaw; F; S; Son; 1507; Yes; Yes
1549; Fulton; m; 9; Miss. Choctaw; F; S; Son; 1508; Yes; Yes

1550; Eunice; f; 43; Miss. Choctaw; F; Wd; Head; 1509; Yes; Yes
1551; Susie; f; 20; Miss. Choctaw; F; S; Dau; 1510; Yes; Yes
1552; Henry; m; 18; Miss. Choctaw; F; S; Son; 1511; Yes; Yes
1553; Celia; f; 17; Miss. Choctaw; F; S; Dau; 1512; Yes; Yes
1554; Austin; m; 6; Miss. Choctaw; F; S; Son; 1513; Yes; Yes

1555; Rachel; f; 48; Miss. Choctaw; F; Wd; Head; 1514; Yes; Yes
1556; Leona; f; 19; Miss. Choctaw; F; S; Dau; 1515; Yes; Yes

1557; Columbus; m; 23; Miss. Choctaw; F; M; Head; 1516; Yes; Yes

Census of the **Mississippi Choctaws** reservation of the **Choctaw Agency** jurisdiction, as of **April 1**, 19**33**, taken by **A. C. Hector**, Superintendent.

KEY; Surname; Census Number; Given Name; Sex; Age at Last Birthday; Tribe; Degree of Blood; Marital Status; Relationship to Head of Family; Last Census Roll Number; At Jurisdiction Where Enrolled (Yes/No); At Another Jurisdiction; Post Office, County, State (if given); Ward (Yes/No)

1558; Essie; f; 21; Miss. Choctaw; F; M; Wife; 1517; Yes; Yes

1559; Stenot; m; 25; Miss. Choctaw; F; M; Head; 1518; Yes; Yes
1560; Annie; f; 20; Miss. Choctaw; F; M; Wife; 1519; Yes; Yes
1561; Alton; m; 13; Miss. Choctaw; F; S; Orphan; 1520; Yes; Yes

WARNER

1562; Johnnie L; m; 21; Miss. Choctaw; F; S; Alone; 1521; Yes; Yes

WESLEY

1563; Sidney; m; 68; Miss. Choctaw; F; Wd; Alone; 1522; Yes; Yes

1564; Cameron; m; 43; Miss. Choctaw; F; M; Head; 1523; Yes; Yes
1565; Julie; f; 29; Miss. Choctaw; F; M; Wife; 1524; Yes; Yes
1566; Bennie; m; 16; Miss. Choctaw; F; S; Son; 1525; Yes; Yes
1567; John; m; 8; Miss. Choctaw; F; S; Son; 1526; Yes; Yes
1568; Willie B; m; 5; Miss. Choctaw; F; Son; 1527; Yes; Yes

WICKSON

1569; Jim; m; 25; Miss. Choctaw; F; Wd; Alone; 1528; Yes; Yes

WILEY

1570; Lizzie; f; 63; Miss. Choctaw; F; S; Alone; 1530; Yes; Yes

WILLIAMS

1571; Jonas; m; 58; Miss. Choctaw; F; M; Head; 1531; Yes; Yes
1572; Maggie; f; 48; Miss. Choctaw; F; M; Wife; 1532; Yes; Yes
1573; Tony; m; 24; Miss. Choctaw; F; S; Son; 1533; Yes; Yes

Census of the **Mississippi Choctaws** reservation of the **Choctaw Agency** jurisdiction, as of **April 1**, 19**33**, taken by **A. C. Hector**, Superintendent.

KEY; Surname; Census Number; Given Name; Sex; Age at Last Birthday; Tribe; Degree of Blood; Marital Status; Relationship to Head of Family; Last Census Roll Number; At Jurisdiction Where Enrolled (Yes/No); At Another Jurisdiction; Post Office, County, State (if given); Ward (Yes/No)

1574; Rufus; m; 26; Miss. Choctaw; F; M; Head; 1534; Yes; Yes
1575; Nellie; f; 32; Miss. Choctaw; F; M; Wife; 1535; Yes; Yes
1576; Evan; m; 11; Miss. Choctaw; F; S; Son; 1536; Yes; Yes
1577; Phillip; m; 10; Miss. Choctaw; F; S; Son; 1537; Yes; Yes
1578; Fillman; m; 6; Miss. Choctaw; F; S; Son; 1538; Yes; Yes
1579; Coy; m; 4; Miss. Choctaw; F; S; Son; 1539; Yes; Yes

1580; Jennie; f; 89: Miss. Choctaw; F; Wd; Head; 1540; Yes; Yes
1581; Fate; m; 44; Miss. Choctaw; F; S; Son; 1541; Yes; Yes

1582; Lewis; m; 56; Miss. Choctaw; F; M; Head; 1542; Yes; Yes
1583; Mamie; f; 34; Miss. Choctaw; F; M; Wife; 1543; Yes; Yes
1584; Mary Ann; f; 8; Miss. Choctaw; F; S; Dau; 1544; Yes; Yes
1585; Sarah; f; 4; Miss. Choctaw; F; S; Dau; 1545; Yes; Yes
1586; Carter; m; 2; Miss. Choctaw; F; S; Son; 1546; Yes; Yes
1587; **Lewis**, Johnnie; m; 35; Miss. Choctaw; F; Wd; Brother-in-law; 976; Yes; Yes

WILLIAMSON

1588; Mack; m; 58; Miss. Choctaw; F; M; Head; 1547; Yes; Yes
1589; Ida; f; 58; Miss. Choctaw; F; M; Wife; 1548; Yes; Yes
1590; Arnold; m; 14; Miss. Choctaw; F; S; Son; 1549; Yes; Yes
1591; **Lewis**, Marceline; f; 9; Miss. Choctaw; F; S; Grand-dau; 1550; Yes; Yes

1592; Bike; m; 41; Miss. Choctaw; F; M; Head; 1551; Yes; Yes
1593; Effie; f; 29; Miss. Choctaw; F; M; Wife; 1552; Yes; Yes
1594; Mary; f; 13; Miss. Choctaw; F; S; Dau; 1553; Yes; Yes
1595; Lallis; f; 11; Miss. Choctaw; F; S; Dau; 1554; Yes; Yes

WILLIS

1596; Bill; m; 37; Miss. Choctaw; F; M; Head; 1555; Yes; Yes

Census of the **Mississippi Choctaws** reservation of the **Choctaw Agency** jurisdiction, as of **April 1**, 19**33**, taken by **A. C. Hector**, Superintendent.

KEY; Surname; Census Number; Given Name; Sex; Age at Last Birthday; Tribe; Degree of Blood; Marital Status; Relationship to Head of Family; Last Census Roll Number; At Jurisdiction Where Enrolled (Yes/No); At Another Jurisdiction; Post Office, County, State (if given); Ward (Yes/No)

1597; Savenie; f; 31; Miss. Choctaw; F; M; Wife; 1556; Yes; Yes
1598; Claud Y; m; 14; Miss. Choctaw; F; S; Son; 1557; Yes; Yes
1599; Elsie; f; 13; Miss. Choctaw; F; S; Dau; 1558; Yes; Yes
1600; William B; m; 10; Miss. Choctaw; F; S; Son; 1559; Yes; Yes

1601; Nath; m; 26; Miss. Choctaw; F; M; Head; 1560; Yes; Yes
1602; Esther; f; 30; Miss. Choctaw; F; M; Wife; 1561; Yes; Yes
1603; Sylvia; f; 5; Miss. Choctaw; F; S; Dau; 1562; Yes; Yes
1604; Joe; m; 3; Miss. Choctaw; F; S; Son; 1563; Yes; Yes

1605; Ike; m; 26; Miss. Choctaw; F; M; Head; 1564; Yes; Yes
1606; Ellen; f; 24; Miss. Choctaw; F; M; Wife; 1565; Yes; Yes
1607; Adam; m; 7; Miss. Choctaw; F; S; Son; 1566; Yes; Yes
1608; Jasper; m; 4; Miss. Choctaw; F; S; Son; 1567; Yes; Yes

1609; Robert; m; 45; Miss. Choctaw; F; M; Head; 1568; Yes; Yes
1610; Celie; f; 32; Miss. Choctaw; F; M; Wife; 1569; Yes; Yes
1611; Mollie; f; 21; Miss. Choctaw; F; S; Dau; 1570; Yes; Yes
1612; **Ben**, Wilson; m; 13; Miss. Choctaw; F; S; Orphan; 1571; Yes; Yes

1613; Finis; m; 31; Miss. Choctaw; F; M; Head; 1572; Yes; Yes
1614; Nora; f; 26; Miss. Choctaw; F; M; Wife; 1573; Yes; Yes
1615; Leona; f; 4; Miss. Choctaw; F; S; Dau; 1574; Yes; Yes
1616; Sarah; f; 2; Miss. Choctaw; F; S; Dau; 1575; Yes; Yes

1617; John; m; 27; Miss. Choctaw; F; M; Head; 1576; Yes; Yes
1618; Susana; f; 19; Miss. Choctaw; F; M; Wife; 1577; Yes; Yes

1619; Johnson; m; 68; Miss. Choctaw; F; Wd; Alone; 1578; Yes; Yes

1620; Gus; m; 60; Miss. Choctaw; F; M; Head; 1579; Yes; Yes
1621; Rainey; f; 36; Miss. Choctaw; F; M; Wife; 1580; Yes; Yes
1622; Hester; m; 6; Miss. Choctaw; F; S; Son; 1581; Yes; Yes
1623; Lester; m; 2; Miss. Choctaw; F; S; Son; 1582; Yes; Yes

Census of the **Mississippi Choctaws** reservation of the **Choctaw Agency** jurisdiction, as of **April 1**, 19**33**, taken by **A. C. Hector**, Superintendent.

KEY; Surname; Census Number; Given Name; Sex; Age at Last Birthday; Tribe; Degree of Blood; Marital Status; Relationship to Head of Family; Last Census Roll Number; At Jurisdiction Where Enrolled (Yes/No); At Another Jurisdiction; Post Office, County, State (if given); Ward (Yes/No)

1624; **Isaac**, William; m; 20; Miss. Choctaw; F; S; Step-son; 1586; Yes; Yes

1625; **Isaac**, Nannie; f; 15; Miss. Choctaw; F; S; Step-dau; 1583; Yes; Yes

1626; **Isaac**, Eunice; f; 13; Miss. Choctaw; F; S; Step-dau; 1584; Yes; Yes

1627; **Isaac**, Rose; m; 9; Miss. Choctaw; F; S; Step-dau; 1585; Yes; Yes

1628; Gamblin; m; 33; Miss. Choctaw; F; M; Head; 1587; Yes; Yes
1629; Ellen; f; 35; Miss. Choctaw; F; M; Wife; 1588; Yes; Yes
1630; Mattie; f; 15; Miss. Choctaw; F; S; Dau; 1589; Yes; Yes
1631; G. C; m; 12; Miss. Choctaw; F; S; Son; 1590; Yes; Yes
1632; Eula; f; 10; Miss. Choctaw; F; S; Dau; 1591; Yes; Yes
1633; Maruice[sic]; f; 9; Miss. Choctaw; F; S; Dau; 1592; Yes; Yes
1634; Marabelle; f; 4; Miss. Choctaw; F; S; Dau; 1593; Yes; Yes
1635; Earl; m; 2; Miss. Choctaw; F; S; Son; 1594; Yes; Yes

1636; Ed; m; 62; Miss. Choctaw; F; Wd; Alone; 1595; Yes; Yes

1637; Joe; m; 64; Miss. Choctaw; F; M; Head; 1597; Yes; Yes
1638; Adaline; f; 61; Miss. Choctaw; F; M; Wife; 1598; Yes; Yes
1639; Nannie; f; 23; Miss. Choctaw; F; S; Grand-dau; 1599; Yes; Yes

1640; Ellis; m; 30; Miss. Choctaw; F; S; Alone; 1600; Yes; Yes

1641; Jim; m; 55; Miss. Choctaw; F; m: Head; 1601; Yes; Yes
1642; Louisa; f; 53; Miss. Choctaw; F; M; Wife; 1602; Yes; Yes
1643; Tom; m; 31; Miss. Choctaw; F; S; Son; 1603; Yes; Yes
1644; Dennis; m; 29; Miss. Choctaw; F; S; 1604; Yes; Yes
1645; Waggoner; m; 24; Miss. Choctaw; F; S; Son; 1605; Yes; Yes
1646; Dailey; f; 22; Miss. Choctaw; F; S; Dau; 1606; Yes; Yes
1647; Dora; f; 21; Miss. Choctaw; F; S; Dau; 1607; Yes; Yes
1648; Smith; m; 18; Miss. Choctaw; F; S; Son; 1609; Yes; Yes

Census of the **Mississippi Choctaws** reservation of the **Choctaw Agency** jurisdiction, as of **April 1**, 19 **33**, taken by **A. C. Hector**, Superintendent.

KEY; Surname; Census Number; Given Name; Sex; Age at Last Birthday; Tribe; Degree of Blood; Marital Status; Relationship to Head of Family; Last Census Roll Number; At Jurisdiction Where Enrolled (Yes/No); At Another Jurisdiction; Post Office, County, State (if given); Ward (Yes/No)

1649; Woodrow Wilson; m; 13; Miss. Choctaw; F; S; Son; 1610; Yes; Yes
1650; Rose; f; 19; Miss. Choctaw; F; S; Dau; 1608; Yes; Yes

1651; Edmond; m; 25; Miss. Choctaw; F; M; Head; 1611; Yes; Yes
1652; Sallie; f; 20; Miss. Choctaw; F; M; Wife; 1612; Yes; Yes
1653; John; m; 4; Miss. Choctaw; F; S; Son; 1613; Yes; Yes
1654; Hayward; m; 2; Miss. Choctaw; F; S; Son; 1614; Yes; Yes

1655; Elie; m; 32; Miss. Choctaw; F; M; Head; 1615; Yes; Yes
1656; Odie; f; 26; Miss. Choctaw; F; M; Wife; 1616; Yes; Yes
1657; Vanola; f; 13; Miss. Choctaw; F; S; Dau; 1617; Yes; Yes
1658; Flora; f; 11; Miss. Choctaw; F; S; Dau; 1618; Yes; Yes
1659; Kitty; f; 10; Miss. Choctaw; F; S; Dau; 1619; Yes; Yes
1660; Bonnie; m[sic]; 8; Miss. Choctaw; F; S; Son; 1620; Yes; Yes
1661; Robert R; m; 11/12; Miss. Choctaw; F; S; Son; Yes; Yes

1662; Cohen; m; 35; Miss Choctaw; F; M; Head; 1621; Yes; Yes
1663; Sissey; f; 31; Miss. Choctaw; F; M; Wife; 1622; Yes; Yes
1664; Ance; f; 15; Miss. Choctaw; F; S; Dau; 1623; Yes; Yes
1665; Una; f; 13; Miss. Choctaw; F; S; Dau; 1624; Yes; Yes
1666; Sallie; f; 10; Miss. Choctaw; F; S; Dau; 1625; Yes; Yes
1667; Harrison; m; 8; Miss. Choctaw; F; S; Son; 1626; Yes; Yes
1668; A. J; m; 5; Miss. Choctaw; F; S; Son; 1627; Yes; Yes
1669; Arline; f; 6/12; Miss. Choctaw; F; S; Dau; Yes; Yes

1670; Hugh; m; 50; Miss. Choctaw; F; S; Head; 1628; Yes; Yes
1671; Mollie; f; 47; Miss. Choctaw; F; S; Wife; 1629; Yes; Yes
1672; Thompson; m; 18; Miss. Choctaw; F; S; Son; 1630; Yes; Yes
1673; Clemon; m; 16; Miss. Choctaw; F; S; Son; 1631; Yes; Yes
1674; J. C; m; 12; Miss. Choctaw; F; S; Son; 1632; Yes; Yes
1675; Collins; m; 10; Miss. Choctaw; F; S; Son; 1633; Yes; Yes
1676; Lillie; f; 9; Miss. Choctaw; F; S; Dau; 1634; Yes; Yes
1677; Walter; m; 8; Miss. Choctaw; F; S; Son; 1635; Yes; Yes

Census of the **Mississippi Choctaws** reservation of the **Choctaw Agency** jurisdiction, as of **April 1**, 19**33**, taken by **A. C. Hector**, Superintendent.

KEY; Surname; Census Number; Given Name; Sex; Age at Last Birthday; Tribe; Degree of Blood; Marital Status; Relationship to Head of Family; Last Census Roll Number; At Jurisdiction Where Enrolled (Yes/No); At Another Jurisdiction; Post Office, County, State (if given); Ward (Yes/No)

1678; Lola; f; 7; Miss. Choctaw; F; S; Dau; 1636; Yes; Yes
1679; Beaman; m; 2; Miss. Choctaw; F; S; Yes; Yes
Omitted on previous census

1680; Spinks; m; 43; Miss. Choctaw; F; M; Head; 1637; Yes; Yes
1681; Susie; f; 34; Miss. Choctaw; F; M; Wife; 1638; Yes; Yes
1682; Wilson; m; 14; Miss. Choctaw; F; S; Son; 1639; Yes; Yes
1683; Flennie; f; 11; Miss. Choctaw; F; S; Dau; 1640; Yes; Yes

1684; Wesley; m; 67; Miss. Choctaw; F; F; Wd; Head; 1641; Yes; Yes
1685; Meley; f; 9; Miss. Choctaw; F; S; Dau; 1642; Yes; Yes
1686; John Banks; m; 6; Miss. Choctaw; F; S; Son; 1643; Yes; Yes
1687; Leighton; m; 3; Miss. Choctaw; F; S; Son; 1644; Yes; Yes

1688; Salum; m; 28; Miss. Choctaw; F; S; Alone; 1645; Yes; Yes

WILSON

1689; John; m; 38; Miss. Choctaw; F; M; Head; 1646; Yes; Yes
1690; Eva; f; 30; Miss. Choctaw; F; M; Wife; 1647; Yes; Yes
1691; Silman; m; 14; Miss. Choctaw; F; S; Son; 1648; Yes; Yes
1692; Mollie; f; 12; Miss. Choctaw; F; S; Dau; 1649; Yes; Yes
1693; Sidney; m; 11; Miss. Choctaw; F; S; Son; 1650; Yes; Yes
1694; Leo; m; 8; Miss. Choctaw; F; S; Son; 1651; Yes; Yes
1695; Edna; f; 3; Miss. Choctaw; F; S; Dau; 1652; Yes; Yes
1696; Martha; f; 85; Miss. Choctaw; F; Wd; Mother; 1653; Yes; Yes

1697; Will; m; 45; Miss. Choctaw; F; M; Head; 1653; Yes; Yes
1698; Martha; f; 39; Miss. Choctaw; F; M; Wife; 1654; Yes; Yes
1699; Sammie; m; 12; Miss. Choctaw; F; S; Son; 1655; Yes; Yes
1700; Linnie; f; 11; Miss. Choctaw; F; S; Dau; 1656; Yes; Yes
1701; Louisana; f; 10; Miss. Choctaw; F; S; Dau; 1657; Yes; Yes
1702; R. L; m; 4; Miss. Choctaw; F; S; Son; 1658; Yes; Yes
1703; Jim; m; 3; Miss. Choctaw; F; S; Son; 1659; Yes; Yes

Census of the __Mississippi Choctaws__ reservation of the __Choctaw Agency__ jurisdiction, as of __April 1__, 19_33_, taken by __A. C. Hector__, Superintendent.

KEY; Surname; Census Number; Given Name; Sex; Age at Last Birthday; Tribe; Degree of Blood; Marital Status; Relationship to Head of Family; Last Census Roll Number; At Jurisdiction Where Enrolled (Yes/No); At Another Jurisdiction; Post Office, County, State (if given); Ward (Yes/No)

1704; Neil Milber; m; 1; Miss. Choctaw; F; S; Son; Yes; Yes

WISHORK

1705; Alpha; f; 31; Miss. Choctaw; F; Wd; Head; 1660; Yes; Yes
1706; Zelia; f; 12; Miss. Choctaw; F; S; Dau; 1661; Yes; Yes
1707; Evelyn; f; 11; Miss. Choctaw; F; S; Dau; 1662; Yes; Yes
1708; Nuga; f; 8; Miss. Choctaw; F; S; Dau; 1663; Yes; Yes
1709; Lyn Presley; m; 4; Miss. Choctaw; F; S; Son; 1664; Yes; Yes
1710; Sampson; m; 69; Miss. Choctaw; F; S; Father-in-law; 1665; Yes; Yes

YORK

1711; Ben; m; 42; Miss. Choctaw; F; M; Head; 1667; Yes; Yes
1712; Louella; f; 48; Miss. Choctaw; F; M; Wife; 1668; Yes; Yes
1713; Hester; m; 11; Miss. Choctaw; F; S; Son; 1670; Yes; Yes

1714; Bennett; m; 43; Miss. Choctaw; F; M: Head; 1674; Yes; Yes
1715; Lacie; f; 25; Miss. Choctaw; F; M; Wife; 1675; Yes; Yes
1716; G. B; m; 7; Miss. Choctaw; F; S; Son; 1676; Yes; Yes
1717; Colie; f; 6; Miss. Choctaw; F; S; Dau; 1677; Yes; Yes
1718; Scott; m; 78; Miss. Choctaw; F; Wd; Father; 1671; Yes; Yes
1719; Berkley; m; 21; Miss. Choctaw; F; S; Nephew; 1673; No; Chilocco; Chilocco, Kay, Okla; Yes

1720; Emmett; m; 29; Miss. Choctaw; F; M; Head; 1684; Yes; Yes
1721; Indiana; f; 18; Miss. Choctaw; F; M; Wife; 1685; Yes; Yes
1722; Florence; f; 3/12; Miss. Choctaw; F; S; Dau; Yes; Yes
1723; Necie; f; 45; Miss. Choctaw; F; S; Mother; 1678; Yes; Yes
1724; Baxter; m; 26; Miss. Choctaw; F; S; Bro; 1679; No; Chilocco; Chilocco, Kay, Okla; Yes
1725; Addie; f; 24; Miss. Choctaw; F; S; Sis; 1680; No; Santa Fe, Santa Fe, N. Mex; Yes

Census of the **Mississippi Choctaws** reservation of the **Choctaw Agency** jurisdiction, as of **April 1**, 19**33**, taken by **A. C. Hector**, Superintendent.

KEY; Surname; Census Number; Given Name; Sex; Age at Last Birthday; Tribe; Degree of Blood; Marital Status; Relationship to Head of Family; Last Census Roll Number; At Jurisdiction Where Enrolled (Yes/No); At Another Jurisdiction; Post Office, County, State (if given); Ward (Yes/No)

1726; Gasler; m; 21; Miss. Choctaw; F; S; Bro; 1681; No; Chilocco; Chilocco, Kay, Okla; Yes

1727; Eunice; f; 19; Miss. Choctaw; F; S; Sis; 1682; No; Chilocco; Chilocco, Kay, Okla; Yes

1728; Beaman; m; 16; Miss. Choctaw; F; S; Bro; 1683; No; Chilocco; Chilocco, Kay, Okla; Yes

1729; **Jackson**, Floyd F; M; 18; Miss. Choctaw; F; S; Orphan; 774; Yes; Yes

Census of the **Mississippi Choctaws** reservation of the **Choctaw Agency** jurisdiction, as of **April 1**, 19**33**, taken by **A. C. Hector**, Superintendent.

KEY; Census Number; Surname, Given Name; Sex; Age at Last Birthday; Tribe; Degree of Blood; Marital Status; Relationship to Head of Family; Last Census Roll Number (if given); At Jurisdiction Where Enrolled (Yes/No); At Another Jurisdiction; Post Office, County, State (if given); Ward (Yes/No)

ADDED BECAUSE OMITTED FROM PREVIOUS CENSUS ROLL

154;   Bell, Mandy; f; 65; Miss. Choctaw; F; Wd; Head; Yes; Yes
155;   Bell, Tony; m; 18; Miss. Choctaw; F; S; Son; Yes; Yes

635;   Frazier, Wesley; m; 70; Miss. Choctaw; F; Wd; Head; Yes; Yes
636;   Frazier, Ella; f; 25; Miss. Choctaw; F; S; Dau; Yes; Yes

884;   Joe, Nichols; m; 2; Miss. Choctaw; F; S; Son; Yes; Yes
964;   Johnson, Ellen; f; 17; Miss. Choctaw; F; M; Wife; Yes; Yes

262;   Lewis, Houston; m; 16; Miss. Choctaw; F; S; Orphan; Yes; Yes

1117; Morris, Chester; m; 3; Miss. Choctaw; F; S; Son; Yes; Yes

1190; Robinson, Mary; f; 3; Miss. Choctaw; F; S; Dau; Yes; Yes

1679; Willis, Beaman; m; 2; Miss. Choctaw; F; S; Son; Yes; Yes

DUPLICATION ON LAST CENSUS ROLL - 1932.
140
144;   Bell, Geneva; f; 22; Miss. Choctaw; F; M; Wife; 1345; Yes; Yes

1591; Lewis, Marceline; f; 9; Miss. Choctaw; F; S; Grand-dau; 1550; Yes; Yes

ADDED ON ACCOUNT OF ERROR IN SEX ON LAST CENSUS ROLL.

117;   Bell, Tom; m; 13; Miss. Choctaw; F; S; Son; 147; Yes; Yes
198;   Billy, Earl; m; 7; Miss. Choctaw; F; S; Grand-son; 192; Yes; Yes
640;   Gipson, Pearl; f; 8; Miss. Choctaw; F; S; Dau; 640; Yes; Yes
778;   Isaac, Lester; m; 9; Miss. Choctaw; F; S; Son; 764; Yes; Yes
880;   Joe, Widge; m; 12; Miss. Choctaw; F; S; Son; 858; Yes; Yes

Census of the **Mississippi Choctaws** reservation of the **Choctaw Agency** jurisdiction, as of **April 1**, 19**33**, taken by **A. C. Hector**, Superintendent.

KEY; Census Number; Surname, Given Name; Sex; Age at Last Birthday; Tribe; Degree of Blood; Marital Status; Relationship to Head of Family; Last Census Roll Number (if given); At Jurisdiction Where Enrolled (Yes/No); At Another Jurisdiction; Post Office, County, State (if given); Ward (Yes/No)

 897;   Joe, Claud; m; 5; Miss. Choctaw; F; S; Son; 874; Yes; Yes
 921;   John, Ruby; f; 12; Miss. Choctaw; F; S; Dau; 898; Yes; Yes
1102;   Morris, Eddie; m; 9; Miss. Choctaw; F; S; Son; 1079; Yes; Yes
1144;   Nickey, Cozette; m; 14; Miss. Choctaw; F; S; Son; 1119; Yes; Yes
1221;   Sam, Lonie; m; 9; Miss. Choctaw; F; S; Son; 1192; Yes; Yes
1377;   Thompson, Alice; m; 8; Miss. Choctaw; F; S; Son; 1342; Yes; Yes
1707;   Wishork, Nuga; f; 8; Miss. Choctaw; F; S; Dau; 1663; Yes; Yes

DEDUCTIONS ON ACCOUNT OF ERROR IN SEX ON LAST CENSUS ROLL.

 117;   Bell, Tom; f; 13; Miss. Choctaw; F; S; Son; 147; Yes; Yes
 198;   Billy, Earl; f; 7; Miss. Choctaw; F; S; Grand-son; 192; Yes; Yes
 640;   Gipson, Pearl; m; 8; Miss. Choctaw; F; S; Son; 640; Yes; Yes
 778;   Isaac, Lester; f; 9; Miss. Choctaw; F; S; Dau; 764; Yes; Yes
 880;   Joe, Widge; f; 12; Miss. Choctaw; F; S; Dau; 868; Yes; Yes
 897;   Joe, Claud; f; 5; Miss. Choctaw; F; S; Dau; 874; Yes; Yes
 921;   John, Ruby; m; 12; Miss. Choctaw; F; S; Son; 898; Yes; Yes
1102;   Morris, Eddie; f; 9; Miss. Choctaw; F; S; Dau; 1079; Yes; Yes
1144;   Nickey, Cozette; f; 14; Miss. Choctaw; F; S; Dau; 1119; Yes; Yes
1221;   Sam, Lonie; f; 9; Miss. Choctaw; F; S; Dau; 1192; Yes; Yes
1377;   Thompson, Alice; f; 8; Miss. Choctaw; F; S; Dau; 1342; Yes; Yes
1708;   Wishork, Nuga; m; 8; Miss. Choctaw; F; S; Son; 1663; Yes; Yes

Mississippi Choctaw Census

as of April 1, 1934

and Additional Information

taken by A. C. Hector, Superintendent

Census of the **Mississippi Choctaws** reservation of the **Choctaw Agency** jurisdiction, as of **April 1**, 19**34**, taken by **A. C. Hector**, Superintendent.

KEY; Surname; Stamped Census Number; Typed Census Number; Given Name; Sex; Age at Last Birthday; Tribe; Degree of Blood; Marital Status; Relationship to Head of Family; Last Census Roll Number (if given); At Jurisdiction Where Enrolled (Yes/No); At Another Jurisdiction; Post Office, County, State (if given); Ward (Yes/No)

[Note: 1934 Census has an extra stamped census number beside the typed number giving each individual 2 roll numbers. There is no explanation why this was done. There is a 26 number separation for the final entry for Beaman York (1792 and 1818)]

ALEX

1; 1; Cooper; m; 24; Miss. Choctaw; F; S; Head; 1; Yes; Yes
Married Sallie Mae B. Alex #236

2; 2; Missie; f; 54; Miss. Choctaw; F; Wd; Head; 2; Yes; Yes
3; 3; Nelson; m; 10; Miss. Choctaw; F; S; Son; 3; Yes; Yes

ALLEN

4; 4; Willis; M; 39; Miss; M; Head; 4; Yes; Yes
5; 5; Bessie; f; 39; Miss. Choctaw; F; Wife; 5; Yes; Yes
6; 6; Bob; m; 17; Miss. Choctaw; F; S; Son; 6; Yes; Yes
7; 7; Sulum; m; 13; Miss. Choctaw; F; S; Son; 7; Yes; Yes
8; 8; Maggie; f; 11; Miss. Choctaw; F; S; Dau; 8; Yes; Yes
9; 9; Huston; m; 10; Miss. Choctaw; F; S; Son; 9; Yes; Yes
10; 10; Nell; f; 9; Miss. Choctaw; F; S; Dau; 10; Yes; Yes
11; 11; Willie; f[sic]; 6; Miss. Choctaw; F; S; Son; 11; Yes; Yes
12; 12; Wilbert; m; 1-8/12; Miss. Choctaw; F; S; Son; 12; Yes; Yes
13; 13; Herbert; m; 1-8/12; Miss. Choctaw; F; S; Son; 13; Yes; Yes

14; 14; Jim; m; 48; Miss. Choctaw; F; M; Head; 14; Yes; Yes
15; 15; Manda; f; 50; Miss. Choctaw; F; M; Wife; 15; Yes; Yes
16; 16; I. C; m; 20; Miss. Choctaw; F; S; Son; 16; Yes; Yes
17; 17; Annie Mae; f; 20; Miss. Choctaw; F; S; Dau; 17; Yes; Yes
18; 18; J. C; m; 19; Miss. Choctaw; F; S; Son; 18; Yes; Yes
Married Mattie Willis Allen #1691
19; 19; R. G; m; 18; Miss. Choctaw; F; S; Son; 19; Yes; Yes

Census of the **Mississippi Choctaws** reservation of the **Choctaw Agency** jurisdiction, as of **April 1**, 19**34**, taken by **A. C. Hector**, Superintendent.

KEY; Surname; Stamped Census Number; Typed Census Number; Given Name; Sex; Age at Last Birthday; Tribe; Degree of Blood; Marital Status; Relationship to Head of Family; Last Census Roll Number (if given); At Jurisdiction Where Enrolled (Yes/No); At Another Jurisdiction; Post Office, County, State (if given); Ward (Yes/No)

20; 20; Will; m; 11; Miss. Choctaw; F; S; Son; 20; Yes; Yes

21; 21; Joseph; m; 41; Miss. Choctaw; F; S; Head; 21; Yes; Yes

22; 22; Lacey; m; 40; Miss. Choctaw; F; S; Head; 22; Yes; Yes

AMOS

23; 23; Sebbie; f; 56; Miss. Choctaw; F; Wd; Head; 23; Yes; Yes
24; 24; Albert; m; 30; Miss. Choctaw; F; S; Nep; 24; Yes; Yes

25; 25; Griffin; m; 46; Miss. Choctaw; F; M; Head; 25; Yes; Yes
26; 26; Sallie; f; 42; Miss. Choctaw; F; M; Wife; 26; Yes; Yes
27; 27; Beauty; f; 24; Miss. Choctaw; F; S; Dau; 27; Yes; Yes
28; 28; Julia; f; 22; Miss. Choctaw; F; S; Dau; 28; Yes; Yes
29; 29; Land; m; 18; Miss. Choctaw; F; S; Son; 29; Yes; Yes
30; 30; Fulton; m; 13; Miss. Choctaw; F; S; Son; 30; Yes; Yes
31; 31; Floyd; m; 13; Miss. Choctaw; F; S; Son; 31; Yes; Yes
32; 32; Mose; m; 12; Miss. Choctaw; F; S; Son; 32; Yes; Yes

33; 33; John; m; 20; Miss. Choctaw; F; M; Head; 33; Yes; Yes
34; 34; Ruth; f; 16; Miss. Choctaw; F; M; Wife; 34; Yes; Yes

35; 35; Lampkin; m; 56; Miss. Choctaw; F; M: Head; 35; Yes; Yes
36; 36; Ann; f; 56; Miss. Choctaw; F; M; Wife; 36; Yes; Yes
37; 37; Lilly; f; 17; Miss. Choctaw; F; S; Dau; 38; Yes; Yes
38; 38; **Isom**, Mary; f; 7; Miss. Choctaw; F; S; Grand-dau; 39; Yes; Yes

ANDERSON

39; 39; Bob; m; 49; Miss. Choctaw; F; M; Head; 40; Yes; Yes
40; 40; Ella; f; 46; Miss. Choctaw; F; M; Wife; 41; Yes; Yes

Census of the **Mississippi Choctaws** reservation of the **Choctaw Agency** jurisdiction, as of **April 1**, 19**34**, taken by **A. C. Hector**, Superintendent.

KEY; Surname; Stamped Census Number; Typed Census Number; Given Name; Sex; Age at Last Birthday; Tribe; Degree of Blood; Marital Status; Relationship to Head of Family; Last Census Roll Number (if given); At Jurisdiction Where Enrolled (Yes/No); At Another Jurisdiction; Post Office, County, State (if given); Ward (Yes/No)

41; 41; A. J; m; 22; Miss. Choctaw; F; S; Son; 42; Yes; Yes
42; 42; Trudie; f; 16; Miss. Choctaw; F; S; Dau; 43; Yes; Yes
43; 43; Josephine; f; 12; Miss. Choctaw; F; S; Dau; 44; Yes; Yes
44; 44; Sallie Mae; f; 9; Miss. Choctaw; F; S; Dau; 45; Yes; Yes
45; 45; Burnice; f; 6; Miss. Choctaw; F; S; Dau; 46; Yes; Yes

46; 46; John; m; 66; Miss. Choctaw; F; M; Head; 47; Yes; Yes
47; 47; Sallie; f; 31; Miss. Choctaw; F; M; Wife; 48; Yes; Yes
48; 48; J. C; m; 9; Miss. Choctaw; F; S; Son; 49; Yes; Yes
49; 49; Amy; f; 1-24 da; Miss. Choctaw; F; S; Dau; 50; Yes; Yes

50; 50; Mattie; f; 64; Miss. Choctaw; F; Wd; Head; 51; Yes; Yes
51; 51; Ike; m; 32; Miss. Choctaw; F; S; Son; 52; Yes; Yes
52; 52; Vada; f; 28; Miss. Choctaw; F; S; Dau; 53; Yes; Yes

53; 53; Irvin; m; 30; Miss. Choctaw; F; M; Head; 54; Yes; Yes
54; 54; Thelma; f; 18; Miss. Choctaw; F; M; Wife; 55; Yes; Yes

55; 55; Ray; m; 38; Miss. Choctaw; F; M; Head; 56; Yes; Yes
56; 56; Lonie; f; 34; Miss. Choctaw; F; M; Wife; 57; Yes; Yes
57; 57; Frances B; f; 5; Miss. Choctaw; F; S; Dau; 58; Yes; Yes
58; 58; Lillie Mae; f; 3/12; Miss. Choctaw; F; S; Dau; Yes; Yes

59; 59; Ollie; m; 48; Miss. Choctaw; F; M; Head; 59; Yes; Yes
60; 60; Kate; f; 53; Miss. Choctaw; F; M; Wife; 60; Yes; Yes
61; 61; Grace; f; 11; Miss. Choctaw; F; S; Dau; 61; Yes; Yes

62; 62; Oliver; m; 48; Miss. Choctaw; F; M; Head; 62; Yes; Yes
63; 63; Sallie; f; 41; Miss. Choctaw; F; M; Wife; 63; Yes; Yes
64; 64; Hinton; m; 20; Miss. Choctaw; F; S; Son; 64; Yes; Yes
65; 65; Tonnie[sic]; m; 19; Miss. Choctaw; F; S; Son; 65; Yes; Yes
66; 66; Phillip; m; 15; Miss. Choctaw; F; S; Son; 66; Yes; Yes
67; 67; Houston; m; 13; Miss. Choctaw; F; S; Son; 67; Yes; Yes

Census of the **Mississippi Choctaws** reservation of the **Choctaw Agency** jurisdiction, as of **April 1**, 19**34**, taken by **A. C. Hector**, Superintendent.

KEY; Surname; Stamped Census Number; Typed Census Number; Given Name; Sex; Age at Last Birthday; Tribe; Degree of Blood; Marital Status; Relationship to Head of Family; Last Census Roll Number (if given); At Jurisdiction Where Enrolled (Yes/No); At Another Jurisdiction; Post Office, County, State (if given); Ward (Yes/No)

68; 68; Lucille; f; 11; Miss. Choctaw; F; S; Dau; 68; Yes; Yes

69; 69; Abel; m; 28; Miss. Choctaw; F; M; Head; 69; Yes; Yes
70; 70; Nancy; f; 48; Miss. Choctaw; F; M; Wife; 70; Yes; Yes
71; 71; **Farmer**, Allie; f; 18; Miss. Choctaw; F; S; Step-dau; 71; Yes; Yes
72; 72; **Farmer**, Ella Mae; f; 12; Miss. Choctaw; F; S; Step-dau; 72; Yes; Yes
73; 73; **Farmer**, Annie Mae; f; 10; Miss. Choctaw; F; S; Step-dau; 73; Yes; Yes

BELL

74; 74; Hugh; m; 54; Miss. Choctaw; F; Wd; Head; 74; Yes; Yes
75; 75; Mamie; f; 8; Miss. Choctaw; F; S; Dau; 75; Yes; Yes
~~76~~; Mary Jane; f; 84; Miss. Choctaw; F; Wd; Mother; 466 Died 8-25-33

76; 77; John; m; 43; Miss. Choctaw; F; M; Head; 76; Yes; Yes
77; 78; Lillian; f; 44; Miss. Choctaw; F; M; Wife; 77; Yes; Yes
78; 79; Hattie; f; 13; Miss. Choctaw; F; S; Dau; 78; Yes; Yes
79; 80; Eva; f; 9; Miss. Choctaw; F; S; Dau; 79; Yes; Yes
80; 81; Ola; f; 7; Miss. Choctaw; F; S; Dau; 80; Yes; Yes

81; 82; Sallie; f; 44; Miss. Choctaw; F; Wd; Head; 81; Yes; Yes
82; 83; Emma; f; 22; Miss. Choctaw; F; S; Dau; 82; Yes; Yes Married Albert Lewis #1069
83; 84; Effie; f; 15; Miss. Choctaw; F; S; Dau; 83; Yes; Yes
84; 85; Idie; f; 1-8/12; Miss. Choctaw; F; S; Dau; 84; Yes; Yes

85; 86; Junus; m; 37; Miss. Choctaw; F; M; Head; 85; Yes; Yes
86; 87; Winnie; f; 32; Miss. Choctaw; F; M; Wife; 86; Yes; Yes

Census of the **Mississippi Choctaws** reservation of the **Choctaw Agency** jurisdiction, as of **April 1**, 19**34**, taken by **A. C. Hector**, Superintendent.

KEY; Surname; Stamped Census Number; Typed Census Number; Given Name; Sex; Age at Last Birthday; Tribe; Degree of Blood; Marital Status; Relationship to Head of Family; Last Census Roll Number (if given); At Jurisdiction Where Enrolled (Yes/No); At Another Jurisdiction; Post Office, County, State (if given); Ward (Yes/No)

87; 88; Ronie; f; 17; Miss. Choctaw; F; S; Dau; 87; Yes; Yes
    Married Jimmie Teach Robinson #1228
88; 89; Woods; m; 14; Miss. Choctaw; F; S; Son; 88; Yes; Yes
89; 90; Minnie; f; 12; Miss. Choctaw; F; S; Dau; 89; Yes; Yes
90; 91; Edmond; m; 9; Miss. Choctaw; F; S; Son; 90; Yes; Yes
91; 92; George; m; 7; Miss. Choctaw; F; S; Son; 91; Yes; Yes

92; 93; Evans; m; 32; Miss. Choctaw; F; M; Head; 92; Yes; Yes
93; 94; Willie; f; 22; Miss. Choctaw; F; M; Wife; 93; Yes; Yes
94; 95; Homer; m; 7; Miss. Choctaw; F; S; Son; 94; Yes; Yes
95; 96; Nancy L; f; 5; Miss. Choctaw; F; S; Dau; 95; Yes; Yes
96; 97; Hester; f; 1-20 da; Miss. Choctaw; F; S; Dau; 96; Yes;
97; 98; Mandy; f; 66; Miss. Choctaw; F; Wd; Mother; 154; Yes; Yes

98; 99; Mack; m; 29; Miss. Choctaw; F; M; Head; 97; Yes; Yes
99; 100; Lena; f; 20; Miss. Choctaw; F; M; Wife; 98; Yes; Yes
100; 101; James Cook; m; 6; Miss. Choctaw; F; S; Son; 99; Yes; Yes
101; 102; Herbert H; m; 2; Miss. Choctaw; F; S; Son; 100; Yes; Yes

102; 103; Thompson; m; 36; Miss. Choctaw; F; M; Head; 101; Yes; Yes
103; 104; Ellen; f; 36; Miss. Choctaw; F; M; Wife; Yes; Yes
104; 105; Frank K; m; 20; Miss. Choctaw; F; S; Son; 103; Yes; Yes

105; 106; Nicholas; m; 34; Miss. Choctaw; F; M; Head; 104; Yes; Yes
106; 107; Cleddie; f; 21; Miss. Choctaw; F; M; Wife; 105; Yes; Yes
107; 108; Ruby; f; 4; Miss. Choctaw; F; S; Dau; 106; Yes; Yes
108; 109; Bonnie K; f; 3; Miss. Choctaw; F; S; Dau; 107; Yes; Yes
109; 110; Franklin; m; 1-3/12; Miss. Choctaw; F; S; Son; 108; Yes; Yes

110; 111; Gipson; m; 21; Miss. Choctaw; F; M; Head; 109; Yes; Yes
111; 112; Lucy; f; 21; Miss. Choctaw; F; M; Wife; 110; Yes; Yes
112; 113; Gipson, Jr; m; 2; Miss. Choctaw; F; S; Son; 111; Yes; Yes

Census of the **Mississippi Choctaws** reservation of the **Choctaw Agency** jurisdiction, as of **April 1**, 19**34**, taken by **A. C. Hector**, Superintendent.

KEY; Surname; Stamped Census Number; Typed Census Number; Given Name; Sex; Age at Last Birthday; Tribe; Degree of Blood; Marital Status; Relationship to Head of Family; Last Census Roll Number (if given); At Jurisdiction Where Enrolled (Yes/No); At Another Jurisdiction; Post Office, County, State (if given); Ward (Yes/No)

113; 114; Amon; m; 32; Miss. Choctaw; F; M; Head; 112; Yes; Yes
114; 115; Alice; f; 31; Miss. Choctaw; F; M; Wife; 113; Yes; Yes

115; 116; Jim; m; 64; Miss. Choctaw; F; S; Alone; 114; Yes; Yes

116; 117; Joe; m; 42; Miss. Choctaw; F; M; Head; 115; Yes; Yes
117; 118; Susie; f; 34; Miss. Choctaw; F; M; Wife; 116; Yes; Yes
118; 119; Tom; m; 14; Miss. Choctaw; F; S; Son; 117; Yes; Yes
119; 120; Bill; m; 10; Miss. Choctaw; F; S; Son; 118; Yes; Yes
120; 121; Henry; m; 8; Miss. Choctaw; F; S; Son; 119; Yes; Yes
121; 122; Polly Ann; f; 6; Miss. Choctaw; F; S; Dau; 120; Yes; Yes
122; 123; Sallie; f; 57; Miss. Choctaw; F; Wd; Mother-in-law; 121; Yes; Yes

123; 124; Boston; m; 49; Miss. Choctaw; F; M; Head; 122; Yes; Yes
124; 125; Lela; f; 34; Miss. Choctaw; F; M; Wife; 123; Yes; Yes
125; 126; Sophia; f; 26; Miss. Choctaw; F; S; Dau; 124; Yes; Yes
126; 127; Ola; f; 24; Miss. Choctaw; F; S; Dau; 125; Yes; Yes
127; 128; Effie; f; 22; Miss. Choctaw; F; S; Dau; 126; Yes; Yes
128; 129; John; m; 12; Miss. Choctaw; F; S; Son; 127; Yes; Yes
129; 130; Emma; f; 10; Miss. Choctaw; F; S; Dau; 128; Yes; Yes
130; 131; Emmett; m; 9; Miss. Choctaw; F; S; Son; 129; Yes; Yes
131; 132; Marshall; m; 4; Miss. Choctaw; F; S; Son; 130; Yes; Yes

132; 133; Cornelius; m; 76; Miss. Choctaw; F; Wd; Head; 131; Yes; Yes
133; 134; John; m; 27; Miss. Choctaw; F; S; Son; 132; Yes; Yes

134; 135; Jim; m; 72; Miss. Choctaw; F; S; Alone; 133; Yes; Yes

135; 136; Lish; m; 44; Miss. Choctaw; F; M; Head; 134; Yes; Yes
136; 137; Martha; f; 39; Miss. Choctaw; F; M; Wife; 135; Yes; Yes
137; 138; Willie; m; 19; Miss. Choctaw; F; S; Son; 136; Yes; Yes

Census of the **Mississippi Choctaws** reservation of the **Choctaw Agency** jurisdiction, as of **April 1**, 19**34**, taken by **A. C. Hector**, Superintendent.

KEY; Surname; Stamped Census Number; Typed Census Number; Given Name; Sex; Age at Last Birthday; Tribe; Degree of Blood; Marital Status; Relationship to Head of Family; Last Census Roll Number (if given); At Jurisdiction Where Enrolled (Yes/No); At Another Jurisdiction; Post Office, County, State (if given); Ward (Yes/No)

138; 139; Houston; m; 14; Miss. Choctaw; F; S; Son; 137; Yes; Yes
139; 140; Minnie; f; 13; Miss. Choctaw; F; S; Dau; 138; Yes; Yes
140; 141; Less C; m; 11; Miss. Choctaw; F; S; Son; 139; Yes; Yes
141; 142; Gene D; m; 9; Miss. Choctaw; F; S; Son; 140; Yes; Yes
142; 143; Jay; m; 7; Miss. Choctaw; F; S; Son; 141; Yes; Yes
143; 144; Gaston; m; 25; Miss. Choctaw; F; S; Bro; 142; Yes; Yes
144; 145; Isaac Wampler; m; 1; Choctaw Miss.; F; S; Son; Yes; Yes

145; 146; Bob; m; 24; Choctaw Miss.; F; M; Head; 143; Yes; Yes
146; 147; Geneva; m[sic]; 23; Choctaw Miss.; F; M; Wife; 144; Yes; Yes
147; 149; Naomi Ruth; f; 2; Choctaw Miss.; F; S; Dau; 146; Yes; Yes
148; 148; Sadie; f; 4; Choctaw Miss.; F; S; Dau; 145; Yes; Yes
149; 150; Bobby Sam; m; 6/12; Choctaw Miss.; F; S; Son; Yes; Yes

150; 151; Lish; m; 53; Choctaw Miss.; F; M; Head; 147; Yes; Yes
151; 152; Maggie; f; 53; Choctaw Miss.; F; M; Wife; 148; Yes; Yes
152; 153; Minnie; f; 26; Choctaw Miss.; F; S; Dau; 149; Yes; Yes
153; 154; Lula; f; 18; Choctaw Miss.; F; S; Dau; 150; Yes; Yes
154; 155; Tom; m; 28; Choctaw Miss.; F; S; 151; Yes; Yes
155; 156; Bon; m; 24; Choctaw Miss.; F; S; Son; 152; Yes; Yes;
156; 157; Basin; m; 9; Choctaw Miss.; F; S; 153; Yes; Yes

157; 158; Tony; m; 19; Choctaw Miss.; F; S; Head; 155; [?]; [?]

BEN

158; 159; Olin; m; 34; Miss. Choctaw; F; M; Head; 156; Yes; Yes
159; 160; Neva; f; 27; Miss. Choctaw; F; M; Wife; 157; Yes; Yes
160; 161; Nannie Mae; f; 10; Miss. Choctaw; F; S; Dau; 158; Yes; Yes
161; 162; Annie Laura; f; 8; Miss. Choctaw; F; S; Dau; 159; Yes; Yes
162; 163; Mattie Lou; f; 6; Miss. Choctaw; F; S; Dau; 160; Yes; Yes

Census of the **Mississippi Choctaws** reservation of the **Choctaw Agency** jurisdiction, as of **April 1**, 19**34**, taken by **A. C. Hector**, Superintendent.

KEY; Surname; Stamped Census Number; Typed Census Number; Given Name; Sex; Age at Last Birthday; Tribe; Degree of Blood; Marital Status; Relationship to Head of Family; Last Census Roll Number (if given); At Jurisdiction Where Enrolled (Yes/No); At Another Jurisdiction; Post Office, County, State (if given); Ward (Yes/No)

163; 164; **Isaac**, Coline; f; 15; Miss. Choctaw; F; S; Sister-in-law; 161; Yes; Yes

164; 165; Wyatt; m; 66; Miss. Choctaw; F; M; Head; 162; Yes; Yes
165; 166; Ellen; f; 62; Miss. Choctaw; F; M; Wife; 163; Yes; Yes

166; 167; Lula; f; 50; Miss. Choctaw; F; Wd; Head; 164; Yes; Yes
167; 168; Jimpson; m; 28; Miss. Choctaw; F; S; Son; 165; Yes; Yes
168; 169; Wilson; m; 17; Miss. Choctaw; F; S; Son; 166; Yes; Yes

169; 170; Otho; m; 20; Miss. Choctaw; F; M; Head; 167; Yes; Yes
170; 171; Lessie Isaac; f; 21; Miss. Choctaw; F; M; Wife; 168; Yes; Yes
171; 172; Chester; m; 6/12; Miss. Choctaw; F; S; Yes; Yes

172; 173; Tom; m; 39; Miss. Choctaw; F; M: Head; 169; Yes; Yes
173; 174; Gladys; f; 28; Miss. Choctaw; F; M; Wife; 170; Yes; Yes
174; 175; Fannie Lou; f; 9; Miss. Choctaw; F; S; Dau; 171; Yes; Yes
175; 176; Hubert; m; 7; Miss. Choctaw; F; S; Son; 172; Yes; Yes
176; 177; Henry Ford; m; 5; Miss. Choctaw; F; S; Son; 173; Yes; Yes
177; 178; Helen Marie; f; 1-6/12; Miss. Choctaw; F; S; Dau; 174; Yes; Yes

178; 179; Charlie; m; 35; Miss. Choctaw; F; M; Head; 175; Yes; Yes
179; 180; Emeline; f; 27; Miss. Choctaw; F; M; Wife; 176; Yes; Yes
180; 181; Opal Grace; f; 2; Miss. Choctaw; F; S; Dau; 177; Yes; Yes

181; 182; Jim; m; 58; Miss. Choctaw; F; Wd; Alone; 178; Yes; Yes

182; 183; Monroe; m; 23; Miss. Choctaw; F; M; Head; 179; Yes; Yes
183; 184; Lilly May; f; 23; Miss. Choctaw; F; M; Wife; 180; Yes; Yes

Census of the **Mississippi Choctaws** reservation of the **Choctaw Agency** jurisdiction, as of **April 1**, 19**34**, taken by **A. C. Hector**, Superintendent.

KEY; Surname; Stamped Census Number; Typed Census Number; Given Name; Sex; Age at Last Birthday; Tribe; Degree of Blood; Marital Status; Relationship to Head of Family; Last Census Roll Number (if given); At Jurisdiction Where Enrolled (Yes/No); At Another Jurisdiction; Post Office, County, State (if given); Ward (Yes/No)

BILLY

184; 185; Lum; m; 49; Miss. Choctaw; F; M; Head; 181; Yes; Yes
185; 186; Minnie; f; 51; Miss. Choctaw; F; M; Wife; 182; Yes; Yes
186; 187; **Charles**, James; m; 36; Miss. Choctaw; F; S; Brother-in-law; Yes; Yes

187; 188; Tom; m; 23; Miss. Choctaw; F; M; Head; 184; Yes; Yes
188; 189; Sallie Stoliby; f; 24; Miss. Choctaw; F; M; Wife; 185; Yes; Yes
189; 190; Robert; m; 6; Miss. Choctaw; F; S; Son; 186; Yes; Yes
190; 191; James; m; 3; Miss. Choctaw; F; S; Son; 187; Yes; Yes
191; 192; Rosaulee[sic]; f; 6/12; Miss. Choctaw; F; S; Dau; Yes; Yes

192; 193; Will; m; 57; Miss. Choctaw; F; S; Alone; 188; Yes; Yes

193; 194; Williston; m; 40; Miss. Choctaw; F; M; Head; 189; Yes; Yes
194; 195; Jessie; f; 30; Miss. Choctaw; F; M; Wife; 190; Yes; Yes
195; 196; Melton; m; 13; Miss. Choctaw; F; S; Son; 191; Yes; Yes
196; 197; Beaman; m; 10; Miss. Choctaw; F; S; Son; 192; Yes; Yes
197; 198; Maurice; m; 8; Miss. Choctaw; F; S; Son; 193; Yes; Yes
198; 199; Horace; m; 7; Miss. Choctaw; F; S; Son; 194; Yes; Yes
199; 200; Betty Jean; f; 3; Miss. Choctaw; F; S; Dau; 195; Yes; Yes
200; 201; Mary; f; 1; Miss. Choctaw; F; S; Dau; Yes; Yes

201; 202; Nicy; f; 74; Miss. Choctaw; F; Wd; Head; 196; Yes; Yes
202; 203; Leona; f; 34; Miss. Choctaw; F; S; Dau; 197; Yes; Yes
203; 204; Earl; m; 8; Miss. Choctaw; F; S; Grand-son; 198; Yes; Yes

204; 205; Ike; m; 24; Miss. Choctaw; F; M; Head; 199; Yes; Yes
205; 206; Jennie C; f; 22; Miss. Choctaw; F; M; Wife; 200; Yes; Yes
206; 207; Kate; f; 1-6/12; Miss. Choctaw; F; S; Dau; 201; Yes; Yes
207; 208; John; m; 3/12; Miss. Choctaw; F; S; Son; Yes; Yes

Census of the **Mississippi Choctaws** reservation of the **Choctaw Agency** jurisdiction, as of **April 1**, 19**34**, taken by **A. C. Hector**, Superintendent.

KEY; Surname; Stamped Census Number; Typed Census Number; Given Name; Sex; Age at Last Birthday; Tribe; Degree of Blood; Marital Status; Relationship to Head of Family; Last Census Roll Number (if given); At Jurisdiction Where Enrolled (Yes/No); At Another Jurisdiction; Post Office, County, State (if given); Ward (Yes/No)

208; 209; Lorene; f; 24; Miss. Choctaw; F; Wd; Head; 202; Yes; Yes
209; 210; Cicero L; m; 2; Miss. Choctaw; F; S; Son; 203; Yes; Yes

210; 211; Johnson; m; 68; Miss. Choctaw; F; M; Head; 204; Yes; Yes
211; 212; Belaria; f; 53; Miss. Choctaw; F; M; Wife; 205; Yes; Yes
212; 213; Gipson; m; 23; Miss. Choctaw; F; S; Son; 206; Yes; Yes
213; 214; Ike; m; 22; Miss. Choctaw; F; S; Son; 207; Yes; Yes
~~215; Maude; f; 21; Miss. Choctaw; F; S; Dau; 208; Yes; Yes~~
214; 216; Wilson; m; 17; Miss. Choctaw; F; S; Son; 209; Yes; Yes
215; 217; Greer; m; 15; Miss. Choctaw; F; S; Son; 210; Yes; Yes
216; 218; Frank; m; 10; Miss. Choctaw; F; S; Son; 211; Yes; Yes
217; 219; Phillip; m; 4; Miss. Choctaw; F; S; Grand-son; 212; Yes; Yes

218; 220; Lewis; m; 29; Miss. Choctaw; F; M; Head; 213; Yes; Yes
219; 221; Zelma; f; 29; Miss. Choctaw; F; M; Wife; 214; Yes; Yes
220; 222; Clennie; f; 14; Miss. Choctaw; F; S; Step-dau; 215; Yes; Yes
221; 223; Mamie; f; 12; Miss. Choctaw; F; S; Step-dau; 216; Yes; Yes
222; 224; Frank; m; 8; Miss. Choctaw; F; S; Son; 217; Yes; Yes
223; 225; Annie; f; 5; Miss. Choctaw; F; S; Dau; 218; Yes; Yes
224; 226; Will; m; 46; Miss. Choctaw; F; M; Head; 219; Yes; Yes
225; 227; Alice; f; 44; Miss. Choctaw; F; M; Wife; 220; Yes; Yes
226; 228; William; m; 19; Miss. Choctaw; F; S; Son; 221; Yes; Yes
227; 229; Lee; m; 18; Miss. Choctaw; F; S; Son; 222; Yes; Yes
228; 230; Rose; f; 15; Miss. Choctaw; F; S; Dau; 223; Yes; Yes
229; 231; Irene; f; 12; Miss. Choctaw; F; S; Dau; 224; Yes; Yes
230; 232; Joe; m; 11; Miss. Choctaw; F; S; Son; 225; Yes; Yes
231; 233; Will, Jr; m; 7; Miss. Choctaw; F; S; Son; 226; Yes; Yes
232; 234; Marchie; f; 6; Miss. Choctaw; F; S; Dau; 227; Yes; Yes
233; 235; Charlie; m; 4; Miss. Choctaw; F; S; Son; 228; Yes; Yes
234; 236; Tommy Jean; f; 6/12; Miss. Choctaw; F; S; Dau; Yes; Yes

~~237~~; Jordan; m; 49; Miss. Choctaw; F; M: Head; 229
Died 8-1-33

Census of the **Mississippi Choctaws** reservation of the **Choctaw Agency** jurisdiction, as of **April 1**, 19**34**, taken by **A. C. Hector**, Superintendent.

KEY; Surname; Stamped Census Number; Typed Census Number; Given Name; Sex; Age at Last Birthday; Tribe; Degree of Blood; Marital Status; Relationship to Head of Family; Last Census Roll Number (if given); At Jurisdiction Where Enrolled (Yes/No); At Another Jurisdiction; Post Office, County, State (if given); Ward (Yes/No)

235; 238; Lillie; f; 31; Miss. Choctaw; F; M; Wife; 230; Yes; Yes
236; 239; Sallie Mae; f; 16; Miss. Choctaw; F; S; Dau; 231; Yes; Yes
    Married Cooper Alex #1
237; 240; Nellie; f; 13; Miss. Choctaw; F; S; Dau; 232; Yes; Yes
238; 241; Jim; m; 8; Miss. Choctaw; F; S; Son; 233; Yes; Yes
239; 242; Mary Lou; 6; Miss. Choctaw; F; S; Dau; 234; Yes; Yes
240; 243; Paul; m; 3; Miss. Choctaw; F; S; Son; Yes; Yes
    ~~244~~; Peter Cooper; m; 1-11/12; Miss. Choctaw; F; S; Son; 236; Yes; Yes   Died 7-13-33

241; 245; Richard; m; 23; Miss. Choctaw; F; M; Head; 237; Yes; Yes
242; 246; Cassie; f; 19; Miss. Choctaw; F; M: Wife; 238; Yes; Yes
243; 247; Duley; f; 2; Miss. Choctaw; F; M[sic]; Dau; 239; Yes; Yes
244; 248; Sarah; f; 1-6 da; Miss. Choctaw; F; S; Dau; 240; Yes; Yes

245; 249; Wade; m; 55; Miss. Choctaw; F; M: Head; 241; Yes; Yes
246; 250; Lina; f; 37; Miss. Choctaw; F; M; Wife; 242; Yes; Yes
247; 251; Sienna; f; 1-26 da; Miss. Choctaw; F; S; Dau; 243; Yes; Yes
248; 252; **Lewis**, (McMillan), Mary; f; 14; Miss. Choctaw; F; S; Step-dau; 244; Yes; Yes

BOB

249; 253; Simon; m; 64; Miss. Choctaw; F; S; Alone; 245; Yes; Yes

BOX

250; 254; Illiman; m; 28; Miss. Choctaw; F; M; Head; 246; Yes; Yes
251; 255; Rosie; f; 22; Miss. Choctaw; F; M; Wife; 247; Yes; Yes

252; 256; Lillie; f; 46; Miss. Choctaw; F; Wd; Head; 248; Yes; Yes
253; 257; Ollie T; m; 19; Miss. Choctaw; F; S; Son; 249; Yes; Yes
254; 258; Bathie; f; 11; Miss. Choctaw; F; S; Dau; 250; Yes; Yes

Census of the **Mississippi Choctaws** reservation of the **Choctaw Agency** jurisdiction, as of **April 1**, 19**34**, taken by **A. C. Hector**, Superintendent.

KEY; Surname; Stamped Census Number; Typed Census Number; Given Name; Sex; Age at Last Birthday; Tribe; Degree of Blood; Marital Status; Relationship to Head of Family; Last Census Roll Number (if given); At Jurisdiction Where Enrolled (Yes/No); At Another Jurisdiction; Post Office, County, State (if given); Ward (Yes/No)

255; 259; Bethy; f; 9; Miss. Choctaw; F; S; Dau; 251; Yes; Yes
256; 260; **Joe**, Emly; f; 74; Miss. Choctaw; F; Wd; Mother; 253; Yes; Yes

257; 261; Ola; f; 19; Miss. Choctaw; F; S; Orphan; 254; Yes; Yes

258; 262; Eula; f; 11; Miss. Choctaw; F; S; Orphan; 255; Yes; Yes

BRISCOE

259; 263; Jim; m; 19; Miss. Choctaw; F; M; Head; 1040; Yes; Yes
260; 264; Elsie Y; F; 18; Miss. Choctaw; F; M; Wife; 1041; Yes; Yes
261; 265; George Ann; f; 6/12; Miss. Choctaw; F; S; Dau; Yes; Yes

262; 266; Tom; m; 33; Miss. Choctaw; F; M; Head; 256; Yes; Yes
263; ~~267; Lucy; f; 51; Miss. Choctaw; F; M; Wife; 257; Yes; Yes~~
    Died May 8, 1935

264; 268; Stephens; m; 25; Miss. Choctaw; F; M; Hear[sic]; 258; Yes; Yes
265; 269; Maggie Gipson; f; 26; Miss. Choctaw; F; M; Wife; 259; Yes; Yes
~~266; 270; J. Claud; m; 2; Miss. Choctaw; F; S; Son; 260; Yes; Yes~~
    Died 4/2/34
267; 271; Calton; m; 6/12; Miss. Choctaw; F; S; Son; Yes; Yes

BULL

268; 272; Pink; m; 56; Miss. Choctaw; F; Wd; Head; 261; Yes; Yes
269; 273; **Lewis**, Houston; m; 17; Miss. Choctaw; F; S; Orphan; 262; Yes; Yes

270; 274; George; m; 60; Miss. Choctaw; F; M; Head; 263; Yes; Yes

Census of the **Mississippi Choctaws** reservation of the **Choctaw Agency** jurisdiction, as of **April 1**, 19**34**, taken by **A. C. Hector**, Superintendent.

KEY; Surname; Stamped Census Number; Typed Census Number; Given Name; Sex; Age at Last Birthday; Tribe; Degree of Blood; Marital Status; Relationship to Head of Family; Last Census Roll Number (if given); At Jurisdiction Where Enrolled (Yes/No); At Another Jurisdiction; Post Office, County, State (if given); Ward (Yes/No)

271; 275; Sissy; f; 52; Miss. Choctaw; F; M; Wife; 264; Yes; Yes

272; 276; Foreman; m; 31; Miss. Choctaw; F; M; Head; 265; Yes; Yes
273; 277; Sarah; f; 30; Miss. Choctaw; F; M; Wife; 266; Yes; Yes

CAMPBELL

274; 278; Wiley; m; 33; Miss. Choctaw; F; M; Head; 267; Yes; Yes
275; 279; Vennie Comby; f; 18; Miss. Choctaw; F; Wife[sic]; Wife; Yes
    Died 6/8/34   Omitted on last census
276; 280; Jimmie; m; 1/12; Miss. Choctaw; F; S; Son; Yes; Yes
    Died 6/10/34

CATES

277; 281; Susan; f; 56; Miss. Choctaw; F; Wd; Head; 268; Yes; Yes
278; 282; Enis; m; 29; Miss. Choctaw; F; S; Son; 269; Yes; Yes
279; 283; Essie; f; 26; Miss. Choctaw; F; S; Dau; 270; Yes; Yes
280; 284; John; m; 22; Miss. Choctaw; F; S; Son; 271; Yes; Yes
281; 285; Lonie; f; 21; Miss. Choctaw; F; S; Dau; 272; Yes; Yes
282; 286; Molpus; m; 20; Miss. Choctaw; F; Son; 273; Yes; Yes
283; 287; Iona; f; 16; Miss. Choctaw; F; S; Dau; 274; Yes; Yes
284; 288; John; m; 6; Miss. Choctaw; F; S; Grand-son; 275; Yes; Yes

285; 289; Oscar; m; 24; Miss. Choctaw; F; S; Alone; 276; Yes; Yes

286; 290; Alice; f; 29[sic]; Miss. Choctaw; F; Wd; Head; 277; Yes; Yes
287; 291; Dock; m; 32; Miss. Choctaw; F; S; Step-son; 278; Yes; Yes
288; 292; Dee; m; 26; Miss. Choctaw; F; S; Son; 279; Yes; Yes

289; 293; Ned; m; 36; Miss. Choctaw; F; M; Head; 280; Yes; Yes
290; 294; Janie; f; 32; Miss. Choctaw; F; M; Wife; 281; Yes; Yes
291; 295; Susan Mabel; f; 17; Miss. Choctaw; F; S; Dau; 282; Yes; Yes

Census of the **Mississippi Choctaws** reservation of the **Choctaw Agency** jurisdiction, as of **April 1**, 19**34**, taken by **A. C. Hector**, Superintendent.

KEY; Surname; Stamped Census Number; Typed Census Number; Given Name; Sex; Age at Last Birthday; Tribe; Degree of Blood; Marital Status; Relationship to Head of Family; Last Census Roll Number (if given); At Jurisdiction Where Enrolled (Yes/No); At Another Jurisdiction; Post Office, County, State (if given); Ward (Yes/No)

292; 296; Emma; f; 17; Miss. Choctaw; F; S; Dau; 283; Yes; Yes
293; 297; Tubby; m; 16; Miss. Choctaw; F; S; Son; 284; Yes; Yes
294; 298; Henry M; m; 14; Miss. Choctaw; F; S; Son; 285; Yes; Yes
295; 299; Willie F; m; 11; Miss. Choctaw; F; S; Son; 286; Yes; Yes
296; 300; Nannie; f; 9; Miss. Choctaw; F; S; Dau; 287; Yes; Yes
297; 301; Julia; f; 8; Miss. Choctaw; F; S; Dau; 288; Yes; Yes

CHAPMAN

298; 302; Will; m; 47; Miss. Choctaw; F; M; Head; 289; Yes; Yes
299; 303; Bettie; f; 50; Miss. Choctaw; F; M; Wife; 290; Yes; Yes
300; 304; Asa; m; 17; Miss. Choctaw; F; S; Son; 291; Yes; Yes
301; 305; Ralston; m; 15; Miss. Choctaw; F; S; Son; 292; Yes; Yes
302; 306; Hattie; f; 11; Miss. Choctaw; F; S; Dau; 293; Yes; Yes
303; 307; Ronie; f; 10; Miss. Choctaw; F; S; Dau; 294; Yes; Yes
304; 308; Lilly; f; 9; Miss. Choctaw; F; S; Dau; 295; Yes; Yes
305; 309; Raymond; m; 8; Miss. Choctaw; F; S; Son; 296; Yes; Yes
306; 310; Christ; m; 7; Miss. Choctaw; F; S; Son; 297; Yes; Yes
307; 311; Minnie; f; 6; Miss. Choctaw; F; S; Dau; 298; Yes; Yes

CHARLIE

308; 312; William; m; 83; Miss. Choctaw; F; M; Head; 299; Yes; Yes
309; 313; Fannie; f; 69; Miss. Choctaw; F; M; Wife; 300; Yes; Yes
310; 314; **McMillen**, Nola; f; 29; Miss. Choctaw; F; Wd; Dau; 301; Yes; Yes
311; 315; **McMillen**, A. G; m; 12; Miss. Choctaw; F; S; Grand-son; 302; Yes; Yes
312; 316; **McMillen**, Odie Mae; f; 10; Miss. Choctaw; F; S; Grand-dau; 303; Yes; Yes
313; 317; **McMillen**, John; m; 7; Miss. Choctaw; F; S; Grand-son; 304; Yes; Yes

Census of the **Mississippi Choctaws** reservation of the **Choctaw Agency** jurisdiction, as of **April 1**, 19**34**, taken by **A. C. Hector**, Superintendent.

KEY; Surname; Stamped Census Number; Typed Census Number; Given Name; Sex; Age at Last Birthday; Tribe; Degree of Blood; Marital Status; Relationship to Head of Family; Last Census Roll Number (if given); At Jurisdiction Where Enrolled (Yes/No); At Another Jurisdiction; Post Office, County, State (if given); Ward (Yes/No)

314; 318; **McMillen**, Mattie; f; 3; Miss. Choctaw; F; S; Grand-dau; 305; Yes; Yes

315; 319; John; m; 40; Miss. Choctaw; F; M; Head; 306; Yes; Yes
316; 320; Mary; f; 32; Miss. Choctaw; F; M; Wife; 307; Yes; Yes
317; 321; Elsie; f; 15; Miss. Choctaw; F; S; Dau; 308; Yes; Yes

318; 322; Coyt; m; 18; Miss. Choctaw; F; M; Head; Yes; Yes
  Omitted on last census
319; 323; Sina Davis; f; 22; Miss. Choctaw; F; M; Wife; 428; Yes; Yes
320; 324; Baby; f; 7/12; Miss. Choctaw; F; S; Dau; Yes; Yes

CHICKAWAY

321; 325; Sim; m; 36; Miss. Choctaw; F; M; Head; 309; Yes; Yes
322; 326; Maggie; f; 33; Miss. Choctaw; F; M; Wife; 310; Yes; Yes
323; 327; Clemon; m; 15; Miss. Choctaw; F; S; Son; 311; Yes; Yes
324; 328; Nellie; f; 13; Miss. Choctaw; F; S; Dau; 312; Yes; Yes
325; 329; Agnes; f; 11; Miss. Choctaw; F; S; Dau; 313; Yes; Yes
326; 330; Albert; m; 8; Miss. Choctaw; F; S; Son; 314; Yes; Yes
327; 331; Maggie Kate; f; 6; Miss. Choctaw; F; S; Dau; 315; Yes; Yes
328; 332; Kate; f; 3; Miss. Choctaw; F; S; Dau; 316; Yes; Yes
329; 333; John Study; m; 1-9/12; Miss. Choctaw; F; S; Son; 317; Yes; Yes

~~330; 334; Isabell; f; 72; Miss. Choctaw; F; Wd; Head; 318; Yes; Yes~~
  Died 11/16/34
331; 335; Ola; f; 27; Miss. Choctaw; F; S; Dau; 319; Yes; Yes

332; 336; Jim; m; 31; Miss. Choctaw; F; M; Head; 320; Yes; Yes
333; 337; Eunice; f; 28; Miss. Choctaw; F; M; Wife; 321; Yes; Yes
334; 338; John Hester; m; 6; Miss. Choctaw; F; S; Son; 322; Yes; Yes
335; 339; Henry; m; 3; Miss. Choctaw; F; S; Son; 323; Yes; Yes

Census of the **Mississippi Choctaws** reservation of the **Choctaw Agency** jurisdiction, as of **April 1**, 19**34**, taken by **A. C. Hector**, Superintendent.

KEY; Surname; Stamped Census Number; Typed Census Number; Given Name; Sex; Age at Last Birthday; Tribe; Degree of Blood; Marital Status; Relationship to Head of Family; Last Census Roll Number (if given); At Jurisdiction Where Enrolled (Yes/No); At Another Jurisdiction; Post Office, County, State (if given); Ward (Yes/No)

336; 340; **Scott**, Rosie Lee; f; 12; Miss. Choctaw; F; S; Step-dau; 324; Yes; Yes

~~341~~; Kelly; m; 41; Miss. Choctaw; F; M; Head; 325; Yes; Yes Died 6-24-33
337; 342; Lilla; f; 32; Miss. Choctaw; F; M; Wife; 326; Yes; Yes
338; 343; Micheal[sic]; m; 11; Miss. Choctaw; F; S; Son; 327; Yes; Yes
339; 344; Anna; f; 9; Miss. Choctaw; F; S; Dau; 328; Yes; Yes
340; 345; Jane; f; 7; Miss. Choctaw; F; S; Dau; 329; Yes; Yes

341; 346; Rufus; m; 32; Miss. Choctaw; F; M: Head; 330; Yes; Yes
342; 347; Bessie; f; 29; Miss. Choctaw; F; M; Wife; 331; Yes; Yes
343; 348; Ross C; m; 6; Miss. Choctaw; F; S; Son; 332; Yes; Yes
344; 349; Elizabeth; f; 4; Miss. Choctaw; F; S; Dau; 333; Yes; Yes

CHITTO

345; 350; Joe; m; 34; Miss. Choctaw; F; M; Head; 334; Yes; Yes
346; 351; Callie; f; 34; Miss. Choctaw; F; M; Wife; 335; Yes; Yes
347; 352; Leo Clifton; m; 6; Miss. Choctaw; F; S; Son; 336; Yes; Yes

348; 353; Pat; m; 57; Miss. Choctaw; F; Wd; Head; 337; Yes; Yes
349; 354; Henrietta; f; 19; Miss. Choctaw; F; S; Dau; 338; Yes; Yes
350; 355; Jefferson; m; 17; Miss. Choctaw; F; S; Son; 339; Yes; Yes
351; 356; Erma; f; 12; Miss. Choctaw; F; S; Dau; 340; Yes; Yes
352; 357; Isom; m; 10; Miss. Choctaw; F; S; Son; 341; Yes; Yes

353; 358; John; m; 44; Miss. Choctaw; F; M; Head; 342; Yes; Yes
354; 359; Sallie; f; 43; Miss. Choctaw; F; M; Wife; 343; Yes; Yes
355; 360; Minnie; f; 23; Miss. Choctaw; F; S; Dau; 344; Yes; Yes
356; 361; Hattie; f; 16; Miss. Choctaw; F; S; Dau; 345; Yes; Yes
357; 362; Allie Nora; f; 14; Miss. Choctaw; F; S; Dau; 346; Yes; Yes
358; 363; Ella; f; 12; Miss. Choctaw; F; S; Dau; 347; Yes; Yes

Census of the **Mississippi Choctaws** reservation of the **Choctaw Agency** jurisdiction, as of **April 1**, 19**34**, taken by **A. C. Hector**, Superintendent.

KEY; Surname; Stamped Census Number; Typed Census Number; Given Name; Sex; Age at Last Birthday; Tribe; Degree of Blood; Marital Status; Relationship to Head of Family; Last Census Roll Number (if given); At Jurisdiction Where Enrolled (Yes/No); At Another Jurisdiction; Post Office, County, State (if given); Ward (Yes/No)

359; 364; Lum Billy; m; 8; Miss. Choctaw; F; S; Son; 348; Yes; Yes

CLEMONS

360; 365; Phillip; m; 39; Miss. Choctaw; F; S; Alone; 349; Yes; Yes
    Died Mar 2/1935

CLEMONS or COWED

361; 366; Jim; m; 29; Miss. Choctaw; F; M; Head; 350; Yes; Yes
362; 367; Bessie; f; 27; Miss. Choctaw; F; M; Wife; 351; Yes; Yes
363; 368; Margie; f; 6; Miss. Choctaw; F; S; Dau; 352; Yes; Yes
364; 369; Lewisman; m; 4; Miss. Choctaw; F; S; Son; 353; Yes; Yes
365; 370; Leonard; m; 1; Miss. Choctaw; F; S; Son; Yes; Yes

CLARK

366; 371; Stella; f; 39; Miss. Choctaw; F; S; Alone; 354; Yes; Yes

CLEMONS

367; 372; Jeff; m; 37; Miss. Choctaw; F; M; Head; 355; Yes; Yes
368; 373; Cora Frazier; f; 33; Miss. Choctaw; F; M: Wife; 356; Yes; Yes
369; 374; Mattie; f; 12; Miss. Choctaw; F; S; Dau; 357; Yes; Yes
370; 375; Irsal[sic]; m; 12; Miss. Choctaw; F; S; Son; Yes; Yes
    Left off of last Census roll
371; 376; Ethel; f; 11; Miss. Choctaw; F; S; Dau; 358; Yes; Yes
   ~~377~~; Letha; f; 9; Miss. Choctaw; F; S; Dau; 359; Yes; Yes
    Died 9-12-33
372; 378; John; m; 8; Miss. Choctaw; F; S; Son; 360; Yes; Yes
373; 379; Rena Mae; f; 6; Miss. Choctaw; F; S; Dau; 361; Yes; Yes
374; 380; Prince; m; 1; Miss. Choctaw; F; S; Son; Yes; Yes

Census of the **Mississippi Choctaws** reservation of the **Choctaw Agency** jurisdiction, as of **April 1**, 19**34**, taken by **A. C. Hector**, Superintendent.

KEY; Surname; Stamped Census Number; Typed Census Number; Given Name; Sex; Age at Last Birthday; Tribe; Degree of Blood; Marital Status; Relationship to Head of Family; Last Census Roll Number (if given); At Jurisdiction Where Enrolled (Yes/No); At Another Jurisdiction; Post Office, County, State (if given); Ward (Yes/No)

375; 381; Munch; m; 51; Miss. Choctaw; F; M; Head; 362; Yes; Yes
376; 382; Nellie; f; 44; Miss. Choctaw; F; M; Wife; 363; Yes; Yes
377; 383; Bathia; f; 15; Miss. Choctaw; F; S; Dau; 364; Yes; Yes
378; 384; Mollie; f; 13; Miss. Choctaw; F; S; Dau; 365; Yes; Yes

COMBY

379; 385; Alma; f; 42; Miss. Choctaw; F; Wd; Head; 366; Yes; Yes
380; 386; **McMillan**, Jimmie; m; 23; Miss. Choctaw; F; S; Son; 367; Yes; Yes   Married Maggie Farmer #504
381; 387; **McMillan**, Jimpson; m; 21; Miss. Choctaw; F; S; Son;; 368; Yes; Yes
382; 388; **McMillan**, Ella; f; 19; Miss. Choctaw; F; S; Dau; 369; Yes; Yes
383; 389; **McMillan**, Jordan; m; 4; Miss. Choctaw; F; S; Grand-son; 370; Yes; Yes

384; 390; Arbin; m; 46; Miss. Choctaw; F; Wd; Head; 371; Yes; Yes
385; 391; Gilbert; m; 22; Miss. Choctaw; F; S; Son; 372; Yes; Yes
386; 392; Rosella; f; 14; Miss. Choctaw; F; S; Dau; 373; Yes; Yes
387; 393; Maudell; f; 11; Miss. Choctaw; F; S; Dau; 374; Yes; Yes

388; 394; Seymour; m; 33; Miss. Choctaw; F; M; Head; 375; Yes; Yes
389; 395; Edna Ben; f; 28; Miss. Choctaw; F; M; Wife; 376; Yes; Yes
390; 396; W. C; m; 12; Miss. Choctaw; F; S; Son; 377; Yes; Yes
391; 397; B. F; m; 10; Miss. Choctaw; F; S; Son; 378; Yes; Yes
392; 398; Leroy; m; 8; Miss. Choctaw; F; S; Son; 379; Yes; Yes
393; 399; Vina Rayburn; f; 3/12; Miss. Choctaw; F; S; Dau; Yes; Yes

394; 400; Allie; f; 29; Miss. Choctaw; F; Wd; Head; 380; Yes; Yes
395; 401; Jonas; m; 10; Miss. Choctaw; F; S; Son; 381; Yes; Yes
396; 402; Irene; f; 8; Miss. Choctaw; F; S; Dau; 382; Yes; Yes
397; 403; Joyce Ann; f; 6; Miss. Choctaw; F; S; Dau; 252; Yes; Yes

Census of the **Mississippi Choctaws** reservation of the **Choctaw Agency** jurisdiction, as of **April 1**, 19**34**, taken by **A. C. Hector**, Superintendent.

KEY; Surname; Stamped Census Number; Typed Census Number; Given Name; Sex; Age at Last Birthday; Tribe; Degree of Blood; Marital Status; Relationship to Head of Family; Last Census Roll Number (if given); At Jurisdiction Where Enrolled (Yes/No); At Another Jurisdiction; Post Office, County, State (if given); Ward (Yes/No).

398; 404; R. L; m; 4; Miss. Choctaw; F; S; Son; 383; Yes; Yes
399; 405; **Chitto**, Mary; f; 35; Miss. Choctaw; F; S; Sister; 384; Yes; Yes

400; 406; Ben; m; 72; Miss. Choctaw; F; M; Head; 385; Yes; Yes
401; 407; Maude Billy; f; 21; Miss. Choctaw; F; M; Wife; 208; Yes; Yes
    Also listed under Maude Billy No. 215. duplication
402; 408; **Billy**, Clarence; m; 8/12; Miss. Choctaw; F; S; Son; Yes; Yes

403; 409; Olmon; m; 56; Miss. Choctaw; F; M; Head; 386; Yes; Yes
404; 410; Laura; f; 53; Miss. Choctaw; F; M; Wife; 387; Yes; Yes

COOPER

405; 411; Dixon; m; 33; Miss. Choctaw; F; M; Head; 388; Yes; Yes
406; 412; Leona; f; 26; Miss. Choctaw; F; M; Wife; 389; Yes; Yes
    Married Newt Jefferson #1047

407; 413; Gaston; m; 48; Miss. Choctaw; F; M; Head; 390; Yes; Yes
408; 414; Ada; f; 50; Miss. Choctaw; F; M; Wife; 391; Yes; Yes
409; 415; Fannie; f; 16; Miss. Choctaw; F; S; Dau; 392; Yes; Yes
    Married Henry Farmer #1082
410; 416; Hubert; m; 13; Miss. Choctaw; F; S; Son; 393; Yes; Yes
411; 417; Christine; f; 10; Miss. Choctaw; F; S; Dau; 394; Yes; Yes
412; 418; Alma; f; 7; Miss. Choctaw; F; S; Dau; 395; Yes; Yes

COTTON

413; 419; John; m; 24; Miss. Choctaw; F; S; Alone; 396; Yes; Yes

414; 420; George; m; 34; Miss. Choctaw; F; M; Head; 397; Yes; Yes
415; 421; Ellen; f; 33; Miss. Choctaw; F; M; Wife; 398; Yes; Yes
416; 422; Minnie; f 8; Miss. Choctaw; F; M[sic]; Dau; 399; Yes; Yes

Census of the **Mississippi Choctaws** reservation of the **Choctaw Agency** jurisdiction, as of **April 1**, 19**34**, taken by **A. C. Hector**, Superintendent.

KEY; Surname; Stamped Census Number; Typed Census Number; Given Name; Sex; Age at Last Birthday; Tribe; Degree of Blood; Marital Status; Relationship to Head of Family; Last Census Roll Number (if given); At Jurisdiction Where Enrolled (Yes/No); At Another Jurisdiction; Post Office, County, State (if given); Ward (Yes/No)

417; 423; **Crenshaw**, Amos; m; 22; Miss. Choctaw; F; S; Orphan; 400; Yes; Yes

418; 424; **Crenshaw**, Austin; m; 18; Miss. Choctaw; F; S; Orphan; 401; Yes; Yes

DAN

419; 425; Williston; m; 37; Miss. Choctaw; F; M; Head; 402; Yes; Yes
420; 426; Dinah; f; 22; Miss. Choctaw; F; M; Wife; 403; Yes; Yes
421; 427; Rose Ida; f; 12; Miss. Choctaw; F; S; Dau; 404; Yes; Yes

DANSBY

422; 428; Jacob; m; 62; Miss. Choctaw; F; M; Head; 405; Yes; Yes
~~423; 429; Jennie; f; 49; Miss. Choctaw; F; m; Wife; 406; Yes; Yes~~
Died 7/23/34

424; 430; **Tubby**, R. B; m; 27; Miss. Choctaw; F; S; Brother-in-law; 407; Yes; Yes

~~425; 431; **Tubby**, Jim; m; 61; Miss. Choctaw; F; S; Brother-in-law; 408; Yes; Yes~~ Died 2/3/1935

DAVIS

426; 432; Alyne; f; 24; Miss. Choctaw; F; M; Wife; 409; No; Ft. Definance[sic]; Ft. Definance, Ariz; Yes

427; 433; Leona; f; 58; Miss. Choctaw; F; Wd; Head; 410; Yes; Yes
428; 434; Hobbie; m; 28; Miss. Choctaw; F; S; Son; 411; Yes; Yes
Married Mary McMillan #1108

429; 435; Will; m; 60; Miss. Choctaw; F; M; Head; 412; Yes; Yes
~~436~~; Mattie; f; 32; Miss. Choctaw; F; M; Wife; 413; Yes; Yes
Died 10-6-33

Census of the **Mississippi Choctaws** reservation of the **Choctaw Agency** jurisdiction, as of **April 1**, 19**34**, taken by **A. C. Hector**, Superintendent.

KEY; Surname; Stamped Census Number; Typed Census Number; Given Name; Sex; Age at Last Birthday; Tribe; Degree of Blood; Marital Status; Relationship to Head of Family; Last Census Roll Number (if given); At Jurisdiction Where Enrolled (Yes/No); At Another Jurisdiction; Post Office, County, State (if given); Ward (Yes/No)

430; ~~437; Annie; f; 15; Miss. Choctaw; F; S; Dau; 414; Yes; Yes~~
   Died Mar. 11, 1935
431; 438; John; m; 12; Miss. Choctaw; F; S; Son; 415; Yes; Yes
432; 439; Mary; f; 6; Miss. Choctaw; F; Dau; 416; Yes; Yes
433; 440; Mack; m; 5; Miss. Choctaw; F; Son; 417; Yes; Yes
434; 441; Lewis; m; 3; Miss. Choctaw; F; S; 418; Yes; Yes
435; 442; William; m; 1-8/12; Miss. Choctaw; F; S; Son; 419; Yes; Yes

436; 443; Sidney; m; 46; Miss. Choctaw; F; Wd; Head; 420; Yes; Yes
437; 444; Elamer; f; 25; Miss. Choctaw; F; S; Dau; 421; Yes; Yes
438; 445; Mabel; f; 22; Miss. Choctaw; F; S; Dau; 422; Yes; Yes
439; 446; Anna; f; 14; Miss. Choctaw; F; S; Dau; 423; Yes; Yes
440; 447; Johnnie; m; 12; Miss. Choctaw; F; S; Son; 424; Yes; Yes

441; 448; Malissie; f; 64; Miss. Choctaw; F; Wd; Head; 425; Yes; Yes
442; 449; Alice; f; 37; Miss. Choctaw; F; S; Dau; 426; Yes; Yes
443; 450; Ada Francis; f; 14; Miss. Choctaw; F; S; Grand-dau; 429; Yes; Yes

444; 451; Tom; m; 34; Miss. Choctaw; F; Wd; Head; 431; Yes; Yes
445; 452; Millie; f; 14; Miss. Choctaw; F; S; Dau; 432; Yes; Yes
446; 453; Henderson; m; 12; Miss. Choctaw; F; S; Son; 433; Yes; Yes

DENSON

447; 454; Lilly; f; 46; Miss. Choctaw; F; Wd; Head; 434; Yes; Yes
448; 455; Hendrix; m; 17; Miss. Choctaw; F; S; Son; 435; Yes; Yes
449; 456; Emma; f; 14; Miss. Choctaw; F; 14; S; Dau; 436; Yes; Yes
450; 457; Charley; m; 11; Miss. Choctaw; F; S; Son; 437; Yes; Yes
451; 458; David; m; 9; Miss. Choctaw; F; S; Son; 438; Yes; Yes

452; 459; Pete; m; 46; Miss. Choctaw; F; M; Head; 440; Yes; Yes

Census of the **Mississippi Choctaws** reservation of the **Choctaw Agency** jurisdiction, as of **April 1**, 19**34**, taken by **A. C. Hector**, Superintendent.

KEY; Surname; Stamped Census Number; Typed Census Number; Given Name; Sex; Age at Last Birthday; Tribe; Degree of Blood; Marital Status; Relationship to Head of Family; Last Census Roll Number (if given); At Jurisdiction Where Enrolled (Yes/No); At Another Jurisdiction; Post Office, County, State (if given); Ward (Yes/No)

453; 460; Rosie Wickson; f; 33; Miss. Choctaw; F; M; Wife; 441; Yes; Yes
454; 461; Jeffie; f; 16; Miss. Choctaw; F; S; Dau; 443; Yes; Yes
455; 462; Edna; f; 11; Miss. Choctaw; F; S; Dau; 444; Yes; Yes
456; 463; Nancy; f; 5; Miss. Choctaw; F; S; Dau; 445; Yes; Yes
457; 464; Jennie E; f; 2; Miss. Choctaw; F; S; Dau; 446; Yes; Yes
458; 465; Odie Mae; f; 1; Miss. Choctaw; F; S; Dau; Yes; Yes

459; 466; Willie; m; 26; Miss. Choctaw; F; M; Head; 447; Yes; Yes
460; 467; Beauty; f; 22; Miss. Choctaw; F; M; Wife; 448; Yes; Yes
461; 468; Hector; m; 1-8/12; Miss. Choctaw; F; S; Son; 449; Yes; Yes

462; 469; Ezell; m; 22; Miss. Choctaw; F; M: Head; 450; Yes; Yes
463; 470; Beauty; f; 22; Miss. Choctaw; F; M; wife; 451; Yes; Yes
464; 471; Ruth; f; 3; Miss. Choctaw; F; S; Dau; 452; Yes; Yes
465; 472; Louise; f; 1-24 da; Miss. Choctaw; F; S; Dau; 453; Yes; Yes

DIXON

466; 473; Nannie; f; 54; Miss. Choctaw; F; Wd; Head; 454; Yes; Yes
467; 474; **Sam**, Charlie; m; 19; Miss. Choctaw; F; S; Nephew; 455; Yes; Yes

468; 475; Jim; m; 33; Miss. Choctaw; F; M; Head; 456; Yes; Yes
469; 476; Sarah Jimmy; f; 31; Miss. Choctaw; F; M; Wife; 457; Yes; Yes
470; 477; Marie; f; 11; Miss. Choctaw; F; S; Dau; 458; Yes; Yes
471; 478; Imogene; f; 8; Miss. Choctaw; F; S; Dau; 459; Yes; Yes
472; 479; Ellen; f; 6; Miss. Choctaw; F; S; Dau; 460; Yes; Yes
473; 480; Mable C; f; 3; Miss. Choctaw; F; S; Dau; 461; Yes; Yes
474; 481; Arthur Aiken; m; 6/12; Miss. Choctaw; F; S; Son; Yes; Yes

475; 482; Jess; m; 56; Miss. Choctaw; F; M; Head; 462; Yes; Yes

Census of the __Mississippi Choctaws__ reservation of the __Choctaw Agency__ jurisdiction, as of __April 1__, 19__34__, taken by __A. C. Hector__, Superintendent.

KEY; Surname; Stamped Census Number; Typed Census Number; Given Name; Sex; Age at Last Birthday; Tribe; Degree of Blood; Marital Status; Relationship to Head of Family; Last Census Roll Number (if given); At Jurisdiction Where Enrolled (Yes/No); At Another Jurisdiction; Post Office, County, State (if given); Ward (Yes/No)

476; 483; Callie; f; 64; Miss. Choctaw; F; M; Wife; 463; Yes; Yes
477; 484; Young; m; 17; Miss. Choctaw; F; S; Son; 464; Yes; Yes
478; 485; Lilly; f; 14; Miss. Choctaw; F; S; Dau; 465; Yes; Yes

479; 486; Scott; m; 23; Miss. Choctaw; F; M; Head; 467; Yes; Yes
480; 487; Essie; f; 27; Miss. Choctaw; F; M; Wife; 468; Yes; Yes
481; 488; Nola; f; 1-6/12; Miss. Choctaw; F; S; Dau; 469; Yes; Yes

482; 489; Horace; m; 28; Miss. Choctaw; F; M; Head; 470; Yes; Yes
483; 490; Esther; f; 27; Miss. Choctaw; F; M; Wife; 471; Yes; Yes
484; 491; Calonia; f; 7; Miss. Choctaw; F; S; Dau; 472; Yes; Yes

485; 492; Edmond; m; 26; Miss. Choctaw; F; M; Head; 473; Yes; Yes
486; 493; Julia; f; 25; Miss. Choctaw; F; M; Wife; 474; Yes; Yes
487; 494; Addie Mae; f; 4; Miss. Choctaw; F; S; Dau; 475; Yes; Yes
488; 495; Anita; f; 1-24 da; Miss. Choctaw; F; S; Dau; 476; Yes; Yes

489; 496; Wilson; m; 75; Miss. Choctaw; F; M; Head; 477; Yes; Yes
490; 497; Hope; f; 48; Miss. Choctaw; F; M; Wife; 478; Yes; Yes

491; 498; Kanis; m; 42; Miss. Choctaw; F; Wd; Head; 479; Yes; Yes
492; 499; Jim; m; 29; Miss. Choctaw; F; S; Son; 482; Yes; Yes
493; 500; Wade; m; 19; Miss. Choctaw; F; S; Son; 483; Yes; Yes

EVANS

494; 501; John; m; 59; Miss. Choctaw; F; Wd; Head; 484; Yes; Yes
495; 502; **Wickson**, Kelly; m; 9; Miss. Choctaw; F; S; Son; 485; Yes; Yes

FARMER

496; 503; Silmon; m; 60; Miss. Choctaw; F; Wd; Head; 486; Yes; Yes

Census of the **Mississippi Choctaws** reservation of the **Choctaw Agency** jurisdiction, as of **April 1**, 19**34**, taken by **A. C. Hector**, Superintendent.

KEY; Surname; Stamped Census Number; Typed Census Number; Given Name; Sex; Age at Last Birthday; Tribe; Degree of Blood; Marital Status; Relationship to Head of Family; Last Census Roll Number (if given); At Jurisdiction Where Enrolled (Yes/No); At Another Jurisdiction; Post Office, County, State (if given); Ward (Yes/No)

497; 504; Henry; m; 22; Miss. Choctaw; F; S; Son; 487; Yes; Yes
498; 505; Bennie; f; 16; Miss. Choctaw; F; S; Dau; 488; Yes; Yes
499; 506; Corine; f; 13; Miss. Choctaw; F; S; Dau; 489; Yes; Yes

500; 507; Ishman; m; 89; Miss. Choctaw; F; M; Head; 490; Yes; Yes
501; 508; Sweeter; f; 61; Miss. Choctaw; F; M; Wife; 491; Yes; Yes
502; 509; Emma; f; 31; Miss. Choctaw; F; S; Dau; 492; Yes; Yes
503; 510; Marshall; m; 29; Miss. Choctaw; F; S; Son; 493; Yes; Yes
504; 511; Maggie; f; 24; Miss. Choctaw; F; S; Dau; 494; Yes; Yes
    Married Jimmie McMillan #380
505; 512; Lena; f; 21; Miss. Choctaw; F; S; Dau; 495; Yes; Yes
506; 513; Bill; m; 18; Miss. Choctaw; F; S; Son; 496; Yes; Yes
507; 514; Renee; f; 14; Miss. Choctaw; F; S; Dau; 497; Yes; Yes

508; 515; Moses; m; 34; Miss. Choctaw; F; M; Head; 498; Yes; Yes
509; 516; Lottie; f; 26; Miss. Choctaw; F; M; Wife; 499; Yes; Yes
510; 517; Mealie; f; 3; Miss. Choctaw; F; S; Dau; 500; Yes; Yes

511; 518; Thomas; m; 68; Miss. Choctaw; F; M; Head; 501; Yes; Yes
    Died 12/7/1934
512; 519; Melissa; f; 61; Miss. Choctaw; F; M; Wife; 502; Yes; Yes

513; 520; Howard; m; 22; Miss. Choctaw; F; M; Head; 503; Yes; Yes
514; 521; Lonie Dixon; f; 20; Miss. Choctaw; F; M; Wife; 504; Yes; Yes
515; 522; Eula Mae; f; 3; Miss. Choctaw; F; S; Dau; 439; Yes; Yes
516; 523; Wilton; m; 1; Miss. Choctaw; F; S; Son; Yes; Yes

FARVE

517; 524; Bennett; m; 41; Miss. Choctaw; F; S; Alone; 505; Yes; Yes

518; 525; Paul; m; 46; Miss. Choctaw; F; M; Head; 506; Yes; Yes
519; 526; Renia; f; 29; Miss. Choctaw; F; M; Wife; 507; Yes; Yes

Census of the **Mississippi Choctaws** reservation of the **Choctaw Agency** jurisdiction, as of **April 1**, 19**34**, taken by **A. C. Hector**, Superintendent.

KEY; Surname; Stamped Census Number; Typed Census Number; Given Name; Sex; Age at Last Birthday; Tribe; Degree of Blood; Marital Status; Relationship to Head of Family; Last Census Roll Number (if given); At Jurisdiction Where Enrolled (Yes/No); At Another Jurisdiction; Post Office, County, State (if given); Ward (Yes/No)

520; 527; Phillip; m; 10; Miss. Choctaw; F; S; Son; 508; Yes; Yes
521; 528; Eula Mae; f; 8; Miss. Choctaw; F; S; Dau; 509; Yes; Yes
522; 529; Estelle; f; 6; Miss. Choctaw; F; S; Dau; 510; Yes; Yes
523; 530; Viola; f; 4; Miss. Choctaw; F; S; Dau; 511; Yes; Yes
524; 531; Anna Rose; f; 1; Miss. Choctaw; F; S; Dau; Yes; Yes

525; 532; Joseph; m; 22; Miss. Choctaw; F; M; Head; 512; Yes; Yes
526; 533; Bessie Davis; f; 24; Miss. Choctaw; F; M; Wife; 427; Yes; Yes
527; 534; Baby; f; 6/12; Miss. Choctaw; F; S; Dau; Yes; Yes

528; 535; Rachel; f; 55; Miss. Choctaw; F; S; Head; 513; Yes; Yes

529; 536; Western; m; 44; Miss. Choctaw; F; Wd; Head; 514; Yes; Yes
530; 537; Chester; m; 29; Miss. Choctaw; F; S; Son; 515; Yes; Yes
531; 538; Josie; f; 26; Miss. Choctaw; F; S; Dau; 516; Yes; Yes
532; 539; John; m; 26; Miss. Choctaw; F; S; Son; 517; Yes; Yes
533; 540; Lillian; f; 23; Miss. Choctaw; F; S; Dau; 518; Yes; Yes
534; 541; Ima; f; 18; Miss. Choctaw; F; S; Dau; 519; Yes; Yes
535; 542; Hilda; f; 10; Miss. Choctaw; F; S; Dau; 520; Yes; Yes

536; 543; Antwine; m; 57; Miss. Choctaw; F; M; Head; 521; Yes; Yes
537; 544; Liseeda; f; 60; Miss. Choctaw; F; M; Wife; 522; Yes; Yes
538; 545; Edna; f; 24; Miss. Choctaw; F; S; Dau; 523; Yes; Yes
539; 546; Cecilia; f; 22; Miss. Choctaw; F; S; Dau; 524; Yes; Yes
540; 547; Isileen; f; 21; Miss. Choctaw; F; S; Dau; 525; Yes; Yes
541; 548; Earl; m; 16; Miss. Choctaw; F; S; Son; 526; Yes; Yes
542; 549; Mamie; f; 14; Miss. Choctaw; F; S; Dau; 527; Yes; Yes
543; 550; Corbrin; m; 11; Miss. Choctaw; F; S; Son; 528; Yes; Yes

544; 551; Dave; m; 56; Miss. Choctaw; F; Wd; Head; 529; Yes; Yes
545; 552; Lena; f; 34; Miss. Choctaw; F; S; Dau; 530; Yes; Yes
546; 554; Georgia; f; 15; Miss. Choctaw; F; Dau; 532; Yes; Yes
547; 554; Sarah Alma; f; 23; Miss. Choctaw; F; S; Dau; 531; Yes; Yes

Census of the **Mississippi Choctaws** reservation of the **Choctaw Agency** jurisdiction, as of **April 1**, 19**34**, taken by **A. C. Hector**, Superintendent.

KEY; Surname; Stamped Census Number; Typed Census Number; Given Name; Sex; Age at Last Birthday; Tribe; Degree of Blood; Marital Status; Relationship to Head of Family; Last Census Roll Number (if given); At Jurisdiction Where Enrolled (Yes/No); At Another Jurisdiction; Post Office, County, State (if given); Ward (Yes/No)

548; 555; John; m 12; Miss. Choctaw; F; S; Son; 533; Yes; Yes
549; 556; William; m; 33; Miss. Choctaw; F; Wd; Alone; 534; Yes; Yes

550; 557; Rosine H; m; 51; Miss. Choctaw; F; M; Head; 535; Yes; Yes
551; 558; Winona; f; 56; Miss. Choctaw; F; M; Wife; 536; Yes; Yes

552; 559; Charles; m; 46; Miss. Choctaw; F; M; Head; 537; Yes; Yes
553; 560; Edwina; f; 43; Miss. Choctaw; F; M; Wife; 538; Yes; Yes
554; 561; Retha; f; 16; Miss. Choctaw; F; S; Dau; 539; Yes; Yes
555; 562; Alvin; m; 14; Miss. Choctaw; F; S; Son; 540; Yes; Yes
556; 563; Irvin; m; 12; Miss. Choctaw; F; S; Son; 541; Yes; Yes
557; 564; Audrey; f; 9; Miss. Choctaw; F; S; Dau; 542; Yes; Yes
558; 565; Vivian; f; 8; Miss. Choctaw; F; S; Dau; 543; Yes; Yes

559; 566; Thomas; m; 52; Miss. Choctaw; F; M; Head; 544; Yes; Yes
560; 567; Mary; f; 36; Miss. Choctaw; F; M; Wife; 545; Yes; Yes
561; 568; Hazel; f; 16; Miss. Choctaw; F; S; Dau; 546; Yes; Yes
562; 569; Robert; m; 15; Miss. Choctaw; F; S; Son; 547; Yes; Yes
563; 570; Gertrude; f; 13; Miss. Choctaw; F; S; Dau; 548; Yes; Yes
564; 571; Ruth; f; 10; Miss. Choctaw; F; S; Dau; 549; Yes; Yes
565; 572; Sylvester; m; 46; Miss. Choctaw; F; S; Alone; 550; Yes; Yes

566; 573; Joe Tole; m; 69; Miss. Choctaw; F; M; Head; 551; Yes; Yes
567; 574; Lola; f; 66; Miss. Choctaw; F; M; Wife; 552; Yes; Yes
568; 575; Dora; f; 41; Miss. Choctaw; F; S; Dau; 553; Yes; Yes
569; 576; Victoria; f; 34; Miss. Choctaw; F; S; Dau; 554; Yes; Yes

570; 577; Gilmore; m; 32; Miss. Choctaw; F; M; Head; 555; Yes; Yes
571; 578; Gertrude; f; 30; Miss. Choctaw; F; M; Wife; 556; Yes; Yes

572; 579; Joe; m; 28; Miss. Choctaw; F; M; Head; 557; Yes; Yes
573; 580; Lillian; f; 25; Miss. Choctaw; F; M; wife; 558; Yes; Yes

Census of the **Mississippi Choctaws** reservation of the **Choctaw Agency** jurisdiction, as of **April 1**, 19**34**, taken by **A. C. Hector**, Superintendent.

KEY; Surname; Stamped Census Number; Typed Census Number; Given Name; Sex; Age at Last Birthday; Tribe; Degree of Blood; Marital Status; Relationship to Head of Family; Last Census Roll Number (if given); At Jurisdiction Where Enrolled (Yes/No); At Another Jurisdiction; Post Office, County, State (if given); Ward (Yes/No)

574; 581; Besie[sic]; m; 23; Miss. Choctaw; F; S; Alone; 559; Yes; Yes
575; 582; Jessie; f; 22; Miss. Choctaw; F; S; Alone; 560; Yes; Yes

576; 583; Corrine; m; 39; Miss. Choctaw; F; M; Head; 561; Yes; Yes
577; 584; Viola; f; 37; Miss. Choctaw; F; M; Wife; 562; Yes; Yes
578; 585; William; m; 18; Miss. Choctaw; F; S; Son; 563; Yes; Yes
579; 586; Francis; m; 12; Miss. Choctaw; F; S; Son; 564; Yes; Yes
580; 587; J. C; m; 10; Miss. Choctaw; F; S; Son; 565; Yes; Yes
581; 588; Wilma; f; 8; Miss. Choctaw; F; S; Dau; 566; Yes; Yes

582; 589; John Tole; m; 51; Miss. Choctaw; F; S; Alone; 567; Yes; Yes

583; 590; Charles T; m; 50; Miss. Choctaw; F; M; Head; 568; Yes; Yes
584; 591; Alfonsine; f; 36; Miss. Choctaw; F; M; Wife; 569; Yes; Yes

585; 592; Emeline; f; 44; Miss. Choctaw; F; S; Alone; 570; Yes; Yes

586; 593; Mary; f; 38; Miss. Choctaw; F; S; Alone; 571; Yes; Yes

587; 594; Julia; f; 49; Miss. Choctaw; F; S; Alone; 572; Yes; Yes

588; 595; R. C; m; 33; Miss. Choctaw; F; S; Alone; 573; Yes; Yes

589; 596; Dennis; m; 46; Miss. Choctaw; F; S; Alone; 574; Yes; Yes

590; 597; Western; m; 54; Miss. Choctaw; F; S; Alone; 575; Yes; Yes

591; 598; Noah; m; 42; Miss. Choctaw; F; S; Alone; 576; Yes; Yes

592; 599; Bennett; m; 40; Miss. Choctaw; F; S; Alone; 577; Yes; Yes

593; 600; William; m; 36; Miss. Choctaw; F; S; Alone; 578; Yes; Yes

Census of the **Mississippi Choctaws** reservation of the **Choctaw Agency** jurisdiction, as of **April 1**, 19**34**, taken by **A. C. Hector**, Superintendent.

KEY; Surname; Stamped Census Number; Typed Census Number; Given Name; Sex; Age at Last Birthday; Tribe; Degree of Blood; Marital Status; Relationship to Head of Family; Last Census Roll Number (if given); At Jurisdiction Where Enrolled (Yes/No); At Another Jurisdiction; Post Office, County, State (if given); Ward (Yes/No)

594; 601; Seman; m; 68; Miss. Choctaw; F; S; Alone; 579; Yes; Yes

595; 602; Elinor; f; 40; Miss. Choctaw; F; S; Alone; 580; Yes; Yes

596; 603; Joe; m; 61; Miss. Choctaw; F; S; Alone; 581; Yes; Yes

597; 604; Lucille; f; 31; Miss. Choctaw; F; S; Alone; 584; Yes; Yes

598; 605; Albert; m; 53; Miss. Choctaw; F; M; Head; 582; Yes; Yes
599; 606; Iktial; f; 51; Miss. Choctaw; F; M; Wife; 583; Yes; Yes

600; 607; Ethel; f; 30; Miss. Choctaw; F; S; Alone; 585; Yes; Yes

601; 608; Ida; f; 54; Miss. Choctaw; F; S; Alone; 586; Yes; Yes

602; 609; Rosella; f; 58; Miss. Choctaw; F; S; Alone; 587; Yes; Yes

603; 610; Amelia; f; 40; Miss. Choctaw; F; S; Alone; 588; Yes; Yes

604; 611; Henrietta; f; 36; Miss. Choctaw; F; S; Alone; 589; Yes; Yes

605; 612; Ray Turner; m; 29; Miss. Choctaw; F; S; Alone; 590; Yes; Yes

606; 613; Ceciline; m; 28; Miss. Choctaw; F; S; Alone; 591; Yes; Yes

607; 614; Charles; m; 54; Miss. Choctaw; F; S; Alone; 592; Yes; Yes

FORBES

608; 615; Wesley; m; 70; Miss. Choctaw; F; M; Head; 593; Yes; Yes
609; 616; Sallie; f; 69; Miss. Choctaw; F; M; Wife; 594; Yes; Yes
610; 617; Ella; f; 23; Miss. Choctaw; F; S; Dau; 595; Yes; Yes

Census of the **Mississippi Choctaws** reservation of the **Choctaw Agency** jurisdiction, as of **April 1**, 19**34**, taken by **A. C. Hector**, Superintendent.

KEY; Surname; Stamped Census Number; Typed Census Number; Given Name; Sex; Age at Last Birthday; Tribe; Degree of Blood; Marital Status; Relationship to Head of Family; Last Census Roll Number (if given); At Jurisdiction Where Enrolled (Yes/No); At Another Jurisdiction; Post Office, County, State (if given); Ward (Yes/No)

FORBES (FRAZIER)

611; 618; Clint; m; 32; Miss. Choctaw; F; M; Head; 596; Yes; Yes
612; 619; Josey Tubby; f; 33; Miss. Choctaw; F; M; Wife; 597; Yes; Yes
613; 620; Ida Mae; f; 16; Miss. Choctaw; F; S; Dau; 598; Yes; Yes
614; 621; Gaston; m; 12; Miss. Choctaw; F; S; Son; 599; Yes; Yes
615; 622; Henry; m; 4; Miss. Choctaw; F; S; Son; 600; Yes; Yes
616; 623; Hazel; f; 1; Miss. Choctaw; F; S; Dau; Yes; Yes

FRAZIER

617; 624; Mollie; f; 59; Miss. Choctaw; F; Wd; Head; 601; Yes; Yes
618; 625; John; m; 23; Miss. Choctaw; F; S; Son; 602; Yes; Yes

~~626~~; West; m; 26; Miss. Choctaw; F; M; Head; 603; Yes; Yes
Died 12-17-33

619; 627; Mamie; f; 25; Miss. Choctaw; F; M; Wife; 604; Yes; Yes
620; 628; Marshall; m; 5; Miss. Choctaw; F; S; 605; Yes; Yes
621; 629; Martha; f; 4; Miss. Choctaw; F; S; Dau; Yes; Yes
Left of last Census.
622; 630; Doris; f; 1; Miss. Choctaw; F; S; Dau; Yes; Yes

623; 631; Forbes; m; 33; Miss. Choctaw; F; M; Head; 606; Yes; Yes
624; 632; Iam; f; 29; Miss. Choctaw; F; M; Wife; 607; Yes; Yes
625; 633; Homer; m; 10; Miss. Choctaw; F; Son; 608; Yes; Yes
626; 634; **Box**, Sam Davis; m; 11; Miss. Choctaw; F; S; Step-son; 609; Yes; Yes

627; 635; Will; m; 35; Miss. Choctaw; F; M; Head; 610; Yes; Yes
628; 636; Lavena; f; 31; Miss. Choctaw; F; M; Wife; 611; Yes; Yes

629; 637; Seale; m; 64; Miss. Choctaw; F; M; Head; 612; Yes; Yes

Census of the **Mississippi Choctaws** reservation of the **Choctaw Agency** jurisdiction, as of **April 1**, 19**34**, taken by **A. C. Hector**, Superintendent.

KEY; Surname; Stamped Census Number; Typed Census Number; Given Name; Sex; Age at Last Birthday; Tribe; Degree of Blood; Marital Status; Relationship to Head of Family; Last Census Roll Number (if given); At Jurisdiction Where Enrolled (Yes/No); At Another Jurisdiction; Post Office, County, State (if given); Ward (Yes/No)

~~630; 638; Eliza; f; 79; Miss. Choctaw; F; M; Wife; 613; Yes; Yes~~
    Died 6/8/34
631; 639; Willie; f; 9; Miss. Choctaw; F; S; Grand-dau; 614; Yes; Yes

632; 640; Jim; m; 28; Miss. Choctaw; F; M; Head; 615; Yes; Yes
633; 641; Nannie Leben[sic]; f; 30; Miss. Choctaw; F; M; Wife; 616; Yes; Yes
634; 642; A. B; m; 7; Miss. Choctaw; F; S; Son; 617; Yes; Yes
635; 643; Henry; m; 8; Miss. Choctaw; F; S; Son; 618; Yes; Yes
636; 644; Nancy; f; 5; Miss. Choctaw; F; S; Dau; 619; Yes; Yes
637; 645; Caspeen; f; 6/12; Miss. Choctaw; F; S; Dau; Yes; Yes

638; 646; Ligman; m; 40; Miss. Choctaw; F; M; Head; 620; Yes; Yes
639; 647; Sina Jackson; f; 25; Miss. Choctaw; F; M; Wife; 621; Yes; Yes
640; 648; Edmond; m; 12; Miss. Choctaw; F; S; Son; 622; Yes; Yes
641; 649; Sallie; f; 10; Miss. Choctaw; F; S; Dau; 623; Yes; Yes
642; 650; Annie; f; 4; Miss. Choctaw; F; S; Dau; Yes; Yes
    Omitted from last census
643; 651; Emma; f; 1½; Miss. Choctaw; F; S; Dau; Yes; Yes
    Omitted from last census
644; 652; Cecile; f; 1; Miss. Choctaw; F; S; Dau; Yes; Yes

645; 653; Emma; f; 36; Miss. Choctaw; F; Wd; Head; 624; Yes; Yes
646; 654; Susie; f; 18; Miss. Choctaw; F; S; Dau; 625; Yes; Yes
~~655~~; Simpson; m; 14; Miss. Choctaw; F; S; Don; 626; Yes; Yes
    Died 8-28-33
647; 656; Herman; m; 13; Miss. Choctaw; F; S; Son; 627; Yes; Yes
648; 657; Frazier; m; 11; Miss. Choctaw; F; S; Son; 628; Yes; Yes
649; 658; Velma; f; 9; Miss. Choctaw; F; S; Dau; 629; Yes; Yes

650; 659; Henson; m; 66; Miss. Choctaw; F; M: Head; 630; Yes; Yes
651; 660; Fenie; f; 64; Miss. Choctaw; F; M; Wife; 631; Yes; Yes
652; 661; Lucy; f; 16; Miss. Choctaw; F; S; Dau; 632; Yes; Yes

Census of the **Mississippi Choctaws** reservation of the **Choctaw Agency** jurisdiction, as of **April 1**, 19**34**, taken by **A. C. Hector**, Superintendent.

KEY; Surname; Stamped Census Number; Typed Census Number; Given Name; Sex; Age at Last Birthday; Tribe; Degree of Blood; Marital Status; Relationship to Head of Family; Last Census Roll Number (if given); At Jurisdiction Where Enrolled (Yes/No); At Another Jurisdiction; Post Office, County, State (if given); Ward (Yes/No)

653; 662; Wade; m; 16; Miss. Choctaw; F; S; Son; 633; Yes; Yes
654; 663; Jake; m; 12; Miss. Choctaw; F; S; Son; 634; Yes; Yes

655; 664; Wesley; m; 61; Miss. Choctaw; F; Wd; Head; 635; Yes; Yes
656; 665; Ella; f; 26; Miss. Choctaw; F; S; Dau; 636; Yes; Yes

GARDNER

657; 666; Jim; m; 35; Miss. Choctaw; F; M; Head; 637; Yes; Yes
658; 667; Celia; f; 30; Miss. Choctaw; F; M; Wife; 638; Yes; Yes
659; 668; Arleta; f; 13; Miss. Choctaw; F; S; Dau; 639; Yes; Yes
660; 669; Alton; m; 7; Miss. Choctaw; F; S; Don; 640; Yes; Yes

GIPSON

661; 670; Bart; m; 58; Miss. Choctaw; F; M: Head; 641; Yes; Yes
662; 671; Lucy; f; 54; Miss. Choctaw; F; M; Wife; 642; Yes; Yes

663; 672; **Tubby**, Mollie; f; 31; Miss. Choctaw; F; S; Alone; 1430; Yes; Yes

664; 673; Homer; m; 21; Miss. Choctaw; F; M; Head; 643; Yes; Yes
~~665; 674; Sophie; f; 21; Miss. Choctaw; F; M; Wife; 644; Yes; Yes~~
    Died Mar. 23, 1935

666; 675; Hensley; m; 23; Miss. Choctaw; F; M; Head; 645; Yes; Yes
667; 676; Elizabeth; f; 23; Miss. Choctaw; F; M; Wife; 646; Yes; Yes
668; 677; Henrietta; f; 2; Miss. Choctaw; F; S; Dau; 647; Yes; Yes
669; 678; Hensley; m; 23; Miss. Choctaw; F; M; Head; 648; Yes; Yes
670; 679; Esther; f; 21; Miss. Choctaw; F; M; Wife; 649; Yes; Yes

671; 680; Gus; m; 25; Miss. Choctaw; F; S; Alone; 650; Yes; Yes

Census of the **Mississippi Choctaws** reservation of the **Choctaw Agency** jurisdiction, as of **April 1**, 19**34**, taken by **A. C. Hector**, Superintendent.

KEY; Surname; Stamped Census Number; Typed Census Number; Given Name; Sex; Age at Last Birthday; Tribe; Degree of Blood; Marital Status; Relationship to Head of Family; Last Census Roll Number (if given); At Jurisdiction Where Enrolled (Yes/No); At Another Jurisdiction; Post Office, County, State (if given); Ward (Yes/No).

672; 681; Nolie; m; 32; Miss. Choctaw; F; M; Head; 651; Yes; Yes
673; 682; Frances; f; 34; Miss. Choctaw; F; M; Wife; 652; Yes; Yes
674; 683; Paul; m; 9; Miss. Choctaw; F; S; Son; 653; Yes; Yes
675; 684; Clay; m; 8; Miss. Choctaw; F; S; Son; 654; Yes; Yes
676; 685; Annie; f; 5; Miss. Choctaw; F; S; Dau; 655; Yes; Yes
677; 686; Fannie; f; 1-11/12; Miss. Choctaw; F; S; Dau; 656; Yes; Yes

678; 687; Steve; m; 70; Miss. Choctaw; F; M; Head; 657; Yes; Yes
679; 688; Jennie; f; 66; Miss. Choctaw; F; M; Wife; 658; Yes; Yes
680; 689; Ikey; f; 31; Miss. Choctaw; F; S; Dau; 659; Yes; Yes
681; 690; Fannie; f; 26; Miss. Choctaw; F; S; Dau; 661; Yes; Yes
682; 691; Annie; f; 25; Miss. Choctaw; F; S; Dau; 661; Yes; Yes
683; 692; Willie; m; 16; Miss. Choctaw; F; S; Son; 662; Yes; Yes
684; 693; Hugh; m; 8; Miss. Choctaw; F; S; Grand-son; 663; Yes; Yes
685; 694; Aron; m; 7; Miss. Choctaw; F; S; Grand-son; 664; Yes; Yes

HALL

686; 695; Langford; m; 39; Miss. Choctaw; F; M; Head; 665; Yes; Yes
687; 696; Lou; f; 29; Miss. Choctaw; F; M; Wife; 666; Yes; Yes
688; 697; Travis; m; 11; Miss. Choctaw; F; S; Sn; 667; Yes; Yes
689; 698; Arlone; f; 10; Miss. Choctaw; F; S; Dau; 668; Yes; Yes
690; 699; Frank; m; 8; Miss. Choctaw; F; S; Son; 669; Yes; Yes
691; 700; Francis; f; 2; Miss. Choctaw; F; S; Dau; 670; Yes; Yes

HARPER

692; 701; Lena; f; 22; Miss. Choctaw; F; S; Alone; 671; Yes; Yes

HARRIS

693; 702; Elamore[sic]; f; 26; Miss. Choctaw; F; S; Alone; 672; Yes; Yes

Census of the Mississippi Choctaws reservation of the Choctaw Agency jurisdiction, as of April 1 , 19 34 , taken by A. C. Hector , Superintendent.

KEY; Surname; Stamped Census Number; Typed Census Number; Given Name; Sex; Age at Last Birthday; Tribe; Degree of Blood; Marital Status; Relationship to Head of Family; Last Census Roll Number (if given); At Jurisdiction Where Enrolled (Yes/No); At Another Jurisdiction; Post Office, County, State (if given); Ward (Yes/No)

HAWKINS

694; 703; Alice; f; 52; Miss. Choctaw; F; Wd; Head; 673; Yes; Yes

~~695; 704; Shoemaker, Mary; f; 23; Miss. Choctaw; F; S; Dau; 674; Yes; Yes~~ Died 12/8/35

HENRY

696; 705; Albert; m; 56; Miss. Choctaw; F; M; Head; 675; Yes; Yes
697; 706; Martha; f; 46; Miss. Choctaw; F; M; Wife; 676; Yes; Yes
698; 707; Guiser; f; 30; Miss. Choctaw; F; S; Dau; 677; Yes; Yes
699; 708; Beulah; f; 26; Miss. Choctaw; F; S; Dau; 678; Yes; Yes
700; 709; Liege; m; 24; Miss. Choctaw; F; S; Son; 679; Yes; Yes
701; 710; Melvin; m; 21; Miss. Choctaw; F; S; Son; 680; Yes; Yes
702; 711; Nettie; f; 19; Miss. Choctaw; F; S; Dau; 681; Yes; Yes
703; 712; Sis; f; 16; Miss. Choctaw; F; S; Dau; 682; Yes; Yes
704; 713; Susie; f; 14; Miss. Choctaw; F; S; Dau; 683; Yes; Yes
705; 714; R. D; m; 12; Miss. Choctaw; F; S; Son; 684; Yes; Yes
706; 715; Ellen; f; 5; Miss. Choctaw; F; S; Grand-dau; 685; Yes; Yes
Daughter of Guiser Henry

707; 716; Jim; m; 31; Miss. Choctaw; F; M; Head; 686; Yes; Yes
708; 717; Sallie; f; 29; Miss. Choctaw; F; M; Wife; 687; Yes; Yes
709; 718; Frank; m; 7; Miss. Choctaw; F; S; Son; 688; Yes; Yes
710; 719; Wicks; m; 5; Miss. Choctaw; F; Son; 689; Yes; Yes
~~711; 720; Joy June; f; 1 4/12; Miss. Choctaw; F; S; Dau; 690; Yes; Yes~~
Died 7/5/34

712; 721; Robert; m; 60; Miss. Choctaw; F; M; Head; 691; Yes; Yes
713; 722; Nellie; f; 50; Miss. Choctaw; F; M: Wife; 692; Yes; Yes
714; 723; Bob; m; 26; Miss. Choctaw; F; S; Son; 693; Yes; Yes
715; 724; Mattie; f; 23; Miss. Choctaw; F; S; Dau; 694; Yes; Yes

Census of the __Mississippi Choctaws__ reservation of the __Choctaw Agency__ jurisdiction, as of __April 1__, 19__34__, taken by __A. C. Hector__, Superintendent.

KEY; Surname; Stamped Census Number; Typed Census Number; Given Name; Sex; Age at Last Birthday; Tribe; Degree of Blood; Marital Status; Relationship to Head of Family; Last Census Roll Number (if given); At Jurisdiction Where Enrolled (Yes/No); At Another Jurisdiction; Post Office, County, State (if given); Ward (Yes/No)

716; 725; Jasper; m; 17; Miss. Choctaw; F; S; Son; 695; Yes; Yes
717; 726; Dolphus; m; 14; Miss. Choctaw; F; S; Son; 696; Yes; Yes

HICKMAN

718; 727; Billy; m; 48; Miss. Choctaw; F; M; Head; 697; Yes; Yes
719; 728; Rose; f; 50; Miss. Choctaw; F; M; Wife; 698; Yes; Yes
720; 729; Sim; m; 22; Miss. Choctaw; F; S; Son; 699; Yes; Yes
721; 730; Susan; f; 16; Miss. Choctaw; F; S; Dau; 700; Yes; Yes
722; 731; Lula; f; 14; Miss. Choctaw; F; S; Dau; 701; Yes; Yes
723; 732; **Hall**, Eliza; f; 81; Miss. Choctaw; F; Wd; Mother; Yes; Yes
Omitted on last Census

724; 733; Willie; m; 24; Miss. Choctaw; F; M; Head; 702; Yes; Yes
725; 734; Lodie Mae; f; 26; Miss. Choctaw; F; M; Wife; 703; Yes; Yes

726; 735; Ellis; m; 64; Miss. Choctaw; F; M; Head; 704; Yes; Yes
727; 736; Susuan[sic]; f; 58; Miss. Choctaw; F; M; Wife; 705; Yes; Yes
728; 737; **Bell**, Burton; m; 14; Miss. Choctaw; F; S; Grand-son; 706; Yes; Yes
729; 738; **Bell**, Henry; m; 12; Miss. Choctaw; F; S; Grand-son; 707; Yes; Yes

730; 739; Johnkin; m; 34; Miss. Choctaw; F; M; Head; 708; Yes; Yes
731; 740; Minnie; f; 29; Miss. Choctaw; F; M; Wife; 709; Yes; Yes
732; 741; Will; m; 4; Miss. Choctaw; F; S; Son; Yes; Yes
Ommitted[sic] from last Census roll

733; 742; Enoch; m; 60; Miss. Choctaw; F; M; Head; 710; Yes; Yes
734; 743; Malinda; f; 58; Miss. Choctaw; F; M; Wife; 711; Yes; Yes
735; 744; Sallie; f; 24; Miss. Choctaw; F; S; Dau; 712; Yes; Yes
736; 745; Sadie; f; 23; Miss. Choctaw; F; S; Dau; 713; Yes; Yes
737; 746; Tubby; m; 21; Miss. Choctaw; F; S; Son; 714; Yes; Yes

Census of the **Mississippi Choctaws** reservation of the **Choctaw Agency** jurisdiction, as of **April 1**, 19**34**, taken by **A. C. Hector**, Superintendent.

KEY; Surname; Stamped Census Number; Typed Census Number; Given Name; Sex; Age at Last Birthday; Tribe; Degree of Blood; Marital Status; Relationship to Head of Family; Last Census Roll Number (if given); At Jurisdiction Where Enrolled (Yes/No); At Another Jurisdiction; Post Office, County, State (if given); Ward (Yes/No)

738; 747; Aliza Jane; f; 20; Miss. Choctaw; F; S; Dau; 715; Yes; Yes
739; 748; Mary Long; f; 18; Miss. Choctaw; F; S; Dau; 716; Yes; Yes
740; 749; Annie; f; 13; Miss. Choctaw; F; S; Dau; 717; Yes; Yes
741; 750; Wm. Penn; m; 12; Miss. Choctaw; F; S; Son; 718; Yes; Yes
742; 751; Varderman; m; 10; Miss. Choctaw; F; S; Son; 719; Yes; Yes
743; 752; John; m; 9; Miss. Choctaw; F; S; Son; 720; Yes; Yes

744; 753; Wallace; m; 28; Miss. Choctaw; F; M; Head; 721; Yes; Yes
745; 754; Dona; f; 25; Miss. Choctaw; F; M; Wife; 722; Yes; Yes
746; 755; Robinson; m; 8; Miss. Choctaw; F; S; Son; 723; Yes;
747; 756; Pearl; f; 1-3/12; Miss. Choctaw; F; S; Dau; 724; Yes; Yes

748; 757; Stennis; m; 30; Miss. Choctaw; F; M; Head; 725; Yes; Yes
749; 758; Winnie T; f; 29; Miss. Choctaw; F; M; Wife; 726; Yes; Yes
750; 759; Eula; f; 7; Miss. Choctaw; F; S; Dau; 727; Yes; Yes
751; 760; Snooks; m; 6; Miss. Choctaw; F; S; Son; 728; Yes; Yes
752; 761; George; m; 3; Miss. Choctaw; F; S; Son; Yes; Yes
 Omitted from last census roll
753; 762; Sabelia; f; 1; Miss. Choctaw; F; S; Dau; Yes; Yes
 Omitted from last census roll
754; 763; Edd Davis; m; 3/12; Miss. Choctaw; F; S; Son; Yes; Yes

755; 764; Mary; f; 78; Miss. Choctaw; F Wd; Head; 729; Yes; Yes
 Died 8/25/34
756; 765; **Charlie**, Beckie; f; 17; Miss. Choctaw; F; S; Grand-dau; 730; Yes; Yes

HUDSON

757; 766; Celia; f; 27; Miss. Choctaw; F; S; Alone; 731; Yes; Yes

Census of the **Mississippi Choctaws** reservation of the **Choctaw Agency** jurisdiction, as of **April 1**, 19**34**, taken by **A. C. Hector**, Superintendent.

KEY; Surname; Stamped Census Number; Typed Census Number; Given Name; Sex; Age at Last Birthday; Tribe; Degree of Blood; Marital Status; Relationship to Head of Family; Last Census Roll Number (if given); At Jurisdiction Where Enrolled (Yes/No); At Another Jurisdiction; Post Office, County, State (if given); Ward (Yes/No)

ISAAC

758; 767; Jim; m; 39; Miss. Choctaw; F; M; Head; 732; Yes; Yes
759; 768; Bessie; f; 33; Miss. Choctaw; F; M; Wife; 733; Yes; Yes
760; 769; Steve; m; 79; Miss. Choctaw; F; Wd; Father; 734; Yes; Yes
      Died May 14, 1935

761; 770; Byrd; m; 38; Miss. Choctaw; F; M; Head; 735; Yes; Yes
762; 771; Pauline Jim; f; 22; Miss. Choctaw; F; M; Wife; 736; Yes; Yes
763; 772; Odie Mae; f; 18; Miss. Choctaw; F; S; Dau; 737; Yes; Yes
      Died 6/25/34
764; 773; Bernice; f; 16; Miss. Choctaw; F; S; Dau; 738; Yes; Yes
765; 774; Catherine; f; 14; Miss. Choctaw; F; S; Dau; 739; Yes; Yes
766; 775; Edwin; m; 7; Miss. Choctaw; F; S; Son; 740; Yes; Yes
767; 776; Jesse A; m; 2; Miss. Choctaw; F; S; Son; 741; Yes; Yes
768; 777; Paul; m; 6/12; Miss. Choctaw; F; S; Son; Yes; Yes
769; 778; **Hall**, Herbert H; m; 5; Miss. Choctaw; F; S; Step-son; Yes; Yes

770; 779; Hickman; m; 27; Miss. Choctaw; F; S; Alone; 743; Yes; Yes
      Died 8/18/34

771; 780; Simon; m; 50; Miss. Choctaw; F; M; Head; 744; Yes; Yes
772; 781; Nannie; f; 53; Miss. Choctaw; F; M; Wife; 745; Yes; Yes
773; 782; Effie; f; 11; Miss. Choctaw; F; S; Grand-dau; 746; Yes; Yes
774; 783; Lillie Mae; f; 9; Miss. Choctaw; F; S; Grand-dau; 747; Yes; Yes

775; 784; Hugh; m; 24; Miss. Choctaw; F; M; Head; 748; Yes; Yes
776; 785; Celia Farmer; f; 25; Miss. Choctaw; F; M; Wife; 749; Yes; Yes
777; 786; Beneda; f; 3; Miss. Choctaw; F; S; Dau; 750; Yes; Yes
778; 787; Anita; f; 3/12; Miss. Choctaw; F; S; Dau; Yes; Yes

Census of the **Mississippi Choctaws** reservation of the **Choctaw Agency** jurisdiction, as of **April 1**, 19**34**, taken by **A. C. Hector**, Superintendent.

KEY; Surname; Stamped Census Number; Typed Census Number; Given Name; Sex; Age at Last Birthday; Tribe; Degree of Blood; Marital Status; Relationship to Head of Family; Last Census Roll Number (if given); At Jurisdiction Where Enrolled (Yes/No); At Another Jurisdiction; Post Office, County, State (if given); Ward (Yes/No)

779; 788; Isaac; m; 33; Miss. Choctaw; F; M; Head; 751; Yes; Yes
780; 789; Maggie A; f; 25; Miss. Choctaw; F; M; Wife; 752; Yes; Yes
781; 790; Claudine; f; 12; Miss. Choctaw; F; S; Dau; 753; Yes; Yes
782; 791; Wilbur N; m; 10; Miss. Choctaw; F; S; Son; 754; Yes; Yes
783; 792; Claud Preston; m; 6; Miss. Choctaw; F; S; Son; 755; Yes; Yes
784; 793; Enochs; m; 5; Miss. Choctaw; F; S; Son; 756; Yes; Yes
785; 794; Delphia; f; 1-11/12; Miss. Choctaw; F; S; Dau; 757; Yes; Yes
786; 795; Mary Lou; f; 2/12; Miss. Choctaw; F; S; Dau; Yes; Yes
787; 796; Will; m; 36; Miss. Choctaw; F; M; Head; 758; Yes; Yes
788; 797; Louisa; f; 35; Miss. Choctaw; F; M; Wife; 759; Yes; Yes
789; 798; Annie; f; 16; Miss. Choctaw; F; S; Dau; 760; Yes; Yes
790; 799; Cornelia; f; 7; Miss. Choctaw; F; S; Dau; 761; Yes; Yes

791; 800; Wilson; m; 80; Miss. Choctaw; F; M; Head; 762; Yes; Yes
801; Martha; f; 67; Miss. Choctaw; F; M; Wife; 763; Yes; Yes
Died 5-19-33
792; 802; John Day; m; 21; Miss. Choctaw; F; S; Son; 764; Yes; Yes
793; 803; **Sam**, Edna; f; 12; Miss. Choctaw; F; S; Orphan; 765; Yes; Yes

794; 804; Jackson; m; 29; Miss. Choctaw; F; M: Head; 766; Yes; Yes
795; 805; Eva; f; 20; Miss. Choctaw; F; M; wife; 767; Yes; Yes
796; 806; Lawrence C; m; 1; Miss. Choctaw; F; S; Son; Yes; Yes
Died 8/25/34

797; 807; David; m; 27; Miss. Choctaw; F; M: Head; 768; Yes; Yes
798; 808; Lesper; f; 26; Miss. Choctaw; F; M; Wife; 769; Yes; Yes
799; 809; Joe Day; m; 7; Miss. Choctaw; F; S; Son; 770; Yes; Yes
800; 810; Franklin; m; 5; Miss. Choctaw; F; S; Son; 771; Yes; Yes
801; 811; Wansey; f; 3; Miss. Choctaw; F; S; Dau; 772; Yes; Yes
Died 8/13/34   See letter 4/30/36 Etherine on Death Roll

802; 812; Dixon; m; 82; Miss. Choctaw; F; M; Head; 773; Yes; Yes

Census of the **Mississippi Choctaws** reservation of the **Choctaw Agency** jurisdiction, as of **April 1**, 19**34**, taken by **A. C. Hector**, Superintendent.

KEY; Surname; Stamped Census Number; Typed Census Number; Given Name; Sex; Age at Last Birthday; Tribe; Degree of Blood; Marital Status; Relationship to Head of Family; Last Census Roll Number (if given); At Jurisdiction Where Enrolled (Yes/No); At Another Jurisdiction; Post Office, County, State (if given); Ward (Yes/No)

803; 813; Lou; f; 29; Miss. Choctaw; F; M; Wife; 774; Yes; Yes
804; 814; Elsie; f; 16; Miss. Choctaw; F; S; Dau; 775; Yes; Yes
805; 815; Rainey; f; 13; Miss. Choctaw; F; S; Dau; 776; Yes; Yes
806; 816; Manda; f; 11; Miss. Choctaw; F; S; Dau; 777; Yes; Yes
807; 817; Lester; m; 10; Miss. Choctaw; F; S; Son; 778; Yes; Yes
808; 818; **Billy**, Emma; f; 28; Miss. Choctaw; F; S; Sister-in-law; 779; Yes; Yes

ISOM

809; 819; Willie; m; 20; Miss. Choctaw; F; S; Alone; 780; Yes; Yes

810; 820; Isom; m; 34; Miss. Choctaw; F; S; Alone; 781; Yes; Yes

JACKSON

811; 821; Betty; f; 58; Miss. Choctaw; F; Wd; Head; 782; Yes; Yes
812; 822; Rose; f; 22; Miss. Choctaw; F; S; Dau; 783; Yes; Yes
813; 823; Nancie; f; 20; Miss. Choctaw; F; S; Dau; 784; Yes; Yes
814; 824; Carlson; m; 14; Miss. Choctaw; F; S; Son; 785; Yes; Yes

815; 825; Lena; f; 46; Miss. Choctaw; F; Wd; Head; 786; Yes; Yes
816; 826; Ella; f; 20; Miss. Choctaw; F; S; Dau; 787; Yes; Yes
817; 827; **Bell** (Jackson), Floyd F; M; 19; Miss. Choctaw; F; S; Son; 1729; Yes; Yes
818; 828; Carson; m; 16; Miss. Choctaw; F; S; Son; 788; Yes; Yes
819; 829; Emmett; m; 14; Miss. Choctaw; F; S; Son; 789; Yes; Yes
820; 830; Lucille; f; 13; Miss. Choctaw; F; S; Dau; 790; Yes; Yes

821; 831; Tom; m; 46; Miss. Choctaw; F; M; Head; 791; Yes; Yes
822; 832; Mamie; f; 42; Miss. Choctaw; F; M; Wife; 792; Yes; Yes
823; 833; Woodrow; m; 15; Miss. Choctaw; F; S; Son; 793; Yes; Yes
824; 834; Eva; f; 14; Miss. Choctaw; F; S; Dau; 794; Yes; Yes

Census of the **Mississippi Choctaws** reservation of the **Choctaw Agency** jurisdiction, as of **April 1**, 19**34**, taken by **A. C. Hector**, Superintendent.

KEY; Surname; Stamped Census Number; Typed Census Number; Given Name; Sex; Age at Last Birthday; Tribe; Degree of Blood; Marital Status; Relationship to Head of Family; Last Census Roll Number (if given); At Jurisdiction Where Enrolled (Yes/No); At Another Jurisdiction; Post Office, County, State (if given); Ward (Yes/No)

825; 835; Sam; m; 50; Miss. Choctaw; F; M; Head; 795; Yes; Yes
826; 836; Martha; f; 51; Miss. Choctaw; F; M; Wife; 796; Yes; Yes

827; 837; Tubby; m; 24; Miss. Choctaw; F; M; Head; 797; Yes; Yes
828; 838; Missie; f; 24; Miss. Choctaw; F; M; Wife; 798; Yes; Yes

829; 839; Prentiss; m; 31; Miss. Choctaw; F; M; Head; 799; Yes; Yes
830; 840; Mary; f; 31; Miss. Choctaw; F; M; Wife; 800; Yes; Yes

~~831; 841; Mike; m; 33; Miss. Choctaw; F; S; Alone; 801; Yes; Yes~~
       Died 12/12/35

JEFFERSON

832; 842; Braxton; m; 28; Miss. Choctaw; F; Wd; Alone; 802; Yes; Yes

833; 843; Amos; m; 27; Miss. Choctaw; F; M; Head; 803; Yes; Yes
834; 844; Ida; f; 22; Miss. Choctaw; F; M; Wife; 804; Yes; Yes
835; 845; Leon; m; 1; Miss. Choctaw; F; S; Son; 805; Yes; Yes
836;   Baby; f; 4/12; Miss. Choctaw; F; S; Dau; Yes; Yes

837; 846; Willis; m; 59; Miss. Choctaw; F; S; Head; 806; Yes; Yes
838; 847; Elsie; f; 47; Miss. Choctaw; F; S; Sister; 807; Yes; Yes

839; 848; Oscar; m; 29; Miss. Choctaw; F; M; Head; 808; Yes; Yes
840; 849; Saline; f; 27; Miss. Choctaw; F; M; Wife; 809; Yes; Yes
841; 850; Malcolm; m; 8; Miss. Choctaw; F; S; Son; 810; Yes; Yes
842; 851; Eva Nell; f; 4; Miss. Choctaw; F; S; Dau; Yes; Yes
       Omitted from last Census

843; 853; Otis; m; 31; Miss. Choctaw; F; M; Head; 811; Yes; Yes
844; 852; Onie; f; 29; Miss. Choctaw; F; M; Wife; 812; Yes; Yes
845; 854; Otho; m; 9; Miss. Choctaw; F; S; Son; 813; Yes; Yes

Census of the **Mississippi Choctaws** reservation of the **Choctaw Agency** jurisdiction, as of **April 1**, 19**34**, taken by **A. C. Hector**, Superintendent.

KEY; Surname; Stamped Census Number; Typed Census Number; Given Name; Sex; Age at Last Birthday; Tribe; Degree of Blood; Marital Status; Relationship to Head of Family; Last Census Roll Number (if given); At Jurisdiction Where Enrolled (Yes/No); At Another Jurisdiction; Post Office, County, State (if given); Ward (Yes/No)

846; 855; Andy; m; 8; Miss. Choctaw; F; S; Son; 814; Yes; Yes
847; 856; Victoria; f; 3; Miss. Choctaw; F; S; Dau; Yes; Yes
   Omitted from last Census
848; 857; Otis; m; 2; Miss. Choctaw; F; S; Son; Yes; Yes
   Omitted; from last Census
849;   Baby; m; 9/12; Miss. Choctaw; F; Son; Yes; Yes

JIM

850; 858; George; m; 66; Miss. Choctaw; F; M; Head; 815; Yes; Yes
851; 859; Eliza; f; 56; Miss. Choctaw; F; M; Wife; 816; Yes; Yes
852; 860; Lee; m; 28; Miss. Choctaw; F; S; Son; 817; Yes; Yes
853; 861; Sidney; m; 18; Miss. Choctaw; F; S; Son; 818; Yes; Yes

854; 862; Cooley; m; 64; Miss. Choctaw; F; M: Head; 819; Yes; Yes
855; 863; Lorena; f; 36; Miss. Choctaw; F; M; Wife; 820; Yes; Yes
856; 864; William; m; 13; Miss. Choctaw; F; S; Son; 821; Yes; Yes
857; 865; Tom; m; 11; Miss. Choctaw; F; S; Son; 822; Yes; Yes

858; 866; John; m; 28; Miss. Choctaw; F; M; Head; 823; Yes; Yes
859; 867; Bessie; f; 25; Miss. Choctaw; F; M; Wife; 824; Yes; Yes
860; 868; Susie Ann; f; 3; Miss. Choctaw; F; S; Dau; 825; Yes; Yes
861; 869; Corrine; f; 1-11/12; Miss. Choctaw; F; S; Dau; 826; Yes; Yes

862; 870; Henry; m; 49; Miss. Choctaw; F; M; Head; 827; Yes; Yes
863; 871; Mollie; f; 62; Miss. Choctaw; F; M; Wife; 828; Yes; Yes

864; 872; Harvey; m; 19; Miss. Choctaw; F; M; Head; 829; Yes; Yes
865; 873; Mattie; f; 36; Miss. Choctaw; F; M; Wife; 830; Yes; Yes
866; 874; **Hall**, Henrietta; f; 6; Miss. Choctaw; F; S; Niece; 831; Yes; Yes
867; 875; **Thomas**, Lula; f; 20; Miss. Choctaw; F; S; Sister-in-law; 832; Yes; Yes

Census of the **Mississippi Choctaws** reservation of the **Choctaw Agency** jurisdiction, as of **April 1**, 19**34**, taken by **A. C. Hector**, Superintendent.

KEY; Surname; Stamped Census Number; Typed Census Number; Given Name; Sex; Age at Last Birthday; Tribe; Degree of Blood; Marital Status; Relationship to Head of Family; Last Census Roll Number (if given); At Jurisdiction Where Enrolled (Yes/No); At Another Jurisdiction; Post Office, County, State (if given); Ward (Yes/No)

868; 876; **Thomas**, George; ; 85; Miss. Choctaw; F; Wd; Father-in-law; 833; Yes; Yes

869; 877; Ben; m; 56; Miss. Choctaw; F; M; Head; 834; Yes; Yes
870; 878; Dora; f; 44; Miss. Choctaw; F; M; Wife; 835; Yes; Yes
871; 879; Annie Mae; f; 20; Miss. Choctaw; F; S; Dau; 836; Yes; Yes
872; 880; Rena; f; 12; Miss. Choctaw; F; S; Dau; 837; Yes; Yes
873; 881; Christine; f; 2; Miss. Choctaw; F; S; Dau; 838; Yes; Yes
874; 882; Frank; m; 6; Miss. Choctaw; F; S; Grand-son; 839; Yes; Yes
875; 883; Bobbie Sue; f; 5; Miss. Choctaw; F; S; Grand-dau; 840; Yes; Yes

876; 884; Logan; m; 86; Miss. Choctaw; F; Wd; Alone; 841; Yes; Yes

877; 885; Amon; m; 57; Miss. Choctaw; F; M: Head; 842; Yes; Yes
878; 886; Lucy; f; 49; Miss. Choctaw; F; M; Wife; 843; Yes; Yes
879; 887; Opal; f; 14; Miss. Choctaw; F; S; Dau; 844; Yes; Yes
880; 888; Carter; m; 5; Miss. Choctaw; F; S; Son; 845; Yes; Yes
881; 889; Wm. Murray; m; 2; Miss. Choctaw; F; S; Son; 846; Yes; Yes

882; 890; Goodman; m; 69; Miss. Choctaw; F; M; Head; 847; Yes; Yes
883; 891; Leona; f; 32; Miss. Choctaw; F; M; Wife; 848; Yes; Yes
884; 892; Frank McKinley; m; 8; Miss. Choctaw; F; S; Son; 849; Yes; Yes
885; 893; Claud Yeates; m; 6; Miss. Choctaw; F; S; Son; 850; Yes; Yes
886; 894; Betty Lou; f; 7/12; Miss. Choctaw; F; S; Dau; 851; Yes; Yes
887; 895; **Farmer**, Sallie; f; 79; Miss. Choctaw; F; Wd; Sister; 852; Yes; Yes

888; 896; Albert; m; 27; Miss. Choctaw; F; M; Head; 853; Yes; Yes
889; 897; Dora; f; 26; Miss. Choctaw; F; M; Wife; 854; Yes; Yes
890; 898; Grace; f; 4; Miss. Choctaw; F; S; Dau; 855; Yes; Yes

Census of the __Mississippi Choctaws__ reservation of the __Choctaw Agency__ jurisdiction, as of __April 1__, 19__34__, taken by __A. C. Hector__, Superintendent.

KEY; Surname; Stamped Census Number; Typed Census Number; Given Name; Sex; Age at Last Birthday; Tribe; Degree of Blood; Marital Status; Relationship to Head of Family; Last Census Roll Number (if given); At Jurisdiction Where Enrolled (Yes/No); At Another Jurisdiction; Post Office, County, State (if given); Ward (Yes/No)

891; 899; Gordon G; m; 1-6/12; Miss. Choctaw; F; S; Son; 856; Yes; Yes

892; 900; Henry; m; 34; Miss. Choctaw; F; m: Head; 857; Yes; Yes
893; 901; Maggie; f; 40; Miss. Choctaw; F; M; Wife; 858; Yes; Yes

894; 902; Winston; m; 24; Miss. Choctaw; F; S; Alone; 859; Yes; Yes

895; 903; Victor; M; 33; Miss. Choctaw; F; M; Head; 860; Yes; Yes
896; 904; Lena; f; 24; Miss. Choctaw; F; M; Wife; 861; Yes; Yes
897; 905; Foy; m; 8; Miss. Choctaw; F; S; Son; 862; Yes; Yes
898; 906; Egbert; m; 4; Miss. Choctaw; F; S; Son; 863; Yes; Yes

JIMMIE

899; 907; Mary; f; 27; Miss. Choctaw; F; Wd; Head; 864; Yes; Yes
900; 908; Ona C; f; 6; Miss. Choctaw; F; S; Dau; 865; Yes; Yes
901; 909; Delores; f; 4; Miss. Choctaw; F; S; Dau; 866; Yes; Yes

902; 910; Frank M; m; 22; Miss. Choctaw; F; S; Alone; 867; No; Chilocco; Chilocco, Kay, Okla; [blank]

903; 911; Ike; m; 64; Miss. Choctaw; F; S; Alone; 868; Yes; Yes

904; 912; Will; m; 54; Miss. Choctaw; F; M: Head; 869; Yes; Yes
905; 913; Hester; f; 52; Miss. Choctaw; F; M; Wife; 870; Yes; Yes
906; 914; Mack; m; 28; Miss. Choctaw; F; S; Dau; 871; Yes; Yes

907; 915; Homer; m; 25; Miss. Choctaw; F; M; Head; 872; Yes; Yes
908; 916; Lela; f; 26; Miss. Choctaw; F; M; Wife; 873; Yes; Yes
909; 917; **Dan**, Irene; f; 8; Miss. Choctaw; F; S; Step-son; 874; Yes; Yes
910; 918; **Dan**, Albert R; m; 4; Miss. Choctaw; F; S; Step-son; 875; Yes; Yes

Census of the **Mississippi Choctaws** reservation of the **Choctaw Agency** jurisdiction, as of **April 1**, 19**34**, taken by **A. C. Hector**, Superintendent.

KEY: Surname; Stamped Census Number; Typed Census Number; Given Name; Sex; Age at Last Birthday; Tribe; Degree of Blood; Marital Status; Relationship to Head of Family; Last Census Roll Number (if given); At Jurisdiction Where Enrolled (Yes/No); At Another Jurisdiction; Post Office, County, State (if given); Ward (Yes/No)

JOE

911; 919; Nicholas; m; 44; Miss. Choctaw; F; M; Head; 876; Yes; Yes
912; 920; Ella; f; 39; Miss. Choctaw; F; M; Wife; 877; Yes; Yes
913; 921; Auston; m; 20; Miss. Choctaw; F; S; Son; 878; Yes; Yes
914; 922; Henry; m; 16; Miss. Choctaw; F; S; Son; 879; Yes; Yes
915; 923; Widge; m; 13; Miss. Choctaw; F; S; Son; 880; Yes; Yes
916; 924; Bessie; f; 11; Miss. Choctaw; F; S; Dau; 881; Yes; Yes
917; 925; Billie Joe; m; 10; Miss. Choctaw; F; S; Son; 882; Yes; Yes
918; 926; Mary; f; 4; Miss. Choctaw; F; S; Dau; 883; Yes; Yes
919; 927; Nichols; m; 3; Miss. Choctaw; F; S; Son; 884; Yes; Yes
920; 928; **Lewis**, Susie; f; 10; Miss. Choctaw; F; S; Step-dau; 885; Yes; Yes
921; 929; **Lewis**, Elsie; f; 9; Miss. Choctaw; F; S; Step-dau; 886; Yes; Yes

922; 930; Jasper; m; 46; Miss. Choctaw; F; M; Head; 887; Yes; Yes
923; 931; Sallie; f; 41; Miss. Choctaw; F; M; Wife; 888; Yes; Yes
924; 932; Lula; f; 21; Miss. Choctaw; F; S; Dau; 889; Yes; Yes
925; 933; Houston; m; 16; Miss. Choctaw; F; S; Son; 890; Yes; Yes
926; 934; Watkins; m; 12; Miss. Choctaw; F; S; Son; 891; Yes; Yes

927; 935; Emily; f; 78; Miss. Choctaw; F; Wd; Alone; 892; Yes; Yes

928; 936; John; m; 35; Miss. Choctaw; F; M; Head; 893; Yes; Yes
929; 937; Emma; f; 34; Miss. Choctaw; F; M; Wife; 894; Yes; Yes
930; 938; Bessie; f; 13; Miss. Choctaw; F; S; Dau; 895; Yes; Yes
931; 939; Killie; f; 9; Miss. Choctaw; F; S; Dau; 896; Yes; Yes
932; 940; Claud; m; 6; Miss. Choctaw; F; S Son; 897; Yes; Yes

933; 941; Langley; m; 87; Miss. Choctaw; F; Wd; Alone; 898; Yes; Yes

Census of the **Mississippi Choctaws** reservation of the **Choctaw Agency** jurisdiction, as of **April 1**, 19**34**, taken by **A. C. Hector**, Superintendent.

KEY; Surname; Stamped Census Number; Typed Census Number; Given Name; Sex; Age at Last Birthday; Tribe; Degree of Blood; Marital Status; Relationship to Head of Family; Last Census Roll Number (if given); At Jurisdiction Where Enrolled (Yes/No); At Another Jurisdiction; Post Office, County, State (if given); Ward (Yes/No)

934; 942; **Denson**, Joe; m; 80; Miss. Choctaw; F; S; Alone; 899; Yes; Yes

JOHN

935; 943; Mike; m; 61; Miss. Choctaw; F; M; Head; 900; Yes; Yes
936; 944; Lizzie; f; 76; Miss. Choctaw; F; M; Wife; 901; Yes; Yes
937; 945; **Willis**, Dina; f; 20; Miss. Choctaw; F; S; Grand-dau; 902; Yes; Yes

938; 946; Josh; m; 58; Miss. Choctaw; F; Wd; Alone; 903; Yes; Yes

939; 947; Anderson; m; 57; Miss. Choctaw; F; M; Head; 904; Yes; Yes
940; 948; Bettie; f; 45; Miss. Choctaw; F; M; Wife; 905; Yes; Yes
941; 949; L. E; f; 19; Miss. Choctaw; F; S; Dau; 906; Yes; Yes
942; 950; Hubert; m; 16; Miss. Choctaw; F; S; Son; 907; Yes; Yes
943; 951; Oden; m; 13; Miss. Choctaw; F; S; Son; 908; Yes; Yes
944; 952; Wilson; m; 6; Miss. Choctaw; F; S; Son; 909; Yes; Yes

945; 953; Bennett; m; 25; Miss. Choctaw; F; M; Head; 910; Yes; Yes
946; 954; Lena Pearl; f; 19; Miss. Choctaw; F; M; Wife; 911; Yes; Yes
947; 955; Egbart[sic]; m; 3; Miss. Choctaw; F; S; Son; 912; Yes; Yes
948; 956; Hamilton; m; 1; Miss. Choctaw; F; S; Son; Yes; Yes

949; 957; Clint; m; 43; Miss. Choctaw; F; S; Alone; 913; Yes; Yes

950; 958; Ira; m; 29; Miss. Choctaw; F; M; Head; 914; Yes; Yes
951; 959; Ovetta; f; 21; Miss. Choctaw; F; M; Wife; 915; Yes; Yes
952; 960; Mercy Lee; f; 4; Miss. Choctaw; F; S; Dau; 916; Yes; Yes
    Died 6/19/34
953; 961; Harry; m; 1-6/12; Miss. Choctaw; F; S; Son; 917; Yes; Yes

954; 962; Bob; m; 60; Miss. Choctaw; F; M: Head; 918; Yes; Yes
955; 963; Onie; f; 49; Miss. Choctaw; F; M; Wife; 919; Yes; Yes

Census of the **Mississippi Choctaws** reservation of the **Choctaw Agency** jurisdiction, as of **April 1**, 19**34**, taken by **A. C. Hector**, Superintendent.

KEY; Surname; Stamped Census Number; Typed Census Number; Given Name; Sex; Age at Last Birthday; Tribe; Degree of Blood; Marital Status; Relationship to Head of Family; Last Census Roll Number (if given); At Jurisdiction Where Enrolled (Yes/No); At Another Jurisdiction; Post Office, County, State (if given); Ward (Yes/No)

956; 964; Oliver; m; 19; Miss. Choctaw; F; S; Son; 920; Yes; Yes
957; 965; Ruby; f; 13; Miss. Choctaw; F; S; Dau; 921; Yes; Yes
958; 966; Rose; f; 11; Miss. Choctaw; F; S; Dau; 922; Yes; Yes

959; 967; Otis; m; 17; Miss. Choctaw; F; M; Head; 923; Yes; Yes
960; 968; Annie Mitch; f; 15; Miss. Choctaw; F; M; Wife; 924; Yes; Yes
961; 969; Grady; m; 3/12; Miss. Choctaw; F; S; Son; Yes; Yes

962; 970; Jack; m; 60; Miss. Choctaw; F; M: Head; 925; Yes; Yes
963; 971; Amanda; f; 39; Miss. Choctaw; F; M; Wife; 926; Yes; Yes
964; 972; Jefferson; m; 12; Miss. Choctaw; F; S; Son; 927; Yes; Yes
965; 973; Mary; f; 10; Miss. Choctaw; F; S; Dau; 928; Yes; Yes
966; 974; **Box**, Mamie; f; 12; Miss. Choctaw; F; S; Orphan; 929; Yes; Yes

967; 975; Bilsy; f; 36; Miss. Choctaw; F; Wd; Head; 930; Yes; Yes
968; 976; Bilbo; m; 17; Miss. Choctaw; F; S; Son; 931; Yes; Yes
969; 977; Mable; f; 14; Miss. Choctaw; F; S; Dau; 932; Yes; Yes
970; 978; Renie; f; 12; Miss. Choctaw; F; S; Dau; 933; Yes; Yes
971; 979; Varderman; m; 9; Miss. Choctaw; F; S; Son; 934; Yes; Yes
972; 980; Smith; m; 7; Miss. Choctaw; F; S; Son; 935; Yes; Yes
973; 981; Lisette H; f; 4; Miss. Choctaw; F; S; Dau; 936; Yes; Yes
974; 982; Elizabeth; f; 6/12; Miss. Choctaw; F; S; Dau; Yes; Yes
975; 983; Margaret; f; 6/12; Miss. Choctaw; F; S; Dau; Yes; Yes

JOHNSON

~~976; 984; Celia; f; 76; Miss. Choctaw; F; Wd; Head; Yes; Yes~~
    Died 8/5/34   Omitted on last Census
977; 985; **Stephens**, Pheobe[sic]; f; 14; Miss. Choctaw; F; S; Grandchild; 1258; Yes; Yes

978; 986; Whitman; m; 23; Miss. Choctaw; F; M; Head; 937; Yes; Yes

Census of the **Mississippi Choctaws** reservation of the **Choctaw Agency** jurisdiction, as of **April 1**, 19**34**, taken by **A. C. Hector**, Superintendent.

KEY; Surname; Stamped Census Number; Typed Census Number; Given Name; Sex; Age at Last Birthday; Tribe; Degree of Blood; Marital Status; Relationship to Head of Family; Last Census Roll Number (if given); At Jurisdiction Where Enrolled (Yes/No); At Another Jurisdiction; Post Office, County, State (if given); Ward (Yes/No)

979; 987; Viola; f; 22; Miss. Choctaw; F; M; Wife; 938; Yes; Yes
980; 988; Priscilla Study; f; 1; Miss. Choctaw; F; S; Dau; Yes; Yes

981; 989; Will; m; 62; Miss. Choctaw; F; M; Head; 939; Yes; Yes
982; 990; Dixie; f; 40; Miss. Choctaw; F; M; Wife; 940; Yes; Yes
983; 991; **Comby**, Gus; m; 9; Miss. Choctaw; F; S; Step-son; 941; Yes; Yes
984; 992; Sallie; f; 79; Miss. Choctaw; F; Wd; Mother; 942; Yes; Yes

985; 993; Afton; m; 30; Miss. Choctaw; F; M; Head; 943; Yes; Yes
986; 994; Savannia; f; 28; Miss. Choctaw; F; M; Wife; 944; Yes; Yes
987; 995; Thelma; f; 5; Miss. Choctaw; F; S; Dau; 945; Yes; Yes
988; 996; Ralph; m; 1-9/12; Miss. Choctaw; F; S; Son; 946; Yes; Yes
989; 997; **Denson**, Zula; f; 10; Miss. Choctaw; F; S; Step-dau; Yes; Yes
Omitted from last Census

990; 998; Edgar; m; 35; Miss. Choctaw; F; M; Head; 947; Yes; Yes
991; 999; Beatrice; f; 31; Miss. Choctaw; F; M; Wife; 948; Yes; Yes
992;1000; Callie; f; 11; Miss. Choctaw; F; S; Dau; 949; Yes; Yes
993;1001; Frances; f; 9; Miss. Choctaw; F; S; Dau; 950; Yes; Yes
994;1002; Egbert; m; 7; Miss. Choctaw; F; S; Son; 951; Yes; Yes
995;1003; Neva; f; 3; Miss. Choctaw; F; S; Dau; 952; Yes; Yes
996;1004; Beverly; f; 1-2 da; Miss. Choctaw; F; S; Dau; 953; Yes; Yes

997;1005; Frank; m; 42; Miss. Choctaw; F; M: Head; 954; Yes; Yes
998;1006; Lorine Solomon; f; 34; Miss. Choctaw; F; M: Wife; 955; Yes; Yes
999;1007; Athens; m; 16; Miss. Choctaw; F; S; Son; 956; Yes; Yes
1000;1008; Sadie; f; 14; Miss. Choctaw; F; S; Dau; 957; Yes; Yes
Married Beaman Charley #1323
1001;1009; Bertha; f; 12; Miss. Choctaw; F; S; Dau; 958; Yes; Yes
1002;1010; Nathan; m; 10; Miss. Choctaw; F; S; Son; 959; Yes; Yes
1003;1011; Hattie; f; 8; Miss. Choctaw; F; S; Dau; 960; Yes; Yes

Census of the __Mississippi Choctaws__ reservation of the __Choctaw Agency__ jurisdiction, as of __April 1__, 19__34__, taken by __A. C. Hector__, Superintendent.

KEY; Surname; Stamped Census Number; Typed Census Number; Given Name; Sex; Age at Last Birthday; Tribe; Degree of Blood; Marital Status; Relationship to Head of Family; Last Census Roll Number (if given); At Jurisdiction Where Enrolled (Yes/No); At Another Jurisdiction; Post Office, County, State (if given); Ward (Yes/No)

1004;1012; Bena; f; 6; Miss. Choctaw; F; S; Dau; 961; Yes; Yes
1005;1013; Marvin; m; 3; Miss. Choctaw; F; S; Son; 962; Yes; Yes
1006;1014; G. O; m; 1; Miss. Choctaw; F; S; Son; Yes; Yes

1007;1015; Otho; m; 18; Miss. Choctaw; F; M; Head; 963; Yes; Yes
Married Juinata[sic] Charley #1324
~~1016~~; Mary Davis; f; 18; Miss. Choctaw; F; M; Wife; 964; Yes; Yes
Died 10-15-33
~~1017~~; Mary; f; 6/12; Miss. Choctaw; F; S; Dau; Yes; Yes
Died 10-15-33

JOSHUA

1008;1018; Jennie; f; 64; Miss. Choctaw; F; Wd; Head; 965; Yes; Yes
1009;1019; **John**, Callie; f; 23; Miss. Choctaw; F; S; Grand-dau; 966; Yes; Yes
1010;1020; **John**, Edison; m; 6; Miss. Choctaw; F; S; Grand-son; 967; Yes; Yes

KING

1011;1021; John W; m; 74; Miss. Choctaw; F; Wd; Head; 968; Yes; Yes
1012;1022; Mollie; f; 31; Miss. Choctaw; F; S; Dau; 969; Yes; Yes
1013;1023; Enis; m; 22; Miss. Choctaw; F; S; Son; 970; Yes; Yes
1014;1024; Varman; m; 22; Miss. Choctaw; F; S; Son; 971; Yes; Yes
1015;1025; John Lee; m; 20; Miss. Choctaw; F; S; Great-nephew; 972; Yes; Yes
1016;1026; Lavenia; f; 15; Miss. Choctaw; F; S; Great-niece; 973; Yes; Yes

1017;1027; Clay; m; 28; Miss. Choctaw; F; M; Head; 974; Yes; Yes
1018;1028; Alice; f; 31; Miss. Choctaw; F; M; Wife; 975; Yes; Yes

Census of the **Mississippi Choctaws** reservation of the **Choctaw Agency** jurisdiction, as of **April 1**, 19**34**, taken by **A. C. Hector**, Superintendent.

KEY; Surname; Stamped Census Number; Typed Census Number; Given Name; Sex; Age at Last Birthday; Tribe; Degree of Blood; Marital Status; Relationship to Head of Family; Last Census Roll Number (if given); At Jurisdiction Where Enrolled (Yes/No); At Another Jurisdiction; Post Office, County, State (if given); Ward (Yes/No)

1019;1029; Betsie; f; 52; Miss. Choctaw; F; Wd; Head; 976; Yes; Yes
1020;1030; Christine; f; 24; Miss. Choctaw; F; S; Dau; 977; Yes; Yes
1021;1031; Joseph; m; 17; Miss. Choctaw; F; S; Son; 978; Yes; Yes
1022;1032; Joe; m; 15; Miss. Choctaw; F; S; Son; 979; Yes; Yes
1023;1033; Barkum; m; 13; Miss. Choctaw; F; S; Son; 980; Yes; Yes
1024;1034; Banks; m; 29; Miss. Choctaw; F; S; Son; 981; Yes; Yes
1025;1035; Betsie; f; 38; Miss. Choctaw; F; M; Daughter-in-law; 982; Yes; Yes

LEBAN

1026;1036; Ben; m; 62; Miss. Choctaw; F; M; Head; 983; Yes; Yes
1027;1037; Lena; f; 61; Miss. Choctaw; F; M; Wife; 984; Yes; Yes
1028;1038; Mary; f; 33; Miss. Choctaw; F; S; Dau; 985; Yes; Yes

LEFLORE

1029;1039; John; m; 63; Miss. Choctaw; F; M; Head; 986; Yes; Yes
1030;1040; Emma; f; 54; Miss. Choctaw; F; M; Wife; 987; Yes; Yes
1031;1041; Richard; m; 41; Miss. Choctaw; F; S; Son; 988; Yes; Yes
1032;1042; S. D; m; 28; Miss. Choctaw; F; S; Son; 989; Yes; Yes
1033;1043; Willie; f; 30; Miss. Choctaw; F; S; Dau; 990; Yes; Yes
1034;1044; Bertha Lee; f; 25; Miss. Choctaw; F; S; Dau; 991; Yes; Yes
1035;1045; John; m; 23; Miss. Choctaw; F; S; Son; 992; Yes; Yes
1036;1046; Lewis; m; 22; Miss. Choctaw; Yes; Yes 993; Yes; Yes Yes

LEWIS

1037;1047; Fannie Davis; f; 44; Miss. Choctaw; F; Wd; Head; 994; Yes; Yes
1038;1048; Hector Archie; m; 1; Miss. Choctaw; F; S; Son; Yes; Yes
 1049; **Wickson**, Alma; f; 19; Miss. Choctaw; F; Wd; Dau; 995; Yes; Yes Died in June 1933

Census of the **Mississippi Choctaws** reservation of the **Choctaw Agency** jurisdiction, as of **April 1**, 19**34**, taken by **A. C. Hector**, Superintendent.

KEY; Surname; Stamped Census Number; Typed Census Number; Given Name; Sex; Age at Last Birthday; Tribe; Degree of Blood; Marital Status; Relationship to Head of Family; Last Census Roll Number (if given); At Jurisdiction Where Enrolled (Yes/No); At Another Jurisdiction; Post Office, County, State (if given); Ward (Yes/No)

1039;1050; Adam; m; 29; Miss. Choctaw; F; M; Head; 996; Yes; Yes
1040;1051; Celia; f; 28; Miss. Choctaw; F; M: Wife; 997; Yes; Yes
1041;1052; Nannie; f; 6; Miss. Choctaw; F; S; Dau; 998; Yes; Yes
1042;1053; Mamie; f; 4; Miss. Choctaw; F; S; Dau; 999; Yes; Yes
1043;1054; Jacob; m; 1-6/12; Miss. Choctaw; F; S; Son; 1000; Yes; Yes
1044;1055; Tom; m; 8; Miss. Choctaw; F; S; Step-son; 1001; Yes; Yes

1045;1056; Elon; m; 53; Miss. Choctaw; F; M; Head; 1002; Yes; Yes
1046;1057; Inla; f; 56; Miss. Choctaw; F; M; Wife; 1003; Yes; Yes
1047;1058; **Jefferson**, Newt; m; 18; Miss. Choctaw; F; S; Step-son; 1004; Yes; Yes Married Leona Nickey Cooper #406

1048;1059; Marshall; m; 59; Miss. Choctaw; F; M: Head; 1005; Yes; Yes
1049;1060; Martha; f; 48; Miss. Choctaw; F; M; Wife; 1006; Yes; Yes
1050;1061; Belfa; f; 18; Miss. Choctaw; F; S; Dau; 1007; Yes; Yes
1051;1062; Houston; m; 15; Miss. Choctaw; F; S; Son; 1008; Yes; Yes;
1052;1063; Lee; m; 13; Miss. Choctaw; F; S; Son; 1009; Yes; Yes
1053;1064; Esther; f; 10; Miss. Choctaw; F; S; Dau; 1010; Yes; Yes
1054;1065; Hodges; m; 7; Miss. Choctaw; F; S; Son; 1011; Yes; Yes
1055;1066; Leon; m; 6; Miss. Choctaw; F; S; Son; 1012; Yes; Yes
1056;1067; Lucille; f; 4; Miss. Choctaw; F; S; Dau; 1013; Yes; Yes
1057;1068; Prentiss; m; 2; Miss. Choctaw; F; S; Son; 1014; Yes; Yes
1058;1069; **Denson**, Wintson[sic]; m; 19; Miss. Choctaw; F; M; Son-in-law; 1015; Yes; Yes
1059;1070; **Denson**, Eliza; f; 19; Miss. Choctaw; F; M; Dau; 1016; Yes; Yes
1060; **Denson**, Baby; m; 1/12; Miss. Choctaw; F; S; Son; Yes; Yes Child of Winston Denson and Eliza Lewis

1061;1071; Joe; m; 60; Miss. Choctaw; F; Wd; Alone; 1017; Yes; Yes

1062;1072; Lennis; m; 27; Miss. Choctaw; F; M; Head; 1018; Yes; Yes
1063;1073; Ola; f; 22; Miss. Choctaw; F; M; Wife; 1019; Yes; Yes

Census of the **Mississippi Choctaws** reservation of the **Choctaw Agency** jurisdiction, as of **April 1**, 19**34**, taken by **A. C. Hector**, Superintendent.

KEY; Surname; Stamped Census Number; Typed Census Number; Given Name; Sex; Age at Last Birthday; Tribe; Degree of Blood; Marital Status; Relationship to Head of Family; Last Census Roll Number (if given); At Jurisdiction Where Enrolled (Yes/No); At Another Jurisdiction; Post Office, County, State (if given); Ward (Yes/No)

1064;1074; Nervie; f; 5; Miss. Choctaw; F; S; Dau; 1020; Yes; Yes

1065;1075; Edd; m; 60; Miss. Choctaw; F; M; Head; 1021; Yes; Yes
1066;1076; Edna; f; 52; Miss. Choctaw; F; M; Wife; 1022; Yes; Yes
1067;1077; Hollis; m; 18; Miss. Choctaw; F; S; Son; 1023; Yes; Yes

~~1078~~; Reuben; m; 74; Miss. Choctaw; F; Wd; Head; 1024; Yes; Yes
Died 4-23-33
1068;1079; Amos; m; 21; Miss. Choctaw; F; S; Grand-son; 1025; Yes; Yes

1069;1080; Albert; m; 40; Miss. Choctaw; F; M; Head; 1026; Yes; Yes
Married Emma Bell Lewis #82
~~1070;1081; Mollie; f; 37; Miss. Choctaw; F; M; Wife; 1027; Yes; Yes~~
Died 6/21/34
1071;1082; Bernice; f; 17; Miss. Choctaw; F; S; Dau; 1028; Yes; Yes
1072;1083; Eastland; m; 15; Miss. Choctaw; F; S; Son; 1029; Yes; Yes
1073;1084; Ivena; f; 13; Miss. Choctaw; F; S; Dau; 1030; Yes; Yes

1074;1085; Jim; m; 31; Miss. Choctaw; F; M; Head; 1031; Yes; Yes
1075;1086; Jennie Willis; f; 26; Miss. Choctaw; F; M; Wife; 1032; Yes; Yes
1076;1087; Jennie Lin; f; 5; Miss. Choctaw; F; S; Dau; 1033; Yes; Yes
1077;1088; Willie; m; 2; Miss. Choctaw; F; S; Son; 1034; Yes; Yes
~~1078;1089; Rosie Mae; f; 1; Miss. Choctaw; F; S; Dau; Yes; Yes~~
Died 9/25/34

1079;1090; Duffie; m; 38; Miss. Choctaw; F; M; Head; 1035; Yes; Yes
1080;1091; Lilly; f; 54; Miss. Choctaw; F; M; Wife; 1036; Yes; Yes
1081;1092; **Briscoe**, Egbert; m; 11; Miss. Choctaw; F; S; Step-son; 1037; Yes; Yes

Census of the **Mississippi Choctaws** reservation of the **Choctaw Agency** jurisdiction, as of **April 1**, 19**34**, taken by **A. C. Hector**, Superintendent.

KEY; Surname; Stamped Census Number; Typed Census Number; Given Name; Sex; Age at Last Birthday; Tribe; Degree of Blood; Marital Status; Relationship to Head of Family; Last Census Roll Number (if given); At Jurisdiction Where Enrolled (Yes/No); At Another Jurisdiction; Post Office, County, State (if given); Ward (Yes/No)

1082;1093; **Farmer**, Henry; m; 23; Miss. Choctaw; F; S; Nephew; 1038; Yes; Yes Married Fannie Cooper #409
1083;1094; **Wickson**, Yates; m; 5; Miss. Choctaw; F; S; Nephew; 1039; Yes; Yes

MARTIN

1084;1095; Willie; m; 44; Miss. Choctaw; F; M; Head; 1042; Yes; Yes
1085;1096; Mary Steve; f; 38; Miss. Choctaw; F; M; Wife; 1043; Yes; Yes
1086;1097; Raymond; m; 14; Miss. Choctaw; F; S; Son; 1044; Yes; Yes
1087; 1098; Edmond J; m; 11; Miss. Choctaw; F; S; Son; 1045; Yes; Yes
1088;1099; Phillip; m; 8; Miss. Choctaw; F; S; Son; 1046; Yes; Yes
1089;1100; Annie Mae; f; 6; Miss. Choctaw; F; S; Dau; 1047; Yes; Yes
1090;1101; Harry M; m; 3; Miss. Choctaw; F; S; Son; 1048; Yes; Yes
~~1102~~; Catheline[sic]; f; 3/12; Miss. Choctaw; F; S; Dau; Yes; Yes Died 2-14-34

1091;1103; Ennis; m; 25; Miss. Choctaw; F; M; Head; 1049; Yes; Yes
~~1092;1104; Nancy Steve; f; 24; Miss. Choctaw; F; M; Wife; 1050; Yes; Yes~~ Died 6/4/34
1093;1105; Thomas; m; 4; Miss. Choctaw; F; S; Son; 1051; Yes; Yes Died 2/17/35
1094;1106; **Alex**, Herbert; m; 7; Miss. Choctaw; F; S; Step-son; 1052; Yes; Yes
1095;1107; Robert John; m; 1/12; Miss. Choctaw; F; S; Son; Yes; Yes

McMILLEN

1096;1108; Sorsby; m; 58; Miss. Choctaw; F; Wd; Head; 1053; Yes; Yes
1097;1109; Mary; f; 20; Miss. Choctaw; F; S; Dau; 1054; Yes; Yes
1098;1110; Emma; f; 19; Miss. Choctaw; F; S; Dau; 1055; Yes; Yes
1099;1111; Clarence; m; 17; Miss. Choctaw; F; S; Son; 1056; Yes; Yes
1100;1112; Bessie; f; 15; Miss. Choctaw; F; S; Dau; 1057; Yes; Yes

Census of the **Mississippi Choctaws** reservation of the **Choctaw Agency** jurisdiction, as of **April 1**, 19**34**, taken by **A. C. Hector**, Superintendent.

KEY; Surname; Stamped Census Number; Typed Census Number; Given Name; Sex; Age at Last Birthday; Tribe; Degree of Blood; Marital Status; Relationship to Head of Family; Last Census Roll Number (if given); At Jurisdiction Where Enrolled (Yes/No); At Another Jurisdiction; Post Office, County, State (if given); Ward (Yes/No)

1101;1113; Gipson; m; 10; Miss. Choctaw; F; S; Son; 1058; Yes; Yes
1102;1114; Pauline; f; 6; Miss. Choctaw; F; S; Dau; 1059; Yes; Yes

1103;1115; Lemmie; m; 24; Miss. Choctaw; F; M; Head; 1060; Yes; Yes
1104;1116; Maggie; f; 25; Miss. Choctaw; F; M; Wife; 1061; Yes; Yes
1105; **Star**, Baby; f; 6/12; Miss. Choctaw; F; S; Dau; Yes; Yes
Father Summer Star #1352

1106;1117; Cephus; m; 52; Miss. Choctaw; F; M; Head; 1062; Yes; Yes
1107;1118; Mina; f; 40; Miss. Choctaw; F; M; Wife; 1063; Yes; Yes
1108;1119; Mary; f; 21; Miss. Choctaw; F; S; Dau; 1064; Yes; Yes
Married Hobbie Davis #428
1109;1120; Willie; m; 18; Miss. Choctaw; F; S; Son; 1065; Yes; Yes
Married Mallie (Mollie) Willis #1672
1110;1121; Enochs; m; 6; Miss. Choctaw; F; S; Son; 1066; Yes; Yes
1111;1122; Lurline; f; 2; Miss. Choctaw; F; S; Dau; 1067; Yes; Yes
1112;1123; **Billy**, Clemon; m; 20; Miss. Choctaw; F; S; Step-son; 1068; Yes; Yes

1113;1124; Anthony; m; 26; Miss. Choctaw; F; M; Head; 1069; Yes; Yes
1114;1125; Venie; f; 18; Miss. Choctaw; F; M; Wife; 1070; Yes; Yes
1115;1126; Marie Theresa; f; 1; Miss. Choctaw; F; S; Dau; Yes; Yes

1116;1127; Oscar; m; 40; Miss. Choctaw; F; M; Head; 1071; Yes; Yes
1117;1128; Bennie Davis; f; 35; Miss. Choctaw; F; M; Wife; 1072; Yes; Yes
1118;1129; Arnold; m; 20; Miss. Choctaw; F; S; Son; 1073; Yes; Yes
1119;1130; Leslie; f; 12; Miss. Choctaw; F; S; Dau; 1074; Yes; Yes
1120;1131; Bert; m; 10; Miss. Choctaw; F; S; Son; 1075; Yes; Yes
1121;1132; Frances; f; 8; Miss. Choctaw; F; S; Dau; 1076; Yes; Yes
1122;1133; John; m; 5; Miss. Choctaw; F; S; Son; 1077; Yes; Yes
1123;1134; Jean; f; 3; Miss. Choctaw; F; S; Dau; 1078; Yes; Yes
1124;1135; Augustine; m; 8/12; Miss. Choctaw; F; S; Son; Yes; Yes

Census of the **Mississippi Choctaws** reservation of the **Choctaw Agency** jurisdiction, as of **April 1**, 19**34**, taken by **A. C. Hector**, Superintendent.

KEY; Surname; Stamped Census Number; Typed Census Number; Given Name; Sex; Age at Last Birthday; Tribe; Degree of Blood; Marital Status; Relationship to Head of Family; Last Census Roll Number (if given); At Jurisdiction Where Enrolled (Yes/No); At Another Jurisdiction; Post Office, County, State (if given); Ward (Yes/No)

MINGO

~~1136~~; Rich; m; 29; Miss. Choctaw; F; M: Head; 1079; Yes; Yes
   Died 10-16-34
1125;1137; Annie; f; 30; Miss. Choctaw; F; M; Wife; 1080; Yes; Yes
1126;1138; Davidson; m; 11; Miss. Choctaw; F; S; Son; 1081; Yes; Yes
1127;1139; Effie; f; 10; Miss. Choctaw; F; S; Dau; 1082; Yes; Yes

1128;1140; John; m; 58; Miss. Choctaw; F; M; Head; 1083; Yes; Yes
1129;1141; Hattie; f; 32; Miss. Choctaw; F; M: Wife; 1084; Yes; Yes
1130;1142; Arch; m; 12; Miss. Choctaw; F; S; Son; 1085; Yes; Yes
1131;1143; Otis; m; 9; Miss. Choctaw; F; S; Son; 1086; Yes; Yes
1132;1144; Sarah; f; 7; Miss. Choctaw; F; S; Dau; 1087; Yes; Yes
1133;1145; Mary; f; 4; Miss. Choctaw; F; S; Dau; 1088; Yes; Yes

1134;1146; Lilly; f; 56; Miss. Choctaw; F; Wd; Head; 1089; Yes; Yes
1135;1147; Olin; m; 16; Miss. Choctaw; F; S; Son; 1091; Yes; Yes
1136;1148; Nettie; f; 13; Miss. Choctaw; F; S; Dau; 1092; Yes; Yes

1137;1149; Jim; m; 19; Miss. Choctaw; F; M; Head; 1090; Yes; Yes
1138;1150; Sally Bell; f; 19; Miss. Choctaw; F; M; Wife; Yes; Yes
   Omitted from last census.

1139;1151; Oscar; m; 24; Miss. Choctaw; F; M; Head; 1093; Yes; Yes
1140;1152; Lena Tubby; f; 30; Miss. Choctaw; F; M; Wife; 1094; Yes; Yes

MITCH

1141;1153; Sarah; f; 50; Miss. Choctaw; F; Wd; Head; 1095; Yes; Yes
1142;1154; Elea; m; 33; Miss. Choctaw; F; S; Son; 1096; Yes; Yes
1143;1155; Divan; m; 30; Miss. Choctaw; F; S; Son; 1097; Yes; Yes
1144;1156; Wilson; m; 28; Miss. Choctaw; F; S; Son; 1098; Yes; Yes

Census of the __Mississippi Choctaws__ reservation of the __Choctaw Agency__ jurisdiction, as of __April 1__, 19__34__, taken by __A. C. Hector__, Superintendent.

KEY; Surname; Stamped Census Number; Typed Census Number; Given Name; Sex; Age at Last Birthday; Tribe; Degree of Blood; Marital Status; Relationship to Head of Family; Last Census Roll Number (if given); At Jurisdiction Where Enrolled (Yes/No); At Another Jurisdiction; Post Office, County, State (if given); Ward (Yes/No)

1145;1157; Gilmore; m; 19; Miss. Choctaw; F; S; Son; 1099; Yes; Yes

MORRIS

1146;1158; Julis[sic]; m; 32; Miss. Choctaw; F; M; Head; 1100; Yes; Yes
1147;1159; Beauty; f; 29; Miss. Choctaw; F; M; Wife; 1101; Yes; Yes
1148;1160; Eddie; m; 10; Miss. Choctaw; F; S; Son; 1102; Yes; Yes
1149;1161; Lena; f; 7; Miss. Choctaw; F; S; Dau; 1103; Yes; Yes
1150;1162; Water Olin; m; 4; Miss. Choctaw; F; S; Son; 1104; Yes; Yes

1151;1163; Moseley; m; 68; Miss. Choctaw; F; M; Head; Yes; Yes
1152;1164; Ida; f; 53; Miss. Choctaw; F; M; Wife; 1106; Yes; Yes
1153;1165; Lilly; f; 34; Miss. Choctaw; F; S; Dau; 1107; Yes; Yes
1154;1166; Wilson; m; 30; Miss. Choctaw; F; S; Son; 1109; Yes; Yes
1155;1167; Joe; m; 20; Miss. Choctaw; F; S; Son; 1110; Yes; Yes
1156;1168; **Wesley**, Sue Morris; f; 32; Miss. Choctaw; F; Wd; Grand-dau; 1108; Yes; Yes
1157;1169; **Wesley**, Rufus; m; 9; Miss. Choctaw; F; S; Son[sic]; 1111; Yes; Yes

1158;1170; Dempsey; m; 33; Miss. Choctaw; F; M; Head; 1112; Yes; Yes
1159;1171; Janie; f; 32; Miss. Choctaw; F; M; Wife; 1113; Yes; Yes
1160;1172; Ora; f; 13; Miss. Choctaw; F; S; Dau; 1114; Yes; Yes
1161;1173; Bethany; m; 10; Miss. Choctaw; F; S; Son; 1115; Yes; Yes
1162;1174; Printeas[sic]; m; 8; Miss. Choctaw; F; S; Son; 1116; Yes; Yes
1163;1175; Chester; m; 4; Miss. Choctaw; F; S; Son; 1117; Yes; Yes
1164;1176; Champ; m; 6; Miss. Choctaw; F; S; Son; 1118; Yes; Yes
1165;1177; Lester; m; 1-7/12; Miss. Choctaw; F; S; Son; 1119; Yes; Yes

1166;1178; Sallie; f; 65; Miss. Choctaw; F; Wd; Head; 1120; Yes; Yes
1167;1179; Seward; m; 33; Miss. Choctaw; F; S; Son; 1121; Yes; Yes
1168;1180; Howard; m; 27; Miss. Choctaw; F; M; Head; 1122; Yes; Yes
1169;1181; Bertie; f; 24; Miss. Choctaw; F; M; Wife; 1123; Yes; Yes

Census of the **Mississippi Choctaws** reservation of the **Choctaw Agency** jurisdiction, as of **April 1**, 19**34**, taken by **A. C. Hector**, Superintendent.

KEY; Surname; Stamped Census Number; Typed Census Number; Given Name; Sex; Age at Last Birthday; Tribe; Degree of Blood; Marital Status; Relationship to Head of Family; Last Census Roll Number (if given); At Jurisdiction Where Enrolled (Yes/No); At Another Jurisdiction; Post Office, County, State (if given); Ward (Yes/No)

1170;1182; Jimmie; m; 8; Miss. Choctaw; F; S; Son; 1124; Yes; Yes

1171;1183; Huston; m; 28; Miss. Choctaw; 1/4; M; Head; 1125; Yes; Yes
1172;1184; Bertha; f; 26; Miss. Choctaw; 1/4; M; Wife; 1126; Yes; Yes
1173;1185; **Hays**, Velma; f; 25; Miss. Choctaw; 1/4; M; Sister; 1127; Yes; Yes

1174;1186; Boston; m; 31; Miss. Choctaw; 1/4; M; Head; 1128; Yes; Yes
1175;1187; Nola; f; 29; Miss. Choctaw; 1/4; M; Wife; 1129; Yes; Yes

MOSES

1176;1188; Alma; f; 23; Miss. Choctaw; F; S; Alone; 1130; Yes; Yes

1177;1189; Allen; m; 28; Miss. Choctaw; F; M; Head; 1131; Yes; Yes
1178;1190; Florence; f; 28; Miss. Choctaw; F; M; Wife; 1132; Yes; Yes

NICKEY

1179;1191; Sam; m; 49; Miss. Choctaw; F; M; Head; 1133; Yes; Yes
1180;1192; Malessie[sic]; f; 47; Miss. Choctaw; F; M; Wife; 1134; Yes; Yes
1181;1193; Dora; f; 19; Miss. Choctaw; F; S; Dau; 1135; Yes; Yes
1182;1194; Sherman; m; 12; Miss. Choctaw; F; S; Son; 1136; Yes; Yes
1183;1195; Copeland; m; 6; Miss. Choctaw; F; S; Son; 1137; Yes; Yes

1184;1196; Billy; m; 51; Miss. Choctaw; F; M; Head; 1138; Yes; Yes
1185;1197; Fronie; f; 54; Miss. Choctaw; F; M; Wife; 1139; Yes; Yes
1186;1198; Ode; f; 25; Miss. Choctaw; F; S; Dau; 1140; Yes; Yes
1187;1199; Zelma; f; 22; Miss. Choctaw; F; S; Dau; 1141; Yes; Yes
1188;1200; Hughie; m; 19; Miss. Choctaw; F; S; Son; 1142; Yes; Yes
1189;1201; Zona; f; 17; Miss. Choctaw; F; S; Dau; 1143; Yes; Yes
 Married Riley Thomas #1403

Census of the **Mississippi Choctaws** reservation of the **Choctaw Agency** jurisdiction, as of **April 1**, 19**34**, taken by **A. C. Hector**, Superintendent.

KEY; Surname; Stamped Census Number; Typed Census Number; Given Name; Sex; Age at Last Birthday; Tribe; Degree of Blood; Marital Status; Relationship to Head of Family; Last Census Roll Number (if given); At Jurisdiction Where Enrolled (Yes/No); At Another Jurisdiction; Post Office, County, State (if given); Ward (Yes/No)

1190;1202; Cozette; m; 15; Miss. Choctaw; F; S; Son; 1144; Yes; Yes
1191;1203; Thomas; m; 11; Miss. Choctaw; F; S; Son; 1145; Yes; Yes

NOAH

1192;1204; Elizabeth; f; 62; Miss. Choctaw; F; Wd; Alone; 1146; Yes; Yes

1193;1205; Lizzie; f; 44; Miss. Choctaw; F; Wd; Head; 1147; Yes; Yes
1194;1206; Nancie; f; 18; Miss. Choctaw; F; S; Dau; 1148; Yes; Yes
1195;1207; Annie; f; 15; Miss. Choctaw; F; S; Dau; 1149; Yes; Yes

NUBBY

1196;1208; Billy; m; 74; Miss. Choctaw; F; M; Head; 1150; Yes; Yes
1197;1209; Lilly; f; 54; Miss. Choctaw; F; M; Wife; 1151; Yes; Yes

PHILLIPS

1198;1210; Riley; m; 27; Miss. Choctaw; F; M; Head; 1152; Yes; Yes
1199;1211; Lester; f; 21; Miss. Choctaw; F; M; Wife; 1153; Yes; Yes
1200;1212; Chas. Geo; m; 1-1/12; Miss. Choctaw; F; S; Son; 1154; Yes; Yes
1201;1213; Edmond; m; 7; Miss. Choctaw; F; S; Son; 1155; Yes; Yes
1202;1214; Empsey; m; 5; Miss. Choctaw; F; S; Son; 1156; Yes; Yes

POLK

1203;1215; Henry; m; 26; Miss. Choctaw; F; M: Head; 1157; Yes; Yes
1204;1216; Susie; f; 32; Miss. Choctaw; F; M; Wife; 1158; Yes; Yes
1205;1217; Sula; f; 5; Miss. Choctaw; F; S; Dau; 1159; Yes; Yes
1201218; Hudson; m; 3; Miss. Choctaw; F; S; Son; 1160; Yes; Yes

Census of the **Mississippi Choctaws** reservation of the **Choctaw Agency** jurisdiction, as of **April 1**, 19**34**, taken by **A. C. Hector**, Superintendent.

KEY; Surname; Stamped Census Number; Typed Census Number; Given Name; Sex; Age at Last Birthday; Tribe; Degree of Blood; Marital Status; Relationship to Head of Family; Last Census Roll Number (if given); At Jurisdiction Where Enrolled (Yes/No); At Another Jurisdiction; Post Office, County, State (if given); Ward (Yes/No)

1207;1219; George; m; 72; Miss. Choctaw; F; Wd; Alone; 1161; Yes; Yes

1208;1220; Francis; m; 24; Miss. Choctaw; F; M; Head; 1162; Yes; Yes
1209;1221; Odell; f; 21; Miss. Choctaw; F; M; Wife; 1163; Yes; Yes
~~1222~~; Baby; f; 6/12; Miss. Choctaw; F; S; Dau; Yes; Yes
    Died 9-12-34

1210;1223; Josie; m; 53; Miss. Choctaw; F; M; Head; 1164; Yes; Yes
1211;1224; Lennie; f; 54; Miss. Choctaw; F; M; Wife; 1165; Yes; Yes
1212;1225; Ada; f; 16; Miss. Choctaw; F; S; Dau; 1166; Yes; Yes
1213;1226; Frances; f; 15; Miss. Choctaw; F; S; Dau; 1167; Yes; Yes

1214;1227; Tom; f[sic]; 56; Miss. Choctaw; F; Wd; Head; 1168; Yes; Yes
1215;1228; Comelia[sic]; m; 24; Miss. Choctaw; F; S; Son; 1169; Yes; Yes
1216;1229; Alma; f; 20; Miss. Choctaw; F; S; Dau; 1170; Yes; Yes
1217;1230; Osborn; m; 18; Miss. Choctaw; F; S; Son; 1171; Yes; Yes

POULSON

1218;1231; Allie; f; 61; Miss. Choctaw; F; S; Alone; 1172; Yes; Yes
1219;1232; Julius; m; 27; Miss. Choctaw; F; S; Alone; 1173; Yes; Yes
1220;1233; Frank; m; 34; Miss. Choctaw; F; M: Head; 1174; Yes; Yes
1221;1234; Mary; f; 32; Miss. Choctaw; F; M; Wife; 1175; Yes; Yes

1222;1235; Eddie M; m; 27; Miss. Choctaw; F; M; Head; 1176; Yes; Yes
1223;1236; Cornelia; f; 30; Miss. Choctaw; F; M; Wife; 1177; Yes; Yes

1224;1237; Johnnie; m; 25; Miss. Choctaw; F; S; Alone; 1178; Yes; Yes

1225;1238; Charlie; m; 22; Miss. Choctaw; F; S; Alone; 1179; Yes; Yes

Census of the **Mississippi Choctaws** reservation of the **Choctaw Agency** jurisdiction, as of **April 1**, 19**34**, taken by **A. C. Hector**, Superintendent.

KEY; Surname; Stamped Census Number; Typed Census Number; Given Name; Sex; Age at Last Birthday; Tribe; Degree of Blood; Marital Status; Relationship to Head of Family; Last Census Roll Number (if given); At Jurisdiction Where Enrolled (Yes/No); At Another Jurisdiction; Post Office, County, State (if given); Ward (Yes/No)

ROBINSON

1226;1239; Thomas; m; 44; Miss. Choctaw; F; M: Head; 1180; Yes; Yes
1227;1240; Syble; f; 39; Miss. Choctaw; F; M; Wife; 1181; Yes; Yes
1228;1241; Jimmie; m; 20; Miss. Choctaw; F; S; Son; 1182; Yes; Yes
  Married Ronie Bell #87
1229;1242; Georgie; f; 18; Miss. Choctaw; F; S; Dau; 1183; Yes; Yes
1230;1243; Sallie; f; 17; Miss. Choctaw; F; S; Dau; 1184; Yes; Yes
1231;1244; Carl; m; 16; Miss. Choctaw; F; S; Son; 1185; Yes; Yes
1232;1245; Mamie; f; 14; Miss. Choctaw; F; S; Dau; 1186; Yes; Yes
1233;1246; Betsey; f; 12; Miss. Choctaw; F; S; Dau; 1187; Yes; Yes
1234;1247; Homer; m; 10; Miss. Choctaw; F; S; Son; 1188; Yes; Yes
1235;1248; Teach; m; 5; Miss. Choctaw; F; S; Son; 1189; Yes; Yes
1236;1249; Mary; f; 4; Miss. Choctaw; F; S; Dau; 1190; Yes; Yes

1237;1250; Belia; f; 27; Miss. Choctaw; F; Wd; Head; 1191; Yes; Yes
1238;1251; Campbell; m; 7; Miss. Choctaw; F; S; Son; 1192; Yes; Yes

RUTHERFORD

1239;1252; Henrietta; f; 36; Miss. Choctaw; F; S; Alone; 1193; Yes; Yes

SAM

1240;1253; Truman; m; 25; Miss. Choctaw; F; M; Head; 1194; Yes; Yes
1241;1254; Sina; f; 22; Miss. Choctaw; F; M; Wife; 1195; Yes; Yes
1242;1255; Beaman; m; 6/12; Miss. Choctaw; F; S; Son; Yes; Yes

1243;1256; Raymond; m; 53; Miss. Choctaw; F; S; Alone; 1196; Yes; Yes

1244;1257; Oscar; m; 80; Miss. Choctaw; F; M; Head; 1197; Yes; Yes
1245;1258; Mattie; f; 54; Miss. Choctaw; F; M; Wife; 1198; Yes; Yes
1246;1259; Seer; m; 20; Miss. Choctaw; F; S; Grand-son; 1199; Yes; Yes

Census of the **Mississippi Choctaws** reservation of the **Choctaw Agency** jurisdiction, as of **April 1**, 19**34**, taken by **A. C. Hector**, Superintendent.

KEY; Surname; Stamped Census Number; Typed Census Number; Given Name; Sex; Age at Last Birthday; Tribe; Degree of Blood; Marital Status; Relationship to Head of Family; Last Census Roll Number (if given); At Jurisdiction Where Enrolled (Yes/No); At Another Jurisdiction; Post Office, County, State (if given); Ward (Yes/No)

1247;1260; Lavade; f; 22; Miss. Choctaw; F; S; Grand-dau; 1200; Yes; Yes
1248;1261; Ruth Ann; f; 1-7/12; Miss. Choctaw; F; S; Great Grand-dau; 1201; Yes; Yes

1249;1262; Jimpson; m; 31; Miss. Choctaw; F; M; Head; 1202; Yes; Yes
1250;1263; Louisiana; f; 29; Miss. Choctaw; F; M; Wife; 1203; Yes; Yes
1251;1264; Etta Lee; f; 4/12; Miss. Choctaw; F; S; Dau; Yes; Yes

1252;1265; Walter; m; 44; Miss. Choctaw; F; Wd; Head; 1204; Yes; Yes
1253;1266; Grace; f; 17; Miss. Choctaw; F; S; Dau; 1205; Yes; Yes
1254;1267; Tom; m; 15; Miss. Choctaw; F; S; Son; 1206; Yes; Yes
1255;1268; Edna; f; 12; Miss. Choctaw; F; S; Dau; 1207; Yes; Yes
1256;1269; Manzie; f; 10; Miss. Choctaw; F; S; Dau; 1208; Yes; Yes

1257;1270; Fontaine; m; 48; Miss. Choctaw; F; M; Head; 1209; Yes; Yes
1258;1271; Emily; f; 44; Miss. Choctaw; F; M; Wife; 1210; Yes; Yes
1259;1272; Leona; f; 12; Miss. Choctaw; F; S; Dau; 1211; Yes; Yes
1260;1273; Elis; m; 9; Miss. Choctaw; F; S; Son; 1212; Yes; Yes
1261;1274; Fannie; f; 8; Miss. Choctaw; F; S; Dau; 1213; Yes; Yes
1262;1275; Ella Ruth; f; 6; Miss. Choctaw; F; S; Dau; 1214; Yes; Yes
1263;1276; Armond; m; 4; Miss. Choctaw; F; S; Son; 1215; Yes; Yes
1264;1277; Beaman; m; 14; Miss. Choctaw; F; S; Nephew; 1216; Yes; Yes

1265;1278; Willie; m; 35; Miss. Choctaw; F; M; Head; 1217; Yes; Yes
1266;1279; Eva; f; 33; Miss. Choctaw; F; M; Wife; 1218; Yes; Yes
1267;1280; Nettie; f; 13; Miss. Choctaw; F; S; Dau; 1219; Yes; Yes
1268;1281; Abel; m; 12; Miss. Choctaw; F; S; Son; 1220; Yes; Yes
1269;1282; Lonie; m; 10; Miss. Choctaw; F; S; Son; 1221; Yes; Yes
1270;1283; Grisaline; f; 4; Miss. Choctaw; F; S; Dau; 1222; Yes; Yes
1271;1284; Susan; f; 1-6/12; Miss. Choctaw; F; S; Dau; 1223; Yes; Yes

Census of the **Mississippi Choctaws** reservation of the **Choctaw Agency** jurisdiction, as of **April 1**, 19**34**, taken by **A. C. Hector**, Superintendent.

KEY; Surname; Stamped Census Number; Typed Census Number; Given Name; Sex; Age at Last Birthday; Tribe; Degree of Blood; Marital Status; Relationship to Head of Family; Last Census Roll Number (if given); At Jurisdiction Where Enrolled (Yes/No); At Another Jurisdiction; Post Office, County, State (if given); Ward (Yes/No)

SCOTT

1272;1285; Marshall; m; 64; Miss. Choctaw; F; M; Head; 1224; Yes; Yes
1273;1286; Lonie Tubby; f; 29; Miss. Choctaw; F; M; Wife; 1225; Yes; Yes
1274;1287; Rachel; f; 8; Miss. Choctaw; F; S; Dau; 1226; Yes; Yes
1275;1288; Maggie Mary; f; 1/12; Miss. Choctaw; F; S; Dau; Yes; Yes

SHOEMAKER

1276;1289; Susan; f; 34; Miss. Choctaw; F; Wd; Head; 1227; Yes; Yes Married Jim Wickson #1622
1277;1290; Dempsey; m; 13; Miss. Choctaw; F; S; Son; 1228; Yes; Yes
1278;1291; Layman; m; 11; Miss. Choctaw; F; S; Son; 1229; Yes; Yes
1279;1292; Ruben; m; 8; Miss. Choctaw; F; S; Son; 1230; Yes; Yes
1280;1293; Noleen; f; 5; Miss. Choctaw; F; S; Dau; 1231; Yes; Yes

1281;1294; Buck; m; 49; Miss. Choctaw; F; M; Head; 1232; Yes; Yes
1282; 1295; Annie; f; 34; Miss. Choctaw; F; M; Wife; 1233; Yes; Yes
1283;1296; Leona; f; 14; Miss. Choctaw; F; S; Dau; 1234; Yes; Yes
1284;1297; Eliza; f; 12; Miss. Choctaw; F; S; Dau; 1235; Yes; Yes
1285;1298; Martha; f; 10; Miss. Choctaw; F; S; Dau; 1236; Yes; Yes
1286;1299; Daisy; f; 8; Miss. Choctaw; F; S; Dau; 1237; Yes; Yes
1287;1300; Carrie Mae; f; 7; Miss. Choctaw; F; S; Dau; 1238; Yes; Yes
1288;1301; Hubert; m; 3; Miss. Choctaw; F; S; Son; 1239; Yes; Yes
1289;1302; Edmond; m; 1-9/12; Miss. Choctaw; F; S; Son; 1240; Yes; Yes

SIMPSON

1290;1303; John; m; 56; Miss. Choctaw; F; M; Head; 1241; Yes; Yes
1291;1304; Sallie; f; 54; Miss. Choctaw; F; M; Wife; 1242; Yes; Yes

Census of the **Mississippi Choctaws** reservation of the **Choctaw Agency** jurisdiction, as of **April 1**, 19**34**, taken by **A. C. Hector**, Superintendent.

KEY; Surname; Stamped Census Number; Typed Census Number; Given Name; Sex; Age at Last Birthday; Tribe; Degree of Blood; Marital Status; Relationship to Head of Family; Last Census Roll Number (if given); At Jurisdiction Where Enrolled (Yes/No); At Another Jurisdiction; Post Office, County, State (if given); Ward (Yes/No)

1292;1305; Pauline; f; 18; Miss. Choctaw; F; S; Dau; 1243; Yes; Yes
1293;1306; Celia; f; 15; Miss. Choctaw; F; S; Dau; 1244; Yes; Yes

SMITH

1294;1307; George; m; 62; Miss. Choctaw; F; M: Head; 1245; Yes; Yes
1295;1308; Mandy; f; 48; Miss. Choctaw; F; M; Wife; 1246; Yes; Yes
1296;1309; **Farmer**, Lilly Kate; f; 14; Miss. Choctaw; F; S; Step-dau; 1247; Yes; Yes
1297;1310; **Farmer**, Grace; f; 11; Miss. Choctaw; F; S; Step-dau; 1248; Yes; Yes
1298;1311; **Farve**, Mary Lou; f; 17; Miss. Choctaw; F; Wd; Step-dau; 1249; Yes; Yes

1299;1312; Sebe; m; 44; Miss. Choctaw; F; M; Head; 1250; Yes; Yes
1300;1313; Sinie; f; 43; Miss. Choctaw; F; M; Wife; 1251; Yes; Yes
1301;1314; Clemont; m; 15; Miss. Choctaw; F; S; Son; 1252; Yes; Yes

1302;1315; John W; m; 59; Miss. Choctaw; F; M; Head; 1253; Yes; Yes
1303;1316; Mary; f; 74; Miss. Choctaw; F; M; Wife; 1254; Yes; Yes

1304;1317; Minnie; f; 39; Miss. Choctaw; F; Wd; Head; 1255; Yes; Yes
1305;1318; Melton; m; 8; Miss. Choctaw; F; S; Son; 1256; Yes; Yes
1306;1319; Elton; m; 6; Miss. Choctaw; F; S; Son; 1257; Yes; Yes
1307;1320; **Isom**, Bailey; m; 14; Miss. Choctaw; F; S; Son; Yes; Yes
Omitted from last census.

1308;1321; Clay; m; 29; Miss. Choctaw; F; M: Head; 1259; Yes; Yes
1309;1322; Mattie; f; 32; Miss. Choctaw; F; M; Wife; 1260; Yes; Yes

SOCKEY

1310;1323; Irvin; m; 52; Miss. Choctaw; F; M; Head; 1261; Yes; Yes

Census of the **Mississippi Choctaws** reservation of the **Choctaw Agency** jurisdiction, as of **April 1**, 19**34**, taken by **A. C. Hector**, Superintendent.

KEY; Surname; Stamped Census Number; Typed Census Number; Given Name; Sex; Age at Last Birthday; Tribe; Degree of Blood; Marital Status; Relationship to Head of Family; Last Census Roll Number (if given); At Jurisdiction Where Enrolled (Yes/No); At Another Jurisdiction; Post Office, County, State (if given); Ward (Yes/No)

1311;1324; Lula; f; 39; Miss. Choctaw; F; M; Wife; 1262; Yes; Yes;
1312;1325; Benny; m; 26; Miss. Choctaw; F; S; Son; 1263; Yes; Yes
               Married Alphia Wishork #1768
1313;1326; Homer; m; 11; Miss. Choctaw; F; S; Son; 1264; Yes; Yes
1314;1327; Ill; m; 6; Miss. Choctaw; F; S; Son; 1265; Yes; Yes

1315;1328; Mike; m; 32; Miss. Choctaw; F; M; Head; 1266; Yes; Yes
1316;1329; Nephus; f; 31; Miss. Choctaw; F; M; Wife; 1267; Yes; Yes
1317;1330; Varelia; f; 12; Miss. Choctaw; F; S; Dau; 1268; Yes; Yes
1318;1331; Odell; m; 10; Miss. Choctaw; F; S; Son; 1269; Yes; Yes
1319;1332; Enochs; m; 7; Miss. Choctaw; F; S; Son; 1270; Yes; Yes
1320;1333; Reba; f; 1-8/12; Miss. Choctaw; F; S; Dau; 1271; Yes; Yes

SOLOMON

1321;1334; Willie; m; 50; Miss. Choctaw; F; M; Head; 1272; Yes; Yes
1322;1335; Onie; f; 48; Miss. Choctaw; F; M; Wife; 1273; Yes; Yes
1323;1336; **Charlie**, Beaman; m; 19; Miss. Choctaw; F; S; Step-son; 1274; Yes; Yes Married Sudie[sic] Johnson #1000
1324;1337; **Charlie**, Juanita; f; 14; Miss. Choctaw; F; S; Step-dau; 1275; Yes; Yes Married Otho Johnson #1007
1325;1338; **Charlie**, Charlie C; m; 12; Miss. Choctaw; F; S; Step-son; 1276; Yes; Yes

1326;1339; Marshall; m; 30; Miss. Choctaw; F; M; Head; 1277; Yes; Yes
1327;1340; Addie; f; 25; Miss. Choctaw; F; M; Wife; 1278; Yes; Yes
1328;1341; Johnson; m; 1-7/12; Miss. Choctaw; F; S; Son; 1279; Yes; Yes

1329;1342; Willie; m; 71; Miss. Choctaw; F; M; Head; 1280; Yes; Yes
1330;1343; Winnie L; f; 29; Miss. Choctaw; F; M; Wife; 1281; Yes; Yes
1331;1344; Mollie Lee; f; 5; Miss. Choctaw; F; S; Dau; 1282; Yes; Yes

Census of the **Mississippi Choctaws** reservation of the **Choctaw Agency** jurisdiction, as of **April 1**, 19**34**, taken by **A. C. Hector**, Superintendent.

KEY; Surname; Stamped Census Number; Typed Census Number; Given Name; Sex; Age at Last Birthday; Tribe; Degree of Blood; Marital Status; Relationship to Head of Family; Last Census Roll Number (if given); At Jurisdiction Where Enrolled (Yes/No); At Another Jurisdiction; Post Office, County, State (if given); Ward (Yes/No)

1332;1345; Raymond; m; 40; Miss. Choctaw; F; M: Head; 1283; Yes; Yes
1333;1346; Bessie; f; 40; Miss. Choctaw; F; M; Wife; 1284; Yes; Yes
1334;1347; Earnest; m; 18; Miss. Choctaw; F; S; Son; 1285; Yes; Yes
1335;1348; Murphy; m; 15; Miss. Choctaw; F; S; Son; 1286; Yes; Yes
1336;1349; Mollie; f; 12; Miss. Choctaw; F; S; Dau; 1287; Yes; Yes

STAR

1337;1350; Lucy; f; 56; Miss. Choctaw; F; Wd; Alone; 1288; Yes; Yes

1338;1351; Bill; m; 45; Miss. Choctaw; F; Wd; Head; 1289; Yes; Yes
1339;1352; Summer; m; 18; Miss. Choctaw; F; S; Son; 1290; Yes; Yes
1340;1353; Edna; f; 16; Miss. Choctaw; F; S; Dau; 1291; Yes; Yes
1341;1354; Nannie; f; 12; Miss. Choctaw; F; S; Dau; 1292; Yes; Yes
1342;1355; Mary; f; 11; Miss. Choctaw; F; S; Dau; 1293; Yes; Yes

STEPHENS

1343;1356; Nathan; m; 31; Miss. Choctaw; F; m: Head; 1294; Yes; Yes
1344;1357; Annie; f; 36; Miss. Choctaw; F; m: Wife; 1295; Yes; Yes
1345;1358; Maxton; m; 9; Miss. Choctaw; F; S; Son; 1296; Yes; Yes
1346;1359; Cutie Mae; f; 7; Miss. Choctaw; F; S; Dau; 1297; Yes; Yes
1347;1360; Dorthy D; f; 6; Miss. Choctaw; F; S; Dau; 1298; Yes; Yes
1348;1361; Bonnie B; f; 4; Miss. Choctaw; F; S; Dau; 1299; Yes; Yes
1349;1362; Franklin; m; 1-6/12; Miss. Choctaw; F; S; Son; 1300; Yes; Yes

1350;1363; Tom; m; 71; Miss. Choctaw; F; Wd; Head; 1301; Yes; Yes
1351;1364; Cornelia; f; 28; Miss. Choctaw; F; S; Dau; 1302; Yes; Yes
1352;1365; Willie; m; 24; Miss. Choctaw; F; S; Son; 1303; Yes; Yes

1353;1366; Felix; m; 29; Miss. Choctaw; F; M; Head; 1304; Yes; Yes

Census of the **Mississippi Choctaws** reservation of the **Choctaw Agency** jurisdiction, as of **April 1**, 19**34**, taken by **A. C. Hector**, Superintendent.

KEY; Surname; Stamped Census Number; Typed Census Number; Given Name; Sex; Age at Last Birthday; Tribe; Degree of Blood; Marital Status; Relationship to Head of Family; Last Census Roll Number (if given); At Jurisdiction Where Enrolled (Yes/No); At Another Jurisdiction; Post Office, County, State (if given); Ward (Yes/No)

1354;1367; Martha Farmer; f; 26; Miss. Choctaw; F; M; Wife; 1305; Yes; Yes
1355;1368; Martha Lee; f; 4; Miss. Choctaw; F; S; Dau; 1306; Yes; Yes
1356;1369; Mary Frances; f; 3; Miss. Choctaw; F; S; Dau; 1307; Yes; Yes
1357;1370; Agnes; f; 6/12; Miss. Choctaw; F; S; Dau; Yes; Yes

STEVE

~~1358;1371; Murphy; m; 60; Miss. Choctaw; F; Wd; Head; 1308; Yes; Yes~~ Died 12/9/34
1359;1372; Helen; f; 7; Miss. Choctaw; F; S; Dau; 1309; Yes; Yes
1360;1373; Winston; m; 4; Miss. Choctaw; F; S; Son; 1310; Yes; Yes
1361;1374; Josie; m; 32; Miss. Choctaw; F; M; Head; 1311; Yes; Yes
1362;1375; Maggie; f; 25; Miss. Choctaw; F; M; Wife; 1312; Yes; Yes
1363;1376; Ruby; f; 8; Miss. Choctaw; F; S; Dau; 1313; Yes; Yes
1364;1377; Jane; f; 7; Miss. Choctaw; F; S; Dau; 1314; Yes; Yes
1365;1378; Joan; f; 1-2/12; Miss. Choctaw; F; S; Dau; 1315; Yes; Yes

1366;1379; Eunis; m; 25; Miss. Choctaw; F; M; Head; 1316; Yes; Yes
1367;1380; Callie Bell; f; 22; Miss. Choctaw; F; M; Wife; 1317; Yes; Yes
1368;1381; Berniece[sic]; f; 1; Miss. Choctaw; F; S; Dau; Yes; Yes
1369;1382; **Morris**, Irene; f; 7; Miss. Choctaw; F; S; Step-dau; 1318; Yes; Yes

1370;1383; Houston; m; 46; Miss. Choctaw; F; M; Head; 1319; Yes; Yes
1371;1384; Lena; f; 42; Miss. Choctaw; F; M; Wife; 1320; Yes; Yes
1372;1385; McKinley; m; 15; Miss. Choctaw; F; S; Son; 1321; Yes; Yes
1373;1386; Yates; m; 11; Miss. Choctaw; F; S; Son; 1322; Yes; Yes
1374;1387; Marabelle; f; 7; Miss. Choctaw; F; S; Dau; 1323; Yes; Yes

1375;1388; Bobo; m; 27; Miss. Choctaw; F; M; Head; 1324; Yes; Yes
1376;1389; Lucille; f; 22; Miss. Choctaw; F; M; Wife; 1325; Yes; Yes
1377;1390; Maurice; m; 8; Miss. Choctaw; F; S; Son; 1326; Yes; Yes

Census of the **Mississippi Choctaws** reservation of the **Choctaw Agency** jurisdiction, as of **April 1**, 19**34**, taken by **A. C. Hector**, Superintendent.

KEY; Surname; Stamped Census Number; Typed Census Number; Given Name; Sex; Age at Last Birthday; Tribe; Degree of Blood; Marital Status; Relationship to Head of Family; Last Census Roll Number (if given); At Jurisdiction Where Enrolled (Yes/No); At Another Jurisdiction; Post Office, County, State (if given); Ward (Yes/No)

1378;1391; Audrey; f; 6; Miss. Choctaw; F; S; Dau; 1327; Yes; Yes
1379;1392; Vivian; f; 4; Miss. Choctaw; F; S; Dau; 1328; Yes; Yes
1380;1393; Maraurite; f; 3; Miss. Choctaw; F; S; Dau; 1329; Yes; Yes
1381;1394; Lauratina; f; 1-17 da; Miss. Choctaw; F; S; Dau; 1330; Yes; Yes

1382;1395; Smith; m; 40; Miss. Choctaw; F; M; Head; 1331; Yes; Yes
1383;1396; Winnie Smith; f; 37; Miss. Choctaw; F; M; Wife; 1332; Yes; Yes
1384;1397; Tonie; f; 14; Miss. Choctaw; F; S; Dau; 1333; Yes; Yes
1385;1398; Pauline; f; 13; Miss. Choctaw; F; S; Dau; 1334; Yes; Yes
1386;1399; Mollie; f; 9; Miss. Choctaw; F; S; Dau; 1335; Yes; Yes
1387;1400; Aileen; f; 5; Miss. Choctaw; F; S; Dau; 1336; Yes; Yes
1388;1401; Rebecca; f; 3; Miss. Choctaw; F; S; Dau; 1337; Yes; Yes
1389;1402; Curtis; m; 6/12; Miss. Choctaw; F; S; Son; Yes; Yes

STOLIBY

1390;1403; Tom; m; 31; Miss. Choctaw; F; S; Head; 1338; Yes; Yes
1391;1404; Elum Ferum; m; 8; Miss. Choctaw; F; S; Nephew; 1339; Yes; Yes

1392;1405; John; m; 44; Miss. Choctaw; F; Wd; Head; 1340; Yes; Yes
1393;1406; Nancy; f; 23; Miss. Choctaw; F; S; Dau; 1341; Yes; Yes
1394;1407; Will Banks; m; 15; Miss. Choctaw; F; S; Son; 1342; Yes; Yes
1395;1408; Otis; m; 13; Miss. Choctaw; F; S; Son; 1343; Yes; Yes
1396;1409; Zona Miller; f; 9; Miss. Choctaw; F; S; Dau; 1344; Yes; Yes

STRIBLING

1397;1410; Malissie; f; 62; Miss. Choctaw; F; Wd; Alone; 1345; Yes; Yes

Census of the **Mississippi Choctaws** reservation of the **Choctaw Agency** jurisdiction, as of **April 1**, 19**34**, taken by **A. C. Hector**, Superintendent.

KEY; Surname; Stamped Census Number; Typed Census Number; Given Name; Sex; Age at Last Birthday; Tribe; Degree of Blood; Marital Status; Relationship to Head of Family; Last Census Roll Number (if given); At Jurisdiction Where Enrolled (Yes/No); At Another Jurisdiction; Post Office, County, State (if given); Ward (Yes/No)

THOMAS

1398;1411; Lewis; m; 50; Miss. Choctaw; F; M; Head; 1346; Yes; Yes
1399;1412; Mamie; f; 47; Miss. Choctaw; F; M; Wife; 1347; Yes; Yes
1400;1413; Newman; m; 15; Miss. Choctaw; F; S; Son; 1348; Yes; Yes
1401;1414; Isaac; m; 11; Miss. Choctaw; F; S; Son; 1349; Yes; Yes
1402;1415; Mina; f; 9; Miss. Choctaw; F; S; Dau; 1350; Yes; Yes

1403;1416; Riley; m; 29; Miss. Choctaw; F; S; Alone; 1351; Yes; Yes
   Married Nona (Zona) Nickey #1189

1404;1417; Cleve; m; 31; Miss. Choctaw; F; M; Head; 1352; Yes; Yes
1405;1418; Phoebe; f; 26; Miss. Choctaw; F; M; Wife; 1353; Yes; Yes

1406;1419; Wilman; m; 34; Miss. Choctaw; F; M; Head; 1354; Yes; Yes
1407;1420; Sallie; f; 33; Miss. Choctaw; F; M; Wife; 1355; Yes; Yes
1408;1421; Woodrow; m; 15; Miss. Choctaw; F; S; Son; 1356; Yes; Yes
1409;1422; Mollie; f; 13; Miss. Choctaw; F; S; Dau; 1357; Yes; Yes
1410;1423; Golden; m; 11; Miss. Choctaw; F; S; Son; 1358; Yes; Yes
1411;1424; Amos; m; 9; Miss. Choctaw; F; S; Son; 1359; Yes; Yes
1412;1425; Single; m; 5; Miss. Choctaw; F; S; Son; 1360; Yes; Yes
1413;1426; Linnie Helen; f; 3; Miss. Choctaw; F; S; Dau; 1361; Yes; Yes

1414;1427; Lester; m; 25; Miss. Choctaw; F; M; Head; 1362; Yes; Yes
1415;1428; Rosie; f; 23; Miss. Choctaw; F; M; Wife; 1363; Yes; Yes

1416;1429; Rosie; f; 39; Miss. Choctaw; F; S; Alone; 1364; Yes; Yes

1417;1430; Leona*; f; 34; Miss. Choctaw; F; M; Head; 1365; Yes; Yes

1418;1431; Evaline*; f; 38; Miss. Choctaw; F; M; Wife; 1366; Yes; Yes
*Leona and Evaline Thomas listed above are married to white men -- no children.

Census of the __Mississippi Choctaws__ reservation of the __Choctaw Agency__ jurisdiction, as of __April 1__, 19__34__, taken by __A. C. Hector__, Superintendent.

KEY; Surname; Stamped Census Number; Typed Census Number; Given Name; Sex; Age at Last Birthday; Tribe; Degree of Blood; Marital Status; Relationship to Head of Family; Last Census Roll Number (if given); At Jurisdiction Where Enrolled (Yes/No); At Another Jurisdiction; Post Office, County, State (if given); Ward (Yes/No)

THOMPSON

1419;1432; Will; m; 30; Miss. Choctaw; F; M; Head; 1367; Yes; Yes
1420;1433; Sina; f; 27; Miss. Choctaw; F; M; Wife; 1368; Yes; Yes
1421;1434; Otis; m; 10; Miss. Choctaw; F; S; Son; 1369; Yes; Yes
1422;1435; Claudine; f; 7; Miss. Choctaw; F; S; Dau; 1370; Yes; Yes
1423;1436; Henry; m; 5; Miss. Choctaw; F; S; Son; 1371; Yes; Yes
1434;1437; Oneva; f; 3; Miss. Choctaw; F; S; Dau; 1372; Yes; Yes
1435;1438; Maxine; f; 1/12; Miss. Choctaw; F; S; Dau; Yes; Yes

1426;1439; Cephus; m; 44; Miss. Choctaw; F; M; Head; 1373; Yes; Yes
~~1440~~; Beckie; f; 29; Miss. Choctaw; F; M; Wife; Yes; Yes
    Died 2-16-34
1427;1441; Dixon; m; 20; Miss. Choctaw; F; S; Son; 1375; Yes; Yes
1428;1442; Tommy; m; 11; Miss. Choctaw; F; S; Son; 1376; Yes; Yes
1429;1443; Ellis; m; 9; Miss. Choctaw; F; S; Son; 1377; Yes; Yes
1430;1444; Annie; f; 6; Miss. Choctaw; F; S; Dau; 1378; Yes; Yes
~~1431;1445; Daniel E; m; 1 4/12; Miss. Choctaw; F; S; Son; 1379; Yes;~~
    ~~Yes~~ Died 7-18-34

1432;1446; Malinda; f; 69; Miss. Choctaw; F; Wd; Alone; 1380; Yes; Yes

1433;1447; Mose; m; 37; Miss. Choctaw; F; M; Head; 1381; Yes; Yes
1434;1448; Jean; f; 38; Miss. Choctaw; F; M; Wife; 1382; Yes; Yes
1435;1449; Jim; m; 14; Miss. Choctaw; F; S; Son; 1383; Yes; Yes
1436;1450; Annie; f; 11; Miss. Choctaw; F; S; Dau; 1384; Yes; Yes
1437;1451; Therman; m; 8; Miss. Choctaw; F; S; Son; 1385; Yes; Yes
1438;1452; Steve; m; 7; Miss. Choctaw; F; S; Son; 1386; Yes; Yes

1439;1453; John; m; 42; Miss. Choctaw; F; M; Head; 1387; Yes; Yes
1440;1454; Ludie; f; 40; Miss. Choctaw; F; M; Wife; 1388; Yes; Yes
1441;1455; Tom; m; 7; Miss. Choctaw; F; S; Son; 1391; Yes; Yes

Census of the **Mississippi Choctaws** reservation of the **Choctaw Agency** jurisdiction, as of **April 1**, 19**34**, taken by **A. C. Hector**, Superintendent.

KEY; Surname; Stamped Census Number; Typed Census Number; Given Name; Sex; Age at Last Birthday; Tribe; Degree of Blood; Marital Status; Relationship to Head of Family; Last Census Roll Number (if given); At Jurisdiction Where Enrolled (Yes/No); At Another Jurisdiction; Post Office, County, State (if given); Ward (Yes/No)

1442;1456; Tommie; m; 35; Miss. Choctaw; F; M; Head; 1392; Yes; Yes
1443;1457; Bonnie; f; 32; Miss. Choctaw; F; M; Wife; 1393; Yes; Yes
~~1458~~; Morine; f; 13; Miss. Choctaw; F; S; Dau; 1389; Yes; Yes Died 2-13-34
~~1459~~; Perry Priest; m; 2/12; Miss. Choctaw; F; S; Grand-~~dau~~ son; Yes; Yes Died 2-15-34
~~1460~~; Onie; f; 12; Miss. Choctaw; F; S; Dau; 1390; Yes; Yes Died 2-13-34
1444;1461; Nathan; m; 3; Miss. Choctaw; F; S; Son; 1394; Yes; Yes
1445;1462; Louise; f; 1-1/12; Miss. Choctaw; F; S; Dau; 1395; Yes; Yes

TUBBY

1446;1463; Dan; m; 32; Miss. Choctaw; F; M; Head; 1396; Yes; Yes
1447;1464; Lola; f; 38; Miss. Choctaw; F; M; Wife; 1397; Yes; Yes
1448;1465; Mable; f; 1/9/12[sic]; Miss. Choctaw; F; S; Dau; 1398; Yes; Yes
1449;1466; **Lewis**, Lum; m; 8; Miss. Choctaw; F; S; Step-son; 1399; Yes; Yes

1450;1467; George; m; 26; Miss. Choctaw; F; M; Head; 1400; Yes; Yes
1451;1468; Mary; f; 23; Miss. Choctaw; F; M; Wife; 1401; Yes; Yes
1452;1469; Thomas; m; 5; Miss. Choctaw; F; S; Son; 1402; Yes; Yes
1453;1470; Annie Lee; f; 1-11/12; Miss. Choctaw; F; S; Dau; 1403; Yes; Yes
1454;1471; Jennie; f; 16; Miss. Choctaw; F; S; Sister; 1404; Yes; Yes
~~1472; Comby, Vennie; f; 17; Miss. Choctaw; F; S; Step-dau; Yes; Yes~~ Omitted from last census.

1455;1473; Lefus; m; 41; Miss. Choctaw; F; M; Head; 1405; Yes; Yes
1456;1474; Frances; f; 34; Miss. Choctaw; F; M; Wife; 1406; Yes; Yes
1457;1475; Ina; f; 12; Miss. Choctaw; F; S; Dau; 1407; Yes; Yes
1458;1476; Irene; f; 10; Miss. Choctaw; F; S; Dau; 1408; Yes; Yes

Census of the **Mississippi Choctaws** reservation of the **Choctaw Agency** jurisdiction, as of **April 1**, 19**34**, taken by **A. C. Hector**, Superintendent.

KEY: Surname; Stamped Census Number; Typed Census Number; Given Name; Sex; Age at Last Birthday; Tribe; Degree of Blood; Marital Status; Relationship to Head of Family; Last Census Roll Number (if given); At Jurisdiction Where Enrolled (Yes/No); At Another Jurisdiction; Post Office, County, State (if given); Ward (Yes/No)

1459;1477; Leona; f; 7; Miss. Choctaw; F; S; Dau; 1409; Yes; Yes
1460;1478; Robert; m; 2; Miss. Choctaw; F; S; Son; 1410; Yes; Yes
1461;1479; **Ben,** Rufus; m; 16; Miss. Choctaw; F; S; Step-son; 1411; Yes; Yes
1462;1480; Sidney; m; 34; Miss. Choctaw; F; M; Head; 1412; Yes; Yes
1463;1481; Kate; f; 33; Miss. Choctaw; F; M; Wife; 1413; Yes; Yes
1464;1482; Rufus; m; 15; Miss. Choctaw; F; S; Son; 1414; Yes; Yes
1465;1483; Phelia; f; 12; Miss. Choctaw; F; S; Son; 1415; Yes; Yes
1466;1484; Eva Kate; f; 9; Miss. Choctaw; F; S; Dau; 1416; Yes; Yes
1467;1485; Edmond; m; 6; Miss. Choctaw; F; S; Son; 1417; Yes; Yes
1468;1486; Paul; m; 6/12; Miss. Choctaw; F; S; Son; Yes; Yes

1469;1487; Annis; m; 55; Miss. Choctaw; F; M; Head; 1418; Yes; Yes
1470;1488; Annie; f; 34; Miss. Choctaw; F; M; Wife; 1419; Yes; Yes

1471;1489; Edgar; m; 34; Miss. Choctaw; F; M; Head; 1420; Yes; Yes
1472;1490; Annie; f; 32; Miss. Choctaw; F; M; Wife; 1421; Yes; Yes
1473;1491; Steve; m; 13; Miss. Choctaw; F; S; Son; 1422; Yes; Yes
1474;1492; Willie; m; 12; Miss. Choctaw; F; S; Son; 1423; Yes; Yes
1475;1493; Odie; m; 10; Miss. Choctaw; F; S; Son; 1424; Yes; Yes
1476;1494; Pauline; f; 7; Miss. Choctaw; F; S; Dau; 1425; Yes; Yes

1477;1495; Dick; m; 63; Miss. Choctaw; F; M; Head; 1426; Yes; Yes
1478;1496; Eline; f; 54; Miss. Choctaw; F; M; Wife; 1427; Yes; Yes
1479; 1497; Jeff; m; 28; Miss. Choctaw; F; s; Nephew; 1428; Yes; Yes

~~1498~~; Allan; m; 78; Miss. Choctaw; F; Wd; Head; 1429; Yes; Yes
    Died 9-11-33

1480;1499; Pat; m; 40; Miss. Choctaw; F; M; Head; 1432; Yes; Yes
1481;1500; Frances; f; 40; Miss. Choctaw; F; M; Wife; 1433; Yes; Yes
1482;1501; Vernal; m; 22; Miss. Choctaw; F; S; Son; 1434; Yes; Yes
    Married Ana (Anna) Willis #1725

Census of the **Mississippi Choctaws** reservation of the **Choctaw Agency** jurisdiction, as of **April 1**, 19**34**, taken by **A. C. Hector**, Superintendent.

KEY; Surname; Stamped Census Number; Typed Census Number; Given Name; Sex; Age at Last Birthday; Tribe; Degree of Blood; Marital Status; Relationship to Head of Family; Last Census Roll Number (if given); At Jurisdiction Where Enrolled (Yes/No); At Another Jurisdiction; Post Office, County, State (if given); Ward (Yes/No)

1483;1502; Earnest; m; 14; Miss. Choctaw; F; S; Son; 1435; Yes; Yes
1484;1503; Loraine; f; 12; Miss. Choctaw; F; S; Dau; 1436; Yes; Yes
1485;1504; Alice; f; 10; Miss. Choctaw; F; S; Dau; 1437; Yes; Yes
1486;1505; Aileen; f; 7; Miss. Choctaw; F; S; Dau; 1438; Yes; Yes
1487;1506; Lysander; m; 46; Miss. Choctaw; F; M; Head; 1439; Yes; Yes

1488;1507; Moley; m; 31; Miss. Choctaw; F; M; Head; 1440; Yes; Yes
1489;1508; Sallie; f; 27; Miss. Choctaw; F; M; Wife; 1441; Yes; Yes
1490;1509; Grace; f; 1-9/12; Miss. Choctaw; F; S; Dau; 1442; Yes; Yes

1491;1510; Adam; m; 32; Miss. Choctaw; F; S; Alone; 1443; Yes; Yes

1492;1511; Dewitt; m; 27; Miss. Choctaw; F; M; Head; 1444; Yes; Yes
1493;1512; Katie; f; 28; Miss. Choctaw; F; M; Wife; 1445; Yes; Yes
1494;1513; Cicero L; m; 1-6/12; Miss. Choctaw; F; S; Son; 1446; Yes; Yes

~~1514~~; Rainey; f; 65; Miss. Choctaw; F; Wd; Head; 1447; Yes; Yes Died 9-11-33
1495;1515; Lena; f; 34; Miss. Choctaw; F; S; Dau; 1448; Yes; Yes
1496;1516; Mollie; f; 29; Miss. Choctaw; F; S; Dau; 1449; Yes; Yes
1497;1517; Herbert; m; 26; Miss. Choctaw; F; S; Son; 1450; Yes; Yes

~~1498;1518; Jimpson; m; 70; Miss. Choctaw; F; Wd; Alone; 1451; Yes; Yes~~ Died 9/6/35

1499;1519; Anderson; m; 34; Miss. Choctaw; F; M; Head; 1452; Yes; Yes
1500;1520; Nancy; f; 24; Miss. Choctaw; F; M; Wife; 1453; Yes; Yes
1501;1521; Jim; m; 10; Miss. Choctaw; F; S; Son; 1454; Yes; Yes
1502;1522; Isa; f; 8; Miss. Choctaw; F; S; Dau; 1455; Yes; Yes
1503;1523; Buracy; f; 6; Miss. Choctaw; F; S; Dau; 1456; Yes; Yes
1504;1524; Etolye; f; 4; Miss. Choctaw; F; S; Dau; 1457; Yes; Yes

Census of the **Mississippi Choctaws** reservation of the **Choctaw Agency** jurisdiction, as of **April 1**, 19**34**, taken by **A. C. Hector**, Superintendent.

KEY; Surname; Stamped Census Number; Typed Census Number; Given Name; Sex; Age at Last Birthday; Tribe; Degree of Blood; Marital Status; Relationship to Head of Family; Last Census Roll Number (if given); At Jurisdiction Where Enrolled (Yes/No); At Another Jurisdiction; Post Office, County, State (if given); Ward (Yes/No)

1505;1525; Evan; m; 41; Miss. Choctaw; F; m: Head; 1458; Yes; Yes
1506;1526; Jennie; f; 46; Miss. Choctaw; F; M; Wife; 1459; Yes; Yes
1507;1527; Annie; f; 11; Miss. Choctaw; F; S; Dau; 1460; Yes; Yes
1508;1528; Charlie; m; 38; Miss. Choctaw; F; M: Head; 1461; Yes; Yes
1509;1529; Betsey Scott; f; 33; Miss. Choctaw; F; M; Wife; 1462; Yes; Yes
1510;1530; Alice; f; 11; Miss. Choctaw; F; S; Dau; 1463; Yes; Yes
1511;1531; Jack; m; 9; Miss. Choctaw; F; S; Son; 1464; Yes; Yes
1512;1532; J. C; m; 7; Miss. Choctaw; F; S; Son; 1465; Yes; Yes
1513;1533; Colleen; f; 7; Miss. Choctaw; F; S; Dau; 1466; Yes; Yes
1514;1534; Bessie; f; 2; Miss. Choctaw; F; S; Dau; 1467; Yes; Yes
1515;1535; Kate; f; 13; Miss. Choctaw; F; S; Step-dau; 1468; Yes; Yes
1516;1536; Ellis; m; 10; Miss. Choctaw; F; S; O4phan[sic]; 1469; Yes; Yes
~~1537~~; Jane; f; 3/12; Miss. Choctaw; F; S; Dau; Yes; Yes
Died 2-5-34
~~1538~~; Jean; f; 3/12; Miss. Choctaw; F; S; Dau; Yes; Yes
Died 2-6-34

1517;1539; Henderson; m; 41; Miss. Choctaw; F; M; Head; 1470; Yes; Yes
1518;1540; Maggie; f; 29; Miss. Choctaw; F; M; Wife; 1471; Yes; Yes
1519;1541; Otis; f; 11; Miss. Choctaw; F; S; Dau; 1472; Yes; Yes
1520;1542; W. C; m; 9; Miss. Choctaw; F; S; Son; 1473; Yes; Yes
1521;1543; Gladys; f; 7; Miss. Choctaw; F; S; Dau; 1474; Yes; Yes
1522;1544; Finis; m; 7; Miss. Choctaw; F; S; Son; 1475; Yes; Yes
1523;1545; Martha Lee; f; 3; Miss. Choctaw; F; S; Dau; 1476; Yes; Yes
1524;1546; James H; m; 1-9/12; Miss. Choctaw; F; S; Son; 1477; Yes; Yes

1525;1547; Clemon; m; 59; Miss. Choctaw; F; M: Head; 1478; Yes; Yes
1526;1548; Alice; f; 59; Miss. Choctaw; F; M; Wife; 1479; Yes; Yes
1527;1549; Joe; m; 25; Miss. Choctaw; F; S; Son; 1480; Yes; Yes

Census of the **Mississippi Choctaws** reservation of the **Choctaw Agency** jurisdiction, as of **April 1**, 19**34**, taken by **A. C. Hector**, Superintendent.

KEY; Surname; Stamped Census Number; Typed Census Number; Given Name; Sex; Age at Last Birthday; Tribe; Degree of Blood; Marital Status; Relationship to Head of Family; Last Census Roll Number (if given); At Jurisdiction Where Enrolled (Yes/No); At Another Jurisdiction; Post Office, County, State (if given); Ward (Yes/No)

1528;1550; Elias; m; 8; Miss. Choctaw; F; S; Great-nephew; 1481; Yes; Yes

1529;1551; Sarah; f; 7; Miss. Choctaw; F; S; Great-niece; 1482; Yes; Yes

1530;1552; Jackson; m; 26; Miss. Choctaw; F; M; Head; 1483; Yes; Yes
1531;1553; Malissa; f; 27; Miss. Choctaw; F; M: Wife; 1484; Yes; Yes
1532;1554; Coleman; m; 1-5/12; Miss. Choctaw; F; S; Son; 1485; Yes; Yes

1533;1555; Nichols; m; 36; Miss. Choctaw; F; M; Head; 1486; Yes; Yes
1534;1556; Esther; f; 31; Miss. Choctaw; F; M; Wife; 1487; Yes; Yes
1535;1557; Sullivan; m; 12; Miss. Choctaw; F; S; Son; 1488; Yes; Yes
1536;1558; Alice; f; 11; Miss. Choctaw; F; S; Dau; 1489; Yes; Yes
1537;1559; Minnie; f; 9; Miss. Choctaw; F; S; Dau; 1490; Yes; Yes
1538;1560; Catherine; f; 7; Miss. Choctaw; F; S; Dau; 1491; Yes; Yes

1539;1561; Alice; f; 44; Miss. Choctaw; F; Wd; Head; 1492; Yes; Yes
1540;1562; **Johnson**, Lee; m; 22; Miss. Choctaw; F; S; Son; 1493; Yes; Yes

1541;1563; Tom; m; 25; Miss. Choctaw; F; M: Head; 1494; Yes; Yes
1542;1564; Marceline; f; 27; Miss. Choctaw; F; M: Wife; 1495; Yes; Yes
1543;1565; Inis; m; 4; Miss. Choctaw; F; S; Son; 1496; Yes; Yes
1544;1566; Leonard; m; 1-6/12; Miss. Choctaw; F; S; Son; 1497; Yes; Yes
1545;1567; Joseph; m; 7; Miss. Choctaw; F; S; Son; 1498; Yes; Yes

1546;1568; Anderson; m; 42; Miss. Choctaw; F; M; Head; 1499; Yes; Yes
1547;1569; Lousiana; f; 44; Miss. Choctaw; F; M; Wife; 1500; Yes; Yes
1548;1570; Hazel; f; 20; Miss. Choctaw; F; S; Dau; 1501; Yes; Yes
1549;1571; Smith; m; 18; Miss. Choctaw; F; S; Son; 1502; Yes; Yes
1550;1572; Icy; f; 16; Miss. Choctaw; F; S; Dau; 1503; Yes; Yes

Census of the __Mississippi Choctaws__ reservation of the __Choctaw Agency__ jurisdiction, as of __April 1__, 19__34__, taken by __A. C. Hector__, Superintendent.

KEY; Surname; Stamped Census Number; Typed Census Number; Given Name; Sex; Age at Last Birthday; Tribe; Degree of Blood; Marital Status; Relationship to Head of Family; Last Census Roll Number (if given); At Jurisdiction Where Enrolled (Yes/No); At Another Jurisdiction; Post Office, County, State (if given); Ward (Yes/No)

1551;1573; John; m; 14; Miss. Choctaw; F; S; Son; 1504; Yes; Yes

1552;1574; Simpson; m; 74; Miss. Choctaw; F; M; Head; Yes; Yes
1553;1575; Minnie; f; 41; Miss. Choctaw; F; M; Wife; 1506; Yes; Yes
1554;1576; Ike; m; 22; Miss. Choctaw; F; S; Son; 1507; Yes; Yes
1555;1577; Henry; m; 21; Miss. Choctaw; F; S; Son; 1508; Yes; Yes
1556;1578; Lewis; m; 17; Miss. Choctaw; F; S; Son; 1509; Yes; Yes
1557;1579; McKinley; m; 14; Miss. Choctaw; F; S; Son; 1510; Yes; Yes
1558;1580; Hudson; m; 11; Miss. Choctaw; F; S; Son; 1511; Yes; Yes
1559;1581; Sullivan; m; 10; Miss. Choctaw; F; S; Son; 1512; Yes; Yes
1560;1582; Callie; f; 8; Miss. Choctaw; F; S; Dau; 1513; Yes; Yes
1561;1583; Nellie; f; 7; Miss. Choctaw; F; S; Dau; 1514; Yes; Yes

1562;1584; D; m; 33; Miss. Choctaw; F; M; Head; Yes; Yes
Omitted from last census.
1563;1585; Lilly Allen; f; 29; Miss. Choctaw; F; M; Wife; Yes; Yes
Omitted from last census.
1564;1586; Susie Anne; f; 26; Miss. Choctaw; F; S; Sister; Yes; Yes
Omitted from last census.
1565;1587; R. B; m; 3; Miss. Choctaw; F; S; Son; Yes; Yes
Omitted from last census.

TUCKALOO

1566;1588; Frances; f; 71; Miss. Choctaw; F; Wd; Head; 1515; Yes; Yes
1567;1589; **Tubby**, Wesley; m; 15; Miss. Choctaw; F; S; Grand-son; 1516; Yes; Yes
1568;1590; Mason; m; 20; Miss. Choctaw; F; S; Grand-son; 1517; Yes; Yes
1569;1591; Enia; m; 10; Miss. Choctaw; F; S; Grand-son; 1518; Yes; Yes
1570;1592; Alice; f; 9; Miss. Choctaw; F; S; Grand-dau; 1519; Yes; Yes
1571;1593; Sarah; f; 8; Miss. Choctaw; F; S; Grand-dau; 1520; Yes; Yes

Census of the **Mississippi Choctaws** reservation of the **Choctaw Agency** jurisdiction, as of **April 1**, 19**34**, taken by **A. C. Hector**, Superintendent.

KEY; Surname; Stamped Census Number; Typed Census Number; Given Name; Sex; Age at Last Birthday; Tribe; Degree of Blood; Marital Status; Relationship to Head of Family; Last Census Roll Number (if given); At Jurisdiction Where Enrolled (Yes/No); At Another Jurisdiction; Post Office, County, State (if given); Ward (Yes/No)

VAUGHN

1572;1594; John; m; 69; Miss. Choctaw; F; Wd; Alone; 1521; Yes; Yes
    Died Oct. 19, 1935
1573;1595; Greer; m; 59; Miss. Choctaw; F; M; Head; 1522; Yes; Yes
1574;1596; Jane; f; 54; Miss. Choctaw; F; M; Wife; 1523; Yes; Yes
1575;1597; Agnes; f; 8; Miss. Choctaw; F; S; Dau; 1524; Yes; Yes

1576;1598; Cooksie; m; 67; Miss. Choctaw; F; M; Head; 1525; Yes; Yes
1577;1599; Susan; f; 62; Miss. Choctaw; F; M; Wife; 1526; Yes; Yes
    Died 4/12/35
1578;1600; Lena; f; 39; Miss. Choctaw; F; S; Dau; 1527; Yes; Yes
1579;1601; Ludie; f; 27; Miss. Choctaw; F; S; Dau; 1528; Yes; Yes

1580;1602; Silmon; m; 22; Miss. Choctaw; F; M; Head; 1529; Yes; Yes
1581;1603; Seta; f; 18; Miss. Choctaw; F; M; Wife; 1530; Yes; Yes

1582;1604; Howard; m; 32; Miss. Choctaw; F; M; Head; 1531; Yes; Yes
1583;1605; Bessie; f; 32; Miss. Choctaw; F; M; Wife; 1532; Yes; Yes
1584;1606; Clifton; m; 8; Miss. Choctaw; F; S; 1533; Yes; Yes
    1607; Mary Rose; f; 6; Miss. Choctaw; F; S; Dau; 1534; Yes; Yes
    Died 3-23-34
1585;1608; Monroe; m; 8/12; Miss. Choctaw; F; S; Son; Yes; Yes

1586;1609; John; m; 28; Miss. Choctaw; F; M; Head; 1535; Yes; Yes
1587;1610; Melissa; f; 41; Miss. Choctaw; F; M; Wife; 1536; Yes; Yes
1588;1611; Mollie; d; 21; Miss. Choctaw; F; S; Step-dau; 1537; Yes; Yes
1589;1612; Annie; f; 16; Miss. Choctaw; F; S; Step-dau; 1538; Yes; Yes

WAITER

1590;1613; Gipson; m; 71; Miss. Choctaw; F; Wd; Alone; 1539; Yes; Yes

Census of the **Mississippi Choctaws** reservation of the **Choctaw Agency** jurisdiction, as of **April 1**, 19**34**, taken by **A. C. Hector**, Superintendent.

KEY; Surname; Stamped Census Number; Typed Census Number; Given Name; Sex; Age at Last Birthday; Tribe; Degree of Blood; Marital Status; Relationship to Head of Family; Last Census Roll Number (if given); At Jurisdiction Where Enrolled (Yes/No); At Another Jurisdiction; Post Office, County, State (if given); Ward (Yes/No)

1591;1614; Minnie; f; 58; Miss. Choctaw; F; Wd; Alone; 1540; Yes; Yes

1592;1615; Lonnie; m; 29; Miss. Choctaw; F; M; Head; 1541; Yes; Yes
1593;1616; Sue; f; 24; Miss. Choctaw; F; M; Wife; 1542; Yes; Yes
1594;1617; Cora Mae; f; 3; Miss. Choctaw; F; S; Dau; 1543; Yes; Yes
1595;1618; Baby; f; 9/12; Miss. Choctaw; F; S; Dau; Yes; Yes

WALLACE

1596;1619; Comby; m; 62; Miss. Choctaw; F; M; Head; 1544; Yes; Yes
1597;1620; Betty Dixon; f; 58; Miss. Choctaw; F; M; Wife; 1545; Yes; Yes
1598;1621; Maggie; f; 17; Miss. Choctaw; F; S; Dau; 1547; Yes; Yes
1599;1622; Tom; m; 13; Miss. Choctaw; F; S; Son; 1548; Yes; Yes
1600;1623; Fulton; m; 10; Miss. Choctaw; F; S; Son; 1549; Yes; Yes
1601;1624; Amy; f; 19; Miss. Choctaw; F; S; Dau; Yes; Yes
Omitted from last census

1602;1625; Eunice; f; 44; Miss. Choctaw; F; Wd; Head; 1550; Yes; Yes
1603;1626; Susie; f; 21; Miss. Choctaw; F; S; Dau; 1551; Yes; Yes
1604;1627; Henry; m; 19; Miss. Choctaw; F; S; Son; 1552; Yes; Yes
1605;1628; Celia; f; 18; Miss. Choctaw; F; S; Dau; 1553; Yes; Yes
1606;1629; Austin; m; 7; Miss. Choctaw; F; S; Son; 1554; Yes; Yes

WALLACE (WILLIS)

1607;1630; Columbus; m; 24; Miss. Choctaw; F; M; Head; 1557; Yes; Yes
1608;1631; Emma Dixon; f; 22; Miss. Choctaw; F; M; Wife; 1558; Yes; Yes
~~1632~~; Richard; m; 2/12; Miss. Choctaw; F; S; Son; Yes; Yes
Died 3-1-34

Census of the **Mississippi Choctaws** reservation of the **Choctaw Agency** jurisdiction, as of **April 1**, 19**34**, taken by **A. C. Hector**, Superintendent.

KEY: Surname; Stamped Census Number; Typed Census Number; Given Name; Sex; Age at Last Birthday; Tribe; Degree of Blood; Marital Status; Relationship to Head of Family; Last Census Roll Number (if given); At Jurisdiction Where Enrolled (Yes/No); At Another Jurisdiction; Post Office, County, State (if given); Ward (Yes/No)

WALLACE

1609;1633; Stenot; m; 26; Miss. Choctaw; F; M; Head; 1559; Yes; Yes
1610;1634; Annie; f; 21; Miss. Choctaw; F; M; Wife; 15605[sic]; Yes; Yes
1611;1635; Houston; m; 14; Miss. Choctaw; F; S; Orphan; 1561; Yes; Yes
1612;1636; Brigam[sic]; m; 1½; Miss. Choctaw; F; S; Son; Yes; Yes
Omitted from last census

WARNER (GIPSON)

1613;1637; Johnnie L; m; 22; Miss. Choctaw; F; S; Alone; 1562; Yes; Yes

WESLEY

1614;1638; Sidney; m; 69; Miss. Choctaw; F; Wd; Alone; 1563; Yes; Yes

1615;1639; Cameron; m; 44; Miss. Choctaw; F; M; Head; 1564; Yes; Yes
1616;1640; Julie Bell; f; 30; Miss. Choctaw; F; M; Wife; 1565; Yes; Yes
1617;1641; John; m; 9; Miss. Choctaw; F; S; Son; 1567; Yes; Yes
1618;1642; Willie B; m; 6; Miss. Choctaw; F; S; Son; 1568; Yes; Yes
1619;1643; Hubert; m; 8/12; Miss. Choctaw; F; S; Son; Yes; Yes

1620;1644; Bennie; m; 17; Miss. Choctaw; F; M; Head; 1566; Yes; Yes
1621;1645; Leona Willis; f; 19; Miss. Choctaw; F; M; Wife; 1556; Yes; Yes

WICKSON

1622;1646; Jim; m; 26; Miss. Choctaw; F; Wd; Alone; 1569; Yes; Yes
Married Susan Davis Shoemaker #1276

Census of the **Mississippi Choctaws** reservation of the **Choctaw Agency** jurisdiction, as of **April 1**, 19**34**, taken by **A. C. Hector**, Superintendent.

KEY; Surname; Stamped Census Number; Typed Census Number; Given Name; Sex; Age at Last Birthday; Tribe; Degree of Blood; Marital Status; Relationship to Head of Family; Last Census Roll Number (if given); At Jurisdiction Where Enrolled (Yes/No); At Another Jurisdiction; Post Office, County, State (if given); Ward (Yes/No)

WILEY

1623;1647; Lizzie; f; 64; Miss. Choctaw; F; S; Alone; 1570; Yes; Yes

WILLIAMS

1624;1648; Jonas; m; 59; Miss. Choctaw; F; M; Head; 1571; Yes; Yes
1625;1649; Maggie; f; 49; Miss. Choctaw; F; M; Wife; 1572; Yes; Yes

1626;1650; Tony; m; 25; Miss. Choctaw; F; M; Head; 1573; Yes; Yes
1627;1651; Mary Alice D; f; 19; Miss. Choctaw; F; M; Wife; 442; Yes; Yes
1628;1652; Johnson; m; 9/12; Miss. Choctaw; F; S; Son; Yes; Yes

1629;1653; Rufus; m; 27; Miss. Choctaw; F; M; Head; 1574; Yes; Yes
1630;1654; Nellie Sullivan; f; 33; Miss. Choctaw; F; M; Wife; 1575; Yes; Yes
1631;1655; Rufus; m; 3/12; Miss. Choctaw; F; S; Son; Yes; Yes
1632;1657; Phillip; m; 11; Miss. Choctaw; F; S; Son; 1577; Yes; Yes
1633;1656; Evan; m; 12; Miss. Choctaw; F; S; Son; 1576; Yes; Yes
1634;1658; Fillman; m; 7; Miss. Choctaw; F; S; Son; 1578; Yes; Yes
1635;1659; Coy; m; 5; Miss. Choctaw; F; S; Son; 1579; Yes; Yes

1636;1660; Jennie; f; 90; Miss. Choctaw; F; Wd; Head; 1580; Yes; Yes
1637;1661; Fate; m; 45; Miss. Choctaw; F; S; Son; 1581; Yes; Yes

1638;1662; Lewis; m; 57; Miss. Choctaw; F; M; Head; 1582; Yes; Yes
1639;1663; Mamie Smith; f; 35; Miss. Choctaw; F; M; Wife; 1583; Yes; Yes
1640;1664; Mary Ann; f; 9; Miss. Choctaw; F; S; Dau; 1584; Yes; Yes
1641;1665; Sarah; f; 5; Miss. Choctaw; F; S; Dau; 1585; Yes; Yes
1642;1666; Carter; m; 3; Miss. Choctaw; F; S; Son; 1586; Yes; Yes
1643;1667; Lurline; f; 6/12; Miss. Choctaw; F; S; Dau; Yes; Yes

Census of the **Mississippi Choctaws** reservation of the **Choctaw Agency** jurisdiction, as of **April 1**, 19**34**, taken by **A. C. Hector**, Superintendent.

KEY; Surname; Stamped Census Number; Typed Census Number; Given Name; Sex; Age at Last Birthday; Tribe; Degree of Blood; Marital Status; Relationship to Head of Family; Last Census Roll Number (if given); At Jurisdiction Where Enrolled (Yes/No); At Another Jurisdiction; Post Office, County, State (if given); Ward (Yes/No)

1644;1668; **Lewis**, Johnnie; m; 36; Miss. Choctaw; F; Wd; Brother-in-law; 1587; Yes; Yes

WILLIAMSON

1645;1669; Mack; m; 59; Miss. Choctaw; F; M; Head; 1588; Yes; Yes
1646;1670; Ida; f; 59; Miss. Choctaw; F; M; Wife; 1589; Yes; Yes
1647;1671; Arnold; m; 15; Miss. Choctaw; F; S; Son; 1590; Yes; Yes
1648;1672; **Lewis**, Marceline; f; 10; Miss. Choctaw; F; S; Grand-dau; 1591; Yes; Yes

1649;1673; Bike; m; 42; Miss. Choctaw; F; M; Head; 1592; Yes; Yes
1650;1674; Effie; f; 30; Miss. Choctaw; F; M; Wife; 1593; Yes; Yes
1651;1675; Mary; f; 14; Miss. Choctaw; F; S; Dau; 1594; Yes; Yes
1652;1676; Lallie; f; 12; Miss. Choctaw; F; S; Dau; 1595; Yes; Yes

WILLIS

1653;1677; Bill; m; 38; Miss. Choctaw; F; M; Head; 1596; Yes; Yes
1654;1678; Savenie Smith; f; 32; Miss. Choctaw; F; M; Wife; 1597; Yes; Yes
1655;1679; Claud Y; m; 15; Miss. Choctaw; F; S; Son; 1598; Yes; Yes
1656;1680; Elsie; f; 14; Miss. Choctaw; F; S; Dau; 1599; Yes; Yes
1657;1681; William B; m; 11; Miss. Choctaw; F; S; Son; 1600; Yes; Yes
1658;1682; John Joseph; m; 6/12; Miss. Choctaw; F; S; Son; Yes; Yes

1659;1683; Nath; m; 27; Miss. Choctaw; F; M; Head; 1601; Yes; Yes
1660;1684; Esther; f; 31; Miss. Choctaw; F; M; Wife; 1602; Yes; Yes
1661;1685; Sylvia; f; 6; Miss. Choctaw; F; S; Dau; 1603; Yes; Yes
1662;1686; Josie; m; 5; Miss. Choctaw; F; S; Son; 1604; Yes; Yes
1663;1687; Given; m; 4; Miss. Choctaw; F; S; Son; Yes; Yes
Omitted from last Census
1664;1688; Ike; m; 27; Miss. Choctaw; F; M: Head; 1605; Yes; Yes

Census of the **Mississippi Choctaws** reservation of the **Choctaw Agency** jurisdiction, as of **April 1**, 19**34**, taken by **A. C. Hector**, Superintendent.

KEY; Surname; Stamped Census Number; Typed Census Number; Given Name; Sex; Age at Last Birthday; Tribe; Degree of Blood; Marital Status; Relationship to Head of Family; Last Census Roll Number (if given); At Jurisdiction Where Enrolled (Yes/No); At Another Jurisdiction; Post Office, County, State (if given); Ward (Yes/No)

1665;1689; Ellen; f; 25; Miss. Choctaw; F; M; Wife; 1606; Yes; Yes
1666;1690; Allen; m; 8; Miss. Choctaw; F; S; Son; 1607; Yes; Yes
1667;1691; Chester; m; 5; Miss. Choctaw; F; S; Son; 1608; Yes; Yes
1668;1692; Leo; m; 4; Miss. Choctaw; F; S; Son; Yes; Yes
    Omitted from last census
1669;1693; Sina; f[sic]; 2; Miss. Choctaw; F; S; Son; Yes; Yes
    Omitted from last census

1670;1694; Robert; m; 46; Miss. Choctaw; F; M; Head; 1609; Yes; Yes
1671;1695; Celie; f; 33; Miss. Choctaw; F; M; wife; 1610; Yes; Yes
1672;1696; Mollie; f; 22; Miss. Choctaw; F; S; Dau; 1611; Yes; Yes
    Married Willie McMillan #1109
1673;1697; **Ben**, Wilson; m; 14; Miss. Choctaw; F; S; Orphan; 1612; Yes; Yes

1674;1698; Finis; m; 32; Miss. Choctaw; F; M; Head; 1613; Yes; Yes
1675;1699; Nora; f; 27; Miss. Choctaw; F; M; Wife; 1614; Yes; Yes
1676;1700; Leona; f; 5; Miss. Choctaw; F; S; Dau; 1615; Yes; Yes
1677;1701; Sarah; f; 3; Miss. Choctaw; F; S; Dau; 1616; Yes; Yes

1678;1702; John; m; 28; Miss. Choctaw; F; M; Head; 1617; Yes; Yes
1679;1703; Susana; f; 20; Miss. Choctaw; F; M; Wife; 1618; Yes; Yes

1680;1704; Johnson; m; 69; Miss. Choctaw; F; Wd; Alone; 1619; Yes; Yes   Died July 27, 1934

1681;1705; Gus; m; 61; Miss. Choctaw; F; M; Head; 1620; Yes; Yes
1682;1706; Rainey; f; 37; Miss. Choctaw; F; M; Wife; 1621; Yes; Yes
1683;1707; Hester; m; 7; Miss. Choctaw; F; S; Son; 1622; Yes; Yes
1684;1708; Lester; m; 3; Miss. Choctaw; F; S; Son; 1623; Yes; Yes
1685;1709; **Isaac**, William; m; 21; Miss. Choctaw; F; S; Step-son; 1624; Yes; Yes

Census of the **Mississippi Choctaws** reservation of the **Choctaw Agency** jurisdiction, as of **April 1**, 19**34**, taken by **A. C. Hector**, Superintendent.

KEY; Surname; Stamped Census Number; Typed Census Number; Given Name; Sex; Age at Last Birthday; Tribe; Degree of Blood; Marital Status; Relationship to Head of Family; Last Census Roll Number (if given); At Jurisdiction Where Enrolled (Yes/No); At Another Jurisdiction; Post Office, County, State (if given); Ward (Yes/No)

1686;1710; **Isaac**, Nannie; f; 17; Miss. Choctaw; F; S; Step-dau; 1625; Yes; Yes
1687;1711; **Isaac**, Eunice; f; 14; Miss. Choctaw; F; S; Step-dau; 1626; Yes; Yes
1688;1712; **Isaac**, Rose; f; 10; Miss. Choctaw; F; S; Step-dau; 1627; Yes; Yes

1689;1713; Gamblin; m; 34; Miss. Choctaw; F; M; Head; 1628; Yes; Yes
1690;1714; Ellen Hickman; f; 36; Miss. Choctaw; F; M; Wife; 1629; Yes; Yes
1691;1715; Mattie; f; 16; Miss. Choctaw; F; S; Dau; 1630; Yes; Yes
Married J. C. Allen #18
~~1716~~; Jake; m; 3/12; Miss. Choctaw; F; S; Son; Yes; Yes
Died 3-25-34
1692;1718; Eula; f; 11; Miss. Choctaw; F; S; Dau; 1632; Yes; Yes
1693;1717; G. C; m; 13; Miss. Choctaw; F; S; Son; 1631; Yes; Yes
1694;1719; Maurice; f[sic]; 10; Miss. Choctaw; F; S; Dau; 1633; Yes; Yes
1695;1720; Marabelle; f; 5; Miss. Choctaw; F; S; Dau; 1634; Yes; Yes
1696;1721; Earl; m; 3; Miss. Choctaw; F; S; Son; 1635; Yes; Yes

1697;1722; Ed; m; 63; Miss. Choctaw; F; Wd; Alone; 1636; Yes; Yes

1698;1723; Joe; m; 65; Miss. Choctaw; F; M; Head; 1637; Yes; Yes
1699;1724; Adaline; f; 62; Miss. Choctaw; F; M; Wife; 1638; Yes; Yes
1700;1725; Nannie; f; 424[sic]; Miss. Choctaw; F; S; Grand-dau; 1639; Yes; Yes

1701;1726; Ellis; m; 31; Miss. Choctaw; F; S; Alone; 1640; Yes; Yes

1702;1727; Jim; m; 56; Miss. Choctaw; F; M; Head; 1641; Yes; Yes
1703;1728; Louisa; f; 54; Miss. Choctaw; F; M; Wife; 1642; Yes; Yes
1704;1729; Tom; m; 32; Miss. Choctaw; F; S; Son; 1643; Yes; Yes
1705;1730; Dennis; m; 30; Miss. Choctaw; F; S; Son; 1644; Yes; Yes

Census of the **Mississippi Choctaws** reservation of the **Choctaw Agency** jurisdiction, as of **April 1**, 19 **34**, taken by **A. C. Hector**, Superintendent.

KEY; Surname; Stamped Census Number; Typed Census Number; Given Name; Sex; Age at Last Birthday; Tribe; Degree of Blood; Marital Status; Relationship to Head of Family; Last Census Roll Number (if given); At Jurisdiction Where Enrolled (Yes/No); At Another Jurisdiction; Post Office, County, State (if given); Ward (Yes/No)

1706;1731; Waggoner; m; 25; Miss. Choctaw; F; S; Son; 1645; Yes; Yes
1707;1732; Dailey; f; 23; F[sic] S[sic]; F; S; Dau; 1646; Yes; Yes
1708;1733; Dora; f; 22; F[sic] S[sic]; F; S; Dau; 1647; Yes; Yes
1709;1734; Smith; m; 19; Miss. Choctaw; F; S; Son; 1648; Yes; Yes
1710;1735; Woodrow Wilson; m; 14; Miss. Choctaw; F; S; Son; Yes; Yes
1711;1736; Rose; f; 20; Miss. Choctaw; F; S; Dau; 1650; Yes; Yes

1712;1737; Edmond; m; 26; Miss. Choctaw; F; M; Head; 1651; Yes; Yes
1713;1738; Sallie; f; 21; Miss. Choctaw; F; M; Wife; 1652; Yes; Yes
1714;1739; John; m; 5; Miss. Choctaw; F; S; Son; 1653; Yes; Yes
1715;1740; Hayward; m; 3; Miss. Choctaw; F; S; Son; 1654; Yes; Yes

1716;1741; Elie; m; 33; Miss. Choctaw; F; M; Head; 1655; Yes; Yes
1717;1742; Odie; f; 27; Miss. Choctaw; F; M; Wife; 1656; Yes; Yes
1718;1743; Vanola; f; 14; Miss. Choctaw; F; S; Dau; 1657; Yes; Yes
1719;1744; Flora; f; 12; Miss. Choctaw; F; S; Dau; 1658; Yes; Yes
1720;1745; Kitty; f; 11; Miss. Choctaw; F; S; Dau; 1659; Yes; Yes
1721;1746; Bonnie; m; 9; Miss. Choctaw; F; S; Son; 1660; Yes; Yes
1722;1747; Robert R; m; 1-11/12; Miss. Choctaw; F; S; Son; 1661; Yes; Yes

1723;1748; Cohen; m; 36; Miss. Choctaw; F; M; Head; 1662; Yes; Yes
1724;1749; Sissey; f; 32; Miss. Choctaw; F; M; Wife; 1663; Yes; Yes
1725;1750; Ance; f; 16; Miss. Choctaw; F; S; Dau; 1664; Yes; Yes
 Married Vernon (Tubby) Jim #1482
1726;1751; Una; f; 13; Miss. Choctaw; F; S; Dau; 1665; Yes; Yes
1727;1752; Sallie; f; 11; Miss. Choctaw; F; S; Dau; 1666; Yes; Yes
1728;1753; Harrison; m; 9; Miss. Choctaw; F; S; Son; 1667; Yes; Yes
1729;1754; A. J; m; 6; Miss. Choctaw; F; S; Son; 1668; Yes; Yes
1730;1755; Arline; f; 1-6/12; Miss. Choctaw; F; S; Dau; 1669; Yes; Yes

1731;1756; Hugh; m; 51; Miss. Choctaw; F; S[sic]; Head; 1670; Yes; Yes
1732;1757; Mollie; f; 48; Miss. Choctaw; F; S[sic]; Wife; 1671; Yes; Yes

Census of the **Mississippi Choctaws** reservation of the **Choctaw Agency** jurisdiction, as of **April 1**, 19**34**, taken by **A. C. Hector**, Superintendent.

KEY; Surname; Stamped Census Number; Typed Census Number; Given Name; Sex; Age at Last Birthday; Tribe; Degree of Blood; Marital Status; Relationship to Head of Family; Last Census Roll Number (if given); At Jurisdiction Where Enrolled (Yes/No); At Another Jurisdiction; Post Office, County, State (if given); Ward (Yes/No)

1733;1758; Thompson; m; 19; Miss. Choctaw; F; S; Son; 1672; Yes; Yes
1734;1759; Clemon; m; 17; Miss. Choctaw; F; S; Son; 1673; Yes; Yes
1735;1760; J. C; m; 13; Miss. Choctaw; F; S; Son; 1674; Yes; Yes
1736;1761; Collins; m; 11; Miss. Choctaw; F; S; Son; 1675; Yes; Yes
1737;1762; Lillie; f; 10; Miss. Choctaw; F; S; Dau; 1676; Yes; Yes
1738;1763; Walter; m; 9; Miss. Choctaw; F; S; Son; 1677; Yes; Yes
1739;1764; Lola; f; 8; Miss. Choctaw; F; S; Dau; 1678; Yes; Yes
1740;1765; Beaman; m; 3; Miss. Choctaw; F; S; Son; 1679; Yes; Yes

1741;1766; Spinks; m; 44; Miss. Choctaw; F; M; Head; 1680; Yes; Yes
1742;1767; Susie; f; 35; Miss. Choctaw; F; M; Wife; 1681; Yes; Yes
1743;1768; Wilson; m; 15; Miss. Choctaw; F; S; Son; 1682; Yes; Yes
1744;1769; Flennie; f; 12; Miss. Choctaw; F; S; Dau; 1683; Yes; Yes
1745;1770; Willie B; f; 10/12; Miss. Choctaw; F; S; Dau; Yes; Yes

1746;1771; Wesley; m; 68; Miss. Choctaw; F; Wd; Head; 1684; Yes; Yes
1747;1772; Meley; f; 10; Miss. Choctaw; F; S; Dau; 1685; Yes; Yes
1748;1773; John Banks; m; 7; Miss. Choctaw; F; S; Son; 1686; Yes; Yes
1749;1774; Leighton; m; 4; Miss. Choctaw; F; S; Son; 1687; Yes; Yes

1750;1775; Salum; m; 29; Miss. Choctaw; F; S; Alone; 1688; Yes; Yes

1751;1776; Rachel; f; 49; Miss. Choctaw; F; Wd; Head; 1555; Yes; Yes

WILSON

1752;1777; John; m; 39; Miss. Choctaw; F; M; Head; 1689; Yes; Yes
1753;1778; Eva Barnett; f; 31; Miss. Choctaw; F; M; Wife; 1690; Yes; Yes
1754;1779; Silman; m; 15; Miss. Choctaw; F; S; Son; 1691; Yes; Yes
1755;1780; Mollie; f; 13; Miss. Choctaw; F; S; Dau; 1692; Yes; Yes
1756;1781; Sidney; m; 12; Miss. Choctaw; F; S; Son; 1693; Yes; Yes
1757;1782; Leo; m; 9; Miss. Choctaw; F; S; Son; 1694; Yes; Yes
1758;1783; Edna; f; 5; Miss. Choctaw; F; S; Dau; 1695; Yes; Yes

Census of the **Mississippi Choctaws** reservation of the **Choctaw Agency** jurisdiction, as of **April 1**, 19**34**, taken by **A. C. Hector**, Superintendent.

KEY; Surname; Stamped Census Number; Typed Census Number; Given Name; Sex; Age at Last Birthday; Tribe; Degree of Blood; Marital Status; Relationship to Head of Family; Last Census Roll Number (if given); At Jurisdiction Where Enrolled (Yes/No); At Another Jurisdiction; Post Office, County, State (if given); Ward (Yes/No)

1759;1784; Martha; f; 86; Miss. Choctaw; F; Wd; Mother; 1696; Yes; Yes

~~1784~~; Gordon; m; 7/12; Miss. Choctaw; F; S; Son; Yes; Yes
Died 8-22-33

1760;1786; Will; m; 46; Miss. Choctaw; F; M; Head; 1697; Yes; Yes
1761;1787; Martha; f; 40; Miss. Choctaw; F; M; Wife; 1698; Yes; Yes
1762;1788; Sammie; m; 13; Miss. Choctaw; F; S; Son; 1699; Yes; Yes
1763;1789; Linnie; f; 12; Miss. Choctaw; F; S; Dau; 1700; Yes; Yes
1764;1790; Lou8sana[sic]; f; 11; Miss. Choctaw; F; S; Dau; 1701; Yes; Yes
1765;1791; R. L; m; 5; Miss. Choctaw; F; S; Son; 1702; Yes; Yes
1766;1792; Jim; m; 4; Miss. Choctaw; F; S; Son; 1703; Yes; Yes
1767;1793; Neil Milber; m; 2; Miss. Choctaw; F; S; Son; 1704; Yes; Yes

WISHORK

1768;1794; Alpha; f; 32; Miss. Choctaw; F; Wd; Head; 1705; Yes; Yes
Married Bennett Sackey #1312
1769;1795; Zelia; f; 13; Miss. Choctaw; F; S; Dau; 1706; Yes; Yes
1770;1796; Evelyn; f; 12; Miss. Choctaw; F; S; Dau; 1707; Yes; Yes
1771;1797; Nuga; f; 9; Miss. Choctaw; F; S; Dau; 1708; Yes; Yes
1772;1798; Lun Presley; m; 5; Miss. Choctaw; F; S; Son; 1709; Yes; Yes
1773;1799; Sampson; m; 70; Miss. Choctaw; F; S; Father-in-law; 1710; Yes; Yes
1774;1800; Ruth; f; 10/12; Miss. Choctaw; F; S; Dau; Yes; Yes

YORK

1775;1801; Ben; m; 43; Miss. Choctaw; F; M; Head; 1711; Yes; Yes
1776;1802; Louella; f; 49; Miss. Choctaw; F; M; Wife; 1712; Yes; Yes
1777;1803; Hester; m; 12; Miss. Choctaw; F; S; Son; 1713; Yes; Yes

1778;1804; Bennett; m; 44; Miss. Choctaw; F; M; Head; 1714; Yes; Yes

Census of the **Mississippi Choctaws** reservation of the **Choctaw Agency** jurisdiction, as of **April 1**, 19**34**, taken by **A. C. Hector**, Superintendent.

KEY; Surname; Stamped Census Number; Typed Census Number; Given Name; Sex; Age at Last Birthday; Tribe; Degree of Blood; Marital Status; Relationship to Head of Family; Last Census Roll Number (if given); At Jurisdiction Where Enrolled (Yes/No); At Another Jurisdiction; Post Office, County, State (if given); Ward (Yes/No)

1779;1805; Lacie; f; 26; Miss. Choctaw; F; M; Wife; 1715; Yes; Yes
1780;1806; G. B; m; 8; Miss. Choctaw; F; S; Son; 1716; Yes; Yes
1781;1807; Colie; f; 7; Miss. Choctaw; F; S; Dau; 1717; Yes; Yes
1782;1808; Scott; m; 79; Miss. Choctaw; F; Wd; Father; 1718; Yes; Yes
1783;1809; Berkley; m; 22; Miss. Choctaw; F; S; Nephew; 1719; No; Chilocco; Chilocco, Kay, Okla; Yes

1784;1810; Emmett; m; 30; Miss. Choctaw; F; M; Head; 1720; Yes; Yes
1785;1811; Indiana; f; 19; Miss. Choctaw; F; M: Wife; 1721; Yes; Yes
1786;1812; Florence; f; 1-3/12; Miss. Choctaw; F; S; Dau; 1722; Yes; Yes
1787;1813; Necie; f; 46; Miss. Choctaw; F; Wd; Mother; 1723; Yes; Yes
1788;1814; Baxter; m; 27; Miss. Choctaw; F; S; Bro; 1724; No; Tulsa; Tulsa, Tulsa, Okla; Yes
1789;1815; Addie; f; 25; Miss. Choctaw; F; S; Sis; 1725; No; Santa Fe; Santa Fe, N.Mex.
1790;1816; Gasler; m; 22; Miss. Choctaw; F; S; Bro; 1726; No; Chilocco; Chilocco, Kay, Okla; Yes
1791;1817; Eunice; f; 20; Miss. Choctaw; F; S; Sis; 1717; No; Chilocco; Chilocco, Kay, Okla; Yes
1792;1818; Beaman; m; 17; Miss. Choctaw; F; S; B5o[sic]; 1728; No; Chilocco; Chilocco, Kay, Okla; Yes

Census of the **Mississippi Choctaws** reservation of the **Choctaw Agency** jurisdiction, as of **April 1**, 19**34**, taken by **A. C. Hector**, Superintendent.

KEY; Extra Census Number (if given); Census Number (if given); Surname; Given Name; Sex; Age at Last Birthday; Tribe; Degree of Blood; Marital Status; Relationship to Head of Family; Last Census Roll Number (if given); At Jurisdiction Where Enrolled (Yes/No); At Another Jurisdiction; Post Office, County, State (if given); Ward (Yes/No)

OMITTED FROM PREVIOUS CENSUS ROLL

275; 279; Campbell, Vennie Comby; f; 18; Miss. Choctaw; F; M; Wife; Yes; Yes

318; 322; Charlie, Coyt; m; 18; Miss. Choctaw; F; M; Head; Yes; Yes

370; 375; Clemons, Irsal[sic]; m; 12; Miss. Choctaw; F; S; Son; Yes; Yes

621; 629; Frazier, Martha; f; 4; Miss. Choctaw; F; S; Dau; Yes; Yes

642; 650; Frazier, Annie; f; 4; Miss. Choctaw; F; S; Dau; Yes; Yes

643; 651; Frazier, Emma; f; 1½; Miss. Choctaw; F; S; Dau; Yes; Yes

723; 732; Hall, Eliza; f; 81; Miss. Choctaw; F; Wd; Mother; Yes; Yes

732; 741; Hickman, Will; m; 4; Miss. Choctaw; F; S; Son; Yes; Yes

752; 761; Hickman, George; m; 3; Miss. Choctaw; F; S; Son; Yes; Yes
753; 762; Hickman, Sabelia; f; 1; Miss. Choctaw; F; S; Dau; Yes; Yes

842; 851; Jefferson, Eva Nell; f; 4; Miss. Choctaw; F; S; Dau; Yes; Yes
847; 856; Jefferson, Victoria; f; 3; Miss. Choctaw; F; S; Dau; Yes; Yes
848; 857; Jefferson, Otis; m; 2; Miss. Choctaw; F; S; Son; Yes; Yes

976; 984; Johnson, Celia; f; 76; Miss. Choctaw; F; Wd; Head; Yes; Yes

989; 997; Denson, Zila; f; 10; Miss. Choctaw; F; S; Step-dau; Yes; Yes

1138;1150; Mingo, Sally Bell; f; 19; Miss. Choctaw; F; M; Wife; Yes; Yes

1307;1320; Isom, Bailey; m; 14; Miss. Choctaw; F; S; Son; Yes; Yes

Census of the __Mississippi Choctaws__ reservation of the __Choctaw Agency__ jurisdiction, as of __April 1__, 19__34__, taken by __A. C. Hector__, Superintendent.

KEY: Extra Census Number (if given); Census Number (if given); Surname; Given Name; Sex; Age at Last Birthday; Tribe; Degree of Blood; Marital Status; Relationship to Head of Family; Last Census Roll Number (if given); At Jurisdiction Where Enrolled (Yes/No); At Another Jurisdiction; Post Office, County, State (if given); Ward (Yes/No)

1562;1584; Tubby, D; m; 33; Miss. Choctaw; F; M; Head; Yes; Yes
1563;1585; Tubby, Lilly Allen; f; 29; Miss. Choctaw; F; M; Wife; Yes; Yes
1564;1586; Tubby, Susie Anne; f; 26; Miss. Choctaw; F; S; Sister; Yes; Yes
1565;1587; Tubby, R. B; m; 3; Miss. Choctaw; F; S; Son; Yes; Yes

1601;1624; Wallace, Amy; f; 19; Miss. Choctaw; F; S; Dau; Yes; Yes

1612;1636; Wallace, Brigam; m; 1½; Miss. Choctaw; F; S; Son; Yes; Yes

1663;1687; Willis, Given; m; 4; Miss. Choctaw; F; S; Son; Yes; Yes

1668;1692; Willis, Leo; m; 4; Miss. Choctaw; F; S; Son; Yes; Yes
1669;1693; Willis, Sina; f; 2; Miss. Choctaw; F; S; Son[sic]; Yes; Yes

DUPLICATIONS LAST CENSUS

514; 521; Farmer, Lonie Dixon; f; 20; Miss. Choctaw; F; M; Wife; 481, 504; Yes; Yes

667; 676; Gipson, Esby or Elizabeth; f; 23; Miss. Choctaw; F; M; Wife; 480, 646; Yes; Yes

~~1016~~; Johnson, Mary Davis; f; 18; Miss. Choctaw; F; M; Wife; 430, 964; Yes; Yes   Died 10-15-33

1140;1152; Mingo, Lilly Tubby; f; 30; Miss. Choctaw; F; M; Wife; 1431, 1094; Yes; Yes

1443;1457; Thompson, Bonnie Amos; f; 23; Miss. Choctaw; F; M; Wife; 37, 1393; Yes; Yes

Census of the **Mississippi Choctaws** reservation of the **Choctaw Agency** jurisdiction, as of **April 1**, 19**34**, taken by **A. C. Hector**, Superintendent.

KEY: Extra Census Number (if given); Census Number (if given); Surname; Given Name; Sex; Age at Last Birthday; Tribe; Degree of Blood; Marital Status; Relationship to Head of Family; Last Census Roll Number (if given); At Jurisdiction Where Enrolled (Yes/No); At Another Jurisdiction; Post Office, County, State (if given); Ward (Yes/No)

1608;1631; Wallace (Willis), Emma Dixon; f; 22; Miss. Choctaw; F; M; Wife; 1546, 1558; Yes; Yes

ADDED TO MALES ON ACCOUNT OF ERROR IN SEX

65; Anderson, Tonnie[sic]; m; 19; Miss. Choctaw; F; S; Son; 65; Yes; Yes

Frazier, Simpson; m; 14; Miss. Choctaw; F; S; Son; 626; Yes; Yes

674; Gipson, Paul; m; 9; Miss. Choctaw; F; S; Son; 653; Yes; Yes

DEDUCTIONS FROM FEMALES ON ACCOUNT OF ERROR IN SEX

65; Anderson, Tonnie; m; 19; Miss. Choctaw; F; S; Son; 65; Yes; Yes

Frazier, Simpson; m; 14; Miss. Choctaw; F; S; Son; 626; Yes; Yes

674; Gipson, Paul; m; 9; Miss. Choctaw; F; S; Son; 653; Yes; Yes

DEDUCTIONS FROM MALES ON ACCOUNT OF ERROR IN SEX

Thompson, Morine; f; 13; Miss. Choctaw; F; S; Dau; 1389; Yes; Yes

ADDED TO FEMALES ON ACCOUNT OF ERROR IN SEX

Thompson, Morine; f; 13; Miss. Choctaw; F; S; Dau; 1389; Yes; Yes

Census of the _____ reservation of the **Choctaw Indian Agency** jurisdiction, as of **January 1, 1935**, 19___, taken by **A. C. Hector**, Superintendent. SUPPLEMENTAL ROLL

KEY; Number (if given); Surname; Given Name; Sex; Date of Birth & Age at Last Birthday (if given); Tribe; Degree of Blood; Marital Status; Relationship to Head of Family; Last Census Roll Number (if given); At Jurisdiction Where Enrolled (Yes/No); At Another Jurisdiction; Post Office, County, State (if given); Ward (Yes/No)

SUPPLEMENTAL TO THE 1934 CENSUS ROLL

    Bell, Tony; 157   [No other information given]
1; Bell, Fanny; f; 2-4-34 & 10/12; Choctaw; F; S; Daughter; Yes; Yes

    Ben, Olin; 157   [No other information given]
2; Ben, Harrison; m; 11-10-34 & 1/12; Choctaw; F; S; Son; Yes; Yes

    Ben, Charlie; 178   [No other information given]
3; Ben, James Charles; m; 9-10-34 & 3/12; Choctaw; F; S; Son; Yes; Yes

    Billy, Richard; 241   [No other information given]
4; Billy, Wilson; m; 7-29-34 & 5/12; Choctaw; F; S; Son; Yes; Yes

    Chitto, Joe; 345   [No other information given]
5; Chitto, Dewy Davis; m; 4-10-34 & 8/12; Choctaw; F; S; Son; Yes; Yes

    Denson, Willie; 459   [No other information given]
6; Denson, Baby; f; 7-7-34 & 5/12; Choctaw; F; S; Daughter; Yes; Yes

    Frazier, Frazier (Bob); 648   [No other information given]
7; Frazier, LeRoy; m; 7-21-34 & 5/12; Choctaw; F; S; Son; Yes; Yes

    Gipson; Nolie; 672   [No other information given]
8; Gipson, Josephine; f; 9-16-34 & 3/12; Choctaw; F; S; Daughter; Yes; Yes

Census of the _____ reservation of the **Choctaw**
Indian Agency jurisdiction, as of **January 1, 1935**, 19___, taken by **A. C. Hector**, Superintendent. SUPPLEMENTAL ROLL

KEY; Number (if given); Surname; Given Name; Sex; Date of Birth & Age at Last Birthday (if given); Tribe; Degree of Blood; Marital Status; Relationship to Head of Family; Last Census Roll Number (if given); At Jurisdiction Where Enrolled (Yes/No); At Another Jurisdiction; Post Office, County, State (if given); Ward (Yes/No)

  Hall, Langford; 686 [No other information given]
9; Hall, Lena; f; 11-30-34 & 1/12; Choctaw; F; S; Daughter; Yes; Yes

  Isaac, David; 797 [No other information given]
~~10; Isaac; David, Jr; m; 8-5-34 & 4/12; Choctaw; F; S; Son; Yes; Yes~~
Died Aug. 5, 1935

  Isaac, Will; 787 [No other information given]
11; Isaac, Juanita; f; 6-17-34 & 6/12; Choctaw; F; S; Daughter; Yes; Yes

  Jim, Goodman; 882 [No other information given]
12; Jim, Goodman, Jr; m; 9-13-34 & 3/12; Choctaw; F; S; Son; Yes; Yes

  Jim, Victor; 895 [No other information given]
13; Jim, Perry; m; 6-13-34 & 6/12; Choctaw; F; S; Son; Yes; Yes

  John, Ira; 950 [No other information given]
14; John, Willie; m; 6-21-34 & 1/12; Choctaw; F; S; Son; Yes; Yes

  McMillan, Anthony; 1113 [No other information given]
15; McMillan, Rita; f; 2-17-34 & 2/12; Choctaw; F; S; Daughter; Yes; Yes

  Mingo, Olin; 1135 [No other information given]
16; Mingo, Robert Bruce; m; 4-11-34 & 8/12; Choctaw; F; S; Son; Yes; Yes

  Morris, Dempsey; 1158 [No other information given]
17; Morris, Alice; f; 6-12-34 & 6/12; Choctaw; F; S; Daughter; Yes; Yes

Census of the _____ reservation of the __Choctaw__
__Indian Agency__ jurisdiction, as of __January 1, 1935__, 19__, taken
by __A. C. Hector__, Superintendent. SUPPLEMENTAL ROLL

KEY; Number (if given); Surname; Given Name; Sex; Date of Birth & Age at Last Birthday (if given); Tribe; Degree of Blood; Marital Status; Relationship to Head of Family; Last Census Roll Number (if given); At Jurisdiction Where Enrolled (Yes/No); At Another Jurisdiction; Post Office, County, State (if given); Ward (Yes/No);

  Sam, Willie; 1265 [No other information given]
18; Sam, Claude; m; 7-17-34 & 5/12; Choctaw; F; S; Son; Yes; Yes

  Shoemake, Buck; 1281 [No other information given]
19; Shoemake, Edburn; m; 4-26-34 & 8/12; Choctaw; F; S; Son; Yes; Yes

  Thomas, Wilmon; 1406 [No other information given]
20; Thomas, Gordon; m; 9-2-34 & 3/12; Choctaw; F; S; Son; Yes; Yes

  Thomas, Cleve; 1404 [No other information given]
21; Thomas, Sam; m; 7-26-34 & 5/12; Choctaw; F; S; Son; Yes; Yes

  Farmer, Moses; 508 [No other information given]
22; Tuffomah, Latima; f; 5-8-34 & 7/12; Choctaw; F; S; Daughter; Yes; Yes

  Willis, Cohen; 1723 [No other information given]
23; Willis, Bead C; m; 7-11-34 & 5/12; Choctaw; F; S; Son; Yes; Yes

  Willis, Nathan; 1659 [No other information given]
24; Willis, Richard; m; 5-31-34 & 7/12; Choctaw; F; S; Son; Yes; Yes

  Wilson, John; 1752 [No other information given]
25; Wilson, Caroline; f; 8-9-34 & 4/12; Choctaw; F; S; Daughter; Yes; Yes

  York, Emmett; 1784 [No other information given]
26; York, Theodore; m; 8-24-34 & 4/12; Choctaw; F; S; Son; Yes; Yes

Census of the _____ reservation of the **Choctaw Indian Agency** jurisdiction, as of **January 1, 1935**, 19__, taken by **A. C. Hector**, Superintendent. DEDUCTION ROLL

KEY; 1934 Census Number; Surname; Given Name; Sex; Age at Last Birthday; Tribe; Degree of Blood; Marital Status; Relationship to Head of Family; At Jurisdiction Where Enrolled (Yes/No); At Another Jurisdiction; Post Office, County, State (if given); Ward (Yes/No)

DEDUCTION ROLL FOR APRIL 1 to DECEMBER 31, 1934

266; Briscoe, John Claude; m; 3; Choctaw; F; S; Son; Yes; Yes
276; Campbell, Jimmie; m; 3/12; Choctaw; F; S; Son; Yes; Yes
275; Campbell, Venie; f; 17; Choctaw; F; M; Wife; Yes; Yes
Died before enrollment   Charlie; Baby; m; Choctaw; F; S; Son; Yes; Yes
330; Chickaway, Isabel; f; 72; Choctaw; F; Wd; Head; Yes; Yes
423; Dansby, Jennie; f; 52; Choctaw; F; M; Wife; Yes; Yes
630; Frazier, Eliza; f; 79; Choctaw; F; M; Wife; Yes; Yes
755; Hickman, Mary; f; 91; Choctaw; F; Wd; Head; Yes; Yes
711; Henry, Joy; f; 1; Choctaw; F; S; Daughter; Yes; Yes
801; Isaac, Etherine or Nansey; f; 2; Choctaw; F; S; Daughter; Yes; Yes   See letter 4/30/36
770; Isaac, Hickman; m; 26; Choctaw; F; S; Alone; Yes; Yes
796; Isaac, Lawrence; m; 1; Choctaw; F; S; Son; Yes; Yes
763; Isaac, Odie Mae; f; 18; Choctaw; F; S; Daughter; Yes; Yes
952; John, Marcy Lee; f; 4; Choctaw; F; S; Daughter; Yes; Yes
976; Johnson, Celia; f; 71; Choctaw; F; Wd; Head; Yes; Yes
Died before enrollment   Lewis, Billy; m; 10; Choctaw; F; S; Son; Yes; Yes
1070; Lewis, Mollie; f; 37; Choctaw; F; M; Wife; Yes; Yes
1078; Lewis, Rosie Mae; f; 1; Choctaw; F; S; Daughter; Yes; Yes
1092; Martin, Nancy; f; 26; Choctaw; F; M; Wife; Yes; Yes
Died before enrollment   Mingo, Betty; f; 1; Choctaw; F; S; Daughter; Yes; Yes
Died before enrollment   Sam, Griffin; m; 7/12; Choctaw; F; S; Son; Yes; Yes
1358; Steve, Murphy; m; 60; Choctaw; F; Wd; Head; Yes; Yes
Died before enrollment   Starr, Allie Lou; f; 11/12; Choctaw; F; S; Daughter; Yes; Yes
1431; Thompson, Daniel; m; [blank]; Choctaw; F; S; Son; Yes; Yes

Census of the _____ reservation of the **Choctaw Indian Agency** jurisdiction, as of **January 1, 1935**, 19__, taken by **A. C. Hector**, Superintendent. DEDUCTION ROLL

KEY; 1934 Census Number; Surname; Given Name; Sex; Age at Last Birthday; Tribe; Degree of Blood; Marital Status; Relationship to Head of Family; At Jurisdiction Where Enrolled (Yes/No); At Another Jurisdiction; Post Office, County, State (if given); Ward (Yes/No)

Died before enrollment   Tubby, Baby; f; [blank]; Choctaw; F; S; Daughter; Yes; Yes

Died before enrollment   Tubby, Levi; m; [blank]; Choctaw; F; S; Son; Yes; Yes

Died before enrollment   Tubby, Mike; m; [blank]; Choctaw; F; S; Son

Died before enrollment   Vaughn, Luke; m; 10; Choctaw; F; S; Son; Yes; Yes

Died beofre[sic] enrollment   Williams, Rufus; m; 5/12; Choctaw; F; S; Son; Yes; Yes

SUPPLEMENTAL

to the 1935 CENSUS ROLL

as of January 1, 1936

taken by A. C. Hector

Census of the _____ reservation of the **Choctaw Indian Agency** jurisdiction, as of **January 1, 1936**, 19__, taken by **A. C. Hector**, Superintendent.

KEY; Census Number; Surname, Given Name; Sex; Date of Birth (if given) & Age at Last Birthday; Tribe; Degree of Blood; Marital Status; Relationship to Head of Family; Last Census Roll Number (if given); At Jurisdiction Where Enrolled (Yes/No); At Another Jurisdiction; Post Office, County, State (if given); Ward (Yes/No)

SUPPLEMENTAL TO THE 1935 CENSUS

1825; Alex, Cooper; m; 25; Choctaw; F; M; Head; 1; Yes; Yes
Alex, Rosemary; f; 1-2-35 & 1; Choctaw; F; S; Dau; Yes; Yes

1826; Allen, J. C; m; 21; Choctaw; F; M; Head; 18; Yes; Yes
Allen, Stella Virginia; f; 3-22-35 & 3/12; Choctaw; F; S; Dau; Yes; Yes

1827; Anderson, John; m; 68; Choctaw; F; M; Head; 46; Yes; Yes
Anderson, Lola Mae; f; 9-24-35 & 3/12; Choctaw; F; S; Dau; Yes; Yes

1828; Bell, Junus; m; 39; Choctaw; F; M; Head; 85; Yes; Yes
Bell, Claud; f; 3-15-35 & 7/12; Choctaw; F; S; Dau; Yes; Yes

1829; Bell, Bob; m; 26; Choctaw; F; M; Head; 145; Yes; Yes
Bell, Evaline; f; 4-14-35 & 8/12; Choctaw; F; S; Dau; Yes; Yes

1830; Bell, Joe; m; 44; Choctaw; F; M; Head; 116; Yes; Yes
Bell, Floyd; m; 5-2-35 & 7/12; Choctaw; F; S; Son; Yes; Yes

1831; Bell, Gibson; m; 23; Choctaw; F; M; Head; 110; Yes; Yes
Bell, Zoe; f; 3-23-35 & 9/12; Choctaw; F; S; Dau; Yes; Yes

1832; Bell, Nicholas; m; 36; Choctaw; F; M; Head; 105; Yes; Yes
Bell, Will Rogers; m; 8-11-35 & 4/12; Choctaw; F; S; Son; Yes; Yes

1833; Ben, Tom; m; 41; Choctaw; F; M; Head; 172; Yes; Yes
Ben, Tom Comby, Jr; m; 11-15-35 & 2/12; Choctaw; F; S; Son; Yes; Yes

Census of the _____ reservation of the **Choctaw Indian Agency** jurisdiction, as of **January 1, 1936**, 19__, taken by **A. C. Hector**, Superintendent.

KEY; Census Number; Surname, Given Name; Sex; Date of Birth (if given) & Age at Last Birthday; Tribe; Degree of Blood; Marital Status; Relationship to Head of Family; Last Census Roll Number (if given); At Jurisdiction Where Enrolled (Yes/No); At Another Jurisdiction; Post Office, County, State (if given); Ward (Yes/No)

1834; Charley, Beaman; m; 21; Choctaw; F; M; Head; 1323; Yes; Yes
Charley, Mary Lou; f; 9-10-35 & 3/12; Choctaw; F; S; Dau; Yes; Yes

1835; Chickaway, Sim; m; 38; Choctaw; F; Head; 332; Yes; Yes
Chickaway, Allie; f; 2-14-35 & 10/12; Choctaw; F; S; Dau; Yes; Yes

1836; Chickaway, Jim; m; 33; Choctaw; F; M; Head; 332; Yes; Yes
Chickaway, Sallie; f; 2-20-35 & 10/12; Choctaw; F; S; Dau; Yes; Yes

1837; Davis, Hobbie; m; 30; Choctaw; F; M; Head; 428; Yes; Yes
Davis, Zina; f; 3-18-35 & 9/12; Choctaw; F; S; Dau; Yes; Yes

1838; Denson, Pete; m; 48; Choctaw; F; M; Head; 452; Yes; Yes
Denson, Lola; f; 12-2-35 & 1/12; Choctaw; F; S; Dau; Yes; Yes

1839; Dixon, Edmond; m; 28; Choctaw; F; M; Head; 485; Yes; Yes
Dixon, Claudine; f; 3-23-35 & 9/12; Choctaw; F; S; Dau; Yes; Yes

1840; Farmer, Henry; m; 24; Choctaw; F; M; Head; 1082; Yes; Yes
Farmer, Robert Joseph; m; 11-21-35 & 2/12; Choctaw; F; S; Son; Yes; Yes

1841; Farve, Paul; m; 48; Choctaw; F; M; Head; 518; Yes; Yes
Farve, Albert Clifton; m; 9-3-35 & 3/12; Choctaw; F; S; Son; Yes; Yes

1842; Farve, Joseph; m; 24; Choctaw; F; M; Head; 525; Yes; Yes
Farve, Hughey; m; 10-11-35 & 2/12; Choctaw; F; S; Son; Yes; Yes

Census of the _____ reservation of the __Choctaw Indian__ __Agency__ jurisdiction, as of __January 1, 1936__, 19__, taken by __A. C. Hector__, Superintendent.

KEY; Census Number; Surname, Given Name; Sex; Date of Birth (if given) & Age at Last Birthday; Tribe; Degree of Blood; Marital Status; Relationship to Head of Family; Last Census Roll Number (if given); At Jurisdiction Where Enrolled (Yes/No); At Another Jurisdiction; Post Office, County, State (if given); Ward (Yes/No)

	Gardner, Jim; m; 37; Choctaw; F; M; Head; 657; Yes; Yes
1843;	Gardner, Floyd; m; 4-9-35 & 8/12; Choctaw; F; S; Son; Yes; Yes
	Gipson, Nolie; m; 34; Choctaw; F; M; Head; 672; Yes; Yes
1844;	Gipson, Doreen; f; 12-26-35 & 26/265; Choctaw; F; S; Dau; Yes; Yes
	Gipson, Homer; m; 23; Choctaw; F; M; Head; 664; Yes; Yes
1845;	Gipson, William; m; 3-8-35 & 9/12; Choctaw; F; S; Son; Yes; Yes
	Hickman, Enoch (Edmond); m; 62; Choctaw; F; M: Head; 733; Yes; Yes
1846;	Hickman, John; m; 10-4-35 & 2/12; Choctaw; F; S; Son; Yes; Yes
	Isaac, Jackson; m; 31; Choctaw; F; M: Head; 794; Yes; Yes
~~1847;~~	Isaac, Ann Marie; f; 11-20-35 & 1/12; Choctaw; F; S; Dau; Yes; Yes
	Jefferson, Otis; m; 33; Choctaw; F; M; Head; 843; Yes; Yes
1848;	Jefferson, Arthur; m; 9-27-35 & 3/12; Choctaw; F; S; Son; Yes; Yes
	Jefferson, Newt; m; 20; Choctaw; F; M; Head; 1047; Yes; Yes
1849;	Jefferson, Franklin; m; 11-20-35 & 1/12; Choctaw; F; S; Son; Yes; Yes
	Jefferson, Oscar; m; 31; Choctaw; F; M; Head; 839; Yes; Yes
1850;	Jefferson, Lula Lane; f; 10-29-35 & 2/12; Choctaw; F; S; Dau; Yes; Yes

Census of the _____ reservation of the **Choctaw Indian Agency** jurisdiction, as of **January 1, 1936**, 19__, taken by **A. C. Hector**, Superintendent.

KEY; Census Number; Surname, Given Name; Sex; Date of Birth (if given) & Age at Last Birthday; Tribe; Degree of Blood; Marital Status; Relationship to Head of Family; Last Census Roll Number (if given); At Jurisdiction Where Enrolled (Yes/No); At Another Jurisdiction; Post Office, County, State (if given); Ward (Yes/No)

           Jim, Albert; m; 29; Choctaw; F; M; Head; 888; Yes; Yes
1851;   Jim, Effie Mae; f; 12-29-35 & 2/265[sic]; Choctaw; F; S; Dau; Yes; Yes

           Jim (Tubby), Vernon; m; 24; Choctaw; F; M; Head; 1482; Yes; Yes
1852;   Jim, Sallie Mae; f; 12-15-35 & 16/365; Choctaw; F; S; Dau; Yes; Yes

           Johnson, Otho; m; 20; Choctaw; F; M; Head; 1007; Yes; Yes
1853;   Johnson, Allie Nora; f; 9-12-35 & 3/12; Choctaw; F; S; Dau; Yes; Yes

           Johnson, Afton; m; 32; Choctaw; F; M; Head; 985; Yes; Yes
1854;   Johnson, Jack Denson; m; 11-15-35 & 1/12; Choctaw; F; S; Son; Yes; Yes

           Johnson, DeWitt (Whitman); m; 25; Choctaw; F; M; Head; 978; Yes; Yes
1855;   Johnson, Lorraine; f; 9-18-35 & 3/12; Choctaw; F; S; Dau; Yes; Yes

           Johnson, Edgar; m; 37; Choctaw; F; M; Head; 990; Yes; Yes
1856;   Johnson, Olive Mae; f; 6-10-35 & 6/12; Choctaw; F; S; Dau; Yes; Yes

           Lewis, Albert; m; 42; Choctaw; F; M; Head; 1069; Yes; Yes
Died—~~Lewis, Allone; f; 10-1-35 & 2/12/ Choctaw; F; S; Dau; Yes; Yes~~

           Lewis, Jim; m; 33; Choctaw; F; M; Head; 1074; Yes; Yes
1858;   Lewis, Baby; m; 8-4-35 & 4/12; Choctaw; F; S; Son; Yes; Yes

Census of the _____ reservation of the **Choctaw Indian** **Agency** jurisdiction, as of **January 1, 1936**, 19__, taken by **A. C. Hector**, Superintendent.

KEY; Census Number; Surname, Given Name; Sex; Date of Birth (if given) & Age at Last Birthday; Tribe; Degree of Blood; Marital Status; Relationship to Head of Family; Last Census Roll Number (if given); At Jurisdiction Where Enrolled (Yes/No); At Another Jurisdiction; Post Office, County, State (if given); Ward (Yes/No)

1859;   McMillan, Willie; m; 20; Choctaw; F; M; Head; 1109; Yes; Yes
McMillan, Henry Lee; m; 11-17-35 & 2/12; Choctaw; F; S; Son; Yes; Yes

1860;   McMillan, Jimmie; m; 25; Choctaw; F; M; Head; 380; Yes; Yes
McMillan, Leo Otho McM; m; 6-15-35 & 6/12; Choctaw; F; Son; Yes; Yes

1861;   McMillan, Ella; f; 21; Choctaw; F; S; Head; 382; Yes; Yes
McMillan, Redy Isaam; m; 12-21-35 & 21/265; Choctaw; F; S; Dau[sic]; Yes; Yes

1862;   Martin, Willie; m; 46; Choctaw; F; M; Head; 1084; Yes; Yes
Martin, Anthony; m; 6-13-35 & 6/12; Choctaw; F; S; Son; Yes; Yes

1863;   Mingo, Jim; m; 21; Choctaw; F; M: Head; 1137; Yes; Yes
Mingo, Otho; m; 4-18-35 & 8/12; Choctaw; F; S; Son; Yes; Yes

Phillips, Lonie; f; [blank]; Choctaw; F; Wd; Head; Omitted on P.C; Yes; Yes
1864;   Phillips, Baby; m; 11-35 & 2/12; Choctaw; F; S; Son; Yes; Yes

1865;   Phillips, Riley; m; 29; Choctaw; F; M; Head; 1198; Yes; Yes
Phillips, D. C; m; 4-17-35 & 8/12; Choctaw; F; S; Son; Yes; Yes

Robinson, Jimmie Teach; m; 22; Choctaw; F; M: Head; 1228; Yes; Yes
1866;   Robinson, Josephine Teach; f; 7-3-35 & 5/12; Choctaw; F; S; Dau; Yes; Yes

Sam, Truman; m; 27; Choctaw; F; M; Head; 1240; Yes; Yes
1867;   San[sic], Baby; m; 8-7-35 & 4/12; Choctaw; F; S; Son; Yes; Yes

Census of the _____ reservation of the **Choctaw Indian Agency** jurisdiction, as of **January 1, 1936**, 19__, taken by **A. C. Hector**, Superintendent.

KEY; Census Number; Surname, Given Name; Sex; Date of Birth (if given) & Age at Last Birthday; Tribe; Degree of Blood; Marital Status; Relationship to Head of Family; Last Census Roll Number (if given); At Jurisdiction Where Enrolled (Yes/No); At Another Jurisdiction; Post Office, County, State (if given); Ward (Yes/No)

1868; Sockey, Bennett; m; 28; Choctaw; F; M; Head; 1312; Yes; Yes
Sockey, Harman; m; 4-7-35 & 8/12; Choctaw; F; S; Son; Yes; Yes

1869; Sockey, Valaria; f; 14; Choctaw; F; S; Head; Yes; Yes
Sockey, Janette; f; 12-7-35 & 24/365; Choctaw; F; S; Dau; Yes; Yes

1870; Steve, Bobo; m; 29; Choctaw; F; M: Head; 1375; Yes; Yes
Steve, Claud; m; 4-21-35 & 8/12; Choctaw; F; S; Son; Yes; Yes

1871; Thomas, Riley; m; 31; Choctaw; M: Head; 1403; Yes; Yes
Thomas, Dorsey; m; 1-29-35 & 11/12; Choctaw; S; Son; Yes; Yes

1872; Thompson, Tommie; m; 37; Choctaw; F; M; Head; 1442; Yes; Yes
Thompson, Bobo; m; 7-31-35 & 5/12; Choctaw; F; S; Son; Yes; Yes

1873; Tubby, Charlie; m; 40; Choctaw; M: Head; 1508; Yes; Yes
Tubby, Claud; m; 4-15-35 & 8/12; Choctaw; F; S; Son; Yes; Yes

1874; Tubby, Dan; m; 34; Choctaw; F; M: Head; 1446; Yes; Yes
Tubby, Dean Culver; m; 11-22-35 & 1/12; Choctaw; F; S; Son; Yes; Yes

1875; Tubby, Henderson; m; 43; Choctaw; F; M; Head; 1517; Yes; Yes
Tubby, Eugene; m; 9-26-35 & 3/12; Choctaw; F; S; Son; Yes; Yes

Census of the _____ reservation of the **Choctaw Indian Agency** jurisdiction, as of **January 1, 1936**, 19__, taken by **A. C. Hector**, Superintendent.

KEY: Census Number; Surname, Given Name; Sex; Date of Birth (if given) & Age at Last Birthday; Tribe; Degree of Blood; Marital Status; Relationship to Head of Family; Last Census Roll Number (if given); At Jurisdiction Where Enrolled (Yes/No); At Another Jurisdiction; Post Office, County, State (if given); Ward (Yes/No)

1876; Tubby, DeWitt; m; 29; Choctaw; F; M; Head; 1492; Yes; Yes
Tubby, May Belle; f; 8-20-35 & 4/12; Choctaw; F; S; Dau; Yes; Yes

1877; Waiter, Lonnie; m; 31; Choctaw; F; M; Head; 1592; Yes; Yes
Waiter, Otho Helen; f; 12-16-35 & 15/365; Choctaw; F; S; Dau; Yes; Yes

1878; Wickson, Jim; m; 28; Choctaw; M; Head; 1622; Yes; Yes
Wickson, Mary Jane; f; 7-23-35 & 5/12; Choctaw; F; S; Dau; yes; Yes

1879; Willis, John; m; 30; Choctaw; F; M; Head; 1678; Yes; Yes
Willis, Baby; m; 4-21-35 & 8/12; Choctaw; F; S; Son; Yes; Yes

1880; Willis, Gamblin; m; 36; Choctaw; F; M; Head; 1689; Yes; Yes
Willis, Zan; m; 4-22-35 & 8/12; Choctaw; F; S; Son; Yes; Yes

1857; Jim, John; m; 30; Choctaw; F; M; Head; 858; Yes; Yes
Jim, Pearl; f; 3-22-34 & 1-9/12; Choctaw; F; S; Dau; Yes; Yes

DBE 1881; Chitto, Joe; m; 36; Choctaw; F; M; Head; 345; Yes; Yes
Chitto, Dewey Wesley; m; [blank]; Choctaw; F; S; Son; Yes; Yes

DBE 1882; Frazier, Jim; m; 30; Choctaw; F; M; Head; 632; Yes; Yes
Frazier, Maxine; f; [blank]; Choctaw; F; S; Dau; Yes; Yes

DBE 1883; Gibson, Nolie (Noah); m; 34; Choctaw; F; M; Head; 672; Yes; Yes
Gibson, Josie; f; 10-16-34 & 1-2/12; Choctaw; F; S; Daughter; Yes; Yes

Mississippi Choctaw Census

as of

January 1, 1937

taken by A. C. Hector, Superintendent

Census of the **Mississippi Choctaws** reservation of the **Choctaw Agency** jurisdiction, as of **January 1, 1937**, 19__, taken by **A. C. Hector**, Superintendent.

KEY; Surname; Present Census Number; Last Census Number; Given Name; Sex; Age at Last Birthday; Tribe; Degree of Blood; Marital Status; Relationship to Head of Family; At Jurisdiction Where Enrolled (Yes/No); At Another Jurisdiction; Post Office, County, State (if given); Ward (Yes/No)

ALEX

1;   1; Cooper; m; 27; Miss. Choctaw; F; M; Head; Yes; Yes
2; 236; Sally Mae Cooper; f; 20; Miss. Choctaw; F; Wife; Yes; Yes
   Died 7-11-38
3;1825; Mary Rose; f; 2; Miss. Choctaw; F; S; Dau; Yes; Yes
4;   Theresa; f; 5/12; Miss. Choctaw; F; S; Dau; Yes; Yes
   Born 7-9-36
5; 235; **Billy**, Lillie; f; 34; Miss. Choctaw; F; Wd; Mo-in-law; Yes; Yes
6; 237; **Billy**, Nellie; f; 16; Miss. Choctaw; F; S; Sis-in-law; Yes; Yes
7; 238; **Billy**, Jim; m; 11; Miss. Choctaw; F; S; Bro-in-law; Yes; Yes
8; 239; **Billy**, Mary Lou; f; 9; Miss. Choctaw; F; S; Sis-in-law; Yes; Yes
9; 240; **Billy**, Paul; m; 6; Miss. Choctaw; F; S; Bro-in-law; Yes; Yes

10;   2; Missie; f; 57; Miss. Choctaw; F; Wd; Head; Yes; Yes
11;   3; Nelson; m; 13; Miss. Choctaw; F; S; Son; Yes; Yes

ALLEN

12; 14; Jim; m; 51; Miss. Choctaw; F; M; Head; Yes; Yes
13; 15; Manda; f; 53; Miss. Choctaw; F; M; Wife; Yes; Yes
   16; I. C; m; 22; Miss. Choctaw; F; S; Son; Yes; Yes
   Died 1935 - Unreported
14; 17; Annie Mae; f; 23; Miss. Choctaw; F; S; Dau; Yes; Yes
15; 18; J. C; m; 22; Miss. Choctaw; F; M; Son; Yes; Yes
16;1691; Mattie Willis; f; 20; Miss. Choctaw; F; M; Dau-in-law; Yes; Yes
17;1826; Stella Virginia; f; 2; Miss. Choctaw; F; S; Grand-dau; Yes; Yes
18; 19; R. G; m; 21; Miss. Choctaw; F; S; Son; Yes; Yes
   Died Jan. 18, 1937
19; 20; William; m; 14; Miss. Choctaw; F; S; Son; Yes; Yes

Census of the **Mississippi Choctaws** reservation of the **Choctaw Agency** jurisdiction, as of **January 1, 1937**, 19__, taken by **A. C. Hector**, Superintendent.

KEY; Surname; Present Census Number; Last Census Number; Given Name; Sex; Age at Last Birthday; Tribe; Degree of Blood; Marital Status; Relationship to Head of Family; At Jurisdiction Where Enrolled (Yes/No); At Another Jurisdiction; Post Office, County, State (if given); Ward (Yes/No)

20; 9; Houston; m; 14; Miss. Choctaw; F; S; Son; Yes; Yes
21;   Ralph; m; 1/12; Miss. Choctaw; F; S; Son; Yes; Yes
        Born 12-30-36

22; 21; Joseph; m; 44; Miss. Choctaw; F; S; Head; Yes; Yes
23; 22; Lacey; m; 43; Miss. Choctaw; F; S; Bro; Yes; Yes
24;1390; **Stoliby**, Tom; m; 34; Miss. Choctaw; F; S; Half-bro; Yes; Yes

25; 4; Willis; m; 42; Miss. Choctaw; F; M; Head; Yes; Yes
26; 5; Bessie; f; 42; Miss. Choctaw; F; M; Wife; Yes; Yes
27; 6; Bob; m; 20; Miss. Choctaw; F; S; Son; Yes; Yes
28; 7; Salem (Sulum); m; 16; Miss. Choctaw; F; S; Son; Yes; Yes
29; 8; Maggie; f; 14; Miss. Choctaw; F; S; Dau; Yes; Yes
30; 10; Nell; f; 12; Miss. Choctaw; F; S; Dau; Yes; Yes
    11; ~~Willie; m; 9; Miss. Choctaw; F; S; Son; Yes; Yes~~
        Died 1936 - Unreported
31; 12; Hubert (Wilbert); m; 4; Miss. Choctaw; F; S; Son; Yes; Yes
32; 13; Hubbard (Herbert); m; 4; Miss. Choctaw; F; S; Son; Yes; Yes

AMOS

    25; ~~Griffin; m; 49; Miss. Choctaw; F; M; Head; Yes; Yes~~
        Died 3-24-36
33; 26; Lena (Sallie); f; 45; Miss. Choctaw; F; M; Wife; Yes; Yes
34; 27; Mollie (Beauty); f; 27; Miss. Choctaw; F; S; Dau; Yes; Yes
35; 28; Julia; f; 25; Miss. Choctaw; F; S; Dau; Yes; Yes
36; 30; Fulton; m; 16; Miss. Choctaw; F; S; Son; Yes; Yes
37; 31; Floyd; m; 16; Miss. Choctaw; F; S; Son; Yes; Yes
38; 32; Mose; m; 15; Miss. Choctaw; F; S; Son; Yes; Yes
39;1588; **Vaughn**, Mollie; f; 24; Miss. Choctaw; F; S; Sis-in-law; Yes; Yes
40;1589; **Vaughn**, Annie; f; 19; Miss. Choctaw; F; S; Sis-in-law; Yes; Yes

Census of the **Mississippi Choctaws** reservation of the **Choctaw Agency** jurisdiction, as of **January 1, 1937**, 19__, taken by **A. C. Hector**, Superintendent.

KEY; Surname; Present Census Number; Last Census Number; Given Name; Sex; Age at Last Birthday; Tribe; Degree of Blood; Marital Status; Relationship to Head of Family; At Jurisdiction Where Enrolled (Yes/No); At Another Jurisdiction; Post Office, County, State (if given); Ward (Yes/No)

41; 33; John; m; 23; Miss. Choctaw; F; M; Head; Yes; Yes
42; 34; Ruth; f; 19; Miss. Choctaw; F; M; Wife; Yes; Yes

43; 35; Lampkin; m; 59; Miss. Choctaw; F; M; Head; Yes; Yes
44; 36; Ann; f; 59; Miss. Choctaw; F; M; Wife; Yes; Yes
45; 271; **Bull**, Lizzy (Sissy); f; 55; Miss. Choctaw; F; Wd; Sis; Yes; Yes

46; 23; Sebbie; f; 59; Miss. Choctaw; F; Wd; Head; Yes; Yes
47; 24; Albert; m; 33; Miss. Choctaw; F; S; Nep; Yes; Yes

48; 29; Willie Lester (Land); m; 21; Miss. Choctaw; F; M; Head; Yes; Yes
49; 812; Rose Jackson; f; 25; Miss. Choctaw; F; M; Wife; Yes; Yes

ANDERSON

50; 41; A. J; m; 25; Miss. Choctaw; F; M; Head; Yes; Yes
51; 72; Ella Mae Farmer; f; 21; Miss. Choctaw; F; M; Wife; Yes; Yes
    Died 9-13-1938
52;   Sarah Ann; f; 11/12; Miss. Choctaw; F; S; Dau; Yes; Yes
    Born 1-29-36

53; 69; Abel; m; 31; Miss. Choctaw; F; M; Head; Yes; Yes
    70; Nancy; f; 51; Miss. Choctaw; F; M; Wife; Yes; Yes
    Died 3-1-36
54; 502; Emma Farmer; f; 34; Miss. Choctaw; F; M; Wife; Yes; Yes

55; 39; Bob; m; 52; Miss. Choctaw; F; M; Head; Yes; Yes
56; 40; Ella; f; 49; Miss. Choctaw; F; M; Wife; Yes; Yes
57; 42; Judie (Trudie); f; 19; Miss. Choctaw; F; S; Dau; Yes; Yes
58; 43; Josephine; f; 15; Miss. Choctaw; F; S; Dau; Yes; Yes
59; 44; Sallie Mae; f; 12; Miss. Choctaw; F; S; Dau; Yes; Yes
60; 45; Berniece; f; 9; Miss. Choctaw; F; S; Dau; Yes; Yes

Census of the __Mississippi Choctaws__ reservation of the __Choctaw Agency__ jurisdiction, as of __January 1, 1937__, 19__, taken by __A. C. Hector__, Superintendent.

KEY; Surname; Present Census Number; Last Census Number; Given Name; Sex; Age at Last Birthday; Tribe; Degree of Blood; Marital Status; Relationship to Head of Family; At Jurisdiction Where Enrolled (Yes/No); At Another Jurisdiction; Post Office, County, State (if given); Ward (Yes/No)

61; 64; Hinton; m; 23; Miss. Choctaw; F; M; Head; Yes; Yes
62;1001; Belthie Johnson; f; 15; Miss. Choctaw; F; Wife; Yes; Yes

63; 51; Ike; m; 35; Miss. Choctaw; F; M; Head; Yes; Yes
64;1016; Lavenia King; f; 18; Miss. Choctaw; F; M; Wife; Yes; Yes

65; 53; Irvin; m; 33; Miss. Choctaw; F; M; Head; Yes; Yes
66; 54; Thelma Ben; f; 21; Miss. Choctaw; F; M; Wife; Yes; Yes
~~Baby; m; [blank]; Miss. Choctaw; F; S; Son; Yes; Yes~~
Born 2-7-36   Died 2-11-36

~~67; 46; John; m; 69; Miss. Choctaw; F; M; Head; Yes; Yes~~
Died 4-19-1938
68; 47; Sallie; f; 34; Miss. Choctaw; F; M; Wife; Yes; Yes
69; 48; J. C; m; 12; Miss. Choctaw; F; S; Son; Yes; Yes
70; 49; Amy; f; 4; Miss. Choctaw; F; S; Dau; Yes; Yes
~~1827; Lola Mae; f; "2{sic}; Miss. Choctaw; F; S; Dau; Yes; Yes~~
Died 7-12-36

71; 65; Lonnie; m; 22; Miss. Choctaw; F; M; Head; Yes; Yes
72;1409; Mollie Thomas; f; 16; Miss. Choctaw; F; M; Wife; Yes; Yes

73; 50; Mattie; f; 67; Miss. Choctaw; F; Wd; Alone; Yes; Yes

74; 59; Ollie; m; 51; Miss. Choctaw; F; M; Head; Yes; Yes
75; 60; Kate; f; 56; Miss. Choctaw; F; M; Wife; Yes; Yes
76; 61; Grace; f; 14; Miss. Choctaw; F; S; Dau; Yes; Yes

77; 62; Oliver; m; 51; Miss. Choctaw; F; M; Head; Yes; Yes
78; 63; Sallie; f; 44; Miss. Choctaw; F; M; Wife; Yes; Yes
79; 66; Phillip; m; 18; Miss. Choctaw; F; S; Son; Yes; Yes
80; 67; Houston; m; 16; Miss. Choctaw; F; S; Son; Yes; Yes
81; 68; Lucille; f; 14; Miss. Choctaw; F; S; Dau; Yes; Yes

Census of the **Mississippi Choctaws** reservation of the **Choctaw Agency** jurisdiction, as of **January 1, 1937**, 19__, taken by **A. C. Hector**, Superintendent.

KEY; Surname; Present Census Number; Last Census Number; Given Name; Sex; Age at Last Birthday; Tribe; Degree of Blood; Marital Status; Relationship to Head of Family; At Jurisdiction Where Enrolled (Yes/No); At Another Jurisdiction; Post Office, County, State (if given); Ward (Yes/No)

82; 55; Roy; m; 41; Miss. Choctaw; F; M; Head; Yes; Yes
83; 56; Lonie; f; 37; Miss. Choctaw; F; M; Wife; Yes; Yes
84; 57; Frances; f; 8; Miss. Choctaw; F; S; Dau; Yes; Yes
85; 58; Lillie Mae; f; #3[sic]; Miss. Choctaw; F; S; Dau; Yes; Yes

AULKER

Pete; m; White; None; M; Head;
86;1417; Leona Thomas; f; 37; Miss. Choctaw; F; M; Wife; Yes; Yes

BELL

87; 113; Amon; m; 35; Miss. Choctaw; F; M; Head; Yes; Yes
88; 114; Alice; f; 34; Miss. Choctaw; F; M; Wife; Yes; Yes

89; 145; Bob; m; 27; Miss. Choctaw; F; M; Head; Yes; Yes
90; 146; Geneva; f; 26; Miss. Choctaw; F; M: Wife; Yes; Yes
91; 147; Rose (Naomi Ruth); f; 5; Miss. Choctaw; F; S; Dau; Yes; Yes
92; 148; Sudie (Sadie); f; 7; Miss. Choctaw; F; S; Dau; Yes; Yes
93; 149; Bobby Sam; m; 3; Miss. Choctaw; F; S; Son; Yes; Yes
94;1829; Evaline; f; 2; Miss. Choctaw; F; S; Dau; Yes; Yes

~~123; Boston; m; 52; Miss. Choctaw; F; M; Head; Yes; Yes~~
Died 1934 - Unreported
95; 124; Lela; f; 37; Miss. Choctaw; F; M; Wife; Yes; Yes
96; 127; Effie; f; 25; Miss. Choctaw; F; S; Dau; Yes; Yes
97; 128; John; m; 15; Miss. Choctaw; F; S; Son; Yes; Yes
98; 129; Emma; f; 13; Miss. Choctaw; F; S; Dau; Yes; Yes
99;1587; **Vaughn**, Melissa Bell; f; 43; Miss. Choctaw; F; Wd; Dau; Yes; Yes
100; **Vaughn**, Johnny; m; 1; Miss. Choctaw; F; S; Grand-son; Yes; Yes   Born 1935 - Unreported
101; 130; Emmett; m; 12; Miss. Choctaw; F; S; Son; Yes; Yes

Census of the __Mississippi Choctaws__ reservation of the __Choctaw Agency__ jurisdiction, as of __January 1, 1937__, 19__, taken by __A. C. Hector__, Superintendent.

KEY; Surname; Present Census Number; Last Census Number; Given Name; Sex; Age at Last Birthday; Tribe; Degree of Blood; Marital Status; Relationship to Head of Family; At Jurisdiction Where Enrolled (Yes/No); At Another Jurisdiction; Post Office, County, State (if given); Ward (Yes/No)

102; Tom; m; 10; Miss. Choctaw; F; S; Son; Yes; Yes
Omitted from previous census
103; Aline; f; 8; Miss. Choctaw; F; S; Dau; Yes; Yes
Omitted from previous census
104; Levi; m; 7; Miss. Choctaw; F; S; Son; Yes; Yes
Omitted from previous census
105; 131; Marshall; m; 7; Miss. Choctaw; F; S; Son; Yes; Yes
106; Leona; f; 5; Miss. Choctaw; F; S; Dau; Yes; Yes
Omitted from previous census

107; 85; Chalmers (Junus); m; 40; Miss. Choctaw; F; M; Head; Yes; Yes
108; 86; Winnie; f; 35; Miss. Choctaw; F; M; Wife; Yes; Yes
109; 88; Woods; m; 17; Miss. Choctaw; F; S; Son; Yes; Yes
110; 89; Minnie; f; 15; Miss. Choctaw; F; S; Dau; Yes; Yes
111; 90; Edmond; m; 12; Miss. Choctaw; F; S; Son; Yes; Yes
112; 91; George; m; 10; Miss. Choctaw; F; S; Son; Yes; Yes
113; Jessie; f; 6; Miss. Choctaw; F; S; Dau; Yes; Yes
Omitted from previous census
114; 1828; Claud; f; 2; Miss. Choctaw; F; S; Dau[sic]; Yes; Yes

115; 132; Cornelius; m; 79; Miss. Choctaw; F; Wd; Head; Yes; Yes
116; 133; John; m; 30; Miss. Choctaw; F; M; Son; Yes; Yes
117; 813; Nancy Jackson; f; 23; Miss. Choctaw; F; M; Dau-in-law; Yes; Yes
118; Rosenbaum; m; 1; Miss. Choctaw; F; S; Grand-son; Yes; Yes
Boen 1935 - Unreported

119; 92; Evan; m; 35; Miss. Choctaw; F; M; Head; Yes; Yes
120; 93; Willie; f; 25; Miss. Choctaw; F; M; Wife; Yes; Yes
121; 94; Homer; m; 10; Miss. Choctaw; F; S; Son; Yes; Yes
122; 95; Nancy L; f; 8; Miss. Choctaw; F; S; Dau; Yes; Yes
123; Edna; f; 6; Miss. Choctaw; F; S; Dau; Yes; Yes
Omitted from previous census

Census of the **Mississippi Choctaws** reservation of the **Choctaw Agency** jurisdiction, as of **January 1, 1937**, 19__, taken by **A. C. Hector**, Superintendent.

KEY; Surname; Present Census Number; Last Census Number; Given Name; Sex; Age at Last Birthday; Tribe; Degree of Blood; Marital Status; Relationship to Head of Family; At Jurisdiction Where Enrolled (Yes/No); At Another Jurisdiction; Post Office, County, State (if given); Ward (Yes/No)

124; 96; Hester; f; 3; Miss. Choctaw; F; S; Dau; Yes; Yes
125; Inez; f; 2; Miss. Choctaw; F; S; Dau; Yes; Yes
Born 7-2-35 - Unreported
126; 97; Mandy; f; 69; Miss. Choctaw; F; Wd; Mother; Yes; Yes

127; 143; Gaston; m; 28; Miss. Choctaw; F; S; Alone; Yes; Yes

128; 110; Gipson; m; 24; Miss. Choctaw; F; M; Head; Yes; Yes
129; 111; Lucy; f; 24; Miss. Choctaw; F; M; Wife; Yes; Yes
130; 112; Lynch (Gipson, Jr); m; 5; Miss. Choctaw; F; S; Son; Yes; Yes
131;1831; Nellie (Zoe); f; 2; Miss. Choctaw; F; S; Dau; Yes; Yes

132; 138; Houston; m; 17; Miss. Choctaw; F; M; Head; Yes; Yes
133; 37; Lilly Amos; f; 21; Miss. Choctaw; F; M; Wife; Yes; Yes

134; 74; Hugh; m; 57; Miss. Choctaw; F; Wd; Head; Yes; Yes
135; 75; Mamie; f; 11; Miss. Choctaw; F; S; Dau; Yes; Yes

~~115; Jim; m; 67; Miss. Choctaw; F; S; Alone; Yes; Yes~~
Died 1933 - Unreported
134; Jim; m; 67; Miss. Choctaw; F; S; Alone; Yes; Yes
Duplication of 115 now deceased

136;1527; (Tubby), Joe; m; 28; Miss. Choctaw; F; M; Head; Yes; Yes
137;1550; Isa; f; 19; Miss. Choctaw; F; M; Wife; Yes; Yes
~~128;1830; Floyd Jarlus; m; 2; Miss. Choctaw; F; S; Son; Yes; Yes~~
Died May 6, 1937

139; 116; Joe; m; 45; Miss. Choctaw; F; M; Head; Yes; Yes
140; 117; Bessie Susie; f; 37; Miss. Choctaw; F; M; Wife; Yes; Yes
141; 118; Tom Mack; m; 17; Miss. Choctaw; F; S; Son; Yes; Yes
142; 119; Bill; m; 13; Miss. Choctaw; F; S; Son; Yes; Yes
143; 120; Henry Sam; m; 11; Miss. Choctaw; F; S; Son; Yes; Yes
144; 121; Nellie (Pollie Ann); f; 9; Miss. Choctaw; F; S; Dau; Yes; Yes

Census of the **Mississippi Choctaws** reservation of the **Choctaw Agency** jurisdiction, as of **January 1, 1937**, 19__, taken by **A. C. Hector**, Superintendent.

KEY; Surname; Present Census Number; Last Census Number; Given Name; Sex; Age at Last Birthday; Tribe; Degree of Blood; Marital Status; Relationship to Head of Family; At Jurisdiction Where Enrolled (Yes/No); At Another Jurisdiction; Post Office, County, State (if given); Ward (Yes/No)

145; 122; Sallie; f; 60; Miss. Choctaw; F; Wd; Mo-in-law; Yes; Yes

146; 76; John; m; 46; Miss. Choctaw; F; M; Head; Yes; Yes
147; 77; Lillian; f; 47; Miss. Choctaw; F; M; Wife; Yes; Yes
148; 78; Hattie; f; 16; Miss. Choctaw; F; S; Dau; Yes; Yes
149; 79; Eva; f; 12; Miss. Choctaw; F; S; Dau; Yes; Yes
150; 80; Ola; f; 10; Miss. Choctaw; F; S; Dau; Yes; Yes

151; 135; Lish; m; 44; Miss. Choctaw; F; M; Head; Yes; Yes
152; 136; Martha; f; 42; Miss. Choctaw; F; M; Wife; Yes; Yes
153; 137; Willie; m; 22; Miss. Choctaw; F; M; Son; Yes; Yes
154;1737; Lillie Willis; f; 13; Miss. Choctaw; F; M; Dau-in-law; Yes; Yes
155; 139; Minnie; f; 16; Miss. Choctaw; F; S; Dau; Yes; Yes
156; 140; Less C; m; 14; Miss. Choctaw; F; S; Son; Yes; Yes
157; 141; Gene D; m; 12; Miss. Choctaw; F; S; Son; Yes; Yes
158; 142; Jay; m; 10; Miss. Choctaw; F; S; Son; Yes; Yes
159; Christine; f; 16; Miss. Choctaw; F; S; Dau; Yes; Yes
Omitted from previous census
160; 144; Odie (Isaac Wampler); m; 4; Miss. Choctaw; F; S; Son; Yes; Yes
161; Susan; f; 9/12; Miss. Choctaw; F; S; Dau; Yes; Yes
Born 3-14-36

162; 150; Lish; m; 56; Miss. Choctaw; F; M; Head; Yes; Yes
163; 151; Maggie; f; 56; Miss. Choctaw; F; S; Dau; Yes; Yes
164; 152; Minnie; f; 29; Miss. Choctaw; F; S; Dau; Yes; Yes
165; 153; Lula; f; 21; Miss. Choctaw; F; S; Dau; Yes; Yes
166; 156; Basin; m; 12; Miss. Choctaw; F; S; Son; Yes; Yes

167; 98; Mack; m; 32; Miss. Choctaw; F; M; Hd[sic]; Yes; Yes

168; 105; Nicholas; m; 37; Miss. Choctaw; F; M; Head; Yes; Yes
169; 106; Cleddie; f; 24; Miss. Choctaw; F; M; Wife; Yes; Yes

Census of the **Mississippi Choctaws** reservation of the **Choctaw Agency** jurisdiction, as of **January 1, 1937**, 19__, taken by **A. C. Hector**, Superintendent.

KEY; Surname; Present Census Number; Last Census Number; Given Name; Sex; Age at Last Birthday; Tribe; Degree of Blood; Marital Status; Relationship to Head of Family; At Jurisdiction Where Enrolled (Yes/No); At Another Jurisdiction; Post Office, County, State (if given); Ward (Yes/No)

170; 107; Ruby; f; 7; Miss. Choctaw; F; S; Dau; Yes; Yes
171; 108; Bonnie K; f; 6; Miss. Choctaw; F; S; Dau; Yes; Yes
172; 109; Franklin; m; 4; Miss. Choctaw; F; S; Son; Yes; Yes
173;1832; Will Rogers; m; 2; Miss. Choctaw; F; S; Son; Yes;

174; 154; Tom; m; 31; Miss. Choctaw; F; M; Head; Yes; Yes
175; 715; Mattie Henry; f; 26; Miss. Choctaw; F; M; Wife; Yes; Yes
176; Allie Mae; f; 9/12; Miss. Choctaw; F; S; Dau; Yes; Yes
Born 3-4-36

177; 102; Thompson; m; 39; Miss. Choctaw; F; M: Head; Yes; Yes
178; 103; Ellen; f; 39; Miss. Choctaw; F; M; Wife; Yes; Yes
179; 104; Frank K; m; 23; Miss. Choctaw; F; S; Son; Yes; Yes

180; 157; Tony; m; 22; Miss. Choctaw; F; M: Head; Yes; Yes
~~181; 99; Bell (Lena Mingo); f; 23; Miss. Choctaw; F; M; Wife; Yes; Yes~~ Died 9-6-1938
182; 101; Herbert H; m; 5; Miss. Choctaw; F; S; Step-son; Yes; Yes
183;1793; Fannie; f; 3; Miss. Choctaw; F; S; Dau; Yes; Yes
184; Henry; m; 2; Miss. Choctaw; F; S; Son; Yes; Yes
Born 8-1-35 - Unreported

BEN

185; 178; Charlie; m; 38; Miss. Choctaw; F; M Head; Yes; Yes
186; 179; Emeline; f; 30; Miss. Choctaw; F; M; Wife; Yes; Yes
187; 180; Opal Grace; f; 5; Miss. Choctaw; F; S; Dau; Yes; Yes
188;1795; Robert (James Clark); m; 2; Miss. Choctaw; F; S; Son; Yes; Yes

189; 181; Jim; m; 61; Miss. Choctaw; F; Wd; Head; Yes; Yes
190; Mike; m; 20; Miss. Choctaw; F; S; Son; Yes; Yes
Omitted from previous census

Census of the __Mississippi Choctaws__ reservation of the __Choctaw Agency__ jurisdiction, as of __January 1, 1937__, 19__, taken by __A. C. Hector__, Superintendent.

KEY; Surname; Present Census Number; Last Census Number; Given Name; Sex; Age at Last Birthday; Tribe; Degree of Blood; Marital Status; Relationship to Head of Family; At Jurisdiction Where Enrolled (Yes/No); At Another Jurisdiction; Post Office, County, State (if given); Ward (Yes/No)

191; 166; Lula; f; 53; Miss. Choctaw; F; Wd; Head; Yes; Yes
192; 167; Jimpson; m; 31; Miss. Choctaw; F; S; Son; Yes; Yes
193; 168; Wilson; m; 20; Miss. Choctaw; F; S; Son; Yes; Yes

194; 182; Monroe; m; 26; Miss. Choctaw; F; M; Head; Yes; Yes
195; 208; Lorene McMillian; f; 27; Miss. Choctaw; F; M; Wife; Yes; Yes
196; 209; **Billy**, Cicero L; m; 5; Miss. Choctaw; F; S; Step-son; Yes; Yes
197;   Eileene[sic]; f; 9/12; Miss. Choctaw; F; S; Dau; Yes; Yes Born 3-16-36

198; 158; Olin; m; 37; Miss. Choctaw; F; M; Head; Yes; Yes
199; 159; Neva; f; 30; Miss. Choctaw; F; M; Wife; Yes; Yes
200; 160; Nannie Mae; f; 13; Miss. Choctaw; F; S; Dau; Yes; Yes
201; 161; Annie Laura; f; 11; Miss. Choctaw; F; S; Dau; Yes; Yes
202; 162; Mattie Lou; f; 9; Miss. Choctaw; F; S; Dau; Yes; Yes
203;1794; Harrison; m; 2; Miss. Choctaw; F; S; Son; Yes; Yes

204; 169; Otho; m; 23; Miss. Choctaw; F; M; Head; Yes; Yes
205; 170; Lessie Isaac; f; 24; Miss. Choctaw; F; M; Wife; Yes; Yes
206; 171; Chester; m; 3; Miss. Choctaw; F; S; Son; Yes; Yes
207;   Brantley Arthur; m; 8/12; Miss. Choctaw; F; S; Son; Yes; Yes Born 4-18-36

~~208;1461; Rufus; m; 19; Miss. Choctaw; F; M; Head; Yes; Yes~~
Died 5-9-38
209; 163; Colleen Isaac; f; 18; Miss. Choctaw; F; M; Wife; Yes; Yes

210; 172; Tom; m; 42; Miss. Choctaw; F; M; Head; Yes; Yes
211; 173; Gladys; f; 31; Miss. Choctaw; F; M; Wife; Yes; Yes
212; 174; Fannie Lou; f; 12; Miss. Choctaw; F; S; Dau; Yes; Yes
213; 175; Hubert; m; 10; Miss. Choctaw; F; S; Son; Yes; Yes
214; 176; Henry Ford; m; 8; Miss. Choctaw; F; S; Son; Yes; Yes

Census of the **Mississippi Choctaws** reservation of the **Choctaw Agency** jurisdiction, as of **January 1, 1937**, 19__, taken by **A. C. Hector**, Superintendent.

KEY; Surname; Present Census Number; Last Census Number; Given Name; Sex; Age at Last Birthday; Tribe; Degree of Blood; Marital Status; Relationship to Head of Family; At Jurisdiction Where Enrolled (Yes/No); At Another Jurisdiction; Post Office, County, State (if given); Ward (Yes/No)

215; 177; Helen Marie; f; 4; Miss. Choctaw; F; S; Dau; Yes; Yes
216;1833; Tom Comby, Jr; m; 2; Miss. Choctaw; F; S; Son; Yes; Yes

~~217; 164; Wyatt; m; 69; Miss. Choctaw; F; M; Head; Yes; Yes~~
      Died 1932
218; 165; Ellen; f; 64; Miss. Choctaw; F; M; Wife; Yes; Yes

BILLY

~~219;1112; Clement; m; 23; Miss. Choctaw; F; M; Head; Yes; Yes~~
      Died 9-25-38
220;1351; Cornelia Stephens; f; 31; Miss. Choctaw; F; M; Wife; Yes; Yes
221;1094; **Alex**, Herbert; m; 10; Miss. Choctaw; F; S; Orphan; Yes; Yes

222; 215; Greer; m; 18; Miss. Choctaw; F; M; Head; Yes; Yes
223;1259; Leona Sam; f; 15; Miss. Choctaw; F; M; Wife; Yes; Yes

224; 204; Ike; m; 27; Miss. Choctaw; F; M; Head; Yes; Yes
225; 205; Jennie C; f; 25; Miss. Choctaw; F; M; Wife; Yes; Yes
226; 206; Kate; f; 4; Miss. Choctaw; F; S; Dau; Yes; Yes
227; 207; John; m; 3; Miss. Choctaw; F; S; Son; Yes; Yes
228;   John Cephus; m; 2; Miss. Choctaw; F; S; Son; Yes; Yes
      Born 1-26-34 - Unreported
229;   Lillie; f; 3/12; Miss. Choctaw; F; S; Dau; Yes; Yes
      Born 9-10-36
230; 203; Earl; m; 11; Miss. Choctaw; F; S; Neph; Yes; Yes

231; 210; Johnson; m; 71; Miss. Choctaw; F; M; Head; Yes; Yes
232; 211; Velaria; f; 56; Miss. Choctaw; F; M; Wife; Yes; Yes
233; 212; Gipson; m; 26; Miss. Choctaw; F; S; Son; Yes; Yes
234; 213; Ike; m; 25; Miss. Choctaw; F; S; Son; Yes; Yes
235; 214; Woodrow (Wilson); m; 20; Miss. Choctaw; F; S; Son; Yes; Yes

Census of the **Mississippi Choctaws** reservation of the **Choctaw Agency** jurisdiction, as of **January 1, 1937**, 19__, taken by **A. C. Hector**, Superintendent.

KEY; Surname; Present Census Number; Last Census Number; Given Name; Sex; Age at Last Birthday; Tribe; Degree of Blood; Marital Status; Relationship to Head of Family; At Jurisdiction Where Enrolled (Yes/No); At Another Jurisdiction; Post Office, County, State (if given); Ward (Yes/No)

236; 216; Frank; m; 13; Miss. Choctaw; F; S; Son; Yes; Yes
237;1713; **Willis**, Sallie; f; 24; Miss. Choctaw; F; S; Wd; Dau; Yes; Yes
238;1714; **Willis**, John; m; 8; Miss. Choctaw; F; S; Grand-son; Yes; Yes
239;1715; **Willis**, Hayward; m; 6; Miss. Choctaw; F; S; Grand-son; Yes; Yes

240; 227; Lee; m; 21; Miss. Choctaw; F; M: Head; Yes; Yes
241; 349; Heniretta[sic] Chitto; f; 22; Miss. Choctaw; F; M; Wife; Yes; Yes
242; Robert Lee; m; 2/12; Miss. Choctaw; F; S; Son; Yes; Yes Born 10-27-36

243; 218; Lewis; m; 32; Miss. Choctaw; F; M; Head; Yes; Yes
244; 219; Zelma; f; 32; Miss. Choctaw; F; M; Wife; Yes; Yes
245; 220; Clennis Willis; f; 17; Miss. Choctaw; F; S; Step-dau; Yes; Yes
246; **Willis**, Henry; m; 10/12; Miss. Choctaw; F; S; Step-grand-son; Yes; Yes   Born 2-26-36
247; 221; Mamie; f; 15; Miss. Choctaw; F; S; Step-dau; Yes; Yes
248; 222; Frank; m; 11; Miss. Choctaw; F; S; Step-son; Yes; Yes
249; 223; Annie; f; 9; Miss. Choctaw; F; S; Step-dau; Yes; Yes

250; 184; Lum; m; 52; Miss. Choctaw; F; M; Head; Yes; Yes
251; 185; Minnie; f; 54; Miss. Choctaw; F; M; Wife; Yes; Yes
252; 186; **Charles**, James; m; 59; Miss. Choctaw; F; S; Bro-in-law; Yes; Yes

~~2; Billie, Mary; f; 99; Miss. Choctaw; F; Wd; Alone; Yes; Yes~~
Omitted on previous census. Died 7-11-36

~~253; 201; Nicey; f; 77; Miss. Choctaw; F; Wd; Head; Yes; Yes~~
Died Dec. 27, 1937

254; 187; Tom; m; 26; Miss. Choctaw; F; M; Head; Yes; Yes
255; 188; Sallie Stoliby; f; 27; Miss. Choctaw; F; M; Wife; Yes; Yes

Census of the **Mississippi Choctaws** reservation of the **Choctaw Agency** jurisdiction, as of **January 1, 1937**, 19__, taken by **A. C. Hector**, Superintendent.

KEY; Surname; Present Census Number; Last Census Number; Given Name; Sex; Age at Last Birthday; Tribe; Degree of Blood; Marital Status; Relationship to Head of Family; At Jurisdiction Where Enrolled (Yes/No); At Another Jurisdiction; Post Office, County, State (if given); Ward (Yes/No)

256; 189; Robert; m; 9; Miss. Choctaw; F; S; Son; Yes; Yes
257; 190; James; m; 6; Miss. Choctaw; F; S; Son; Yes; Yes
258; 191; Rosaulee[sic]; f; 3; Miss. Choctaw; F; S; Dau; Yes; Yes
259; Lorraine; f; 6/12; Miss. Choctaw; F; S; Dau; Yes; Yes
Born 6-18-36

260; 192; Will; m; 60; Miss. Choctaw; F; S; Alone; Yes; Yes

261; 224; Will; m; 49; Miss. Choctaw; F; M; Head; Yes; Yes
262; 225; Alice; f; 47; Miss. Choctaw; F; M; Wife; Yes; Yes
263; 226; William; m; 22; Miss. Choctaw; F; S; Son; Yes; Yes
264; 228; Rose; f; 18; Miss. Choctaw; F; S; Dau; Yes; Yes
265; 229; Irene; f; 15; Miss. Choctaw; F; S; Dau; Yes; Yes
266; 230; Joe; m; 14; Miss. Choctaw; F; S; Son; Yes; Yes
~~231; Will, Jr; m; 10; Miss. Choctaw; F; S; Son; Yes; Yes~~
Died 1931 or 1932 - Unreported
267; 232; Marchie; f; 9; Miss. Choctaw; F; S; Dau; Yes; Yes
268; 233; Charlie; m; 7; Miss. Choctaw; F; S; Son; Yes; Yes
269; 234; Tommy Jean; f; 3; Miss. Choctaw; F; S; Dau; Yes; Yes

270; 241; Richard; m; 26; Miss. Choctaw; F; M; Head; Yes; Yes
271; 242; Eva (Cassie); f; 22; Miss. Choctaw; F; M; Wife; Yes; Yes
272; 243; Duley; f; 5; Miss. Choctaw; F; S; Dau; Yes; Yes
273; 244; Sarah; f; 4; Miss. Choctaw; F; S; Dau; Yes; Yes
274; 1796; Wilson; m; 3; Miss. Choctaw; F; S; Son; Yes; Yes
275; Reta; f; 10/12; Miss. Choctaw; F; S; Dau; Yes; Yes
Born 2-9-36

276; 245; Wade; m; 58; Miss. Choctaw; F; M; Head; Yes; Yes
277; 246; Lina; f; 40; Miss. Choctaw; F; M; Wife; Yes; Yes
278; 247; Sienna; f; 4; Miss. Choctaw; F; S; Dau; Yes; Yes
279; 248; **McMillan**, Mary Lewis; f; 17; Miss. Choctaw; F; S; Stepdau; Yes; Yes

Census of the __Mississippi Choctaws__ reservation of the __Choctaw Agency__ jurisdiction, as of __January 1, 1937__, 19__, taken by __A. C. Hector__, Superintendent.

KEY; Surname; Present Census Number; Last Census Number; Given Name; Sex; Age at Last Birthday; Tribe; Degree of Blood; Marital Status; Relationship to Head of Family; At Jurisdiction Where Enrolled (Yes/No); At Another Jurisdiction; Post Office, County, State (if given); Ward (Yes/No)

280; 193; Williston; m; 43; Miss. Choctaw; F; M; Head; Yes; Yes
281; 194; Jessie; f; 33; Miss. Choctaw; F; M; Wife; Yes; Yes
282; 195; Melton; m; 16; Miss. Choctaw; F; S; Son; Yes; Yes
283; 196; Finis (Beaman); m; 13; Miss. Choctaw; F; S; Son; Yes; Yes
~~197; Maurice; m; 11; Miss. Choctaw; F; S; Son; Yes; Yes~~
    Dead - Unreported
284; 198; Horace; m; 10; Miss. Choctaw; F; S; Son; Yes; Yes
285; 199; Betty Jean; f; 5; Miss. Choctaw; F; S; Dau; Yes; Yes
287;   Beaman; m; 8/12; Miss. Choctaw; F; S; Son; Yes; Yes
    Born 4-27-36

BOB

288; 249; Simon; m; 67; Miss. Choctaw; F; S; Alone; Yes; Yes

BRISCOE

289; 259; Jim; m; 22; Miss. Choctaw; F; M; Head; Yes; Yes
290; 260; Elsie Y; f; 21; Miss. Choctaw; F; M; Wife; Yes; Yes
291; 261; George Ann; f; 3; Miss. Choctaw; F; S; Dau; Yes; Yes
~~292;   Charlie; m; 3/12; Miss. Choctaw; F; S; Son; Yes; Yes~~
    Born 9-26-36 Died March 12, 1937

293; 264; Stephen; m; 28; Miss. Choctaw; F; M; Head; Yes; Yes
294; 265; Maggie Gipson; f; 29; Miss. Choctaw; F; M: Wife; Yes; Yes
295; 267; Colton; m; 4; Miss. Choctaw; F; S; Son; Yes; Yes

296; 262; Tom; m; 36; Miss. Choctaw; F; Wd; Alone; Yes; Yes

BULL

~~268; Pink; m; 59; Miss. Choctaw; F; Wd; Head; Yes; Yes~~
    Died 4-15-36 in Oklahoma

Census of the **Mississippi Choctaws** reservation of the **Choctaw Agency** jurisdiction, as of **January 1, 1937**, 19__, taken by **A. C. Hector**, Superintendent.

KEY; Surname; Present Census Number; Last Census Number; Given Name; Sex; Age at Last Birthday; Tribe; Degree of Blood; Marital Status; Relationship to Head of Family; At Jurisdiction Where Enrolled (Yes/No); At Another Jurisdiction; Post Office, County, State (if given); Ward (Yes/No)

297; 269; **Lewis**, Houston; m; 20; Miss. Choctaw; F; S; Orphan; Yes; Yes

298; 272; Foreman; m; 34; Miss. Choctaw; F; M; Head; Yes; Yes
299; 273; Sarah; f; 33; Miss. Choctaw; F; M; Wife; Yes; Yes
300;1567; **Tubby**, Wesley; m; 18; Miss. Choctaw; F; S; Step-son; Yes; Yes

~~270; George; m; 63; Miss. Choctaw; F; M; Head; Yes; Yes~~
Died 4-13-36

BULLOCHE

Clayton; m; [blank]; White; None; M; Head
301;1418; Evaline Thomas; f; 41; Miss. Choctaw; F; M; Wife; Yes; Yes

CAMPBELL

302; 274; Wiley; m; 36; Miss. Choctaw; F; M[sic]; Alone; Yes; Yes

CATES

288; **(Tubby)**, D; m; 29; Miss. Choctaw; F; M; Son; Yes; Yes
Duplication of 1562-34

291; Susan Mabel; f; 21; Miss. Choctaw; F; S; Slone; Yes; Yes
Duplication of 1563-34

CARVER

George; m; [blank]; White; None; M; Head; Yes; Yes
303; 586; Mary Farve; f; 41; Miss. Choctaw; F; M; Wife; Yes; Yes

Census of the **Mississippi Choctaws** reservation of the **Choctaw Agency** jurisdiction, as of **January 1, 1937**, 19__, taken by **A. C. Hector**, Superintendent.

KEY; Surname; Present Census Number; Last Census Number; Given Name; Sex; Age at Last Birthday; Tribe; Degree of Blood; Marital Status; Relationship to Head of Family; At Jurisdiction Where Enrolled (Yes/No); At Another Jurisdiction; Post Office, County, State (if given); Ward (Yes/No)

Mr; m; [blank]; White; None; M; Head; Yes; Yes
304; 587; Julia Farve; f; 52; Miss. Choctaw; F; M; Wife; Yes; Yes

CHAPMAN

305; 300; Asa; m; 20; Miss. Choctaw; F; M; Head; Yes; Yes
306;1097; Mary McMillan; f; 23; Miss. Choctaw; F; M; Wife; Yes; Yes

307; 298; Will; m; 50; Miss. Choctaw; F; M; Head; Yes; Yes
308; 299; Bettie; f; 53; Miss. Choctaw; F; M; Wife; Yes; Yes
309; 301; Ralston; m; 18; Miss. Choctaw; F; S; Son; Yes; Yes
310; 302; Hattie; f; 14; Miss. Choctaw; F; S; Dau; Yes; Yes
311; 303; Ronie; f; 13; Miss. Choctaw; F; S; Dau; Yes; Yes
312; 304; Lilly; f; 12; Miss. Choctaw; F; S; Dau; Yes; Yes
313; 305; Raymond; m; 11; Miss. Choctaw; F; S; Son; Yes; Yes
314; 306; Christ; m; 10; Miss. Choctaw; F; S; Son; Yes; Yes
315; 307; Minnie; f; 9; Miss. Choctaw; F; S; Dau; Yes; Yes

CHARLIE

316; 318; Coyt; m; 21; Miss. Choctaw; F; M; Head; Yes; Yes
317; 319; Sina Davis; f; 25; Miss. Choctaw; F; M; Wife; Yes; Yes
318; 320; Irene; f; 3; Miss. Choctaw; F; S; Dau; Yes; Yes
319; Louey; m; 10/12; Miss. Choctaw; F; S; Son; Yes; Yes
Born 2-9-36

320; 315; John; m; 43; Miss. Choctaw; F; M: Head; Yes; Yes
321; 316; Mary; f; 35; Miss. Choctaw; F; M; Wife; Yes; Yes
322; 317; Elsie; f; 18; Miss. Choctaw; F; S; Dau; Yes; Yes

323; 308; William; m; 86; Miss. Choctaw; F; M; Head; Yes; Yes
Died 5-26-38
324; 309; Fannie; f; 72; Miss. Choctaw; F; M; Wife; Yes; Yes
Died Nov. 23, 1937

Census of the **Mississippi Choctaws** reservation of the **Choctaw Agency** jurisdiction, as of **January 1, 1937**, 19__, taken by **A. C. Hector**, Superintendent.

KEY; Surname; Present Census Number; Last Census Number; Given Name; Sex; Age at Last Birthday; Tribe; Degree of Blood; Marital Status; Relationship to Head of Family; At Jurisdiction Where Enrolled (Yes/No); At Another Jurisdiction; Post Office, County, State (if given); Ward (Yes/No)

CHAUVET

Paul; m; White; None; M; Head; Yes[sic]; Yes[sic]
325; 601; Ida Farve; f; 57; Miss. Choctaw; F; M; Wife; Yes; Yes

CHICKAWAY

326; 332; Jim; m; 34; Miss. Choctaw; F; M; Head; Yes; Yes
327; 333; Eunice; f; 31; Miss. Choctaw; F; M; Wife; Yes; Yes
328; 334; John Hester; m; 9; Miss. Choctaw; F; S; Son; Yes; Yes
329; 335; Henry; m; 6; Miss. Choctaw; F; S; Son; Yes; Yes
330;1836; Sallie (Rejina); f; 2; Miss. Choctaw; F; S; Dau; Yes; Yes
331; 336; **Wilson**, Rosie Lee; f; 15; Miss. Choctaw; F; S; Step-dau; Yes; Yes

332; 331; Ola; f; 30; Miss. Choctaw; F; S; Alone; Yes; Yes

333; 341; Rufus; m; 35; Miss. Choctaw; F; M; Head; Yes; Yes
 Died July 12, 1937
334; 342; Bessie; f; 32; Miss. Choctaw; F; M; Wife; Yes; Yes
335; 343; Ross C; m; 9; Miss. Choctaw; F; S; Son; Yes; Yes
336; 344; Elizabeth; f; 7; Miss. Choctaw; F; S; Dau; Yes; Yes
337; Mary Frances; f; 4; Miss. Choctaw; F; S; Dau; Yes; Yes
 Born 8-3-32 - Unreported
338; Josephine Berniece; f; 3/12; Miss. Choctaw; F; S; Dau; Yes; Yes Born 9-29-36

339; 321; Sim; m; 29; Miss. Choctaw; F; M; Head; Yes; Yes
340; 322; Maggie; f; 36; Miss. Choctaw; F; M; Wife; Yes; Yes
341; 323; Clemon; m; 18; Miss. Choctaw; F; S; Son; Yes; Yes
342; 324; Mollie (Nellie); f; 16; Miss. Choctaw; F; S; Dau; Yes; Yes
343; 325; Agnes; f; 14; Miss. Choctaw; F; S; Dau; Yes; Yes
344; 326; Maggie Kate; f; 9; Miss. Choctaw; F; S; Dau; Yes; Yes
346; 327; Kate; f; 6; Miss. Choctaw; F; S; Dau; Yes; Yes

Census of the **Mississippi Choctaws** reservation of the **Choctaw Agency** jurisdiction, as of **January 1, 1937**, 19__, taken by **A. C. Hector**, Superintendent.

KEY; Surname; Present Census Number; Last Census Number; Given Name; Sex; Age at Last Birthday; Tribe; Degree of Blood; Marital Status; Relationship to Head of Family; At Jurisdiction Where Enrolled (Yes/No); At Another Jurisdiction; Post Office, County, State (if given); Ward (Yes/No)

347; 329; John Study; m; 4; Miss. Choctaw; F; S; Son; Yes; Yes
348;1835; Allie; f; 2; Miss. Choctaw; F; S; Dau; Yes; Yes

CHITTO

349; 345; Joe; m; 37; Miss. Choctaw; F; M; Head; Yes; Yes
350; 346; Callie; f; 37; Miss. Choctaw; F; M; Wife; Yes; Yes
351; 347; Leo Clifton; m; 9; Miss. Choctaw; F; S; Son; Yes; Yes
~~1797; Dewey Davis; m; 3; Miss. Choctaw; F; S; Son; Yes; Yes~~
    Died 8-2-35 - Unreported
352; 399; Mary; f; 38; Miss. Choctaw; F; S; Sister; Yes; Yes

353; 353; John; m; 47; Miss. Choctaw; F; M; Head; Yes; Yes
354; 354; Sallie; f; 46; Miss. Choctaw; F; M; Wife; Yes; Yes
355; 356; Hattie; f; 19; Miss. Choctaw; F; S; Dau; Yes; Yes
356; 357; Allie Nora; f; 17; Miss. Choctaw; F; S; Dau; Yes; Yes
357; 358; Ella; f; 15; Miss. Choctaw; F; S; Dau; Yes; Yes
    359; Lum Billy; m; 11; Miss. Choctaw; F; S; Son; Yes; Yes
    Duplication of 1449-34;

358; 348; Pat; m; 60; Miss. Choctaw; F; Wd; Head; Yes; Yes
359; 350; Jefferson; m; 20; Miss. Choctaw; F; S; Son; Yes; Yes
360; 351; Iren (Erma); f; 15; Miss. Choctaw; F; S; Dau; Yes; Yes
361; 352; Isom; m; 13; Miss. Choctaw; F; S; Son; Yes; Yes

CLARK

362; 366; Stella; f; 42; Miss. Choctaw; F; S; Alone; Yes; Yes

CLEMONS

363; 367; Jeff; m; 40; Miss. Choctaw; F; M; Head; Yes; Yes
364; 368; Cora Frazier; f; 36; Miss. Choctaw; F; M; Wife; Yes; Yes

Census of the **Mississippi Choctaws** reservation of the **Choctaw Agency** jurisdiction, as of **January 1, 1937**, 19__, taken by **A. C. Hector**, Superintendent.

KEY; Surname; Present Census Number; Last Census Number; Given Name; Sex; Age at Last Birthday; Tribe; Degree of Blood; Marital Status; Relationship to Head of Family; At Jurisdiction Where Enrolled (Yes/No); At Another Jurisdiction; Post Office, County, State (if given); Ward (Yes/No)

~~365; 369; Mattie; f; 15; Miss. Choctaw; F; S; Dau; Yes; Yes~~
    Died 1936
~~366; 370; Irsal[sic]; m; 15; Miss. Choctaw; F; S; Son; Yes; Yes~~
    Died 1936
367; 371; Ethel; f; 14; Miss. Choctaw; F; S; Dau; Yes; Yes
368; 372; Sim (John); m; 6; Miss. Choctaw; F; S; Son; Yes; Yes
369; 373; Emma (Rena Mae); f; 9; Miss. Choctaw; F; S; Dau; Yes; Yes
370; 374; Prince; m; 4; Miss. Choctaw; F; S; Son; Yes; Yes

371; 361; Jim; m; 32; Miss. Choctaw; F; M; Had; Yes; Yes
372; 362; Bessie; f; 30; Miss. Choctaw; F; M; Wife; Yes; Yes
~~_____; 363; Margie; f; 9; Miss. Choctaw; F; S; Dau; Yes; Yes~~
    Died 1934 - Unreported
373; 364; Lewisman; m; 7; Miss. Choctaw; F; S; Son; Yes; Yes
374; 365; Leonard; m; 4; Miss. Choctaw; F; S; Son; Yes; Yes
375;   Winnie; f; 1; Miss. Choctaw; F; S; Dau; Yes; Yes
    Born 1936 - Unreported

~~_____; 375; Munch; m; 54; Miss. Choctaw; F; M; Head; Yes; Yes~~
    Died 1936 - Unreported
376; 376; Nellie; f; 47; Miss. Choctaw; F; M; Wife; Yes; Yes
377;   Ruth; f; 20; Miss. Choctaw; F; S; Dau; Yes; Yes
    Omitted from previous census
378; 377; Bathia; f; 18; Miss. Choctaw; F; S; Dau; Yes; Yes
379;   Bates; m; 17; Miss. Choctaw; F; S; Son; Yes; Yes
    Omitted from previous census
380; 378; Mollie; f; 16; Miss. Choctaw; F; S; Dau; Yes; Yes
381;   Stennis; m; 12; Miss. Choctaw; F; S; Son; Yes; Yes
    Omitted from previous census
382;   Baby; f; 4; Miss. Choctaw; F; S; Dau; Yes; Yes
    Omitted from previous census

Census of the **Mississippi Choctaws** reservation of the **Choctaw Agency** jurisdiction, as of **January 1, 1937**, 19__, taken by **A. C. Hector**, Superintendent.

KEY; Surname; Present Census Number; Last Census Number; Given Name; Sex; Age at Last Birthday; Tribe; Degree of Blood; Marital Status; Relationship to Head of Family; At Jurisdiction Where Enrolled (Yes/No); At Another Jurisdiction; Post Office, County, State (if given); Ward (Yes/No)

COMBY

383; 394; Allie; f; 32; Miss. Choctaw; F; Wd; Head; Yes; Yes
384; 395; Jonas; m; 13; Miss. Choctaw; F; S; Son; Yes; Yes
385; 396; Irene; f; 11; Miss. Choctaw; F; S; Dau; Yes; Yes
386; 397; Joyce Ann; f; 9; Miss. Choctaw; F; S; Dau; Yes; Yes
387; 398; R. L (William); m; 7; Miss. Choctaw; F; S; Son; Yes; Yes
388; 403; Olmon; m; 59; Miss. Choctaw; F; M; Step-father; Yes; Yes
389; 404; Laura; f; 56; Miss. Choctaw; F; M; Mother; Yes; Yes

390; 379; Alma; f; 45; Miss. Choctaw; F; Wd; Head; Yes; Yes
391; 381; **McMillan**, Jimpson; m; 24; Miss. Choctaw; F; S; Son; Yes; Yes
392; 894; **Lewis (Jim)**, Winston; m; 26; Miss. Choctaw; F; M; Son-in-law; Yes; Yes
~~393; 382; **Lewis**, Ella McMillan; f; 22; Miss. Choctaw; F; M; Dau; Yes; Yes~~ Died 7-13-38
394; 1861; **Lewis**, Redy Isaam; m; 2; Miss. Choctaw; F; S; Grand-son; Yes; Yes
395; 383; Jordan McMillan; m; 7; Miss. Choctaw; F; S; Grand-son; Yes; Yes

396; 384; Arbin; m; 49; Miss. Choctaw; F; Wd; Head; Yes; Yes
397; 385; Gilbert; m; 24; Miss. Choctaw; F; S; Son; Yes; Yes
~~386; Rosella; f; 17; Miss. Choctaw; F; S; Dau; Yes; Yes~~ Died 3-2-36
~~387; Maudell; f; 14; Miss. Choctaw; F; S; Dau; Yes; Yes~~ Died 3-14-36

398; 400; Ben; m; 75; Miss. Choctaw; F; M; Head; Yes; Yes
399; 401; Maude Billy; f; 24; Miss. Choctaw; F; M; Wife; Yes; Yes
400; 217; Philip; m; 7; Miss. Choctaw; F; S; Son; Yes; Yes
401; 402; Clarence Billy; m; 3; Miss. Choctaw; F; S; Son; Yes; Yes

Census of the **Mississippi Choctaws** reservation of the **Choctaw Agency** jurisdiction, as of **January 1, 1937**, 19__, taken by **A. C. Hector**, Superintendent.

KEY; Surname; Present Census Number; Last Census Number; Given Name; Sex; Age at Last Birthday; Tribe; Degree of Blood; Marital Status; Relationship to Head of Family; At Jurisdiction Where Enrolled (Yes/No); At Another Jurisdiction; Post Office, County, State (if given); Ward (Yes/No)

402; 388; Seymour; m; 36; Miss. Choctaw; F; M; Head; Yes; Yes
403; 389; Edna Ben; f; 31; Miss. Choctaw; F; M; Wife; Yes; Yes
404; 390; W. C; m; 15; Miss. Choctaw; F; S; Son; Yes; Yes
405; 391; B. F; m; 13; Miss. Choctaw; F; S; Son; Yes; Yes
406; 392; LeRoy; m; 11; Miss. Choctaw; F; S; Son; Yes; Yes
407; 393; Vina Rayburn; f; 3; Miss. Choctaw; F; S; Dau; Yes; Yes

COOPER

408; 407; Gaston; m; 51; Miss. Choctaw; F; M; Head; Yes; Yes
409; 408; Ada; f; 53; Miss. Choctaw; F; M; Wife; Yes; Yes
410; 410; Hubert; m; 13; Miss. Choctaw; F; S; Son; Yes; Yes
411; 411; Christine; f; 13; Miss. Choctaw; F; S; Dau; Yes; Yes
412; 412; Alma; f; 10; Miss. Choctaw; F; S; Dau; Yes; Yes

COTTON

413; 414; George; m; 37; Miss. Choctaw; F; M; Head; Yes; Yes
414; 415; Ellen; f; 36; Miss. Choctaw; F; M; Wife; Yes; Yes
415; 294; **(Cates)**, Henry; m; 17; Miss. Choctaw; F; S; Son; Yes; Yes
416; 416; Minnie; f; 11; Miss. Choctaw; F; S; Dau; Yes; Yes
417; Emma; f; 2; Miss. Choctaw; F; S; Dau; Yes; Yes
Born 1935 - Unreported

418; 285; **(Cates)**, Oscar; m; 27; Miss. Choctaw; F; M; Head; Yes; Yes
419; Zula; f; 26; Miss. Choctaw; F; M; Wife; Yes; Yes
Omitted from previous census
420; Henry; m; 4; Miss. Choctaw; F; S; Son; Yes; Yes
Omitted from previous census
421; Effie; f; 3; Miss. Choctaw; F; S; Dau; Yes; Yes
Omitted from previous census
422; Zula; f; 1; Miss. Choctaw; F; S; Dau; Yes; Yes
Omitted from previous census

Census of the __Mississippi Choctaws__ reservation of the __Choctaw Agency__ jurisdiction, as of __January 1, 1937__, 19__, taken by __A. C. Hector__, Superintendent.

KEY; Surname; Present Census Number; Last Census Number; Given Name; Sex; Age at Last Birthday; Tribe; Degree of Blood; Marital Status; Relationship to Head of Family; At Jurisdiction Where Enrolled (Yes/No); At Another Jurisdiction; Post Office, County, State (if given); Ward (Yes/No)

423; 277; **(Cates)**, Susan; f; 59; Miss. Choctaw; F; Wd; Head; Yes; Yes
424; 278; **(Cates)**, Ennis; m; 31; Miss. Choctaw; F; S; Son; Yes; Yes
425; 280; **(Cates)**, John; m; 25; Miss. Choctaw; F; S; Son; Yes; Yes
426; 281; **(Cates)**, Lonie; f; 24; Miss. Choctaw; F; S; Dau; Yes; Yes
427; 282; **(Cates)**, Molpus; m; 23; Miss. Choctaw; F; S; Son; Yes; Yes
428; 283; **(Cates)**, Iona; f; 19; Miss. Choctaw; F; S; Dau; Yes; Yes
429; 284; **(Cates)**, John; m; 9; Miss. Choctaw; F; S; Grand-son; Yes; Yes

CRENSHAW

430; 417; Amos; m; 25; Miss. Choctaw; F; S; Head; Yes; Yes
431; 418; Austin; m; 21; Miss. Choctaw; F; S; Orphan; Yes; Yes

CHITTO

1881; Dewey Wesley; m; 1; Miss. Choctaw; F; S; Son; Yes; Yes
Duplication of 1797-34 Supple.

355; Minnie; f; 26; Miss. Choctaw; F; S; Alone; Yes; Yes
Duplication of 1700-34

DAN

432; 419; Williston; m; 40; Miss. Choctaw; F; M; Head; Yes; Yes
433; 420; Dinah; f; 25; Miss. Choctaw; F; M; Wife; Yes; Yes
~~421; Rose Ida; f; 15; Miss. Choctaw; F; S; Dau; Yes; Yes~~
Died 12-3-36

DANSBY

~~434; 422; Jacob; m; 65; Miss. Choctaw; F; M; Head; Yes; Yes~~
Died Nov. 13, 1937

Census of the **Mississippi Choctaws** reservation of the **Choctaw Agency** jurisdiction, as of **January 1, 1937**, 19__, taken by **A. C. Hector**, Superintendent.

KEY; Surname; Present Census Number; Last Census Number; Given Name; Sex; Age at Last Birthday; Tribe; Degree of Blood; Marital Status; Relationship to Head of Family; At Jurisdiction Where Enrolled (Yes/No); At Another Jurisdiction; Post Office, County, State (if given); Ward (Yes/No)

DAVIS

    Ansleum; m; Navajo; [blank]; M; Head; No; Ft. Definance[sic], Ft. Definance, Ariz; [blank]
435; 426; Alyne; f; 27; Miss. Choctaw; F; M; Wife; No; Ft. Definance, Ft. Definance, Ariz; [blank]

436; 428; Hobbie; m; 30; Miss. Choctaw; F; M; Head; Yes; Yes
437;1108; Mary McMillan; f; 25; Miss. Choctaw; F; M; Wife; Yes; Yes
438;1837; Berniece (Zina); f; 2; Miss. Choctaw; F; S; Dau; Yes; Yes

439; 441; Malissie; f; 67; Miss. Choctaw; F; Wd; Head; Yes; Yes
440; 442; Alice; f; 40; Miss. Choctaw; F; S; Dau; Yes; Yes
~~443; Ada Frances; f; 14; Miss. Choctaw; F; S; Grand-dau; Yes; Yes~~ Died 1934 - Unreported

441; 436; Sidney; m; 49; Miss. Choctaw; F; Wd; Head; Yes; Yes
442; 437; Elamer; f; 28; Miss. Choctaw; F; S; Dau; Yes; Yes
443; 438; Mabel; f; 25; Miss. Choctaw; F; S; Dau; Yes; Yes
444; 439; Anna; f; 17; Miss. Choctaw; F; S; Dau; Yes; Yes
445; 440; Johnnie; m; 15; Miss. Choctaw; F; S; Son; Yes; Yes

446; 444; Tom; m; 37; Miss. Choctaw; F; M; Head; Yes; Yes
447; 310; Nola McMillan; f; 32; Miss. Choctaw; F; M; Wife; Yes; Yes
448; 445; Millie; f; 17; Miss. Choctaw; F; S; Dau; Yes; Yes
449; 446; Henderson; m; 15; Miss. Choctaw; F; S; Son; Yes; Yes
450;   Lonie; m; 2; Miss. Choctaw; F; S; Son; Yes; Yes Born 1935 - Unreported
451; 311; **McMillan**, A. G; m; 15; Miss. Choctaw; F; S; Step-son; Yes; Yes
452; 312; **McMillan**, Odie Mae; f; 13; Miss. Choctaw; F; S; Step-dau; Yes; Yes
453; 313; **McMillan**, John; m; 10; Miss. Choctaw; F; S; Step-son; Yes; Yes

Census of the **Mississippi Choctaws** reservation of the **Choctaw Agency** jurisdiction, as of **January 1, 1937**, 19__, taken by **A. C. Hector**, Superintendent.

KEY; Surname; Present Census Number; Last Census Number; Given Name; Sex; Age at Last Birthday; Tribe; Degree of Blood; Marital Status; Relationship to Head of Family; At Jurisdiction Where Enrolled (Yes/No); At Another Jurisdiction; Post Office, County, State (if given); Ward (Yes/No)

454; 314; **McMillan**, Mattie; f; 6; Miss. Choctaw; F; S; Step-dau; Yes; Yes

455; 429; Will; m; 63; Miss. Choctaw; F; Wd; Head; Yes; Yes
456; 431; John; m; 15; Miss. Choctaw; F; S; Son; Yes; Yes
457; 432; Mary; f; 9; Miss. Choctaw; F; S; Dau; Yes; Yes
458; 433; Mack; m; 8; Miss. Choctaw; F; S; Son; Yes; Yes
459; 434; Lewis; m; 6; Miss. Choctaw; F; S; Son; Yes; Yes
460; 435; William; m; 4; Miss. Choctaw; F; S; Son; Yes; Yes

DENSON

461; 462; Ezell; m; 25; Miss. Choctaw; F; M; Head; Yes; Yes
462; 463; Beauty; f; 25; Miss. Choctaw; F; M; Wife; Yes; Yes
463; 464; Ruth; f; 6; Miss. Choctaw; F; S; Dau; Yes; Yes
463; 465; Louise; f; 4; Miss. Choctaw; F; S; Dau; Yes; Yes

465; 448; Hendrix; m; 20; Miss. Choctaw; F; M; Head; Yes; Yes
466; 824; Eva Jackson; f; 17; Miss. Choctaw; F; M; Wife; Yes; Yes
Died 3-1-38
467; John; m; 5/12; Miss. Choctaw; F; S; Son; Yes; Yes
Born 7-30-36

468; 447; Lilly; f; 49; Miss. Choctaw; F; F; Wd; Head; Yes; Yes
469; 449; Emma; f; 17; Miss. Choctaw; F; S; Dau; Yes; Yes
470; 450; Charley; m; 14; Miss. Choctaw; F; S; Son; Yes; Yes
471; 451; David; m; 12; Miss. Choctaw; F; S; Son; Yes; Yes

472; 452; Pete; m; 49; Miss. Choctaw; F; M; Head; Yes; Yes
473; 453; Rosie Wickson; f; 36; Miss. Choctaw; F; M; Wife; Yes; Yes
474; 455; Edna; f; 14; Miss. Choctaw; F; S; Dau; Yes; Yes
475; 456; Nancy; f; 8; Miss. Choctaw; F; S; Dau; Yes; Yes
476; 457; Jennie E; f; 5; Miss. Choctaw; F; S; Dau; Yes; Yes
477; 458; Odie Mae; f; 4; Miss. Choctaw; F; S; Dau; Yes; Yes

Census of the **Mississippi Choctaws** reservation of the **Choctaw Agency** jurisdiction, as of **January 1, 1937**, 19__, taken by **A. C. Hector**, Superintendent.

KEY; Surname; Present Census Number; Last Census Number; Given Name; Sex; Age at Last Birthday; Tribe; Degree of Blood; Marital Status; Relationship to Head of Family; At Jurisdiction Where Enrolled (Yes/No); At Another Jurisdiction; Post Office, County, State (if given); Ward (Yes/No)

478; 1838; Lola; f; 2; Miss. Choctaw; F; S; Dau; Yes; Yes

479; 459; Willie; m; 29; Miss. Choctaw; F; M; Head; Yes; Yes
480; 460; Beauty; f; 25; Miss. Choctaw; F; M; Wife; Yes; Yes
481; 461; Silmon (Hector); m; 4; Miss. Choctaw; F; S; Son; Yes; Yes
482; 1798; Una; f; 3; Miss. Choctaw; F; S; Dau; Yes; Yes
483; Marguerite; f; 6/12; Miss. Choctaw; F; S; Dau; Yes; Yes
Born 6-20-36

484; 1058; Winston; m; 22; Miss. Choctaw; F; M; Head; Yes; Yes
~~1059; Eliza Lewis; f; 22; Miss. Choctaw; F; M; Wife; Yes; Yes~~
Died 3-18-36
485; 1050; Belfa Lewis; f; 21; Miss. Choctaw; F; M; Wife; Yes; Yes

DIXON

486; 485; Edmond; m; 29; Miss. Choctaw; F; M; Head; Yes; Yes
487; 486; Julia; f; 28; Miss. Choctaw; F; M; Wife; Yes; Yes
488; 487; Addie Mae; f; 7; Miss. Choctaw; F; S; Dau; Yes; Yes
489; 488; Anita; f; 4; Miss. Choctaw; F; S; Dau; Yes; Yes
490; 1839; Claudine; f; 2; Miss. Choctaw; F; S; Dau; Yes; Yes
491; Williston; m; 1/12; Miss. Choctaw; F; S; Son; Yes; Yes
Born 12-22-36

492; 482; Horace; m; 31; Miss. Choctaw; F; M; Head; Yes; Yes
493; 483; Esther; f; 30; Miss. Choctaw; F; M; Wife; Yes; Yes
494; 484; Calonia; f; 10; Miss. Choctaw; F; S; Dau; Yes; Yes

~~475; Jess; m; 59; Miss. Choctaw; F; M; Head; Yes; Yes~~
Died 11-8-36
495; 476; Callie; f; 67; Miss. Choctaw; F; M; Wife; Yes; Yes
496; 477; Young; m; 20; Miss. Choctaw; F; M; Son; Yes; Yes
497; 1621; Leona Willis Wesley; f; 21; Miss. Choctaw; F; M; Dau-in-law; Yes; Yes

Census of the **Mississippi Choctaws** reservation of the **Choctaw Agency** jurisdiction, as of **January 1, 1937**, 19__, taken by **A. C. Hector**, Superintendent.

KEY; Surname; Present Census Number; Last Census Number; Given Name; Sex; Age at Last Birthday; Tribe; Degree of Blood; Marital Status; Relationship to Head of Family; At Jurisdiction Where Enrolled (Yes/No); At Another Jurisdiction; Post Office, County, State (if given); Ward (Yes/No)

498; 478; Lilly; f; 17; Miss. Choctaw; F; S; Dau; Yes; Yes

499; 468; Jim; m; 37; Miss. Choctaw; F; m: Head; Yes; Yes
500; 469; Sarah Jimmie; f; 34; Miss. Choctaw; F; M; Wife; Yes; Yes
501; 470; Marie; f; 14; Miss. Choctaw; F; S; Dau; Yes; Yes
502; 471; Imogene; f; 11; Miss. Choctaw; F; S; Dau; Yes; Yes
503; 472; Ellen; f; 9; Miss. Choctaw; F; S; Dau; Yes; Yes
504; 473; Mable C; f; 6; Miss. Choctaw; F; S; Dau; Yes; Yes
505; 474; Morris (Arthur Aiken); m; 3; Miss. Choctaw; F; S; Son; Yes; Yes
506; David Clem; m; 2/12; Miss. Choctaw; F; S; Son; Yes; Yes
Born 10-22-36

507; 492; Jim; m; 32; Miss. Choctaw; F; M; Head; Yes; Yes
508; 202; Leona Billy; f; 19; Miss. Choctaw; F; M; Wife; Yes; Yes
509; James; m; 5; Miss. Choctaw; F; S; Son; Yes; Yes
Omitted on previous census
510; Cora; f; 3; Miss. Choctaw; F; S; Dau; Yes; Yes
Omitted on previous census
511; Baby; m; 2; Miss. Choctaw; F; S; Son; Yes; Yes
Born 5-15-35 - Unreported

~~491; Kanis; m; 45; Miss. Choctaw; F; SM; Alone; Yes; Yes~~
Died 1934 - Unreported

512; 479; Scott; m; 26; Miss. Choctaw; F; M; Head; Yes; Yes
513; 480; Essie; f; 30; Miss. Choctaw; F; M; Wife; Yes; Yes
514; 481; Nola; f; 4; Miss. Choctaw; F; S; Dau; Yes; Yes

515; 493; Wade; m; 22; Miss. Choctaw; F; S; Alone; Yes; Yes

516; 489; Wilson; m; 78; Miss. Choctaw; F; M; Head; Yes; Yes
517; 490; Hope; f; 51; Miss. Choctaw; F; M; Wife; Yes; Yes

Census of the **Mississippi Choctaws** reservation of the **Choctaw Agency** jurisdiction, as of **January 1, 1937**, 19__, taken by **A. C. Hector**, Superintendent.

KEY; Surname; Present Census Number; Last Census Number; Given Name; Sex; Age at Last Birthday; Tribe; Degree of Blood; Marital Status; Relationship to Head of Family; At Jurisdiction Where Enrolled (Yes/No); At Another Jurisdiction; Post Office, County, State (if given); Ward (Yes/No)

EVANS

518; 494; John; m; 62; Miss. Choctaw; F; Wd; Head; Yes; Yes
519; 495; **Wickson**, Kelly; m; 12; Miss. Choctaw; F; S; Son; Yes; Yes

ELLIS

       George; m; [blank]; White; None; M; Head; Yes; Yes
520; 603; Amelia Farve; f; 43; Miss. Choctaw; F; M; Wife; Yes; Yes

FARMER

521;1082; Henry; m; 25; Miss. Choctaw; F; M; Head; Yes; Yes
~~522; 409; Fannie Cooper; f; 19; Miss. Choctaw; F; M; Wife; Yes; Yes~~
       Died April 29, 1937
523;1840; Robert Joseph; m; 2; Miss. Choctaw; F; S; Son; Yes; Yes

     497; Henry; m; 25; Miss. Choctaw; F; M: Head; Yes; Yes
       Duplication of 1082-34

524; 513; Howard; m; 25; Miss. Choctaw; F; M; Head; Yes; Yes
525; 514; Lonie Dixon; f; 23; Miss. Choctaw; F; M; Wife; Yes; Yes
526; 515; Eula Mae; f; 6; Miss. Choctaw; F; S; Dau; Yes; Yes
527; 516; Wilton; m; 4; Miss. Choctaw; F; S; Son; Yes; Yes
528; 512; Melissa; f; 64; Miss. Choctaw; F; Wd; Mother; Yes; Yes

~~529; 500; Ishman; m; 92; Miss. Choctaw; F; M: Head; Yes; Yes~~
       Died 12-4-38
530; 501; Suela; f; 64; Miss. Choctaw; F; M; Wife; Yes; Yes
531; 503; Marshall; m; 32; Miss. Choctaw; F; S; Son; Yes; Yes
532; 505; Lena; f; 24; Miss. Choctaw; F; S; Dau; Yes; Yes
533; 506; Bell; m; 21; Miss. Choctaw; F; S; Son; Yes; Yes
534; 507; Renee; f; 17; Miss. Choctaw; F; S; Dau; Yes; Yes

Census of the __Mississippi Choctaws__ reservation of the __Choctaw Agency__ jurisdiction, as of __January 1, 1937__, 19__, taken by __A. C. Hector__, Superintendent.

KEY; Surname; Present Census Number; Last Census Number; Given Name; Sex; Age at Last Birthday; Tribe; Degree of Blood; Marital Status; Relationship to Head of Family; At Jurisdiction Where Enrolled (Yes/No); At Another Jurisdiction; Post Office, County, State (if given); Ward (Yes/No)

535; 508; Moses; m; 37; Miss. Choctaw; F; M; Head; Yes; Yes
~~536; 509; Lottie; f; 29; Miss. Choctaw; F; M; Wife; Yes; Yes~~
    Died 8-4-38
537; 510; Mealie; f; 6; Miss. Choctaw; F; S; Dau; Yes; Yes
538;1814; Latima; f; 3; Miss. Choctaw; F; S; Dau; Yes; Yes

539; 496; Silmon; m; 63; Miss. Choctaw; F; Wd; Head; Yes; Yes
540; 498; Venie; f; 19; Miss. Choctaw; F; S; Dau; Yes; Yes
541;   Hester (Clark Gable); m; 10/12; Miss. Choctaw; F; S; Grand-son; Yes; Yes   Born 2-11-36
542; 499; Corine; f; 16; Miss. Choctaw; F; S; Dau; Yes; Yes

FARVE

543; 536; Antwine; m; 60; Miss. Choctaw; F; M; Head; Yes; Yes
544; 537; Liseeda; f; 63; Miss. Choctaw; F; M; Wife; Yes; Yes
545; 538; Edna; f; 27; Miss. Choctaw; F; S; Dau; Yes; Yes
546; 539; Cecelia; f; 25; Miss. Choctaw; F; S; Dau; Yes; Yes
547; 540; Isileen; f; 24; Miss. Choctaw; F; S; Dau; Yes; Yes
548; 541; Earl; m; 19; Miss. Choctaw; F; S; Son; Yes; Yes
549; 542; Mamie; f; 17; Miss. Choctaw; F; S; Dau; Yes; Yes
550; 543; Corbrin; m; 14; Miss. Choctaw; F; S; Son; Yes; Yes

551; 598; Albert; m; 56; Miss. Choctaw; F; M: Head; Yes; Yes
552; 599; Iktial; f; 54; Miss. Choctaw; F; M; Wife; Yes; Yes

553; 574; Basil; m; 26; Miss. Choctaw; F; S; Alone; Yes; Yes

554; 605; Bay Turner; m; 32; Miss. Choctaw; F; S; Alone; Yes; Yes

555; 517; Bennett; m; 44; Miss. Choctaw; F; S; Alone; Yes; Yes

556; 576; Cameron; m; 42; Miss. Choctaw; F; M; Head; Yes; Yes
557; 577; Viola; f; 40; Miss. Choctaw; F; M; Wife; Yes; Yes

Census of the **Mississippi Choctaws** reservation of the **Choctaw Agency** jurisdiction, as of **January 1, 1937**, 19__, taken by **A. C. Hector**, Superintendent.

KEY; Surname; Present Census Number; Last Census Number; Given Name; Sex; Age at Last Birthday; Tribe; Degree of Blood; Marital Status; Relationship to Head of Family; At Jurisdiction Where Enrolled (Yes/No); At Another Jurisdiction; Post Office, County, State (if given); Ward (Yes/No)

558; 578; William; m; 21; Miss. Choctaw; F; S; Son; Yes; Yes
559; 579; Francis; m; 15; Miss. Choctaw; F; S; Son; Yes; Yes
560; 580; J. C; m; 13; Miss. Choctaw; F; S; Son; Yes; Yes
561; 581; Wilma; f; 11; Miss. Choctaw; F; S; Dau; Yes; Yes

562; 606; Ceciline; m; 31; Miss. Choctaw; F; S; Alone; Yes; Yes

563; 583; Charles T; m; 53; Miss. Choctaw; F; M; Head; Yes; Yes
564; 584; Alfonsine; f; 39; Miss. Choctaw; F; M; Wife; Yes; Yes

565; 607; Charles; m; 57; Miss. Choctaw; F; S; Alone; Yes; Yes

566; 552; Charles; m; 49; Miss. Choctaw; F; M; Head; Yes; Yes
567; 553; Edwina; f; 46; Miss. Choctaw; F; M; Wife; Yes; Yes
568; 554; Retha; f; 19; Miss. Choctaw; F; S; Dau; Yes; Yes
569; 555; Alvin; m; 17; Miss. Choctaw; F; S; Son; Yes; Yes
570; 556; Irvin; m; 15; Miss. Choctaw; F; S; Son; Yes; Yes
571; 557; Audrey; f; 12; Miss. Choctaw; F; S; Dau; Yes; Yes
572; 558; Vivian; f; 11; Miss. Choctaw; F; S; Dau; Yes; Yes

~~573; 544; Dave; m; 59; Miss. Choctaw; F; Wd; Head; Yes; Yes~~
         Died - 1934
574; 545; Lena; f; 37; Miss. Choctaw; F; S; Dau; Yes; Yes
575; 546; Georgia; f; 18; Miss. Choctaw; F; S; Dau; Yes; Yes
576; 547; Sarah Alma; f; 26; Miss. Choctaw; F; S; Dau; Yes; Yes
577; 548; John; m; 15; Miss. Choctaw; F; S; Son; Yes; Yes

578; 589; Dennis; m; 49; Miss. Choctaw; F; S; Alone; Yes; Yes

579; 595; Eleanor; f; 43; Miss. Choctaw; F; S; Alone; Yes; Yes

580; 500; Ethel; f; 33; Miss. Choctaw; F; S; Alone; Yes; Yes

Census of the __Mississippi Choctaws__ reservation of the __Choctaw Agency__ jurisdiction, as of __January 1, 1937__, 19__, taken by __A. C. Hector__, Superintendent.

KEY; Surname; Present Census Number; Last Census Number; Given Name; Sex; Age at Last Birthday; Tribe; Degree of Blood; Marital Status; Relationship to Head of Family; At Jurisdiction Where Enrolled (Yes/No); At Another Jurisdiction; Post Office, County, State (if given); Ward (Yes/No)

581; 570; Gilmore; m; 35; Miss. Choctaw; F; M; Head; Yes; Yes
582; 571; Gertrude; f; 33; Miss. Choctaw; F; M; Wife; Yes; Yes

583; 575; Jessie; f; 25; Miss. Choctaw; F; S; Alone; Yes; Yes

584; 572; Joe; m; 31; Miss. Choctaw; F; M; Head; Yes; Yes
585; 573; Lillian; f; 28; Miss. Choctaw; F; M; Wife; Yes; Yes

586; 596; Joe; m; 64; Miss. Choctaw; F; S; Alone; Yes; Yes

587; 566; Joe Tole; m; 72; Miss. Choctaw; F; M; Head; Yes; Yes
588; 567; Ora Lee; f; 69; Miss. Choctaw; F; M; Wife; Yes; Yes
589; 568; Dora; f; 44; Miss. Choctaw; F; S; Dau; Yes; Yes

590; 582; John Tole; m; 54; Miss. Choctaw; F; S; Alone; Yes; Yes

591; 525; Joseph; m; 25; Miss. Choctaw; F; M; Head; Yes; Yes
592; 526; Bessie Davis; f; 27; Miss. Choctaw; F; M; Wife; Yes; Yes
593; 527; Baby; f; 3; Miss. Choctaw; F; S; Dau; Yes; Yes
594;1842; Hughey; m; 2; Miss. Choctaw; F; S; Son; Yes; Yes

Lem; m; [blank]; White; None; M; Head; Yes; Yes
595; 602; Rosella; f; 61; Miss. Choctaw; F; M; Wife; Yes; Yes

596; 597; Lucille; f; 34; Miss. Choctaw; F; S; Alone; Yes; Yes

597; 591; Noah; m; 45; Miss. Choctaw; F; S; Alone; Yes; Yes

598; 518; Paul; m; 49; Miss. Choctaw; F; M; Head; Yes; Yes
599; 519; Renie; f; 32; Miss. Choctaw; F; M; Wife; Yes; Yes
600; 520; Phillip; m; 13; Miss. Choctaw; F; S; Son; Yes; Yes
601; 521; Eula Mae; f; 11; Miss. Choctaw; F; S; Dau; Yes; Yes
602; 522; Estelle; f; 9; Miss. Choctaw; F; S; Dau; Yes; Yes
603; 523; Viola; f; 7; Miss. Choctaw; F; S; Dau; Yes; Yes

Census of the **Mississippi Choctaws** reservation of the **Choctaw Agency** jurisdiction, as of **January 1, 1937**, 19__, taken by **A. C. Hector**, Superintendent.

KEY; Surname; Present Census Number; Last Census Number; Given Name; Sex; Age at Last Birthday; Tribe; Degree of Blood; Marital Status; Relationship to Head of Family; At Jurisdiction Where Enrolled (Yes/No); At Another Jurisdiction; Post Office, County, State (if given); Ward (Yes/No)

604; 524; Anna Rose; f; 4; Miss. Choctaw; F; S; Dau; Yes; Yes
605;1841; Albert Clifton; m; 2; Miss. Choctaw; F; S; Son; Yes; Yes

606; 528; Rachel; f; 58; Miss. Choctaw; F; S; Head; Yes; Yes

607; 588; R. C; m; 36; Miss. Choctaw; F; S; Alone; Yes; Yes

608; 550; Rosine H; m; 54; Miss. Choctaw; F; M; Head; Yes; Yes
609; 551; Winona; f; 59; Miss. Choctaw; F; M; Wife; Yes; Yes

610; 565; Sylvester; m; 49; Miss. Choctaw; F; S; Alone; Yes; Yes

611; 559; Thomas; m; 55; Miss. Choctaw; F; M; Head; Yes; Yes
612; 560; Mary; f; 39; Miss. Choctaw; F; M; Wife; Yes; Yes
613; 561; Hazel; f; 19; Miss. Choctaw; F; S; Dau; Yes; Yes
614; 562; Robert; m; 18; Miss. Choctaw; F; S; Son; Yes; Yes
615; 563; Gertrude; f; 16; Miss. Choctaw; F; S; Dau; Yes; Yes
616; 564; Ruth; f; 13; Miss. Choctaw; F; S; Dau; Yes; Yes

617; 529; Western; m; 47; Miss. Choctaw; F; Wd; Head; Yes; Yes
618; 530; Chester; m; 32; Miss. Choctaw; F; S; Son; Yes; Yes
619; 531; Josie; f; 29; Miss. Choctaw; F; S; Dau; Yes; Yes
620; 532; John; m; 29; Miss. Choctaw; F; S; Son; Yes; Yes
621; 533; Lillian; f; 26; Miss. Choctaw; F; S; Dau; Yes; Yes
622; 534; Ima; f; 21; Miss. Choctaw; F; S; Dau; Yes; Yes
623; 535; Hilda; f; 13; Miss. Choctaw; F; S; Dau; Yes; Yes

624; 590; Western; m; 57; Miss. Choctaw; F; S; Alone; Yes; Yes

625; 549; William; m; 36; Miss. Choctaw; F; Wd; Alone; Yes; Yes

626; 593; William; m; 39; Miss. Choctaw; F; S; Alone; Yes; Yes

627; 594; Seman; m; 71; Miss. Choctaw; F; S; Alone; Yes; Yes

Census of the **Mississippi Choctaws** reservation of the **Choctaw Agency** jurisdiction, as of **January 1, 1937**, 19__, taken by **A. C. Hector**, Superintendent.

KEY; Surname; Present Census Number; Last Census Number; Given Name; Sex; Age at Last Birthday; Tribe; Degree of Blood; Marital Status; Relationship to Head of Family; At Jurisdiction Where Enrolled (Yes/No); At Another Jurisdiction; Post Office, County, State (if given); Ward (Yes/No)

FORBES

~~609; Sallie; f; 62; Miss. Choctaw; F; M: Head; Yes; Yes~~
Dead 6 years - Unreported

FRAZIER

628; 611; (Forbes); Clint; m; 35; Miss. Choctaw; F; M; Head; Yes; Yes
629; 612; Josey Tubby; f; 36; Miss. Choctaw; F; M; Wife; Yes; Yes
630; 613; Ida Mae; f; 19; Miss. Choctaw; F; S; Dau; Yes; Yes
631; 614; Gaston; m; 15; Miss. Choctaw; F; S; Son; Yes; Yes
632;   Inez; f; 11; Miss. Choctaw; F; S; Dau; Yes; Yes
          Omitted from previous census
633; 615; (Forbes), Henry; m; 7; Miss. Choctaw; F; S; Son; Yes; Yes
634; 616; (Forbes), Hazel; f; 4; Miss. Choctaw; F; S; Dau; Yes; Yes
635;   Isral[sic]; m; 3; Miss. Choctaw; F; S; Son; Yes; Yes
          Born 1934 - Unreported
~~636; 655; Wesley; m; 73; Miss. Choctaw; F; Wd; Father; Yes; Yes~~
          Died Dec. 27, 1937

637; 623; Forbes; m; 36; Miss. Choctaw; F; M; Head; Yes; Yes
638;1247; Lavada Sam; f; 25; Miss. Choctaw; F; M; Wife; Yes; Yes
639;1248; **Sam**, Ruth Ann; f; 4; Miss. Choctaw; F; S; Step-Dau; Yes; Yes
640;1799; LeRoy (Quitman); m; 3; Miss. Choctaw; F; S; Son; Yes; Yes
641;   Julian; m; 8/12; Miss. Choctaw; F; S; Son; Yes; Yes
          Born 4-22-36
~~626; Box, Sam Davis; m; 14; Miss. Choctaw; F; S; Step-son; Yes; Yes~~ Dead - Unreported

642; 650; Henson; m; 69; Miss. Choctaw; F; M; Head; Yes; Yes
~~643; 651; Fannie; f; 67; Miss. Choctaw; F; M: Wife; Yes; Yes~~
          Died Aug. 16, 1937

Census of the __Mississippi Choctaws__ reservation of the __Choctaw Agency__ jurisdiction, as of __January 1, 1937__, 19__, taken by __A. C. Hector__, Superintendent.

KEY; Surname; Present Census Number; Last Census Number; Given Name; Sex; Age at Last Birthday; Tribe; Degree of Blood; Marital Status; Relationship to Head of Family; At Jurisdiction Where Enrolled (Yes/No); At Another Jurisdiction; Post Office, County, State (if given); Ward (Yes/No)

644; 652; Agnes (Lucy); F; 19; Miss. Choctaw; F; S; Grand-dau; Yes; Yes
645; 653; Wade; m; 19; Miss. Choctaw; F; S; Grand-son; Yes; Yes
646; 654; Jake; m; 15; Miss. Choctaw; F; S; Grand-son; Yes; Yes

604; **Farve**, Henrietta; f; 36; Miss. Choctaw; F; S; Alone; Yes; Yes
Duplication of 1239-34

647; 632; Jim; m; 31; Miss. Choctaw; F; M; Head; Yes; Yes
648; 633; Nannie Leben; f; 33; Miss. Choctaw; F; M; Wife; Yes; Yes
~~634; A. B; m; 10; Miss. Choctaw; F; S; Son; Yes; Yes~~
Dead 5 years - Unreported
650; 636; Nancy; f; 8; Miss. Choctaw; F; S; Dau; Yes; Yes
651; 637; Josephine (Caspeen); f; 3; Miss. Choctaw; F; S; Dau; Yes; Yes

652; 638; Ligman; m; 43; Miss. Choctaw; F; M; Head; Yes; Yes
653; 639; Sina Jackson; f; 28; Miss. Choctaw; F; M; Wife; Yes; Yes
654; 640; Edmond; m; 15; Miss. Choctaw; F; S; Son; Yes; Yes
655; 641; Sallie; f; 13; Miss. Choctaw; F; S; Dau; Yes; Yes
656; 631; Willie Rose; f; 12; Miss. Choctaw; F; S; Dau; Yes; Yes
657; 642; Annie; f; 7; Miss. Choctaw; F; S; Dau; Yes; Yes
658; 643; Emma; f; 4; Miss. Choctaw; F; S; Dau; Yes; Yes
659; 644; Cecile; f; 4; Miss. Choctaw; F; S; Dau; Yes; Yes
660; Clemon; m; 9/12; Miss. Choctaw; F; S; Son; Yes; Yes
Born 3-30-36

661; 617; Mollie; f; 62; Miss. Choctaw; F; Wd; Head; Yes; Yes
662; 618; John; m; 26; Miss. Choctaw; F; S; Son; Yes; Yes
663;1583; **Vaughn**, Bessie; f; 35; Miss. Choctaw; F; Wd; Dau; Yes; Yes
664;1584; **Vaughn**, Clifton; m; 11; Miss. Choctaw; F; S; Grand-son; Yes; Yes
~~665;1585; **Vaughn**, Monroe; m; 3; Miss. Choctaw; F; S; Grand-son; Yes; Yes~~ Died - 1935

Census of the **Mississippi Choctaws** reservation of the **Choctaw Agency** jurisdiction, as of **January 1, 1937**, 19__, taken by **A. C. Hector**, Superintendent.

KEY; Surname; Present Census Number; Last Census Number; Given Name; Sex; Age at Last Birthday; Tribe; Degree of Blood; Marital Status; Relationship to Head of Family; At Jurisdiction Where Enrolled (Yes/No); At Another Jurisdiction; Post Office, County, State (if given); Ward (Yes/No)

666; 627; Will; m; 38; Miss. Choctaw; F; M; Head; Yes; Yes
667; 628; Lavena; f; 34; Miss. Choctaw; F; M: Wife; Yes; Yes

    608; Wesley; m; 73; Miss. Choctaw; F; Wd; Alone; Yes; Yes
    Duplication of 655-34
    610; **Forbes**, Ella; f; 23; Miss. Choctaw; F; S; Dau; Yes; Yes
    Duplication of 656-34

    645; Emma Dixon; f; 39; Miss. Choctaw; F; Wd; Head; Yes; Yes
    Duplication of 1608-34

    592; **Farve**, Bennett; m; 43; Miss. Choctaw; F; S; Alone; Yes; Yes
    Duplication of 517-34

GARDNER

668; 657; Jim; m; 38; Miss. Choctaw; F; M; Head; Yes; Yes
669; 658; Celia; f; 33; Miss. Choctaw; F; M: Wife; Yes; Yes
670; 660; Alton; m; 1-; Miss. Choctaw; F; S; Son; Yes; Yes

671; 413; (Cotton); John; m; 27; Miss. Choctaw; F; M; Head; Yes; Yes
672; 656; Ella; g; 27; Miss. Choctaw; F; M; Wife; Yes; Yes
673;1843; Floyd; m; 2; Miss. Choctaw; F; S; Son; Yes; Yes

GIPSON

674; 669; Andrew; m; 32; Miss. Choctaw; F; M; Head; Yes; Yes
675; 670; Esther; f; 24; Miss. Choctaw; F; M; Wife; Yes; Yes

676; 661; Bart; m; 61; Miss. Choctaw; F; M; Head; Yes; Yes
677; 662; Lucy; f; 57; Miss. Choctaw; F; M; Wife; Yes; Yes

Census of the **Mississippi Choctaws** reservation of the **Choctaw Agency** jurisdiction, as of **January 1, 1937**, 19__, taken by **A. C. Hector**, Superintendent.

KEY; Surname; Present Census Number; Last Census Number; Given Name; Sex; Age at Last Birthday; Tribe; Degree of Blood; Marital Status; Relationship to Head of Family; At Jurisdiction Where Enrolled (Yes/No); At Another Jurisdiction; Post Office, County, State (if given); Ward (Yes/No)

678; 671; Gus; m; 28; Miss. Choctaw; F; M: Head; Yes; Yes
679;1651; Mary Williamson; f; 17; Miss. Choctaw; F; M; Wife; Yes; Yes
680; Leona; f; 3; Miss. Choctaw; F; S; Dau; Yes; Yes
Born 11-24-34 - Unreported
~~681; Irene (Annie Maud); f; 2/12; Miss. Choctaw; F; M[sic]; Dau; Yes; Yes~~ Born 10-6-36 Died 5-7-38

682; 666; Hensley m; 26; Miss. Choctaw; F; M; Head; Yes; Yes
683; 667; Elizabeth; f; 26; Miss. Choctaw; F; M; Wife; Yes; Yes
684; 668; Henrietta; f; 5; Miss. Choctaw; F; S; Dau; Yes; Yes

685; 664; Homer; m; 24; Miss. Choctaw; F; M; Head; Yes; Yes
686;1296; Lilly Farmer; f; 17; Miss. Choctaw; F; M; Wife; Yes; Yes
687; Willie D; m; 5/12; Miss. Choctaw; F; S; Son; Yes; Yes
Born 7-30-36

688;1015; Johnny Lee; m; 22; Miss. Choctaw; F; M; Head; Yes; Yes
689; 71; Allie Farmer; f; 21; Miss. Choctaw; F; M; wife; Yes; Yes
690; Mary L; f; 2; Miss. Choctaw; F; S; Dau; Yes; Yes
Born 1935 - Unreported
691; Lora Ann; f; 1; Miss. Choctaw; F; S; Dau; Yes; Yes
Born 1936 - Unreported
692; 73; **Farmer**, Annie Mae; f; 13; Miss. Choctaw; F; S; Sis-in-law; Yes; Yes

693; 672; Nolie; m; 35; Miss. Choctaw; F; M; Head; Yes; Yes
694; 673; Frances; f; 37; Miss. Choctaw; F; M; Wife; Yes; Yes
695; 674; Paul; m; 12; Miss. Choctaw; F; S; Son; Yes; Yes
696; 675; Clay; m; 11; Miss. Choctaw; F; S; Son; Yes; Yes
697; 676; Annie; f; 8; Miss. Choctaw; F; S; Dau; Yes; Yes
698; 677; Fannie; f; 4; Miss. Choctaw; F; S; Dau; Yes; Yes
699;1844; Doreen; f; 2; Miss. Choctaw; F; S; Dau; Yes; Yes

Census of the __Mississippi Choctaws__ reservation of the __Choctaw Agency__ jurisdiction, as of __January 1, 1937__, 19__, taken by __A. C. Hector__, Superintendent.

KEY; Surname; Present Census Number; Last Census Number; Given Name; Sex; Age at Last Birthday; Tribe; Degree of Blood; Marital Status; Relationship to Head of Family; At Jurisdiction Where Enrolled (Yes/No); At Another Jurisdiction; Post Office, County, State (if given); Ward (Yes/No)

700; 678; Steve; m; 73; Miss. Choctaw; F; M; Head; Yes; Yes
701; 679; Jennie; f; 69; Miss. Choctaw; F; M; Wife; Yes; Yes
702; 680; Ikey; f; 34; Miss. Choctaw; F; S; Dau; Yes; Yes
703; 681; Fannie; f; 29; Miss. Choctaw; F; S; Dau; Yes; Yes
704; 682; Annie; f; 28; Miss. Choctaw; F; S; Dau; Yes; Yes
705; 683; Willie; m; 19; Miss. Choctaw; F; S; Son; Yes; Yes
706;   Minnie; f; 21; Miss. Choctaw; F; S; Dau; Yes; Yes
        Omitted on previous census
707; 684; Hugh; m; 11; Miss. Choctaw; F; S; Son; Yes; Yes
708; 685; Aron; m; 10; Miss. Choctaw; F; S; Son; Yes; Yes

HALL

709; 686; Langford; m; 42; Miss. Choctaw; F; M; Head; Yes; Yes
710; 687; Lou; f; 32; Miss. Choctaw; F; M; Wife; Yes; Yes
711; 688; Travis; m; 14; Miss. Choctaw; F; S;; Son; Yes; Yes
712; 689; Arlone; f; 13; Miss. Choctaw; F; S; Dau; Yes; Yes
713; 690; Frank; m; 11; Miss. Choctaw; F; S; Son; Yes; Yes
714; 691; Frances; f; 5; Miss. Choctaw; F; S; Dau; Yes; Yes
715;1801; Lena; f; 3; Miss. Choctaw; F; S; Dau; Yes; Yes

HARPER

716; 692; Lena; f; 25; Miss. Choctaw; F; S; Alone; Yes; Yes

HARRIS

717; 693; Elsmore; f; 29; Miss. Choctaw; F; S; Alone; Yes; Yes

HAYS

718;1173; Velma; f; 28; Miss. Choctaw; F; ¼; S; Alone; Yes; Yes

Census of the **Mississippi Choctaws** reservation of the **Choctaw Agency** jurisdiction, as of **January 1, 1937**, 19__, taken by **A. C. Hector**, Superintendent.

KEY; Surname; Present Census Number; Last Census Number; Given Name; Sex; Age at Last Birthday; Tribe; Degree of Blood; Marital Status; Relationship to Head of Family; At Jurisdiction Where Enrolled (Yes/No); At Another Jurisdiction; Post Office, County, State (if given); Ward (Yes/No)

HENRY

719; 696; Albert; m; 59; Miss. Choctaw; F; M: Head; Yes; Yes
720; 697; Martha; f; 49; Miss. Choctaw; F; M; Wife; Yes; Yes
721; 698; Guiser; f; 33; Miss. Choctaw; F; S; Dau; Yes; Yes
722; 699; Beulah; f; 29; Miss. Choctaw; F; S; Dau; Yes; Yes
723; 700; Liege; m; 27; Miss. Choctaw; F; S; Son; Yes; Yes
724; 701; Melvin; m; 24; Miss. Choctaw; F; S; Son; Yes; Yes
725; 702; Nettie; f; 22; Miss. Choctaw; F; S; Dau; Yes; Yes
726; 703; Sis; f; 19; Miss. Choctaw; F; S; Dau; Yes; Yes
727; 704; Susie; f; 17; Miss. Choctaw; F; S; Dau; Yes; Yes
728; 705; R. D; m; 15; Miss. Choctaw; F; S; Son; Yes; Yes
729; 706; Ellen; f; 8; Miss. Choctaw; F; S; Grand-dau; Yes; Yes

730; 707; Jim; m; 34; Miss. Choctaw; F; M; Head; Yes; Yes
731; 708; Sallie; f; 32; Miss. Choctaw; F; M; Wife; Yes; Yes
732; 709; Frank; m; 10; Miss. Choctaw; F; S; Son; Yes; Yes
733; 710; Wick; m; 8; Miss. Choctaw; F; S; Son; Yes; Yes
734; Cornelia; f; 6/12; Miss. Choctaw; F; S; Dau; Yes; Yes
Born 6-14-36

735; 712; Robert; m; 63; Miss. Choctaw; F; M; Head; Yes; Yes
736; 713; Nellie; f; 53; Miss. Choctaw; F; M; Wife; Yes; Yes
737; 714; Bob; m; 29; Miss. Choctaw; F; M; Son; Yes; Yes
738; 716; Jasper; m; 20; Miss. Choctaw; F; S; Son; Yes; Yes
739; 717; Dolphus; m; 17; Miss. Choctaw; F; S; Son; Yes; Yes
740;1071; Berniece Lewis; f; 20; Miss. Choctaw; F; M; Dau-in-law;
Yes; Yes   Wife of Bob Henry

HICKMAN

741; 718; Billy; m; 51; Miss. Choctaw; F; M; Head; Yes; Yes
742; 719; Rose; f; 53; Miss. Choctaw; F; M; Wife; Yes; Yes
743; 721; Susan; f; 19; Miss. Choctaw; F; S; Dau; Yes; Yes

Census of the **Mississippi Choctaws** reservation of the **Choctaw Agency** jurisdiction, as of **January 1, 1937**, 19__, taken by **A. C. Hector**, Superintendent.

KEY; Surname; Present Census Number; Last Census Number; Given Name; Sex; Age at Last Birthday; Tribe; Degree of Blood; Marital Status; Relationship to Head of Family; At Jurisdiction Where Enrolled (Yes/No); At Another Jurisdiction; Post Office, County, State (if given); Ward (Yes/No)

744; 722; Lula; f; 17; Miss. Choctaw; F; S; Dau; Yes; Yes

~~723; Hall, Eliza; f; 84; Miss. Choctaw; F; Wd; Mo-in-law; Yes; Yes~~ Died 11-4-36

745; Edmond; m; 27; Miss. Choctaw; F; M; Head; Yes; Yes
Omitted on previous census
746; Jane; f; 23; Miss. Choctaw; F; M; Wife; Yes; Yes
Omitted on previous census
747; Onie; f; 6; Miss. Choctaw; F; S; Dau; Yes; Yes
Omitted on previous census
748;1846; John; m; 3; Miss. Choctaw; F; S; Son; Yes; Yes
749; Tony; m; 1; Miss. Choctaw; F; S; Son; Yes; Yes
Born 1936 - Unreported

750; 726; Ellis; m; 67; Miss. Choctaw; F; M; Head; Yes; Yes
751; 727; Susan; f; 61; Miss. Choctaw; F; M; Wife; Yes; Yes
752; 748; Stenis; m; 37; Miss. Choctaw; F; Wd; Son; Yes; Yes
753; 912; **Joe**, Ella; f; 42; Miss. Choctaw; F; Wd; Dau; Yes; Yes
754; 917; **Joe**, Shone (Billie); m; 13; Miss. Choctaw; F; S; Grand-son; Yes; Yes
755; 918; **Joe**, Susan (Mary); f; 7; Miss. Choctaw; F; S; Grand-dau; Yes; Yes
756; 919; **Joe**, John (Nichols); m; 6; Miss. Choctaw; F; S; Grand-son; Yes; Yes
757; **Joe**, June; f; 5; Miss. Choctaw; F; S; Grand-dau; Yes; Yes
Omitted on previous census
758; 920; **Lewis**, Susie; f; 13; Miss. Choctaw; F; S; Grand-dau; Yes; Yes
759; 921; **Lewis**, Elsie; f; 12; Miss. Choctaw; F; S; Grand-dau; Yes; Yes
760; 728; **Bell**, Burton; m; 17; Miss. Choctaw; F; S; Grand-son; Yes; Yes
761; 729; **Bell**, Henry; m; 15; Miss. Choctaw; F; S; Grand-son; Yes; Yes

Census of the **Mississippi Choctaws** reservation of the **Choctaw Agency** jurisdiction, as of **January 1, 1937**, 19__, taken by **A. C. Hector**, Superintendent.

KEY; Surname; Present Census Number; Last Census Number; Given Name; Sex; Age at Last Birthday; Tribe; Degree of Blood; Marital Status; Relationship to Head of Family; At Jurisdiction Where Enrolled (Yes/No); At Another Jurisdiction; Post Office, County, State (if given); Ward (Yes/No)

762; 155; **Bell**, Bob; m; 24; Miss. Choctaw; F; Wd; Grand-son; Yes; Yes

~~763; 733; Enoch; m; 63; Miss. Choctaw; F; M; Head; Yes; Yes~~
   Died Feb. 28, 1937
764; 734; Malinda; f; 61; Miss. Choctaw; F; M; Wife; Yes; Yes
765; 735; Sallie; f; 27; Miss. Choctaw; F; S; Dau; Yes; Yes
766; 736; Sadie; f; 26; Miss. Choctaw; F; S; Dau; Yes; Yes
767; 737; Tubby; m; 24; Miss. Choctaw; F; S; Son; Yes; Yes
~~738; Eliza Jane; f; 23; Miss. Choctaw; F; S; Dau; Yes; Yes~~
   Died 1933 - unreported
768; 739; Mary Long; f; 21; Miss. Choctaw; F; S; Dau; Yes; Yes
769; 740; Annie; f; 16; Miss. Choctaw; F; S; Dau; Yes; Yes
770; 741; Willie (Wm. Penn); m; 15; Miss. Choctaw; F; S; Son; Yes; Yes
771; 742; Bobby (Vardeman); m; 13; Miss. Choctaw; F; S; Son; Yes; Yes
772; 743; John; m; 12; Miss. Choctaw; F; S; Son; Yes; Yes

773; 258; (Box), Eula; f; 14; Miss. Choctaw; F; S; Alone; Yes; Yes

774; 250; (Box), Illiman; m; 31; Miss. Choctaw; F; M; Head; Yes; Yes
775; 251; (Box), Rosie; f; 25; Miss. Choctaw; F; M; Wife; Yes; Yes

~~730; Johnkin; m; 43; Miss. Choctaw; F; M; Head; Yes; Yes~~
   Died 1-17-36

776; 252; (Box), Lillie; f; 49; Miss. Choctaw; F; Wd; Head; Yes; Yes
777; 254; (Box), Lizzie (Bathie); f; 14; Miss. Choctaw; F; S; Dau; Yes; Yes
778; 255; (Box), Lula (Bethy); f; 12; Miss. Choctaw; F; S; Dau; Yes; Yes
~~779; 256; (Box), Emelia (Emly); f; 77; Miss. Choctaw; F; Wd; Mo; Yes; Yes~~   Died 5-16-38

Census of the __Mississippi Choctaws__ reservation of the __Choctaw Agency__ jurisdiction, as of __January 1, 1937__, 19__, taken by __A. C. Hector__, Superintendent.

KEY; Surname; Present Census Number; Last Census Number; Given Name; Sex; Age at Last Birthday; Tribe; Degree of Blood; Marital Status; Relationship to Head of Family; At Jurisdiction Where Enrolled (Yes/No); At Another Jurisdiction; Post Office, County, State (if given); Ward (Yes/No)

780; 966; (Box), Mamie; f; 15; Miss. Choctaw; F; S; Alone; Yes; Yes

781; 757; **Hudson**, Celia; f; 30; Miss. Choctaw; F; S; Alone; Yes; Yes

782; 257; (Box), Ola; f; 22; Miss. Choctaw; F; S; Alone; Yes; Yes

783; 253; Ollie T; m; 22; Miss. Choctaw; F; M; Head; Yes; Yes
784; 624; Iama[sic] Frazier; f; 32; Miss. Choctaw; F; M; Wife; Yes; Yes
785; 625; **Frazier**, Homer; m; 13; Miss. Choctaw; F; S; Step-son; Yes; Yes

786; 720; Sim; m; 25; Miss. Choctaw; F; M; Head; Yes; Yes
787; 52; Vada Anderson; f; 31; Miss. Choctaw; F; M; Wife; Yes; Yes

788; 744; Wallace; m; 31; Miss. Choctaw; F; M; Head; Yes; Yes
789; 745; Dona; f; 28; Miss. Choctaw; F; M; Wife; Yes; Yes
790; 746; Robinson; m; 11; Miss. Choctaw; F; S; Son; Yes; Yes
791; 747; Hickman; f; 4; Miss. Choctaw; F; S; Dau; Yes; Yes

792; 724; Willie; m; 27; Miss. Choctaw; F; M; Head; Yes; Yes
793; 725; Lodie Mae; f; 29; Miss. Choctaw; F; M; Wife; Yes; Yes
794; **Davis**, Francis; m; 2; Miss. Choctaw; F; S; Orphan; Yes; Yes Born 1935 - Unreported

ISAAC

795; 761; Byrd; m; 41; Miss. Choctaw; F; M; Head; Yes; Yes
796; 762; Pauline Jim; f; 25; Miss. Choctaw; F; M; Wife; Yes; Yes
797; 764; Berniece; f; 19; Miss. Choctaw; F; S; Dau; Yes; Yes
798; 765; Catherine; f; 17; Miss. Choctaw; F; S; Dau; Yes; Yes
799; 766; Edwin; m; 10; Miss. Choctaw; F; S; Son; Yes; Yes
800; 767; Jesse A; M; 5; Miss. Choctaw; F; S; Son; Yes; Yes
801; 768; Calvin (Paul); m; 3; Miss. Choctaw; F; S; Son; Yes; Yes

Census of the __Mississippi Choctaws__ reservation of the __Choctaw Agency__ jurisdiction, as of __January 1, 1937__, 19__, taken by __A. C. Hector__, Superintendent.

KEY; Surname; Present Census Number; Last Census Number; Given Name; Sex; Age at Last Birthday; Tribe; Degree of Blood; Marital Status; Relationship to Head of Family; At Jurisdiction Where Enrolled (Yes/No); At Another Jurisdiction; Post Office, County, State (if given); Ward (Yes/No)

802; 797; David; m; 30; Miss. Choctaw; F; M; Head; Yes; Yes
803; 798; Lester; f; 29; Miss. Choctaw; F; M; Wife; Yes; Yes
804; 799; Joe D; m; 10; Miss. Choctaw; F; S; Son; Yes; Yes
805; 800; Preston (Franklin); m; 8; Miss. Choctaw; F; S; Son; Yes; Yes
806; 801; Wansey; f; 6; Miss. Choctaw; F; S; Dau; Yes; Yes
~~806;1802; Dave, Jr; m; 3; Miss. Choctaw; F; S; Son; Yes; Yes~~
 Reported dead 1934 Supple. (Alive, shown as Omission)

807; 775; Hugh; m; 27; Miss. Choctaw; F; M; Head; Yes; Yes
808; 776; Celia Farmer; f; 28; Miss. Choctaw; F; M; Wife; Yes; Yes
809; 777; Vanida; f; 6; Miss. Choctaw; F; S; Dau; Yes; Yes
810; 778; Anada[sic]; f; 3; Miss. Choctaw; F; S; Dau; Yes; Yes
~~811; Alice Marie; f; 8/12; Miss. Choctaw; F; S; Dau; Yes; Yes~~
 Born 4-19-36   Died Oct. 5, 1937

812; 779; Isaac; m; 36; Miss. Choctaw; F; M; Head; Yes; Yes
813; 780; Maggie A; F; 28; Miss. Choctaw; F; M; Wife; Yes; Yes
814; 781; Claudine; f; 15; Miss. Choctaw; F; S; Dau; Yes; Yes
815; 782; Wilbur N; m; 14; Miss. Choctaw; F; S; Son; Yes; Yes
816; 784; Edmond (Enochs); m; 9; Miss. Choctaw; F; S; Son; Yes; Yes
817; 785; Delphia; f; 4; Miss. Choctaw; F; S; Dau; Yes; Yes
818; 786; Mary Lou; f; 3; Miss. Choctaw; F; S; Dau; Yes; Yes
819; Sarene; f; 5; Miss. Choctaw; F; S; Dau; Yes; Yes
 Omitted on previous census

820; 794; Jackson; m; 32; Miss. Choctaw; F; M; Head; Yes; Yes
821; 795; Eva; f; 23; Miss. Choctaw; F; M; Wife; Yes; Yes
822;1803; Juanita; f; 3; Miss. Choctaw; F; S; Dau; Yes; Yes
823;1847; Ann Marie; f; 2; Miss. Choctaw; F; S; Dau; Yes; Yes

824; 758; Jim; m; 42; Miss. Choctaw; F; M; Head; Yes; Yes
825; 759; Bessie; f; 36; Miss. Choctaw; F; M; Wife; Yes; Yes

826; 771; Simon; m; 53; Miss. Choctaw; F; M; Head; Yes; Yes

Census of the **Mississippi Choctaws** reservation of the **Choctaw Agency** jurisdiction, as of **January 1, 1937**, 19__, taken by **A. C. Hector**, Superintendent.

KEY; Surname; Present Census Number; Last Census Number; Given Name; Sex; Age at Last Birthday; Tribe; Degree of Blood; Marital Status; Relationship to Head of Family; At Jurisdiction Where Enrolled (Yes/No); At Another Jurisdiction; Post Office, County, State (if given); Ward (Yes/No)

827; 772; Nannie; f; 56; Miss. Choctaw; F; M; Wife; Yes; Yes
828; 773; Effie; f; 14; Miss. Choctaw; F; S; Dau; Yes; Yes
829; 774; Lillie Mae; f; 12; Miss. Choctaw; F; S; Grand-dau; Yes; Yes
830;1177; **Moses**, Allen; m; 31; Miss. Choctaw; F; SM; Son-in-law; Yes; Yes
831;1178; **Moses**, Florence; f; 31; Miss. Choctaw; F; M; Dau; Yes; Yes
832; 783; Claud Preston; m; 9; Miss. Choctaw; F; S; Grand-son; Yes; Yes   Son of Isaac Isaac

833; 787; Will; m; 39; Miss. Choctaw; F; M; Head; Yes; Yes
834; 788; Louisa; f; 38; Miss. Choctaw; F; M; Wife; Yes; Yes
835; 789; Annie; f; 19; Miss. Choctaw; F; S; Dau; Yes; Yes
836; 790; Cornelia; f; 10; Miss. Choctaw; F; S; Dau; Yes; Yes

~~791; Wilson; m; 83; Miss. Choctaw; F; M; Head; Yes; Yes~~
Died 2-3-36
837; 792; John Day; m; 24; Miss. Choctaw; F; S; Son; Yes; Yes

ISOM

838; 810; Isom; m; 37; Miss. Choctaw; F; S; Alone; Yes; Yes

839; 809; Willie; m; 23; Miss. Choctaw; F; M; Head; Yes; Yes
840;1791; Eunice York; f; 23; Miss. Choctaw; F; M; Wife; Yes; Yes
841;   Salina; f; 1/12; Miss. Choctaw; F; S; Dau; Yes; Yes
Born 12-10-36

JACKSON

~~811; Betty; f; 61; Miss. Choctaw; F; Wd; Head; Yes; Yes~~
Died 5-31-36
842; 814; Carlson; m; 17; Miss. Choctaw; F; S; Son; Yes; Yes

Census of the **Mississippi Choctaws** reservation of the **Choctaw Agency** jurisdiction, as of **January 1, 1937**, 19__, taken by **A. C. Hector**, Superintendent.

KEY; Surname; Present Census Number; Last Census Number; Given Name; Sex; Age at Last Birthday; Tribe; Degree of Blood; Marital Status; Relationship to Head of Family; At Jurisdiction Where Enrolled (Yes/No); At Another Jurisdiction; Post Office, County, State (if given); Ward (Yes/No)

843; 815; Lena; f; 49; Miss. Choctaw; F; Wd; Head; Yes; Yes
844; 816; Ellen Bell; f; 23; Miss. Choctaw; F; S; Dau; Yes; Yes
845; 817; Floyd Bell; f; 22; Miss. Choctaw; F; S; Son; Yes; Yes
846; 818; Carson; m; 19; Miss. Choctaw; F; S; Son; Yes; Yes
847; 819; Emmett; m; 17; Miss. Choctaw; F; S; Son; Yes; Yes
848; 820; Lucille; f; 16; Miss. Choctaw; F; S; Dau; Yes; Yes
849;1369; **Morris**, Irene; f; 10; Miss. Choctaw; F; S; Grand-dau; Yes; Yes

850; 825; Sam; m; 53; Miss. Choctaw; F; M; Head; Yes; Yes
851; 826; Martha; f; 54; Miss. Choctaw; F; M; Wife; Yes; Yes

852; 829; Prentiss; m; 34; Miss. Choctaw; F; M; Head; Yes; Yes
853; 830; Mary; f; 34; Miss. Choctaw; F; M; Wife; Yes; Yes

854; 821; Tom; m; 49; Miss. Choctaw; F; M; Head; Yes; Yes
855; 822; Mamie Lewis; f; 45; Miss. Choctaw; F; M; Wife; Yes; Yes

856; 827; Tubby; m; 27; Miss. Choctaw; F; M; Head; Yes; Yes
857; 828; Missie; f; 27; Miss. Choctaw; F; M; Wife; Yes; Yes
858; William; m; 7; Miss. Choctaw; F; S; Son; Yes; Yes
　　　Omitted on previous census
859; Katherine; f; 4; Miss. Choctaw; F; S; Dau; Yes; Yes
　　　Omitted on previous census
860; Colman; m; 3; Miss. Choctaw; F; S; Son; Yes; Yes
　　　Omitted on previous census
861; Rosaline; f; 1; Miss. Choctaw; F; S; Dau; Yes; Yes
　　　Born 11-24-35 - Unreported

862; 823; Woodrow; m; 18; Miss. Choctaw; F; M; Head; Yes; Yes;
863; 871; Anne Mae Jim; f; 23; Miss. Choctaw; F; M; Wife; Yes; Yes
864; Lorraine; f; 2; Miss. Choctaw; F; S; Dau; Yes; Yes
　　　Born 1935 - Unreported

Census of the **Mississippi Choctaws** reservation of the **Choctaw Agency** jurisdiction, as of **January 1, 1937**, 19__, taken by **A. C. Hector**, Superintendent.

KEY; Surname; Present Census Number; Last Census Number; Given Name; Sex; Age at Last Birthday; Tribe; Degree of Blood; Marital Status; Relationship to Head of Family; At Jurisdiction Where Enrolled (Yes/No); At Another Jurisdiction; Post Office, County, State (if given); Ward (Yes/No)

JEFFERSON

865; 833; Amos; m; 30; Miss. Choctaw; F; M; Head; Yes; Yes
866; 834; Ida; f; 25; Miss. Choctaw; F; M; Wife; Yes; Yes
867; 835; Goldman (Leon); m; 4; Miss. Choctaw; F; S; Son; Yes; Yes
868; 836; Mary Sallie; f; 3; Miss. Choctaw; F; S; Dau; Yes; Yes
869; Hubert; m; 1; Miss. Choctaw; F; S; Son; Yes; Yes
Born 1936 - Unreported

870; 832; Braxton; m; 31; Miss. Choctaw; F; M; Head; Yes; Yes
871;1181; Dora Nickey; f; 32; Miss. Choctaw; F; M; Wife; Yes; Yes

872;1047; Newt; m; 21; Miss. Choctaw; F; M; Head; Yes; Yes
873; 406; Leona Nickey Cooper; f; 30; Miss. Choctaw; F; M; Wife; Yes; Yes
874;1849; Franklin; m; 2; Miss. Choctaw; F; S; Son; Yes; Yes

~~875; 839; Oscar; m; 32; Miss. Choctaw; F; M; Head; Yes; Yes~~
Died Sept. 12, 1937
876; 840; Saline; f; 30; Miss. Choctaw; F; M; Wife; Yes; Yes
877; 841; Malcolm; m; 11; Miss. Choctaw; F; S; Son; Yes; Yes
878; 842; Eva Nell; f; 7; Miss. Choctaw; F; S; Dau; Yes; Yes
879;1850; Luline[sic] Jane; f; 2; Miss. Choctaw; F; S; Dau; Yes; Yes
880; Irvin; m; 3; Miss. Choctaw; F; S; Son; Yes; Yes
Omitted on previous census

881; 843; Otis; m; 34; Miss. Choctaw; F; M; Head; Yes; Yes
882; 844; Onie; f; 32; Miss. Choctaw; F; M; Wife; Yes; Yes
883; 845; Otho; m; 12; Miss. Choctaw; F; S; Son; Yes; Yes
884; 846; Andy; m; 11; Miss. Choctaw; F; S; Son; Yes; Yes
885; 847; Victoria; f; 6; Miss. Choctaw; F; S; Dau; Yes; Yes
886; 848; Otis; m; 5; Miss. Choctaw; F; S; Son; Yes; Yes
887; 849; Grady; m; 3; Miss. Choctaw; F; S; Son; Yes; Yes

Census of the **Mississippi Choctaws** reservation of the **Choctaw Agency** jurisdiction, as of **January 1, 1937**, 19__, taken by **A. C. Hector**, Superintendent.

KEY; Surname; Present Census Number; Last Census Number; Given Name; Sex; Age at Last Birthday; Tribe; Degree of Blood; Marital Status; Relationship to Head of Family; At Jurisdiction Where Enrolled (Yes/No); At Another Jurisdiction; Post Office, County, State (if given); Ward (Yes/No)

~~888;1848; Arthur; m; 2; Miss. Choctaw; F; S; Son; Yes; Yes~~
     Died 1-15-38

889; 837; Willis; m; 62; Miss. Choctaw; F; S; Head; Yes; Yes
890; 838; Elsie; f; 50; Miss. Choctaw; F; S; Sis; Yes; Yes

JIM

891; 888; Albert; m; 30; Miss. Choctaw; F; M; Head; Yes; Yes
892; 889; Dora Bell; f; 29; Miss. Choctaw; F; M; Wife; Yes; Yes
893; 890; Grace; f; 7; Miss. Choctaw; F; S; Dau; Yes; Yes
894; 891; Gordon G; m; 4; Miss. Choctaw; F; S; Son; Yes; Yes
895;1851; Effie Mae; f; 2; Miss. Choctaw; F; S; Dau; Yes; Yes

~~877; Amon; m; 60; Miss. Choctaw; F; M; Head; Yes; Yes~~
     Died 10-14-36
896; 878; Lucy; f; 52; Miss. Choctaw; F; M; Head; Yes; Yes
897; 879; Opal; f; 17; Miss. Choctaw; F; S; Dau; Yes; Yes
898; 880; Odie Moore (Carter); m; 8; Miss. Choctaw; F; S; Son; Yes; Yes
899; 881; Ed (Wm. Murray); m; 5; Miss. Choctaw; F; S; Son; Yes; Yes

900; 869; Ben; m; 59; Miss. Choctaw; F; M: Head; Yes; Yes
~~870; Dora; f; 47; Miss. Choctaw; F; M; Wife; Yes; Yes~~
     Died 7-26-36
901; 876; Logan; m; 89; Miss. Choctaw; F; Wd; Bro; Yes; Yes

902; 854; Cooley; m; 67; Miss. Choctaw; F; M; Head; Yes; Yes
903; 855; Lorena; f; 39; Miss. Choctaw; F; M; Wife; Yes; Yes
904; 856; William; m; 16; Miss. Choctaw; F; S; Son; Yes; Yes
905; 857; Tom; m; 14; Miss. Choctaw; F; S; Son; Yes; Yes

~~906; 802; (Isaac), Dixon; m; 85; Miss. Choctaw; F; M; Head; Yes; Yes~~
     Died Dec. 9, 1937

Census of the **Mississippi Choctaws** reservation of the **Choctaw Agency** jurisdiction, as of **January 1, 1937**, 19__, taken by **A. C. Hector**, Superintendent.

KEY; Surname; Present Census Number; Last Census Number; Given Name; Sex; Age at Last Birthday; Tribe; Degree of Blood; Marital Status; Relationship to Head of Family; At Jurisdiction Where Enrolled (Yes/No); At Another Jurisdiction; Post Office, County, State (if given); Ward (Yes/No)

907; 803; (Isaac), Lou; f; 32; Miss. Choctaw; F; M; Wife; Yes; Yes
908; 804; (Isaac), Elsie; f; 19; Miss. Choctaw; F; S; Dau; Yes; Yes
909; 805; (Isaac), Rainey; f 16; Miss. Choctaw; F; S; Dau; Yes; Yes
910; 806; (Isaac), Manda; f; 14; Miss. Choctaw; F; S; Dau; Yes; Yes
911; 807; (Isaac), Lester; f; 14; Miss. Choctaw; F; S; Dau; Yes; Yes
912; 808; **Billy**, Emma; f; 31; Miss. Choctaw; F; S; Sis-in-law; Yes; Yes

913; 850; George; m; 69; Miss. Choctaw; F; M; Head; Yes; Yes
914; 851; Eliza; f; 59; Miss. Choctaw; F; M; Wife; Yes; Yes
915; 852; Lee; m; 31; Miss. Choctaw; F; S; Son; Yes; Yes
916; 769; **Hall**, Herbert; m; 8; Miss. Choctaw; F; S; Grand-son; Yes; Yes

~~917; 882; Goodman; m; 72; Miss. Choctaw; F; M; Head; Yes; Yes~~
   Died 9-21-38
918; 883; Leona; f; 35; Miss. Choctaw; F; M; Wife; Yes; Yes
919; 884; Frank McKinley; m; 11; Miss. Choctaw; F; S; Son; Yes; Yes
920; 885; Claud Yates; m; 9; Miss. Choctaw; F; S; Son; Yes; Yes
921; 886; Mary Lou; f; 3; Miss. Choctaw; F; S; Dau; Yes; Yes
922;1804; Fillie[sic] (Goodman, Jr); m; 3; Miss. Choctaw; F; S; Son; Yes; Yes
~~923;   Frances; f; 9/12; Miss. Choctaw; F; S; Dau; Yes; Yes~~
   Born 4-11-36   Died March 20, 1937
924;   Frank; m; 9/12; Miss. Choctaw; F; S; Son; Yes; Yes
   Born 4-11-36
925; 887; **Farmer**, Sallie; f; 82; Miss. Choctaw; F; Wd; Sis; Yes; Yes

926; 864; Harvey; m; 22; Miss. Choctaw; F; M; Head; Yes; Yes
927; 865; Mattie; f; 39; Miss. Choctaw; F; M; Wife; Yes; Yes
928; 866; **Hall**, Henrietta; f; 9; Miss. Choctaw; F; S; Niece; Yes; Yes
929; 868; **Thomas**, George; m; 88; Miss. Choctaw; F; Wd; Father-in-law; Yes; Yes

930; 862; Henry; m; 52; Miss. Choctaw; F; M; Head; Yes; Yes

Census of the **Mississippi Choctaws** reservation of the **Choctaw Agency** jurisdiction, as of **January 1, 1937**, 19__, taken by **A. C. Hector**, Superintendent.

KEY; Surname; Present Census Number; Last Census Number; Given Name; Sex; Age at Last Birthday; Tribe; Degree of Blood; Marital Status; Relationship to Head of Family; At Jurisdiction Where Enrolled (Yes/No); At Another Jurisdiction; Post Office, County, State (if given); Ward (Yes/No)

931; 863; Mollie; f; 65; Miss. Choctaw; F; M; Wife; Yes; Yes
932; 873; Christine; f; 5; Miss. Choctaw; F; S; Orphan; Yes; Yes
933; 874; Frank; m; 9; Miss. Choctaw; F; S; Orphan; Yes; Yes
934; 875; Bobbie Sue; f; 8; Miss. Choctaw; F; S; Orphan; Yes; Yes
935; 405; **Cooper**, Wickson Dee; m; 38; Miss. Choctaw; F; Wd; Nephew; Yes; Yes

936; 858; John; m; 31; Miss. Choctaw; F; M; Head; Yes; Yes
937; 859; Bessie; f; 28; Miss. Choctaw; F; M; Wife; Yes; Yes
938; 860; Susie Ann; f; 6; Miss. Choctaw; F; S; Dau; Yes; Yes
939; 861; Corrine; f; 4; Miss. Choctaw; F; S; Dau; Yes; Yes
940;1857; Pearl; f; 2; Miss. Choctaw; F; S; Dau; Yes; Yes
941; Otho; m; 9/12; Miss. Choctaw; F; S; Son; Yes; Yes
Born 3-25-36

942; 853; Sidney; m; 21; Miss. Choctaw; F; M; Head; Yes; Yes
~~943; 867; Lula Thomas; f; 23; Miss. Choctaw; F; M; Wife; Yes; Yes~~
Died 1-29-38
944; Richard; m; 9/12; Miss. Choctaw; F; S; Son; Yes; Yes
Born 3-15-36

945; 892; Henry; m; 37; Miss. Choctaw; F; M; Head; Yes; Yes
946; 893; Maggie; f; 43; Miss. Choctaw; F; M: Wife; Yes; Yes

947;1482; (Tubby), Vernon; m; 24; Miss. Choctaw; F; SM; Head; Yes; Yes
948;1725; Ance Willis (Anna); f; 20; Miss. Choctaw; F; M; Wife; Yes; Yes
~~1852; Sallie Mae; f; 2; Miss. Choctaw; F; S; Dau; Yes; Yes~~
Died 6-21-36

949; 895; Victor; m; 36; Miss. Choctaw; F; M; Head; Yes; Yes
950; 896; Lena; f; 27; Miss. Choctaw; F; M; Wife; Yes; Yes
951; 897; Fay; m; 11; Miss. Choctaw; F; S; Son; Yes; Yes

Census of the __Mississippi Choctaws__ reservation of the __Choctaw Agency__ jurisdiction, as of __January 1, 1937__, 19__, taken by __A. C. Hector__, Superintendent.

KEY; Surname; Present Census Number; Last Census Number; Given Name; Sex; Age at Last Birthday; Tribe; Degree of Blood; Marital Status; Relationship to Head of Family; At Jurisdiction Where Enrolled (Yes/No); At Another Jurisdiction; Post Office, County, State (if given); Ward (Yes/No)

952; 898; Cicero (Egbert); m; 7; Miss. Choctaw; F; S; Son; Yes; Yes
953; 1805; Perry; m; 3; Miss. Choctaw; F; S; Son; Yes; Yes
954; Lesley; m; 5½; Miss. Choctaw; F; S; Son; Yes; Yes
Omitted on previous census
955; Anderson; m; 1; Miss. Choctaw; F; S; Son; Yes; Yes
Born 3-9-36

JIMMIE

956; 902; Frank; m; 25; Miss. Choctaw; F; M; Head; Yes; Yes
957; 659; Arleta Gardner; f; 16; Miss. Choctaw; F; M; Wife; Yes; Yes

958; 907; Homer; m; 29; Miss. Choctaw; F; M; Head; Yes; Yes
959; 908; Lela; f; 29; Miss. Choctaw; F; M; Wife; Yes; Yes
960; 909; **Dan**, Irene; f; 11; Miss. Choctaw; F; S; Step-dau; Yes; Yes
961; 910; **Dan**, Bonnie (Albert R); m; 7; Miss. Choctaw; F; S; Step-son; Yes; Yes

962; 903; Ike; m; 67; Miss. Choctaw; F; S; Alone; Yes; Yes

963; 899; Mary; f; 30; Miss. Choctaw; F; Wd; Head; Yes; Yes
964; 900; Ona C; f; 9; Miss. Choctaw; F; S; Dau; Yes; Yes
965; 901; Delores; f; 9; Miss. Choctaw; F; S; Dau; Yes; Yes

966; 904; Will; m; 57; Miss. Choctaw; F; M; Head; Yes; Yes
967; 905; Hester; f; 55; Miss. Choctaw; F; M; Wife; Yes; Yes
968; 906; Mack; m; 31; Miss. Choctaw; F; S; Son; Yes; Yes

JOE

969; 914; Henry; m; 19; Miss. Choctaw; F; M; Head; Yes; Yes
979; 126; Alma Bell; f; 27; Miss. Choctaw; F; M; Wife; Yes; Yes

~~Jane; f; 8/12; Miss. Choctaw; F; S; Dau; Yes; Yes~~

Census of the **Mississippi Choctaws** reservation of the **Choctaw Agency** jurisdiction, as of **January 1, 1937**, 19__, taken by **A. C. Hector**, Superintendent.

KEY; Surname; Present Census Number; Last Census Number; Given Name; Sex; Age at Last Birthday; Tribe; Degree of Blood; Marital Status; Relationship to Head of Family; At Jurisdiction Where Enrolled (Yes/No); At Another Jurisdiction; Post Office, County, State (if given); Ward (Yes/No)

Born 4-27-36 Died 4-27-36
971;   Sallie; f; 8/12; Miss. Choctaw; F; S; Dau; Yes; Yes
Born 4-27-36

972; 922; Jasper; m; 49; Miss. Choctaw; F; M; Head; Yes; Yes
973; 923; Sallie; f; 44; Miss. Choctaw; F; M; Wife; Yes; Yes
974; 924; Lula; f; 24; Miss. Choctaw; F; S; Dau; Yes; Yes
975; 925; Houston; m; 19; Miss. Choctaw; F; S; Son; Yes; Yes
976; 926; Watkins; m; 15; Miss. Choctaw; F; S; Son; Yes; Yes
977;   John; m; 13; Miss. Choctaw; F; S; Son; Yes; Yes
Omitted from previous census
978;   Sarah; f; 13; Miss. Choctaw; F; S; Dau; Yes; Yes
Omitted from previous census
979;   Tom; m; 9; Miss. Choctaw; F; S; Son; Yes; Yes
Omitted from previous census
980;   Ronie; m; 7; Miss. Choctaw; F; S; Son; Yes; Yes
Omitted from previous census

981; 928; John; m; 38; Miss. Choctaw; F; M; Head; Yes; Yes
982; 929; Emma; f; 37; Miss. Choctaw; F; M; Wife; Yes; Yes
983; 930; Bessie; f; 16; Miss. Choctaw; F; S; Dau; Yes; Yes
984; 931; Lillie; f; 12; Miss. Choctaw; F; S; Dau; Yes; Yes
985; 932; Claud; m; 9; Miss. Choctaw; F; S; Son; Yes; Yes
986;   Clark; m; 2; Miss. Choctaw; F; S; Son; Yes; Yes
Born 1935 - Unreported

~~933; Langley; m; 90; Miss. Choctaw; F; Wd; Alone; Yes; Yes~~
Died 3-10-36
~~934; Denson, Joe; m; 83; Miss. Choctaw; F; S; Alone; Yes; Yes~~
Died 1934 - Unreported

~~911; Nicholas; m; 47; Miss. Choctaw; F; M; Head; Yes; Yes~~
Dead - Unreported
987; 913; Auston; m; 23; Miss. Choctaw; F; S; Son; Yes; Yes

Census of the **Mississippi Choctaws** reservation of the **Choctaw Agency** jurisdiction, as of **January 1, 1937**, 19__, taken by **A. C. Hector**, Superintendent.

KEY; Surname; Present Census Number; Last Census Number; Given Name; Sex; Age at Last Birthday; Tribe; Degree of Blood; Marital Status; Relationship to Head of Family; At Jurisdiction Where Enrolled (Yes/No); At Another Jurisdiction; Post Office, County, State (if given); Ward (Yes/No)

988; 915; Wedge; m; 16; Miss. Choctaw; F; S; Son; Yes; Yes
989; 916; Bessie; f; 14; Miss. Choctaw; F; S; Dau; Yes; Yes

JOHN

990; 939; Anderson; m; 60; Miss. Choctaw; F; M; Head; Yes; Yes
991; 940; Bettie; f; 48; Miss. Choctaw; F; M; Wife; Yes; Yes
992; 941; Ella (L.E.); f; 22; Miss. Choctaw; F; S; Dau; Yes; Yes
993; 942; Hubert; m; 19; Miss. Choctaw; F; S; Son; Yes; Yes
994; 943; Owen; m; 16; Miss. Choctaw; F; S; Son; Yes; Yes
995; 944; Wilson; m; 9; Miss. Choctaw; F; S; Son; Yes; Yes
996; Mico; m; 5; Miss. Choctaw; F; S; Son; Yes; Yes
　　Omitted on previous census
997; Jarvis; m; 7; Miss. Choctaw; F; S; Son; Yes; Yes
　　Omitted on previous census

998; 945; Bennett; m; 28; Miss. Choctaw; F; M; Head; Yes; Yes
999; 946; Lena Pearl; f; 22; Miss. Choctaw; F; M; Wife; Yes; Yes
1000; 947; Albert; m; 6; Miss. Choctaw; F; S; Son; Yes; Yes
1001; 948; Hamilton; m; 4; Miss. Choctaw; F; S; Son; Yes; Yes

1002; 967; Bilsy; f; 39; Miss. Choctaw; F; Wd; Head; Yes; Yes
1003; 968; Bilbo; m; 20; Miss. Choctaw; F; M; Son; Yes; Yes
~~1393; Nancy Stoliby; f; 26; Miss. Choctaw; F; M; Dau-in-law; Yes; Yes~~ Died 11-15-36
1004; Nancy Lou; f; 7/12; Miss. Choctaw; F; S; Grand-dau; Yes; Yes　Born 5-5-36
1005; 969; Mable; f; 17; Miss. Choctaw; F; S; Dau; Yes; Yes
1006; 970; Renie; f; 15; Miss. Choctaw; F; S; Dau; Yes; Yes
1007; 971; Vardeman; m; 12; Miss. Choctaw; F; S; Son; Yes; Yes
1008; 972; Smith; m; 10; Miss. Choctaw; F; S; Son; Yes; Yes
1009; 973; Lisette H; f; 7; Miss. Choctaw; F; S; Dau; Yes; Yes
1010; 974; Elizabeth; f; 3; Miss. Choctaw; F; S; Dau; Yes; Yes
1011; 975; Margaret; f; 3; Miss. Choctaw; F; S; Dau; Yes; Yes

Census of the **Mississippi Choctaws** reservation of the **Choctaw Agency** jurisdiction, as of **January 1, 1937**, 19__, taken by **A. C. Hector**, Superintendent.

KEY; Surname; Present Census Number; Last Census Number; Given Name; Sex; Age at Last Birthday; Tribe; Degree of Blood; Marital Status; Relationship to Head of Family; At Jurisdiction Where Enrolled (Yes/No); At Another Jurisdiction; Post Office, County, State (if given); Ward (Yes/No)

1012; 954; Bob; m; 63; Miss. Choctaw; F; M; Head; Yes; Yes
1013; 955; Onie; f; 52; Miss. Choctaw; F; M; Wife; Yes; Yes
1014; 956; Albert (Oliver); m; 22; Miss. Choctaw; F; S; Son; Yes; Yes
1015; 957; Ruby; m; 16; Miss. Choctaw; F; S; Son; Yes; Yes
1016; 958; Rosa; f; 14; Miss. Choctaw; F; S; Dau; Yes; Yes
1017;1201; **Phillips**, Edmond; m; 10; Miss. Choctaw; F; S; Grand-son; Yes; Yes
1018;1202; **Phillips**, M. C. (Emsey); m; 8; Miss. Choctaw; F; S; S[sic]; Yes; Yes

1019; 949; Clint; m; 46; Miss. Choctaw; F; M; Head; Yes; Yes
1010;1246; Suella; f; 22; Miss. Choctaw; F; M; Wife; Yes; Yes
1021; Molpus; m; 6; Miss. Choctaw; F; S; Son; Yes; Yes
Omitted on previous census

1022; 990; Edgar; m; 38; Miss. Choctaw; F; M; Head; Yes; Yes
1023; 991; Beatrice; f; 34; Miss. Choctaw; F; M; Wife; Yes; Yes
1024; 992; Callie; f; 14; Miss. Choctaw; F; S; Dau; Yes; Yes
1025; 993; Frances; f; 12; Miss. Choctaw; F; S; Dau; Yes; Yes
1026; 994; Johnson, Egbert; m; 10; Miss. Choctaw; F; S; Son; Yes; Yes
Died - 1933
1027; 995; Neva; f; 6; Miss. Choctaw; F; S; Dau; Yes; Yes
1028; 996; Beverly; f; 4; Miss. Choctaw; F; S; Dau; Yes; Yes
Johnson, Iva May
1029;1856; Olive Mae; f; 2; Miss. Choctaw; F; S; Dau; Yes; Yes
Died May 11, 1937

1030; 962; Jack; m; 63; Miss. Choctaw; F; M; Head; Yes; Yes
1031; 963; Amanda; f; 42; Miss. Choctaw; F; M; Wife; Yes; Yes
1032; 964; Jefferson; m; 15; Miss. Choctaw; F; S; Son; Yes; Yes
1033; 965; Annie Mae (Mary); f; 13; Miss. Choctaw; F; S; Dau; Yes; Yes

1034; 950; Ira; m; 32; Miss. Choctaw; F; M; Head; Yes; Yes
1035; 951; Oretta; f; 24; Moss; M; Wife; Yes; Yes
1036; 953; Harry; m; 4; Miss. Choctaw; F; S; Son; Yes; Yes

Census of the **Mississippi Choctaws** reservation of the **Choctaw Agency** jurisdiction, as of **January 1, 1937**, 19__, taken by **A. C. Hector**, Superintendent.

KEY; Surname; Present Census Number; Last Census Number; Given Name; Sex; Age at Last Birthday; Tribe; Degree of Blood; Marital Status; Relationship to Head of Family; At Jurisdiction Where Enrolled (Yes/No); At Another Jurisdiction; Post Office, County, State (if given); Ward (Yes/No)

1037;1806; Willie; m; 3; Miss. Choctaw; F; S; Son; Yes; Yes

1038; 935; Mike; m; 64; Miss. Choctaw; F; M; Head; Yes; Yes
1039; 936; Lizzie; f; 79; Miss. Choctaw; F; M; Wife; Yes; Yes
——— 937; ~~Polk (Willis), Dina; f; 23; Miss. Choctaw; F; S; Grand-dau; Yes; Yes~~ Died 10-21-36

——— 938; ~~Josh; m; 61; Miss. Choctaw; F; Wd; Alone; Yes; Yes~~
 Died 5-4-35 - Unreported

——— 959; ~~Otis; m; 20; Miss. Choctaw; F; M; Head; Yes; Yes~~
 Died 8-7-36
1040; 960; Anne Mitch; f; 18; Miss. Choctaw; F; M: Wife; Yes; Yes
1041; 961; Grady; m; 3; Miss. Choctaw; F; S; Son; Yes; Yes
1042; Gladdis (Reta); f; 8/12; Miss. Choctaw; F; S; Dau; Yes; Yes
 Born 4-11-36

JOHNSON

1043; 999; Athens; m; 19; Miss. Choctaw; F; M; Head; Yes; Yes
1044;1384; Tonie Steve; f; 17; Miss. Choctaw; F; M; Wife; Yes; Yes

1045; 985; Afton; m; 33; Miss. Choctaw; F; M; Head; Yes; Yes
1046; 986; Savannia; f; 31; Miss. Choctaw; F; M; Wife; Yes; Yes
1047; 987; Velma (Thelma); f; 8; Miss. Choctaw; F; S; Dau; Yes; Yes
1048; 988; Hubert (Ralph); m; 4; Miss. Choctaw; F; S; Son; Yes; Yes
1049; 989; Zula Denson; f; 13; Miss. Choctaw; F; S; Step-dau; Yes; Yes
1050;1854; Jack Denson; m; 2; Miss. Choctaw; F; S; Son; Yes; Yes
1051; 977; **Stephens**, Pheobe[sic]; f; 17; Miss. Choctaw; F; S; Niece; Yes; Yes

1052; 997; Frank; m; 45; Miss. Choctaw; F; M; Head; Yes; Yes
1053; 998; Lorine Solomon; f; 27; Miss. Choctaw; F; M; Wife; Yes; Yes
1054;1002; Nathan; m; 13; Miss. Choctaw; F; S; Son; Yes; Yes

Census of the **Mississippi Choctaws** reservation of the **Choctaw Agency** jurisdiction, as of **January 1, 1937**, 19__, taken by **A. C. Hector**, Superintendent.

KEY; Surname; Present Census Number; Last Census Number; Given Name; Sex; Age at Last Birthday; Tribe; Degree of Blood; Marital Status; Relationship to Head of Family; At Jurisdiction Where Enrolled (Yes/No); At Another Jurisdiction; Post Office, County, State (if given); Ward (Yes/No)

1055;1003; Hattie; f; 11; Miss. Choctaw; F; S; Dau; Yes; Yes
1056;1004; Cathie (Bona); f; 9; Miss. Choctaw; F; S; Dau; Yes; Yes
~~1005; Marvin; m; 6; Miss. Choctaw; F; S; Don; Yes; Yes~~
    Dead 1933 - Unreported
1057;1006; Jadee (G.O.); m; 4; Miss. Choctaw; F; S; Son; Yes; Yes

1058;1007; Otho; m; 20; Miss. Choctaw; F; M; Head; Yes; Yes
1059;1324; Jaunita Charley; f; 18; Miss. Choctaw; F; M; Wife; Yes; Yes
1060;1853; Allie Nora; f; 2; Miss. Choctaw; F; S; Dau; Yes; Yes

1061; 978; Whitman; m; 26; Miss. Choctaw; F; M; Head; Yes; Yes
1062; 979; Viola; f; 25; Miss. Choctaw; F; M; Wife; Yes; Yes
1063; 980; Priscella Study; f; 4; Miss. Choctaw; F; S; Dau; Yes; Yes
1064;1855; Lorraine; f; 2; Miss. Choctaw; F; S; Dau; Yes; Yes

1065; 981; Will; m; 65; Miss. Choctaw; F; M; Head; Yes; Yes
1066; 982; Dixie; f; 43; Miss. Choctaw; F; M; Wife; Yes; Yes
1067; 983; Gus; m; 12; Miss. Choctaw; F; S; Son; Yes; Yes
1068; 100; **Bell**, James; m; 9; Miss. Choctaw; F; S; Orphan; Yes; Yes

JOSHUA

1069;1008; Jane (Jennie); f; 67; Miss. Choctaw; F; Wd; Head; Yes; Yes
1070;1009; (John), Carrie; f; 26; Miss. Choctaw; F; S; Grand-dau; Yes; Yes
1071;1010; Hollis (Edison); m; 9; Miss. Choctaw; F; S; Grand-son; Yes; Yes

~~976; Johnson, Celia; f; 79; Miss. Choctaw; F; Wd; Alone; Yes; Yes~~   Died 1934 - Unreported

   984; **Johnson**, Sallie; f; 79; Miss. Choctaw; F; Wd; Alone; Yes; Yes   Duplication of 976-34

Census of the __Mississippi Choctaws__ reservation of the __Choctaw Agency__ jurisdiction, as of __January 1, 1937__, 19__, taken by __A. C. Hector__, Superintendent.

KEY; Surname; Present Census Number; Last Census Number; Given Name; Sex; Age at Last Birthday; Tribe; Degree of Blood; Marital Status; Relationship to Head of Family; At Jurisdiction Where Enrolled (Yes/No); At Another Jurisdiction; Post Office, County, State (if given); Ward (Yes/No)

927; **Joe**, Emily; f; 81; Miss. Choctaw; F; Wd; Alone; Yes; Yes
Duplication of 256-34

KING

1072;1019; Betsie; f; 55; Miss. Choctaw; F; Wd; Head; Yes; Yes
1073;1024; Banks; m; 32; Miss. Choctaw; F; M; Son; Yes; Yes
1074;1025; Betsie; f; 41; Miss. Choctaw; F; M; Dau-in-law; Yes; Yes
1075;1020; Christine; f; 29; Miss. Choctaw; F; S; Dau; Yes; Yes
1076;1021; Joseph; m; 20; Miss. Choctaw; F; S; Son; Yes; Yes
1077;1022; Joe; m; 19; Miss. Choctaw; F; S; Son; Yes; Yes
1078;1023; Korkum; m; 16; Miss. Choctaw; F; S; Son; Yes; Yes

1079;1017; Clay; m; 31; Miss. Choctaw; F; M; Head; Yes; Yes
1080;1018; Alice; f; 34; Miss. Choctaw; F; M; Wife; Yes; Yes

~~1011; John W; m; 77; Miss. Choctaw; F; Wd; Head; Yes; Yes~~
Died 6-12-33 - Unreported
1081;1012; Mollie; f; 34; Miss. Choctaw; F; S; Dau; Yes; Yes
1082;1013; Enis; m; 25; Miss. Choctaw; F; S; Son; Yes; Yes
1083;1014; Vardman; m; 25; Miss. Choctaw; F; S; Son; Yes; Yes

LADNER

Sidney; m; [blank]; White; None; M; Head; Yes; Yes
1084;1026; Rosie Thomas; f; 42; Miss. Choctaw; F; M; Wife; yes;

LEBEN

1085;1026[sic]; Ben; m; 65; Miss. Choctaw; F; M; Head; Yes; Yes
1086;1027; Lena; f; 64; Miss. Choctaw; F; M; Wife; Yes; Yes
1087;1028; Mary; f; 36; Miss. Choctaw; F; S; Dau; Yes; Yes
1088; Hester; f; 3; Miss. Choctaw; F; S; Grand-dau; Yes; Yes
Born 1933 - Unreported

Census of the __Mississippi Choctaws__ reservation of the __Choctaw Agency__ jurisdiction, as of __January 1, 1937__, 19__, taken by __A. C. Hector__, Superintendent.

KEY; Surname; Present Census Number; Last Census Number; Given Name; Sex; Age at Last Birthday; Tribe; Degree of Blood; Marital Status; Relationship to Head of Family; At Jurisdiction Where Enrolled (Yes/No); At Another Jurisdiction; Post Office, County, State (if given); Ward (Yes/No)

LEFLORE

1089;1029; John; m; 65; Miss. Choctaw; F; M; Head; Yes; Yes
1090;1030; Emma; f; 57; Miss. Choctaw; F; M; Wife; Yes; Yes
1091;1031; Richard; m; 44; Miss. Choctaw; F; S; Son; Yes; Yes
1092;1032; S. D; m; 31; Miss. Choctaw; F; S; Son; Yes; Yes
1093;1033; Willie; f; 33; Miss. Choctaw; F; S; Dau; Yes; Yes
1093;1034; Bertha Lee; f; 28; Miss. Choctaw; F; S; Dau; Yes; Yes
1095;1035; John; m; 26; Miss. Choctaw; F; S; Son; Yes; Yes
1096;1036; Lewis; m; 25; Miss. Choctaw; F. S; Son; Yes; Yes

LEWIS

1097;1039; Adam; m; 32; Miss. Choctaw; F; M; Head; Yes; Yes
1098;1040; Celia; f; 31; Miss. Choctaw; F; M; Wife; Yes; Yes
1099;1041; Nannie; f; 9; Miss. Choctaw; F; S; Dau; Yes; Yes
1100;1042; Nema (Mamie); f; 7; Miss. Choctaw; F; S; Dau; Yes; Yes
1101;1043; Jacob; m; 4; Miss. Choctaw; F; S; Son; Yes; Yes
1102;1044; Tom; m; 11; Miss. Choctaw; F; S; Step-son; Yes; Yes
1103; Lucy Mae; f; 3; Miss. Choctaw; F; S; Dau; Yes; Yes
Born 1934 - Unreported

1104;1069; Albert; m; 43; Miss. Choctaw; F; M; Head; Yes; Yes
1105; 82; Emma Bell; f; 26; Miss. Choctaw; F; M; Wife; Yes; Yes
1106;1072; Eastland; m; 18; Miss. Choctaw; F; S; Son; Yes; Yes
1107;1073; Ivena; f; 16; Miss. Choctaw; F; S; Dau; Yes; Yes

~~1108;1079; Duffie; m; 41; Miss. Choctaw; F; M; Head; Yes; Yes~~
Died 4-28-38
1109;1080; Lilly; f; 57; Miss. Choctaw; F; M; Wife; Yes; Yes
1110;1081; Egbert; m; 14; Miss. Choctaw; F; S; Step-son; Yes; Yes
1111;1083; **Wickson**, Yates; m; 8; Miss. Choctaw; F; S; Nephew; Yes; Yes

Census of the **Mississippi Choctaws** reservation of the **Choctaw Agency** jurisdiction, as of **January 1, 1937**, 19__, taken by **A. C. Hector**, Superintendent.

KEY; Surname; Present Census Number; Last Census Number; Given Name; Sex; Age at Last Birthday; Tribe; Degree of Blood; Marital Status; Relationship to Head of Family; At Jurisdiction Where Enrolled (Yes/No); At Another Jurisdiction; Post Office, County, State (if given); Ward (Yes/No)

1112;1065; Edd; m; 63; Miss. Choctaw; F; M; Head; Yes; Yes
1113;1066; Edna; f; 55; Miss. Choctaw; F; M: Wife; Yes; Yes
1114;1067; Hollis; m; 21; Miss. Choctaw; F; S; Son; Yes; Yes
1115; 81; **Bell**, Sallie; f; 47; Miss. Choctaw; F; Wd; Boarder; Yes; Yes
1116; 83; **Bell**, Effie; f; 18; Miss. Choctaw; F; S; Dau-of Boarder; Yes; Yes
1117; 84; **Bell**, Ardie; f; 3; Miss. Choctaw; F; S; Dau-of Boarder; Yes; Yes
1118; **Bell**, Edith Rae; f; 10/12; Miss. Choctaw; F; S; Grand-dau of Board[sic]; Yes; Yes   Born 2-2-36   Daughter of Effie Bell

1119;1045; Elon; m; 56; Miss. Choctaw; F; M; Head; Yes; Yes
1120;1046; Lula; f; 59; Miss. Choctaw; F; M; Wife; Yes; Yes

1121;1061; Joe; m; 63; Miss. Choctaw; F; Wd; Alone; Yes; Yes

1122;1644; Johnnie; m; 39; Miss. Choctaw; F; Wd; Alone; Yes; Yes

1123;1062; Leonard (Lennis); m; 30; Miss. Choctaw; F; M; Head; Yes; Yes
1124;1063; Ola; f; 25; Miss. Choctaw; F; M; Wife; Yes; Yes
1125;1064; Nervie; f; 8; Miss. Choctaw; F; M[sic]; Dau; Yes; Yes
1126; Marguerite; f; 5; Miss. Choctaw; F; S; Dau; Yes; Yes
Omitted from previous census
1127; Hazel; f; 1; Miss. Choctaw; F; S; Dau; Yes; Yes
Born 1936 - Unreported
1128; 629; **Frazier**, Seale; m; 67; Miss. Choctaw; F; Wd; Father-in-law; Yes; Yes

1129;1074; Jim; m; 34; Miss. Choctaw; F; M; Head; Yes; Yes
1130;1075; Jennie Willis; f; 29; Miss. Choctaw; F; M; Wife; Yes; Yes
1131;1076; Jennie Lin; f; 8; Miss. Choctaw; F; S; Dau; Yes; Yes
1132;1077; Willie; m; 5; Miss. Choctaw; F; S; Son; Yes; Yes

Census of the **Mississippi Choctaws** reservation of the **Choctaw Agency** jurisdiction, as of **January 1, 1937**, 19__, taken by **A. C. Hector**, Superintendent.

KEY; Surname; Present Census Number; Last Census Number; Given Name; Sex; Age at Last Birthday; Tribe; Degree of Blood; Marital Status; Relationship to Head of Family; At Jurisdiction Where Enrolled (Yes/No); At Another Jurisdiction; Post Office, County, State (if given); Ward (Yes/No)

~~1858; Kenneth; m; 1; Miss. Choctaw; F; S; Son; Yes; Yes~~
    Died 9-7-36

1133;1048; Marshall; m; 62; Miss. Choctaw; F; M; Head; Yes; Yes
1134;1049; Martha; f; 51; Miss. Choctaw; F; M; Wife; Yes; Yes
1135;1051; Houston; m; 18; Miss. Choctaw; F; M; Son; Yes; Yes
1136; 793; Edna Sam; f; 15; Miss. Choctaw; F; M; Dau-in-law; Yes; Yes
1137;1052; Lee; m; 16; Miss. Choctaw; F; S; Son; Yes; Yes
1138;1053; Esther; f; 13; Miss. Choctaw; F; S; Dau; Yes; Yes
1139;1054; Horace (Hodges); m; 10; Miss. Choctaw; F; S; Son; Yes; Yes
1140;1055; Bart (Leon); m; 9; Miss. Choctaw; F; S; Son; Yes; Yes
1141;1056; Rosalind (Lucille); f; 7; Miss. Choctaw; F; S; Dau; Yes; Yes
1142;1057; Prentiss; m; 5; Miss. Choctaw; F; S; Son; Yes; Yes
1143;1060; **Denson**, Bonnie Lee; m; 4; Miss. Choctaw; F; S; Grand-son; Yes; Yes   Child of Eliza and Winston Denson
1144;   **Denson**, Loretta; f; 10/12; Miss; S; Grand-dau; Yes; Yes
    Child of Eliza and Winston Denson

MARTIN

1145;1091; Ennis; m; 29; Miss. Choctaw; F; M; Head; Yes; Yes
1146; 337; Lylie Chickaway; f; 35; Miss. Choctaw; F; M; Wife; Yes; Yes
1147; 338; **Chickaway**, Michael; m; 14; Miss. Choctaw; F; S; Step-son; Yes; Yes
1148; 339; **Chickaway**, Anna; f; 12; Miss. Choctaw; F; S; Step-dau; Yes; Yes
1149; 340; **Chickaway**, Jane; f; 10; Miss. Choctaw; F; S; Step-dau; Yes; Yes
1150;1095; Robert John; m; 3; Miss. Choctaw; F; S; Son; Yes; Yes

~~1151;1084; Willis; m; 47; Miss. Choctaw; F; M; Head; Yes; Yes~~
    Died Dec. 25, 1937
1152;1085; Mary Steve; f; 41; Miss. Choctaw; F; M; Wife; Yes; Yes
1153;1086; Raymond; m; 17; Miss. Choctaw; F; S; Son; Yes; Yes

Census of the __Mississippi Choctaws__ reservation of the __Choctaw Agency__ jurisdiction, as of __January 1, 1937__, 19__, taken by __A. C. Hector__, Superintendent.

KEY; Surname; Present Census Number; Last Census Number; Given Name; Sex; Age at Last Birthday; Tribe; Degree of Blood; Marital Status; Relationship to Head of Family; At Jurisdiction Where Enrolled (Yes/No); At Another Jurisdiction; Post Office, County, State (if given); Ward (Yes/No)

1154;1087; Edmond J; m; 14; Miss. Choctaw; F; S; Son; Yes; Yes
1155;1088; Phillip; m; 11; Miss. Choctaw; F; S; Son; Yes; Yes
1156;1089; Annie Mae; f; 9; Miss. Choctaw; F; S; Dau; Yes; Yes
1157;1090; Harry M; m; 5; Miss. Choctaw; F; S; Son; Yes; Yes
1158;1862; Anthony; m; 2; Miss. Choctaw; F; S; Son; Yes; Yes

McMILLAN

1159;1113; Anthony; m; 31; Miss. Choctaw; F; M; Head; Yes; Yes
1160;1114; Venie Comby; f; 21; Miss. Choctaw; F; M; Wife; Yes; Yes
1161;1115; Marie Theresa; f; 4; Miss. Choctaw; F; S; Dau; Yes; Yes
1162;1807; Rita; f; 3; Miss. Choctaw; F; S; Dau; Yes; Yes
1163; Leonard Yates; m; 6/12; Miss. Choctaw; F; S; Son; Yes; Yes Born 6-13-36

1164;1106; Cephus; m; 55; Miss. Choctaw; F; M; Head; Yes; Yes
1165;1107; Mina; f; 42; Miss. Choctaw; F; M: Wife; Yes; Yes
1166;1110; Enochs; m; 9; Miss. Choctaw; F; S; Son; Yes; Yes
1167;1111; Lurline; f; 5; Miss. Choctaw; F; S; Dau; Yes; Yes
1168;1859; Henry Lee; m; 2; Miss. Choctaw; F; S; Grand-son; Yes; Yes

1169; 380; Jimmie; m; 26; Miss. Choctaw; F; M: Head; Yes; Yes
1170; 504; Maggie Farmer; f; 28; Miss. Choctaw; F; M; Wife; Yes; Yes
1171;1860; Lee Otho; m; 2; Miss. Choctaw; F; S; Son; Yes; Yes

1172;1103; Lemmie; m; 27; Miss. Choctaw; F; M: Head; Yes; Yes
1173; 756; Becky Charlie f; 20; Miss. Choctaw; F; M; Wife; Yes; Yes
1174; 427; **Davis**, Leona; f; 61; Miss. Choctaw; F; Wd; Mother; Yes; Yes

1175;1096; Sorsby; m; 61; Miss. Choctaw; F; Wd; Head; Yes; Yes
1176;1098; Emma; f; 22; Miss. Choctaw; F; S; Dau Yes; Yes
1177;1099; Clarence; m; 20; Miss. Choctaw; F; S; Son; Yes; Yes
1178;1100; Bessie; f; 18; Miss. Choctaw; F; Son; Dau; Yes; Yes

Census of the __Mississippi Choctaws__ reservation of the __Choctaw Agency__ jurisdiction, as of __January 1, 1937__, 19__, taken by __A. C. Hector__, Superintendent.

KEY; Surname; Present Census Number; Last Census Number; Given Name; Sex; Age at Last Birthday; Tribe; Degree of Blood; Marital Status; Relationship to Head of Family; At Jurisdiction Where Enrolled (Yes/No); At Another Jurisdiction; Post Office, County, State (if given); Ward (Yes/No)

1179;1101; Gipson; m; 13; Miss. Choctaw; F; S; Son; Yes; Yes
1180;1102; Pauline; f; 9; Miss. Choctaw; F; S; Dau; Yes; Yes

~~1181;1116; Oscar; m; 43; Miss. Choctaw; F; M; Head; Yes; Yes~~
              Died March 14, 1937
1182;1117; Bonnie Davis; f; 38; Miss. Choctaw; F; M; Wife; Yes; Yes
1183;1118; Arnold; m; 23; Miss. Choctaw; F; S; Son; Yes; Yes
1184;1119; Leslie; f; 15; Miss. Choctaw; F; S; Dau; Yes; Yes
1185;1120; Bert; m; 13; Miss. Choctaw; F; S; Son; Yes; Yes
1186;1121; Frances; f; 11; Miss. Choctaw; F; S; Dau; Yes; Yes
1187;1122; Joe (John); m; 8; Miss. Choctaw; F; S; Son; Yes; Yes
1188;1123; Jean; f; 5; Miss. Choctaw; F; S; Dau; Yes; Yes
1189;1124; Augusta; m; 3; Miss. Choctaw; F; S; Son; Yes; Yes

1190;1109; Willis; m; 21; Miss. Choctaw; F; M: Head; Yes; Yes
1191;1672; Mallie Willis; f; 26; Miss. Choctaw; F; M; Wife; Yes; Yes

MINGO

1192;1137; Jim; m; 22; Miss. Choctaw; F; M; Head; Yes; Yes
1193;1138; Sally Bell; f; 22; Miss. Choctaw; F; M; Wife; Yes; Yes
~~   1863; Otho; m; 2; Miss. Choctaw; F; S; Son; Yes; Yes~~
              Died 6-30-36

1194;1128; John; m; 61; Miss. Choctaw; F; M; Head; Yes; Yes
1195;1129; Hattie; f; 35; Miss. Choctaw; F; M; Wife; Yes; Yes
1196;1130; Arch; m; 15; Miss. Choctaw; F; S; Son; Yes; Yes
1197;1131; Otis; m; 12; Miss. Choctaw; F; S; Son; Yes; Yes
1198;1132; Sarah; f; 10; Miss. Choctaw; F; S; Dau; Yes; Yes
1199;1133; Mary; f; 7; Miss. Choctaw; F; S; Dau; Yes; Yes

1200;1134; Lilly; f; 59; Miss. Choctaw; F; Wd; Alone; Yes; Yes

1201;1135; Olin; m; 19; Miss. Choctaw; F; M; Head; Yes; Yes

Census of the **Mississippi Choctaws** reservation of the **Choctaw Agency** jurisdiction, as of **January 1, 1937**, 19__, taken by **A. C. Hector**, Superintendent.

KEY; Surname; Present Census Number; Last Census Number; Given Name; Sex; Age at Last Birthday; Tribe; Degree of Blood; Marital Status; Relationship to Head of Family; At Jurisdiction Where Enrolled (Yes/No); At Another Jurisdiction; Post Office, County, State (if given); Ward (Yes/No)

1202;1125; Annie Mingo (Renie Cotton); f; 33; Miss. Choctaw; F; M; Wife; Yes; Yes
1203;1126; Davidson; m; 14; Miss. Choctaw; F; S; Step-son; Yes; Yes
1204;1127; Effie; f; 13; Miss. Choctaw; F; S; Step-dau; Yes; Yes
1205;1808; Robert Bruce; m; 3; Miss. Choctaw; F; S; Step-son; Yes; Yes
1206;   Baby; f; 2/12; Miss. Choctaw; F; S; Dau; Yes; Yes
           Born 10-21-36

MITCH

1207;1145; Gilmore; m; 22; Miss. Choctaw; F; M; Head; Yes; Yes
1208; 183; Lillie Mae Ben; f; 26; Miss. Choctaw; F; M; Wife; Yes; Yes

1209;1141; Sarah; f; 53; Miss. Choctaw; F; Wd; Head; Yes; Yes
1210;1142; Elea; m; 35; Miss. Choctaw; F; S; Son; Yes; Yes
1211;1144; Wilson; m; 31; Miss. Choctaw; F; S; Son; Yes; Yes

MORRIS

1212;1174; Boston; m; 34; Miss. Choctaw; ¼; M; Head; Yes; Yes
1213;1176; Nola; f; 42; Miss. Choctaw; F; ¼; M; Wife; Yes; Yes

1214;1158; Dempsey; m; 36; Miss. Choctaw; F; M; Head; Yes; Yes
           (Children shown on page [231])
1215;1159; Jane Donie; f; 35; Miss. Choctaw; F; M; Wife; Yes; Yes
1216;1160; Ora; f; 16; Miss. Choctaw; F; S; Dau; Yes; Yes
1217;1161; Bethany; m; 13; Miss. Choctaw; F; S; Son; Yes; Yes

1218;1168; Howard; m; 30; Miss. Choctaw; F; M; Head; Yes; Yes
1219;1169; Bertie; f; 27; Miss. Choctaw; F; M; Wife; Yes; Yes
1220;1170; Jimmie; m; 11; Miss. Choctaw; F; S; Son; Yes; Yes

1221;1171; Houston; m; 30; Miss. Choctaw; ¼; M; Head; Yes; Yes
1222;1172; Bertha; f; 29; Miss. Choctaw; F; M; Wife; Yes; Yes

Census of the **Mississippi Choctaws** reservation of the **Choctaw Agency** jurisdiction, as of **January 1, 1937**, 19__, taken by **A. C. Hector**, Superintendent.

KEY; Surname; Present Census Number; Last Census Number; Given Name; Sex; Age at Last Birthday; Tribe; Degree of Blood; Marital Status; Relationship to Head of Family; At Jurisdiction Where Enrolled (Yes/No); At Another Jurisdiction; Post Office, County, State (if given); Ward (Yes/No)

1223;1155; Joe; m; 23; Miss. Choctaw; F; M; Head; Yes; Yes
1224; 749; Winnie T. Hickman; f; 32; Miss. Choctaw; F; M; Wife; Yes; Yes
1225; 750; **Hickman**, Eula; f; 10; Miss. Choctaw; F; S; Step-dau; Yes; Yes
1226; 751; **Hickman**, Smokey (Snooks); F; S; Step-son; Yes; Yes
1227;752; **Hickman**, George; m; 6; Miss. Choctaw; F; S; Step-son; Yes; Yes

1230;1146; Julius; m; 35; Miss. Choctaw; F; M; Head; Yes; Yes
1231;1147; Beauty; f; 32; Miss. Choctaw; F; M; Wife; Yes; Yes
1232;1148; Edna (Eddie); f; 13; Miss. Choctaw; F; S; Dau; Yes; Yes
1233;1149; Lena; f; 10; Miss. Choctaw; F; S; Dau; Yes; Yes
1234;1150; Walter Olin; m; 7; Miss. Choctaw; F; S; Son; Yes; Yes
1235; Maude; f; 4; Miss. Choctaw; F; S; Dau; Yes; Yes
    Omitted from previous census
1236; Phelix; m; 2; Miss. Choctaw; F; S; Son; Yes; Yes
    Omitted from previous census

1237;1151; Mosley; m; 71; Miss. Choctaw; F; M; Head; Yes; Yes
~~1238;1152; Ida; f; 56; Miss. Choctaw; F; M; Wife; Yes; Yes~~
    Died Feb. 19, 1937
1239;1153; Lilly; f; 37; Miss. Choctaw; F; S; Dau; Yes; Yes
1240;1154; Wilson; m; 33; Miss. Choctaw; F; S; Son; Yes; Yes
1241;1156; **Wesley**, Sue Morris; f; 35; Miss. Choctaw; F; Wd; Dau; Yes; Yes
1242;1157; **Wesley**, Rufus; m; 12; Miss. Choctaw; F; S; Grand-son; Yes; Yes

1243;1162; Printeas[sic]; m; 11; Miss. Choctaw; F; S; Son; Yes; Yes
    Child of Dempsey Morris shown on page [230]
1244;1163; Chester; m; 7; Miss. Choctaw; F; S; Son; Yes; Yes
    Child of Dempsey Morris shown on page [230]

Census of the **Mississippi Choctaws** reservation of the **Choctaw Agency** jurisdiction, as of **January 1, 1937**, 19__, taken by **A. C. Hector**, Superintendent.

KEY; Surname; Present Census Number; Last Census Number; Given Name; Sex; Age at Last Birthday; Tribe; Degree of Blood; Marital Status; Relationship to Head of Family; At Jurisdiction Where Enrolled (Yes/No); At Another Jurisdiction; Post Office, County, State (if given); Ward (Yes/No)

1245;1164; Champ; m; 9; Miss. Choctaw; F; S; Son; Yes; Yes
    Child of Dempsey Morris shown on page [230]
1246;1165; Lester; m; 4; Miss. Choctaw; F; S; Son; Yes; Yes
    Child of Dempsey Morris shown on page [230]
1247;1809; Alice (Salina); f; 7; Miss. Choctaw; F; S; Dau; Yes; Yes
    Child of Dempsey Morris shown on page [230]
1248; Mazelle; f; 7/12; Miss. Choctaw; F; S; Dau; Yes; Yes
  Born 5-21-36 Child of Dempsey Morris shown on page [230]

1249;1166; Sallie; f; 68; Miss. Choctaw; F; Wd; Head; Yes; Yes
1250;1167; Seward; m; 36; Miss. Choctaw; F; S; Son; Yes; Yes

MOSES

1251;1176; Alma; f; 26; Miss. Choctaw; F; S; Alone; Yes; Yes

NERASIE

    Cloza; m; [blank]; White; None; M; Head; Yes; Yes
1252; 585; Emeline Farve; f; 47; Miss. Choctaw; F; M; Wife; Yes; Yes

NICKEY

1253;1184; Billy; m; 53; Miss. Choctaw; F; M; Head; Yes; Yes
1254;1185; Fronie; f; 56; Miss. Choctaw; F; M; Wife; Yes; Yes
1255;1186; Ode; f; 28; Miss. Choctaw; F; S; Dau; Yes; Yes
1256;1187; Zima (Zelma); f; 25; Miss. Choctaw; F; S; Dau; Yes; Yes
1257;1190; Cozette; m; 18; Miss. Choctaw; F; S; Son; Yes; Yes
1258;1191; Thomas; m; 14; Miss. Choctaw; F; S; Son; Yes; Yes

1259;1188; Hughey; m; 22; Miss. Choctaw; F; M; Head; Yes; Yes
~~1260; 872; Rena Jim; f; 15; Miss. Choctaw; F; M; Wife; Yes; Yes~~
    Died 1-9-38

Census of the Mississippi Choctaws reservation of the Choctaw Agency jurisdiction, as of January 1, 1937 , 19__, taken by A. C. Hector , Superintendent.

KEY; Surname; Present Census Number; Last Census Number; Given Name; Sex; Age at Last Birthday; Tribe; Degree of Blood; Marital Status; Relationship to Head of Family; At Jurisdiction Where Enrolled (Yes/No); At Another Jurisdiction; Post Office, County, State (if given); Ward (Yes/No)

1261;   John Joseph; m; 11/12; Miss. Choctaw; F; S; Son; Yes; Yes
           Born 1-20-36

1262;1179; Sam; m; 52; Miss. Choctaw; F; M; Head; Yes; Yes
1263;1180; Lizzie (Malissie); f; 50; Miss. Choctaw; F; M; Wife; Yes; Yes
1264;1182; Sherman; m; 15; Miss. Choctaw; F; S; Son; Yes; Yes
1265;1183; Copeland; m; 9; Miss. Choctaw; F; S; Son; Yes; Yes

NOAH

1266;1192; Elizabeth; f; 65; Miss. Choctaw; F; Wd; Alone; Yes; Yes

1267;1193; Lizzie; f; 47; Miss. Choctaw; F; Wd; Head; Yes; Yes
1268;1194; Nancie; f; 21; Miss. Choctaw; F; S; Dau; Yes; Yes
1269;1195; Annie; f; 18; Miss. Choctaw; F; S; Dau; Yes; Yes

NUBBY

1270;1196; Billy; m; 77; Miss. Choctaw; F; M; Head; Yes; Yes
1271;1197; Lilly; f; 57; Miss. Choctaw; F; M; Wife; Yes; Yes

PHILLIPS

1272;1198; Riley; m; 30; Miss. Choctaw; F; M; Head; Yes; Yes
1273;1199; Lester Smith; f; 24; Miss. Choctaw; F; M; Wife; Yes; Yes
1274;1200; Roy Lee (Chas. Geo); m; 4; Miss. Choctaw; F; S; Son; Yes; Yes
1275;1865; D. C; m; 2; Miss. Choctaw; F; S; Son; Yes; Yes
1276; 694; **Hawkins**, Alice; f; 55; Miss. Choctaw; F; Wd; Mo-in-law; Yes; Yes

POLK

1277;1208; Francis; m; 27; Miss. Choctaw; F; M; Head; Yes; Yes

Census of the **Mississippi Choctaws** reservation of the **Choctaw Agency** jurisdiction, as of **January 1, 1937**, 19__, taken by **A. C. Hector**, Superintendent.

KEY; Surname; Present Census Number; Last Census Number; Given Name; Sex; Age at Last Birthday; Tribe; Degree of Blood; Marital Status; Relationship to Head of Family; At Jurisdiction Where Enrolled (Yes/No); At Another Jurisdiction; Post Office, County, State (if given); Ward (Yes/No)

1278;1209; Odell; f; 24; Miss. Choctaw; F; M; Wife; Yes; Yes

~~1207; George; m; 75; Miss. Choctaw; F; Wd; Alone; Yes; Yes~~
Died 12-23-36

1279;1203; Henry; m; 29; Miss. Choctaw; F; M; Head; Yes; Yes
1280;1204; Susie; f; 35; Miss. Choctaw; F; M; Wife; Yes; Yes
1281;1205; Sula; f; 8; Miss. Choctaw; F; S; Dau; Yes; Yes
1282;1206; Hudson; m; 6; Miss. Choctaw; F; S; Son; Yes; Yes

1283; Herman; m; 23; Miss. Choctaw; F; M; Head; Yes; Yes
Omitted from previous census
1284; Susie Ben; f; 40; Miss. Choctaw; F; M; Wife; Yes; Yes
Omitted from previous census
1285; Jim; m; 2/12; Miss. Choctaw; F; S; Son; Yes; Yes
Born 11 2 36

1286;1210; Josie; m; 56; Miss. Choctaw; F; M: Head; Yes; Yes
~~1211; Lena (Lennie); f; 57; Miss. Choctaw; F; M; Wife; Yes; Yes~~
Died 1936 - Unreported
1287;1212; Ada; f; 19; Miss. Choctaw; F; S; Dau; Yes; Yes
1288;1213; Frances; f; 18; Miss. Choctaw; F; S; Dau; Yes; Yes

1289;1214; Tom; m; 59; Miss. Choctaw; F; Wd; Head; Yes; Yes
1290;1215; Cornelia; m; 27; Miss. Choctaw; F; S; Son; Yes; Yes
1291;1216; Alma; f; 23; Miss. Choctaw; F; S; Dau; Yes; Yes
1292;1217; Osborn; m; 21; Miss. Choctaw; F; S; Son; Yes; Yes

POULSON

1293;1218; Allie; f; 64; Miss. Choctaw; F; S; Alone; Yes; Yes
1294;1219; Julius; m; 30; Miss. Choctaw; F; S; Alone; Yes; Yes

1295;1225; Charlie; m; 25; Miss. Choctaw; F; S; Alone; Yes; Yes

Census of the **Mississippi Choctaws** reservation of the **Choctaw Agency** jurisdiction, as of **January 1, 1937**, 19__, taken by **A. C. Hector**, Superintendent.

KEY; Surname; Present Census Number; Last Census Number; Given Name; Sex; Age at Last Birthday; Tribe; Degree of Blood; Marital Status; Relationship to Head of Family; At Jurisdiction Where Enrolled (Yes/No); At Another Jurisdiction; Post Office, County, State (if given); Ward (Yes/No)

1296;1222; Eddie M; m; 30; Miss. Choctaw; F; M; Head; Yes; Yes
1297;1223; Cornelia; f; 33; Miss. Choctaw; F; M; Wife; Yes; Yes

1298;1220; Frank; m; 37; Miss. Choctaw; F; M; Head; Yes; Yes
1299;1221; Mary; f; 35; Miss. Choctaw; F; M; Wife; Yes; Yes

1300;1224; Johnnie; m; 28; Miss. Choctaw; F; S; Alone; Yes; Yes

PHILLIPS

1301;1884; Lonie; f; 40; Miss. Choctaw; F; Wd; Head; Yes; Yes
1302;1864; Baby; m; 2; Miss. Choctaw; F; S; Son; Yes; Yes

ROBINSON

1303;1237; Belia; f; 30; Miss. Choctaw; F; Wd; Head; Yes; Yes
1304;1238; Campbell; m; 10; Miss. Choctaw; F; S; Son; Yes; Yes

1305;1228; Jimmie; m; 23; Miss. Choctaw; F; M; Head; Yes; Yes
1306; 87; Bonnie Bell; f; 21; Miss. Choctaw; F; M; Wife; Yes; Yes
1307;1866; Josephine Teach; f; 2; Miss. Choctaw; F; S; Dau; Yes; Yes

1308;1226; Thomas; m; 47; Miss. Choctaw; F; M; Head; Yes; Yes
1309;1227; Syble; f; 42; Miss. Choctaw; F; M; Wife; Yes; Yes
1310;1229; Georgia; f; 21; Miss. Choctaw; F; S; Dau; Yes; Yes
1311;1230; Sallie; f; 20; Miss. Choctaw; F; S; Dau; Yes; Yes
1312;1231; Carl; m; 19; Miss. Choctaw; F; S; Son; Yes; Yes
1313;1232; Mamie; f; 17; Miss. Choctaw; F; S; Dau; Yes; Yes
1314;1233; Betsey; f; 15; Miss. Choctaw; F; S; Dau; Yes; Yes
1315;1234; Homer; m; 13; Miss. Choctaw; F; S; Son; Yes; Yes
1316;1235; Teach; m; 9; Miss. Choctaw; F; S; Son; Yes; Yes
1317;1236; Mary; f; 7; Miss. Choctaw; F; S; Dau; Yes; Yes
1318; Billie; m; 2; Miss. Choctaw; F; S; Son; Yes; Yes
Born 1935 - Unreported

Census of the __Mississippi Choctaws__ reservation of the __Choctaw Agency__ jurisdiction, as of __January 1, 1937__, 19__, taken by __A. C. Hector__, Superintendent.

KEY; Surname; Present Census Number; Last Census Number; Given Name; Sex; Age at Last Birthday; Tribe; Degree of Blood; Marital Status; Relationship to Head of Family; At Jurisdiction Where Enrolled (Yes/No); At Another Jurisdiction; Post Office, County, State (if given); Ward (Yes/No)

RUTHERFORD

            John; m; [blank]; White; None; M; Head; Yes; Yes
1319;1239; Henrietta; f; 39; Miss. Choctaw; F; M; Wife; Yes; Yes

SAM

1320;1257; Fontaine; m; 51; Miss. Choctaw; F; M: Head; Yes; Yes
1321;1258; Emily; f; 47; Miss. Choctaw; F; M; Wife; Yes; Yes
1322;1260; Ellis; m; 12; Miss. Choctaw; F; S; Son; Yes; Yes
1323;1261; Fannie; f; 11; Miss. Choctaw; F; S; Dau; Yes; Yes
1324;1262; Ella Ruth; f; 9; Miss. Choctaw; F; S; Dau; Yes; Yes
1325;1263; Armond; m; 7; Miss. Choctaw; F; S; Son; Yes; Yes
1326;1264; Beaman; m; 17; Miss. Choctaw; F; S; Nephew; Yes; Yes

1327;1249; Jimpson; m; 34; Miss. Choctaw; F; M; Head; Yes; Yes
1328;1250; Louisiana; f; 32; Miss. Choctaw; F; M; Wife; Yes; Yes
1329;1251; Etta Lee; f; 3; Miss. Choctaw; F; S; Dau; Yes; Yes
            Jimpson; m; 6/12; Miss. Choctaw; F; S; Son; Yes; Yes
            Born 6-3-36   Died 7-12-36

1330;1244; Oscar; m; 83; Miss. Choctaw; F; M; Head; Yes; Yes
1331;1245; Mattie; f; 57; Miss. Choctaw; F; M: Wife; Yes; Yes

1332;1243; Raymond; m; 56; Miss. Choctaw; F; S; Alone; Yes; Yes

1333; 467; Charlie; m; 22; Miss. Choctaw; F; S; Alone; Yes; Yes

1334;1240; Truman; m; 28; Miss. Choctaw; F; M; Head; Yes; Yes
1335;1241; Sina John; f; 25; Miss. Choctaw; F; M; Wife; Yes; Yes
1336;1242; Beaman; m; 3; Miss. Choctaw; F; S; Son; Yes; Yes
1337;1867; Baby; m; 2; Miss. Choctaw; F; S; Son; Yes; Yes

Census of the **Mississippi Choctaws** reservation of the **Choctaw Agency** jurisdiction, as of **January 1, 1937**, 19__, taken by **A. C. Hector**, Superintendent.

KEY; Surname; Present Census Number; Last Census Number; Given Name; Sex; Age at Last Birthday; Tribe; Degree of Blood; Marital Status; Relationship to Head of Family; At Jurisdiction Where Enrolled (Yes/No); At Another Jurisdiction; Post Office, County, State (if given); Ward (Yes/No)

~~1252; Walter; m; 47; Miss. Choctaw; F; Wd; Head; Yes; Yes~~
    Died 11-23-36
1338;1253; Grace; f; 20; Miss. Choctaw; F; S; Dau; Yes; Yes
1339;1254; Tom; m; 18; Miss. Choctaw; F; S; Son; Yes; Yes
1340;1255; Edna; f; 15; Miss. Choctaw; F; S; Dau; Yes; Yes
1341;1256; Manzie; f; 13; Miss. Choctaw; F; S; Dau; Yes; Yes

1342;1265; Willie; m; 38; Miss. Choctaw; F; M: Head; Yes; Yes
1343;1266; Eva; f; 36; Miss. Choctaw; F; M; Wife; Yes; Yes
1344;1267; Nettie; f; 16; Miss. Choctaw; F; S; Dau; Yes; Yes
1345;1268; Abel; m; 15; Miss. Choctaw; F; S; Son; Yes; Yes
1346;1269; Louie; m; 13; Miss. Choctaw; F; S; Son; Yes; Yes
1347;1270; Griscelina; f; 7; Miss. Choctaw; F; S; Dau; Yes; Yes
1348;1271; Susie; f; 4; Miss. Choctaw; F; S; Dau; Yes; Yes
1349;1810; Claud; m; 3; Miss. Choctaw; F; S; Son; Yes; Yes
1350;   Edward; m; 1/12; Miss. Choctaw; F; S; Son; Yes; Yes
    Born 11-28-36

SAUCIER

    Stanley; m; [blank]; White; None; M; Head; Yes; Yes
1351; 569; Victoria Farve; f; 37; Miss. Choctaw; F; M; Wife; Yes; Yes

SCOTT

1352;1272; Marshall; m; 67; Miss. Choctaw; F; M; Head; Yes; Yes
1353;1273; Lonie Tubby; f; 32; Miss. Choctaw; F; M; Wife; Yes; Yes
1354;1274; Rachel; f; 11; Miss. Choctaw; F; S; Dau; Yes; Yes
1355;1275; Maggie Mary; f; 3; Miss. Choctaw; F; S; Dau; Yes; Yes
1356;1139; **Mingo**, Oscar; m; 27; Miss. Choctaw; F; M; Nephew; Yes; Yes
1357;1140; **Mingo**, Lena Tubby; f; 33; Miss. Choctaw; F; M; Niece; Yes; Yes

Census of the **Mississippi Choctaws** reservation of the **Choctaw Agency** jurisdiction, as of **January 1, 1937**, 19__, taken by **A. C. Hector**, Superintendent.

KEY; Surname; Present Census Number; Last Census Number; Given Name; Sex; Age at Last Birthday; Tribe; Degree of Blood; Marital Status; Relationship to Head of Family; At Jurisdiction Where Enrolled (Yes/No); At Another Jurisdiction; Post Office, County, State (if given); Ward (Yes/No)

SHOEMAKE

1358;1281; Buck; m; 52; Miss. Choctaw; F; M; Head; Yes; Yes
1359;1282; Annie; f; 37; Miss. Choctaw; F; M; Wife; Yes; Yes
1360;1283; Leona; f; 17; Miss. Choctaw; F; S; Dau; Yes; Yes
1361;1284; Eliza; f; 15; Miss. Choctaw; F; S; Dau; Yes; Yes
1362;1285; Martha; f; 13; Miss. Choctaw; F; S; Dau; Yes; Yes
1363;1286; Daisy; f; 11; Miss. Choctaw; F; S; Dau; Yes; Yes
1364;1287; Carrie Mae; f; 10; Miss. Choctaw; F; S; Dau; Yes; Yes
1365;1288; Hubert; m; 6; Miss. Choctaw; F; S; Son; Yes; Yes
1366;1289; Edmond; m; 4; Miss. Choctaw; F; S; Son; Yes; Yes
1367;1811; Edburn; m; 3; Miss. Choctaw; F; S; Son; Yes; Yes

SIMPSON

1368;1290; John; m; 59; Miss. Choctaw; F; M; Head; Yes
1369;1291; Sallie; f; 57; Miss. Choctaw; F; M; Wife; Yes; Yes
~~1292; Pauline; f; 21; Miss. Choctaw; F; S; Dau; Yes; Yes~~
 Died 6-19-36
1370;1293; Celie; f; 19; Miss. Choctaw; F; S; Dau; Yes; Yes
1371; Franklin Lee; m; 8/12; Miss. Choctaw; F; S; Grand-son; Yes; Yes   Born 4-7-36   Son of Celie

SMITH

1372;1308; Clay; m; 32; Miss. Choctaw; F; M; Head; Yes; Yes
~~1373;1309; Mattie; f; 35; Miss. Choctaw; F; M; Wife; Yes; Yes~~
 Died Dec. 5, 1937
1374;1647; **Williamson**, Arnold; m; 18; Miss. Choctaw; F; S; Nephew; Yes; Yes
1375;1648; **Lewis**, Marceline; f; 13; Miss. Choctaw; F; S; Niece; Yes; Yes

1376;1301; Clement; m; 18; Miss. Choctaw; F; M; Head; Yes; Yes
1377;1336; Mollie Solomon; f; 15; Miss. Choctaw; F; M; Wife; Yes; Yes

Census of the **Mississippi Choctaws** reservation of the **Choctaw Agency** jurisdiction, as of **January 1, 1937**, 19__, taken by **A. C. Hector**, Superintendent.

KEY; Surname; Present Census Number; Last Census Number; Given Name; Sex; Age at Last Birthday; Tribe; Degree of Blood; Marital Status; Relationship to Head of Family; At Jurisdiction Where Enrolled (Yes/No); At Another Jurisdiction; Post Office, County, State (if given); Ward (Yes/No)

1378;1294; George; m; 65; Miss. Choctaw; F; M; Head; Yes; Yes
~~1295; Mandy; f; 51; Miss. Choctaw; F; M; Wife; Yes; Yes~~
    Died 6-4-36
1379;1297; **Farmer**, Grace; f; 14; Miss. Choctaw; F; S; Step-dau; Yes; Yes
1380;   **Farmer**, Franklin; m; 3/12; Miss. Choctaw; F; S; Grand stepson; Yes; Yes   Born 9-2-36   Son of Grace
1381;1298; **Farve** (Farmer), Mary Lou; f; 20; Miss. Choctaw; F; Wd; Step-dau; Yes; Yes
1382;   **Farve**, Cecil Eugene; m; 2/12; Miss. Choctaw; F; S; Step-grand son; Yes; Yes   Born 10-20-36   Son of Mary Lou

1383;1302; John W; m; 62; Miss. Choctaw; F; M; Head; Yes; Yes
1384;1303; Mary; f; 77; Miss. Choctaw; F; M; Wife; Yes; Yes

1385;1304; Minnie; f; 42; Miss. Choctaw; F; Wd; Head; Yes; Yes
1386;1305; Melton; m; 11; Miss. Choctaw; F; S; Son; Yes; Yes
1387;1306; Elton; m; 9; Miss. Choctaw; F; S; Son; Yes; Yes
1388;1307; **Isom**, Bailey; m; 17; Miss. Choctaw; F; S; Son; Yes; Yes

1389;1299; Sebe; m; 47; Miss. Choctaw; F; M; Head; Yes; Yes
1390;1300; Sinie; f; 46; Miss. Choctaw; F; M; Wife; Yes; Yes
1391;1845; **Gipson**, William; m; 2; Miss. Choctaw; F; S; Grand-son; Yes; Yes   Son of Homer Gipson

SOCKEY

1392;1312; Bennett; m; 29; Miss. Choctaw; F; M; Head; Yes; Yes
1393;1768; Alpha Wishork; f; 36; Miss. Choctaw; F; M; Wife; Yes; Yes
1394;1769; **Wishork**, Zelia; f; 16; Miss. Choctaw; F; S; Step-dau; Yes; Yes
1395;1770; **Wishork**, Evelyn; f; 15; Miss. Choctaw; F; S; Step-dau; Yes; Yes

Census of the __Mississippi Choctaws__ reservation of the __Choctaw Agency__ jurisdiction, as of __January 1, 1937__, 19__, taken by __A. C. Hector__, Superintendent.

KEY; Surname; Present Census Number; Last Census Number; Given Name; Sex; Age at Last Birthday; Tribe; Degree of Blood; Marital Status; Relationship to Head of Family; At Jurisdiction Where Enrolled (Yes/No); At Another Jurisdiction; Post Office, County, State (if given); Ward (Yes/No)

1396;1771; **Wishork**, Nuga; f; 12; Miss. Choctaw; F; S; Step-dau; Yes; Yes
1397;1772; **Wishork**, Lun Presley; m; 8; Miss. Choctaw; F; S; Step-son; Yes; Yes
1398;1774; **Wishork**, Ruth; f; 3; Miss. Choctaw; F; S; Step-dau; Yes; Yes
~~1868; Harmon; m; 2; Miss. Choctaw; F; S; Son; Yes; Yes~~
    Died 3-1-36

1399;1310; Irvin; m; 55; Miss. Choctaw; F; M; Head; Yes; Yes
1400;1311; Lela; f; 42; Miss. Choctaw; F; M; Wife; Yes; Yes
1401;1313; Homer; m; 14; Miss. Choctaw; F; S; Son; Yes; Yes

1402;1315; Mike; m; 35; Miss. Choctaw; F; M; Head; Yes; Yes
1403;1316; Nephus; f; 34; Miss. Choctaw; F; M; Wife; Yes; Yes
1404;1317; Varelia; f; 15; Miss. Choctaw; F; S; Dau; Yes; Yes
1405;1869; Janette; f; 2; Miss. Choctaw; F; S; Grand-dau; Yes; Yes
    Daughter of Varelia
1406;1318; Odell; m; 13; Miss. Choctaw; F; S; Son; Yes; Yes
1407;1319; Enochs; m; 10; Miss. Choctaw; F; S; Son; Yes; Yes
1408;1320; Reba; f; 4; Miss. Choctaw; F; S; Dau; Yes; Yes
1409;   Ruth; f; 4/12; Miss. Choctaw; F; S; Dau; Yes; Yes
    Born 8-9-36

SOLOMON

1410;1334; Ernest; m; 21; Miss. Choctaw; F; M; Head; Yes; Yes
1411; 454; Jeffry Denson; f; 19; Miss. Choctaw; F; M; Wife; Yes; Yes
1412;   Mattie (Bettie Lee); f; 4/12; Miss. Choctaw; F; S; Dau; Yes; Yes Born 8-2-36

1413;1326; Marshall; m; 33; Miss. Choctaw; F; M; Head; Yes; Yes
1414;1327; Addie; f; 28; Miss. Choctaw; F; M; Wife; Yes; Yes
1415;1328; Brunson (Johnson); m; 4; Miss. Choctaw; F; S; Son; Yes; Yes

Census of the **Mississippi Choctaws** reservation of the **Choctaw Agency** jurisdiction, as of **January 1, 1937**, 19__, taken by **A. C. Hector**, Superintendent.

KEY; Surname; Present Census Number; Last Census Number; Given Name; Sex; Age at Last Birthday; Tribe; Degree of Blood; Marital Status; Relationship to Head of Family; At Jurisdiction Where Enrolled (Yes/No); At Another Jurisdiction; Post Office, County, State (if given); Ward (Yes/No)

~~————————— Baby; m; 8/12; Miss. Choctaw; F; S; Son; Yes; Yes~~
Born 4-27-36   Died 5-2-36

~~————— 1332; Raymond; m; 43; Miss. Choctaw; F; M; Head; Yes; Yes~~
Died 11-22-36
1416;1333; Bessie; f; 43; Miss. Choctaw; F; M; Wife; Yes; Yes
1417;1335; Murphy; m; 18; Miss. Choctaw; F; S; Son; Yes; Yes

1418;1329; Willie; m; 74; Miss. Choctaw; F; M: Head; Yes; Yes
1419;1330; Winnie L; f; 32; Miss. Choctaw; F; M; Wife; Yes; Yes
1420;1331; Mollie Lee; f; 8; Miss. Choctaw; F; S; Dau; Yes; Yes

1421;1321; Willie; m; 53; Miss. Choctaw; F; M; Head; Yes; Yes
1422;1322; Onie; f; 51; Miss. Choctaw; F; M; Wife; Yes; Yes
1423;1323; Beaman; m; 22; Miss. Choctaw; F; M; Step-son; Yes; Yes
1424;1000; Sudie Johnson; f; 18; Miss. Choctaw; F; M; Step-da-in-law; Yes; Yes
1425;1834; Mary Lou; f; 2; Miss. Choctaw; F; S; Step-grand-dau; Yes; Yes
1426;1325; **Charlie**, Charlie C; m; 15; Miss. Choctaw; F; S; Stepson; Yes; Yes
~~1427;1364; **Steve**, Jennie; f; 10; Miss. Choctaw; F; S; Step-grand-dau; Yes; Yes~~   Died 9-18-138   Daughter of Josie Steve

STARR

1428;1338; Bill; m; 48; Miss. Choctaw; F; Wd; Head; Yes; Yes
1429;1340; Edna; f; 19; Miss. Choctaw; F; S; Dau; Yes; Yes
1430;1341; Nannie; f; 15; Miss. Choctaw; F; S; Dau; Yes; Yes
1431;1342; Mary; f; 14; Miss. Choctaw; F; S; Dau; Yes; Yes

1432;1337; Lucy; f; 59; Miss. Choctaw; F; Wd; Alone; Yes; Yes

1433;1339; Summer; m; 21; Miss. Choctaw; F; M; Head; Yes; Yes

Census of the **Mississippi Choctaws** reservation of the **Choctaw Agency** jurisdiction, as of **January 1, 1937**, 19__, taken by **A. C. Hector**, Superintendent.

KEY; Surname; Present Census Number; Last Census Number; Given Name; Sex; Age at Last Birthday; Tribe; Degree of Blood; Marital Status; Relationship to Head of Family; At Jurisdiction Where Enrolled (Yes/No); At Another Jurisdiction; Post Office, County, State (if given); Ward (Yes/No)

1434;1104; Maggie McMillan; f; 28; Miss. Choctaw; F; M: Wife; Yes; Yes
1435; Wanira[sic]; f; 11/12; Miss. Choctaw; F; S; Dau; Yes; Yes
Born 1-1-36

STEPHENS

1436;1353; Felix; m; 32; Miss. Choctaw; F; M: Head; Yes; Yes
1437;1354; Martha Farmer; f; 29; Miss. Choctaw; F; M: Wife; Yes; Yes
1438;1355; Zena (Martha Lee); f; 7; Miss. Choctaw; F; S; Dau; Yes; Yes
1439;1356; Mary Frances; f; 6; Miss. Choctaw; F; S; Dau; Yes; Yes
1440;1357; Hazel Agnes; f; 3; Miss. Choctaw; F; S; Dau; Yes; Yes
1441; Lee Mack; m; 8/12; Miss. Choctaw; F; S; Son; Yes; Yes
Born 4-19-36

1442;1343; Nathan; m; 34; Miss. Choctaw; F; M; Head; Yes; Yes
1443;1344; Annie; f; 39; Miss. Choctaw; F; M; Wife; Yes; Yes
1444;1345; Maxton; m; 12; Miss. Choctaw; F; S; Son; Yes; Yes
1445;1346; Cutie Mae; f; 10; Miss. Choctaw; F; S; Dau; Yes; Yes
1446;1347; Dorthy D; f; 9; Miss. Choctaw; F; S; Dau; Yes; Yes
1447;1348; Sarah (Bonnie B.); f; 7; Miss. Choctaw; F; S; Dau; Yes; Yes
1448;1349; Franklin; m; 4; Miss. Choctaw; F; S; Son; Yes; Yes

1449;1350; Tom; m; 74; Miss. Choctaw; F; Wd; Head; Yes; Yes
Died 1934
1450;1352; Willie; m; 27; Miss. Choctaw; F; S; Son; Yes; Yes

STEVE

1451;1375; Bobo; m; 30; Miss. Choctaw; F; M; Head; Yes; Yes
1452;1376; Lucille; f; 25; Miss. Choctaw; F; M; Wife; Yes; Yes
1453;1377; Maurice; m; 11; Miss. Choctaw; F; S; Son; Yes; Yes
1454;1378; Odie (Audrey); f; 9; Miss. Choctaw; F; S; Dau; Yes; Yes
1455;1379; Vivian; f; 7; Miss. Choctaw; F; S; Dau; Yes; Yes

Census of the **Mississippi Choctaws** reservation of the **Choctaw Agency** jurisdiction, as of **January 1, 1937**, 19__, taken by **A. C. Hector**, Superintendent.

KEY; Surname; Present Census Number; Last Census Number; Given Name; Sex; Age at Last Birthday; Tribe; Degree of Blood; Marital Status; Relationship to Head of Family; At Jurisdiction Where Enrolled (Yes/No); At Another Jurisdiction; Post Office, County, State (if given); Ward (Yes/No)

1456;1380; Marguerite; f; 6; Miss. Choctaw; F; S; Dau; Yes; Yes
1457;1381; Lauralina; f; 4; Miss. Choctaw; F; S; Dau; Yes; Yes
~~------;1870; Claud; m; 2; Miss. Choctaw; F; S; Son; Yes; Yes~~
        Died 8-24-36
1458; Sallie; f; 8/12; Miss. Choctaw; F; S; Dau; Yes; Yes
        Born 4-17-36

1459;1366; Ennis; m; 28; Miss. Choctaw; F; M; Head; Yes; Yes
1460;1367; Callie Bell; f; 25; Miss. Choctaw; F; M; Wife; Yes; Yes
~~------;1368; Berniece; f; 4; Miss. Choctaw; F; S; Dau; Yes; Yes~~
        Died 1935 - Unreported
1461; Gladys Eva; f; 11/12; Miss. Choctaw; F; S; Dau; Yes; Yes
        Born 1-20-36

1462;1370; Houston; m; 49; Miss. Choctaw; F; M; Head; Yes; Yes
1463;1371; Lena; f; 45; Miss. Choctaw; F; M; Wife; Yes; Yes
1464;1372; McKinley; m; 18; Miss. Choctaw; F; S; Son; Yes; Yes
1465;1373; Yates; m; 14; Miss. Choctaw; F; S; Son; Yes; Yes
1466;1374; Minnie (Marabelle); f; 10; Miss. Choctaw; F; S; Dau; Yes; Yes
1467;1359; Helen; f; 10; Miss. Choctaw; F; S; Niece; Yes; Yes
1468;1360; Winston John; m; 7; Miss. Choctaw; F; S; Nephew; Yes; Yes

1469;1361; Josie; m; 35; Miss. Choctaw; F; M; Head; Yes; Yes
1470;1362; Maggie; f; 28; Miss. Choctaw; F; M; Wife; Yes; Yes
1471;1363; Ruby; f; 11; Miss. Choctaw; F; S; Dau; Yes; Yes
1472;1365; Catherine; f; 4; Miss. Choctaw; F; S; Dau; Yes; Yes
1473; Clyde; m; 4/12; Miss. Choctaw; F; S; Son; Yes; Yes
        Born 8-19-36

1474;1382; Smith; m; 43; Miss. Choctaw; F; M; Head; Yes; Yes
1475;1383; Winnie Smith; f; 40; Miss. Choctaw; F; M; Wife; Yes; Yes
1476;1385; Pauline; f; 16; Miss. Choctaw; F; S; Dau; Yes; Yes
1477;1386; Mollie; f; 12; Miss. Choctaw; F; S; Dau; Yes; Yes

Census of the **Mississippi Choctaws** reservation of the **Choctaw Agency** jurisdiction, as of **January 1, 1937**, 19__, taken by **A. C. Hector**, Superintendent.

KEY; Surname; Present Census Number; Last Census Number; Given Name; Sex; Age at Last Birthday; Tribe; Degree of Blood; Marital Status; Relationship to Head of Family; At Jurisdiction Where Enrolled (Yes/No); At Another Jurisdiction; Post Office, County, State (if given); Ward (Yes/No)

1478;1387; Aileen; f; 8; Miss. Choctaw; F; S; Dau; Yes; Yes
1479;1388; Rebecca; f; 6; Miss. Choctaw; F; S; Dau; Yes; Yes
1480;1389; Curtis; m; 3; Miss. Choctaw; F; S; Son; Yes; Yes

STOLIBY

1481;1392; John; m; 47; Miss. Choctaw; F; Wd; Head; Yes; Yes
1482;1394; Will Banks; m; 18; Miss. Choctaw; F; S; Son; Yes; Yes
1483;1395; Otis; m; 16; Miss. Choctaw; F; S; Son; Yes; Yes
1484;1396; Zona Miller; f; 12; Miss. Choctaw; F; S; Dau; Yes; Yes

STRIBLING

1485;1397; Malissie; f; 65; Miss. Choctaw; F; Wd; Alone; Yes; Yes

    1314; **Sockey**, III; m; 9; Miss. Choctaw; F; S; Son; Yes; Yes
    Duplication of 230-34

    1105; **Starr**, Baby; f; 3; Miss. Choctaw; F; S; Dau; Yes; Yes
    Duplication of 1822-34 Suppl.

    ~~1822; Starr, Allie Lou; f; 3; Miss. Choctaw; F; S; Dau; Yes; Yes~~
    Shown as dead on 1934 Supple. Roll

THOMAS

1486;1404; Cleve; m; 34; Miss. Choctaw; F; M; Head; Yes; Yes
1487;1548; Hazel Tubby; f; 23; Miss. Choctaw; F; M; Wife; Yes; Yes
1488;1813; Sam; m; 3; Miss. Choctaw; F; S; Son; Yes; Yes

1489;1398; Lewis; m; 53; Miss. Choctaw; F; M; Head; Yes; Yes
1490;1399; Mamie; f; 50; Miss. Choctaw; F; M; Wife; Yes; Yes
1491;1400; Newman; m; 18; Miss. Choctaw; F; S; Son; Yes; Yes
1492;1401; Isaac; m; 14; Miss. Choctaw; F; S; Son; Yes; Yes

Census of the **Mississippi Choctaws** reservation of the **Choctaw Agency** jurisdiction, as of **January 1, 1937**, 19__, taken by **A. C. Hector**, Superintendent.

KEY; Surname; Present Census Number; Last Census Number; Given Name; Sex; Age at Last Birthday; Tribe; Degree of Blood; Marital Status; Relationship to Head of Family; At Jurisdiction Where Enrolled (Yes/No); At Another Jurisdiction; Post Office, County, State (if given); Ward (Yes/No)

1493;1402; Mina; f; 12; Miss. Choctaw; F; S; Dau; Yes; Yes

1494;1414; Lester; m; 28; Miss. Choctaw; F; M; Head; Yes; Yes
1495;1415; Rosie; f; 26; Miss. Choctaw; F; M; Wife; Yes; Yes

1496;1403; Riley; m; 32; Miss. Choctaw; F; M; Head; Yes; Yes
1497;1189; Zona Nickey; f; 21; Miss. Choctaw; F; M; Wife; Yes; Yes
1497;1871; Dorsey; m; 2; Miss. Choctaw; F; S; Son; Yes; Yes

~~1499;1406; Wilmon; m; 37; Miss. Choctaw; F; M; Head; Yes; Yes~~
 Died 1-25-36
1500;1407; Sallie; f; 36; Miss. Choctaw; F; M; Wife; Yes; Yes
1501;1408; Woodrow; m; 18; Miss. Choctaw; F; S; Son; Yes; Yes
1502;1410; Golden; m; 14; Miss. Choctaw; F; S; Son; Yes; Yes
1503;1411; Amos; m; 12; Miss. Choctaw; F; S; Son; Yes; Yes
1504;1412; Singleton; m; 8; Miss. Choctaw; F; S; Son; Yes; Yes
1505;1413; Dora (Linnie Helen); f; 6; Miss. Choctaw; F; S; Dau; Yes; Yes
1506;1812; Gordon; m; 3; Miss. Choctaw; F; S; Son; Yes; Yes

THOMPSON

1507;1426; Cephus; m; 47; Miss. Choctaw; F; Wd; Head; Yes; Yes
1508;1428; Tommy; m; 14; Miss. Choctaw; F; S; Son; Yes; Yes
1509;1429; Ellis; m; 12; Miss. Choctaw; F; S; Son; Yes; Yes
1510;1430; Annie; f; 8; Miss. Choctaw; F; S; Dau; Yes; Yes

1511;1427; Dixon; m; 20; Miss. Choctaw; F; M; Head; Yes; Yes
1512; 279; Elsie Cotton (Cates); f; 29; Miss. Choctaw; F; M; Wife; Yes; Yes
1513; Baby; m; 1/12; Miss. Choctaw; F; S; Son; Yes; Yes
 Born 11-2-36

1514;1439; John; m; 45; Miss. Choctaw; F; M: Head; Yes; Yes

Census of the __Mississippi Choctaws__ reservation of the __Choctaw Agency__ jurisdiction, as of __January 1, 1937__, 19__, taken by __A. C. Hector__, Superintendent.

KEY; Surname; Present Census Number; Last Census Number; Given Name; Sex; Age at Last Birthday; Tribe; Degree of Blood; Marital Status; Relationship to Head of Family; At Jurisdiction Where Enrolled (Yes/No); At Another Jurisdiction; Post Office, County, State (if given); Ward (Yes/No)

1515;1440; Ludie; f; 43; Miss. Choctaw; F; M; Wife; Yes; Yes

1516;1432; Malinda; f; 72; Miss. Choctaw; F; Wd; Alone; Yes; Yes

1517;1433; Mose; m; 40; Miss. Choctaw; F; M; Head; Yes; Yes
1518;1434; Jean; f; 41; Miss. Choctaw; F; M; Wife; Yes; Yes
1519;1435; Jim; m; 17; Miss. Choctaw; F; S; Son; Yes; Yes
1520;1436; Annie; f; 14; Miss. Choctaw; F; S; Dau; Yes; Yes
1521;1437; (Chickaway), Therman; m; 11; Miss. Choctaw; F; S; Son; Yes; Yes
1522;1438; Steve; m; 10; Miss. Choctaw; F; S; Son; Yes; Yes
1523; Hector; m; 3; Miss. Choctaw; F; S; Son; Yes; Yes
Omitted on previous census

1524; 289; (Cates), Ned; m; 39; Miss. Choctaw; F; M; Head; Yes; Yes
1525; 290; (Cates), Janie; f; 35; Miss. Choctaw; F; M; Wife; Yes; Yes
1526; 292; (Cates), Lumie (Emma); f; 20; Miss. Choctaw; F; S; Dau; Yes; Yes
1527; 293; (Cates), Tubby; m; 19; Miss. Choctaw; F; S; Son; Yes; Yes
1528; 295; (Cates), Willie f: m; 14; Miss. Choctaw; F; S; Son; Yes; Yes
~~1529; 296; (Cates), Nannie; f; 12; Miss. Choctaw; F; S; Dau; Yes; Yes~~
Died 7-30-38
1530; 297; (Cates), Julia (Jewel); f; 11; Miss. Choctaw; F; S; Dau; Yes; Yes
1531; (Cates), Melvin; m; 2; Miss. Choctaw; F; S; Son; Yes; Yes
Born 1935 - Unreported

1532;1419; Will; m; 33; Miss. Choctaw; F; M; Head; Yes; Yes
1533;1420; Sina; f; 30; Miss. Choctaw; F; M; Wife; Yes; Yes
~~1421; Otis; m; 13; Miss. Choctaw; F; S; Son; Yes; Yes~~
Died 1932 - Unreported
1534;1422; Claudine; f; 10; Miss. Choctaw; F; S; Dau; Yes; Yes
1535;1423; Henry; m; 8; Miss. Choctaw; F; S; Son; Yes; Yes
1536;1424; Oneva; f; 6; Miss. Choctaw; F; S; Dau; Yes; Yes

Census of the __Mississippi Choctaws__ reservation of the __Choctaw Agency__ jurisdiction, as of __January 1, 1937__, 19__, taken by __A. C. Hector__, Superintendent.

KEY; Surname; Present Census Number; Last Census Number; Given Name; Sex; Age at Last Birthday; Tribe; Degree of Blood; Marital Status; Relationship to Head of Family; At Jurisdiction Where Enrolled (Yes/No); At Another Jurisdiction; Post Office, County, State (if given); Ward (Yes/No)

1537;1425; Maxine; f; 3; Miss. Choctaw; F; S; Dau; Yes; Yes

1538;1442; Tommie; m; 38; Miss. Choctaw; F; M; Head; Yes; Yes
1539;1443; Bonnie; f; 35; Miss. Choctaw; F; M; Wife; Yes; Yes
1540;   38; Nola Isom (Mary); f; 11; Miss. Choctaw; F; S; Dau; Yes; Yes
1541;1444; Nathan; m; 6; Miss. Choctaw; F; S; Son; Yes; Yes
1542;1445; Louise; f; 4; Miss. Choctaw; F; M[sic]; Dau; Yes; Yes
1543;1872; Bobo; m; 2; Miss. Choctaw; F; M[sic]; Son; Yes; Yes

TUBBY

1544;1491; Adam; m; 35; Miss. Choctaw; F; S; Head; Yes; Yes
1545;1496; Mollie; f; 32; Miss. Choctaw; F; S; Niece; Yes; Yes
1546;1497; Herbert; m; 29; Miss. Choctaw; F; S; Nephew; Yes; Yes

1547;1539; Alice; f; 47; Miss. Choctaw; F; Wd; Head; Yes; Yes
1548;1540; **Johnson**, Lee; m; 25; Miss. Choctaw; F; S; Son; Yes; Yes

1549; 286; (Cates), Alice; f; 31; Miss. Choctaw; F; Wd; Head; Yes; Yes
1550; 287; (Cates), Dock; m; 35; Miss. Choctaw; F; S; Step-son; Yes; Yes

1551;1499; Anderson; m; 37; Miss. Choctaw; F; M; Head; Yes; Yes
1552;1500; Nancy; f; 27; Miss. Choctaw; F; M; Wife; Yes; Yes
1553;1501; Jim; m; 13; Miss. Choctaw; F; S; Son; Yes; Yes
1554;1502; Odie (Isa); f; 11; Miss. Choctaw; F; S; Dau; Yes; Yes
1555;1503; Bonnie (Buracy); f; 9; Miss. Choctaw; F; S; Dau; Yes; Yes
1556;1504; Cornelia (Etolye); f; 7; Miss. Choctaw; F; S; Dau; Yes; Yes

1557;1546; Anderson; m; 45; Miss. Choctaw; F; M; Head; Yes; Yes
1558;1547; Louisiana; f; 47; Miss. Choctaw; F; M; Wife; Yes; Yes
1559;1549; Smith; m; 21; Miss. Choctaw; F; S; Son; Yes; Yes
~~1560;1551; John; m; 17; Miss. Choctaw; F; S; Son; Yes; Yes~~
    Died 7-11-38

Census of the **Mississippi Choctaws** reservation of the **Choctaw Agency** jurisdiction, as of **January 1, 1937**, 19__, taken by **A. C. Hector**, Superintendent.

KEY; Surname; Present Census Number; Last Census Number; Given Name; Sex; Age at Last Birthday; Tribe; Degree of Blood; Marital Status; Relationship to Head of Family; At Jurisdiction Where Enrolled (Yes/No); At Another Jurisdiction; Post Office, County, State (if given); Ward (Yes/No)

1561;1469; Annis; m; 58; Miss. Choctaw; F; M; Head; Yes; Yes
1562;1470; Annie; f; 37; Miss. Choctaw; F; M; Wife; Yes; Yes

1563;1508; Charlie; m; 41; Miss. Choctaw; F; M; Head; Yes; Yes
1564;1509; Betsey Scott; f; 37; Miss. Choctaw; F; M; Wife; Yes; Yes
1565;1510; Alice; f; 14; Miss. Choctaw; F; S; Dau; Yes; Yes
1566;1511; Jack; m; 12; Miss. Choctaw; F; S; Son; Yes; Yes
1567;1512; J. C; m; 10; Miss. Choctaw; F; S; Son; Yes; Yes
1568;1513; Colleen; f; 10; Miss. Choctaw; F; S; Dau; Yes; Yes
1569;1514; Bessie; f; 5; Miss. Choctaw; F; S; Dau; Yes; Yes
1570;1515; Kate; f; 16; Miss. Choctaw; F; S; Step-dau; Yes; Yes
1571;1516; Ellis; m; 13; Miss. Choctaw; F; S; Orphan; Yes; Yes
1572;1873; Claud; m; 2; Miss. Choctaw; F; S; Son; Yes; Yes

1573;1525; Clemon; m; 62; Miss. Choctaw; F; M; Head; Yes; Yes
1574;1526; Alice; f; 62; Miss. Choctaw; F; M; Wife; Yes; Yes
1575;1528; Elias; m; 11; Miss. Choctaw; F; S; Nephew; Yes; Yes
1576;1529; Sarah; f; 10; Miss. Choctaw; F; S; Great-niece; Yes; Yes

1577;1446; Dan; m; 35; Miss. Choctaw; F; M; Head; Yes; Yes
1578;1447; Lola Chitto; f; 42; Miss. Choctaw; F; M; Wife; Yes; Yes
1579;1448; Mable; f; 4; Miss. Choctaw; F; S; Dau; Yes; Yes
~~   1449; Lewis, Lum Billy; m; 11; Miss. Choctaw; F; S; Step-son; Yes; Yes~~   Died 1934 - Unreported
1580;1874; Dean Culver; m; 2; Miss. Choctaw; F; S; Son; Yes; Yes

1581;1562; Dee; m; 36; Miss. Choctaw; F; M; Head; Yes; Yes
1582;1563; Lilly Allen; f; 32; Miss. Choctaw; F; M; Wife; Yes; Yes
1583;1564; Susie Anne; f; 29; Miss. Choctaw; F; S; Sister; Yes; Yes
1584;1565; R. B; m; 6; Miss. Choctaw; F; S; Son; Yes; Yes
1585; Mary; f; 2; Miss. Choctaw; F; S; Dau; Yes; Yes
Born 1935 - Unreported

1586;1492; Dewitt; m; 30; Miss. Choctaw; F; M: Head; Yes; Yes

Census of the **Mississippi Choctaws** reservation of the **Choctaw Agency** jurisdiction, as of **January 1, 1937**, 19__, taken by **A. C. Hector**, Superintendent.

KEY; Surname; Present Census Number; Last Census Number; Given Name; Sex; Age at Last Birthday; Tribe; Degree of Blood; Marital Status; Relationship to Head of Family; At Jurisdiction Where Enrolled (Yes/No); At Another Jurisdiction; Post Office, County, State (if given); Ward (Yes/No)

1587;1493; Katie; f; 31; Miss. Choctaw; F; M; Wife; Yes; Yes
1588;1494; Cicero L; m; 4; Miss. Choctaw; F; S; Son; Yes; Yes
~~1589;1876; May Belle; f; 2; Miss. Choctaw; F; S; Dau; Yes; Yes~~
 Died Dec. 29, 1937

1590;1477; Dick; m; 66; Miss. Choctaw; F; M; Head; Yes; Yes
1591;1478; Lina Eline; f; 57; Miss. Choctaw; F; M; Wife; Yes; Yes
1592;1479; Jeff; m; 31; Miss. Choctaw; F; S; Nephew; Yes; Yes

1593;1471; Edgar; m; 37; Miss. Choctaw; F; M; Head; Yes; Yes
1594;1472; Annie; f; 35; Miss. Choctaw; F; M; Wife; Yes; Yes
1595;1473; Steve; m; 16; Miss. Choctaw; F; S; Son; Yes; Yes
1596;1474; Willie; m; 15; Miss. Choctaw; F; S; Son; Yes; Yes
1597;1475; Odie; m; 13; Miss. Choctaw; F; S; Son; Yes; Yes
1598;1476; Pauline; f; 10; Miss. Choctaw; F; S; Dau; Yes; Yes

1599;1505; Evan; m; 44; Miss. Choctaw; F; M; Head; Yes; Yes
1600;1506; Jenne[sic]; f; 49; Miss. Choctaw; F; M; Wife; Yes; Yes

1601;1456; Frances; f; 37; Miss. Choctaw; F; Wd; Head; Yes; Yes
1602;1458; Irene; f; 13; Miss. Choctaw; F; S; Dau; Yes; Yes
1603;1143; **Mitch**, Divon; m; 33; Miss. Choctaw; F; S; Boarder; Yes; Yes
1604;1460; Addison (Robert); m; 5; Miss. Choctaw; F; S; Son; Yes; Yes

1605;1450; George; m; 29; Miss. Choctaw; F; M; Head; Yes; Yes
1606;1451; Mary; f; 26; Miss. Choctaw; F; M; Wife; Yes; Yes
1607;1452; Thomas; m; 8; Miss. Choctaw; F; S; Son; Yes; Yes
1608;1453; Annie Lee; f; 4; Miss. Choctaw; F; S; Dau; Yes; Yes
1609; Sarah Ann; f; 2; Miss. Choctaw; F; S; Dau; Yes; Yes
 Born 1935 - Unreported
1610;1454; Jennie; f; 19; Miss. Choctaw; F; S; Sis; Yes; Yes

1611;1517; Henderson; m; 44; Miss. Choctaw; F; M; Head; Yes; Yes

Census of the **Mississippi Choctaws** reservation of the **Choctaw Agency** jurisdiction, as of **January 1, 1937**, 19__, taken by **A. C. Hector**, Superintendent.

KEY; Surname; Present Census Number; Last Census Number; Given Name; Sex; Age at Last Birthday; Tribe; Degree of Blood; Marital Status; Relationship to Head of Family; At Jurisdiction Where Enrolled (Yes/No); At Another Jurisdiction; Post Office, County, State (if given); Ward (Yes/No)

~~1612;1518; Maggie; f; 32; Miss. Choctaw; F; M; Wife; Yes; Yes~~
    Died 7-12-38
1613;1519; Otis; f; 14; Miss. Choctaw; F; S; Dau; Yes; Yes
1614;1520; W. C; m; 12; Miss. Choctaw; F; S; Son; Yes; Yes
1615;1521; Gladys; f; 10; Miss. Choctaw; F; S; Dau; Yes; Yes
1616;1522; Finis; m; 10; Miss. Choctaw; F; S; Son; Yes; Yes
1617;1523; Martha Lee; f; 6; Miss. Choctaw; F; S; Dau; Yes; Yes
1618;1524; James H; m; 4; Miss. Choctaw; F; S; Son; Yes; Yes
1619;1875; Eugene; m; 2; Miss. Choctaw; F; S; Son; Yes; Yes

1620;1530; Jackson; m; 29; Miss. Choctaw; F; M; Head; Yes; Yes
1621;1531; Malissa; f; 30; Miss. Choctaw; F; M; Wife; Yes; Yes
1622;1532; Coleman; m; 4; Miss. Choctaw; F; S; Son; Yes; Yes

   1441; **Thompson**, Tom; m; 10; Miss. Choctaw; F; S; Son; Yes; Yes
       Duplication of 1428-34

1623;1455; Lefus; m; 44; Miss. Choctaw; F; Wd; Head; Yes; Yes
1624;1457; Ina; f; 15; Miss. Choctaw; F; S; Dau; Yes; Yes
1625;1459; Leona; f; 10; Miss. Choctaw; F; S; Dau; Yes; Yes

1626;1495; Lena; f; 37; Miss. Choctaw; F; Wd; Alone; Yes; Yes

1627;1487; Lysander; m; 49; Miss. Choctaw; F; M; Head; Yes; Yes
1628;1037; Fannie Lewis Davis; f; 47; Miss. Choctaw; F; M; Wife; Yes; Yes
1629;1038; **Lewis**, Archie Hector; m; 4; Miss. Choctaw; F; S; Step-son; Yes; Yes

1630;1552; Simpson; m; 77; Miss. Choctaw; F; M; Head; Yes; Yes
1631;1553; Minnie; f; 44; Miss. Choctaw; F; M; Wife; Yes; Yes
1632;1554; Ike; m; 25; Miss. Choctaw; F; S; Son; Yes; Yes
1633;1555; Henry; m; 24; Miss. Choctaw; F; S; Son; Yes; Yes
1634;1556; Lewis; m; 20; Miss. Choctaw; F; S; Son; Yes; Yes

Census of the **Mississippi Choctaws** reservation of the **Choctaw Agency** jurisdiction, as of **January 1, 1937**, 19__, taken by **A. C. Hector**, Superintendent.

KEY; Surname; Present Census Number; Last Census Number; Given Name; Sex; Age at Last Birthday; Tribe; Degree of Blood; Marital Status; Relationship to Head of Family; At Jurisdiction Where Enrolled (Yes/No); At Another Jurisdiction; Post Office, County, State (if given); Ward (Yes/No)

1635;1557; McKinley; m; 17; Miss. Choctaw; F; S; Son; Yes; Yes
1636;1558; Hudson; m; 14; Miss. Choctaw; F; S; Son; Yes; Yes
1637;1559; Sullivan; m; 13; Miss. Choctaw; F; S; Son; Yes; Yes
1638;1560; Callie; f; 11; Miss. Choctaw; F; S; Dau; Yes; Yes
1639;1561; Nellie; f; 10; Miss. Choctaw; F; S; Dau; Yes; Yes

1640;1488; Moley; m; 34; Miss. Choctaw; F; M; Head; Yes; Yes
1641;1489; Sallie; f; 30; Miss. Choctaw; F; M; Wife; Yes; Yes
1642;1490; Grace; f; 4; Miss. Choctaw; F; S; Dau; Yes; Yes
~~Joel Dodson; m; 10/12; Miss. Choctaw; F; S; Son; Yes; Yes~~
Born 2-3-36 Died 4-12-36

1643; 663; Mollie; f; 34; Miss. Choctaw; F; S; Alone; Yes; Yes

1644;1533; Nicholas; m; 39; Miss. Choctaw; F; M; Head; Yes; Yes
1645;1534; Esther; f; 54; Miss. Choctaw; F; M; Wife; Yes; Yes
1646;1535; Sullivan; m; 15; Miss. Choctaw; F; S; Son; Yes; Yes
1647;1536; Alice; f; 14; Miss. Choctaw; F; S; Dau; Yes; Yes
1648;1537; Minnie; f; 12; Miss. Choctaw; F; S; Dau; Yes; Yes
1649;1538; Catherine; f; 10; Miss. Choctaw; F; S; Dau; Yes; Yes

1650;1480; Pat; m; 43; Miss. Choctaw; F; M: Head; Yes; Yes
1651;1481; Frances; f; 43; Miss. Choctaw; F; M; Wife; Yes; Yes
1652;1483; Earnest; m; 17; Miss. Choctaw; F; S; Son; Yes; Yes
1653;1484; Lorraine; f; 15; Miss. Choctaw; F; S; Dau; Yes; Yes
1654;1485; Alice; f; 13; Miss. Choctaw; F; S; Dau; Yes; Yes
1655;1486; Aileen; f; 10; Miss. Choctaw; F; S; Dau; Yes; Yes

1656; 424; R. B; m; 30; Miss. Choctaw; F; M; Head; Yes; Yes
1657;1405; Phoebe Thomas; f; 29; Miss. Choctaw; F; M; Wife; Yes; Yes

1658;1462; Sidney; m; 37; Miss. Choctaw; F; M; Head; Yes; Yes
1659;1463; Kate; f; 36; Miss. Choctaw; F; M; Wife; Yes; Yes
1660;1464; Rufus; m; 18; Miss. Choctaw; F; S; Son; Yes; Yes

Census of the __Mississippi Choctaws__ reservation of the __Choctaw Agency__ jurisdiction, as of __January 1, 1937__, 19__, taken by __A. C. Hector__, Superintendent.

KEY; Surname; Present Census Number; Last Census Number; Given Name; Sex; Age at Last Birthday; Tribe; Degree of Blood; Marital Status; Relationship to Head of Family; At Jurisdiction Where Enrolled (Yes/No); At Another Jurisdiction; Post Office, County, State (if given); Ward (Yes/No)

1661;1465; Philia; f; 15; Miss. Choctaw; F; S; Dau; Yes; Yes
1662;1466; Eva Kate; f; 12; Miss. Choctaw; F; S; Dau; Yes; Yes
1663;1467; Edmond; m; 9; Miss. Choctaw; F; S; Son; Yes; Yes
1664;1468; Paul; m; 3; Miss. Choctaw; F; S; Son; Yes; Yes

1665; R. B; m; 30; Miss. Choctaw; F; M; Head; Yes; Yes
Omitted from previous census
1666; Fillie; f; 28; Miss. Choctaw; F; M; Wife; Yes; Yes
Omitted from previous census

1667;1541; Tom; m; 28; Miss. Choctaw; F; M; Head; Yes; Yes
1668;1542; Marceline; f; 30; Miss. Choctaw; F; M: Head; Yes; Yes
1669;1543; Finis (Inis); m; 7; Miss. Choctaw; F; S; Son; Yes; Yes
1670;1545; Joseph; m; 10; Miss. Choctaw; F; S; Son; Yes; Yes
~~Dixie Lee; f; 1; Miss. Choctaw; F; S; Dau; Yes; Yes~~
Born 3 6 36 Died 3-7-36

TUCKALOO

~~1566; Frances; f; 74; Miss. Choctaw; F; Wd; Head; Yes; Yes~~
Died 6-29-36
1672;1568; Nathan (Mosn[sic]); m; 23; Miss. Choctaw; F; S; Grand-son; No; Oklahoma, Okla; Yes; Yes
1673;1569; Enis; m; 13; Miss. Choctaw; F; S; Grand-son; No; Oklahoma, Okla; Yes
1674;1570 Alice; f; 12; Miss. Choctaw; F; S; Grand-dau; No; Oklahoma, Okla; Yes
1675;1571; Sarah; f; 11; Miss. Choctaw; F; S; Grand-dau; No; Oklahoma, Okla; Yes

VAUGHN

~~1576; Cooksie; m; 70; Miss. Choctaw; F; M; Head; Yes; Yes~~
Died 1-26-36

Census of the **Mississippi Choctaws** reservation of the **Choctaw Agency** jurisdiction, as of **January 1, 1937**, 19__, taken by **A. C. Hector**, Superintendent.

KEY; Surname; Present Census Number; Last Census Number; Given Name; Sex; Age at Last Birthday; Tribe; Degree of Blood; Marital Status; Relationship to Head of Family; At Jurisdiction Where Enrolled (Yes/No); At Another Jurisdiction; Post Office, County, State (if given); Ward (Yes/No)

1676;1573; Greer; m; 62; Miss. Choctaw; F; M; Head; Yes; Yes
1677;1574; Jane; f; 57; Miss. Choctaw; F; M; Wife; Yes; Yes
1678;1575; Agnes; f; 11; Miss. Choctaw; F; S; Dau; Yes; Yes
1679; 619; **Frazier**, Mamie Vaughn; f; 28; Miss. Choctaw; F; Wd; Dau; Yes; Yes
1680; 620; **Frazier**, Marshall; m; 8; Miss. Choctaw; F; S; Grand-son; Yes; Yes
1681; 621; **Frazier**, Malissa (Martha); f; 7; Miss. Choctaw; F; S; Grand-dau; Yes; Yes
1682; 622; **Frazier**, Dollie (Doris); f; 4; Miss. Choctaw; F; S; Grand-dau; Yes; Yes

~~1582; Howard; m; 35; Miss. Choctaw; F; M; Head; Yes; Yes~~
   Died 1935 - Unreported

1683;1586; John; m; 31; Miss. Choctaw; F; M; Head; Yes; Yes
1684; 125; Sopha Bell; f; 29; Miss. Choctaw; F; M; Wife; Yes; Yes

1685;1580; Silmon; m; 25; Miss. Choctaw; F; Head; Yes; Yes
1686;1581; Sadie Hickman; f; 21; Miss. Choctaw; F; M; Wife; Yes; Yes
1687; Bart Riley; m; 2; Miss. Choctaw; F; S; Son; Yes; Yes
   Omitted from previous census
1688; Linnie; f; 5; Miss. Choctaw; F; S; Dau; Yes; Yes
   Omitted from previous census
1689; Eleanor; f; 1; Miss. Choctaw; F; S; Dau; Yes; Yes
   Born 1936 - Unreported
1690;1578; Lena; f; 43; Miss. Choctaw; F; S; Sis; Yes; Yes
1691;1579; Ludie; f; 30; Miss. Choctaw; F; S; Sis; Yes; Yes
1692; 731; **Hickman**, Minnie; f; 32; Miss. Choctaw; F; Wd; Sis-in-law; Yes; Yes
1693; 732; **Hickman**, Will; m; 7; Miss. Choctaw; F; S; Nephew; Yes; Yes

Census of the **Mississippi Choctaws** reservation of the **Choctaw Agency** jurisdiction, as of **January 1, 1937**, 19__, taken by **A. C. Hector**, Superintendent.

KEY; Surname; Present Census Number; Last Census Number; Given Name; Sex; Age at Last Birthday; Tribe; Degree of Blood; Marital Status; Relationship to Head of Family; At Jurisdiction Where Enrolled (Yes/No); At Another Jurisdiction; Post Office, County, State (if given); Ward (Yes/No)

WAITER

1694;1590; Gipson; m; 74; Miss. Choctaw; F; Wd; Alone; Yes; Yes

1695;1592; Lonnie; m; 32; Miss. Choctaw; F; M: Head; Yes; Yes
1696;1593; Sue; f; 27; Miss. Choctaw; F; M; Wife; Yes; Yes
1697;1594; Cora Mae; f; 6; Miss. Choctaw; F; S; Dau; Yes; Yes
1698;1595; Willie Mae; f; 3; Miss. Choctaw; F; S; Dau; Yes; Yes
1699;1877; Otho Helen; f; 2; Miss. Choctaw; F; S; Dau; Yes; Yes

~~1591; Minnie; f; 61; Miss. Choctaw; F; Wd; Alone; Yes; Yes~~
Died 1934 - Unreported

WALLACE

~~1700;1596; Comb~~y; ~~m; 65; Miss. Choctaw; F; M; Head; Yes; Yes~~
Died 1-3-38
1701;1597; Hetty Dixon; f; 61; Miss. Choctaw; F; M; Wife; Yes; Yes
1702;1601; Amy; f; 22; Miss. Choctaw; F; S; Dau; Yes; Yes
1703;1598; Maggie; f; 20; Miss. Choctaw; F; S; Dau; Yes; Yes
1704;1599; Tom; m; 16; Miss. Choctaw; F; S; Son; Yes; Yes
1705;1600; Fulton; m; 13; Miss. Choctaw; F; S; Son; Yes; Yes

1706;1602; Eunice; f; 47; Miss. Choctaw; F; Wd; Head; Yes; Yes
1707;1603; Susie; f; 24; Miss. Choctaw; F; S; Dau; Yes; Yes
1708;1604; Henry; m; 22; Miss. Choctaw; F; S; Son; Yes; Yes
1709;1605; Celia; f; 21; Miss. Choctaw; F; S; Dau; Yes; Yes
1710;1606; Austin; m; 10; Miss. Choctaw; F; S; Son; Yes; Yes

1711;1609; Stenot; m; 29; Miss. Choctaw; F; M; Head; Yes; Yes
1712;1610; Annie; f; 24; Miss. Choctaw; F; M; Wife; Yes; Yes
1713;1611; Houston; m; 17; Miss. Choctaw; F; S; Orphan; Yes; Yes
1714;1612; Ligman (Brigman); m; 4; Miss. Choctaw; F; S; Son; Yes; Yes

Census of the **Mississippi Choctaws** reservation of the **Choctaw Agency** jurisdiction, as of **January 1, 1937**, 19__, taken by **A. C. Hector**, Superintendent.

KEY; Surname; Present Census Number; Last Census Number; Given Name; Sex; Age at Last Birthday; Tribe; Degree of Blood; Marital Status; Relationship to Head of Family; At Jurisdiction Where Enrolled (Yes/No); At Another Jurisdiction; Post Office, County, State (if given); Ward (Yes/No)

1715; Otis; m; 1; Miss. Choctaw; F; S; Son; Yes; Yes
Born 1936 - Unreported

WARNER

1716;1613; (Gipson), Johnnie L; m; 25; Miss. Choctaw; F; S; Alone; Yes; Yes

WESLEY

1717;1620; Ben; m; 21; Miss. Choctaw; F; M; Head; Yes; Yes
1718;1507; Anne Tubby; f; 14; Miss. Choctaw; F; M; Wife; Yes; Yes

1719;1615; Cameron; m; 47; Miss. Choctaw; F; M; Head; Yes; Yes
1720;1616; Julia Bell; f; 33; Miss. Choctaw; F; M; Wife; Yes; Yes
1721;1617; John; m; 12; Miss. Choctaw; F; S; Son; Yes; Yes
1722;1618; Willie B; m; 9; Miss. Choctaw; F; S; Son; Yes; Yes
1723;1619; Robert; m; 3; Miss. Choctaw; F; S; Son; Yes; Yes

~~1724;1614; Sidney; m; 72; Miss. Choctaw; F; Wd; Alone; Yes; Yes~~
Died May 5, 1937

Tom, m; 21; Miss. Choctaw; F; S; Alone; Yes; Yes
Omitted from previous census

WICKSON

1725;1622; Jim; m; 29; Miss. Choctaw; F; M; Head; Yes; Yes
1726;1276; Susan Davis; f; 38; Miss. Choctaw; F; M; Wife; Yes; Yes
1727;1878; Mary Jane; f; 2; Miss. Choctaw; F; S; Dau; Yes; Yes
1728;1277; **Shoemaker**, Dempsey; m; 16; Miss. Choctaw; F; S; Step-son; Yes; Yes
1729;1278; **Shoemaker**, Layman; m; 14; Miss. Choctaw; F; S; Step-son; Yes; Yes

Census of the **Mississippi Choctaws** reservation of the **Choctaw Agency** jurisdiction, as of **January 1, 1937**, 19___, taken by **A. C. Hector**, Superintendent.

KEY; Surname; Present Census Number; Last Census Number; Given Name; Sex; Age at Last Birthday; Tribe; Degree of Blood; Marital Status; Relationship to Head of Family; At Jurisdiction Where Enrolled (Yes/No); At Another Jurisdiction; Post Office, County, State (if given); Ward (Yes/No)

1730;1279; **Shoemaker**, Ruben; m; 11; Miss. Choctaw; F; S; Step-son; Yes; Yes
1731;1280; **Shoemaker**, Noleen; f; 8; Miss. Choctaw; F; S; Step-dau; Yes; Yes

WILEY

1732;1623; Lizzie; f; 67; Miss. Choctaw; F; S; Alone; Yes; Yes

WILLIAMSON

1733;1649; Bike; m; 45 Miss. Choctaw; F; M; Head; Yes; Yes
1734;1650; Effie; f; 33; Miss. Choctaw; F; M; Wife; Yes; Yes
1735;1652; Lallie; f; 15; Miss. Choctaw; F; S; Dau; Yes; Yes

WILLIAMS

1736;1636; Jennie; f; 93; Miss. Choctaw; F; Wd; Head; Yes; Yes
~~1737;1637; Fate; m; 48; Miss. Choctaw; F; S; Son; Yes; Yes~~
    Died 10-7-38

1738;1624; Jonas; m; 62; Miss. Choctaw; F; M; Head; Yes; Yes
1739;1625; Maggie; f; 52; Miss. Choctaw; F; M; Wife; Yes; Yes

~~1740;1638; Lewis; m; 60; Miss. Choctaw; F; M; Head; Yes; Yes~~
    Died 3-17-38
1741;1639; Mamie Smith; f; 38; Miss. Choctaw; F; M; Wife; Yes; Yes
1742;1640; Mary Ann; f; 12; Miss. Choctaw; F; S; Dau; Yes; Yes
1743;1641; Sarah; f; 8; Miss. Choctaw; F; S; Dau; Yes; Yes
1744;1642; Carter; m; 6; Miss. Choctaw; F; S; Son; Yes; Yes
1745;1643; Lurline; f; 3; Miss. Choctaw; F; S; Dau; Yes; Yes

Census of the **Mississippi Choctaws** reservation of the **Choctaw Agency** jurisdiction, as of **January 1, 1937**, 19__, taken by **A. C. Hector**, Superintendent.

KEY; Surname; Present Census Number; Last Census Number; Given Name; Sex; Age at Last Birthday; Tribe; Degree of Blood; Marital Status; Relationship to Head of Family; At Jurisdiction Where Enrolled (Yes/No); At Another Jurisdiction; Post Office, County, State (if given); Ward (Yes/No)

WILLIAMSON

~~1645; Mack; m; 62; Miss. Choctaw; F; M; Head; Yes; Yes~~
 Died 4-3-36
~~1646; Ida; f; 62; Miss. Choctaw; F; M; Wife; Yes; Yes~~
 Died 1935 - Unreported

WILLIAMS

1746;1629; Rufus; m; 30; Miss. Choctaw; F; M; Head; Yes; Yes
1747;1630; Nellie Sullivan; f; 36; Miss. Choctaw; F; M; Wife; Yes; Yes
1748;1633; Irvin (Evan); m; 15; Miss. Choctaw; F; S; Son; Yes; Yes
1749;1632; Phillip; m; 14; Miss. Choctaw; F; S; Son; Yes; Yes
1750;1634; Fillman; m; 10; Miss. Choctaw; F; S; Son; Yes; Yes
1751;1635; Coy; m; 8; Miss. Choctaw; F; S; Son; Yes; Yes
~~1631; Rufus; m; 3; Miss. Choctaw; F; S; Son; Yes; Yes~~
 Died 7-10-34 - Unreported
1752; Peter Jimpson; m; 6/12; Miss. Choctaw; F; S; Son; Yes; Yes
 Born 6-12-36

1753;1626; Tony; m; 28; Miss. Choctaw; F; M; Head; Yes; Yes
1754;1627; Mary Alice D; f; 22; Miss. Choctaw; F; M; Wife; Yes; Yes
1755;1628; Johnson; m; 3; Miss. Choctaw; F; S; Son; Yes; Yes
~~1756; Lamar; m; 4/12; Miss. Choctaw; F; S; Son; Yes; Yes~~
 Born 8-5-35   Died April 24, 1937

WILLIS

~~1699; Adaline; f; 65; Miss. Choctaw; F; Wd; Alone; Yes; Yes~~
 Dead - Unreported

1757;1653; Bill; m; 41; Miss. Choctaw; F; M; Head; Yes; Yes
1758;1654; Savenie Smith; f; 35; Miss. Choctaw; F; M; Wife; Yes; Yes
1759;1655; Claud Y; m; 18; Miss. Choctaw; F; S; Son; Yes; Yes

Census of the **Mississippi Choctaws** reservation of the **Choctaw Agency** jurisdiction, as of **January 1, 1937**, 19__, taken by **A. C. Hector**, Superintendent.

KEY; Surname; Present Census Number; Last Census Number; Given Name; Sex; Age at Last Birthday; Tribe; Degree of Blood; Marital Status; Relationship to Head of Family; At Jurisdiction Where Enrolled (Yes/No); At Another Jurisdiction; Post Office, County, State (if given); Ward (Yes/No)

1760;1656; Elsie; f; 17; Miss. Choctaw; F; S; Dau; Yes; Yes
1761;1657; William B; m; 14; Miss. Choctaw; F; S; Son; Yes; Yes
1762;1658; John Joseph; m; 3; Miss. Choctaw; F; S; Son; Yes; Yes

1763;1607; (Wallace), Columbus; m; 27; Miss. Choctaw; F; M: Head; Yes; Yes
1764;1608; Emma Dixon; f; 25; Miss. Choctaw; F; M; Wife; Yes; Yes
1765; Nephus; m; 8/12; Miss. Choctaw; F; S; Son; Yes; Yes
Born 4-25-36
1766;1751; Racheal; f; 52; Miss. Choctaw; F; Wd; Grand-mo; Yes; Yes
1767; 646; **Frazier**, Susie; f; 24; Miss. Choctaw; F; Wd; Step-dau; Yes; Yes
1768; 647; **Frazier**, Herman; m; 16; Miss. Choctaw; F; S; Gr-son; Yes; Yes
1769; 648; **Frazier**, Bob (Frazier); m; 14; Miss. Choctaw; F; S; Step-son; Yes; Yes
1770; 649; **Frazier**, Velma; f; 12; Miss. Choctaw; F; S; Step-dau; Yes; Yes
1771; **Frazier**, Wage; f; 5; Miss. Choctaw; F; S; Step-dau; Yes; Yes
Omitted from previous census

1772;1712; Edmond; m; 29; Miss. Choctaw; F; M; Head; Yes; Yes
1773;1711; Rose; f; 23; Miss. Choctaw; F; M; Wife; Yes; Yes

1774;1697; Ed; m; 66; Miss. Choctaw; F; M; Head; Yes; Yes
1775; 466; Nannie Dixon; f; 57; Miss. Choctaw; F; M; Wife; Yes; Yes

1776;1716; Elie; m; 36; Miss. Choctaw; F; M: Head; Yes; Yes
1777;1717; Otis; f; 30; Miss. Choctaw; F; M; Wife; Yes; Yes
1778;1718; Plonie; f; 17; Miss. Choctaw; F; S; Dau; Yes; Yes
1779;1719; Flora; f; 15; Miss. Choctaw; F; S; Dau; Yes; Yes
1780;1720; Kitty; f; 14; Miss. Choctaw; F; S; Dau; Yes; Yes
1781;1721; Bonnie; m[sic]; 12; Miss. Choctaw; F; S; Son; Yes; Yes
1782;1722; Robert R; m; 4; Miss. Choctaw; F; S; Son; Yes; Yes

Census of the **Mississippi Choctaws** reservation of the **Choctaw Agency** jurisdiction, as of **January 1, 1937**, 19__, taken by **A. C. Hector**, Superintendent.

KEY; Surname; Present Census Number; Last Census Number; Given Name; Sex; Age at Last Birthday; Tribe; Degree of Blood; Marital Status; Relationship to Head of Family; At Jurisdiction Where Enrolled (Yes/No); At Another Jurisdiction; Post Office, County, State (if given); Ward (Yes/No)

1783;   Gordon Griffiths; m; 7/12; Miss. Choctaw; F; S; Son; Yes; Yes   Born 5-7-36

1784;1701;   Ellis; m; 34; Miss. Choctaw; F; S; Alone; Yes; Yes

1785;1674;   Finis; m; 35; Miss. Choctaw; F; M; Head; Yes; Yes
1786;1675;   Nora; f; 30; Miss. Choctaw; F; M; Wife; Yes; Yes
1787;1676;   Seney (Leona); f; 8; Miss. Choctaw; F; S; Dau; Yes; Yes
1788;1677;   Sarah; f; 6; Miss. Choctaw; F; S; Dau; Yes; Yes
1789;   Willie; m; 2/12; Miss. Choctaw; F; S; Son; Yes; Yes
             Born 10-25-36
1790;   Nettie; f; 3; Miss. Choctaw; F; S; Dau; Yes; Yes
             Omitted from previous census

1791;1689;   Gamblin; m; 37; Miss. Choctaw; F; M; Head; Yes; Yes
1792;1690;   Ellen Hickman; f; 39; Miss. Choctaw; F; M; Wife; Yes; Yes
1793;1692;   Eula; f; 14; Miss. Choctaw; F; S; Dau; Yes; Yes
1794;1693;   J. C; m; 16; Miss. Choctaw; F; S; Son; Yes; Yes
~~1795;1694; Maurice; f[sic]; 13; Miss. Choctaw; F; S; Dau; Yes; Yes~~
             Died 1-17-38
1796;1695;   Marabelle; f; 8; Miss. Choctaw; F; S; Dau; Yes; Yes
1797;1696;   Earl; m; 6; Miss. Choctaw; F; S; Son; Yes; Yes
1798;1880;   Zon; m; 2; Miss. Choctaw; F; S; Son; Yes; Yes

1799;1681;   Gus; m; 64; Miss. Choctaw; F; M; Head; Yes; Yes
1800;1682;   Rainey; f; 40; Miss. Choctaw; F; M; Wife; Yes; Yes
1801;1683;   Hester; m[sic]; 10; Miss. Choctaw; F; S; Son; Yes; Yes
1802;1684;   Lester; m; 6; Miss. Choctaw; F; S; Son; Yes; Yes
1803;1685;   **Isaac**, William; m; 24; Miss. Choctaw; F; S; Step-son; No; Oklahoma; Yes
1804;1686;   **Isaac**, Nannie; f; 20; Miss. Choctaw; F; S; Step-dau; No; Oklahoma; Yes
1805;1687;   **Isaac**, Eunice; f; 17; Miss. Choctaw; F; S; Step-dau; No; Oklahoma; Yes

Census of the **Mississippi Choctaws** reservation of the **Choctaw Agency** jurisdiction, as of **January 1, 1937**, 19__, taken by **A. C. Hector**, Superintendent.

KEY; Surname; Present Census Number; Last Census Number; Given Name; Sex; Age at Last Birthday; Tribe; Degree of Blood; Marital Status; Relationship to Head of Family; At Jurisdiction Where Enrolled (Yes/No); At Another Jurisdiction; Post Office, County, State (if given); Ward (Yes/No)

1806;1688; **Isaac**, Rose; f; 13; Miss. Choctaw; F; S; Step-dau; No; Oklahoma; Yes

1807;1733; Houston (Thompson); m; 22; Miss. Choctaw; F; M; Head; Yes; Yes
1808;1136; Nettie Mingo; f; 16; Miss. Choctaw; F; M; Wife; Yes; Yes

1809;1731; Hugh; m; 54; Miss. Choctaw; F; S[sic]; Head; Yes; Yes
1810;1732; Mollie; f; 52; Miss. Choctaw; F; S[sic]; Wife; Yes; Yes
1811;1734; Clemson; m; 20; Miss. Choctaw; F; S; Son; Yes; Yes
1812;1735; J. C; m; 16; Miss. Choctaw; F; S; Son; Yes; Yes
1813;1736; Collins; m; 14; Miss. Choctaw; F; S; Son; Yes; Yes
1814;1738; Walter; m; 12; Miss. Choctaw; F; S; Son; Yes; Yes
1815;1739; Nola; f; 11; Miss. Choctaw; F; S; Dau; Yes; Yes
1816;1740; Beaman; m; 6; Miss. Choctaw; F; S; Son; Yes; Yes

1817;1702; Jim; m; 59; Miss. Choctaw; F; M; Head; Yes; Yes
1818;1703; Louisa; f; 57; Miss. Choctaw; F; M; Wife; Yes; Yes
1819;1704; Ike (Tom); m; 28; Miss. Choctaw; F; S; Son; Yes; Yes
1820;1705; Dennis; m; 33; Miss. Choctaw; F; S; Son; Yes; Yes
1821;1707; Dera (Dailey); f; 26; Miss. Choctaw; F; S; Dau; Yes; Yes
1822;1708; Dora; f; 25; Miss. Choctaw; F; S; Dau; Yes; Yes
1823;1709; Smith; m; 22; Miss. Choctaw; F; S; Son; Yes; Yes
1824;1710; Woodrow Wilson; m; 17; Miss. Choctaw; F; S; Son; Yes; Yes

1825;1664; Ike; m; 30; Miss. Choctaw; F; M: Head; Yes; Yes
1826;1665; Ellen; f; 28; Miss. Choctaw; F; M; Wife; Yes; Yes
1827;1666; Allen; m; 11; Miss. Choctaw; F; S; Son; Yes; Yes
1828;1667; Chester; m; 8; Miss. Choctaw; F; S; Son; Yes; Yes
1829;1668; Leo; m; 7; Miss. Choctaw; F; S; Son; Yes; Yes
1830;1669; Sina; f; 5; Miss. Choctaw; F; S; Dau; Yes; Yes
1831;1391; **Stoliby**, Boy Willis (Elum Ferum); m; 11; Miss. Choctaw; F; S; Orphan; Yes; Yes

Census of the **Mississippi Choctaws** reservation of the **Choctaw Agency** jurisdiction, as of **January 1, 1937**, 19__, taken by **A. C. Hector**, Superintendent.

KEY; Surname; Present Census Number; Last Census Number; Given Name; Sex; Age at Last Birthday; Tribe; Degree of Blood; Marital Status; Relationship to Head of Family; At Jurisdiction Where Enrolled (Yes/No); At Another Jurisdiction; Post Office, County, State (if given); Ward (Yes/No)

1832;1698; Joe; m; 68; Miss. Choctaw; F; Wd; Alone; Yes; Yes

1833;1678; John; m; 31; Miss. Choctaw; F; M; Head; Yes; Yes
1834;1679; Susana; f; 23; Miss. Choctaw; F; M; Wife; Yes; Yes
1835;1879; Baby; m; 2; Miss. Choctaw; F; S; Son; Yes; Yes

1836;1723; Kohran (Cohen); m; 39; Miss. Choctaw; F; M; Head; Yes; Yes
1837;1724; Molly (Sissey); f; 33; Miss. Choctaw; F; M; Wife; Yes; Yes
1838;1726; Una; f; 16; Miss. Choctaw; F; S; Dau; Yes; Yes
1839;1727; Sallie; f; 14; Miss. Choctaw; F; S; Dau; Yes; Yes
1840;1728; Harrison; m; 12; Miss. Choctaw; F; S; Son; Yes; Yes
1841;1729; A. J; m; 9; Miss. Choctaw; F; S; Son; Yes; Yes
1842;1730; Arline; f; 4; Miss. Choctaw; F; S; Dau; Yes; Yes
1843;1815; Brasie (Bead C); m; 3; Miss. Choctaw; F; S; Son; Yes; Yes

1844;1659; Nathan; m; 30; Miss. Choctaw; F; M: Head; Yes; Yes
1845;1660; Esther; f; 34; Miss. Choctaw; F; M; Wife; Yes; Yes
1846;1661; Norma (Sylvia); f; 9; Miss. Choctaw; F; S; Dau; Yes; Yes
1847;1662; Josie; m; 8; Miss. Choctaw; F; S; Son; Yes; Yes
1848; Louie; m; 5; Miss. Choctaw; F; S; Son; Yes; Yes
Omitted from previous census
1849;1663; Givan; m; 7; Miss. Choctaw; F; S; Son; Yes; Yes
1850;1816; Richard; m; 3; Miss. Choctaw; F; S; Son; Yes; Yes
1851; Ethel; f; 9/12; Miss. Choctaw; F; S; Dau; Yes; Yes
Born 3-28-36

1852;1670; Robert; m; 49; Miss. Choctaw; F; M: Head; Yes; Yes
1853;1671; Sallie (Celie); f; 36; Miss. Choctaw; F; M; Wife; Yes; Yes
1854;1673; **Ben**, Wilson; m; 17; Miss. Choctaw; F; S; Orphan; Yes; Yes

1855;1750; Saleen; m; 32; Miss. Choctaw; F; S; Alone; Yes; Yes

1856;1741; Spinks; m; 47; Miss. Choctaw; F; M; Head; Yes; Yes

Census of the **Mississippi Choctaws** reservation of the **Choctaw Agency** jurisdiction, as of **January 1, 1937**, 19__, taken by **A. C. Hector**, Superintendent.

KEY; Surname; Present Census Number; Last Census Number; Given Name; Sex; Age at Last Birthday; Tribe; Degree of Blood; Marital Status; Relationship to Head of Family; At Jurisdiction Where Enrolled (Yes/No); At Another Jurisdiction; Post Office, County, State (if given); Ward (Yes/No)

1857;1742; Susie; f; 38; Miss. Choctaw; F; M; Wife; Yes; Yes
1858;1743; Julius (Wilson); m; 18; Miss. Choctaw; F; S; Son; Yes; Yes
1859;1744; Nan (Flennie); f; 15; Miss. Choctaw; F; S; Dau; Yes; Yes
1860;1745; Willie B; f; 3; Miss. Choctaw; F; S; Dau; Yes; Yes
1861;1748; John B; m; 9; Miss. Choctaw; F; S; Nephew; Yes; Yes
1862;1747; Mary Lee; f; 13; Miss. Choctaw; F; S; Niece; Yes; Yes
1863;1749; Layton J; m; 7; Miss. Choctaw; F; S; Nephew; Yes; Yes

1864;1706; Waggoner; m; 28; Miss. Choctaw; F; M; Head; Yes; Yes
1865;1700; Nannie; f; 28; Miss. Choctaw; F; M; Wife; Yes; Yes
1866; Bone; m; 6; Miss. Choctaw; F; S; Step-son; Yes; Yes
Omitted from previous census
1867; Frank; m; 4; Miss. Choctaw; F; S; Step-son; Yes; Yes
Omitted from previous census
1868; Fred; m; 3; Miss. Choctaw; F; S; Step-son; Yes; Yes
Omitted from previous census

1869;1746; Wesley; m; 71; Miss. Choctaw; F; Wd; Head; Yes; Yes

WILSON

1870;1752; John; m; 42; Miss. Choctaw; F; M; Head; Yes; Yes
1871;1753; Eva Barnett; f; 34; Miss. Choctaw; F; SM; Wife; 1753; Yes; Yes
1872;1754; Cinnamon (Silmon); m; 18; Miss. Choctaw; F; S; Son; Yes; Yes
1873;1755; Mollie; f; 16; Miss. Choctaw; F; S; Dau; Yes; Yes
1874;1756; Sidney m; 15; Miss. Choctaw; F; S; Son; Yes; Yes
1875;1757; Leo; m; 12; Miss. Choctaw; F; S; Yes; Yes
1876;1758; Edna; f; 8; Miss. Choctaw; F; S; Dau; Yes; Yes
1877; Sillen; m; 5; Miss. Choctaw; F; S; Son; Yes; Yes
Omitted from previous census
~~Stoliby (Wilsons); Martha; f; 89; Miss. Choctaw; F; Wd; Mo; Yes; Yes~~ Died 12-30-34 - Unreported

Census of the **Mississippi Choctaws** reservation of the **Choctaw Agency** jurisdiction, as of **January 1, 1937**, 19__, taken by **A. C. Hector**, Superintendent.

KEY; Surname; Present Census Number; Last Census Number; Given Name; Sex; Age at Last Birthday; Tribe; Degree of Blood; Marital Status; Relationship to Head of Family; At Jurisdiction Where Enrolled (Yes/No); At Another Jurisdiction; Post Office, County, State (if given); Ward (Yes/No)

1878;1817; Caroline; f; 3; Miss. Choctaw; F; S; Dau; Yes; Yes

1879;1760; Will; m; 49; Miss. Choctaw; F; M; Head; Yes; Yes
~~1880;1761; Martha; f; 43; Miss. Choctaw; F; M; Wife; Yes; Yes~~
 Died April 16, 1937
1881;1762; Sammie; m; 16; Miss. Choctaw; F; S; Son; Yes; Yes
1882;1763; Lena (Lennie); f; 16; Miss. Choctaw; F; S; Dau; Yes; Yes
1883;1764; Louisiana; f; 14; Miss. Choctaw; F; S; Dau; Yes; Yes
1884;1765; R. L; m; 8; Miss. Choctaw; F; S; Son; Yes; Yes
1885;1766; Dean (Jim); m; 7; Miss. Choctaw; F; S; Son; Yes; Yes
1886;1767; Wilbur Neil; m; 5; Miss. Choctaw; F; S; Son; Yes; Yes
1887; Silas; m; 2; Miss. Choctaw; F; S; Son; Yes; Yes
 Born 1935 - Unreported

WISHORK

~~1773; Sampson; m; 73; Miss. Choctaw; F; Wd; Alone; Yes; Yes~~
 Dead - Unreported

YORK

1888;1775; Ben; m; 46; Miss. Choctaw; F; M; Head; Yes; Yes
1889;1776; Louella; f; 52; Miss. Choctaw; F; M; Wife; Yes; Yes
1890;1777; Hester; m; 15; Miss. Choctaw; F; S; Son; Yes; Yes
~~1891;1782; Scott; m; 82; Miss. Choctaw; F; Wd; Father; Yes; Yes~~
 Died Aug. 25, 1937

1892;1778; Bennett; m; 47; Miss. Choctaw; F; M; Head; Yes; Yes
1893;1779; Lacie; f; 29; Miss. Choctaw; F; M; Wife; Yes; Yes
1894;1780; J. B; m; 11; Miss. Choctaw; F; S; Son; Yes; Yes
1895;1781; Colie; f; 10; Miss. Choctaw; F; S; Dau; Yes; Yes

1896;1783; Berkley; m; 25; Miss. Choctaw; F; S; Alone; Yes; Yes

Census of the __Mississippi Choctaws__ reservation of the __Choctaw Agency__ jurisdiction, as of __January 1, 1937__, 19__, taken by __A. C. Hector__, Superintendent.

KEY; Surname; Present Census Number; Last Census Number; Given Name; Sex; Age at Last Birthday; Tribe; Degree of Blood; Marital Status; Relationship to Head of Family; At Jurisdiction Where Enrolled (Yes/No); At Another Jurisdiction; Post Office, County, State (if given); Ward (Yes/No)

1897;1784; Emmett; m; 33; Miss. Choctaw; F; M; Head; Yes; Yes
1898;1785; Indiana; f; 22; Miss. Choctaw; F; M; Wife; Yes; Yes
1899;1818; Theodore; m; 3; Miss. Choctaw; F; S; Son; Yes; Yes
1900;1786; Florence; f; 4; Miss. Choctaw; F; S; Dau; Yes; Yes
1901; Merlin; m; 5/12; Miss. Choctaw; F; S; Son; Yes; Yes
Born 7-16-36

1902;1787; Necie; f; 49; Miss. Choctaw; F; Wd; Head; Yes; Yes
1903;1788; Baxter; m; 30; Miss. Choctaw; F; S; Son; Yes; Yes
1904;1789; Addie; f; 28; Miss. Choctaw; F; S; Dau; Yes; Yes
1905;1790; Sasler; m; 25; Miss. Choctaw; F; S; Son; Yes; Yes
1906;1792; Beaman; m; 20; Miss. Choctaw; F; S; Son; Yes; Yes
1907;1068; **Lewis**, Amos (Buddy); m; 24; Miss. Choctaw; F; S; Orphan; Yes; Yes

YARBROUGH

1908; Baker; m; 58; Miss. Choctaw; F; S; Wd[sic]; Yes; Yes
Omitted from previous census

BIRTHS -

January 1, 1932 to December 31, 1938

Choctaw Indian Agency, Mississippi.

State **Mississippi** Reservation **Choctaw Agency** Agency or jurisdiction **Choctaw Agency, Philadelphia, Mississippi** Office of Indian Affairs

Key: Census Roll Number; Surname, Given Name; Date of Birth (Year-Month-Day); Live Births (Yes unless otherwise given); Still Births (blank unless otherwise given); Sex; Tribe; Ward (Yes/No); Degree of Blood (Father; Mother; Child); At Jurisdiction Where Enrolled (Yes/No); (If no - Where)

BIRTHS OCCURRING BETWEEN JANUARY 1 and DECEMBER 31, 1932- UNREPORTED

337; Chickaway, Mary Frances; 1932-8-3; f; Choctaw; Yes; F; F; F; Yes

BIRTHS OCCURRING BETWEEN JANUARY 1 and DECEMBER 31, 1933- UNREPORTED

1088; Laben, Hester; 1933-?-?; f; Choctaw; Yes; F; F; F; Yes

BIRTHS OCCURRING BETWEEN JANUARY 1 and DECEMBER 31, 1934- UNREPORTED

228; Billy, John Cephus; 1934-1-26; m; Choctaw; Yes; F; F; F; Yes
635; Frazier; Isral[sic]; 1934-?-?; m; Choctaw; Yes; F; F; F; Yes
680; Gipson, Leona; 1934-11-24; f; Choctaw; Yes; F; F; F; Yes
1103; Lewis; Lucy Mae; 1934-?-?; f; Choctaw; Yes; F; F; F; Yes

UNREPORTED BIRTHS OCCURRING PRIOR TO APRIL 1, 1934

Died before enrollment 10/133[sic] Mingo, Betty; 1933-1---; F; Choctaw; Yes; F; F; F; Yes
Died before enrollment Sam, Griffin; 1934-1-20; M; Choctaw; Yes; F; F; F; Yes
Died before enrollment Starr, Allie Lou; 1933-9-16; F; Choctaw; Yes; F; F; F; Yes
Died before enrollment Vaughn, Luke; 1933-8-6; M; Choctaw; Yes; F; F; F; Yes
Died before enrollment Williams, Rufus; 1934-2-22; M; Choctaw; Yes; F; F; F; Yes

State __ **Mississippi** ___ Reservation **Choctaw Agency** ___ Agency or jurisdiction **Choctaw Agency, Philadelphia, Mississippi** Office of Indian Affairs

Key: Census Roll Number; Surname, Given Name; Date of Birth (Year-Month-Day); Live Births (Yes unless otherwise given); Still Births (blank unless otherwise given); Sex; Tribe; Ward (Yes/No); Degree of Blood (Father; Mother; Child); At Jurisdiction Where Enrolled (Yes/No); (If no – Where)

BIRTHS OCCURRING BETWEEN APRIL 2 and DECEMBER 31, 1934

1; Bell, Fannie; 1934-7-14; F; Choctaw; Yes; F; F; F; Yes

2; Ben, Harrison; 1934-11-10; M; Choctaw; Yes; F; F; F; Yes

3; Ben, James Charles; 1934-9-10; M; Choctaw; Yes; F; F; F; Yes

4; Billy, Wilson; 1934-7-29; M; Choctaw; Yes; F; F; F; Yes

Died before enrollment   Charlie, Baby; 1934-7-7; M; Choctaw; Yes; F; F; F; Yes

5; Chitto, Dewy Davis; 1934-4-10; M; Choctaw; Yes; F; F; F; Yes

6; Denson, Baby; 1934-7-7; F; Choctaw; Yes; F; F; F; Yes

7; Frazier, LeRoy; 1934-7-21; M; Choctaw; Yes; F; F; F; Yes

8; Gipson, Josephine; 1934-9-16; F; Choctaw; Yes; F; F; F; Yes

9; Hall, Lena; 1934-11-30; F; Choctaw; Yes; F; F; F; Yes

10; Isaac, David, Jr; 1934-8-5; M; Choctaw; Yes; F; F; F; Yes

11; Isaac, Juanita; 1934-6-17; F; Choctaw; Yes; F; F; F; Yes

12; Jim, Goodman, Jr; 1934-9-13; M; Choctaw; Yes; F; F; F; Yes

13; Jim, Perry; 1934-6-13; M; Choctaw; Yes; F; F; F; Yes

14; John, Willie; 1934-11-21; M; Choctaw; Yes; F; F; F; Yes

15; McMillan, Rita; 1934-10-17; F; Choctaw; Yes; F; F; F; Yes

16; Mingo, Robert Bruce; 1934-4-11; M; Choctaw; Yes; F; F; F; Yes

17; Morris, Alice; 1934-6-12; F; Choctaw; Yes; F; F; F; Yes

18; Sam, Claude; 1934-7-17; M; Choctaw; Yes; F; F; F; Yes

19; Shoemake, Edburn; 1934-4-26; M; Choctaw; Yes; F; F; F; Yes

20; Thomas, Gordon; 1934-9-2; M; Choctaw; Yes; F; F; F; Yes

21; Thomas, Sam; 1934-7-26; M; Choctaw; Yes; F; F; F; Yes

Died before enrollment   Tubby, Mike; 1934-4-21; M; Choctaw; Yes; F; F; F; Yes

Died before enrollment   Tubby, Levi; 1934-4-21; M; Choctaw; Yes; F; F; F; Yes

State **Mississippi** Reservation **Choctaw Agency** Agency or jurisdiction **Choctaw Agency, Philadelphia, Mississippi** Office of Indian Affairs

Key: Census Roll Number; Surname, Given Name; Date of Birth (Year-Month-Day); Live Births (Yes unless otherwise given); Still Births (blank unless otherwise given); Sex; Tribe; Ward (Yes/No); Degree of Blood (Father; Mother; Child); At Jurisdiction Where Enrolled (Yes/No); (If no – Where)

Died before enrollment   Tubby, Baby; 1934-4-27; F; Choctaw; Yes; F; F; F; Yes
22; Tuffomah, Latima; 1934-5-8; F; Choctaw; Yes; F; F; F; Yes
23; Willis, Bead C; 1934-7-11; M; Choctaw; Yes; F; F; F; Yes
24; Willis, Richard; 1934-5-31; M; Choctaw; Yes; F; F; F; Yes
25; Wilson, Caroline; 1934-8-9; F; Choctaw; Yes; F; F; F; Yes
26; York, Theodore; 1934-8-24; M; Choctaw; Yes; F; F; F; Yes

Census of the _____ reservation of the __Choctaw__ __Indian Agency__ jurisdiction, as of __January 1, 1935__, 19__, taken by ____A. C. Hector____, Superintendent.

KEY; Number; Surname; Given Name; Sex; Date of Birth & Age at Last Birthday; Tribe; Degree of Blood; Marital Status; Relationship to Head of Family; At Jurisdiction Where Enrolled (Yes/No); At Another Jurisdiction; Post Office, County, State (if given); Ward (Yes/No)

BIRTHS AS OF JANUARY 1, 1935

- 1; Bell, Fannie; f; 7-4-34 & 5/12; Choctaw; F; S; Daughter; Yes; Yes
- 2; Ben, Harrison; m; 11-10-34 & 1/12; Choctaw; F; S; Son; Yes; Yes
- 3; Ben, James Charles; m; 9-10-34 & 3/12; Choctaw; F; S; Son; Yes; Yes
- 4; Billy, Wilson; m; 7-29-34 & 5/12; Choctaw; F; S; Son; Yes; Yes
- DBE Charlie, Baby; m; 7-7-34 & 5/12; Choctaw; F; S; Son; Yes; Yes
- 5; Chitto, Dewy Davis; m; 4-10-34 & 8/12; Choctaw; F; S; Yes; Yes
- 6; Denson, Baby; f; 7-7-34 & 5/12; Choctaw; F; S; Daughter; Yes; Yes
- 7; Frazier, LeRoy; m; 7-21-34 & 5/12; Choctaw; F; S; Son; Yes; Yes
- 8; Gipson, Josephine; f; 9-16-34 & 3/12; Choctaw; F; S; Daughter; Yes; Yes
- 9; Hall, Lena; f; 11-30-34 & 1/12; Choctaw; F; S; Daughter; Yes; Yes
- 10; Isaac; David, Jr; m; 8-5-34 & 1/12; Choctaw; F; S; Son; Yes; Yes
- 11; Isaac, Juanita; f; 6-17-34 & 6/12; Choctaw; F; S; Daughter; Yes; Yes
- 12; Jim, Goodman, Jr; m; 9-13-34 & 3/12; Choctaw; F; S; Son; Yes; Yes
- 13; Jim, Perry; m; 6-13-34 & 6/12; Choctaw; F; S; Son; Yes; Yes
- 14; John, Willie; m; 11-21-34 & 1/12; Choctaw; F; S; Son; Yes; Yes
- 15; McMillan, Rita; f; 10-17-34 & 2/12; Choctaw; F; S; Daughter; Yes; Yes
- 16; Mingo, Robert Bruce; m; 4-11-34 & 8/12; Choctaw; F; S; Son; Yes; Yes
- 17; Morris, Alice; f; 6-12-34 & 2/12; Choctaw; F; S; Daughter; Yes; Yes
- 18; Sam, Claude; m; 7-17-34 & 5/12; Choctaw; F; S; Son; Yes; Yes
- 19; Shoemake, Edburn; m; 1-26-34 & 8/12; Choctaw; F; S; Son; Yes; Yes
- 20; Thomas, Gordon; m; 9-2-34 & 3/12; Choctaw; F; S; Son; Yes; Yes
- 21; Thomas, Sam; m; 7-26-34 & 5/12; Choctaw; F; S; Son; Yes; Yes

Census of the _____ reservation of the **Choctaw Indian Agency** jurisdiction, as of **January 1, 1935**, 19___, taken by **A. C. Hector**, Superintendent.

KEY; Number; Surname; Given Name; Sex; Date of Birth & Age at Last Birthday; Tribe; Degree of Blood; Marital Status; Relationship to Head of Family; At Jurisdiction Where Enrolled (Yes/No); At Another Jurisdiction; Post Office, County, State (if given); Ward (Yes/No)

DBE Tubby, Mike; m; 4-21-34 & 8/12; Choctaw; F; S; Son; Yes; Yes
DBE Tubby, Levi; m; 4-21-34 & 8/12; Choctaw; F; S; Son; Yes; Yes
DBE Tubby, Baby; f; 7-27-34 & 8/12; Choctaw; F; S; Daughter; Yes; Yes
22; Toffomah, Latima; f; 5-8-34 & 7/12; Choctaw; F; S; Daughter; Yes; Yes
23; Willis, Bead C; m; 7-11-34 & 5/12; Choctaw; F; S; Son; Yes; Yes
24; Willis, Richard; m; 5-31-34 & 7/12; Choctaw; F; S; Son; Yes; Yes
25; Wilson, Caroline; f; 8-9-3 & 4/12; Choctaw; F; S; Daughter; Yes; Yes
26; York, Theodore; m; 8-24-34 & 4/12; Choctaw; F; S; Son; Yes; Yes

UNREPORTED BIRTHS OCCURRING PRIOR TO APRIL 1, 1934.

Died before enrollment   Mingo, Betty; f; 10/1933 & 1; Choctaw; F; S; Daughter; Yes; Yes

Died before enrollment   Sam, Griffin; m; 1-20-34 & 11/12; Choctaw; F; S; Son; Yes; Yes

Died before enrollment   Starr, Allie Lou; f; 9-16-33 & 3/12; Choctaw; F; S; Daughter; Yes; Yes

Died before enrollment   Vaughn, Luke; m; 8-6-22 & 4/12; Choctaw; F; S; Son; Yes; Yes

Died before enrollment   Williams, Rufus; m; 2-22-34 & 10/12; Choctaw; F; S; Son; Yes; Yes

OMITTED FROM LAST CENSUS

Died before enrollment   Lewis, Billy; m; 10; Choctaw; F; S; Son; Yes; Yes

State __Mississippi__ Reservation __Choctaw Agency__ Agency or jurisdiction __Choctaw Agency, Philadelphia, Mississippi__ Office of Indian Affairs

Key: Census Roll Number; Surname, Given Name; Date of Birth (Year-Month-Day); Live Births (Yes unless otherwise given); Still Births (blank unless otherwise given); Sex; Tribe; Ward (Yes/No); Degree of Blood (Father; Mother; Child); At Jurisdiction Where Enrolled (Yes/No); (If no – Where)

BIRTHS OCCURRING BETWEEN JANUARY 1, 1935 and DECEMBER 31, 1936 – UNREPORTED

100; Vaughn, Johnny; 1935-?-?; m; Choctaw; Yes; F; F; F; Yes
118; Bell, Rosenbaum; 1935-?-?; m; Choctaw; Yes; F; F; F; Yes
125; Bell, Inez; 1935-7-2; f; Choctaw; Yes; F; F; F; Yes
184; Bell, Henry; 1935-8-1; m; Choctaw; Yes; F; F; F; Yes
417; Cotton, Emma; 1935-?-?; f; Choctaw; Yes; F; F; F; Yes
450; Davis, Lonie; 1935-?-?; m; Choctaw; Yes; F; F; F; Yes
511; Dixon, Baby; 1935-5-15; m; Choctaw; Yes; F; F; F; Yes
690; Gipson, Marie L; 1935-?-?; f; Choctaw; Yes; F; F; F; Yes
794; Davis, Frances; 1935-?-?; m; Choctaw; Yes; F; F; F; Yes
864; Jackson, Lorraine; 1935-?-?; f; Choctaw; Yes; F; F; F; Yes
861; Jackson, Rosaline; 1935-?-?; f; Choctaw; Yes; F; F; F; Yes
986; Joe, Clark; 1935-?-?; m; Choctaw; Yes; F; F; F; Yes
1318; Robinson, Billie; 1935-?-?; m; Choctaw; Yes; F; F; F; Yes
1531; Thompson (Cates), Melvin; 1935-?-?; m; Choctaw; Yes; F; F; F; Yes
1585; Tubby, Mary; 1935-?-?; f; Choctaw; Yes; F; F; F; Yes
1609; Tubby, Sarah Ann; 1935-?-?; f; Choctaw; Yes; F; F; F; Yes
1887; Wilson, Silas; 1935-?-?; m; Choctaw; Yes; F; F; F; Yes

BIRTHS OCCURRING BETWEEN JANUARY 1 and DECEMBER 31, 1936

4; Alex, Theresa; 1936-7-9; f; Choctaw; Yes; F; F; F; Yes
21; Allen, Ralph; 1936-12-30; m; Choctaw; Yes; F; F; F; Yes
52; Anderson, Sarah Ann; 1936-1-29; f; Choctaw; Yes; F; F; F; Yes
DBE Anderson, Baby; 1936-1-29; m; Choctaw; Yes; F; F; F; Yes
161; Bell, Susan; 1936-3-14; f; Choctaw; Yes; F; F; F; Yes

State **Mississippi** Reservation **Choctaw Agency** Agency or jurisdiction **Choctaw Agency, Philadelphia, Mississippi** Office of Indian Affairs

Key: Census Roll Number; Surname, Given Name; Date of Birth (Year-Month-Day); Live Births (Yes unless otherwise given); Still Births (blank unless otherwise given); Sex; Tribe; Ward (Yes/No); Degree of Blood (Father; Mother; Child); At Jurisdiction Where Enrolled (Yes/No); (If no – Where)

176; Bell, Allie Mae; 1936-3-4; f; Choctaw; Yes; F; F; F; Yes
197; Ben, Eileene; 1936-3-6; f; Choctaw; Yes; F; F; F; Yes
207; Ben, Brantley Arthur; 1936-4-8; m; Choctaw; Yes; F; F; F; Yes
229; Billy, Lillie; 1936-9-10; f; Choctaw; Yes; F; F; F; Yes
242; Billy, Robert Lee; 1936-10-27; m; Choctaw; Yes; F; F; F; Yes
246; Willis, Henry; 1936-2-16; m; Choctaw; Yes; F; F; F; Yes
259; Billy, Lorraine; 1936-6-18; f; Choctaw; Yes; F; F; F; Yes
275; Billy, Reta; 1936-2-9; f; Choctaw; Yes; F; F; F; Yes
287; Billy, Beaman; 1936-4-27; m; Choctaw; Yes; F; F; F; Yes
292; Briscoe, Charlie; 1936-9-26; m; Choctaw; Yes; F; F; F; Yes
319; Charlie, Louey; 1936-2-9; m; Choctaw; Yes; F; F; F; Yes
338; Chickaway, Josephine Berniece; 1936-9-29; f; Choctaw; Yes; F; F; F; Yes
467; Denson, John; 1936-7-30; m; Choctaw; Yes; F; F; F; Yes
483; Denson, Marguerite; 1936-6-20; f; Choctaw; Yes; F; F; F; Yes
491; Dixon, Williston; 1936-12-22; m; Choctaw; Yes; F; F; F; Yes
506; Dixon, David Clem; 1936-10-22; m; Choctaw; Yes; F; F; F; Yes
541; Farmer, Hector; 1936-2-11; m; Choctaw; Yes; F; F; F; Yes
641; Frazier, Julian; 1936-4-22; m; Choctaw; Yes; F; F; F; Yes
660; Frazier, Clemon; 1936-3-30; m; Choctaw; Yes; F; F; F; Yes
681; Gipson, Irene; 1936-10-6; f; Choctaw; Yes; F; F; F; Yes
687; Gipson, Willie D; 1936-7-30; m; Choctaw; Yes; F; F; F; Yes
734; Henry, Cornelia; 1936-6-14; f; Choctaw; Yes; F; F; F; Yes
811; Isaac, Alice Marie; 1936-4-19; f; Choctaw; Yes; F; F; F; Yes
841; Isom, Salina; 1936-12-10; f; Choctaw; Yes; F; F; F; Yes
923; Jim; Frances; 1936-4-11; f; Choctaw; Yes; F; F; F; Yes
924; Jim; Frank; 1936-4-11; m; Choctaw; Yes; F; F; F; Yes
941; Jim, Otho; 1936-3-25; m; Choctaw; Yes; F; F; F; Yes
944; Jim, Richard; 1935-3-15; m; Choctaw; Yes; F; F; F; Yes

State __Mississippi__ Reservation __Choctaw Agency__ Agency or jurisdiction __Choctaw Agency, Philadelphia, Mississippi__ Office of Indian Affairs

Key: Census Roll Number; Surname, Given Name; Date of Birth (Year-Month-Day); Live Births (Yes unless otherwise given); Still Births (blank unless otherwise given); Sex; Tribe; Ward (Yes/No); Degree of Blood (Father; Mother; Child); At Jurisdiction Where Enrolled (Yes/No); (If no – Where)

955; Jim, Anderson; 1936-3-9; m; Choctaw; Yes; F; F; F; Yes
DBE Joe, Jane; 1936-4-27; f; Choctaw; Yes; F; F; F; Yes
971; Joe, Sallie; 1936-4-27; f; Choctaw; Yes; F; F; F; Yes
1004; John, Nancy Lou; 1936-5-5; f; Choctaw; Yes; F; F; F; Yes
1042; John, Reta; 1936-4-11; f; Choctaw; Yes; F; F; F; Yes
1118; Bell, Edith Rae; 1936-2-2; f; Choctaw; Yes; F; F; F; Yes
1144; Denson, Loretta; 1936-2-8; f; Choctaw; Yes; F; F; F; Yes
1163; McMillan, Leonard Yates; 1936-6-13; m; Choctaw; Yes; F; F; F; Yes
1206; Mingo, Baby; 1936-10-21; f; Choctaw; Yes; F; F; F; Yes
1248; Morris, Mazelle; 1936-5-21; f; Choctaw; Yes; F; F; F; Yes
1261; Nickey, John Joseph; 1936-1-20; m; Choctaw; Yes; F; F; F; Yes
1285; Polk, Jim; 1936-11-2; m; Choctaw; Yes; F; F; F; Yes
DBE Sam, Jimpson; 1936-6-3; m; Choctaw; Yes; F; F; F; Yes
1350; Sam, Edward; 1936-11-28; m; Choctaw; Yes; F; F; F; Yes
1370; Simpson, Franklin Lee; 1936-4-7; m; Choctaw; Yes; F; F; F; Yes
1380; Farmer, Franklin; 1936-9-2; m; Choctaw; Yes; F; F; F; Yes
1381; Farve (Farmer), Cecil Eugene; 1936-10-20; m; Choctaw; Yes; F; F; F; Yes
1409; Sockey, Ruth; 1936-8-9; f; Choctaw; Yes; F; F; F; Yes
1412; Solomon, Mattie; 1936-8-2; f; Choctaw; Yes; F; F; F; Yes
DBE Solomon, Baby; 1936-4-27; m; Choctaw; Yes; F; F; F; Yes
1435; Starr, Wanira; 1936-1-1; f; Choctaw; Yes; F; F; F; Yes
1441; Stephens, Lee Mack; 1936-4-19; m; Choctaw; Yes; F; F; F; Yes
1458; Steve, Sallie; 1936-4-17; f; Choctaw; Yes; F; F; F; Yes
1461; Steve, Gladys Eva; 1936-1-20; f; Choctaw; Yes; F; F; F; Yes
1473; Steve, Clyde; 1936-8-19; m; Choctaw; Yes; F; F; F; Yes
1513; Thompson, Baby; 1936-11-2; m; Choctaw; Yes; F; F; F; Yes
DBE Tubby, Joel Dodson; 1936-2-4; m; Choctaw; Yes; F; F; F; Yes

State **Mississippi** Reservation **Choctaw Agency** Agency or jurisdiction **Choctaw Agency, Philadelphia, Mississippi** Office of Indian Affairs

Key: Census Roll Number; Surname, Given Name; Date of Birth (Year-Month-Day); Live Births (Yes unless otherwise given); Still Births (blank unless otherwise given); Sex; Tribe; Ward (Yes/No); Degree of Blood (Father; Mother; Child); At Jurisdiction Where Enrolled (Yes/No); (If no – Where)

DBE; Tubby, Dixie Lee; 1936-3-6; f; Choctaw; Yes; F; F; F; Yes
1752; Williams, Peter Jimpson; 1936-6-12; m; Choctaw; Yes; F; F; F; Yes
1756; Williams, Lamar; 1936-8-5; m; Choctaw; Yes; F; F; F; Yes
1765; Willis, Nephus; 1936-4-25; m; Choctaw; Yes; F; F; F; Yes
1783; Willis, Gordon Griffiths; 1936-5-7; m; Choctaw; Yes; F; F; F; Yes
1789; Willis, Willie; 1936-10-25; m; Choctaw; Yes; F; F; F; Yes
1851; Willis, Ethel; 1936-3-28; f; Choctaw; Yes; F; F; F; Yes
1901; York, Marlin; 1936-7-16; m; Choctaw; Yes; F; F; F; Yes

BIRTHS OCCURRING BETWEEN JANUARY 1 and DECEMBER 31, 1936 UNREPORTED

375; Clemons, Winnie; 1936-?-?; f; Choctaw; Yes; F; F; F; Yes
691; Gipson, Lora Ann; 1936-?-?; f; Choctaw; Yes; F; F; F; Yes
749; Hickman, Tony; 1936-?-?; m; Choctaw; Yes; F; F; F; Yes
869; Jefferson, Hubert; 1936-?-?; m; Choctaw; Yes; F; F; F; Yes
1127; Lewis, Hazel; 1936-?-?; f; Choctaw; Yes; F; F; F; Yes
1689; Vaughn, Eleanor; 1936-?-?; f; Choctaw; Yes; F; F; F; Yes
1715; Wallace, Otis; 1936-?-?; m; Choctaw; Yes; F; F; F; Yes

Agency **Choctaw Indian Agency, Philadelphia, Mississippi**
Reservation **Choctaw**

Key: Suppl. Roll Number; Last Census Roll No. of Head of Family; Surname, Given Name; Sex; Date of Birth (Month-Day-Year); Tribe (Choctaw unless stated otherwise); Exact Degree of Blood; Marital Status; Relation To Head of Family; Jurisdiction Where Enrolled; County

LIVE BIRTHS FOR THE CALENDAR YEAR OF 1937
List only additions to the 1937 Census Roll

1; 71; Anderson, Cleveland; m; 5-22-37; F; S; Son; Choctaw; Newton
2; 65; Anderson, Mervia; f; 9-23-37; F; S; Daughter; Choctaw; Newton
3; 168; Bell, Dorothy; f; 8-22-37; F; S; Daughter; Choctaw; Neshoba
4; 119; Bell, Ida Mae; f; 10-10-37; F; S; Daughter; Choctaw; Neshoba
5; 136; Bell, Naomi; f; 3-4-37; F; S; Daughter; Choctaw; Neshoba
6; 174; Bell, Robert Lee; m; 10-20-37; F; S; Son; Choctaw; Neshoba
7; 198; Ben, Baby; f; 7-2-37; F; S; Daughter; Choctaw; Leake
8; 194; Ben, John; m; 11-2-37; F; S; Son; Choctaw; Newton
9; 208; Ben, Ruben; m; 3-15-37; F; S; Son; Choctaw; Leake
10; 222; Billie, Sally Ruth; f; 9-30-37; F; S; Daughter; Choctaw; Leake
11; 276; Billie, Baby; m; 4-20-37; F; S; Son; Choctaw; Neshoba
12; 293; Briscoe, Baby; f; 6-12-37; F; S; Son; Choctaw; Scott
13; 305; Chapman, Thresa; f; 7-28-37; F; S; Daughter; Choctaw; Jasper
14;1423; Charlie, Baby; m; 9-28-37; F; S; Son; Choctaw; Newton
15; 339; Chickaway, Baby; f; 3-2-37; F; S; Daughter; Choctaw; Neshoba
16; 326; Chickaway, Mary; f; 5-3-37; F; S; Daughter; Choctaw; Neshoba
17; 461; Denson, Ceasar; m; 2-15-37; F; S; Son; Choctaw; Newton
18; 484; Denson, Baby; m; 3-22-37; F; S; Son; Choctaw; Leake
19; 507; Dixon, Woodrow; m; 7-21-37; F; S; Son; Choctaw; Leake
20; 535; Farmer, J. C; m; 7-21-37; F; S; Son; Choctaw; Neshoba
21; 591; Farve, Encie; f; 11-5-37; F; S; Daughter; Choctaw; Newton

Agency   **Choctaw Indian Agency, Philadelphia, Mississippi**
Reservation   **Choctaw**

Key: Suppl. Roll Number; Last Census Roll No. of Head of Family; Surname, Given Name; Sex; Date of Birth (Month-Day-Year); Tribe (Choctaw unless stated otherwise); Exact Degree of Blood; Marital Status; Relation To Head of Family; Jurisdiction Where Enrolled; County

22; 688; Gipson, Annie Lee; f; 5-5-37; F; S; Daughter; Choctaw; Newton

23; 737; Henry, Norman; m; 9-1-37; F; S; Son; Choctaw; Neshoba

24; 745; Hickman, Baby; m; 11-14-37; F; S; Son; Choctaw; Neshoba

25; 812; Isaac, Charles; m; 5-5-37; F; S; Son; Choctaw; Neshoba

26; 802; Isaac, David; m; 10-28-37; F; S; Son; Choctaw; Neshoba

27; 802[sic];Isaac, Theresa Mae; f; 3-20-37; F; S; Daughter; Choctaw; Neshoba

28; 856; Jackson, Mollie; f; 5-31-37; F; S; Daughter; Choctaw; Neshoba

29; 870; Jefferson, Baby; m; 6-19-37; F; S; Daughter; Choctaw; Scott

30; 881; Jefferson, Birdie Mae; f; 9-2-37; F; S; Daughter; Choctaw; Newton

31; 865; ~~Jefferson, Shirley; f; 4-30-37; F; S; Daughter; Choctaw; Newton~~ Died 6-4-38

32; 947; Jim, Baby; f; 6-7-37; F; S; Daughter; Choctaw; Neshoba

33; 956; Jimmie, Leonard H; m; 10-7-37; F; S; Son; Choctaw; Neshoba

34; 981; Joe, Claudeece; f; 5-17-37; F; S; Daughter; Choctaw; Neshoba

35;1034; John, Bobbie; m; 7-22-37; F; S; Son; Choctaw; Neshoba

36;1022; Johnson, Baby; f; 5-28-37; F; S; Daughter; Choctaw; Newton

37;1097; Lewis, Maudie Lee; f; 2-24-37; F; S; Daughter; Choctaw; Newton

38;1104; Lewis, Baby; f; 6-6-37; F; S; Daughter; Choctaw; Neshoba

39;1135; Lewis, Baby; f; 5-28-37; F; S; Daughter; Choctaw; Leake

40;1123; Lewis, Waiter; m; 9-8-37; F; S; Son; Choctaw; Neshoba

41;1172; ~~McMillan, Ita Inez; f; 10-14-37; F; S; Daughter; Choctaw; Neshoba~~ Died 9-13-38

42;1190; McMillan, Theodore Nelson; m; 5-16-37; F; S; Son; Choctaw; Neshoba

43;1305; Robinson (Teach), Baby; f; 11-16-37; F; S; Choctaw; Neshoba

Agency   **Choctaw Indian Agency, Philadelphia, Mississippi**
Reservation   Choctaw

Key: Suppl. Roll Number; Last Census Roll No. of Head of Family; Surname, Given Name; Sex; Date of Birth (Month-Day-Year); Tribe (Choctaw unless stated otherwise); Exact Degree of Blood; Marital Status; Relation To Head of Family; Jurisdiction Where Enrolled; County

44;1334;   Sam, Baby; f; 3-14-37; F; S; Daughter; Choctaw; Neshoba
45;1327;   Sam, Baby; m; 8-3-37; F; S; Son; Choctaw; Neshoba
46;1570;   Sam, Donald; m; 9-13-37; F; S; Son; Choctaw; Neshoba
47;1376;   Smith, Clarence; m; 6-19-37; F; S; Son; Choctaw; Newton
48;1392;   Sockey, Margery; f; 4-3-37; F; S; Daughter; Choctaw; Leake
49;1442;   Stephens, Edna Ivey; f; 11-10-37; F; S; Daughter; Choctaw; Newton
50;1442[sic];Stephens, Edward Yates; m; 11-10-37; F; S; Son; Choctaw; Newton
51;1486;   Thomas, Leon; m; 4-24-37; F; S; Son; Choctaw; Neshoba
52;1667;   Tubby, Clenny Mae; f; 4-13-37; F; S; Daughter; Choctaw; Neshoba
53;1586;   Tubby, Aban; m; 4-6-37; F; S; Son; Choctaw; Neshoba
54;1563;   Tubby, Leon; m; 5-3-37; F; S; Son; Choctaw; Neshoba
55;1695;   Waiter, Betty Lee; f; 9-9-37; F; S; Daughter; Choctaw; Neshoba
56;1725;   Wickson, Baby; m; 5-31-37; F; S; Son; Choctaw; Newton
57;1791;   Willis, Baby; f; 7-6-37; F; S; Daughter; Choctaw; Neshoba
58;1807;   Willis, Baby; f; 12-22-37; F; S; Daughter; Choctaw; Neshoba
59;1836;   Willis, Roscoe; m; 8-25-37; F; S; Son; Choctaw; Neshoba
60;1825;   Willis, Harrison; m; 6-26-37; F; S; Son; Choctaw; Leake
61;1856;   Willis, Baby; m; 10-1-37; F; S; Son; Choctaw; Neshoba
62;1864;   Willis, Roger; m; 4-4-37; F; S; Son; Choctaw; Leake
63;1879;   ~~Wilson, Lucille; f; ;7-10-37; F; S; Daughter; Choctaw; Leake~~ Died 5-20-38
64;1873;   Wilson, Grady; m; 2-12-37; F; S; Son; Choctaw; Leake
65;1870;   Wilson, Lecin; f; 9-10-37; F; S; Daughter; Choctaw; Leake
66; 316;   Charlie; Baby; f; 12-28-37; F; S; Daughter; Choctaw; Newton

Agency   **Choctaw Indian Agency, Philadelphia, Mississippi**
Reservation   **Choctaw**

Key: Suppl. Roll Number; Last Census Roll No. of Head of Family; Surname, Given Name; Sex; Date of Birth (Month-Day-Year); Tribe (Choctaw unless stated otherwise); Exact Degree of Blood; Marital Status; Relation To Head of Family; Jurisdiction Where Enrolled; County

OMISSIONS FROM PREVIOUS CENSUS ROLLS
All Other Additions
List only additions to the 1937 Census Roll

DBE; None; Willis, Mary; f; 1854; F; M; Wife; Choctaw; Neshoba
DBE; None; Farve, Frazene; f; 3-17-1878; F; M; Wd; Choctaw; Hancock
DBE; None; Willis, Henry; m; 1833; F; M; Husband; Choctaw; Neshoba

BIRTHS OCCURRING BEFORE JANUARY 1, 1937
UNREPORTED
List only additions to the 1937 Census Roll

1; 293; Briscoe, Scott; m; 1935; F; S; Son; Choctaw; Scott

BIRTHS OCCURRING BEFORE JANUARY 1, 1938 - UNREPORTED
List only additions to the 1938 Census Roll

60;1707-37; Wallace, Barbalette; f; 6-1-37; F; S; Daughter; Miss; Neshoba

OMISSIONS FROM PREVIOUS CENSUS ROLLS
List only additions to the 1938 Census Roll

61; 33-37; Willis, Willis; m; [blank]; F; Head; Son; Miss; Neshoba
62; 33-37; Amos, Wagoner; m; [blank]; F; Head; Son; Miss; Neshoba
63; 62-38; Amos, Tubby; m; 2; F; S; Son of 62-38; Miss; Neshoba
64; 62-38; Amos, Nellie; f; 1; F; S; Dau of 62-38; Miss; Neshoba
65;1442-37; Stephens, Celia Lois; f; 4; F; S; Dau; Miss; Neshoba

State __Mississippi__ Reservation_____ Agency or jurisdiction __Choctaw Indian Agency, Philadelphia, Mississippi__ Office of Indian Affairs

Key: Census Roll Number; Surname, Given Name; Date of Birth (Year-Month-Day); Live Births (Yes unless otherwise given); Still Births (blank unless otherwise given); Sex; Tribe; Ward (Yes/No); Degree of Blood (Father; Mother; Child); At Jurisdiction Where Enrolled (Yes/No); (If no – Where)

BIRTHS OCCURRING BETWEEN JANUARY 1 and DECEMBER 31, 1938

1; Amos, Martha Laner; 1938-10-9; f; Miss. Choctaw; Yes; F; F; F; Yes
2; Anderson, Mary; 1938-2-16; f; Miss. Choctaw; Yes; F; F; F; Yes
3; Anderson, Fronie Mae; 1938-10-23; f; Miss. Choctaw; Yes; F; F; F; Yes
DBE; Bell, Baby; 1938-8-28; m; Miss. Choctaw; Yes; F; F; F; Yes
DBE; Bell, Claud; 1938-2-17; m; Miss. Choctaw; Yes; F; F; F; Yes
4; Bell, Charles; 1938-2-17; m; Miss. Choctaw; Yes; F; F; F; Yes
5; Bell, Dorothy; 1938-3-1; f; Miss. Choctaw; Yes; F; F; F; Yes
6; Bell, Josephine; 1938-11-11; f; Miss. Choctaw; Yes; F; F; F; Yes
7; Ben, Bobby; 1938-3-9; m; Miss. Choctaw; Yes; F; F; F; Yes
8; Ben, Lester; 1938-12-33; m; Miss. Choctaw; Yes; F; F; F; Yes
9; Billie, Collins; 1938-10-4; m; Miss. Choctaw; Yes; F; F; F; Yes
10; Billie, Lewis; 1938-6-15; m; Miss. Choctaw; Yes; F; F; F; Yes
11; Billie, Marguarite; 1938-3-23; f; Miss. Choctaw; Yes; F; F; F; Yes
12; Briscoe, Olivia; 1938-5-19; f; Miss. Choctaw; Yes; F; F; F; Yes
13; Charlie, Elizabeth; 1938-10-14; f; Miss. Choctaw; Yes; F; F; F; Yes
14; Davis, Alice; 1938-4-9; f; Miss. Choctaw; Yes; F; F; F; Yes
DBE; Denson, Baby; 1938-2-28; [blank]; Yes; m; Miss. Choctaw; Yes; F; F; [blank]; [blank]
15; Dixon, Dorothy; 1938-11-11; f; Miss. Choctaw; Yes; F; F; F; Yes
16; Dixon, Melba; 1938-5-28; f; Miss. Choctaw; Yes; F; F; F; Yes
17; Farmer, Robert Lee; 1938-11-11; m; Miss. Choctaw; Yes; F; F; F; Yes
18; Frazier, Betsy Ann; 1938-2-15; f; Miss. Choctaw; Yes; F; F; F; Yes
19; Gibson, Granville; 1938-6-17; m; Miss. Choctaw; Yes; F; F; F; Yes
20; Gibson, Stephen; 1938-6-19; m; Miss. Choctaw; Yes; F; F; F; Yes
21; Henry, Jeanette; 1038-12-12; f; Miss. Choctaw; Yes; F; F; F; Yes
22; Isaac, Bradley; 1938-5-4; m; Miss. Choctaw; Yes; F; F; F; Yes
23; Isaac, George; 1938-2-22; m; Miss. Choctaw; Yes; F; F; F; Yes
24; Isaac, Juliva; 1938-1-6; f; Miss. Choctaw; Yes; F; F; F; Yes

State __Mississippi__ Reservation _____ Agency or jurisdiction __Choctaw Indian Agency, Philadelphia, Mississippi__
Office of Indian Affairs

Key: Census Roll Number; Surname, Given Name; Date of Birth (Year-Month-Day); Live Births (Yes unless otherwise given); Still Births (blank unless otherwise given); Sex; Tribe; Ward (Yes/No); Degree of Blood (Father; Mother; Child); At Jurisdiction Where Enrolled (Yes/No); (If no – Where)

25; Isaac, Mills; 1938-12-7; m; Miss. Choctaw; Yes; F; F; F; Yes
26; Jackson, Emma Lee; 1938-7-24; f; Miss. Choctaw; Yes; F; F; F; Yes
27; Jim, Bernice; 1938-9-14; f; Miss. Choctaw; Yes; F; F; F; Yes
28; Jim, Missola; 1938-3-16; f; Miss. Choctaw; Yes; F; F; F; Yes
29; Joe, Baby; 1938-1-17; m; Miss. Choctaw; Yes; F; F; F; Yes
30; Joe, Wayne; 1938-10-16; m; Miss. Choctaw; Yes; F; F; F; Yes
31; John, Semm Lee; 1938-3-22; f; Miss. Choctaw; Yes; F; F; F; Yes
DBE; Johnson, Irvin K. Morris; 1938-9-21; m; Miss. Choctaw; Yes; F; F; F; Yes
32; Johnson, James; 1938-6-13; m; Miss. Choctaw; Yes; F; F; F; Yes
DBE; Lewis, Frank; 1938-3-21; m; Miss. Choctaw; Yes; F; F; F; Yes
33; Lewis, Runner; 1938-3-15; m; Miss. Choctaw; Yes; F; F; F; Yes
34; McMillan, Elinor; 1938-2-12; f; Miss. Choctaw; Yes; F; F; F; Yes
35; McMillan, Ruby; 1948-9-2; f; Miss. Choctaw; Yes; F; F; F; Yes
36; McMillan, Clifton; 1938-8-2; m; Miss. Choctaw; Yes; F; F; F; Yes
37; Morris, Garrett; 1938-5-19; m; Miss. Choctaw; Yes; F; F; F; Yes
DBE; Morris, Ottosella; 1938-3-6; f; Miss. Choctaw; Yes; F; F; F; Yes
38; Polk, Louise; 1938-9-23; f; Miss. Choctaw; Yes; F; F; F; Yes
39; Sam, Nat; 1938-8-18; m; Miss. Choctaw; Yes; F; F; F; Yes
40; Shumake; Mary; 1938-2-22; f; Miss. Choctaw; Yes; F; F; F; Yes
41; Sockey, Major; 1938-3-7; m; Miss. Choctaw; Yes; F; F; F; Yes
42; Sockey, May Bell; 1938-9-24; f; Miss. Choctaw; Yes; F; F; F; Yes
43; Solomon, Thomas Freeman; 1938-11-23; m; Miss. Choctaw; Yes; F; F; F; Yes
44; Starr, Ruben; 1938-3-11; m; Miss. Choctaw; Yes; F; F; F; Yes
45; Stephens, Elizabeth; 1938-4-10; f; Miss. Choctaw; Yes; F; F; F; Yes
46; Steve, Frank; 1938-10-2; m; Miss. Choctaw; Yes; F; F; F; Yes
47; Steve, Katherine; 1938-10-27; f; Miss. Choctaw; Yes; F; F; F; Yes
48; Thompson, Easton; 1938-10-15; m; Miss. Choctaw; Yes; F; F; F; Yes
49; Thompson, Willie Dean; 1938-11-29; f; Miss. Choctaw; Yes; F; F; F; Yes
DBE; Thompson, Jack; 1938-8-16; m; Miss. Choctaw; Yes; F; F; F; Yes

State **Mississippi** Reservation_____Agency or jurisdiction **Choctaw Indian Agency, Philadelphia, Mississippi**
Office of Indian Affairs

Key: Census Roll Number; Surname, Given Name; Date of Birth (Year-Month-Day); Live Births (Yes unless otherwise given); Still Births (blank unless otherwise given); Sex; Tribe; Ward (Yes/No); Degree of Blood (Father; Mother; Child); At Jurisdiction Where Enrolled (Yes/No); (If no – Where)

50; Tubby, Binford Lee; 1938-9-17; m; Miss. Choctaw; Yes; F; F; F; Yes
51; Wickson, Mack; 1938-11-10; m; Miss. Choctaw; Yes; F; F; F; Yes
52; Williams, Wilson; 1938-10-4; m; Miss. Choctaw; Yes; F; F; F; Yes
53; Willis, Bertha; 1938-4-1; f; Miss. Choctaw; Yes; F; F; F; Yes
54; Willis, Fannie Lou; 1938-3-15; f; Miss. Choctaw; Yes; F; F; F; Yes
55; Willis, John Crawford; 1938-7-19; m; Miss. Choctaw; Yes; F; F; F; Yes
56; Willis, Lee Roy; 1938-2-14; m; Miss. Choctaw; Yes; F; F; F; Yes
57; Willis, Susie Jane; 1938-12-27; f; Miss. Choctaw; Yes; F; F; F; Yes
58; Wilson, Jimmie; 1938-3-23; m; Miss. Choctaw; Yes; F; F; F; Yes
59; York, Evelyn; 1938-4-25; f; Miss. Choctaw; Yes; F; F; F; Yes

DEATHS -

January 1, 1932 to December 31, 1938

Choctaw Indian Agency, Mississippi.

State___**Mississippi**___Reservation___Choctaw Agency___Agency or jurisdiction___**Choctaw Agency, Philadelphia, Mississippi**___Office of Indian Affairs

Key: Year and Number Last Census Roll (if given); Surname, Given Name; Date of Death (Year-Month-Day, if given); Age at Death; Sex; Tribe; Ward (Yes/No); Degree of Blood; Cause of Death; At Jurisdiction Where Enrolled (Yes/No); (If no – Where)

DEATHS NOT REPORTED PRIOR TO JANUARY 1, 1939
Deaths Occurring Between January 1, 1933 to December 31, 1937

1937; 217; Ben, Wyatt; 1933; 65; m; Miss. Choctaw; Yes; F; Unknown; Yes

1937; 366; Clemons, Irsal; 1936; 14; Miss. Choctaw; Yes; F; Typhoid; Yes

1937; 365; Clemons, Mattie; 1936; 14; f; Miss. Choctaw; Yes; F; Typhoid; Yes

1937; 573; Farve, Dave; 1934; 56; m; Miss. Choctaw; Yes; F; Unknown; Yes

1937;1026; Johnson, Egbert; 1933; 6; m; Miss. Choctaw; Yes; F; Unknown; Yes

1937;1108; Lewis, Duffie; 1938-4-28; 41; m; Miss. Choctaw; Yes; F; Burned to death; Yes   No certificate

1937;1499; Thomas, Wilmon; 1936-1-25; 36; m; Miss. Choctaw; Yes; F; Unknown; Yes

1937;1449; Stephens, Tom; 1934; 71; m; Miss. Choctaw; Yes; F; Unknown; Yes

1937; 665; Vaughn, Monroe; 1935; 4; m; Miss. Choctaw; Yes; F; Flu; Yes

DEATHS OCCURRING BETWEEN JANUARY 1 and DECEMBER 31, 1938

1937; 2; Alex, Sallie Mae; 1938-7-11; 22; f; Miss. Choctaw; Yes; F; Pulmonary tuberculosis; Yes

1937; 51; Anderson, Ella Mae; 1938-9-13; 23; f; Miss. Choctaw; Yes; F; Pulmonary tuberculosis; Yes

1937; 67; Anderson, John Lish; 1938-4-19; 71; m; Miss. Choctaw; Yes; F; Pulmonary tuberculosis; Yes

DBE; Bell, Claud; 1938-3-5; 29 days; m; Miss. Choctaw; Yes; F; Inanition; Yes   Father #132-37

1937; 181; Bell, Lena Mingo; 1938-9-6; 25; f; Miss. Choctaw; Yes; F; Pulmonary tuberculosis; Yes

State__**Mississippi**__Reservation__**Choctaw Agency**__Agency or jurisdiction__**Choctaw Agency, Philadelphia, Mississippi**__Office of Indian Affairs

Key: Year and Number Last Census Roll (if given); Surname, Given Name; Date of Death (Year-Month-Day, if given); Age at Death; Sex; Tribe; Ward (Yes/No); Degree of Blood; Cause of Death; At Jurisdiction Where Enrolled (Yes/No); (If no – Where)

DBE;	Bell, Baby; 1938-8-30; 2 days; m; Miss. Choctaw; Yes; F; Hemoplulia[sic] of new born; Yes Father #128-37
1937; 208;	Ben, Rufus; 1938-5-9; 21; m; Miss. Choctaw; Yes; F; Shot through abdomen (suicide); Yes
1937; 219;	Billie, Clement; 1938-9-25; 25; m; Miss. Choctaw; Yes; F; Concussion of the brain; Yes
1937; 323;	Charlie, William; 1938;5;26; 88; m; Miss. Choctaw; Yes; F; Strangulated hernia; Yes
1937; 466;	Denson, Eva Jackson; 1938-3-1; 19; f; Miss. Choctaw; Yes; F; Abnormal pregnancy; Yes
	~~DBE; Denson, Baby; 1938-2-28; [blank]; m; Miss. Choctaw; Yes; F; Stillborn; Yes~~ Father #465-37
1937; 529;	Farmer, Ishman; 1938-12-4; 94; m; Miss. Choctaw; Yes; F; Unknown; Yes
1937; 536;	Farmer, Lottie Chickaway; 1938-8-4; 31; f; Miss. Choctaw; Yes; F; Pulmonary tuberculosis; Yes
1937; 681;	Gibson, Annie Maude; 1938-5-7; 1 yr 7 mo; f; Miss. Choctaw; Yes; F; Symtoms[sic] of diarrhea & malnutrition; Yes
1938; 888; Sup.	Jefferson, Arthur; 1938-1-15; 4; m; Miss. Choctaw; Yes; F; Unknown; Yes
1937; 917;	Jim, Goodman; 1938-9-21; 74; m; Miss. Choctaw; Yes; F; Pellagra; Yes
1937; 943;	Jim, Lulu Thomas; 1938-1-29; 25; f; Miss. Choctaw; Yes; F; Pulmonary tuberculosis; Yes
1937; 779;	Joe, Emelia; 1938-5-16; 79; f; Miss. Choctaw; Yes; F; Unknown; Yes
DBE;	Johnson, Irvin K. Morris; 1938-10-21; 1 mo; m; Miss. Choctaw; Yes; F; Unknown; Yes
1937; 393;	Lewis, Ella McMillan; 1938-7-13; 24; f; Miss. Choctaw; Yes; F; Pulmonary tuberculosis; Yes
DBE;	Lewis, Frank; 1938-6-15; 2m & 24d; m; Miss. Choctaw; Yes; F; Lobular pneumonia; Yes Father #392-37

State **Mississippi** Reservation **Choctaw Agency** Agency or jurisdiction **Choctaw Agency, Philadelphia, Mississippi** Office of Indian Affairs

Key: Year and Number Last Census Roll (if given); Surname, Given Name; Date of Death (Year-Month-Day, if given); Age at Death; Sex; Tribe; Ward (Yes/No); Degree of Blood; Cause of Death; At Jurisdiction Where Enrolled (Yes/No); (If no – Where)

1938; 41; McMillan, Ida; 1938-9-13; 10m & 29d; f; Miss. Choctaw; Sup. Yes; F; Diarrhea fermentative; Yes

DBE; Morris, Ottozella; 1938-5-3; 1m & 27d; f; Miss. Choctaw; Yes; F; Symtoms[sic] of pneumonia; Yes Father #1230-37

1937;1260; Nickey, Rena Jim; 1938-1-9; 17; f; Miss. Choctaw; Yes; F; Pulmonary tuberculosis; Yes

1937;1427; Steve, Jean; 1938-9-18; 12; f; Miss. Choctaw; Yes; F; Pulmonary tuberculosis; Yes

DBE; Thompson, Jack; 1938-12-5; 3m & 19d; m; Miss. Choctaw; Yes; F; Collitis[sic] fermentative; Yes Father #1538-37

1937;1529; Thompson, Nonie; 1938-7-30; 14; f; Miss. Choctaw; Yes; F; Embolism; Yes

1937;1560; Tubby, John; 1938-7-11; 19; m; Miss. Choctaw; Yes; F; Symtoms of kidney infection; Yes

1937;1612; Tubby, Maggie; 1938-7-12; 34; f; Miss. Choctaw; Yes; F; Mutiple[sic] arthritis pregnant; Yes

1937;1700; Wallace, Cumby; 1938-1-3; 67; m; Miss. Choctaw; Yes; F; Nephritis, parenchymatous[sic] lobular pnue[sic]; Yes

1937;1737; Williams, Fate; 1938-10-7; 50; m; Miss. Choctaw; Yes; F; Struck by car killed instantly; Yes

1937;1740; Williams, Louis; 1938-3-17; 62; m; Miss. Choctaw; Yes; F; Acute bronchitis & phlebitis; Yes

1938; 63; Wilson, Lucille; 1938-5-20; 7m & 13d; f; Miss. Choctaw; Sup. Yes; F; Chronic bronchitis; Yes

1937; 1795; Willis, Maurice; 1938-1-17; 15; m; Miss. Choctaw; Yes; F; Ruptured appendix; Yes

1937;1898; York, Indiana Lewis; 1938-10-17; f; Miss. Choctaw; Yes; F; Pulmonary tuberculosis; Yes

DEATHS OCCURRING BETWEEN JANUARY 1 and DECEMBER 31, 1937

1936; 18; Allen, R. G; 1937-1-18; 22; m; Yes; Full; Lobar Pneumonia; Yes

State **Mississippi** Reservation Choctaw Agency Agency or jurisdiction **Choctaw Agency, Philadelphia, Mississippi** Office of Indian Affairs

Key: Year and Number Last Census Roll (if given); Surname, Given Name; Date of Death (Year-Month-Day, if given); Age at Death; Sex; Tribe; Ward (Yes/No); Degree of Blood; Cause of Death; At Jurisdiction Where Enrolled (Yes/No); (If no – Where)

1936; 138; Bell, Charles (Floyd Jarlus); 1937-5-6; 2; m; Yes; Full; Bacillary dysentery; Yes

1936; 253; Billy, Nicey; 1937-12-27; 78; f; Yes; Full; Old age; Yes

1936; 292; Briscoe, Charles; 1937-3-12; 2/12; m; Yes; Full; Lobular pneumonia; Yes

DBE; None; Charlie, Billie; 1937-10-13; 16/365; m; Yes; Full; Unknown; Yes

1936; 324; Charlie, Fannie; 1937-11-23; 70; f; Yes; Full; Diabetes; Yes

1936; 333; Chickaway, Rufus; 1937-7-12; m; Yes; Full; Pul. tuberculosis; Yes

1936; 434; Dansby, Jake (Jacob); 1937-11-13; 68; m; Yes; Full; Lobular pneumonia; Yes

1936; 522; Farmer, Fannie Cooper; 1937-4-29; f; Yes; Full; Malaria; Yes

DBE;Omitted Farve, Frazene; 1937-6-13; 65; f; Yes; Full; Maniacal on p. C. exhaustion; Yes

1936; 643; Frazier, Fannie Venie; 1937-8-16; 58; f; Yes; Full; Carcinoma of stomach; Yes

1936; 636; Frazier, Wesley; 1937-12-27; 90; m; Yes; Full; Unknown; Yes

1936; 763; Hickman, Enoch; 1937-2-28; 64; m; Yes; Full; Lobular pneumonia; Yes

1936; 811; Isaac, Alice Marie; 1937-10-5; 1; f; Yes; Full; Whooping cough; Yes

1936; 906; Isaac (Jim), Dixon; 1937-12-9; 83; m; Yes; Full; Lobular pneumonia; Yes

1936; 875; Jefferson, Oscar; 1937-9-12; 35; m; Yes; Full; Fracture skull; Yes

1936; 923; Jim, Frances; 1937-3-20; 11/12; f; Yes; Full; Acute gastre[sic] enteritis; Yes

DBE; None; Johnson, Belfy; 1937-10-20; 4/12; f; Yes; Full; Whooping cough & pne.; Yes

1936; 1029; Johnson, Iva May; 1937-5-11; 1; f; Yes; Full; Fermentative diarrohoea[sic]; Yes

State **Mississippi** Reservation Choctaw Agency Agency or jurisdiction **Choctaw Agency, Philadelphia, Mississippi** Office of Indian Affairs

Key: Year and Number Last Census Roll (if given); Surname, Given Name; Date of Death (Year-Month-Day, if given); Age at Death; Sex; Tribe; Ward (Yes/No); Degree of Blood; Cause of Death; At Jurisdiction Where Enrolled (Yes/No); (If no – Where)

1936; 1151; Martin, Willie; 1937-12-25; 45; m; Yes; Full; Acute alcoholism; Yes

1936; 1181; McMillan, Oscar; 1937-3-14; 46; m; Yes; Full; Pul. tuberculosis; Yes

1936; 1238; Morris, Ida; 1937-2-19; 60; f; Yes; Full; Lobular pneumonia; Yes

1936; 1373; Smith, Mattie; 1937-12-5; 34; f; Yes; Full; Pul. tuberculosis; Yes

1936; 1589; Tubby, May Belle; 1937-12-5; 2; f; Yes; Full; Bronchial pneumonia; Yes

1936; 1724; Wesley, Sidney; 1937-5-5; 78; m; Yes; Full; Diabetes; Yes

1936; 1756; Williams, Lamar; 1937-4-24; 8/12; m; Yes; Full; Pneumonia; Yes

DBE; O.P.C;Willis, Henry; 1937-3-8; 104; m; Yes; Full; Old age; Yes

DBE; O.P.C;Willis, Mary; 1937-3-13; 83; f; Yes; Full; Lobular pneumonia; Yes

DBE; Willis, Roscoe; 1937-11-6; 2/12; m; Yes; Full; Lobular pneumonia; Yes

1936; 1880; Wilson, Martha Allen; 1937-8-16; 43; f; Yes; Full; Pul. tuberculosis; Yes

1936; 1891; York, Scott; 1937-8-25; 85; m; Yes; Full; Acute dilatation of heart; Yes

DEATHS OCCURRING BETWEEN JANUARY 1 and DECEMBER 31, 1936

1934; 25; Amos, Griffin; 1936-3-24; 49; m; Miss. Choctaw; Yes; Full; Unknown; Yes

1934; 70; Anderson (Farmer), Nancy; 1936-3-1; 51; f; Miss. Choctaw; Yes; Full; Tuberculosis; Yes

DBE; DBE; Anderson; Baby; 1936-2-11; 4 days; m; Miss. Choctaw; Yes; Full; Unknown; Yes

State **Mississippi** Reservation **Choctaw Agency** Agency or jurisdiction **Choctaw Agency, Philadelphia, Mississippi** Office of Indian Affairs

Key: Year and Number Last Census Roll (if given); Surname, Given Name; Date of Death (Year-Month-Day, if given); Age at Death; Sex; Tribe; Ward (Yes/No); Degree of Blood; Cause of Death; At Jurisdiction Where Enrolled (Yes/No); (If no – Where)

1934 Supple. 1827;	Anderson, Lola Mae; 1936-7-12; 2; f; Miss. Choctaw; Yes; Full; Unknown; Yes
Omitted on prev. cen.	Billie, Mary; 1936-7-11; 99; f; Miss. Choctaw; Yes; Full; Fractured femur; Yes
1934; 258;	Bull, Pink; 1936-4-15; 59; m; Miss. Choctaw; Yes; Full; Car accident; Yes
1934; 270;	Bull, George; 1936-4-13; 63; m; Miss. Choctaw; Yes; Full; Symptoms of pneumonia; Yes
1934; 386;	Comby, Rousella; 1936-3-2; 17; f; Miss. Choctaw; Yes; Full; Broncho pneumonia; Yes
1934; 387;	Comby, Maudell; 1936-3-14; 14; f; Miss. Choctaw; Yes; Full; Pulmonary tuberculosis; Yes
1934; 421;	Dan, Ida Rose; 1936-12-3; 15; f; Miss. Choctaw; Yes; Full; Tuberculosis; Yes
1934;1059;	Denson, Eliza Lewis; 1936-3-18; 22; f; Miss. Choctaw; Yes; Full; Tuberculosis; Yes
1934; 475;	Dixon, Jess; 1936-11-8; 59; m; Miss. Choctaw; Yes; Full; Atrophic Cirrhosis liver; Yes
1934; 723;	Hall, Eliza; 1936-11-4; 84; f; Miss. Choctaw; Yes; Full; Unknown; Yes
1934; 730;	Hickman, Johnkin; 1936-1-17; 43; m; Miss. Choctaw; Yes; Full; Gun shot fight Meningitis; Yes
1934; 791;	Isaac, Wilson; 1936-2-3; 83; m; Miss. Choctaw; Yes; Full; Brights decease[sic]; Yes
1934; 811;	Jackson, Betty; 1936-5-31; 61; f; Miss. Choctaw; Yes; Full; Unknown; Yes
1934; 877;	Jim, Amon; 1936-10-14; 60; m; Miss. Choctaw; Yes; Full; Acute Alcoholic Poisoning; Yes

State **Mississippi** Reservation Choctaw Agency Agency or jurisdiction **Choctaw Agency, Philadelphia, Mississippi** Office of Indian Affairs

Key: Year and Number Last Census Roll (if given); Surname, Given Name; Date of Death (Year-Month-Day, if given); Age at Death; Sex; Tribe; Ward (Yes/No); Degree of Blood; Cause of Death; At Jurisdiction Where Enrolled (Yes/No); (If no – Where)

1934; 870; Jim, Dora; 1936-7-26; f; Miss. Choctaw; Yes; Full; Cholera Morbuse[sic]; Yes

1935 Supple. 1852; Jim, Sallie Mae; 1936-6-21; f; Miss. Choctaw; Yes; Full; Lobular pneumonia; Yes

DBE; Joe, Jane; 1936-4-27; 8/12; f; Miss. Choctaw; Yes; Full; Unknown; Yes

1934; 933; Joe, Langley; 1936-3-10; 90; m; Miss. Choctaw; Yes; Full; Cardiac decease; Yes

1934;1393; John, Nancy Stoliby; 1936-11-15; 26; f; Miss. Choctaw; Yes; Full; Malaria; Yes

1934; 937; Polk, Dina Willis; 1936-10-21; 21; f; Miss. Choctaw; Yes; Full; Tuberculosis; Yes

1934; 959; John, Otis; 1936-8-7; 20; m; Miss. Choctaw; Yes; Full; Kidney infection; Yes

1935 Supple. 1858; Lewis, Kenneth; 1936-9-7; 1; m; Miss. Choctaw; Yes; Full; Malaria; Yes

1935 Supple. Mingo, Otho; 1936-6-30; 2; m; Miss. Choctaw; Yes; Full; Diarrhea Fermentative; Yes

1934;1207; Polk, George; 1936-12-23; 75; m; Miss. Choctaw; Yes; Full; Mitral insufficiency; Yes

DBE Sam, Jimpson; 1936-7-12; 6/12; m; Miss. Choctaw; Yes; Full; Unknown; Yes

1934;1251; Sam, Walter; 1936-11-23; 47; m; Miss. Choctaw; Yes; Full; Skull fracture; Yes

1934;1292; Simpson, Pauline; 1936-6-19; 21; f; Miss. Choctaw; Yes; Full; Kidney infection; Yes

1934;1295; Smith, Mandy; 1936-6-4; 51; f; Miss. Choctaw; Yes; Full; Apoplexy; Yes

State___**Mississippi**___Reservation_Choctaw Agency_ Agency or jurisdiction_**Choctaw Agency, Philadelphia, Mississippi**___Office of Indian Affairs

Key: Year and Number Last Census Roll (if given); Surname, Given Name; Date of Death (Year-Month-Day, if given); Age at Death; Sex; Tribe; Ward (Yes/No); Degree of Blood; Cause of Death; At Jurisdiction Where Enrolled (Yes/No); (If no – Where)

1935 Supple. 1868; Sockey, Harmon; 1936-3-1; 2; m; Miss. Choctaw; Yes; Full; Lobular pneumonia; Yes

DBE Solomon, Baby; 1936-5-2; 8/12; m; Miss. Choctaw; Yes; Full; Unknown; Yes

1934;1332; Solomon, Raymond; 1936-11-22; 43; m; Miss. Choctaw; Yes; Full; Contused wound on hd.; Yes

1935 Supple. 1870; Steve, Claud; 1936-8-24; 2; m; Miss. Choctaw; Yes; Full; Unknown; Yes

DBE Tubby, Joel Dodson; 1936-4-12; 10/12; m; Miss. Choctaw; Yes; Full; Pneumonia

DBE Tubby, Dixie Lee; 1936-3-7; 1/12; f; Miss. Choctaw; Yes; Full; Premature infant; Yes

1934;1566; Tookaloo, Frances; 1936-6-29; 74; f; Miss. Choctaw; Yes; Full; Carcinoma of stomach; Yes

1934;1576; Vaughn, Cooksie; 1936-1-26; 70; m; Miss. Choctaw; Yes; Full; Unknown; Yes

Omitt. Wesley, Tom; 1936-1-3; 21; m; Miss. Choctaw; Yes; Full; Cancer; Yes

1934;1645; Williamson, Mack; 1936-4-3; 62; m; Miss. Choctaw; Yes; Full; Acute Nephritis; Yes

DEATHS OCCURRING BETWEEN JANUARY 1 and DECEMBER 31, 1936 UNREPORTED

1934; 11; Allen, Willie; 1936-?-?; 9; m; Miss. Choctaw; Yes; Full; Unknown; Yes

1934; 375; Clemons, Munch; 1936-?-?; 54; m; Miss. Choctaw; Yes; Full; Unknown; Yes

State **Mississippi** Reservation **Choctaw Agency** Agency or jurisdiction **Choctaw Agency, Philadelphia, Mississippi** Office of Indian Affairs

Key: Year and Number Last Census Roll (if given); Surname, Given Name; Date of Death (Year-Month-Day, if given); Age at Death; Sex; Tribe; Ward (Yes/No); Degree of Blood; Cause of Death; At Jurisdiction Where Enrolled (Yes/No); (If no – Where)

1934; 1211; Polk, Lena; 1936-?-?; 57; f; Miss. Choctaw; Yes; Full; Unknown; Yes

DEATHS OCCURRING BETWEEN JANUARY 1, 1935 to January 1, 1936

1934; 263; Briscoe, Lucy; 1935-May 8; 47; f; Choctaw; Yes; Full; Tuberculosis; Yes

D.B.E. Chitto, Dewey Wesley; 1935-Aug 2; 1-5/12; m; Choctaw; Yes; Full; Diphtheria; Yes

1934; 360; Clemmons, Philip; 1935-Mar 2; 36; m; Choctaw; Yes; Full; Influenza; Yes

1934; 430; Davis, Anne; 1935-Mar 11; 16; f; Choctaw; Yes; Full; Eclampsia; Yes

D.B.E. Frazier, Maxine; 1935-Feb 9; 9/12; f; Choctaw; Yes; Full; Pneumonia; Yes

D.B.E. Gibson, Josie; 1935-Jan 16; 3/12; f; Choctaw; Yes; Full; Whooping cough; Yes

1934; 665; Gibson, Sophie; 1935-Mar 23; 21; f; Choctaw; Yes; Full; Post Partem infection; Yes

1935; ~~1882~~; Isaac, Dave, Jr; 1935-Aug 4; 1-3/12; m; Choctaw; Yes; Full; Illiocolitis[sic]; Yes   Suppl No. 10

1934; 760; Isaac, Steve; 1935-May 14; 67; m; Choctaw; Yes; Full; Nephritis chronic; Yes

1934; 831; Jackson, Mack (Mike); 1935-Dec 12; 40; m; Choctaw; Yes; Full; Malaria fever; Yes

D.B.E. Lewis, Allone[sic]; 1935-Oct 2; 1/365; f; Choctaw; Yes; Full; Myocarditis; Yes

1934; 1093; Martin, Thomas; 1935-Feb 27; f; m; Choctaw; Yes; Full; Not known; Yes

D.B.E. Sam, Rosaline; 1935-Aug 14; 2/365; f; Choctaw; Yes; Full; Shoulder presentation delivered by version; Yes

1934; 425; Tubby, Jim; 1935-Feb 3; 68; m; Choctaw; Yes; Full; Crushed by car; Yes

State   **Mississippi**   Reservation Choctaw Agency Agency or jurisdiction **Choctaw Agency, Philadelphia, Mississippi**   Office of Indian Affairs

Key: Year and Number Last Census Roll (if given); Surname, Given Name; Date of Death (Year-Month-Day, if given); Age at Death; Sex; Tribe; Ward (Yes/No); Degree of Blood; Cause of Death; At Jurisdiction Where Enrolled (Yes/No); (If no – Where)

1934; 695; Shumaker, Mary Mae; 1935-Dec 8; 23; f; Choctaw; Yes; Full; Tuberculosis, Pul; Yes

1934; 1498; Tubby, Jimpson; 1935-Sept 6; 110; m; Choctaw; Yes; Full; Unknown; Yes

1934; 1572; Vaughn, John; 1935-Oct 19; 84; m; Choctaw; Yes; Full; Pneumonia; Yes

1934; 1577; Vaughn, Susan; 1935-Apr 12; 68; f; Choctaw; Yes; Full; Carceroma[sic] of uterus and bladder; Yes

Omitted on pre- roll   Willis, Vernie; 1935-July 17; 23; f; Choctaw; Yes; Full; Malaria fever; Yes

Omitted on previous roll   Polk, Frank; 1934-Dec 25; 1-1/12; m; Choctaw; Yes; Full; Undetermined; Yes

1934; 511; Farmer, Thomas; 1934-Dec 7; 70; m; Choctaw; Yes; Full; Malaria fever; Yes

1934; 1680; Willis, Johnson; 1934-July 27; 70; m; Choctaw; Yes; Full; Myocarditis and chronic nephritis; Yes

DEATHS OCCURRING BETWEEN JANUARY 1 and DECEMBER 31, 1935
UNREPORTED

1934; 16; Allen, I. C; 1935-?-?; 22; m; Miss. Choctaw; Yes; Full; Unknown; Yes

1934 Supple. 1797;   Chitto, Dewey Davis; 1935-8-2; 3; m; Miss. Choctaw; Yes; Full; Diphtheria; Yes

1934; 938; John, Josh; 1935-5-4; 61; m; Miss. Choctaw; Yes; Full; Unknown; Yes

1934;1368; Steve, Berniece; 1935-?-?; 4; f; Miss. Choctaw; Yes; Full; Unknown; Yes

1934;1582; Vaughn, Howard; 1935-?-?; 35; m; Miss. Choctaw; Yes; Full; Unknown; Yes

State   **Mississippi**   Reservation **Choctaw Agency** Agency or jurisdiction **Choctaw Agency, Philadelphia, Mississippi** Office of Indian Affairs

Key: Year and Number Last Census Roll (if given); Surname, Given Name; Date of Death (Year-Month-Day, if given); Age at Death; Sex; Tribe; Ward (Yes/No); Degree of Blood; Cause of Death; At Jurisdiction Where Enrolled (Yes/No); (If no – Where)

1934;1646;   Williamson, Ida; 1935-?-?; 62; f; Miss. Choctaw; Yes; Full; Unknown; Yes

DEATHS OCCURRING BETWEEN APRIL 1 TO DECEMBER 31, 1934

1934; 266; Briscoe, John Claud; 1934-4-2; 3 yrs; m; Choctaw; Yes; F; Mitral insufficiency; Yes
1934; 276; Campbell, Jimmie; 1934-6-10; 3 ½ mo; m; Choctaw; Yes; F; Innation[sic]; Yes
       275; Campbell, Venie; 1934-5-8; 17 yrs; f; Choctaw; Yes; F; Tuberculosis; Yes
Died before enroll.   Charlie, Baby; 1934-4-27; S.B; m; Choctaw; Yes; F; Stillborn; Yes
       330; Chickaway, Isabel; 1934-11-16; 72 yrs; f; Choctaw; Yes; F; Mitral insufficiency; Yes
       423; Dansby, Jennie; 1934-7-23; 52 yrs; f; Choctaw; Yes; F; Carcinoma of uterus; Yes
       630; Frazier, Eliza; 1934-6-8; 79 yrs; f; Choctaw; Yes; F; Malaria; Yes
       755; Hickman, Mary; 1934-8-25; 91 yrs; f; Choctaw; Yes; F; Cerebral Hemorrhages; Yes
       711; Henry, Joy; 1934-7-5; 1-7/12; f; Choctaw; Yes; F; Pneumonia; Yes
       801; Isaac, Etherine or Nansey; 1934-8-13; 2-5/12; f; Choctaw; Yes; F; Pneumonia; Yes   See letter 4/30/36
       770; Isaac, Hickman; 1934-8-18; 26 yrs; m; Choctaw; Yes; F; External violence; Yes
       796; Isaac, Lawrence; 1934-8-25; 1-2/12; m; Choctaw; Yes; F; Pneumonia; Yes
       763; Isaac, Odie Mae; 1934-6-25; 18 yrs; f; Choctaw; Yes; F; Tuberculosis; Yes
       952; John, Mercy Lee; 1934-6-19; 4 yrs; f; Choctaw; Yes; F; Whooping cough; Yes

State **Mississippi** Reservation Choctaw Agency Agency or jurisdiction **Choctaw Agency, Philadelphia, Mississippi** Office of Indian Affairs

Key: Year and Number Last Census Roll (if given); Surname, Given Name; Date of Death (Year-Month-Day, if given); Age at Death; Sex; Tribe; Ward (Yes/No); Degree of Blood; Cause of Death; At Jurisdiction Where Enrolled (Yes/No); (If no – Where)

976; Johnson, Celia; 1934-8-5; 71 yrs; f; Choctaw; Yes; F; Malaria; Yes

Died before enroll. Lewis, Billy; 1934-9-28; 10 yrs; m; Choctaw; Yes; F; Malaria; Yes

1070; Lewis, Mollie; 1934-6-21; 37 yrs; f; Choctaw; Yes; F; Tuberculosis; Yes

1078; Lewis, Rosie Mae; 1934-9-25; 1½ yrs; f; Choctaw; Yes; F; Whooping cough; Yes

1092; Martin, Nancy; 1934-6-4; 26 yrs; f; Choctaw; Yes; F; Tuberculosis; Yes

Died before enroll. Mingo, Betty; 1934-7-26; 1 yr; f Choctaw; Yes; F; Pneumonia; Yes

Died before enroll. Sam, Griffin; 1034-9-16; 7/12; m; Choctaw; Yes; F; Malaria; Yes

1934; 1358; Steve, Murphy; 1934-12-9; 60 yrs; m; Choctaw; Yes; F; Tuberculosis; Yes

Died before enroll. Starr, Allie Lou; 1934-8-9; 11/12; f; Choctaw; Yes; F; Gastroenteritis; Yes

1431; Thompson, Daniel; 1934-7-18; 2 yrs; m; Choctaw; Yes; F; Pneumonia; Yes

Died before enroll. Tubby, Baby; 1934-4-27; 1 hr; f; Choctaw; Yes; F; Prematurity; Yes

Died before enroll. Tubby, Levi; 1934-4-22; 1 day; m; Choctaw; Yes; F; Prematurity; Yes

Died before enroll. Tubby, Mike; 1934-4-23; 2 day; m; Choctaw; Yes; F; Prematurity; Yes

Died before enroll. Vaughn, Luke; 1934-4-2; m; Choctaw; Yes; F; Pneumonia; Yes

Died before enroll. Williams, Rufus; 1934-7-10; 5/12; m; Choctaw; Yes; F; Innation; Yes

DEATHS OCCURRING BETWEEN JANUARY 1 and DECEMBER 31, 1934 UNREPORTED

State __Mississippi__ Reservation __Choctaw Agency__ Agency or jurisdiction __Choctaw Agency, Philadelphia, Mississippi__ Office of Indian Affairs

Key: Year and Number Last Census Roll (if given); Surname, Given Name; Date of Death (Year-Month-Day, if given); Age at Death; Sex; Tribe; Ward (Yes/No); Degree of Blood; Cause of Death; At Jurisdiction Where Enrolled (Yes/No); (If no – Where)

1934; 123; Bell, Boston; 1934-?-?; 52; m; Miss. Choctaw; Yes; Full; Unknown; Yes

1934; 363; Clemons, Margie; 1934-?-?; 9; f; Miss. Choctaw; Yes; Full; Unknown; Yes

1934; 443; Davis, Ada Frances; 1934-?-?; 14; F; Miss. Choctaw; Yes; Full; Unknown; Yes

1934; 491; Dixon, Kanis; 1934-?-?; 45; m; Miss. Choctaw; Yes; Full; Suicide; Yes

1934; 934; Denson, Joe; 1934-?-?; 83; m; Miss. Choctaw; Yes; Full; Unknown; Yes

1934;1449; Lewis, Lum Billy; 1934-?-?; 11; m; Miss. Choctaw; Yes; Full; Malaria; Yes

1934;1591; Waiter, Minnie; 1934-?-?; 6; f; Miss. Choctaw; Yes; Full; Pulmonary Tuberculosis; Yes

1934;1631; Williams, Rufus; 1934-7-10; 3; m; Miss. Choctaw; Yes; Full; Lack of inamition[sic]; Yes

1934;1759; Stoliby (Wilson), Martha; 1934-12-20; 89; f; Miss. Choctaw; Yes; Full; Unknown; Yes

[Note: The following Years listed for the Last Census Roll are all incorrect. This is the way the original roll appears.]

DEATHS OCCURRING BETWEEN JANUARY 1 and DECEMBER 31, 1933 UNREPORTED

1934; 115; Bell, Jim; 1933-?-?; 67; m; Miss. Choctaw; Yes; Full; Unknown; Yes

1934; 738; Hickman, Eliza; 1933-?-?; 23; f; Miss. Choctaw; Yes; Full; Unknown; Yes

State **Mississippi** Reservation Choctaw Agency Agency or jurisdiction **Choctaw Agency, Philadelphia, Mississippi** Office of Indian Affairs

Key: Year and Number Last Census Roll (if given); Surname, Given Name; Date of Death (Year-Month-Day, if given); Age at Death; Sex; Tribe; Ward (Yes/No); Degree of Blood; Cause of Death; At Jurisdiction Where Enrolled (Yes/No); (If no – Where)

1934;1005; Johnson, Marvin; 1933-?-?; 6; m; Miss. Choctaw; Yes; Full; Unknown; Yes

1934;1011; King, John W; 1933-6-12; 77; m; Miss. Choctaw; Yes; Full; Atrophic Cirrhosis; Yes

DEATHS OCCURRING BETWEEN JANUARY 1 and DECEMBER 31, 1932 UNREPORTED

1934; 231; Billy, Will, Jr; 1932-?-?; 10; m; Miss. Choctaw; Yes; Full; Unknown; Yes

1934; 197; Billy, Maurice; 1932-?-?; 11; m; Miss. Choctaw; Yes; Full; Unknown; Yes

1934; 609; Forbes, Sallie; 1932-?-?; 72; f; Miss. Choctaw; Yes; Full; Unknown; Yes

1934; 626; Box, Sam Davis; 1932-?-?; 14; m; Miss. Choctaw; Yes; Full; Unknown; Yes

1934; 634; Frazier, A. B; 1932-?-?; 10; m; Miss. Choctaw; Yes; Full; Unknown; Yes

1934; 911; Joe, Nicholas; 1932-?-?; 47; m; Miss. Choctaw; Yes; Full; Unknown; Yes

1934;1421; Thompson, Otis; 1932-?-?; 13; m; Miss. Choctaw; Yes; Full; Unknown; Yes

1934;1699; Willis, Adaline; 1932-?-?; 65; f; Miss. Choctaw; Yes; Full; Unknown; Yes

1934;1773; Wishork, Sampson; 1932-?-?; 73; m; Miss. Choctaw; Yes; Full; Unknown; Yes

TRANSFER or ADJUSTMENT ROLL -

as of JANUARY 1, 1939

Choctaw Indian Agency, Mississippi.

Census of the **Choctaw Indian Agency** reservation of the _____ jurisdiction, as of **January 1, 1939**, 19__, taken by **Harvey K. Meyer**, Superintendent.   **Transfer or Adjustment Roll**

KEY; Number; Surname, Given Name; Sex; Age at Last Birthday; Tribe; Degree of Blood; Marital Status; Relationship to Head of Family; At Jurisdiction Where Enrolled (Yes/No)

ADDED TO FEMALES ON ACCOUNT OF ERROR IN SEX

374-37; Clemons, Leonard Rose; f; 6; Miss. Choctaw; F; S; Daughter; Yes

SUBTRACTED FROM MALES ON ACCOUNT OF ERROR IN SEX

374-37; Clemons, Leonard; m; 6; Miss. Choctaw; F; S; Son; Yes

INDIANS RETURNING TO JURISDICTION WHERE ENROLLED

1803-37; Isaac, William; m; 26; Miss. Choctaw; F; S; Head; Yes
1804-37; Isaac, Nannie; f; 22; Miss. Choctaw; F; S; Sister; Yes
1805-37; Isaac, Eunice; f; 19; Miss. Choctaw; S; Sister; Yes
1806-37; Isaac, Rose; f; 15; Miss. Choctaw; F; S; Sister; Yes
All step-children of Gus Willis #1799-37

1672-37; Tookaloo, Nathan; m; 25; Miss. Choctaw; F; S; Head; Yes
1674-37; Tookaloo, Alice; f; 14; Miss. Choctaw; F; S; Sister; Yes
1675-37; Tookaloo, Sarah; f; 13; Miss. Choctaw; F; S; Sister; Yes

MARRIAGES -

1936 - 1938

Choctaw Indian Agency, Mississippi.

Census of the _____ reservation of the **Choctaw Indian Agency** jurisdiction, as of _____, 19__, taken by **A. C. Hector**, Superintendent.   Marriages

KEY; 1934 Census Number; Surname, Given Name; Sex; Age at Last Birthday; Tribe; Degree of Blood; Marital Status; Relationship to Head of Family; At Jurisdiction Where Enrolled (Yes/No); At Another Jurisdiction; Post Office, County, State (if given); Ward (Yes/No)

Marriages as of January 1, 1936

   1; Alex, Cooper; m; 25; Choctaw; F; M; Head; Yes; Yes
236; Alex, Sallie Mae B; f; 18; Choctaw; F; M; Wife; Yes

  18; Allen, J. C; m; 21; Choctaw; F; M; Head; Yes; Yes
1691; Allen, Mattie Willis; f; 18; Choctaw; F; M; Wife; Yes; Yes

1323; Charley, Beaman; m; 21; Choctaw; F; M; Head; Yes; Yes
1000; Charley, Sudie Johnson; f; 16; Choctaw; F; M; Wife; Yes; Yes

428; Davis, Hobbie; m; 30; Choctaw; F; M; Head; Yes; Yes
1108; Davis, Mary McMillan; f; 23; Choctaw; F; M; Wife; Yes; Yes

1082; Farmer, Henry; m; 24; Choctaw; F; M; Head; Yes; Yes
409; Farmer, Fannie Cooper; f; 18; Choctaw; F; M; Wife; Yes; Yes

1047; Jefferson, Newt; m; 20; Choctaw; F; M; Head; Yes; Yes
406; Jefferson, Leona Nickey Cooper; f; 28; Choctaw; F; M; Wife; Yes; Yes

1482; Jim (Tubby), Vernon; m; 24; Choctaw; F; M; Head; Yes; Yes
1725; Jim, Ance (Anna) Willis; f; 18; Choctaw; F; M; Wife; Yes; Yes

1007; Johnson, Otho; m; 20; Choctaw; F; M; Head; Yes; Yes
1324; Johnson, Juanita Charley; f; 16; Choctaw; F; M; Wife; Yes; Yes

1069; Lewis, Albert; m; 42; Choctaw; F; M; Head; Yes; Yes
  82; Lewis, Emma Bell; f; 24; Choctaw; F; M; Wife; Yes; Yes

1109; McMillan, Willie; m; 20; Choctaw; F; M; Head; Yes; Yes
1672; McMillan, Mallie (Mollie) Willis; f; 24; Choctaw; F; M; Wife; Yes; Yes

Census of the_____reservation of the **Choctaw Indian Agency** jurisdiction, as of_____, 19__, taken by **A. C. Hector**, Superintendent.   Marriages

KEY; 1934 Census Number; Surname, Given Name; Sex; Age at Last Birthday; Tribe; Degree of Blood; Marital Status; Relationship to Head of Family; At Jurisdiction Where Enrolled (Yes/No); At Another Jurisdiction; Post Office, County, State (if given); Ward (Yes/No)

1228;   Robinson, Jimmie Teach; m; 22; Choctaw; F; M; Head; Yes; Yes
  87;   Robinson, Ronie Bell; f; 19; Choctaw; F; M; Wife; Yes; Yes

1403;   Thomas, Riley; m; 31; Choctaw; F; M; Head; Yes; Yes
1189;   Thomas, Nona (Zona) Nickey; f; 19; Choctaw; F; M; Wife; Yes; Yes

1312;   Sockey, Bennett; m; 28; Choctaw; F; M; Head; Yes; Yes
1768;   Sockey, Alphia Wishork; f; 34; Choctaw; F; M; Wife; Yes; Yes

1622;   Wickson, Jim; m; 28; Choctaw; F; M; Head; Yes; Yes
1276;   Wickson, Susan Davis Shoemaker; f; 36; Choctaw; F; M; Wife; Yes; Yes

Census of the **Choctaw Indian Agency** reservation of the **Choctaw** jurisdiction, as of _____, 19__, taken by _____, Superintendent.

KEY; Last Census Number; Surname, Given Name; Sex; Age at Last Birthday; Tribe; Degree of Blood; Marital Status; Relationship to Head of Family; At Jurisdiction Where Enrolled (Yes/No); At Another Jurisdiction; Post Office, County, State (if given); Ward (Yes/No)

MARRIAGES - 1937

1507; Thompson, Cephus; m; 48; Choctaw; F; M; Head; Yes; Yes
 896; Jim, Lucy; f; 53; Choctaw; F; M; Wife; Yes; Yes

1623; Tubby, Lefus; m; 45; Choctaw; F; M; Head; Yes; Yes
 897; Jim, Opal; f; 18; Choctaw; F; M; Wife; Yes; Yes

1634; Tubby, Lewis; m; 21; Choctaw; F; M; Head; Yes; Yes
1116; Bell, Effie; f; 19; Choctaw; F; M; Wife; Yes; Yes

1813; Willis, Collins; m; 15; Choctaw; F; M; Head; Yes; Yes
1216; Morris, Ora; f; 17; Choctaw; F; M; Wife; Yes; Yes

1881; Wilson, Sammie; m; 17; Choctaw; F; M; Head; Yes; Yes
 264; Billy, Rose; f; 19; Choctaw; F; M; Wife; Yes; Yes

Census of the **Mississippi Choctaws** reservation of the **Choctaw Indian Agency** jurisdiction, as of **January 1**, 19**39**, taken by **Harvey K. Meyer**, Superintendent.

KEY: Census Number; Surname, Given Name; Sex; Age at Last Birthday; Tribe; Degree of Blood; Marital Status; Relationship to Head of Family; At Jurisdiction Where Enrolled (Yes/No); At Another Jurisdiction; Post Office, County, State (if given); Ward (Yes/No)

MARRIAGES AS OF JANUARY 1, 1939

61-38; Amos, Willis; m; [blank]; Miss. Choctaw; F; Head[sic]; [blank]; Yes   Omitted on previous census previous census

155-37; Amos, Minnie Bell; f; 18; Miss. Choctaw F; M; Wife; Yes Daughter of Lish Bell #151-37

80-37; Anderson, Houston; m; 18; Miss. Choctaw F; M; Head; Yes Father Oliver Anderson #77-37

1375-37; Anderson, Marceline Lewis; f; 15; Miss. Choctaw F; M; Wife; Yes   Niece of Clay Smith #1372-37

179-37; Bell, Frank; m; 25; Miss. Choctaw F; M; Head; Yes Son of Thompson Bell #177-37

1107-37; Bell, Ivena Lewis; f; 18; Miss. Choctaw F; M; Wife; Yes Daughter of Albert Lewis, No. 1104-37

296-37; Briscoe, Tom; m; 38; Miss. Choctaw F; M; Head; Yes

1500-37; Briscoe, Sallie Thomas; f; 38; Miss. Choctaw F; M; Wife; Yes Widow of Wilmon Thomas #1499-37. Now dead.

302-37; Campbell, Wiley; m; 38; Miss. Choctaw F; M; Head; Yes

1002-37; Campbell, Bilsy John; f; 41; Miss. Choctaw F; M; Wife; Yes

533-37; Farmer, Bill; m; 23; Miss. Choctaw; F; M; Head; Yes Son of Ishman & Suela Farmer #529 & 530-37

247-37; Farmer, Mamie Willis (Billy); f; 17; Miss. Choctaw; F; M; Wife; Yes Dau of Zelma Willis Billy #244-37 now married to Lewis Billy #243-37

535-37; Farmer, Mose; m; 39; Miss. Choctaw; F; M; Head; Yes Former wife Lottie Chickaway #536 dead.

245-37; Farmer, Clennis Willis; f; 19; Miss. Choctaw; F; M; Wife; Yes

Census of the **Mississippi Choctaws** reservation of the **Choctaw Indian Agency** jurisdiction, as of **January 1**, 19**39**, taken by **Harvey K. Meyer**, Superintendent.

KEY; Census Number; Surname, Given Name; Sex; Age at Last Birthday; Tribe; Degree of Blood; Marital Status; Relationship to Head of Family; At Jurisdiction Where Enrolled (Yes/No); At Another Jurisdiction; Post Office, County, State (if given); Ward (Yes/No)

      Dau. of Zelma Willis Billy #244-37 now wife of Lewis Billy #243-37

531-37; Farmer, Marshall; m; 34; Miss. Choctaw; F; M; Head; Yes Son of Ishman & Suela Farmer #529 & 530-37

1381-37; Farmer, Mary Lou Farve; f; 22; Miss. Choctaw; F; M; Wife; Yes Dau. of Mandy Smith #1295-34 now dead.

846-37; Jackson, Carson; m; 21; Miss. Choctaw; F; M; Head; Yes Son of Lena Jackson #843-37

1702-37; Jackson, Amy Wallace; f; 24; Miss. Choctaw; F; M; Wife; Yes Dau. of Comby & Betty Dixon Wallace #1700 & 1701-37.

987-37; Joe, Auston; m; 25; Miss. Choctaw; F; M; Had; Yes Son of Nicholas Joe #911-34 now dead.

970-37; Joe, Alma or Ole; f; 29; Miss. Choctaw; F; M; Wife; Yes Dau. of Boston & Lela Bell - 123-34 & 95-37. Shown as wife of Henry Joe on 1937 Census.

969-37; Joe, Henry; m; 21; Miss. Choctaw; F; M; Head; Yes Son of Nicholas & Ella Joe #911-34 & 912-34

96-37; Joe, Effie Bell; f; 27; Miss. Choctaw; F; M; Wife; Yes Dau. of Boston & Lela Bell #123-34 & 95-37. Should have been shown as wife of Henry Joe on 1937 Census.

1122-37; Lewis, Johnnie; m; 41; Miss. Choctaw; F; M; Head; Yes

1741-37; Lewis, Mamie Smith Williams; 40; Miss. Choctaw; F; M; Wife; Yes Former wife of Lewis Williams #1740-37 now dead.

1603-37; Mitch, Divon; m; 35; Miss. Choctaw; F; M; Head; Yes

1602-37; Mitch, Irene Tubby; f; 15; Miss. Choctaw; F; M; Wife; Yes Dau. of Frances Tubby #1601-37

Census of the **Mississippi Choctaws** reservation of the **Choctaw Indian Agency** jurisdiction, as of **January 1**, 19__39__, taken by **Harvey K. Meyer**, Superintendent.

KEY; Census Number; Surname, Given Name; Sex; Age at Last Birthday; Tribe; Degree of Blood; Marital Status; Relationship to Head of Family; At Jurisdiction Where Enrolled (Yes/No); At Another Jurisdiction; Post Office, County, State (if given); Ward (Yes/No)

1211-37; Mitch, Wilson; m; 33; Miss. Choctaw; F; M; Head; Yes
    Son of Sarah Mitch #1209-37.
1601-37; Mitch, Frances Tubby; f; 39; Miss. Choctaw; F; M; Wife; Yes

1290-37; Polk, Cornelia; m; 29; Miss. Choctaw; F; M; Head; Yes
    Son of Tom Polk #1289-37.
1176-37; Polk, Emma McMillan; f; 24; Miss. Choctaw; F; M; Wife; Yes
    Dau. of Sorsby McMillan #1175-37.

1286-37; Polk, Josie; m; 58; Miss. Choctaw; F; M; Head; Yes
    Former husband of Lena Polk #1211-34 now dead
334-37; Polk, Bessie Chickaway; f; 34; Miss. Choctaw; F; M; Wife; Yes   Former wife of Rufus Chickaway #333-37 now dead.

1339-37; Sam, Tom; m; 20 Miss. Choctaw; F; M; Head; Yes
    Son of Walter Sam #1252-34 now dead.
6-37; Sam, Nellie Billy; f; 18; Miss. Choctaw; F; M; Wife; Yes
    Dau. of Lillie Billy #5-37.

1501-37; Thomas, Woodrow; m; 20; Miss. Choctaw; F; M; Head; Yes
    Son of Wilmon & Sallie Thomas #1499 & 1500-37.
542-37; Thomas, Corine Farmer; f; 18; Miss. Choctaw; F; M; Wife; Yes   Dau. of Silmon & Venie Farmer #539 & 540-37.

1507-37; Thompson, Cephus; m; 49; Miss. Choctaw; F; M; Head; Yes
    NOTE: Shown married on 1937 census.
896-37; Thompson, Lucy Jim; f; 54; Miss. Choctaw; F; M; Wife; Yes
    Former wife of Amon Jim #877-34 now dead.

1519-37; Thompson, Jim; m; 19; Miss. Choctaw; F; M; Head; Yes
    Son of Mose & Jean Thompson #1517 & 1518-37.
39-37; Thompson, Mollie Vaughn; f; 26; Miss. Choctaw; F; M; Wife; Yes   Sister of Lena Sallie Amos 33-37.

Census of the **Mississippi Choctaws** reservation of the **Choctaw Indian Agency** jurisdiction, as of **January 1**, 19**39**, taken by **Harvey K. Meyer**, Superintendent.

KEY; Census Number; Surname, Given Name; Sex; Age at Last Birthday; Tribe; Degree of Blood; Marital Status; Relationship to Head of Family; At Jurisdiction Where Enrolled (Yes/No); At Another Jurisdiction; Post Office, County, State (if given); Ward (Yes/No)

1820-37; Willis, Dennis; m; 35; Miss. Choctaw; F; M; Head; Yes
Son of Jim & Louisa Willis #1817 & 1818-37.

704-37; Willis, Annie Gipson; f; 30; Miss. Choctaw; F; M; Wife; Yes
Dau. of Steve & Jennie Gipson #700 & 701-37.

1881-38; Wilson, Sammie; m; 17; Miss. Choctaw; F; M; Head; Yes
Shown married to Rose Billy. An error should have been.

1872-37; Wilson, Silmon; m; 19; Miss. Choctaw; F; M; Head; Yes
Son of John & Eva Barnett Wilson #1870 & 1871-37.

264-37; Wilson, Rose Billy; f; 20; Miss. Choctaw; F; M; Wife; Yes
Dau. of Will & Alice Billy #261- 262-37.

1903-37; York, Baxter; m; 32; Miss. Choctaw; F; M; Head; Yes
Son of Necie York #1902-37.

1338-37; York, Grace Sam; f; 22; Miss. Choctaw; F; M; Wife; Yes
Dau. of Walter Sam #1252-34, now dead.

1905-37; York, Gassler; m; 27; Miss. Choctaw; F; M; Head; Yes
Son of Necie York #1902-37.

1005-37; York, Mable John; f; 19; Miss. Choctaw; F; M; Wife; Yes
Dau. of Bilsy John #1002-37.

Index

ALEX
- Cooper 3,81,91,175,185,319
- Herbert......................47,131,195
- Mary Rose 185
- Missie..................................3,81,185
- Nelson.................................3,81,185
- Rosemary...............................175
- Sallie Mae...............................299
- Sallie Mae B.......................81,319
- Sally Mae Cooper 185
- Theresa.............................185,286

ALLEN
- Annie Mae........................3,81,185
- Bessie................................3,81,186
- Bob 3,81,186
- Herbert..3,81
- Houston...................................186
- Hubbard (Herbert)................186
- Hubert (Wilbert)....................186
- Huston.....................................3,81
- I C.......................................3,81,185,308
- J C................3,81,160,175,185,319
- Jim 3,81,185
- Joseph...............................3,82,186
- Lacey.................................3,82,186
- Maggie..............................3,81,186
- Manda................................3,81,185
- Mattie Willis...............81,185,319
- Nell....................................3,81,186
- R G....................................3,81,185,301
- Ralph................................186,286
- Salem (Sulum).......................186
- Silbert... 3
- Stella Virginia 175,185
- Sulum..3,81
- Wilbert.......................................81
- Will...3,82
- William....................................185
- Willie......................3,81,186,306
- Willis.................................3,81,186

AMOS
- Albert...............................4,82,187
- Ann....................................4,82,187
- Beauty...................................4,82
- Bonnie....................................... 4
- Floyd................................4,82,186
- Fulton..............................4,82,186
- Griffin......................4,82,186,303
- John..................................4,82,187
- Julia..................................4,82,186
- Lampkin..........................4,82,187
- Land................................4,82
- Lena (Sallie) 186
- Lena Sallie...............................324
- Lilly..82
- Lonie... 4
- Martha Laner.........................294
- Minnie Bell..............................322
- Mollie (Beauty)......................186
- Mose 4,82,186
- Nellie..293
- Rose Jackson...........................187
- Ruth 4,82,187
- Sallie 4,82
- Sebbie...............................4,82,187
- Tubby..293
- Wagoner..................................293
- Willie Lester (Land)..............187
- Willis..322

ANDERSON
- Abel 5,84,187
- Amy 5,83,188
- Baby 188,286,303
- Belthie Johnson 188
- Berniece...................................187
- Bob 4,82,187
- Burnice................................4,83
- Chuty...4
- Cleveland................................290
- Ella 4,82,187
- Ella Mae 299
- Ella Mae Farmer....................187
- Emma Farmer........................187
- Evan...5
- Frances 189
- Frances B..............................5,83
- Fronie Mae..............................294
- Grace................................5,83,188
- Hinton 5,83,188
- Houston................5,83,188,322

Ike 5,83,188
Irvin 83,188
A J 4,83,187
J C 5,83,188
John 4,175,188
John Lish 299
Josephine 4,83,187
Judie (Trudie) 187
Juohn 83
Kate 5,83,188
Lavenia King 188
Lillie Mae 83,189
Lola Mae 175,188,304
Lonie 5,83,189
Lonnie 188
Lucille 5,84,188
Marceline Lewis 322
Mary 294
Mattie 5,83,188
Mervia 290
Mollie Thomas 188
Nancy 5,84,187
Oliver 5,83,188,322
Ollie 5,83,188
Phillip 5,83,188
Ray 83
Roy 5,189
Sallie 5,83,188
Sallie Mae 4,83,187
Sarah Ann 187,286
Thelma 5,83
Thelma Ben 188
Tonnie 83,167
Trudie 83
Vada 5,83
ANDERSON (FARMER), Nancy
.... 303
AULKER
Leona Thomas 189
Pete 189
BELL
Alice 7,86,189
Aline 190
Allie Mae 193,287
Amon 7,86,189

Ardie 240
Baby 294,300
Basin 8,87,192
Bell (Lena Mingo) 193
Bessie Susie 191
Bill 7,86,191
Bob 8,87,175,189,223
Bobby Sam 87,189
Bon 87
Bonnie K 7,85,193
Boston 7,86,189,311,323
Burton 32,114,222
Chalmers (Junus) 190
Charles 294,302
Christine 192
Claud 175,190,294,299
Cleddie 7,85,192
Cornelius 8,86,190
Dorothy 290,294
Edith Rae 240,288
Edmond 6,85,190
Edna 190
Effie 6,7,84,86,189,240,321
Ellen 7,85,193
Emma 6,7,84,86,189
Emmett 8,86,189
Eva 6,84,192
Evaline 175,189
Evan 190
Evans 6,85
Fannie 193,282,284
Fanny 168
Floyd 175
Floyd F 118
Floyd Jarlus 191
Frank 322
Frank K 7,85,193
Franklin 7,85,193
Gaston 8,87,191
Gene D 8,87,192
Geneva 8,76,87,189
George 6,85,190
Gibson 175
Gipson 7,85,191
Gipson, Jr 7,85

Index

Hattie 6,84,192
Henry 7,32,86,114,193,222,286
Henry Sam 191
Herbert H 6,85,193
Hester 6,85,191
Homer 6,85,190
Houston 8,87,191
Hugh 6,84,191
Ida Mae 290
Idie 6,84
Inez 191,286
Isa 191
Isaac Wampler 87
Ivena Lewis 322
James 237
James Cook 6,85
Jay 8,87,192
Jessie 190
Jim 7,8,86,191,311
Joe 86,175,191
John 6,7,8,84,86,189,190,192
Josephine 294
Junus 6,84,175
Lela 7,86,189,323
Lena 6,85
Lena Mingo 299
Leona 190
Less C 8,87,192
Levi 190
Lillian 6,84,192
Lillie Willis 192
Lilly Amos 191
Lish 8,86,87,192,322
Lucy 7,85,191
Lula 8,87,192
Lynch (Gipson, Jr) 191
Mack 6,85,192
Maggie 8,87,192
Mamie 6,84,191
Mandy 8,76,85,191
Marshall 8,86,190
Martha 8,86,192
Mary Jane 84
Mattie Henry 193
Minnie 6,8,85,87,190,192

Nancy Jackson 190
Nancy L 6,85,190
Naomi 290
Naomi Ruth 8,87
Nellie (Pollie Ann) 191
Nellie (Zoe) 191
Nicholas 7,85,175,192
Odie (Isaac Wampler) 192
Ola 6,7,84,86,192
Polly Ann 7,86
Robert Lee 290
Ronie 6,85,138
Rose (Naomi Ruth) 189
Rosenbaum 190,286
Ruby 7,85,193
Sadie 8,87
Sallie 6,7,84,86,192,240
Sophia 7,86
Sudie (Sadie) 189
Susan 192,286
Susie 7,86
Thompson 7,85,193,322
Tom 7,8,76,77,86,87,175,
.... 190,193
Tom Comby, Jr 175
Tom Mack 191
Tony 9,76,87,168,193
Will Rogers 175,193
Willie 6,8,85,86,190,192
Winnie 6,84,190
Woods 6,85,190
Zoe 175
BELL (TUBBY), Joe 191
BEN
    Annie Laura 9,87,194
    Baby 290
    Bobby 294
    Brantley Arthur 194,287
    Charlie 9,88,168,193
    Chester 88,194
    Colleen Isaac 194
    Eileene 194,287
    Elle 9
    Ellen 88,195
    Emeline 9,88,193

Fannie Lou 9,88,194
Gladys 9,88,194
Harrison 168,194,282,284
Helen Marie 9,88,195
Henry Ford 9,88,194
Hubert 9,88,194
James Charles 168,282,284
Jim 10,88,193
Jimpson 9,88,194
John 290
Lessie 9
Lessie Isaac 88,194
Lester 294
Lilly May 10,88
Lorene McMillian 194
Lula 9,88,194
Mattie Lou 9,87,194
Mike 193
Monroe 10,88,194
Nannie Mae 9,87,194
Neva 9,87,194
Olin 9,87,168,194
Opal Grace 9,88,193
Otho 9,88,194
Robert (James Clark) 193
Ruben 290
Rufus 62,149,194,300
Tom 9,88,194
Tom Comby, Jr 195
Wilson 9,70,88,159,194,275
Wyatt 9,88,195,299
BILLIE
    Baby 290
    Clement 300
    Collins 294
    Lewis 294
    Marguarite 294
    Mary 196,304
    Sally Ruth 290
BILLY
    Alice 11,90,197,325
    Annie 11,90,196
    Beaman 10,89,198,287
    Belaria 11,90
    Betty Jean 10,89,198

Cassie 12,91
Charlie 11,90,197
Cicero 90
Cicero L 11,194
Clarence 99
Clement 195
Clemon 47,132
Clennie 11,90
Clennis Willis 196
Cornelia Stephens 195
Duley 12,91,197
Earl 10,76,77,89,195
Emma 35,118,230
Eva (Cassie) 197
Finis (Beaman) 198
Frank 11,90,196
Gipson 11,90,195
Greer 11,90,195
Heniretta Chitto 196
Horace 10,89,198
Ike 10,11,89,90,195
Irene 11,90,197
James 10,89,197
Jennie 10
Jennie C 89,195
Jessie 10,89,198
Jim 12,91,185
Joe 11,90,197
John 89,195
John Cephus 195,281
Johnson 11,90,195
Jordan 11,90
Kate 10,89,195
Lee 11,90,196
Leona 10,89
Leona Sam 195
Lewis 11,90,196,322
Lillie 11,91,185,195,287,324
Lina 12,91,197
Lorene 11,90
Lorraine 197,287
Lum 10,89,196
Mamie 11,90,196
Marchie 11,90,197
Mary 89

330

Index

Mary Lou 12,91,185
Maude 11,90
Maurice 10,89,198,312
Melton 10,89,198
Minnie 10,89,196
Nellie 12,91,185
Nicey 196,302
Nicy 10,89
Paul 12,91,185
Peter Cooper 12,91
Phillip 11,90
Reta 197,287
Richard 12,91,168,197
Robert 10,89,197
Robert Lee 196,287
Rosaulee 89,197
Rose 11,90,197,321,325
Sallie 10
Sallie Mae 11,91
Sallie Stoliby 89,196
Sarah 12,91,197
Sienna 12,91,197
Tom 10,89,196
Tommy Jean 90,197
Velaria 195
Wade 12,91,197
Will 10,11,89,90,197,325
Will, Jr 11,90,197,312
William 11,90,197
Williston 10,89,198
Wilson 11,90,168,197,282,284
Woodrow (Wilson) 195
Zelma 11,90,196
Zelma Willis 322,323
BOB, Simon 12,91,198
BOX
   Bathie 12,91
   Bethy 12,92
   Eula 13,92
   Illiman 12,91
   Lillie 12,91
   Mamie 41,125
   Ola 12,92
   Ollie T 12,91
   Rosie 12,91

   Sam Davis 28,109,216,312
BRISCOE
   Baby 290
   Calton 92
   Charles 302
   Charlie 198,287
   Colton 198
   Egbert 46,130
   Elsie 46
   Elsie Y 92,198
   George Ann 92,198
   J Claud 13,92
   Jim 46,92,198
   John Claud 309
   John Claude 171
   Lucy 13,92,307
   Maggie 13
   Maggie Gipson 92,198
   Olivia 294
   Sallie Thomas 322
   Scott 293
   Stephen 198
   Stephens 13,92
   Tom 13,92,198,322
BULL
   Foreman 13,93,199
   George 13,92,199,304
   Lizzy (Sissy) 187
   Pink 13,92,198,304
   Sarah 13,93,199
   Sissy 13,93
BULLOCHE
   Clayton 199
   Evaline Thomas 199
CAMPBELL
   Bilsy John 322
   Jimmie 93,171,309
   Venie 171,309
   Vennie Comby 93,165
   Wiley 13,93,199,322
CARVER
   George 199
   Julia Farve 200
   Mary Farve 199
   Mr 200

Index

CATES
- Alice 14,93
- Dee 14,93
- Dock 14,93
- Emma 14,94
- Enis 13,93
- Essie 13,93
- Henry M 14,94
- Iona 14,93
- Janie 14,93
- John 13,14,93
- Julia 14,94
- Lonie 13,93
- Molpus 93
- Mulpus 14
- Nannie 14,94
- Ned 14,93
- Oscar 14,93
- Susan 13,93
- Susan Mabel 14,93,199
- Tubby 14,94
- Willie F 14,94

CATES (TUBBY), D 199

CHAPMAN
- Asa 14,94,200
- Bettie 14,94,200
- Christ 14,94,200
- Hattie 14,94,200
- Lilly 14,94,200
- Mary McMillan 200
- Minnie 14,94,200
- Ralston 14,94,200
- Raymond 14,94,200
- Ronie 14,94,200
- Thresa 290
- Will 14,94,200

CHARLES, James 10,89,196

CHARLEY
- Beaman 126,176,319
- Juinata 127
- Mary Lou 176
- Sudie Johnson 319

CHARLIE
- Baby 95,171,282,284,290,292,309
- Beaman 56,142
- Beckie 33,115
- Billie 302
- Charlie C 56,142,255
- Coyt 95,165,200
- Elizabeth 294
- Elsie 15,95,200
- Fannie 15,94,200,302
- Irene 200
- John 15,95,200
- Juanita 142
- Juanitas 56
- Louey 200,287
- Mary 15,95,200
- Sina Davis 95,200
- William 15,94,200,300

CHAUVET
- Ida Farve 201
- Paul 201

CHICKAWAY
- Agnes 15,95,201
- Albert 15,95
- Allie 176,202
- Anna 16,96,241
- Baby 290
- Bessie 16,96,201
- Clemon 15,95,201
- Elizabeth 16,96,201
- Eunice 16,95,201
- Henry 16,95,201
- Isabel 171,309
- Isabell 15,95
- Jane 16,96,241
- Jim 16,95,176,201
- John Hester 16,95,201
- John Study 15,95,202
- Josephine Berniece 201,287
- Kate 15,95,201
- Kelly 16,96
- Lilla 16,96
- Lottie 322
- Maggie 15,95,201
- Maggie Kate 15,95,201
- Mary 290
- Mary Frances 201,281
- Michael 241

    Micheal 16,96
    Mollie (Nellie) 201
    Nellie 15,95
    Ola 15,95,201
    Ross C 16,96,201
    Rufus 16,96,201,302,324
    Sallie 176
    Sallie (Rejina) 201
    Sim 15,95,176,201
CHITTO
    Allie Nora 17,96,202
    Callie 16,96,202
    Dewey Davis 202,308
    Dewey Wesley 181,206,307
    Dewy Davis 168,282,284
    Ella 17,96,202
    Erma 16,96
    Hattie 16,96,202
    Henrietta 16,96
    Iren (Erma) 202
    Isom 16,96,202
    Jefferson 16,96,202
    Joe 16,96,168,181,202
    John 16,96,202
    Leo Clifton 16,96,202
    Lum Billy 17,97,202
    Mary 18,99,202
    Minnie 16,96,206
    Pat 16,96,202
    Sallie 16,96,202
CLARK, Stella 17,97,202
CLEMMONS, Philip 307
CLEMONS
    Baby 203
    Bates 203
    Bathia 17,98,203
    Bessie 17,97,203
    Cora 17
    Cora Frazier 97,202
    Emma (Rena Mae) 203
    Ethel 17,97,203
    Irsal 97,165,203,299
    Jef 97
    Jeff 17,202
    Jim 17,97,203

    John 17,97
    Leonard 97,203,315
    Leonard Rose 315
    Letha 17,97
    Lewisman 17,97,203
    Margie 17,97,203,311
    Mattie 17,97,203,299
    Mollie 17,98,203
    Munch 17,98,203,306
    Nellie 17,98,203
    Phillip 17,97
    Prince 97,203
    Rena Mae 17,97
    Ruth 203
    Sim (John) 203
    Stennis 203
    Winnie 203,289
COMBY
    Allie 18,98,204
    Alma 17,98,204
    Arbin 18,98,204
    B C 18
    B F 98,205
    Ben 18,99,204
    Clarence Billy 204
    Edna 18
    Edna Ben 98,205
    Gilbert 18,98,204
    Gus 42,126
    Irene 18,98,204
    Jonas 18,98,204
    Jordan McMillan 204
    Joyce Ann 18,98,204
    Laura 18,99,204
    LeRoy 205
    Leroy 18,98
    Maude Billy 99,204
    Maudell 18,98,204,304
    Olmon 18,99,204
    Philip 204
    R L 18,99
    R L (William) 204
    Rosella 18,98,204
    Rousella 304
    Seymour 18,98,205

Index

Vennie 148
Vina Rayburn 98,205
W C 18,98,205
COOPER
   Ada 19,99,205
   Alma 19,99,205
   Christine 19,99,205
   Dixon 19,99
   Fannie 19,99,131
   Gaston 19,99,205
   Hubert 19,99,205
   Leana 19
   Leona 99
   Wickson Dee 231
COTTON
   Effie 205
   Ellen 19,99,205
   Emma 205,286
   George 19,99,205
   Henry 205
   John 19,99
   Minnie 19,99,205
   Renie 244
   Zula 205
COTTON (CATES)
   Ennis 206
   Henry 205
   Iona 206
   John 206
   Lonie 206
   Molpus 206
   Oscar 205
   Susan 206
COWED
   Bessie 17,97
   Jim 17,97
   Leonard 97
   Lewisman 17,97
   Margie 17,97
CRENSHAW
   Amos 19,100,206
   Austin 19,100,206
DAN
   Albert R 39,122
   Bonnie 232
   Dinah 19,100,206
   Ida Rose 304
   Irene 39,122,232
   Rose Ida 19,100,206
   Williston 19,100,206
DANSBY
   Jacob 19,100,206
   Jake (Jacob) 302
   Jennie 19,100,171,309
DAVIS
   Ada Frances 207,311
   Ada Francis 20,101
   Alice 20,101,207,294
   Alyne 20,100,207
   Anna 20,101,207
   Anne 307
   Annie 20,101
   Ansleum 207
   Berniece (Zina) 207
   Bessie 20
   Elamer 20,101,207
   Frances 286
   Francis 224
   Henderson 21,101,207
   Hobbie ... 20,100,132,176,207,319
   John 20,101,208
   Johnnie 20,101,207
   Leona 20,100,242
   Lewis 20,101,208
   Lonie 207,286
   Mabel 20,101,207
   Mack 20,101,208
   Malissie 20,101,207
   Mary 20,21,101,208
   Mary McMillan 207,319
   Mattie 20,100
   Millie 21,101,207
   Nola McMillan 207
   Sidney 20,101,207
   Sina 20
   Tom 21,101,207
   Will 20,100,208
   William 20,101,208
   Zina 176
DENSON

Index

Baby 129,168,282,284,290, 294,300
Beauty 21,102,208,209
Belfa Lewis 209
Bonnie Lee 241
Ceasar 290
Charley 21,101,208
David 21,101,208
Edna 21,102,208
Eliza 45,129,241
Eliza Lewis 209,304
Emma 21,101,208
Eva Jackson 208,300
Ezell 21,102,208
Hector 21,102
Hendrix 21,101,208
Jeffie 21,102
Jennie E 21,102,208
Joe 40,124,233,311
John 208,287
Lilly 21,101,208
Lola 176,209
Loretta 241,288
Louise 21,102,208
Marguerite 209,287
Mary 21
Nancy 21,102,208
Odie Mae 102,208
Pete 21,101,176,208
Rosie 21
Rosie Wickson 102,208
Ruth 21,102,208
Silmon (Hector) 209
Una 209
Willie 21,102,168,209
Winston 129,209,241
Wintson 45,129
Zila 165
Zula 126

DIXON
Addie Mae 22,103,209
Anita 22,103,209
Arthur Aiken 102
Baby 210,286
Callie 22,103,209
Calonia 22,103,209
Claudine 176,209
Cora 210
David Clem 210,287
Dorothy 294
Edmond 103,176,209
Ellen 22,102,210
Esby 23
Essie 22,103,210
Esther 22,103,209
Hope 22,103,210
Horace 22,103,209
Imogene 22,102,210
James 210
Jess 22,102,209,304
Jim 22,23,102,103,210
Julia 22,103,209
Kanis 103,210,311
Leona Billy 210
Leona Willis Wesley 209
Lilly 22,103,210
Lonie 23
Mable C 22,102,210
Marie 22,102,210
Melba 294
Morris (Arthur Aiken) 210
Nannie 21,102
Nola 22,103,210
Sarah 22
Sarah Jimmie 210
Sarah Jimmy 102
Scott 22,103,210
Wade 23,103,210
Williston 209,287
Wilson 22,103,210
Woodrow 290
Young 22,103,209
DIXON EDMOND 22
DIXON KANIS 22
ELLIS
Amelia Farve 211
George 211
EVANS, John 23,103,211
FARMER
Allie 84

335

Index

Annie Mae 5,84,219
Bell 211
Bennie 23,104
Betsy Ann 294
Bill 23,104,322
Clennis Willis 322
Corine 23,104,212
Ella Mae 5,84
Emma 23,104
Eula Mae 21,104,211
Fannie Cooper 211,302,319
Franklin 253,288
Grace 55,141,253
Hector 287
Henry 23,46,99,104,131,176,
.... 211,319
Hester (Clark Gable) 212
Howard 24,104,211
Ishman ... 23,104,211,300,322,323
J C 290
Latima 212
Lena 23,104,211
Lilly Kate 55,141
Lonie 24
Lonie Dixon 104,166,211
Lottie 23,104,212
Lottie Chickaway 300
Maggie 23,104
Mamie Willis (Billy) 322
Marshall 23,104,211,323
Mary Lou Farve 323
Mealie 23,104,212
Melissa 23,104,211
Mose 322
Moses 23,104,170,212
Rainey 23
Renee 104,211
Robert Joseph 176,211
Robert Lee 294
Sallie 5,38,121,230
Silmon 23,103,212,324
Suela 211,322,323
Sweeter 23,104
Thomas 23,104,308
Venie 212,324

Wilton 104,211
FARVE
Albert 27,108,212
Albert Clifton 176,215
Alfonsine 26,107,213
Alvin 25,106,213
Amelia 27,108
Anna Rose 105,215
Antwine 24,105,212
Audrey 25,106,213
Baby 105,214
Basie 26
Basil 212
Bay Turner 27,212
Bennett 24,26,104,107,212,218
Besie 107
Bessie Davis 105,214
Cameron 212
Cecelia 212
Cecil Eugene 253
Cecilia 24,105
Ceciline 27,108,213
Charles 25,27,106,108,213
Charles T 26,107,213
Chester 24,105,215
Corbrin 24,105,212
Corrine 26,107
Dave 25,105,213,299
Dennis 26,107,213
Dora 25,106,214
Earl 24,105,212
Edna 24,105,212
Edwina 25,106,213
Eleanor 213
Elinor 27,108
Emeline 26,107
Encie 290
Estelle 24,105,214
Ethel 27,108,213
Eula Mae 24,105,214
Francis 26,107,213
Frazene 293,302
Georgia 25,105,213
Gertrude 25,26,106,214,215
Gilmore 25,106,214

Index

Hazel 25,106,215
Henrietta 27,108,217
Hilda 24,105,215
Hughey 176,214
Ida 27,108
Iktial 27,108,212
Ima 24,105,215
Irvin 25,106,213
Isileen 24,105,212
J C 26,107,213
Jessie 26,107,214
Joe 26,27,106,108,214
Joe Tole 25,106,214
John 24,25,105,106,213,215
John Tole 26,107,214
Joseph 24,105,176,214
Josie 24,105,215
Julia 26,107
Lem 214
Lena 25,105,213
Lilliaen 215
Lillian 24,25,105,106,214
Liseeda 24,105,212
Lola 25,106
Lucille 27,108,214
Mamie 24,105,212
Mary 25,26,106,107,215
Mary Lou 55,141
Noah 26,107,214
Ora Lee 214
Paul 24,104,176,214
Phillip 24,105,214
R C 26,107,215
Rachel 24,105,215
Ray Turner 108
Renia 24,104
Renie 214
Retha 25,106,213
Robert 25,106,215
Rosella 27,108,214
Rosine H 25,106,215
Ruth 25,106,215
Sarah Alma 24,105,213
Seman 27,108,215
Sylvester 25,106,215

Thomas 25,106,215
Victoria 25,106
Viola 24,26,105,107,212,214
Vivian 25,106,213
Western 24,26,105,107,215
William 25,26,27,106,107,
.... 213,215
Wilma 26,107,213
Winoa 25
Winona 106,215
FARVE (FARMER)
  Cecil Eugene 288
  Mary Lou 253
FORBES
  Clint 28
  Ella 27,108,218
  Gaston 28
  Henry 28
  Ida Mae 28
  Josey 28
  Sallie 27,108,216,312
  Wesley 27,108
FORBES (FRAZIER)
  Clint 109
  Gaston 109
  Hazel 109
  Henry 109
  Ida Mae 109
  Josey Tubby 109
FRAZIER
  Agnes (Lucy) 217
  Annie 110,165,217
  A B 28,110,217,312
  Bob (Frazier) 272
  Caspeen 110
  Cecile 110,217
  Clemon 217,287
  Dollie (Doris) 267
  Doris 109
  Edmond 29,110,217
  Eliza 28,110,171,309
  Ella 29,76,111
  Emma 29,110,165,217
  Emma Dixon 218
  Fannie 216

Fannie Venie	302	Wesley	29,76,111,216,218,302
Fenie	29,110	West	28,109
Forbes	28,109,216	Will	28,109,218
Frazier	29,110	Willie	28,110
Frazier (Bob)	168	Willie Rose	217

FRAZIER (FORBES)

Clint	216
Hazel	216
Henry	216

Gaston	216		
Henry	28,110		
Henson	29,110,216		
Herman	29,110,272		
Homer	28,109,224		

GARDNER

Alton	29,111,218
Arleta	29,111
Celia	29,111,218
Ella	218
Floyd	177,218
Jim	29,111,177,218

Iam	28,109		
Ida Mae	216		
Inez	216		
Isral	216,281		
Jake	29,111,217		
Jim	28,110,181,217		
John	28,109,217		

GARDNER (COTTON), John ... 218

GIBSON

Annie Maude	300
Granville	294
Josie	181,307
Nolie (Noah)	181
Sophie	307
Stephen	294

Josephine (Caspeen)	217
Josey Tubby	216
Julian	216,287
Lavada Sam	216
Lavena	28,109,218
LeRoy	168,282,284
LeRoy (Quitman)	216
Ligman	29,110,217
Lucy	29,110
Malissa (Martha)	267
Mamie	109
Mamie Vaughn	267
Marshall	28,109,267
Martha	109,165
Maxine	181,307
Mollie	28,109,217
Nancy	28,110,217
Nannie	28
Nannie Leben	110,217
Sallie	29,110,217
Seale	28,109,240
Simpson	29,110,167
Sina	29
Sina Jackson	110,217
Susie	29,110,272
Velma	29,110,272
Wade	29,111,217
Wage	272

GIPSON

Allie Farmer	219
Andrew	30,218
Annie	30,112,219,220
Annie Lee	291
Aron	30,112,220
Bart	111,218
Clay	30,112,219
Doreen	177,219
Elizabeth	30,111,166,219
Esby	166
Esther	30,111,218
Fannie	30,112,219,220
Frances	30,112,219
Gus	30,111,219
Henrietta	30,111,219
Hensley	30,111,219
Homer	30,111,177,219,253
Hugh	30,112,220
Ikey	30,112,220
Irene	287

Irene (Annie Maud) 219
Jennie 30,112,220,325
Johnny Lee 219
Josephine 168,282,284
Leona 219,281
Lilly Farmer........................... 219
Lora Ann 219,289
Lucy 29,111,218
Marie L................................... 286
Mary L 219
Mary Williamson................... 219
Minnie.................................... 220
Nolie............. 30,112,168,177,219
Paul 112,167,219
Pearl 30,76,77
Sophie 30,111
Steve..................... 30,112,220,325
William 177,253
Willie........................... 30,112,220
Willie D....................... 219,287
GIPSON BART................................ 29
GRANT, Rosie Lee 16
HALL
   Arlone....................... 30,112,220
   Eliza.................. 114,165,222,304
   Frances................................... 220
   Francis.............................. 31,112
   Frank........................ 30,112,220
   Henrietta..................... 37,120,230
   Herbert................................... 230
   Herbert H 34,116
   Langford............. 30,112,169,220
   Lena.................... 169,220,282,284
   Lou 30,112,220
   Travis 30,112,220
HARPER, Lena 31,112,220
HARRIS
   Elamore.................................. 112
   Elsmore............................ 31,220
HAWKINS, Alice 31,113,247
HAYS, Velma.................. 50,135,220
HENRY
   Albert........................... 31,113,221
   Berniece Lewis....................... 221
   Beulah......................... 31,113,221

   Bob................. 32,113,221
   Cornelia........................... 221,287
   Dolphus..................... 32,114,221
   Ellen............................ 31,113,221
   Frank........................... 31,113,221
   Guiser........................ 31,113,221
   Jasper......................... 32,114,221
   Jeanette................................. 294
   Jim................................ 31,113,221
   Joy 171,309
   Joy June 32,113
   Liege 31,113,221
   Martha 31,113,221
   Mattie 32,113
   Melvin 31,113,221
   Nellie 32,113,221
   Nettie 31,113,221
   Norman 291
   R D 31,113,221
   Robert 32,113,221
   Sallie 31,113,221
   Sis 31,113,221
   Susie........................... 31,113,221
   Wick 221
   Wicks 31,113
HICKMAN
   Aliza Jane.............................. 115
   Annie 33,115,223
   Baby 291
   Billy 32,114,221
   Bobby (Vardeman)................ 223
   Dona 33,115,224
   Edd Davis 115
   Edmond................................ 222
   Eliza 311
   Eliza Jane........................... 33,223
   Ellis 32,114,222
   Enoch 32,114,223,302
   Enoch (Edmond) 177
   Eula............................. 33,115,245
   George 115,165,245
   Hickman............................... 224
   Iama 224
   Jane 222
   John.............. 33,115,177,222,223

Johnkin	32,114,223,304
Lodie Mae	32,114,224
Lula	32,114,222
Malinda	32,114,223
Mary	33,115,171,309
Mary Long	33,115,223
Minnie	32,114,267
Ollie T	224
Onie	222
Pearl	33,115
Rhodie	32
Robinson	33,115,224
Rose	114,221
Sabelia	115,165
Sadie	32,114,223
Sallie	32,114,223
Sim	32,114,224
Smokey (Snooks)	245
Snooks	33,115
Stenis	222
Stennis	33,115
Susan	32,114,221,222
Susuaj	32
Susuan	114
Tony	222,289
Tubby	32,114,223
Vada Anderson	224
Varderman	33,115
Wallace	33,115,224
Will	114,165,267
Willie	32,114,224
Willie (Wm Penn)	223
Winnie	33,115
Wm Penn	33,115
HICKMAN (BOX)	
Emelia (Emly)	223
Eula	223
Illiman	223
Lillie	223
Lizzie (Bathie)	223
Lula (Bethy)	223
Mamie	224
Ola	224
Rosie	223
HUDSON, Celia	33,115,224

ISAAC

Alice Marie	225,287,302
Anada	225
Anita	116
Ann Marie	177,225
Annie	34,117,226
Beneda	34,116
Bernice	34,116
Berniece	224
Bessie	33,116,225
Bradley	294
Byrd	33,116,224
Calvin (Paul)	224
Catherine	34,116,224
Celia	34
Celia Farmer	116,225
Charles	291
Claud Preston	34,117,226
Claudine	34,117,225
Coline	9,88
Cornelia	34,117,226
Dave, Jr	225,307
David	35,117,169,225,291
David, Jr	169,282,284
Delphia	34,117,225
Dixon	35,117
Edmond (Enochs)	225
Edwin	34,116,224
Effie	34,116,226
Elsie	35,118
Enochs	34,117
Etherine	171
Etherine Or Nansey	309
Eunice	71,160,273,315
Eva	35,117,225
Franklin	35,117
George	294
Hickman	34,116,171,309
Hugh	34,116,225
Isaac	34,117,225,226
Jackson	35,117,177,225
Jesse A	34,116,224
Jim	33,116,225
Joe D	225
Joe Day	35,117

John Day 34,117,226	**JACKSON**
Juanita 169,225,282,284	Amy Wallace 323
Juliva 294	Anne Mae Jim 227
Lawrence 117,171,309	Betty 35,118,226,304
Lesper 35,117	Carlson 35,118,226
Lester 35,76,77,118,225	Carson 118,227,323
Lillie Mae 34,116,226	Colman 227
Lou 35,118	Ella 35,118
Louisa 34,117,226	Ellen Bell 227
Maggie 34,117	Emma Lee 295
Maggie A 225	Emmett 36,118,227
Manda 35,118	Eva 36,118
Martha 34,117	Floyd Bell 227
Mary Lou 117,225	Floyd F 75,118
Mills 295	Jackson 35
Nannie 34,71,116,160,226,	Katherine 227
.... 273,315	Lena 35,118,227,323
Nansey 171	Lorraine 227,286
Odie Mae 33,116,171,309	Lucile 118
Paul 116	Lucille 36,227
Pauline 33	Mack (Mike) 307
Pauline Jim 116,224	Mamie 36,118
Preston (Franklin) 225	Mamie Lewis 227
Rainey 35,118	Martha 36,119,227
Rose 71,160,274,315	Mary 36,119,227
Sarene 225	Mike 36,119
Simon 34,116,225	Missie 36,119,227
Steve 33,116,307	Mollie 291
Theresa Mae 291	Nancie 35,118
Vanida 225	Prentiss 36,119,227
Waney 35	Rosaline 227,286
Wansey 117,225	Rose 35,118
Wilbur 34	Sam 36,119,227
Wilbur N 117,225	Tom 36,118,227
Will 34,117,169,226	Tubby 36,119,227
William 71,159,273,315	William 227
Wilson 34,117,226,304	Woodrow 36,118,227
ISAAC (JIM), Dixon 302	**JEFFERSON**
ISOM	Amos 36,119,228
Bailey 141,165,253	Andy 37,120,228
Eunice York 226	Arthur 177,229,300
Isom 35,118,226	Baby 119,120,291
Mary 4,82	Birdie Mae 291
Salina 226,287	Braxton 36,119,228
Willie 35,118,226	Dora Nickey 228

Index

Elsie 36,119,229
Eva Nell 119,165,228
Franklin 177,228
Goldman (Leon) 228
Grady 228
Hubert............................228,289
Ida 36,119,228
Irvin.......................................228
Leon 36,119
Leona Nickey Cooper 228,319
Lula Lane.................................177
Luline.....................................228
Malcolm............36,119,228
Mary Sallie 228
Newt 99,129,177,228,319
Nute 45
Onie............................37,119,228
Oscar 36,119,177,228,302
Otho 37,119,228
Otis 37,119,120,165,177,228
Saline................36,119,228
Shirley...................................291
Victoria 120,165,228
Willis 36,119,229

JIM
Albert...................38,121,178,229
Amon 38,121,229,304,324
Ance (Anna) Willis................319
Ance Willis (Anna)................231
Anderson.........................232,288
Annie Mae........................38,121
Baby 291
Ben..............................37,121,229
Bernice 295
Bessie........................37,120,231
Betty Lou 38,121
Bobbie Sue................38,121,231
Carter 38,121
Christine 38,121,231
Cicero....................................232
Claud Yates 38,121,230
Cooley 37,120,229
Corrine....................37,120,231
Dora 38,121,229,305
Dora Bell.................................229

Ed (Wm Murray) 229
Effie Mae........................178,229
Egbert 39,122
Eliza 37,120,230
Fay 231
Fillie (Goodman, Jr) 230
Foy 39,122
Frances 230,287,302
Frank............ 38,121,230,231,287
Frank McKinley 38,121,230
George 37,120,230
Goodman 38,121,169,230,300
Goodman, Jr 169,282,284
Gordon G...................38,122,229
Grace............................38,121,229
Harvey......................37,120,230
Henry....... 37,38,120,122,230,231
John.....................37,120,181,231
Lee............................37,120,230
Lena 38,122,231
Leona 38,121,230
Lesley..................................232
Logan..........................38,121,229
Lorena 37,120,229
Lucy 38,121,229,321
Lula Thomas...........................231
Lulu Thomas 300
Maggie.................38,122,231
Mary Lou 230
Mattie 37,120,230
Missola 295
Mollie................37,120,231
Odie Moore (Carter).............229
Opal 38,121,229,321
Otho................................ 231,287
Pearl.............................181,231
Perry 169,232,282,284
Rena 38,121
Richard 231,287
Sallie Mae..................178,231,305
Sidney.........................37,120,231
Susie Ann...................37,120,231
Tom...............................37,120,229
Vernon (Tubby).....................161
Victor 38,122,169,231

William 37,120,229
Winston 38,122
Wm Murray 38,121
JIM (ISAAC)
   Dixon....................................229
   Elsie......................................230
   Lester...................................230
   Lou..230
   Manda..................................230
   Rainey..................................230
JIM (TUBBY), Vernon ..178,231,319
JIMMIE
   Arleta Gardner......................232
   Delores........................39,122,232
   Frank....................................232
   Frank M 39,122
   Hester.........................39,122,232
   Homer........................39,122,232
   Ike...............................39,122,232
   Lela.............................39,122,232
   Leonard H 291
   Mack............................39,122,232
   Mary............................39,122,232
   Ona..232
   Ona C 39,122
   Will..............................39,122,232
JOE
   Alma Bell..............................232
   Alma Or Ole.........................323
   Austin 39
   Auston 123,234,323
   Baby......................................295
   Bessie...............39,40,123,233,234
   Billie Joe 39,123
   Clark.............................233,286
   Claud 40,77,123,233
   Claudeece..............................291
   Effie Bell................................323
   Ella.............................39,123,222,323
   Emelia...................................300
   Emily..........................40,123,238
   Emly 12,92
   Emma.......................40,123,233
   Henry................39,123,232,323
   Houston......................40,123,233

Jane 233,288,305
Jasper........................ 40,123,233
John............................ 40,123,233
John (Nichols)....................... 222
June...................................... 222
Killie 40,123
Langley................ 40,123,233,305
Lillie 233
Lula............................ 40,123,233
Mary 39,123
Nicholas .. 39,40,123,233,312,323
Nichols 76,123
Ronie.................................... 233
Sallie 40,123,233,288
Sarah.................................... 233
Shone (Billie)......................... 222
Susan (Mary) 222
Tom...................................... 233
Watkins 40,123,233
Wayne 295
Wedge 234
Widge 39,76,77,123
JOHN
   Albert................................... 234
   Albert (Oliver)...................... 235
   Amanda..................... 41,125,235
   Anderson 40,124,234
   Anne Mitch........................... 236
   Annie..................................... 41
   Annie Mae (Mary) 235
   Annie Mitch.......................... 125
   Beatrice................................. 235
   Bennett 41,124,234
   Betsie 41
   Bettie 40,124,234
   Beverly 235
   Bilbo........................... 41,125,234
   Bilsy 125,234,325
   Bob............................ 41,124,235
   Bobbie................................... 291
   Callie......................... 43,127,235
   Clint........................... 41,124,235
   Edgar 235
   Edison.............................. 43,127
   Egbart................................... 124

Egbert	41
Elizabeth	125,234
Ella (L E)	234
Frances	235
Gladdis (Reta)	236
Grady	125,236
Hamilton	124,234
Harry	41,124,236
Hubert	41,124,234
Ira	41,124,169,235
Jack	41,125,235
Jarvis	234
Jefferson	41,125,235
Josh	40,124,236,308
L E	41,124
Lena Pearl	41,124,234
Lisette	234
Lisette H	42,125
Lizzie	40,124,236
Mable	41,125,234
Marcy Lee	171
Margaret	125,235
Mary	41,125
Mercy Lee	41,124,309
Mico	234
Mike	40,124,236
Molpus	235
Nancy Lou	234,288
Nancy Stoliby	234,305
Neva	235
Oden	41,124
Olive Mae	235
Oliver	41,125
Onie	41,124,235
Oretta	235
Otis	41,125,236,305
Ovetta	41,124
Owen	234
Renie	42,125,234
Reta	288
Rosa	235
Rose	41,125
Ruby	41,77,125,235
Semm Lee	295
Smith	42,125,234
Suella	235
Vardeman	234
Varderman	42,125
Willie	169,236,282,284
Wilson	41,124,234

JOHNSON

Afton	42,126,178,236
Allie Nora	178,237
Athens	42,126,236
Baby	291
Beatrice	42,126
Belfy	302
Bena	43,127
Bertha	42,126
Beverly	42,126
Callie	42,126
Cathie (Bona)	237
Celia	125,165,171,237,310
DeWitt (Whitman)	178
Dixie	42,126,237
Edgar	42,126,178
Egbert	42,126,235,299
Ellen	43,76
Frances	42,126
Frank	42,126,236
G O	127
Gus	237
Hattie	126,237
Haven	42
Hubert (Ralph)	236
Irvin K Morris	295,300
Iva May	235,302
Jack Denson	178,236
Jadee (G O)	237
James	295
Jaunita Charley	237
Juanita Charley	319
Lee	65,152,261
Lorine	42
Lorine Solomon	126,236
Lorraine	178,237
Marvin	43,127,237,312
Mary	127
Mary Davis	127,166
Nathan	126,237

Neva 42,126
Olive Mae 178
Otho 43,127,142,178,237,319
Priscella Study 237
Priscilla Study 126
Ralph 42,126
Sadie 42,126
Sallie 42,126,237
Savannia 42,126,236
Sudan 43
Sudie 142
Thelma 126
Tonie Steve 236
Velma (Thelma) 236
Viola 42,126,237
Whitman 42,125,237
Will 42,126,237
Zula Denson 236

JOSHUA
  Hollis (Edison) 237
  Jane (Jennie) 237
  Jennie 127
  Jennnie 43
JOSHUA (JOHN), Carrie 237
KING
  Alice 43,127,238
  Banks 44,128,238
  Barkum 43,128
  Betsie 43,44,128,238
  Christine 43,128,238
  Clay 43,127,238
  Enis 43,127,238
  Joe 43,128,238
  John Lee 43,127
  John W 43,127,238,312
  Joseph 43,128,238
  Korkum 238
  Lavenia 43,127
  Mollie 43,127,238
  Vardman 238
  Varman 43,127
LABEN, Hester 281
LADNER
  Rosie Thomas 238
  Sidney 238

LEBAN
  Ben 44,128
  Lena 44,128
  Mary 44,128
LEBEN
  Ben 238
  Hester 238
  Lena 238
  Mary 238
LEFLORE
  Bertha Lee 44,128,239
  Emma 44,128,239
  John 44,128,239
  Lewis 44,128,239
  Richard 44,128,239
  S D 44,128,239
  Willie 44,128,239
LEWIS
  Adam 44,129,239
  Albert 45,84,130,178,239,
  319,322
  Allone 178,307
  Amos 45,130
  Amos (Buddy) 278
  Archie Hector 264
  Baby 178,291
  Bart (Leon) 241
  Belfa 45,129
  Bernice 45,130
  Billy 171,285,310
  Celia 44,129,239
  Duffie 46,130,239,299
  Eastland 45,130,239
  Edd 45,130,240
  Edna 45,130,240
  Edna Sam 241
  Egbert 239
  Eliza 129
  Ella McMillan 204,300
  Elon 44,129,240
  Elsie 40,123,222
  Emma Bell 130,239,319
  Esther 45,129,241
  Fannie 44
  Fannie Davis 128

Index

Frank 295,300
Hazel 240,289
Hector Archie 128
Hodges 45,129
Hollis 45,130,240
Horace (Hodges) 241
Houston 13,45,76,92,129,
.... 199,241
Inla 129
Ivena 46,130,239
Jacob 44,129,239
Jennie 46
Jennie Lin 46,130,240
Jennie Willis 130,240
Jim 46,130,178,240
Joe 45,129,240
Johnnie 69,158,240,323
Kenneth 241,305
Lee 45,129,241
Lennis 45,129
Leon 45,129
Leonard (Lennis) 240
Lilly 46,130,239
Lucille 45,129
Lucy Mae 239,281
Lula 45,240
Lum 61,148
Lum Billy 262,311
Mamie 44,129
Mamie Smith Williams 323
Marceline 69,158,252
Marguerite 240
Marshall 45,129,241
Martha 45,129,241
Marveline 76
Mary 91
Maudie Lee 291
Mollie 45,130,171,310
Nannie 44,129,239
Nema (Mamie) 239
Nervie 45,130,240
Ola 45,129,240
Prentiss 45,129,241
Redy Isaam 204
Reuben 45,130

Rosalind (Lucille) 241
Rosie Mae 130,171,310
Runner 295
Susie 40,123,222
Tom 44,129,239
Waiter 291
Willie 46,130,240
LEWIS (JIM), Winston 204
MARTIN
   Annie Mae 46,131,242
   Anthony 179,242
   Catheline 131
   Edmond 242
   Edmond J 46,131
   Ennis 46,131,241
   Harry M 46,131,242
   Lylie Chickaway 241
   Mary 46
   Mary Steve 131,241
   Nancy 46,171,310
   Nancy Steve 131
   Phillip 46,131,242
   Raymond 46,131,241
   Robert John 131,241
   Thomas 46,131,307
   Willie 46,131,179,303
   Willis 241
MCMILLAN, Sorsby 324
MCMILLAN
   Anthony 169,242
   Arnold 243
   Augusta 243
   Becky Charlie 242
   Bert 243
   Bessie 242
   Bonnie Davis 243
   Cephus 242
   Clarence 242
   Clifton 295
   Elinor 295
   Ella 18,98,179
   Emma 242
   Enochs 242
   Frances 243
   A G 207

Gipson 243
Henry Lee 179,242
Ida 301
Ita Inez 291
Jean 243
Jimmie 18,98,104,179,242
Jimpson 18,98,204
Joe (John) 243
John 207
Jordan 18,98
Lee Otho 242
Lemmie 242
Leo Otho McM 179
Leonard Yates 242,288
Leslie 243
Lurline 242
Maggie Garmer 242
Mallie (Mollie) Willis 319
Mallie Willis 243
Marie Theresa 242
Mary 12,91,100
Mary Lewis 197
Mattie 208
Mina 242
Odie Mae 207
Oscar 243,303
Pauline 243
Redy Isaam 179
Rita 169,242,282,284
Ruby 295
Sorsby 242
Theodore Nelson 291
Venie Comby 242
Willie 159,179,319
Willis 243

MCMILLEN
  Anthony 47,132
  Arnold 47,132
  Augustine 132
  Bennie 47
  Bennie Davis 132
  Bert 47,132
  Bessie 47,131
  Cephus 47,132
  Clarence 47,131

Emma 47,131
Enochs 47,132
Frances 47,132
A G 94
Gipson 47,132
A J 15
Jean 48,132
John 15,48,94,132
Lemmie 47,132
Leslie 47,132
Lurline 47,132
Maggie 47,132
Marie Theresa 132
Mary 47,131,132
Mattie 15,95
Mina 47,132
Nola 15,94
Odie Mae 15,94
Oscar 47,132
Pauline 47,132
Sorsby 47,131
Venie 47,132
Willie 47,132

MINGO
  Annie 48,133
  Annie Mingo 244
  Arch 48,133,243
  Baby 244,288
  Betty 171,281,285,310
  Davidson 48,133,244
  Effie 48,133,244
  Hattie 48,133,243
  Jim 48,133,179,243
  John 48,133,243
  Lena Tubby 133,251
  Lilly 48,133,243
  Lilly Tubby 166
  Linday 48
  Mary 48,133,243
  Nettie 48,133
  Olin 48,133,169,243
  Oscar 48,133,251
  Otho 179,243,305
  Otis 48,133,243
  Rich 48,133

Robert Bruce......169,244,282,284
Sally Bell..................133,165,243
Sarah 133,243
Sister...48
MITCH
   Divan......................................48,133
   Divon 263,323
   Elea..............................48,133,244
   Frances Tubby.......................324
   Gilmore.......................48,134,244
   Irene Tubby...........................323
   Lillie Mae Ben.......................244
   Sarah 48,133,244,324
   Wilson.................48,133,244,324
MORRIS
   Alice 169,282,284
   Alice (Salina)..........................246
   Arwin..58
   Beauty 49,134,245
   Bertha.........................50,135,244
   Bertie..........................49,134,244
   Bethany.......................49,134,244
   Boston 50,135,244
   Champ 49,134,246
   Chester...................49,76,134,245
   Dempsey.............49,134,169,244,
  245,246
   Eddie................................49,77,134
   Edna (Eddie) 245
   Garrett....................................295
   Houston 244
   Howard.......................49,134,244
   Huston 50,135
   Ida 49,134,245,303
   Irene 144,227
   Jane Donie 244
   Janie....................................49,134
   Jimmie.........................49,135,244
   Joe................................49,134,245
   Julis..................................49,134
   Julius.......................................245
   Lena.............................49,134,245
   Lester 49,134,246
   Lilly 49,134,245
   Maude.....................................245

Mazelle............................246,288
Moseley............................49,134
Mosley....................................245
Nola 50,135,244
Ora 49,134,244,321
Ottosella................................295
Ottozella................................301
Phelix.....................................245
Printeas.........................134,245
Printess...................................49
Sallie 49,134,246
Seward.......................49,134,246
Sue 49
Walter Olin 245
Water Olin 49,134
Wilson.........................49,134,245
Winnie T Hickman 245
MOSES
   Allen 50,135,226
   Alma 50,135,246
   Florence......................50,135,226
NERASIE
   Cloza......................................246
   Emeline Farve.......................246
NICKEY
   Annie..51
   Billy.............................50,135,246
   Cop-eland 135
   Copeland............................50,247
   Cozette 50,77,136,246
   Dora 50,135
   Elizabeth 51
   Fronie 50,135,246
   Hughey 246
   Hughie..............................50,135
   John Joseph.....................247,288
   Lizzie..51
   Lizzie (Malissie) 247
   Malessie............................50,135
   Nancie......................................51
   Nona......................................146
   Ode 50,135,246
   Rena Jim........................246,301
   Sam 50,135,247
   Sherman......................50,135,247

Index

Thomas 50,136,246
Zelma 50,135
Zima (Zelma) 246
Zona 50,135,146

NOAH
Annie 51,136,247
Elizabeth 50,136,247
Lizzie 51,136,247
Nancie 51,136,247

NUBBY
Billy 51,136,247
Lilly 51,136,247

PHILLIPS
Baby 179,249
Chas Geo 51,136
D C 179,247
Edmond 51,136,235
Empsey 51,136
Lester 51,136
Lester Smith 247
Lonie 179,249
M C (Emsey) 235
Riley 51,136,179,247
Roy Lee (Chas Geo) 247

POLK
Ada 52,137,248
Alma 52,137,248
Baby 137
Bessie Chickaway 324
Comelia 52,137
Cornelia 248,324
Dina Willis 305
Emma McMillan 324
Frances 52,137,248
Francis 51,137,247
Frank 308
George 51,137,248,305
Henry 51,136,248
Herman 248
Hudson 51,136,248
Jim 248,288
Josie 51,137,248,324
Lena 307,324
Lena (Lennie) 248
Lennie 52,137

Louise 295
Odell 51,137,248
Osborn 52,137,248
Sula 51,136,248
Susie 51,136,248
Susie Ben 248
Tom 52,137,248,324
POLK (WILLIS), Dina 236

POULSON
Allie 52,137,248
Charlie 52,137,248
Cornelia 52,137,249
Eddie M 52,137,249
Frank 52,137,249
Johnnie 52,137,249
Julius 52,137,248
Mary 52,137,249

ROBINSON
Belia 53,138,249
Betsey 52,138,249
Billie 249,286
Bonnie Bell 249
Campbell 53,138,249
Carl 52,138,249
Georgia 249
Georgie 52,138
Homer 53,138,249
Jimmie 52,138,249
Jimmie Teach 85,179,320
Josephine Teach 179,249
Mamie 52,138,249
Mary 53,76,138,249
Ronie Bell 320
Sallie 52,138,249
Syble 52,138,249
Teach 53,138,249
Thomas 52,138,249
ROBINSON (TEACH), Baby 291

RUTHERFORD
Henrietta 53,138,250
John 250
SACKEY, Bennett 163

SAM
Abel 54,139,251
Armond 54,139,250

Baby 250,292
Beaman 54,138,139,250
Charlie 22,102,250
Claud 251
Claude......................170,282,284
Donald 292
Edna 34,53,117,139,251
Edward 251,288
Elis...139
Ella Ruth....................54,139,250
Ellis................................54,250
Emily 54,139,250
Etta Lee 139,250
Eva....................................54,139,251
Fannie 54,139,250
Fontaiine...............................139
Fontaine............................54,250
Grace 53,139,251
Griffin 171,281,285,310
Grisaline 54,139
Griscelina............................251
Jimpson.........53,139,250,288,305
Lavade 53,139
Leona 54,139
Lonie 54,77,139
Louie 251
Louisiana 139,250
Lousiana................................53
Manzie....................53,139,251
Mattie..........................53,138,250
Nat...295
Nellie Billy.............................324
Nettie 54,139,251
Oscar 53,138,250
Raymond...................53,138,250
Rosaline 307
Ruth Ann....................53,139,216
Seer................................53,138
Sina...................................53,138
Sina John........................250
Susan 54,139
Susie 251
Tom 53,139,251,324
Truman...............53,138,179,250
Walter 53,139,251,305,324,325

Willie 54,139,170,251
SAN, Baby...................................179
SAUCIER
  Stanley......................................251
  Victoria Farve 251
SCOTT
  Lonie...54
  Lonie Tubby 140,251
  Maggie Mary 140,251
  Marshall 54,140,251
  Rachel 54,140,251
  Rosie Lee....................................96
SHOEMAKE
  Annie..252
  Buck................................170,252
  Carrie Mae 252
  Daisy..252
  Edburn 170,252,282,284
  Edmond...................................252
  Eliza 252
  Hubert 252
  Leona 252
  Martha....................................252
SHOEMAKER
  Annie..................................54,140
  Buck.....................................54,140
  Carrie Mae 55,140
  Daisy...................................55,140
  Dempsey 54,140,269
  Edmond...................................55,140
  Eliza 55,140
  Hubert 55,140
  Layman 54,140,269
  Leona 54,140
  Martha...............................55,140
  Mary 31,113
  Noleen 54,140,270
  Ruben 54,140,270
  Susan 54,140
  Susan Davis 156
SHUMAKE, Mary......................295
SHUMAKER, Mary Mae...........308
SIMPSON
  Celia 141
  Celie....................................55,252

Franklin Lee 252,288
John 55,140,252
Pauline 55,141,252,305
Sallie 55,140,252

SMITH
Clarence...................................292
Clay 56,141,252,322
Clement 252
Clemon 55
Clemont....................................141
Elton.........................56,141,253
George.......................55,141,253
John W 55,141,253
Mandy..........55,141,253,305,323
Mary..........................55,141,253
Mattie...................56,141,252,303
Melton.......................55,141,253
Minnie.......................55,141,253
Mollie Solomon......................252
Sebe 55,141,253
Sinie..........................55,141,253

SOCKEY
Alpha Wishork 253
Alphia Wishork 320
Bennett.....................180,253,320
Benny............................56,142
Enochs.....................56,142,254
Harman...................................180
Harmon 254,306
Homer.....................56,142,254
Ill..............................56,142,258
Irvin.........................56,141,254
Janette 180,254
Lela..254
Lula 56,142
Major..295
Margery...................................292
May Bell..................................295
Mike........................56,142,254
Nephus...................56,142,254
Odell........................56,142,254
Reba........................56,142,254
Ruth.................................254,288
Valaria....................................180
Varelia...................56,142,254

SOLOMON
Addie..........................56,142,254
Baby 255,288,306
Beaman...................................255
Bessie 57,143,255
Brunson (Johnson) 254
Earnest............................. 57,143
Ernest......................................254
Jeffry Denson......................... 254
Johnson............................ 57,142
Marshall 56,142,254
Mary Lou 255
Mattie 288
Mattie (Bettie Lee).................254
Mollie............................... 57,143
Mollie Lee 57,142,255
Murphy 57,143,255
Onie 56,142,255
Raymond............. 57,143,255,306
Sudie Johnson.........................255
Thomas Freeman 295
Willie 56,57,142,255
Winnie L......................57,142,255

STAR
Baby 132
Bill................................... 57,143
Edna................................ 57,143
Lucy................................ 57,143
Mary................................ 57,143
Nannie............................. 57,143
Summer...................... 132,143
Summers 57

STARR
Allie Lou 171,258,281,285,310
Baby 258
Bill.. 255
Edna.. 255
Lucy 255
Maggie McMillan................... 256
Mary 255
Nannie..................................... 255
Ruben 295
Summer 255
Wanira.......................... 256,288

STEPHENS

Index

Agnes 144
Annie 57,143,256
Bonnie B 57,143
Celia Lois 293
Cornelia 57,143
Cutie Mae 57,143,256
Dorthy D 57,143,256
Edna Ivey 292
Edward Yates 292
Elizabeth 295
Felix 58,143,256
Franklin 57,143,256
Hazel Agnes 256
Lee Mack 256,288
Martha 58
Martha Farmer 144,256
Martha Lee 58,144
Mary Frances 58,144,256
Maxton 57,143,256
Nathan 57,143,256
Pheobe 125,236
Phoebe 56
Sarah (Bonnie B) 256
Tom 57,143,256,299
Willie 57,143,256
Zena (Martha Lee) 256

STEVE
Aileen 59,145,258
Audrey 58,145
Berniece 144,257,308
Bobo 58,144,180,256
Callie 58
Callie Bell 144,257
Catherine 257
Claud 180,257,306
Clyde 257,288
Curtis 145,258
Ennis 58,257
Eunis 144
Frank 295
Gladys Eva 257,288
Helen 58,144,257
Houston 58,144,257
Jane 58,144
Jean 301

Jennie 255
Joan 58,144
Josie 58,144,255,257
Katherine 295
Lauraline 257
Lauratina 59,145
Lena 58,144,257
Lucille 58,144,256
Maggie 58,144,257
Marabelle 58,144
Maraurite 58,145
Marguerite 257
Maurice 58,144,256
McKinley 58,144,257
Minnie (Marabelle) 257
Mollie 59,145,257
Murphy 58,144,171,310
Odie (Audrey) 256
Pauline 59,145,257
Rebecca 59,145,258
Ruby 58,144,257
Sallie 257,288
Smith 59,145,257
Tonie 59,145
Vivian 58,145,256
Winnie 59
Winnie Smith 145,257
Winston 58,144
Winston John 257
Yates 58,144,257

STOLIBY
Boy Willis (Elum Ferum) 274
Elum Ferum 59,145
John 59,145,258
Nancy 59,145
Otis 59,145,258
Tom 59,145,186
Will Banks 59,145,258
Zona Miller 59,145,258

STOLIBY (WILSON), Martha ... 311
STOLIBY (WILSONS), Martha . 276
STRIBLING, Malissie 59,145,258

THOMAS
Amos 60,146,259
Cleve 60,146,170,258

Corine Farmer..........................324
Dora (Linnie Helen) 259
Dorsey.................................180,259
Evaline....................................60,146
George........................37,121,230
Golden 60,146,259
Gordon.............. 170,259,282,284
Hazel Tubby............................258
Isaac..............................59,146,258
Leon 292
Leona 60,146
Lester 60,146,259
Lewis.............................59,146,258
Linnie Helen........................60,146
Lula.......................................37,120
Mamie..........................59,146,258
Mina 59,146,259
Mollie....................................60,146
Newman.....................59,146,258
Nona (Zone) Nickey 320
Phoebe 60,146
Riley 59,135,146,180,259,320
Rosie............................60,146,259
Sallie......................60,146,259,324
Sam......................170,258,282,284
Single 60,146
Singleton..................................259
Wilman 60,146
Wilmon 170,259,299,322,324
Woodrow..............60,146,259,324
Zona Nickey............................259
THOMPSON
 Alice 61,77
 Annie....................61,147,259,260
 Baby 259,288
 Beckie..................................60,147
 Bobo 180,261
 Bonnie.........................61,148,261
 Bonnie Amos...........................166
 Cephus..........60,147,259,321,324
 Claudine.......................60,147,260
 Daniel................................171,310
 Daniel E 61,147
 Dixon..........................61,147,259
 Easton 295

Ellis 147,259
Elsie Cotton (Cates) 259
Farmer 61
Hector 260
Henry........................... 60,147,260
Jack............................... 295,301
Jean 61,147,260,324
Jim......................... 61,147,260,324
John........................... 61,147,259
Louise 61,148,261
Lucy Jim 324
Ludie 147,260
Lula 61
Malinda 61,147,260
Mary Jane.................................. 22
Maxine............................ 147,261
Moline 61
Mollie Vaughn.....................324
Morine............................. 148,167
Mose 61,147,260,324
Nathan........................... 61,148,261
Nola Isom (Mary) 261
Nonie..301
Oneva 60,147,260
Onie 61,148
Otis...................... 60,147,260,312
Perry Priest 148
Sina 60,147,260
Steve 61,147,260
Therman........................... 61,147
Tom 61,147,264
Tommie 61,148,180,261
Tommy 147,259
Will 60,147,260
Willie Dean........................... 295
THOMPSON (CATES)
 Janie 260
 Julia (Jewel)............................ 260
 Lumie (Emma) 260
 Melvin 260,286
 Nannie..................................... 260
 Ned 260
 Tubby 260
 Willie 260
THOMPSON (CHICKAWAY),

Index

Therman.....................260
TOFFOMAH, Latima.................285
TOOKALOO
  Alice 315
  Frances....................306
  Nathan....................315
  Sarah 315
TUBBY
  Aban.......................292
  Adam 63,150,261
  Addison (Robert)...................263
  Aileen.........................63,150,265
  Alice 63,64,65,150,151,152,
 261,262,265
  Allan......................................149
  Allen..62
  Anderson........63,65,150,152,261
  Annie........62,64,149,151,262,263
  Annie Lee 62,148,263
  Annis...........................62,149,262
  Baby 172,283,285,310
  Bessie.............................64,151,262
  Betsey..64
  Betsey Scott 151,262
  Binford Lee.............................296
  Bonnie (Buracy) 261
  Buracy.................................64,150
  Callie...............................66,153,265
  Catherine..............65,152,265
  Charlie 64,151,180,262
  Cicero 263
  Cicero L..............................63,150
  Claud 180,262
  Clemon 64,151,262
  Clenny Mae...............................292
  Coleman 65,152,264
  Colie..64
  Colleen...........................151,262
  Cornelia (Etolye).....................261
  D 153,166
  Dan.......................61,148,180,262
  Dean Culver.....................180,262
  Dee 262
  DeWitt...............................181
  Dewitt 63,150,262

Dick............................ 62,149,263
Dixie Lee 266,289,306
Earnest........................ 63,150,265
Edgar 62,149,263
Edmond...................... 62,149,266
Elias 64,152,262
Eline................................. 62,149
Ellis 64,151,262
Esther........................... 65,152,265
Etolye........................... 64,150
Eugene............................. 180,264
Eva Kate 62,149,266
Evan............................ 64,151,263
Fannie Lewis Davis 264
Fillie 266
Finis 64,151,264
Finis (Inis) 266
Frances 62,63,148,149,263,
.... 265,323
George 61,148,263
Gladys 64,151,264
Grace........................... 63,150,265
Hazel 65,152
Henderson 64,151,180,263
Henry........................... 65,153,264
Herbert 63,150,261
Hudson....................... 65,153,265
Icy 65,152
Ide 65
Ike 153,264
Ina 62,148,264
Inis 65,152
Irene 62,148,263
Isa 150
J C 64,151,262
Jack............................. 64,151,262
Jackson 64,152,264
James H 64,151,264
Jane 151
Jean 151
Jedd 263
Jeff..62,149
Jenne 263
Jennie.............. 62,64,148,151,263
Jim............ 20,63,100,150,261,307

Jimpson 63,308	Oscar 64
Jimpsons 150	Otis 64,151,264
Joe 64,151	Parline 62
Joel Dodson 265,288,306	Pat 63,149,265
John 65,153,261,301	Paul 149,266
Joseph 65,152,266	Pauline 149,263
Kate 62,64,149,151,262,265	Phelia 62,149
Katie 63,150,263	Philia 266
Lefus 62,148,264,321	Phoebe Thomas 265
Lena 63,150,264	R B 20,100,153,166,262,265,266
Leon 292	Rainey 63,150
Leona 62,149,264	Robert 62,149
Leonard 65,152	Rufus 62,149,265
Levi 172,282,285,310	Sallie 63,150,265
Lewis 65,153,264,321	Sarah 64,152,262
Lilly 63	Sarah Ann 263,286
Lilly Allen 153,166,262	Sidney 62,149,265
Lina Eline 263	Simpson 65,153,264
Lola 61,148	Smith 65,152,261
Lola Chitto 262	Steve 62,149,263
Loraine 63,150	Sullivan 65,152,153,265
Lorraine 265	Susie Anne 153,166,262
Louisiana 261	Thomas 62,148,263
Lousiana 65,152	Tom 65,152,266
Lysander 63,150,264	Vernal 63,149
Mabke 262	W C 64,151,264
Mable 61,148	Wesley 66,153,199
Maggie 64,151,264,301	Willie 62,149,263
Malissa 65,152,264	TUBBY (CATES)
Marceline 65,152,266	Alice 261
Martha Lee 64,151,264	Dock 261
Mary 61,63,148,262,263,286	TUCKALOO
May Belle 181,263,303	Alice 66,153,266
McKinley 65,153,265	Enia 66,153
Mike 172,282,285,310	Enis 266
Minnie 65,152,153,264,265	Frances 66,153,266
Moley 63,150,265	Mason 66,153
Mollie 63,150,261,265	Nathan (Mosn) 266
Molly 111	Sarah 66,153,266
Nancy 63,150,261	TUFFOMAH, Latima 170,283
Nellie 66,153,265	VAUGHN
Nicholas 265	Agnes 66,154,267
Nichols 65,152	Annie 67,154,186
Odie 62,149,263	Bart Riley 267
Odie (Isa) 261	Bessie 66,154,217

Index

Clifton 66,154,217
Cooksie 66,154,266,306
Eleanor 267,289
Greer 66,154,267
Howard................. 66,154,267,308
Jane................................ 66,154,267
John 66,67,154,267,308
Johnny 189,286
Lena 66,154,267
Linnie 267
Ludie 66,154,267
Luke 281,285,310
Mary Rose 66,154
Melissa 67,154
Melissa Bell 189
Mollie 67,154,186
Monroe 154,217,299
Sadie Hickman 267
Seta 66,154
Silmon 66,154,267
Sopha Bell 267
Susan 66,154,308
VAUGHT, Luke 172
WAITER
    Baby 155
    Betty Lee 292
    Cora Mae 67,155,268
    Gipson 67,154,268
    Lonnie 67,155,181,268
    Minnie 67,155,268,311
    Otho Helen 181,268
    Sue 67,155,268
    Willie Mae 268
WALLACE
    Alton 68
    Amy 155,166,268
    Annie 68,156,268
    Austin 67,155,268
    Barbalette 293
    Betty 67
    Betty Dixon 155,323
    Brigam 156,166
    Celia 67,155,268
    Columbus 67
    Comby 67,155,268,323

Cumby 301
Emma 67
Essie 68
Eunice 67,155,268
Fulton 67,155,268
Henry 67,155,268
Hetty Dixon 268
Houston 156,268
Leona 67
Ligman (Brigman) 268
Maggie 67,155,268
Otis 269,289
Rachel 67
Stenot 68,156,268
Susie 67,155,268
Tom 67,155,268
WALLACE (WILLIS)
    Columbus 155
    Emma Dixon 155,167
    Richard 155
WARNER, Johnnie L 68
WARNER (GIPSON)
    Johnnie 156
    Johnnie L 269
WESLEY
    Anne Tubby 269
    Ben 269
    Bennie 68,156
    Cameron 68,156,269
    Hubert 156
    John 68,156,269
    Julia Bell 269
    Julie 68
    Julie Bell 156
    Leona Willis 156
    Robert 269
    Rufus 49,134,245
    Sidney 68,156,269,303
    Sue Morris 134,245
    Tom 269,306
    Willie B 68,156,269
WICKSON
    Alma 44,128
    Baby 292
    Jim 68,140,156,181,269,320

Index

Kelly 23,103,211
Mack 296
Mary Jane 181,269
Susan Davis 269
Susan Davis Shoemaker 320
Yates 46,131,239
WILEY, Lizzie 68,157,270
WILLIAMS
   Carter 69,157,270
   Coy 69,157,271
   Evan 69,157
   Fate 69,157,270,301
   Fillman 69,157,271
   Irvin (Evan) 271
   Jennie 69,157,270
   Johnson 157,271
   Jonas 68,157,270
   Lamar 271,289,303
   Lewis 69,157,270,323
   Louis 301
   Lurline 158,270
   Maggie 68,157,270
   Mamie 69
   Mamie Smith 157,270
   Mary Alice D 157,271
   Mary Ann 69,157,270
   Nellie 69
   Nellie Sullivan 157,271
   Peter Jimpson 271,289
   Phillip 69,157,271
   Rufus 69,157,172,271,281,
   285,310,311
   Sarah 69,157,270
   Tony 68,157,271
   Wilson 296
WILLIAMSON
   Arnold 69,158,252
   Bike 69,158,270
   Effie 69,158,270
   Ida 69,158,271,309
   Lallie 158,270
   Lallis 69
   Mack 69,158,271,306
   Mary 69,158
WILLIS

Adaline 71,160,271,312
Adam 70
Alen 274
Allen 159
Ana 149
Ance 72,161
Anna 149
Annie Gipson 325
Arline 72,161,275
Baby 181,275,292
Basie (Bead C) 275
Bead C 170,283,285
Beaman 73,76,162,274
Bertha 296
Bill 69,158,271
Bone 276
Bonnie 72,161,272
Celie 70,159
Chester 159,274
Claud Y 70,158,271
Clemon 72,162
Clemson 274
Cohen 72,161,170
Collins 72,162,274,321
Dailey 71,161
Dennis 71,160,274,325
Dera (Dailey) 274
Dina 40,124
Dora 71,161,274
Earl 71,160,273
Ed 71,160,272
Edmond 72,161,272
Elie 72,161,272
Ellen 70,71,159,274
Ellen Hickman 160,273
Ellis 71,160,273
Elsie 70,158,272
Emma Dixon 272
Esther 70,158,275
Ethel 275,289
Eula 71,160,273
Fannie Lou 296
Finis 70,159,273
Flennie 73,162
Flora 72,161,272

Index

Frank	276
Fred	276
G C	71,160
Gamblin	71,160,181,273
Givan	275
Given	158,166
Gordon Griffiths	273,289
Gus	70,159,273,315
Harris	275
Harrison	72,161,292
Hayward	72,161,196
Henry	196,287,293,303
Hester	70,159,273
Houston (Thompson)	274
Hugh	72,161,274
Ike	70,159,274
Ike (Tom)	274
A J	72,161,275
J C	72,162,273,274
Jake	160
Jasper	70
Jim	71,160,274,325
Joe	70,71,160,275
John	70,72,159,161,181,196,275
John B	276
John Banks	73,162
John Crawford	296
John Joseph	158,272
Johnson	70,159,308
Josie	158,275
Julius (Wilson)	276
Kitty	72,161,272
Kohran (Cohen)	275
Layton J	276
Lee Roy	296
Leighton	73,162
Leo	159,166,274
Leona	70,159
Lester	70,159,273
Lillie	72,162
Lola	73,162
Louie	275
Louisa	71,160,274,325
Mallie	132
Marabelle	71,160,273
Maruice	71
Mary	293,303
Mary Lee	276
Mattie	71,160
Maurice	160,273,301
Meley	73,162
Mollie	70,72,132,159,161,274
Molly (Sissey)	275
Nan (Flennie)	276
Nannie	71,160,276
Nannie Dixon	272
Nath	70,158
Nathan	170,275
Nephus	272,289
Nettie	273
Nettie Mingo	274
Nola	274
Nora	70,159,273
Norma (Sylvia)	275
Odie	72,161
Otis	272
Plonie	272
Racheal	272
Rachel	162
Rainey	70,159,273
Richard	170,275,283,285
Robert	70,159,275
Robert R	72,161,272
Roger	292
Roscoe	292,303
Rose	72,161,272
Saleen	275
Sallie	72,161,196,275
Sallie (Celie)	275
Salum	73,162
Sarah	70,159,273
Savenie	70
Savenie Smith	158,271
Seney (Leona)	273
Sina	159,166,274
Sissey	72,161
Smith	71,161,274
Spinks	73,162,275
Susana	70,159,275
Susie	73,162,276

Susie Jane 296
Sylvai 158
Sylvia 70
Thompson 72,162
Tom 71,160
Una 72,161,275
Vanola 72,161
Vernie 308
Waggoner 71,161,276
Walter 72,162,274
Wesley 73,162,276
William B 70,158,272
Willie 273,289
Willie B 162,276
Willis 293
Wilson 73,162
Woodrow Wilson 72,161,274
Zan 181
Zon 273
WILLIS (WALLACE), Columbus..
.... 272
WILSON
    Caroline 170,277,283,285
    Cinnamon (Silmon) 276
    Dean (Jim) 277
    Edna 73,162,276
    Eva 73
    Eva Barne 276
    Eva Barnett 162,325
    Gordon 163
    Grady 292
    Jim 73,163
    Jimmie 296
    John 73,162,170,276,325
    Lecin 292
    Lena (Lennie) 277
    Lennie 73
    Leo 73,162,276
    Linnie 163
    Lou8sana 163
    Louisana 73
    Louisiana 277
    Lucille 292,301
    Martha 73,163,277
    Martha All3n 303
    Mollie 73,162,276
    Neil Milber 73,163
    R L 73,163,277
    Rose Billy 325
    Rosie Lee 201
    Sammie 73,163,277,321,325
    Sidney 73,162,276
    Silas 277,286
    Sillen 276
    Silman 73,162
    Silmon 325
    Wilbur Neil 277
    Will 73,163,277
WISHORK
    Alpha 74,163
    Alphia 142
    Evelyn 74,163,253
    Lum Presley 254
    Lun Presley 163
    Lyn Presley 74
    Nuga 74,77,163,254
    Ruth 163,254
    Sampson 74,163,277,312
    Zelia 74,163,253
YARBROUGH, Baker 278
YORK
    Addie 74,164,278
    Baxter 74,164,278,325
    Beaman 75,164,278
    Ben 74,163,277
    Bennett 74,163,277
    Berkley 74,164,277
    Colie 74,164,277
    Emmett 74,164,170,278
    Eunice 75,164
    Evelyn 296
    Florence 74,164,278
    G B 74,164
    Gasler 74,164
    Gassler 325
    Grace Sam 325
    Hester 74,163,277
    Indiana 74,164,278
    Indiana Lewis 301
    J B 277

Index

Lacie 74,164,277
Louella 74,163,277
Mable John 325
Marlin 289
Merlin 278
Necie 74,164,278,325
Sasler 278
Scott 74,164,277,303
Theodore 170,278,283,285

www.ingramcontent.com/pod-product-compliance
Lightning Source LLC
Chambersburg PA
CBHW020238030426
42336CB00010B/531